Piedmont Airlines

PIEDMONT AIRLINES

A Complete History, 1948–1989

RICHARD E. ELLER

McFarland & Company, Inc., Publishers
Jefferson, North Carolina, and London

The present work is a reprint of the illustrated case bound edition of Piedmont Airlines: A Complete History, 1948–1989, *first published in 2008 by McFarland.*

The employees of Piedmont Airlines would like to thank Professor Richard Eller for taking on the difficult task of traveling over the many roads on the Piedmont System to gather the stories from a unique group of dedicated employees who became a "Piedmont Family," and in doing so made Piedmont one of the best airlines in North America. Again, we say "thank you" for documenting the legacy of Piedmont.— Captain Paul Snell, Historian, Piedmont Silver Eagles

LIBRARY OF CONGRESS CATALOGUING-IN-PUBLICATION DATA

Eller, Richard E., 1960–
Piedmont Airlines : a complete history, 1948–1989 / Richard E. Eller.
    p.   cm.
Includes bibliographical references and index.

ISBN 978-0-7864-6914-7
softcover : 50# alkaline paper ∞

1. Piedmont Airlines — History.
2. Airlines — United States — History.   I. Title.
HE9803.P53E45   2012   387.7065'73 — dc22   2007050787

BRITISH LIBRARY CATALOGUING DATA ARE AVAILABLE

© 2008 Richard E. Eller. All rights reserved

No part of this book may be reproduced or transmitted in any form or by any means, electronic or mechanical, including photocopying or recording, or by any information storage and retrieval system, without permission in writing from the publisher.

On the cover: A Piedmont DC-3 crew (from left) Purser Stan Brunt, First Officer Tommy Orrell and Captain Sam Parnell (Piedmont Aviation Historical Society, Zeke Saunders collection)

Manufactured in the United States of America

*McFarland & Company, Inc., Publishers
Box 611, Jefferson, North Carolina 28640
www.mcfarlandpub.com*

To the thousands of employees who made a special airline possible, as well as the millions of passengers who recognized the effort being made for their comfort and service. This volume is also dedicated to my good friend Jerry Goodnight, without whose friendship and encouragement this effort might never have been undertaken.

Acknowledgments

In researching and writing a comprehensive volume on Piedmont Airlines, I was struck by the attitude of those encountered. Only once, while producing a documentary on a unique furniture company in Hickory, North Carolina, has this author witnessed this kind of devotion to the company and such personal investment of employees toward the job. Such employee loyalty and enthusiasm was as mystifying to fully explain here as was the case in the previous experience. After observing the genuine love of everyone interviewed for Piedmont Aviation, it became easier to appreciate what they had achieved as well as what they had lost.

In many ways, Tom Davis was the luckiest human being of them all. With his natural ability to put people at ease, he ventured into a business and cultivated a corporate climate that paid him back exponentially. During my association with former Piedmont employees, I had the rare privilege of reliving many experiences with those folks as they relayed insightful details about their work experience on the airline, as well as those for whom they worked. Without exception, everyone went out of their way to show tremendous respect for Mr. Davis. It is for that reason that once he became president of Piedmont, the narrative acknowledges him as Mr. Davis. It was considered necessary by this writer to convey the level of feeling and great esteem that employees had for the man. In much the same way, I also thank him for the company he built.

The same is true of Zeke Saunders. Some younger employees occasionally referred to Mr. Davis' right hand man as Mr. Saunders, but almost everyone else called him Zeke. They have admired him as much as they did Mr. Davis. As Tom Sharpe said, "He was just Zeke." So in the effort to capture the feelings of the employees, I occasionally refer to him as they did. His assistance in this project has been very important to its completion. He welcomed any question and spoke candidly on a variety of issues concerning Piedmont, even when they showed a less than flattering side of the company. His warmth and generosity embellished much of this project. His willingness to share photos that document the airline's history has insured that much of what was special about Piedmont will be preserved.

Likewise, I thank the many employees who took time to answer questions about Piedmont, dig through old photographs and query their fellow employees about specific dates and events to make sure that this story presented the history accurately. All of them were a joy to interview and much like in their work environment, they were helpful, thoughtful and encouraging in the development of this work. Every one of these people provided a piece of the Piedmont puzzle for a clearer picture of the tremendous flight of the Speedbird. A few of those individuals took on the added task of advising on technical and organizational issues, as well as reading the chapters to make sure they essentially told their story. To Ronnie Macklin, Jim Hamilton, Stephanie Hamilton, Paul Snell, and Larry Dudley, I offer my deepest thanks. Several of them also claim membership to the Piedmont Silver Eagles, which served as a catalyst in bringing this book together. Often I felt confident in my inquiries knowing that I had the backing of this wonderful philanthropic organization. Their support has been invaluable in the effort.

At this point, a number of people deserve mention for their assistance with this book. First and foremost, I would like to thank my friend Jerry Goodnight, who worked right alongside me on this project for a period of time before branching off into other topics of research. Together, we talked with many of the unforgettable personalities who populate the text. I thank him for his help and support throughout the project. Also, this book might never have come to fruition without the interest of Piedmont Silver Eagle Paul Snell, who, having read the previous work of Goodnight and Eller, saw us as potential chroniclers for the story. Thank you, Paul, for your help and your trust. In addition, the Piedmont Silver Eagles president Stephanie Hamilton and her husband Jim gave tremendous assistance and encouragement throughout the writing of this history. Both repeatedly said they wanted the story told and facilitated its writing with both encouragement and introductions. They opened a lot of doors for research that might otherwise have stayed closed as they lent their names to the legitimacy of this research. Thank you for a wonderful ride on Piedmont Airlines, Stephanie and Jim.

A number of libraries and librarians provided assistance in researching the myriad of events in which the Speedbird was involved. Probably the most helpful was the research staff, especially Laura Wickstead, Virginia Room Librarian, at the Roanoke Public Library, who contributed remarkable assistance. A huge thanks to Ari Sigal and the Catawba Valley Community College Library is required for assistance in procuring a number of important texts. Also, the North Carolina Room at the Forsyth County Library was a tremendous resource in researching the hometown airline. In addition, appreciation also extends to Diane Devoy, Adult Services Librarian at the Waynesville, Virginia, Public Library; and Jean Palmer at the Syracuse, New York, Public Library, who made expert use of the Internet to give me important documents associated with the Empire acquisition. Also, special thanks to the New Hanover County Library in Wilmington, North Carolina; the Henderson County Library in Hendersonville, North Carolina; the Atlanta–Fulton County Library in Atlanta, Georgia; the Charleston, West Virginia, Public Library; and the Caldwell Community College Library, Hudson, North Carolina.

In dealing with the painful subject of crashes, several individuals were important to the information contained in this work. Richard F. Gaya and Paul Houle have studied specific incidents extensively and were very kind to share their work on the subject. Some readers may object to points made about the causes of such tragedies, but the scholarship of researchers quoted here comes after thorough investigation and the perspective that historical inquiry can give. Interestingly, the work of Mr. Houle resulted in a consideration of the reopening the investigation of the crash of Flight 22 near Hendersonville, N.C. His investigation singlehandedly provoked a reexamination of the causes that led to a tragic collision in July of 1967.

Invaluable help and advice was provided by Walter Turner, historian with the North Carolina Transportation Museum in Spencer, N.C. His previous work on the subject, coupled with his wide knowledge of transportation in the Tar Heel state, proved to be an incredible resource in hunting down many of the small facts that build context for this story. Likewise, to his associates at the NCTM, Martha Battle Jackson and Elizabeth Smith, thanks very much for your support and assistance.

Special commendation should be given to my several readers who took the time to review the text for continuity and meaning. Along with Piedmont folk like Ronnie Macklin and Jim and Stephanie Hamilton, they include Mrs. Lois Ward, and my wonderful wife, Claudia. All were generous with their time and provided many helpful suggestions that aided the clarity and focus of the story. Much help was also provided by several transcribers who took voice interviews and turned them into scripts. They include Marilyn Heinemann, David Hamilton, Jerry Goodnight and Pauline Thomas.

The narrative has been greatly enhanced by the contributions of a number of people who provided images that could be displayed within these pages. The photographs give an indication of what these folks looked like as they were crafting one of the truly unique companies in the airline industry, as well as in American business. I felt images were a vital asset to the text and to the ones who provided or helped secure photos for inclusion in this volume, my thanks.

Deepest appreciation also goes to Laurie Lyda, my primary editor, and Jerry Sain. Their work in a very short period of time has given me confidence to place this book before readers with assurance that my intent has been delivered.

As Tom Davis himself would probably say, one should never overlook the passengers who climbed aboard the Pacemakers and turned a "puddle jumper" into the greatest airline in the U.S. with their support and their ticket purchases. It only became a special airline when customers remembered it as such and though the narrative contains a very few who patronized the airline, reaction from many more who learned about this work was always positive and sometimes a bit rueful that a carrier like this one no longer exists.

Finally, I want to take it back to where it all started, in Winston-Salem. It is my contention that the atmosphere in the Twin Cities gave Tom Davis the opportunity to realize a dream. After being a resident who cherished my days there, I now thank the city for giving me the chance to realize mine.

Table of Contents

Acknowledgments	vii
Preface	1
Introduction: Speedbird	5
1. Winston-Salem Air, 1918–1944	9
2. First Flight, 1944–1948	31
3. Puddle Jumping, 1948–1958	50
4. Speedy Petey, 1958–1968	81
5. Experience Comes with Age, 1968–1977	113
6. The Hazards of Flight, 1959–1988	145
7. The Great Outfit, 1978–1984	173
8. The Last Virgin, 1985–1987	205
9. Another Airline, 1987–1989	226
Afterword: Last Flight Out	246
Epilogue: Flying West	252
Appendix A: The Piedmont Fleet, 1948–1989	259
Appendix B: Piedmont Destinations, 1948–1989	265
Chapter Notes	269
Bibliography	287
Index	301

Preface

Once upon a time in Winston-Salem, North Carolina, there was an airline. Once a week, usually on Fridays, I rode past its headquarters on my way to downtown Winston-Salem, as I accompanied my mother on our weekly shopping trips. With airplanes on both sides of Liberty Street emblazoned with a "Speedbird," I knew that in order to take off, one or another of these Piedmont aircraft had to cross the street. I always kept an eye opened wide for the stoplight that signaled a crossing. As much as I would like to say that one day I was rewarded with the vision of a majestic Martin 404 or a Boeing 737 parading before the windshield of our 1969 Ford XL and that moment marked the start of my admiration for this unique airline, I can't. My timing was never right.

It actually took many more years after my family moved west from Winston-Salem and the airline re-adorned its tailfin with the logo of another airline that my timing got better and my moment to gaze in awe of Piedmont arrived. Since the demise of the airline, efforts had been made to tell the story of the aviation company, its people, its customers, its moment in time. Each took off with hopes of explaining the Piedmont phenomenon, but none had landed on a published page when I received a call from the Piedmont Silver Eagles. The historian for the group enjoyed *The Tarheel Lincoln*, a manuscript on which Jerry Goodnight and I had collaborated. They invited us to ride a flight into Piedmont history. We jumped at the chance. When Jerry was pulled back into the Lincoln controversy with still more aspects to explore, I stayed with Piedmont. In the spring of 2004, a sad reality was dawning on many former Piedmont employees. Year by year, the precious details of the story of Piedmont Airlines were being lost. With the clock already having ticked away 15 years, a documented history with a representative portion of the group who formed the original company had better be gathered quickly. Already many had departed. It was time for action. With tape recorders in hand, we canvassed those who knew the story, or at least some part of it, so that an accurate oral history could be documented. Former employees who had no clue as to the efforts to tell their history received phone calls out of the blue asking for a meeting about their Piedmont experience. The overwhelming majority were gracious and forthcoming with their recollections.

In order to provide a framework for those remembrances, it was necessary to document the highlights (and low points) in the history of the airline. For those purposes, two general sources proved invaluable — the publications from the company and the communities of which Piedmont Aviation was a part. Corporate documents told the story with its best foot forward, as marketing departments are charged to do. The annual reports, prepared as a yearly snapshot of the company, interpreted all the figures and growth to sound as positive as possible since these brochures were intended to boost shareholder confidence in company efforts. Interestingly enough, the numbers regarding revenue, passenger seat miles and expenses offered an intriguing story over the years as the carrier struggled mightily at times to show profit. The annual reports, taken as a whole, revealed the turbulence that could be found in the 41 year ride of Piedmont Airlines. Newspapers added another perspective to the story. The *Winston-Salem Journal* and *Twin City Sentinel*, while proud of the hometown company, did not shy away from company controversy when it arose. Its readers encompassed more than just Piedmont employees, so the stories reflected the good, the bad and the sometimes ugly truth about the city's second largest business behind R.J. Reynolds. Outside of Winston-Salem, stories were less frequent but still mostly impartial when it came to the airline. If a crash occurred, or the airline was moving into their city, papers throughout the Southeast relayed the information readily with as much detail as they could provide. Occasionally, magazines ferreted out some aspect of the airline to tell readers. Those publications, too, helped bring into focus where Piedmont Airlines was heading at a given time. Especially toward the end of the Piedmont era, which coincided with the beginning of the video cassette recorder era, a number of television news stories provided another take on events, like the London flight and the USAir merger.

At times, articles led to new interviews which led back to new dates to check against newspaper accounts as the effort grew to tell the story of Piedmont as accurately as possible. Some records did not always agree with personal recollections. If controversy arose, an attempt was made to acknowledge such and provide both sides of the issue. From the interview side, some subjects were touchy. This was especially true about crashes. The loss of passengers and fellow employees stung everyone associated with the airline since a life and death event was more than a blemish on performance. Each of these historic events meant that close friends and coworkers lost their own in catastrophic moments that were difficult to fathom.

Even with the painful memories, the overriding emotion that emanates from Piedmont people is exuberance over the company they created, the recognition it received and the lasting friendships they shared. Often one person would say, "You've got to talk to..." an old friend and fellow employee, whom they maybe hadn't seen in years. When I mentioned employees whom I had previously interviewed, they always asked how the former coworkers were doing. The interviewees were always generous with their time, memories and even pictures of days with the company. Their welcome and candor made the story tingle with anticipation as they revealed what their life's work meant to them.

As word of the subject matter got out, another group of people occasionally popped up to add a "hurrah" to the account. They were the passengers of Piedmont Airlines. Though they appear only occasionally in the narrative, they were the real reason Tom Davis built the airline he envisioned. Though their recollections about the airline were too numerous to capture here, they helped spur on this effort. One day I took my daughter to get ice cream. In the middle of my large cone of chocolate an elderly woman noticed the Speedbird logo on a t-shirt I was wearing and began to reminisce. She fondly recalled the days when she could fly from Hickory, North Carolina, to any of Piedmont's myriad destinations and enjoy the ride better than any she has flown since. We discussed the little things the airline did to put passengers at ease and the superior level of Piedmont customer service. Her memories were typical of those I encountered from former passengers when the subject of Piedmont Airlines came up. During the writing of this volume they came along periodically to remind me how important Piedmont was as a service company and how significant were the accomplishments of its employees.

A lot of hard work went into making the flights of my ice cream shop friend so pleasurable that, decades later, she fondly remembered her time onboard a Piedmont Pacemaker.

I found in my research that the feeling was mutual. Passengers never knew what was going on behind the scenes while they were enjoying their trip. Piedmont employees always say the effort was worth whatever extra work it took, not that it wasn't challenging, and from time to time, more than they expected. The employees I encountered were uniformly proud of their collective accomplishments, extended praise for the contributions of their fellow employees and would gladly do it all again. With that kind of attitude, a story like theirs was a dream to present.

Introduction: Speedbird

As an aviation achievement and as one of North Carolina's most beloved successes, Piedmont Airlines flew into history. For 41 years, the Winston-Salem based company, housed out of tiny Smith Reynolds Airport, toiled and struggled to become an airline on the verge of being knighted as a major carrier. Like an actor or musician cut down in the prime of life, Piedmont Airlines left many wondering how commercial aviation might have been better if only it had remained intact. This company reflected much of the ingenuity and determination of Orville and Wilbur Wright, who made their famous first flight in the same state. The safe money would have been on neither the Wright Brothers nor founder and longtime president of Piedmont Airlines Tom Davis while each worked to get their respective planes into the air. However, the long shot would have paid off big dividends, at Kitty Hawk as well as in Winston-Salem. Both efforts exemplify the importance of perseverance and each writes vital chapters in the history of flight. The Piedmont story is less celebrated, but nonetheless significant to the history of the development of U.S. commercial aviation.

A chronicle of Piedmont Airlines might seem no more important than that of a taxi service that hauled people from one place to another and then one day ceased operation. However, the Piedmont story encompasses much more than the history of a transportation company. In the post–World War II period, the visionaries, the innovators, the builders, the organizers, and the restless souls looking for adventure could all be found at this local service carrier, named for the region of the Tar Heel state from which it came. More than a chronicle of the airline in its time, the story of the shared experiences of this special group of individuals sets the stage for our own. It tells us of the ethic of their time and leaves us to figure out how those values become what we embrace today. In the effort to become airborne, we can see our own struggles to make our work meaningful, whatever that work may be. Piedmont Aviation, which included an airline as well as other divisions devoted to related aspects of commercial flight, exemplified a group of individuals who came together to earn more than a post–World War II living. They built a company from which they took enormous pride when either they or the company retired. Their achievements are compelling and romantic, something a more disconnected time reflects upon with envy. A funny thing happened as they did it too; they went from looking at their workmates as fellow employees to embracing them as brothers and sisters. Piedmont employees reveal a story of family, not bound by birth, but by ideals and interest. Their bonds were tighter (and have remained so) than many families.

As the patriarch and the founder, Tom Davis sits at the head of the Piedmont table as an American success story. Like Theodore Roosevelt, Tom was a young kid whose asthma kept him from an average childhood. He found freedom in flight and while probing its possibilities, discovered a business acumen that helped him create a company that made the still-novel pursuit of aviation profitable in much the same way that William Paley took a small radio network and turned it into CBS. His imagination was fired by the likes of no less than Charles Lindbergh, the barnstormer who risked his life to fly across the Atlantic and demonstrated that a good airplane was just as reliable as a good horse out on the prairie. Tom Davis followed in the footsteps of Eddie Rickenbacker, the flying ace who started the larger but no less extinct Eastern Airlines. The phenomenal aspect of this story is that Tom Davis never left his hometown to make his mark.

Davis did not however, create his airline alone. Along the way, he met many good people. Actually, he did more than meet them; he recruited them. Most were kindred spirits who also loved aviation. In these people, Tom saw the kinds of skills and attitude that would make his ideas fly, quite literally. As children of the Great Depression, they knew no substitute for hard work, no easy path to opportunity. On top of that, the second war to make the world safe for democracy had dealt these people another helping of sacrifice. Their post-war world guaranteed nothing, and yet they remained optimistic about life, about the future, and about a little transportation company know as Piedmont Aviation. Just as Tom Davis saw something in them, they returned the compliment and stood shoulder to shoulder with him to give the venture every chance for success. The work required persistence and ingenuity with some improvisation thrown in from time to time.

Their endeavor also has a familiar American ring to it. With long hours — sometimes very long — and lower pay than most in the industry, Piedmont employees still took pride in their jobs and worked for more than the money. What's more, they enjoyed each other's company. Indeed, they often put their heads together to solve a problem, laughed at antics of one another, and cried when they lost one. For the most part, the clan was never clannish. They welcomed anyone into the circle as an employee, a customer, and even an enthusiast. Many Piedmont brothers and sisters brought along the next generation to follow the career standards they established. Sometimes it was their own sons and daughters, whom they wanted to work for the "best company on earth."

The age of Piedmont Airlines is now past along with the Speedbird emblem that adorned the tail of all Piedmont planes. The adage goes that in this day and time such an employment circumstance could never occur. The Piedmont story is wrapped up in the work ethic of the World War II generation; and yet with many of those early employees gone, subsequent generations are left to tell the story. They love the company as much as the founding fathers. Sure, over the years as the mythical airline faded farther and farther into the past, it might be remembered more fondly as a nostalgic recollection. However, the record speaks for itself. Having been named "Airline of the Year" in 1984 and being sold for the highest price any airline ever commanded in corporate buyout signify that Piedmont was something special. And it isn't just employees who make the case. Passengers too recall an airline experience that they have seldom since seen. One needs only mention Piedmont Airlines in a community where the Speedbird flew to get a favorable recollection of how flights on Piedmont differed from the others.

Why was Piedmont a special aviation company? The real answer lies in the people, the family, if you will, who banded together for the effort. It wasn't just Thomas H. Davis, or his successor, William R. Howard, though both set the tone for their times. If there was yeast in this company that made it rise to the highest levels of customer service, it was the fraternity within the airline and its sister division, called Fixed Base Operations. Regardless of whatever stock employees may have had in the company, a Piedmont person felt invested in this aviation enterprise from the bottom to the top and back again. From the toilet cleaner to the maintenance department, pilots to the front office, morale boosted performance well beyond what a group of otherwise ordinary individuals should be able to do. Yet collectively, they soared, each contributing his or her key element to the mix. They took pride, they cared, and in the end they elevated an airline to a shining example, reflected in their advertising slogan of, "An example of just how good an airline can be." Those unfamiliar with Piedmont should ask around. Chances are that an acquaintance remembers the airline. When that person is found, gauge the reaction. It will be surprising. Like a sports fanatic's feeling for his or her favorite team, the devotion has remained long after the winning streak ended. In its time, Piedmont folks knew they were part of something special, something they had a hand in developing, and they were not going to relax the standard one inch. They took ownership of Piedmont Aviation right along with the stockholders. Only when it came to the profit to be made from the sale of the company did the two groups part company.

This narrative provides insight on how to create such a company. One need only look for the ways Piedmont management cultivated its employee base. Mr. Davis knew his employees by name. This personal attention meant so much that his employees worked doubly hard for him. Whenever decisions were necessary, executives sought out those who would be affected most by the changes and got their input, which made any resolution easier to implement. When any worker made the wrong decision for the right reason, the correction was handled with understanding and grace. These were fairly simple business practices and each worked well for Piedmont. Since a good idea never goes out of style, the Piedmont brand of management could be (and among some companies has been) drawn upon again.

Managing a group as diverse as a collection of airline employees was no easy task. Some workers were meticulous organizers who knew where every spare part for every aircraft could be located. They contrasted sharply with many of the people who actually flew those collections of parts. If a latter day equivalent for the 19th century cowboy existed, it could be found in the cockpit. The pilot group represented some of the most outrageous and at times heroic individuals found in America, and Piedmont had its share. Not to say that other groups at Piedmont were not both outrageous and heroic, they were. But the stories told about pilots define them as the most adventurous and intrepid souls to be found. Some even began their careers as barnstormers and stunt pilots, flying for pure thrill. For many of them, it was only slightly less exhilarating to take a "real job" and fly the Speedbird. Some risked their lives, some gave them. As one flight trainer noted, pilots were always confident, ready and fearless. They knew their airplane and their own abilities. There was a bit of a swagger in their walk as they departed the crew room to mount up their trusty steed. Add to that confidence the innovative people who served customers face to face as flight attendants and counter personnel, the ground crews who welcomed in every Piedmont Pacemaker (as Tom Davis liked to call his aircraft), the maintenance workers who kept those planes in the best of working order, the reservationists, clerical and administrative folks, and the planners, researchers and support personnel who kept those on the planes going, and the landscape is wide for the personalities it took to keep Piedmont flying.

For all of its efforts, Piedmont was not a perfect airline. Though everyone gave, occasionally their efforts faltered. In remembering the good, some obscure the bad which paints a skewed picture. On four occasions, Speedbirds crashed. The anguish and regret created by those events were felt long after the headlines reported the loss of life. Perhaps the most lamentable error came in the success experienced by the company in the 1980s, for it was in that period that the seeds were sown for its eventual departure. The merger process that culminated in 1989 with the disappearance of the name and identity stuck with everyone, not the least of whom were customers who saw their level of service diminish. For some folks, the change was a financial windfall. Just about everyone made more money under the USAir banner than they did before, but the work environment and the relationships indicated that nothing was the same. Most said they would have given up the bigger paycheck to have their old airline back. In fact, many say they would have followed Mr. Davis to a new airline if he had been willing to start one. The relationship was that strong. In her essay on what constitutes those "kindred spirits of folks who lived and loved Piedmont Airlines," former flight attendant Barbara Jamieson Adams uses the term "Piedmonster" to include people who "worked with the Piedmont family as an employee, were an employee's family member, were a member of the Piedmont family by flying as a passenger on Piedmont Airlines, or became an enthusiast of Piedmont by reading about its rich history."[1]

As one (or several) of the above, count yourself part of the gang, join the Piedmont family, and experience their story.

• 1 •

Winston-Salem Air, 1918–1944

A distinct atmosphere permeated Winston-Salem, North Carolina. In late summer and early autumn, the sweet smell of tobacco leaf saturated the air as tobacco farmers hauled their crop to the warehouses of R.J. Reynolds, the city's largest employer. In the first decade of the twentieth century, the twin cities of Winston and Salem (they would not be officially joined by their golden hyphen until 1913) were North Carolina's largest metropolitan area, eclipsing both the capital city of Raleigh and Charlotte, the state's emerging railroad center. Just before World War I, the "Twin City" solidified its prominence as the birthplace of a national craze: Camel Cigarettes. With a unique blend of leaf and a provocative marketing campaign, the R.J. Reynolds Company surpassed the Duke Family's tobacco operation located down the road in Durham as leading supplier of tobacco products to the nation. Winston-Salem's stature as a tobacco town was such that it quickly received the name of Camel City. As the aroma of curing tobacco filled the air, it also gave rise to an ambitious population, giving them a confidence to indulge their "flights" of fancy.

Of all the heirs to the precedent set at Kitty Hawk by the Wright Brothers, no other North Carolina town embraced the art of aviation like Winston-Salem. Aeroplanes, pilots, and flight intrigued citizens so much that the town became a destination for those who flew. Many came to demonstrate their prowess in planes that still closely resembled the model Orville first took into the air. Winston-Salem always guaranteed a paying crowd for these early aviators and their air shows.

Lincoln Beachy was one of the country's first and most daring aerial exhibitionists. In the spring of 1911, Beachy came to Winston-Salem's Piedmont Park "dipping and gliding gracefully" his aeroplane "completely at the will of the daring operator."[1] Beachy, known as the "Flying Fool," piloted his "Curtiss Air Ship" flawlessly before a Twin City crowd in a drizzling rain. While the weather forced the cancellation of a race against an automobile, the other transportation wonder of the day, Beachy remained in Winston-Salem a second day to take his plane into the sky, again to the marvel of the paying crowd. Interest flowered and the skies of Winston-Salem began to fill with more than just the smell of harvested tobacco.

Thanksgiving Day of 1911 brought an even greater display of aerial acrobatics as the city's newspaper, the *Winston-Salem Journal,* sponsored an aviation meet. Billed as the largest such event in the South, the paper crowed that "no city in North Carolina has yet had two noted aviators on the same day, both in the air at once and [both have] been doing stunts that defy the laws of nature."[2] The day was cold and muddy, which curtailed a few of the "six death defying stunts" promised, but still the spectators came. The *Journal* described the crowd as "flatteringly large" with a banner headline observing, "Flights are Excellent." "Notwithstanding the brisk wind, which made their machines wobble a little dangerously at times, Messrs. Walsh and Witmer, professional bird men of the Curtiss Company amply sustained their remarkable record for daring and successful manipulation of the biplanes."³ The throng loved what they saw and Winston-Salem continued to earn its wings as a preeminent aviation center among cities in the southeast.

Through the years of World War I, folks in Winston-Salem mostly read about the feats of aviators who performed their "tricks" on the battlefields of northern France in the allied effort to defeat the Germans. Once the war was over, however, planes returned to the skies over the Twin City with regularity. One veteran of the war, Roscoe Turner, flew his AVROE 504K into Winston-Salem without the aid of a landing strip. Instead, Turner landed on the lawn of largest estate in town, the new home of the recently deceased tobacco millionaire R.J. Reynolds. The residence was called Reynolda. There to see Roscoe Turner touch down were the Reynolds children, including twelve year old R.J. Jr. (known as Dick) and his eight year old brother Smith. Both became entranced with flying, increasing by two the number of city residents deeply attracted to aviation.

After World War I, returning war heroes stormed the nation looking for audiences to thrill. Called barnstormers, they staged their own shows, sometimes referred to as "flying circuses," with faster and more powerful aircraft to create greater thrills for spectators. Winston-Salem served as an ideal stop. Landing strips blossomed. By 1920, Maynard Field operated southeast of Winston-Salem, followed two years later by Charles Field. The latter was cre-

Just after World War I, flying ace Roscoe Turner flew into Winston-Salem for a visit. Instead of landing at one of several airstrips, he touched down on the front lawn of Reynolda, where he is shown with the Reynolds children (Reynolda House Archives).

ated by hometown aviator Shelly Charles, who "scraped out an area"[4] of his family's farm for an airstrip. Charles, an Army Air Corps pilot, began staging his own barnstorming events for his fellow citizens, thrilling crowds with aerial antics that went well beyond those attempted by aviators ten years before.

Shelly Charles and flyers like him followed a proven formula as they brought spectators in to see just how far a daredevil would go to please his audience. The crowd held its collective breath because airplane antics were a sensation unlike anything experienced before. Brightly colored "open air" biplanes sputtered toward the crowd and paraded by before taking off to engage in a series of loops, dives and tricks. The events demonstrated the dexterity of pilots like Charles to manipulate the controls and show more courage than anything imaginable. Among the standard demonstrations were races, either plane to plane or against automobiles, flying under obstacles, stunt landings, and target bombings with non-combustible objects. Some steel-nerved daredevils went beyond those tricks to include such exploits as crawling out onto the wing and holding on by a hand, a foot, and even teeth to the fear and delight of the audience. Air shows grew into intricate theatrical events with the sky as their stage. On one occasion, a whole cop and robber chase took place in the air with one adventurer pursuing the other and scrambling all over the airplane while dressed in costume.[5]

On the day after Thanksgiving 1922, eleven years after the first *Winston-Salem Journal* air show, Shelly Charles wowed an audience with his crowd-rousing aerial theatrics. These stunts thrilled spectators but also terrified, as it was known that the possibility of death came with any careless mistake, equipment malfunction, or even quick atmospheric change. While the better nature of audiences hoped loss of life was not part of the show, if tragedy did occur most were right there to witness it. Just two months earlier across the Appalachian Mountains from Winston-Salem, in the community of Cleveland, Tennessee, spectators witnessed a young female stunt performer climbing out of the cockpit while her plane flew overhead. She then descended down a rope ladder, readying herself for a jump into a lake below. Disastrously, her hair became entangled in the rope, and when an empty fuel tank required the pilot to land, the plane dragged beautiful, young Eva Moss to her death.[6]

During the November show, Shelly Charles carefully tried to stay away from stunts that might turn calamitous. However, after performing a successful maneuver and landing with the intention of quickly returning to the sky, tragedy struck. Just as Charles's biplane slowed in front of the crowd, William Melchor, a man described in newspaper reports as "feeble," walked in front of the plane where the propeller blades chopped him to pieces. The incident reminded Twin City residents of how dangerous airplanes, even those on the ground, could be. Even so, the calamity did not abate the appetite of aviation fans. After investigation, Shelly Charles was exonerated from responsibility in the death of William Melchor and continued to build his reputation as a renowned stunt flier, as did his younger brother Paul Charles. Both became commercial pilots in the late 1920s, eventually flying for Eastern Air Transport, later Eastern Airlines.[7] Winston-Salem found its first homegrown aviation heroes in the Charles brothers. The city would claim many more as fascination with flight continued its climb.

Aviation, or "aeronautics" as it was called at the time, attracted many around town but few had the financial means to indulge their interest. Among those who could afford it were the young heirs to the R.J. Reynolds tobacco fortune. After watching Roscoe Turner land in their yard, the Reynolds boys dedicated much of their time and some of their wealth to flying. In the wake of the 1918 passing of their father, each stood to inherit up to $28 million by age 28. With such a fortune, both Dick and Smith invested in number of "ships," as the press referred to airplanes in those days.[8] The two millionaires shared a growing passion for flight. They differed only in the way they pursued the sky.

Richard J. Reynolds, Jr., the oldest Reynolds heir, looked for business opportunities and invested heavily in the commercial application. Quoted as saying "Those things that tend to facilitate transportation are the things that advance civilization," Dick believed that aviation would profit from his speculation, just as his father had trusted in the future of tobacco. Following after Charles Lindbergh's historic May 1927 flight across the Atlantic, Dick bought New York's Curtiss Field, where Lindbergh had housed his plane, *The Spirit of St. Louis*, prior to its record-setting Atlantic flight. In doing so, Dick saved Curtiss Field from being consumed by developers. Later that same year, Dick Reynolds started Reynolds Aviation. Based at his new airfield in the Big Apple, Reynolds planned to create his own airline. To that end, his purchase of 13 planes populated the fleet of Reynolds Airways. As Dick's son Patrick pointed out in his family history, *The Gilded Leaf*, his father was in the "right place" to get in on the ground floor of passenger air travel.[9]

Dick Reynolds invested in almost anything connected with flight. Among those ventures was the Plane Speaker Company, a company that outfitted airplanes with speaker systems to be used for broadcasting information. He envisioned a myriad of ways in which this sound delivery system could be helpful to those on the ground. He felt that voicing messages from the air might be handy for airports' incoming flights or maintaining infantry organization on the battlefield. Reynolds also thought plane speakers could also deliver advertising messages to the general public. Once, he brought a Reynolds Airways Ford Trimotor to Winston-Salem equipped with a full set of speakers. To test his idea, Dick Reynolds voiced a personal message to his fellow citizens. Echoing down from the sky, people on the street heard "Warning ... a swarm of killer bees is on the way. Take cover! Warning...." Had Twin City citizens not been so accustomed to airplanes over their heads and the practical jokes of the tobacco heir, they might have panicked.[10]

Dick's enthusiasm for flying dissipated after two setbacks. Following World War I, the Army began delivering mail for the U.S. Postal Service. Calvin Coolidge sought to privatize air mail, and the government began awarding contracts. Along with numerous fledgling airlines, Reynolds Airways pursued the business that would have given Dick Reynolds an instant and sustainable profit. However, instead of winning the run from New York to Chicago, Reynolds lost out to the company that eventually became United Airlines, exemplifying the make or break importance of mail contracts. Dick Reynolds then turned to the next best source of air revenue: people. The novelty of flying was still strong in 1927, even if most Americans still relied on trains to reach distant destinations. Reynolds Airways filled seats for rides around the New York skyline. On the afternoon of September 17, ten passengers boarded a Reynolds Airways Fokker F-VIII in a hard rain at Curtiss Field. The flight turned catastrophic as soon as the plane took off, crashing into an orchard in New Jersey. Five passengers survived the wreck, but the other five were killed, along with the flight's pilot and mechanic. The crash proved fatal to the airline as well. After the incident spawned several lawsuits, the remnants of Reynolds Airways were moved back to Winston-Salem and became a sideline business under the name Reynolds Aviation. Likewise, interest in Curtiss Field waned, and Dick Reynolds eventually sold the property.[11]

Zachary Smith Reynolds, the youngest of the four Reynolds children, loved aviation in a more fundamental way than Dick. Smith flew for the thrill, not for the profit. Following his older brother to New York, he soaked up all he could learn about aviation. Abandoning a formal college education, Smith Reynolds immersed himself in all aspects of flight. High school classmate Egbert Davis, Jr. remarked that Smith "would rather fly than go to school."[12] By the time Smith was 18, he received his Airframe and Engine Mechanics (A & E) license so that he could fix his own plane. He demonstrated his dexterity in the cockpit for the hometown crowd once, participating in acrobatic events that marked the opening of Winston-Salem's Miller Field in 1927.[13] As something of a daredevil, Smith set out to establish speed records in air travel. In 1930, he flew from New York to Los Angeles in twenty-eight hours and five minutes, which was a first.[14] He then made a groundbreaking trip across Europe and Asia in 1931.[15] In her introduction to Smith's flight log of that event, his niece, Barbara Babcock Millhouse, noted that at age 17, Smith was the "youngest transport pilot in the United States."[16] He might have set more records in aviation had his exploits not been curtailed by his untimely death. In the summer of 1932, Smith Reynolds died in what was ruled an accidental shooting at the family home of Reynolda.[17]

Dick Reynolds continued to dabble in aviation investments, more to make money than as an active interest. The will of R.J. Reynolds, Sr. stipulated that heirs receive one dollar for each dollar they earned. Thus, Dick's interest centered not so much on small concerns, but on a much broader pursuit of the aviation business and an expectation of greater financial return. This interest helped a number of aviation companies to get off the ground. Patrick Reynolds wrote of the pivotal role his father played in the life of a number of airlines in the southeast:

> Dick [Reynolds] became the largest stockholder in the underfinanced Eastern Airlines, not merely because he believed in the future of aviation, but also, as with the RJR stock buy, so that he could use his resulting leverage with the company. There was a plan for Eastern to bring regular scheduled service to Winston-Salem. The Z. Smith Reynolds Foundation had pledged money to upgrade the airport but made the grant contingent on regular scheduled passenger service being brought to Winston by a large airline such as Eastern. Winston's negotiations with Eastern took the better part of the next two years. Later in 1940 fledgling Delta Airlines got in trouble and turned to Dick; his purchase of a large block of stock enabled Delta to stay in business.[18]

Both Reynolds brothers first learned the mechanics of flying from the same experienced pilot, Lewin S. McGinnis, known to some friends as "Bud" and as "Mac" to others. A Maryland native, McGinnis worked as an instructor at New York's Curtiss Flying School and when the property came into the hands of Dick Reynolds in the summer of 1927, Mac came with it.[19] In New York, McGinnis gave lessons to both Dick and Smith during the formative days of Reynolds Airways. Smith was only 14 years old when Mac taught him the basics. Dick, at 21, already knew how to fly but refined his skills under Mac's tutelage. In 1928, Dick Reynolds needed a pilot for Reynolds Airways so he selected Mac. In succeeding years, McGinnis would go on to become Dick's personal pilot, eventually running the new version of Reynolds Aviation back in Winston-Salem, which was rechristened as Camel City Flying Service.[20]

In the formative days of commercial aviation, popular connection points were absolutely necessary. Winston-Salem's Miller Field was in a competitive race with another known then as Friendship Airport, 17 miles to the east near Greensboro. Reynolds attempted to win the race for his hometown with strong-arm tactics to pull Eastern Airlines toward the Twin City, including pouring millions of dollars into the upgrade of Miller Field through the philanthropic organization created to honor Dick's younger brother, whose 1932 mysterious shooting death had left the family devastated. Seemingly, the aviation aspirations of the Reynolds family died with Smith. With the exception of renaming Winston-Salem's Miller Field as Z. Smith Reynolds Airport in 1942, the Reynolds family never again became actively involved in the business of flight.

Circa 1923 at Miller Field in Winston-Salem. Aviation was an early fascination for many in the Twin City. The city served to launch a number of airlines, including Camel City Flying Service and its descendent, Piedmont Aviation (courtesy of Reynolda House Archives).

Since Winston-Salem was a beehive of flight, it was no surprise that Charles Lindbergh, after his record breaking crossing of the Atlantic Ocean, stopped off in the Twin City while conducting a nationwide tour promoting aviation. Coincidentally, Mac McGinnis also knew Lindbergh. "Lucky Lindy" had worked with Mac McGinnis in New York and both Dick and Smith Reynolds noted having met Colonel Lindbergh.[21] In those days, while aviation captured the imagination of many, few were able to actually participate. Only the wealthy, who could afford airplanes, and daredevils, who would do anything to fly, were involved. The Reynolds brothers fit into the former category; Lindbergh and Mac were part of the latter. Mac was known as both a gifted pilot and excellent mechanic. The night before Lindbergh left for Europe, McGinnis reportedly helped fine tune *The Spirit of St. Louis* at Curtiss Field.[22] After the success of the ultimate barnstorming trick — flying across the Atlantic — the Daniel Guggenheim Foundation bankrolled a tour around the United States for Charles Lindbergh. Promoting the burgeoning business of flight, the pilot of the now famous *Spirit of St. Louis* flew his aircraft from state to state as part of a 75-city sweep.

On October 14, 1927, Lindbergh touched down in Winston-Salem, where he delivered a well-worn speech in support of airport construction and the development of commercial possibilities involving flight.[23] Lindbergh argued for the benefit of "conducting a progressive air program for your city in order to keep your city in the foreground of American aeronautics." He closed by saying, "I hope that you will devote a pattern of your interest in the future to aviation in relation to your community."[24] Civic leaders in Winston-Salem had already implemented some of the "Lone Eagle's" advice with the creation of the airport where Lindbergh landed. Now, all the city needed was someone among the spectators to carry those dreams further aloft.

Among the crowd of 25,000 who came to Miller Field to hear America's newest hero was Egbert L. Davis and his two sons, Egbert Jr. and Thomas Henry. Nine-year-old Tom considered that moment the beginning of his devotion to aviation and later said, "I think Lindbergh was largely responsible for my interest in flying."[25] That spark of "interest in the future of aviation" instilled in Tom Davis by Charles Lindbergh's visit was fanned by Tom's father, Egbert Sr., who fed his sons' interest by purchasing the boys a *Spirit of St. Louis* model to put together and fly. The kit was one of the first toys of its kind and was made of balsam wood covered with rice paper and powered by a rubber band. The Davis boys used their driveway as a runway. Tom and his brother sent the plane skyward time and time again, watching it land in the pea patch on their side yard while dreaming of larger craft that someday they might pilot.[26]

From childhood, flight permeated Tom's imagination. He doodled in art classes and almost always his subjects were airplanes.[27] At home, his bedroom served as a hangar for an ever-growing "fleet of model airplanes,"[28] as dreams of flying became an obsession. No doubt that when he got his hands on a copy of Lindbergh's autobiography *We*, he voraciously read it. However, Lindbergh's arrival was not Tom's first encounter with flight. His father had taken him to several of the barnstorming events around Winston-Salem that were popular throughout the decade, like the Shelly Charles event in 1922.[29] Born March 16, 1918, Tom grew up during an era when a young boy's greatest hero was an aviator who performed his death defying acts in front of their very eyes.[30] In the words of Tom's brother, outings to see stunt pilots were numerous, and it "wasn't anything special for us to do, because in those days there were plenty of barnstormers."[31]

Tom loved airplanes and flying like no other activity that had ever occupied his mind. As he put it, "I've liked airplanes ever since I was old enough to know what one was."[32] At age eleven, he went up for the first time, remembering it quite well for the rest of his life. "It was with one of those barnstormers, a fellow named Poindexter," said Tom. "He flew me over my house, it was quite a thrill."[33] He continually sneaked into the hangars at Miller Field, just to hang out and hang onto every word he could glean from the experienced flyers. All his allowance money secretly went for lessons from the airport's most influential pilot and best trainer, the same pilot who trained the Reynolds boys and serviced the *Spirit of St. Louis*, Mac McGinnis.

Tom's health drove him toward flying too. His older brother Egbert watched him suffer from asthma, a condition inherited from his mother. "It bothered him tremendously when he was growing up. He was in the bed a lot, missed school a lot, all on account of his asthma." Egbert Jr. remembered how Tom "got despondent in his early teens. He was to the point where he was ready to give up. He couldn't breathe. He couldn't run with the boys. He couldn't play. He couldn't do anything. He just had that asthma."[34] Sending the young man off to a number of locales (including his aunt's in Richmond, Virginia, and boarding school) failed to improve his condition. Because of the asthma, Tom ultimately relied on tutors for most of his elementary and secondary education.[35]

Tom's father recognized his son's growing fascination with flying, which went well beyond model planes and drawings. Tom Davis recalled when the two came to agreement on what would ultimately be his career. "I came home from high school for lunch and my father, Egbert L. Davis, said to me out of the blue, 'Why don't you go out and take a flying lesson this afternoon?' I'll never know whether he had found out that I had been saving my allowance just for that purpose and, in fact, had already secretly taken two or three lessons. In any event, I didn't waste any time in getting back out to the airport."[36] As soon as Tom made the decision to pursue aviation, his father instantly saw the advantage. According to Tom's older brother Egbert Jr., "Daddy had recognized that [in] flying an airplane, all you do is just sit there, you know, and manipulate the controls. It doesn't require a whole lot of breath and breathing. And so it just happened to be something that he could do, and his asthma wouldn't worry him so much."[37] Isolated from the strenuous life, Tom Davis found flying to be a fulfilling alternative. He breathed better when flying, partly because the air was thinner in flight, but also because he gained a sense of accomplishment and exhilaration that could not be found with his limited mobility on the ground.[38]

At the age of 16, Tom Davis soloed "in a Taylor E-2 Cub, with its two seats, a canvas cover and a 37-horsepower engine." Years later, reminiscing about his first flight, he said, "One of the main things that I remember about it was the total surprise at how quickly the airplane would get off the ground and how fast it would climb without the instructor in it. Before the airplane rolled very far, it was off the ground and climbing like a scared duck."[39]

Tom's love of flying never subsided. Years later, after his attention had passed from the Taylor E-2 to a fleet of planes, Tom returned to the joy of that first solo as he diligently sought out the exact same single-engine craft of his first solo flight for his personal collection. He finally found the plane in pieces in Aiken, South Carolina. An antique plane enthusiast owned the disassembled aircraft and had it stored in the basement of his house. Tom wooed the man for a year seeking to buy the Cub. At last his persistence paid off, and he purchased the conglomeration of parts. Eventually Tom oversaw this monument to his passion reassembled and restored to fly again. He was able to recapture the moment when he flew for the first time. His obsession with flying and airplanes stirred within him a drive that would later lead to spectacular achievements in aviation.[40]

By the time Tom graduated from high school, he had logged a considerable number of hours in the air, looking for any excuse to take him there. Among his favorite stories was how he flew to Greensboro on Saturdays for a hamburger. A restaurant beside Lindley Field, 17 miles from Winston-Salem, made his favorite burger. Instead of driving the distance Tom flew in his own Stinson Reliant to the air field, taxied to the eatery, which was located nearby along Highway 421, and pulled up beside the cars. The young pilot parked his airplane and waited for curb service just like the other customers in their automobiles.[41]

Tom Davis's interest in aviation might have been limited to piloting airplanes, had it not been for the encouragement and more importantly, the financial backing of his father, Egbert Sr. The elder Davis had been an integral part of Winston-Salem's largest enterprise, the R.J. Reynolds Tobacco Company. "E.L. Davis was R.J. Reynolds's first tobacco salesman and, upon retirement, added to this success in other business ventures," was the reputation of Egbert Sr. around town.[42] Tom's father seemed to have a Midas touch in all of his business undertakings. While at R.J. Reynolds, the elder Davis took over sales in the Chicago market to handle demand for the company's newest sensation, Camel Cigarettes. Egbert Davis, Sr. led an elite sales management team which helped propel the tobacco company to its ultimate status as the dominant cigarette maker in America.[43] After a brilliant career with R.J. Reynolds, the patriarch of the Davis clan started a successful plumbing, heating and air-conditioning supply company. Then he ventured into the clothing business with his brother, creating a department store that bore the Davis family name. Next, he went to work as a salesman for the small, Greensboro-based Security Life Insurance Company, boosting sales tremendously. Egbert Davis's effort was the catalyst that eventually helped propel the insurance company's transformation into Integon, an auto insurer that merged to become part of General Motors' credit division, GMAC.[44]

Egbert Sr. possessed several traits that he passed on to his sons, not the least of which were his business connections. "Daddy was a good businessman, a very good businessman. He therefore had a lot of very good businessmen as his friends and he helped Tom in that way," asserted Egbert Jr., who also noted that Tom was an apt pupil. "Tom was smart as a whip," he said.[45] Tom Davis also seemed to possess the same affable charm as his father. What gave Egbert Sr. the ability to sell both tobacco and insurance also furnished Tom with the growing reputation as a genial, easygoing young man with a promising future.

The Davis clan came to Winston-Salem from just up the road in Yadkinville, North Carolina. Tom's paternal grandfather, Eli Thomas Davis, owned two farms on the Yadkin River that produced tobacco for various companies in Winston-Salem, including Reynolds. Eli sent his son Egbert to school in Winston-Salem, followed by a course of study at Wake Forest College, located then in Wake Forest, North Carolina. Egbert Sr.'s plans to attend Harvard Law School were interrupted by appendicitis, and "he returned to Winston-Salem in 1906, where he was employed by his former high school principal in the sales department of R.J. Reynolds Tobacco Company."[46] From there he made his reputation and his fortune.

The Davis family had only a modest connection to the Reynolds family but the sons of each family shared a passion for planes. After 1925, the Egbert Davis, Sr. family left their downtown residence to move into a newly constructed, 5,100 square foot home called "Sunnynoll."[47] Living down the street from Reynolda Manor, Egbert Sr.'s sons watched eagerly when any of the Reynolds's family, which also included sister Mary Reynolds, took off from or landed on the family estate. Tom Davis was as enthusiastic as Smith about flying, but the Davis family never possessed the exorbitant wealth of the Reynolds family. They were affluent enough, however, to afford Tom's indulgence in more modest airplanes.

Though flying may have seemed to be Tom Davis's first choice for a profession, and even though his father reportedly said, "Yes Buddy, you can sure do that,"[48] Davis initially gravitated toward a more altruistic pursuit. The struggle with asthma caused Tom to commit himself to study medicine. Flying, he decided, should remain a hobby. After all, there were very few Charles Lindberghs and Davis lacked the resources to sustain a record-setting flight across Eurasia, as Smith Reynolds had done. Tom's empathy for others with the condition he had lived with since the age of two also moved him toward a career of service. He wanted a hands-on occupation where he could make a difference. Maybe he would find a cure for asthma, or become a surgeon.

In the fall of 1935, Tom Davis enrolled at the University of Arizona. The choice derived from an earlier family visit to California where an amazing thing occurred. Older brother Egbert Davis, Jr. said his father noticed "that when we got to Arizona, well Tom was just as free as a daisy. He could run and jump and had no asthma at all, to speak of."[49] Tucson did indeed provide a more arid climate which helped Tom to breathe and presented a more favorable environment for devoting himself to the task of studying medicine. To support the decision, the family purchased a home in Tucson for Tom's comfort. Egbert Jr. watched his brother's health improve dramatically, even during trips from Winston-Salem to Tucson. Tom's brother maintained, "We could help him get on an airplane here. He would have asthma

The home of adolescent Tom Davis, constructed by his father in 1925, was situated on 100 acres of land. From the yard Tom could witness the aerial antics of the Reynolds boys, whose home was less than a mile down the road (Ronnie Macklin Collection).

so much you'd sort of have to help him, hold his arm and so forth for him to get on the plane and he would get out to Arizona, and he would go upstairs and change his clothes right quick and go outside and play a game of basketball. It was a miracle."[50] It just so happened that the Arizona climate also provided excellent year-round flying weather.

Tom's fascination with aviation remained constant during his career at the University of Arizona, but his interest in becoming a doctor did not. Medicine slowly began to lose its appeal while Tom's attraction with flight and planes flourished to become his favored avocation. Flying for Tom replaced his earlier ambition to find a cure for asthma for a number of reasons, not the least of which included his stomach. It was said that "he was unable to stay in the premed program [beyond a bachelor's degree] because of the fumes from the chemicals in the science labs."[51] Life in an airplane provided much more fresh air.

The young collegiate made the most of his situation, despite the changes in his personal attitudes and interests. Having already acquired his commercial pilot's rating, Tom's proficiency in the cockpit proved beneficial while completing his bachelor's degree. Upon contacting the airport operator in Tucson, Tom eagerly accepted part time work giving flying lessons, sometimes even to his fellow university students, for a dollar an hour.[52] The relationship with Tucson's community of airplane pilots grew to the point that Tom assisted regularly in the aerial delivery of newspapers. Remembering the experience well, he said, "We had an open-cockpit plane, with space for two in the front cockpit, one in the rear. We'd put the newspapers in bags and load them into one of the forward seats and then we'd fly to little towns around Tucson, like Benson, Wilcox and Safford, and we'd swoop low and slide the bags off the wing onto the ground."[53]

Tom took advantage of every opportunity to fly, whether it involved instructing new students or delivering papers. He increased his flight hours and his skills as a pilot. His devotion to flight continued to flourish, and a career in flying became a likely alternative to medicine. Trips back and forth between Winston-Salem, North Carolina, and Tucson, Arizona, only added to his comfort in the air. He flew his own four-seat Stinson Reliant, and by the time Tom left the University of Arizona just short of a four year degree, he had actually received an additional and much more useful education in flight.[54] However, the question of how to get into a business connected with airplanes remained unanswered. Unlike medicine, there was no residency, no standard means of entry. Tom would have to make his own breaks in this relatively new but growing field.

Flying back in to Winston-Salem in the spring of 1939, Tom Davis returned with some answers about the direction of his life. He had earned credits toward a pre-med degree but had no desire to become a doctor. His experience in Tucson had not been wasted, though. The dry desert air had strengthened his lungs to the point that he was no longer constantly bothered by asthma. Looking back, he admitted, "I don't think I would have been able to come back here and live all these years in the good health I have enjoyed without those four years in Arizona."[55] The issue of a career choice was simply to follow his desire, which led him back to Miller Field.

What he found was the remnants of the company Dick Reynolds had started just before Lindbergh visited in 1927. Reynolds Aviation sputtered after its mishaps and, by the early thirties, reverted to its original status as a fixed base operator. That meant that the company engaged in the support services of aircraft repair, maintenance and storage, flight training, and charter services. The company was the authorized dealer of both Taylor Cubs (Piper Cubs after 1938), which were small aircraft, and Stinson Reliants, larger, more luxurious planes. The company, however, no longer bore the Reynolds name. Putting the company assets to work under the name Camel City Flying Service, Dick Reynolds had chosen his father's most famous cigarette brand to identify his aviation company. To manage the operation, Dick Reynolds turned to his chief pilot, Mac McGinnis, who had a thorough knowledge of aviation, but no real business experience. According to some, it may have been McGinnis who even proposed the new venture. Either way, McGinnis ran Camel City with assets that were supplied by his boss, Dick Reynolds.

When Tom Davis approached his old flight instructor about a job, he was surprised and delighted to find that Mac had an opening for a salesman. Tom quickly accepted the position. He recalled, "The pre-med training I had received at the University of Arizona was quickly forgotten and I jumped at the chance to be paid to fly rather than having to rent an airplane to build up my flight time."[56] Tom went around the state setting up dealerships and making pitches to potential customers.[57] While the job was a welcome entry into the aviation business, thirty years later he would look back on the position as more of a transition than a destination. Tom remembered clearly his most out-of-the-ordinary sales call, which took place in a cow pasture-turned-landing strip near Mt. Airy, in the fall of 1940:

> After a demonstration flight with my customer, we were sitting on a log just outside the fence and I was giving him the old sales pitch.... I noticed the wings of my airplane rocking back and forth.... There was the biggest black bull I've ever seen pushing the wing tip of my pretty, shiny, bright red Cub Coupe up and down with his horns.... I jumped over the fence and

tried to scare him off by waving my briefcase.... All he did was ... start snorting and pawing the ground as if I were his next target. It occurred to me that the only [way to] frighten him off was [with] the noise of the engine.... There were no starters on most airplanes and to start them you had to pull the propeller through sharply by hand. I ran around to the other side of the airplane, reached in and turned the switch, went back around to the front and pulled that prop ... hoping and praying all the time that the engine would start on the first pull. It did, and ... the bull turned tail and ran.... Without a word to my prospect, I jumped in and took off.... I never got an order from that man. That's about the time I decided I wanted to be an officer instead of a salesman.[58]

The incident with the bull may have dampened Tom's enthusiasm for selling airplanes, but not for building an aviation company. It soon became evident that the business needed his help. As it turned out, Tom became something of a doctor after all and pumped new life into a faltering business. The deal between McGinnis and Reynolds included loans from the tobacco millionaire to establish Camel City Flying Service with planes from the old Reynolds Airways. The company "was the largest aircraft sales and service, repair and flight training operation between Washington and Atlanta."[59] A 1937 *Official Aviation Guide* showed Camel City as the only company providing charter air service (flying Stinson Reliants) in the upper South and one of only six in the entire South.[60] As unique and multifaceted as the operation was, Mac McGinnis had been unable to turn Camel City Flying Service into a profitable enterprise.

Dick Reynolds, who recognized Tom Davis as a "smart and a fine pilot"[61] as well as a "young man of some means," could claim some responsibility for Tom's move into management.[62] The circumstances of their transaction have several versions, including a casual mention and an authorized business proposal. According to a Rotary Club salute to Tom Davis after his death, the connection was made "at a membership dance on the opening of the Old Town Club in 1940." At that event of Winston-Salem's elite, "Dick Reynolds asked Tom's older brother Egbert if Tom might be interested in buying out Dick's interest in the business."[63] Another version described a more formal approach made through Charlie Norfleet, trust department officer with Wachovia Bank. Norfleet also served as commission secretary of what was originally known then as Miller Field, later Z. Smith Reynolds Airport. According to that account, related by Tom himself, "One day, Charlie called me down to his office and asked if I would be interested in becoming more permanently and financially involved in the aviation business and, if so, Dick would like to talk to me. That afternoon, I went by Dick's house and he suggested that if I would pay off Mac's note, he would see that I became principal stockholder of the company. That event led to the dissolution of Camel City Flying Service and the formation of Piedmont Aviation, Inc."[64]

Regardless of which version brought Tom into the ownership picture, he readily jumped at the opportunity. The company Tom Davis bought into had numerous assets he felt could be used as the basis on which to build a successful company. What he got for his investment of $14,487[65] was several airplanes, two small hangars, and office space in an old house at Winston-Salem's Miller Field. Camel City also held distributorship rights for the most popular brands of small planes. At the time of transition, the company employed up to six people.[66] One of those employees was a young man by the name of Eddie Culler. Like Tom Davis, Culler was fascinated with flying. He described himself as an "airport bum" hanging around Miller Field (later Smith Reynolds Airport) after school and on weekends. He helped out any way he could in order to be around airplanes. Mac eventually put him on the payroll making twelve dollars per six day week. More importantly, the young man got 30 min-

Camel City–Piedmont mechanic Ed Culler in front of a Fairchild KR34. Culler began with the airline in 1940, even before Tom Davis bought part interest in the company. Culler spent the next 46 years with Piedmont (Piedmont Aviation Historical Society; from the collection of Ed Culler).

utes of free flying time each week.[67] Culler remembered doing everything from "sweeping hangars to gassing airplanes."[68] Eddie Culler and Tom Davis epitomized the generation of boys brought up on barnstormers and as young men were ready to devote their careers to the possibilities of aviation. Tom Davis took his small but enthusiastic workforce and put them to work.

Before jumping into the venture financially, Tom discussed the opportunity with his father, Egbert Sr., who had demonstrated his own entrepreneurial talents in companies like Davis Department Store and Security Life and Trust Company.[69] The elder Davis contributed more than advice to the decision. Egbert Jr. recalled that his father helped Tom "sell stock and to get some money and put money in it himself."[70] If his baby boy was not going to be a doctor, Egbert Sr. hoped Tom would be a successful businessman, as he himself was.[71] The arrangement made Mac McGinnis and his former pupil equal partners in the venture with each holding from 45 to 48 percent as their share of the company. The remaining company stock was controlled by Camel City's chief pilot Frank Groat, a friend of Mac's, and Milton Fare, accountant for the company.[72]

What did a kid fresh out of college bring to this sputtering endeavor that gave his father hope of success? The fact is that Tom Davis had indomitable leadership qualities that brought success to a failing company soon after he joined. In essence, he embraced three types of skills that served him well. First, he made sure he knew about all aspects of his product. Many employees would later comment on Davis's ability to stop and "talk shop" with them. As friend and associate John G. Medlin put it, "He knew every nook and cranny of that business." Secondly, a college friend who would later work for Tom, Bob Northington, Sr., defined one of Tom's great talents as "vision and integrity," observing that the man "wanted to do business in a fair and progressive way."[73] But maybe his most outstanding ability was in handling people. Northington, Medlin, and just about every person who worked with Tom Davis through the years remarked on his knack with people. According to Medlin, "He was imbued with a sense of caring and that showed through his employees."[74] The investment in Camel City Flying Service gave Tom an opportunity to put those skills to work.

Tom demonstrated his ability to see far into the future when one of his first acts after acquiring almost half of the company was to change its name. Camel City was a clear reference to Winston-Salem. Tom saw the name as a "bit confining"[75] because he had larger landscapes in mind. Since the company handled sales of Piper Cubs and Stinson airplanes throughout North Carolina, the name had to reflect a wider territory for the new venture.

On July 2, 1940, Camel City Flying Service received a corporate charter as Piedmont Aviation, Inc. The new name was the brainchild of the smart, young administrator whose money had resuscitated the company. However, he did not become president of this new incarnation. As part of a compromise, 22 year-old Tom Davis took the seat of vice-president and treasurer for the company, while Mac McGinnis remained president. The new five-member board of directors included the stockholders as well as Tom's older brother, Egbert Jr. This suggestion was probably at the recommendation of their father.[76] Piedmont's two leaders soon concentrated their individual efforts in different parts of the operation, McGinnis in the maintenance area, Davis in flight operations.[77] Mac also continued to serve as pilot for Dick Reynolds when necessary, as he had done during the days of Camel City.[78]

Mac McGinnis and Tom Davis were as different as night and day. Bill Barber, who

The two creators of Piedmont Aviation, Tom Davis (left) and Lewin "Mac" McGinnis. Mac gave flight lessons to Tom as a boy and a job to the young college graduate. When they went into business together, they were a team of "fire and ice." Mac proved to be quick tempered while Tom was the calm, analytical type (Piedmont Aviation Historical Society; from the collection of Zeke Saunders).

worked for both men, described Mac McGinnis as a hothead. "He'd fire me in a minute. Sometimes he'd fire me two or three times a day. And sometimes I'd go three or four days without being fired. But that was the kind of fellow he was."[79] In contrast, he remembered Tom Davis as the calm one who reassured him that he had a job even after dismissal by Mac. In Barber's opinion, "Tom always ran it."[80] Bill Barber felt no real animosity toward his mercurial boss, saying that "McGinnis was a good fellow. He just had a short fuse."[81] Conversely though, he also liked the way Tom Davis did business, saying, "If you went to him with a problem it was solved right there."[82]

The firing incidents were not unique between Bill Barber and Mac McGinnis. Mac engaged in momentary conflict with almost all of his employees. Barber remembered that the head mechanic named Reynolds (a distant relation to the tobacco family) and Mac "fought all the time."[83] Harold K. "Zeke" Saunders had similar experiences with McGinnis, though he admitted that they became good friends years later. "Mac got upset with me one day for the way I was flying an airplane and fired me, but Tom hired me right back."[84] According to Zeke, the incident resulted from "outside looping a P-19. [Mac] said I reamed the bars out on it. He carried on for a while.... The FAA guy was there and he said you couldn't outside loop a P-19. Well, I had been doing it so I knew you could. So he said, 'I'll bet anyone a hundred dollars you can't.' So I said, 'I'll bet you a hundred dollars you can,' and I went up and did it and Mac saw me do it. And he said [I was] trying to tear my [Piedmont's] damned airplanes up, blah, blah, blah. He got kind of hot headed. He got over it."[85] Despite their mercurial relationships with McGinnis, both Zeke Saunders and Bill Barber later became vice presidents for Tom Davis.

Even with the personality conflicts, Tom put his full energy into improving the business. "To help meet the payroll, we also hopped passengers over town on Sunday afternoon sightseeing tours for three dollars a head,"[86] he recalled. From the Winston-Salem base, Piedmont toiled to establish "seventeen sales and repair parts dealerships throughout North Carolina,"[87] which made the company into something of a powerhouse in the southeastern section of the nation. According to Tom, "By the time World War II started, we had more dealers and were selling more aircraft in the state than all our competitors combined. In fact, we had become one of the largest wholesale aircraft distributors in the U.S."[88] Tom stayed very busy, developing plans to construct a new hangar and engine shop in addition to his regular duties.[89]

Those who were a part of the early days of Piedmont saw Tom Davis give the business his full attention, as well as plenty of his sweat; many years later, Tom's work ethic is still remembered. A Piedmont mechanic asserted, "He hasn't forgotten what it was like to get grease under his fingernails reworking the piston heads on a balky Waco bi-plane at 3 [A.M.] so the bright-faced, would-be pilots would have something to fly at 7 in the morning."[90] Giving everything to make the business successful was a principle that permeated the workings of Piedmont Aviation from top management throughout the ranks. The attitude was instilled by Tom Davis. Fellow board member Egbert Davis, Jr. described his little brother: "He knew how to hire good people and keep them happy. They stuck to him like chewing gum."[91] To make Piedmont Aviation a success, Tom Davis was going to need those good people.

Piedmont's most critical early venture was a contract with the United States government to train pilots for combat and serve as an authorized repair facility for military aircraft. By the summer of 1941, Piedmont Aviation's first birthday, the United States War Department was gearing up for another global conflict, the second in twenty-five years. The government needed trained pilots and ground crew ready to fly combat missions. At first, the administration wanted these Civilian Pilot Training (CPT) programs conducted in the academic setting of colleges and universities throughout the United States. However, not enough institutions of higher learning could be secured for instruction and the government opened the program to "non-college training centers." Piedmont's Winston-Salem base was chosen as a site, with the initial training contract secured by Tom Davis.[92] In addition, Piedmont expanded its overhaul and maintenance shops for the government. By 1941 the company "became the first aircraft and engine overhaul shop approved by the Civil Aeronautics Administration between Washington and Atlanta. The employee staff grew from 10 to 100."[93] Piedmont Aviation began to expand.

Among the growing list of Piedmont employees was the occasionally fired but always rehired Zeke Saunders. Another young man spellbound by airplanes, Zeke was managing the Martinsville, Virginia, airport when offered the job as a flight instructor at Piedmont Aviation. Saunders pre-trained cadets in the basics of aeronautics, essentially giving them a background upon which the military could build: "[I] just started them out in a Cub and got them about 50 hours, then they went into the Air Force," he said.[94] Some pupils received more advanced training, depending on their prewar experiences in the cockpit. Zeke stayed ahead of all of them, instructing in a variety of areas. "I taught acrobatics for about a year, I taught cross-country and sensor reliance about another year."[95] The demand for instruction increased as the war revved up in both the European and Pacific theaters. Zeke pointed out that Piedmont was fully engaged in the war effort, with not one, but two schools for pilot training. "We ran the big school in Winston-Salem which included the primary, the acrobatics, the cross-country and the instructors, and in Greensboro, we ran another school,"[96] where the more basic pre-training took place.

In the middle of the Civilian Pilot Training program, the leadership agreement within the Piedmont management structure began to deteriorate. By 1943, Davis's stake in the company had gone up while McGinnis's went down. It wasn't just a personality contest that Tom was winning. According to reports of company records, Mac's stock totaled $11,510 while Tom's had increased to $18,460. No explanation of the disparity has ever been given, but in all likelihood, Mac cashed in some of his stock which Tom then enthusiastically bought. The imbalance gave Tom the leverage he needed to gain control of the company. Tom convinced subordinate company officials Frank Groat and Milton Fare, who owned a small number of shares in the company, to vote for him as the new president of Piedmont Aviation. Subsequently, Mac was relegated to a secondary position.[97] Quickly following the indignity, Mac McGinnis left for service in the military (training pilots) while Tom Davis took full control.[98] Following the shakeup Tom remained guarded about his old flight instructor and business partner and rarely commented on him except to say, "Mac [McGinnis] was a good pilot, a good friend and a wonderful mechanic, but he wasn't much of a businessman."[99] The tension continued until 1946 when McGinnis was denied a seat on the board of directors.[100] He then sold his remaining shares in Piedmont. By that time, he had moved to San Diego to accept a job as pilot for Consolidated Aviation.[101] He later became a test pilot for Bendix Corporation and eventually a technical representative for airplane manufacturer Fairchild.

Mac McGinnis died in 1954 from lung cancer. Before his death, he sought out his old friend and employee Zeke Saunders, who remembered the circumstances of the diagnosis.

> He called me and asked me if I would take him over to the hospital, said he had to have a physical. I told him sure. He had borrowed an airplane from Joe Dyer, who was running Florida Airlines at the time. Joe was from Winston and one of Mac's former students. So I took him to the hospital and told him to call me when he was finished. He called me about 4:30 and I went over and picked him up. He was just chit-chatting and he talked a lot. And I

asked him, how did it work out? He said, "Hell, they tell me I'm going to die in six weeks, said I've got lung cancer." He did.[102]

Once Mac had left from Piedmont, Tom Davis flew into action as the director of Piedmont Aviation's future. Not only was he now company president, but he also continued in the office of treasurer and remained on the board of directors.[103] Because of his leadership position, Tom was becoming Winston-Salem's next aviation hero, putting into action Lindbergh's challenge from years before.

During the World War II years, Piedmont Aviation focused heavily on the CPT program and airplane maintenance operations, while bringing along some of its young talent. Early employees like Eddie Culler were proving themselves valuable to the company. In three short years, Culler had gone from general employee to lead mechanic for Piedmont; he was "one of the youngest in the business."[104] While some of Piedmont's best — like Eddie Culler, Bill Barber, and Zeke Saunders — left to join the armed services, Tom Davis stayed in Winston-Salem. His asthma exempted him from being drafted, so he served where he could, eventually attaining the rank of major in the Civil Air Patrol.[105] More importantly, he served in a

Circa 1943. Mechanics in the engine overhaul shop repair Lycoming engines from a Stinson airplane and a Piper J-3. Left to Right, Ed Culler, Red Willard, Othel Wagner, Cliff Rowe, Bill Swaim, Jason Rowe, and Mr. Wheeler (Piedmont Aviation Historical Society; from the collection of Ed Culler).

vital role as support service for the U.S. government by operating the Civilian Pilot Training program, which continued to expand. As one of only twelve "type A" training schools in the United States, the boys in Winston-Salem were relied upon to handle even greater needs. Increasing numbers of civilians seeking to become pilots, ground crew, or mechanics in the armed forces received reliable training from Tom's crew.

In the summer of 1941, Piedmont Aviation faced its first setback: A fire in the company's new hangar destroyed 15 planes late in the evening of August 13. Six of the aircraft belonged to private owners and were maintained by the fixed base operation while the other nine were used as CPT training planes. Upon discovering the blaze, Piedmont employees heroically managed to wheel three planes to safety as fire leapt from one plane to the next, as gas tanks exploded, which hampered firefighting efforts. The destructive effects of the flames totaled $50,000 in losses. However, damage to the hangar was "superficial," and insurance covered the loss of the aircraft. Several theories were offered about how the fire started, including the possibility of spontaneous combustion, but no official cause was ever assigned.[106] Tom Davis refused to allow an unfortunate event like a fire to quell his burgeoning business. And luckily, his track record with the federal government helped Piedmont to expand through the adversity.

The government's third CPT program contract offered to Piedmont was a greater challenge than any task yet asked of Tom Davis and his employees. The State Department wanted Piedmont's flight school to "train pilots from Central and South American countries."[107] Having

Smith Reynolds Airport from the air during World War II. Rows of tents line the foreground next to Liberty Street. Across the runway is Piedmont Aviation's hangar (courtesy Piedmont Aviation Historical Society; from the collection of Ronnie Macklin).

successfully graduated one class per month under the previous two contracts, Piedmont accepted the offer. Latin-American pilots presented unique problems for Tom and his staff of instructors. The first obstacle was the language barrier. Most students spoke very little, if any, English. "We had an instructor named [Rockwell S.] Boyle who had been raised in Brazil and spoke Portuguese," said Tom. "He worked out a rough sign language for the other instructors to use."[108] Ultimately, Tom's school hired college professors to teach English to these students.[109]

Language was not the only challenge presented by the third contract. There was a second obstacle involving the level of experience these students had, which was mostly none. As a result, some of these students caused minor accidents during their training and several ran their airplanes off the runway.[110] There was also difficulty managing the trainees because, as Zeke Saunders recalled, "They threatened to call [U.S. Secretary of State] Cordell Hull" anytime they were censured.[111] A third major problem in fulfilling the contract was the difference in lifestyle habits of the Winston-Salem trainers and some of the South American trainees. One example involved a student who brought both his wife and his girlfriend, presumably separately, with him when he entered the school. The trainee housed each in rooms at Winston-

The first group of flight instructors for Piedmont Aviation, posing in 1942. These men taught basic flight instruction as part of 13 civilian training facilities nationwide. Zeke Saunders is second from the right on the front row (courtesy Piedmont Aviation Historical Society; from the collection of Zeke Saunders).

Salem's Hotel Robert E. Lee directly adjacent to his room, one on each side. The arrangement, known by all the parties involved, created quite a stir among the folks at Piedmont, to the point that in later years Tom Davis would joke that the loss of his hair was a result of fulfilling the South American contract.[112] The Latin American students ultimately proved to be good pilots and Tom Davis looked back on that third contract with pride. "Many of those South Americans went home to set up training programs for their own air forces.... I still get Christmas cards from some of those folks," he said in 1977.[113]

By any measurement, the Civilian Flight Training Program administered by Piedmont Aviation was a success. Teaching mathematics, navigation, and meteorology to over one thousand students and graduating 18 classes under three separate government contracts had been quite an undertaking, but Piedmont's growing stable of professionals met the challenge. Tom and his trainers adapted well to the situations they encountered, as they did with the South American contract. "The one thing of which we are most proud during this period is our safety record. Of the hundreds of students we trained for the war, not a single one suffered a serious injury."[114]

World War II offered many advantages for Piedmont Aviation but also some disadvantages, at least temporarily. Both Bill Barber and Zeke Saunders left to join the armed services. Bill served stateside from the time he entered the Army Reserves. Zeke joined the Air Force, where he flew over 136 round trip missions, piloting C-47s across the "hump," traversing the forbidding Himalayas from Burma to China. Bob Northington, Howard Cartwright, and Eddie Culler also left to serve their country. All would eventually return. Tom Davis remained in close contact with his employees, even as the absence of some of them going off to war caused a scramble for temporary replacements. Tom knew good people when he found them and refused to let a world war interfere with keeping them. This interest in people was just part of Tom's personal touch that brought many back to the company and eventually made Piedmont into more of a family than a business.[115]

Tom's recognition of great talent was never more evident than with his discovery of Zeke Saunders. Harold K. Saunders grew up a skinny farm boy near the Catawba River about 40 miles west of Winston-Salem. He learned to fly while in high school, following in the footsteps of several older brothers who owned planes. He developed a special affinity for performing acrobatic tricks while in the air. As a flight instructor in Martinsville, Virginia, Saunders met an energetic young man selling Piper and Stinson aircraft. Zeke's whimsical remembrance was that Tom Davis "had to come up to Martinsville about once a week because they didn't have any alcohol stores in North Carolina, so they had to buy their whiskey in Virginia." Zeke bought his first plane, a yellow Piper Cub, from Tom Davis in 1940.[116] The relationship continued to build as Zeke recalled, "About the time the war was starting, he asked me if I would come down there and go to work for him as a flight instructor, which I did."[117]

It was during this period prior to the war when Tom Davis dubbed Harold Saunders "Zeke." The nickname stuck and has become a symbol of respect among those who have known him. Saunders recalled the events leading up to the moment he became "Zeke."

> They [Piedmont] had three of the Fairchilds and two of the Wacos and they had them to teach acrobatics in. They had two instructors assigned to each airplane. One flew it from six in the morning until twelve noon, with students, and then the other one flew it from twelve until six in the afternoon. On winter mornings, it would get awful cold in the back seat of that airplane, even with fur lined suits on. And there was this picture called *Sergeant York* where he [Alvin York] said he was going to get him a piece of bottom land, that it was better than fighting this war [World War I.] So when I got out of the airplane, I had in mind I was

Zeke Saunders boarding his Waco plane at age 19 in Martinsville, Virginia (1941). His stunt flying as a youth led to his work as a trainer for Piedmont Aviation, flying the "Hump" in China during World War II and returning to Piedmont for a long, distinguished career (courtesy Piedmont Aviation Historical Society; from the collection of Zeke Saunders).

> going to quit. I told Tom I could get me a piece of bottom land and make a better living without freezing to death on it. Tom said, "Now 'Zeke,' get back in that airplane." The other instructors heard him and they started calling me Zeke, and that's how I got the name Zeke.[118]

Saunders accepted the new name with ease. Throughout his entire career with Piedmont, those who did not refer to him formally as Mr. Saunders just called him Zeke. Most probably did not know that actually Harold was his given name. In future years, Tom Davis would call upon Zeke regularly to help him keep Piedmont Aviation operating.

By 1944, Piedmont had grown into a large organization but had no way to expand any farther. The end of World War II meant the company would, by necessity, have to return to its pre-war minuscule size. "Toward the end of the war, we recognized the fact that we could not provide jobs for the large number of employees used in our training program if we simply reverted to the fixed base, general aviation sales and service business,"[119] Tom lamented. In fact, the War Department officially informed Piedmont Aviation in January of 1944 that the CPT program was to be shut down.[120] Tom Davis searched for other profitable opportunities. With over 100 people on the payroll, his toughest decision would be whom to let go.

Tom Davis's Piedmont Aviation in 1943 after the departure of Mac McGinnis. All company personnel, including mechanics, office personnel and instructors, pose in front of the aircraft that students took up into the air. In all, over 1000 graduated from the school (courtesy Piedmont Aviation Historical Society; from the collection of Ronnie Macklin).

But Tom Davis was looking much farther into the future than that, saying, "just because the war was over, I didn't want to turn them out in the cold."[121]

He began to consider the future of commercial air travel. Prior to the war, the commercial market had remained small. Potential passengers had any number of reasons to stay away from air travel. An airplane was considered risky, with crashes well publicized. Flights were so expensive that Pan American Airlines offered loans to pay for fares. And connecting points ranged only from one metropolitan area to another. Few medium-sized cities and zero small towns found their way onto flight schedules. Undaunted, Tom began to conceive a scenario in which he might address most, if not all, of these issues as well as provide future employment to his staff. Tom Davis wanted to start an airline.

• 2 •

First Flight, 1944–1948

Skies cleared for takeoff. A group of grey-suited men gathered with coffee cups in the terminal, minutes before 7 A.M. Huddled together, they moved out to a shiny, silver plane. Wearing hats and overcoats, they shivered and talked as the sun began its climb above the landscape. A thin man with a warm smile braved the winter morning without his overcoat, then removed his hat and turned to the others to welcome them, occasionally referencing the aircraft which waited silently on the runway nearby. He acknowledged the hard work and enormous effort which brought them to this point, telling his audience, "It's been a long pull and we're glad to get it started at last."[1]

It was an auspicious day but very cold. The purser welcomed the entourage, and they disappeared beyond the door into the plane as nine sacks of cargo were shoved into the baggage section. Once the passengers were secured, the wheel chocks were kicked away. The captain and co-pilot taxied into takeoff position down the runway. The plane turned to face the long expanse of empty field. It sat there for a moment like a restless bird as its engines came to life with the opening throttles. Suddenly, the DC-3 aircraft surged forward as the brakes released, sending the plane thundering down the runway to lift slowly into the air above Wilmington, North Carolina's Bluethenthal Field. The few people left on the ground waved to the sky; they became dots in the distance as Flight 41 charged into the air. The plane turned, dipping its wings to the group of shivering fans, slowly moving beyond their vision to begin its historic journey. Piedmont Airlines was at last in business and ready to serve the public. Flight captain Leon Fox looked back on the gathering with its small festivities and said, "We didn't start out with a big bang, I guarantee you."[2]

As master of ceremonies for the informal event, Tom Davis had reason to grin. He had waited patiently for this morning, Friday, February 20, 1948, while dodging numerous obstacles that threatened to keep his new enterprise on the ground. A shy, slender man with a rapidly receding hairline, Tom Davis looked much older than his 29 years. He also possessed a charming personality. That morning, Davis chatted with mayors, commissioners and chamber of commerce heads, all dignitaries from the towns through which this flight would pass. He took great satisfaction in seeing this particular flight take off because he knew he had proved many critics wrong.

"When he first mentioned this [starting an airline], some people kind of laughed at the idea," responded an unnamed acquaintance, years later.[3] After all, what was Piedmont Aviation but a few old planes, a couple of hangars, all run out of an old house at a small airport with employees made obsolete by the end of the war? And Tom Davis was a generally untested leader. His fortune during the war could have been chalked up to being in the right place at the right time. Skeptics might have seen him better suited to a return to fixed base operations

Inside a DC-3 with Tom Davis (front left) as he travels his airline with his most important cargo, passengers (courtesy Piedmont Aviation Historical Society).

where his company started. But Tom Davis was no skeptic. He believed in his idea to the point that he analyzed all the possible impediments and then devised solutions to clear his path. Two days after receiving the telegram to end the CPT program, Tom Davis went to his board of directors to pitch an idea for expansion. Present were Tom and his brother Egbert, Jr., Mac McGinnis and Frank Groat. In the minutes of the meeting, Tom was directed "to explore the possibilities of airline, contract freight and airmail pickup operation for the company."4 With that command, a life-altering test for Tom Davis commenced.

Though Tom Davis was not prescient, he was perceptive and optimistic. Several factors supported Tom's confidence. First, though the totals were still small, Americans had begun to embrace air travel in greater numbers after World War II, thanks in part to the wartime experience of millions of soldiers who flew or received air support. These veterans believed in the solidity of the technology and saw no reason to fear flying. Secondly, the post-war economy boomed, making once expensive ticket prices more affordable. With the proliferation of the automobile, Americans began to travel extensively. Piedmont offered a direct alternative to cars and buses for those who wanted to move even faster than the new interstate highway system could take them. Travelers, especially those with business to conduct, looked to the air. Next, Tom Davis chose not to compete against the already established air carriers directly. His interest concerned a smaller piece of the pie, one overlooked by the major commercial haulers. He sought out the "short hop service,"5 and was happy to serve the upper Southeast. Lastly, he already had a number of excellent employees who would again be available after the war. When he told Hoss Dobbins, on a brief stopover at Smith Reynolds Airport during the war, "You boys get all the experience you can because we're going to have an airline after the war," Tom Davis was already starting to pencil in his raft of pilots.[6]

In June of 1944, the *Winston-Salem Journal* reported the news: "Piedmont Aviation Seeks Permit for 9 Local and Feeder Lines." Less than six months after the military notified him that the Civilian Pilot Training program was ending, Tom publicly revealed his intentions and began the process to gain government approval to start an airline. In part, the newspaper account read, "Piedmont Aviation, Inc., has filed application with the Civil Aeronautics Board for a certificate to operate nine local and feeder routes for passenger, mail, express and property pick-up service covering cities and towns with a total population of approximately six and a half million."[7] Though passengers were the objective of this new "Piedmont Airlines," Davis wanted to carry anything he could profitably haul through the air. His application sought permission to also carry mail, express packages and cargo. According to the article, "Planes would stop regularly at the scheduled stops and would stop only when flagged at flag stops. At the pickups, the planes would come in low enough to pick up the mail from automatic pickup devices."[8]

The plan to provide passenger service to the masses had changed dramatically from the time when Piedmont's predecessor, Reynolds Airways, attempted a similar feat almost twenty years earlier. Since then, the United States government had become involved in the process in a big way. Airplane crashes like the one suffered by Reynolds Airways brought a public outcry to protect passengers. The Civil Aeronautics Act of 1938 created a new regulatory body to oversee the airline industry. Since then, the governing body, known as the Civil Aeronautics Board (CAB), authorized every route run by every company in the effort to avoid cutthroat competition. The agency also kept tabs on business performance to make sure that passengers were transported safely. While Congress was at it, they gave the board authority over airmail and air cargo transport, which meant that if anyone wanted to fly anything for profit, the CAB had to approve.[9]

Though Tom Davis prepared his 170-page application to the CAB thoroughly, he had to fight strenuously to win approval. His request numbered just one of many received by the five-member CAB, seeking the certificate to fly routes from as far south as Charleston, South Carolina, to the Ohio Valley. In all, Tom competed against 25 other applicants, who sought a total 45 different routes throughout the United States.[10] Tom brought strong analysis to his proposal, specifically stating how he intended to handle financial aspects of the business. Many of the other applicants left those details vague.[11] Piedmont also had connections in many of the proposed route cities thanks to the sale of Piper and Stinson airplanes at many airports. Opponents were less specific on finances and facilities, saying they planned to deal with such issues after receiving the nod for the certificate. And thanks to the legacy of Camel City Flying Service, Tom and Piedmont sported a proven track record, displaying growth and a good working relationship with the United States government, reflected by contracts to train World War II pilots. The only area Tom Davis didn't thoroughly outline in his plan was his choice of cities served. Although he stated his preference, he left the CAB the latitude to plug the carrier into routes they thought best suited Piedmont.

In the post-war world, the government had opened up the airline business for what it called regional, or "feeder," airlines. The main routes of U.S. air travel were the domain of a core of airlines known as the "Big Four": United, American, Trans-World, and Eastern had all the profitable trips between large cities sewn up. These routes, called "trunk" lines, handled all traffic between the major metropolitan areas. In an effort to spread air travel to more of the nation, the new offering from the CAB granted service rights to applying airlines to carry passengers from smaller cities to ones served by the Big Four. These airlines would gather air travelers from smaller geographical regions and feed them into the routes of the trunk carriers. The plan's design did not challenge the "old boys" but instead supported them. The rights to take these trips were a hot commodity for many operators, like Piedmont, who felt themselves worthy of becoming a small airline.

Tom Davis displayed his ingenuity and innovation with the type of application he submitted. Defying conventional wisdom within the airline industry, he wanted his airline to fly across the Appalachian Mountains instead of around them. Like pioneering settlers from the early days of the republic, the mountain chain effectively blocked travel on a direct east-west basis from most of the Atlantic seaboard. Tom instead embraced the idea of an "air bridge" rather than traveling south to Atlanta or north to Washington, D.C., before crossing back and forth from the east coast to the Midwestern states.[12] He revealed his strategy years later when he noted that "prior to that time all the other airlines had simply followed the railroad up and down the coast. We figured there was a good opportunity for us to get our airline going by giving people direct service across the mountains."[13]

The Piedmont proposal advocated an innovative step that some competitors believed extended beyond the expertise of the folks from Winston-Salem. Tom Davis believed otherwise and said so. "We wanted to do something different so we started flying across the mountains." In retrospect, he also noted, "we were real trailblazers."[14] The new ground across which Piedmont was particularly suited to fly was known in CAB terms as "Route 87." The route took passengers back and forth from the Ohio Valley to the Atlantic coast.[15]

To handle the challenge, Tom Davis needed not only the staff already in place, but personnel who could implement and maintain additional support systems beyond maintaining and flying a fleet of planes. He needed people in reservations, station operations and baggage handling. Many of these people would have to come from the established airlines. Tom plucked several executives from Eastern Airlines, who in turn brought more. R.D. Hager, Lee Golson, Gordon Brown, and R.E. Turbiville all came from Eastern Airlines and brought considerable knowledge about how an airline was supposed to operate. Hager topped the list of qualifications with 17 years' experience. In his new duties at Piedmont, he also served as assistant to the president and as a member of the board of directors.[16] Golson had logged 10 years with Eastern before he came to Winston-Salem to handle sales and traffic. He brought right hand man Gordon Brown along, who served as assistant traffic manager. Turbiville left Eastern as the Winston-Salem station manager to oversee all stations for Piedmont.[17]

Another important find was Thelma Taylor, later Thelma Davis (no relation to Tom) and known by her colleagues as "T." She stepped in to develop a reservation system. A native of Pilot Mountain, just up the road from Winston-Salem, Thelma had worked at Eastern Airlines for a year and a half and knew the reservation process well enough to build one from scratch with the assistance of former Eastern colleague Gordon Brown.[18] Thelma Taylor brought her manuals from Eastern and enjoyed the challenge. She felt very positive about the viability of this new airline. She said, "We all worked together. If the floor needed sweeping we swept it. If the walkway needed to be cleaned, we cleaned it. We did whatever needed to be done because we were extremely interested in the airline getting off the ground."[19] Despite the challenges, enormous as they were, Tom Davis took comfort in the knowledge that he was getting the right people for the right job, a talent for which he would later be acclaimed. With such a skilled supporting staff, he felt the CAB would have no choice but to rule in Piedmont's favor.

The original lineup continued to literally be fleshed out.[20] New and necessary personnel came to the organization in as many different ways as there were individuals. Some, like

A social meeting of Piedmont personnel. Tom Davis talks shop with his colleagues, who include Ed Culler to Tom's right. Behind Culler is Bill McGee (courtesy Piedmont Aviation Historical Society; from the collection of Ed Culler).

Thelma Davis, brought previous airline experience which benefited her new employer. When he could, Tom drew from a talent pool that had been instrumental in securing three wartime contracts for the aviation company, including some, like Zeke Saunders and Bill Barber, who became available after the war. Another fruitful source of talent was the over one thousand well-trained graduates of Piedmont's own flight training school.

In 1946, as Tom made his case for a CAB route, his proposed airline was a business endeavor clouded in uncertainty. One of the original twelve pilots hired by Piedmont spoke explicitly about waiting for the CAB's decision. According to pilot Frank Nicholson, "We were on pins and needles waiting to see if we got the contract."[21] Despite the wait and indecision, gifted individuals continued to commit strongly to Tom Davis's dream and flocked to Winston-Salem, where collectively they set about building a company called Piedmont. Bill McGee, who came on board as superintendent of passengers, summed up the faith those early employees had in Tom Davis, "There was a great deal of confidence when we started."[22]

Among those who arrived early with faith in Piedmont's future success was Captain Bill Taylor. A South Carolina native, Taylor won a scholarship to Piedmont's Civilian Pilot Training school in 1942. Upon graduation in early 1943 and after acquiring his instrument rating in Denver, Colorado, Taylor jumped at the chance to return to Winston-Salem and become part of the human mechanism that would make the airlines prosper. "Before I had completed [instrument training], Tom Davis called saying he was enlarging the flight school. I had a flight instructor's certificate and a commercial [license]. He hired me and Glenn Hendrix over the telephone and we came right on back. We quit United Airlines and came back to work with Tom Davis."[23] He and Glenn Hendrix joined a group that also included Jack Tadlock, a member of Piedmont's first CPT graduating class.[24]

Expansion of the emerging enterprise required a unique ability to blend individuals together for the good of the organization. Tom Davis amassed a group of people he liked and trusted. From that time forward, a share of the burden to grow and improve rested on their shoulders. Zeke Saunders, in addition to becoming a lifelong friend of Tom's, proved to be an indispensable assistant in those days before the launch. He recalled the growing amount of responsibility presented to the company members as they set about establishing themselves in the aviation industry:

> [The job] entailed hiring the pilots, doing all the pilot training, getting the routes approved. Back then, still today, in order to get an airline route you have to write an operation manual: how you are going to operate, what training program you will be using, which airplanes you will be using. Then you have to get the government to ride with you over the routes that you plan. You do approaches and landings of those routes, and call up all your pilots. Each one has to go along and do a landing and take off and fly the route, to get approved on it — that type of work.[25]

As one of Piedmont's first employees, Zeke wore many Piedmont hats, some comfortable, some not. He recognized his limitations and had no problem acknowledging his discomfort or his lack of qualifications in assuming certain tasks. While writing the flight manuals, Zeke soon realized he was not the right man for the job. Quickly, he sought out another former CPT instructor, Bud Gilley, who had recently worked for the government, and as Zeke remembered it, "knew exactly what the government required." Though Zeke had become part of the operation before Bud Gilley and had actually recruited him for employment with the new airline, when the necessity of establishing seniority was mentioned, the two settled the issue like carefree young men: They flipped a coin. "When we set up the seniority list he and I matched for the number one position and I lost. I had the choice of being chief pilot, or being operations manager, so I chose the chief pilot's job."[26] This was how informal the circumstances were as the employees prepared and waited for the opportunities they felt certain lie ahead.

As Zeke mentioned, he then took on the job of hiring the rest of the pilot group. Since thousands had been trained for the cockpit by organizations like Piedmont Aviation, an abundance of well-qualified men were available, so Piedmont had its pick. When Zeke Saunders set about hiring the men who would take Piedmont aloft, he tended to look "for someone who had a lot of instrument flying time. Most of the air transport pilots who were in the military had that qualification. If I remember right, there was one Navy pilot and the rest of the captains were Air Force captains." But beyond the technical ability to take off and land an airplane, Zeke took a studied approach towards who would fit the job best. In a word, he wanted "character."

> When we first started out we tried to hire college people. But we soon found out that that was not the complete answer for an airline at the time. They were flying over; looking at the

same piece of ground day after day and it would get monotonous to them. So if you found a good high school graduate that was sharp and had a good character, he would do better, he would make a better pilot. The others were good pilots but they were too damned smart really. They wanted to do something else instead of look at that same piece of land every day. But we'd normally get our recommendations from the cities. Every city had some ex–Air Force pilot who came from a real nice family. They would call you and say this is a real good guy. You need to take a look at him. We'd get some of them from that and back then you knew most of the pilots around in the area, in North Carolina, Virginia. You usually personally knew them by that time.[27]

A good example that came along just after the airline got underway was Charlie Meacham. A North Carolina boy from Rockingham, like Zeke, he flew the "hump" in China during the war. Coming home, he wanted to stay in aviation and in North Carolina. After flying for a non-scheduled service called "Resort Airlines" he went to Winston-Salem upon hearing that Resort planned to relocate in Florida. The word from eastern North Carolina was that Charlie Meacham would be an asset to the company. When Piedmont Airlines began to expand its stable of pilots, Meacham flew for the airline until his retirement.

As the employee base grew, so did the strain and monotony of waiting to fly the first flight. If Piedmont had received an unfavorable answer to its application, many of these people would have to look elsewhere to find a job, and their trust in Tom Davis would have been ill founded. As an advocate, Davis fought hard for them, as well as for his company. He continued to operate as if his company would indeed, be awarded the flights he'd requested. He embodied the theory that success was contagious, that he must not allow his employees to become pessimistic or doubtful in any manner. Tom was fundamentally an optimist, an indispensable attitude for a man with such high goals.

As point man for the new enterprise, Tom Davis handled all aspects of the business. Securing financial backing proved to be perhaps his most crucial job. Without the necessary cash for "pre-operating expenses,"[28] the airline would remain a dream. Luckily, Tom's friend Charlie Norfleet believed in the future of Piedmont. A loan officer for Wachovia Bank, "Fat Charlie," as he was known by the Reynolds family, shared Tom's interest in flight.[29] Norfleet, at one time, headed Winston-Salem's Airport Commission as president. Tom approached his old friend for money. Knowing the young man, Norfleet felt confident that Tom Davis was a good risk and recommended financial assistance to help Piedmont Aviation. He convinced Wachovia Bank that an investment in an airline made sound financial sense and a loan was quickly approved. By the time Tom began to spend the money, his company counted over $300,000 in its coffers and had a green light to grow.[30] It is likely that Piedmont would never have gotten off the ground without the Wachovia seed money.

In many ways, Charlie Norfleet was the forefather of Piedmont Airlines. He was there at the time of Tom's purchase into Camel City Flying Service, seeing the true potential of Tom Davis's talent probably before anyone outside the Davis family. When the aviation company wanted to start regularly scheduled flights, he again proved to be a catalyst, assisting with financing to keep the venture moving forward. Without Charlie Norfleet, Tom Davis might have remained an airplane salesman and Camel City Flying Service would have crashed into bankruptcy.

The real obstacle to becoming an airline was the CAB certificate. Once in operation, however, government policy virtually assured financial success for an airline. It did so with subsidies. Since air carriers hauled mail as well as what passengers they could attract, they were guaranteed payment from the government for doing the service of transporting government property, U.S. mail. For any company in the business of air travel, the revenue from passenger trips was calculated as almost pure profit. The only catch stipulated by the CAB involved the amount of gain. The more an airline made from passenger and cargo revenue, the less the government paid in subsidies. Since the rate did not go down as fast as profits might go up, the incentive remained to increase the number of passengers as much as possible to maximize revenue. Tom Davis explained the process:

> The rationale behind the regional air carriers, officially recognized by the CAB in 1946, is to provide air service to the smaller cities across the country which don't really generate enough passengers or freight to justify the larger airlines' serving them on a purely profit-motivated basis. To encourage smaller airlines to take on the job, the federal government provides "public service revenues" to help support the service to cities which do not generate sufficient passenger traffic to take care of the cost of providing the service at the smaller points.[31]

Always one to spend his money wisely, another vital component of his success, Tom went looking for airplanes. Since all aircraft manufacturers had given full attention to the war effort, no new commercial passenger planes existed for purchase. They might have been too expensive anyway since Tom Davis had to divide his cash between planes and personnel. Looking for an economical, yet roomy commercial airliner, Piedmont chose the Douglas Commercial 3, or DC-3 for short, a plane designed in the mid–1930s. Douglas Aircraft retooled this plane for the war by making combat versions of the DC-3, designated mostly as the C-47 and C-53. The end of the war brought a glut of military surplus airplanes, which could easily be converted back to civilian passenger carriers, so the DC-3 remained a mainstay of the industry. Following the war, Douglas discontinued production, concentrating on development of the next generation of airplanes. Newer alternatives existed, but Tom Davis chose the cheaper, reliable, 21-passenger DC-3, leasing the first one from Southern Airways. Southern was another CAB applicant based in Birmingham, Alabama, seeking to become a feeder airline in the Deep South.[32]

According to Zeke Saunders, Southern Airways experienced its own logistical problems trying to get off the ground and rented a DC-3 to Piedmont as a trainer for the first group of pilots who would be "flying the line" soon. The next two planes were purchased from Colonial Airlines, a carrier in the northeast. Tom Davis personally selected these first planes for his operation. "Bud Gilley, one of our original pilots and I went to New York and looked the airplanes over," said Davis, looking back over the years. After inspection "[we] decided they were a good opportunity, well maintained, good shape, ready to go on the line. So he flew one back and I flew the other one back, in formation."[33] The cost to Piedmont Aviation: $110,000.[34]

In choosing the DC-3, Tom Davis simply followed in the footsteps of an industry that had grown to love this plane. American Airlines president C.R. Smith called it "the first airplane that could make money just by hauling passengers."[35] An airline historian went further, praising the model as "a well nigh perfect transport, striking a happy balance in speed, gross weight, power, payload space, and wing area."[36] By the time Piedmont began its fleet, the Douglas Aircraft no longer produced the DC-3, which meant that only used craft were available for purchase. This inconvenience did not discourage the growing airline industry from continuing to rely heavily on this particular model of airplane.

Commercial aviation manufacturers like Donald Douglas, whose company designed the original DC-3, knew only too well the drawbacks of a plane which had been designed ten years earlier. Without a pressurized cabin, temperatures could not be controlled easily, which

A Piedmont DC-3 waits at Winston-Salem's Smith Reynolds Airport, much like the two inaugural flights that passed through the home city in early 1948 (Ronnie Macklin Collection).

meant conditions ranged widely for passengers but especially the crew. In addition, the planes only seated 21 passengers, not bad for a flight in 1936 when Americans were still making up their mind about traveling by air, but less than ideal for a post–World War II venture intent on moving the masses. New alternatives provided by aircraft manufacturers, however, did not measure up to the DC-3 in terms of reliability and price. The DC-3 and its combat twin, the C-47, were plentiful after the war and ready for conversion to Piedmont Airline planes. Astutely, Tom Davis built his company around the DC-3.

A happy accident from the purchase of two planes from Colonial Airlines was the resulting archetype for a ready-made logo. As Coca-Cola has become known by its "fluid ribbon device" and Chevrolet by its "bow-tie," Tom Davis needed a symbol for the Piedmont Airlines. According to long-time Piedmont maintenance supervisor Ronnie Macklin, Piedmont found its logo on the side of one of the planes it had purchased. Macklin noted that the Colonial planes were "the guide for the first paint scheme for Piedmont Airlines." The name "Colonial" was removed from the side of the fuselage and over the passenger entry door. "Piedmont," in the same letter style, replaced Colonial. The Piedmont bird was similar to the Colonial insignia but two wings were added.[37] The three-winged bird was in keeping with an earlier logo for Piedmont Aviation. Thus, the symbol of Piedmont Airlines, the "Speedbird," as it was called, was born.

As companies lined up for the race to gain government approval to carry passengers, applicants overwhelmed the Civil Aeronautics Board. Instead of considering each separately, the government agency consolidated all the applications in the southeastern United States into the "Southeastern States Case." Deliberations began in June of 1945, as the war wound down.

A Colonial Airlines DC-3 like those purchased by Piedmont Airlines in 1947. Notice the logo for Colonial. The bird resembles the "Speedbird" later used by Piedmont (Ronnie Macklin Collection).

Throughout 1946, the CAB weighed one request against another, trying to determine which proposal best served the public. For Tom Davis, the process dragged on. Having recently married, Tom later credited his new wife with having played a greater role in gaining governmental approval than he did. He said, "Nancy stuck by me and patiently sat through many long, boring hearings of the CAB when we were battling for those airline routes. In fact, there are times when I am inclined to think she had more to do with our getting those routes than anyone else."[38] While Tom presented his case, answered questions, and waited, the employees of Piedmont continued to prepare for an affirmative answer to Tom's request.

Finally the wheels of bureaucracy ground out a decision on April 4, 1947. Only Piedmont and one other bidder, Southern Airlines from Birmingham, Alabama (the one from which Piedmont had leased its trainer plane), won a "Certificate of Public Convenience and Necessity." The five-member Civil Aeronautics Board granted Piedmont most, but not all, of Tom's request in the original application. Certainly, more than he expected was granted though.[39] The only problem with the certificate was that it was temporary. The board granted Piedmont and Southern two years to prove their worth to the flying public. Piedmont remained the only carrier in the mid–Atlantic region to receive the right to fly commercially, which included passengers, mail, and cargo.[40] It was a signal victory, one that Tom Davis celebrated by getting down to the business of transporting customers.

Preparations accelerated to launch the airline. Top management scheduled planes to begin service by September 1, 1947, but several complications persisted, mostly with the application itself.[41] When Tom Davis made the bid for Route 87, which included a total of nine routes, according to later litigants, he failed to specify concretely what he wanted to haul and where he wanted to go. He left the request open-ended enough to give the CAB room to assign the specific cities which it thought best for Piedmont to travel. However, this caused one of the disappointed applicants, State Airlines, to raise objections. In appealing the decision, State Airlines, a Charlotte, North Carolina–based company with no fleet and only a small employee base, contended that the process by which Piedmont had been awarded its route was inequitable. They complained of the unfairness to both State and other carriers, since in State's application they did not realize Piedmont would be a direct competitor for the same lines for which they were applying. State wanted an opportunity to compete head to head for each route awarded, calling upon officials from route destinations to testify about State's ability to serve more effectively than Piedmont.

Several established carriers also joined the State Airlines protest. Both Delta Airlines and Eastern Airlines saw the Piedmont award as too lucrative for the Winston-Salem company and complained that some of the lines awarded Piedmont looked more like trunk lines than feeder routes. Both Delta and Eastern did not want to see Piedmont grow to the point of challenging the market share that each enjoyed. State Airlines' fragile hopes to overturn the CAB decision blossomed with the assistance of two large airlines like Delta and Eastern.[42]

State, Delta, and Eastern Airlines took Piedmont, and the decision of the CAB, to court. In the United States Court of Appeals for the District of Columbia Circuit, the rejected carrier and its friends argued for a reversal of the decision based on three reasons. First, Piedmont had not filed for specific routes, and as such, rendered its application null and void. Secondly, since State Airlines competed, albeit unknowingly, head-to-head with Piedmont, Hank Gilbert, president of State Airlines, had no opportunity to compare his company directly with Piedmont Airlines.[43] Thirdly, lawyers for State insisted that the decision of the Civil Aeronautics Board was "in the legal sense, arbitrary and capricious and lacked the support of substantial evidence" and that the certificate should be awarded to State Airlines. The legal move kept Piedmont on the ground for the rest of 1947. The court froze Piedmont's first flight, but the Court of Appeals refused to hand over the routes to the plaintiff. With his company, his people and his future on the line, Tom Davis fought back.

An appeal of the appeal swung into action. Both the CAB and Piedmont petitioned the court for a review of the reversal while State asked again to be given the certificate. The question centered on the CAB's right to give routes to applicants. State Airlines argued that the board overstepped its legal authority by awarding the certificate to a company which State saw as an inferior applicant. Lawyers for all three groups quickly found themselves arguing their respective cases to the United States Court of Appeals. While the CAB sought to protect its prerogative to decide among applicants for the federal government, State Airlines had nothing to lose in its effort to gain the routes. But for Piedmont Airlines, time was of the essence. Money had been spent on an airline that, six months after the CAB decision, still could not take off. Litigants argued the case before the appeals court. Ruling somewhat in Piedmont's favor, the Court of Appeals believed the CAB acted within its jurisdiction not to award the certificate to State but would not go so far as to fully sanction Piedmont's right to legitimately hold the certificate. The Court of Appeals returned the right of decision to the CAB, which reiterated its choice of Piedmont Airlines.

Unsatisfied, Hank Gilbert and State Airlines played yet another card. Another appeal took the case to the United States Supreme Court, where the decision of the justices would not be immediate and might prove fatal to Piedmont years down the road if they saw the issue in the same light as Gilbert. Tom Davis had made a substantial investment and needed to get his planes flying. If, at some future date, his airline remained grounded, he would be ruined. The high court agreed to hear the case, but arguments would not be made until two years exactly after the CAB moved forward and issued the "Certificate of Public Convenience and Necessity" to Piedmont on December 12, 1947.[44]

With this dispensation, Tom Davis had his certificate, if only momentarily. However, every time he thought he had the battle won, the State/Delta/Eastern coalition attempted some new roadblock to keep Piedmont from flying. Later, Tom would look back on this application process and court battle as his most trying time. Certainly, everything he and his people were working for hung in the balance. But characteristic optimism punctuated his recollections of the period. He attempted to remain philosophical, noting, "Whatever impedes a man and doesn't stop him, aids his progress." Further, he was "inclined to believe that Piedmont's progress has been largely the result of the fantastic achievements and experience of the Piedmont people and the support of many steadfast friends during that trying experience."[45]

While waiting for the legal wrangling to subside, Tom's airline family continued to live a questionable existence. Always concerned about the welfare of his people, these somewhat idle-by-circumstance employees were kept working and remained occupied with sundry jobs. Zeke Saunders remembered Piedmont's original crew of pilots: "We kept those twelve on the payroll, and we paid them $125 a month [half pay] and they painted the buildings and kept the grounds and did everything else. Jobs were hard to find. There were so many air force pilots; they stayed there from when we hired them in June or July. They stayed there until next February when we ran the airlines."[46]

One of those working was pilot Leon Fox, who remembered, "Well, we'd do most anything. We sanded and painted floors, made up the sidewalks, anything [we] could do to keep busy. We had one airplane that was leased and we'd go out every once in a while and fly it a little bit. But mostly — we had that old army barracks there at the offices, and it required a lot of work. That's mostly what we did."[47]

When former employees look back on those pre-flight days, they say they were just glad to have a job. These men were not deterred by the knowledge that once the airline started flying they would make less, much less, than their trunk airline contemporaries. Pilots for Eastern Airlines like Shelly Charles, the original king of the Winston-Salem barnstormers, earned an average of $800 per month. Piedmont captains were scheduled to gross only about half that in their first year on the job. Co-pilots made even less, earning $240 per month.[48] The commitment of these early employees showed just how much faith they had in Tom Davis's venture.

While the period of waiting and battling had the company in a state of limbo, Tom Davis reorganized his company for greater efficiency and to reflect the new operations Piedmont hoped to begin. Piedmont Aviation, Incorporated, became parent company to two businesses. First, the core operations of fixed base enterprises were grouped together as General Aviation. This arm of the business was the foundation of the company, a place to find parts and mechanics for most major aircraft, along with a sales operation that featured Beechcraft planes and offered airplanes for hire as part of its charter operation. Flight training was still part of the offering and that, too, fell under the auspices of General Aviation. Some of Piedmont's early employees remained under the wing of fixed base operations, including Ed Culler and his brother Joe, who started out as a part-time lineman before turning to airplane sales.[49]

The new branch of the company was designated "Piedmont Airlines," a division that ran everything from scheduling flights to training the all-male flight attendants, known at in that era as stewards or pursers. In many ways, the airline operation grew to overshadow and often, seemingly, to represent the entire company, but this does not describe the true strength of Piedmont Aviation. If Piedmont Airlines had attempted to get off the ground without its fixed

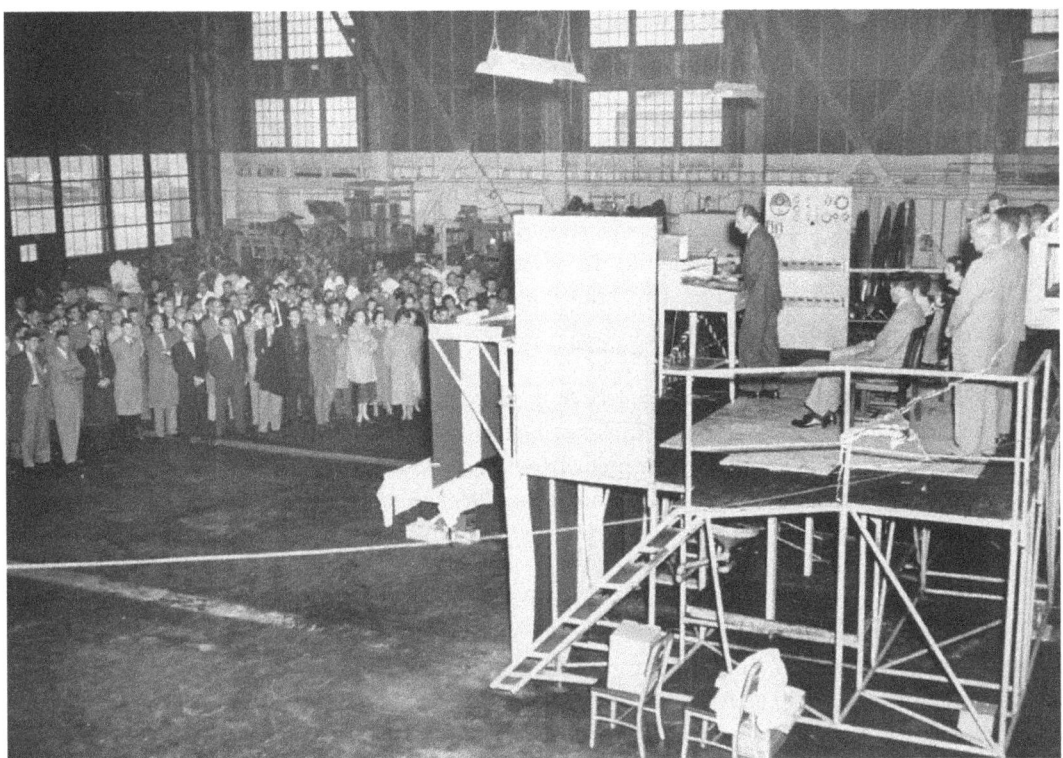

Tom Davis addresses a group of Piedmont employees in the early days of the airline. At the time of the Speedbird's first flight, Davis was only 29 years old (courtesy Piedmont Aviation Historical Society).

base division, success would surely have been much more elusive. Since aircraft needed maintenance, fixed base provided the expertise to draw upon, as well as a handy source for parts to keep planes in the charter and airline divisions flying. Piedmont Airlines needed and would always rely on its General Aviation "big brother," although "each division was to operate autonomously under the corporate structure of Piedmont Aviation, Inc." according to Tom Davis.[50] However, he also recognized the helping hand the fixed based operation could give the fledgling airline. "It was a good thing we had it," Davis admitted. "There were mighty lean pickings back then."[51]

Ironically, the title of Piedmont Airlines once belonged to another transportation company. The Norfolk-Danville Railroad used the name "Piedmont Air Line" to encompass a network of rail lines that stretched through the piedmont section from Richmond to Atlanta in the 1880s. A brochure on the line remarked that the smooth-as-air ride was "often found within sight of the highlands toward the north-west, penetrating and surmounting them at several points by a system of divergent railways seldom surpassed in the history of modern engineering achievements."[52] In constructing the new Piedmont Airlines, Tom Davis sought to do the railroad version of Piedmont Air Lines one better by taking to the skies with his own "modern engineering achievement."

The growing Piedmont family plowed ahead. Route 87, which the CAB had now given them, would allow Piedmont to fly several paths and serve a number of cities. First, trips would originate as far south as Wilmington, North Carolina, move through the state to the

Tri-Cities area of Tennessee, and then across Kentucky and as far North as Cincinnati. A northern route beginning in New Bern, North Carolina (the line expanded in summer to originate from Morehead City), would encompass cities in both Virginia and West Virginia before terminating in Louisville, Kentucky. All or part of six states would be served by Piedmont Airlines, which placed stations in cities such as Goldsboro, Raleigh/Durham, Greensboro/High Point, Winston-Salem, Southern Pines/Pinehurst/Aberdeen, and Asheville in North Carolina. In Virginia, stations were established in the cities of Norfolk, Richmond, Charlottesville, Lynchburg, Roanoke, and Danville. In West Virginia, Piedmont would serve Princeton/Bluefield, Beckley, Charleston, and Huntington. Kentucky included Middlesboro/Harlan, London/Corbin and Lexington, and just across the Ohio River was another station in Portsmouth, Ohio.

As 1948 began, a flurry of activity took place as preparations continued for the much anticipated first flight of Piedmont Airlines. The date was set for February 14, Valentine's Day. In the meantime, schedules were printed, airport counters erected, and the Speedbird posted. A rush of new employees climbed on board, readying themselves and the DC-3s for operation. Training was completed for employees, as were numerous other chores and details essential for the creation of a new company.

As expected, more money was still needed. In addition to the $300,000 capitalization and projected government subsidy, the airline needed further capital not only to cover its initial cost to do business, but also to fund anticipated growth. To solve the problem, Piedmont Aviation announced in early February its plans to issue 675,000 shares of common stock, put forward at one dollar per share. Kirchoffer and Arnold Associates of Raleigh, North Carolina, arranged transactions, designed primarily for Tar Heel investors to help avoid interstate fees.[53]

Each time Tom and the underwriters at Kirchoffer and Arnold planned to roll out the stock offering, complications arose. With the stock prospectus completed, the initial public offering was planned for January 19. The morning headline in papers throughout the state of North Carolina killed the sale, however: State Airlines had gone back to the CAB, requesting it suspend its decision in favor of Piedmont until the five man board could review State's argument that it should be regarded as "the only qualified applicant."[54] Both Tom and the underwriters agreed to withhold the stock offering until the issue reached resolution.

After the CAB denied the rather frivolous State request, Tom and the Kirchoffer-Arnold team announced a public offering date of January 29. Again leaking stories to the press on the eve of the stock sale in an effort to disrupt Tom's further capitalization of his airline, State Airlines once more made headlines across the state, as the failed carrier filed a petition to deny Piedmont its ability to carry U.S. mail on board its planes. Two days later, the CAB turned down State Airlines' latest request.[55]

The third time proved to be the charm for sale of the Piedmont shares. Convinced that the State Airlines petitions were timed to poison Piedmont's stock offering, everyone connected with the offering kept the date secret. Before State Airlines could create more bad press for Tom and his stocks, all 675,000 shares had been sold. Tom admitted how difficult the process had been when he later said, "It seemed like we had two hands tied behind us." With his renowned grin, he went on to observe, "but we had a lot of support from our friends."[56]

Never stooping to trickery as his opponents had, Tom also did not sugarcoat the risk involved with putting money into Piedmont. He said, "We tried to be honest. We did not encourage people to invest who couldn't afford to lose the money. We went to them with an honest, straightforward admission that it was speculative."[57] Interestingly, by the time Tom retired as president of Piedmont, each of those "speculative" one dollar shares being offered at the time proved to be worth 60 times that amount with a number of cash dividends paid in between.

Tom Davis began to take pride in the agility of his operation. As he once remarked, "We managed to complete a successful public stock offering and were in actual operation even before most of the other new airlines got started."[58] The choice by Piedmont to market itself and its stock to North Carolinians is important in understanding the kind of airline Tom Davis wanted to run. He never sought to be the biggest; he just wanted Piedmont to be the best. He felt that he had the tools to build it in his own state. Newspaper articles noted, "Piedmont is purchasing all types of equipment and machinery from local concerns in as far as this is possible."[59] Many of his employees came from the Tar Heel state as well. Tom Davis put supreme confidence in his fellow North Carolinians, as employees, investors, and potential customers. Once Piedmont had its funding and was putting it to use, the only thing that could ground the airline was for the Supreme Court to decide against Piedmont Airlines.[60]

In building his airline, Tom Davis kept close control of expenses, a trait for which he would always be known. While employees waited for the airline to take to the air, the president of the company talked them into building all the ticket counters, baggage carts, and passenger steps the airline planned to use in all the cities it served, saving carpentry costs. Many of the spare parts used on the DC-3s were Army surplus bought after the war. In fact, the VHF radio transmitters used by the company had been bought at a sale of war assets and modified for only "$324 per installation." Piedmont even chose to mimeograph its own operating manuals to avoid printing costs.[61] The effort to conserve resources began a practice of frugality that grew to become a hallmark of the company.

Frantic preparation continued as the flight day approached. Stations in all nineteen cities served by the carrier had to be set up, complete with signs as Piedmont Airlines hung "out its shingle."[62] Lee Golson, general traffic manager, handled the placement of Piedmont's Speedbird logo in airport terminals all the way from Wilmington, North Carolina, to Cincinnati, Ohio. Training continued for the station personnel who would assist passengers with tickets and questions. Ground crews practiced their skills in the effort to perform efficient turnarounds to help keep the airline on schedule. Everyone wanted the first flight to set a standard for Piedmont Airlines that passengers would appreciate. With a "minuscule fleet of flat-tailed DC-3s," as detractors labeled them, the employees were determined to overcome the adversity already faced by this company, which they were increasingly starting to call their own. Unfortunately, Tom Davis had one more hurdle, one he could do nothing about: the weather.[63]

February was not a good time to launch an airline. Through no fault of their own, Piedmont personnel found themselves ready to take off in the middle of an especially icy winter. *The Wilmington Morning Star* called it the worst in fifteen years.[64] Everyone knew that conditions for launching the first flight were less than ideal, but these people also understood the growing burden of delay. To continue to wait meant mounting expenses with no revenue. Most of the Piedmont family accepted the fact that the planes would be flying for a while with few, if any, passengers, as folks who had never before had an option to travel directly over the Appalachian Mountains considered flying as an alternative mode of transportation. So why not go? As Superintendent of Passengers Bill McGee put it, "You didn't make any money sitting on the ground. You did it flying."[65]

Before the first scheduled flight could make it off the ground, though, the originating city, Wilmington, North Carolina, got socked with two ice storms. Each wave brought the coastal city to a standstill. Power and telephone lines were downed, and fuel oil and coal were rationed to keep as many residents warm as possible against the winter's unusual onslaught. The winter of 1948 was proving to be Tom Davis's worst obstacle yet. Ever optimistic, he cancelled the Valentine's Day flight and waited for skies to clear. As one newspaper reported, "They look at it philosophically and say they would rather have trouble before they get started than afterward." *Winston-Salem Journal-Sentinel* reporter Rixie Hunter added his own advice, observing that "an airline official who frets about the weather would soon go crazy."[66] Piedmont people took the journalist's advice. Instead of fretting, they planned for clearer weather.

Forecasts predicted a better week ahead. A new date of Friday, February 20, was set as a target, knowing it too might be postponed if the meteorologists were wrong. As temperatures warmed and the snow, sleet and ice melted, a new problem emerged in Wilmington: flooding. Many rivers, including the Cape Fear, which rolls right past the seaport town as it drains into the Atlantic, were at or near flood stage. Still, the weather allowed the airline to demonstrate its capability to government inspectors through a proving run, also called a "ride out." On Tuesday, February 17, Chief Pilot Zeke Saunders and officials from the Civil Aeronautics Administration flew out of Wilmington to display the ability of the airline to perform for the public. The southern route of Piedmont's service area got its final approval. On the same day, the U.S. Circuit Court of Appeals notified Tom Davis that it had denied a stay to State Airlines, which continued to engage in legal maneuvers to keep Piedmont on the ground. Though the Supreme Court had yet to rule on the case, for the moment, Piedmont still had wings.[67]

As Friday, February 20, approached, plane and personnel were readied for full operation to begin. Tom Davis flew down from Winston-Salem on Thursday afternoon with his executives on board. In fact, Tom piloted the DC-3 himself. The chosen craft would be the *Kanawha River Pacemaker*. In an effort to distinguish aircraft beyond federal numbers, Tom inaugurated his own naming system for the planes. As he himself noted, "From the very beginning, our motto has been 'Piedmont Sets the Pace.' That's why we call our airplanes Pacemakers."[68] Since Piedmont Airlines would augment Davis's motto into the term "Route of the Pacemakers" as a catch-phrase to describe its service, each plane was "commissioned" as a Pacemaker, preceded by the name of a community or area served by the airline. The Kanawha River in West Virginia, over which Piedmont planes would fly many times in the coming years, served as the namesake of the *Kanawha River Pacemaker* craft that flew out to Cincinnati. The DC-3 sported the name just behind the nose on the captain's side. The official designation of NC37468 was noticeable on the tailfin, but the Piedmont name was much easier to remember. This plane was one of the two purchased from Colonial, the other being the *Appalachian Pacemaker*, which was down in New Bern in the capable hands of Zeke Saunders, who prepared to make a proving run over the northern route to Louisville, Kentucky.[69] The reference to planes as "Pacemakers" was designed as something of a tribute to another first flight in North Carolina, that of the Wright Brothers, proving that the Tar Heel state again flew in the forefront of aviation history.[70] The naming of more Pacemakers as they came on line, like "Shenandoah Valley" or "Hampton Roads" paid compliments to areas that welcomed those planes so warmly. It was a way Tom Davis could say thank you to the communities he hoped his airline would serve for years to come.[71]

Coincidentally, as the new airline prepared to make its maiden flight, the last pioneer of heavier-than-air flight was dying. On February 1, the co-inventor of the airplane, Orville Wright, who made the original first flight just 44 years earlier, died in Dayton, Ohio. Tom Davis planned his airline's inaugural flight down the coast less than 200 air miles from where the Wrights conducted their first successful effort to prove that man could leave the ground. Also on February 1, Captain John T. Daniels died; he was the only surviving member of the crew who helped position the plane before takeoff in Kitty Hawk. Reading the obituaries and finding that two of the men who helped make manned flight possible had died on the same day signaled the end of one chapter in aviation history, but for Tom Davis and his crews at Piedmont, a new chapter, a sequel to first flight, was about to unfold.[72]

This first flight was to be much more of an introduction to the communities Piedmont Airlines would serve than a money maker. The trip included company men like Davis's assistant, R.D. Hager, and Superintendent of Passengers Bill McGee. Along for the ride was *Winston-Salem Journal* photographer Frank Jones, and Egbert Davis, Jr., brother of the Piedmont president and still a member of the board of directors. The inaugural Speedbird picked up local dignitaries as Piedmont made its initial stops along its trek. By the time the plane reached its ultimate destination in Cincinnati, the twenty-one seat craft would be full. The trip included only one paying customer, and he was something of a minor celebrity himself. Bill Turner worked as a regional manager for Shell Oil, but more importantly, he was brother of renowned racing pilot and barnstormer Roscoe Turner, the same barnstormer who landed on Winston-Salem's Reynolda Estates three decades earlier.[73] Turner paid a total of $68.70 for the round-trip on the new airline.[74]

Pilots on the *Kanawha River Pacemaker* were already in Wilmington, since their flights would routinely begin and end there. Both Leon Fox and Harold Dobbins, among the first twelve hired by Piedmont, would be stationed out of Wilmington. For this first flight, Fox would serve as captain and "Hoss" Dobbins as first officer. Both men had connections to Piedmont long before its airline days. Leon Fox had completed his flight training during the Civilian Pilot Training Program in 1941, while Dobbins worked as an instructor for the school.

Fox remembered that the issue of seniority among the men at Piedmont had been somewhat of a logistical problem for the new airline. All airlines set up a system for their pilots, the most senior having first choice about assignments and routes. As Fox recalled, "It was suggested that the six captains' names were put in a hat and drawn out and they would be awarded numbers three and up, because one and two would be reserved for Gilley and Saunders. Then the six captains were drawn out and assigned the six numbers. Then the six co-pilots were drawn out, so that we had fourteen."[75] Both Fox and Dobbins got low numbers and chose to establish their base in Wilmington, North Carolina, where they stayed for the rest of their careers.

The plan had been executed, the obstacles were overcome and the weather was clear. Before first light, the men gathered. The air was cold and the ceremony brief and uneventful. Besides well wishes and flowers, which were to be presented to Cincinnati officials, the most important handoff was the nine sacks of mail delivered by the head of Wilmington's Post Office to Piedmont's local manager, R.W. Samuels. New Hanover County Commissioner George Trask and local Chamber of Commerce secretary John H. Farrell represented Wilmington. As passenger Bill Turner got on the plane, *Winston-Salem Journal* photographer Frank Jones snapped a picture. Boarding right behind Turner was Piedmont president Tom Davis. The fact that Turner boarded the plane first spoke volumes about where the head of the company kept his attention focused that day. During the many years that followed, while Tom Davis controlled the airline, he made sure that the paying customers came first. He figured that as long as he gave first consideration to those who paid money to fly on Piedmont, the airline would remain solvent.[76]

With mail and males securely aboard, Leon Fox got the signal from the station manager to take off. The captain and copilot fired up the Pratt and Whitney Twin Wasp engines. As propellers spun, "Flight 41" taxied to the runway and at 7:19 A.M. took off for Pinehurst/Southern Pines, the next stop on what was scheduled to be a four and a half hour trip. As Captain Leon Fox remembered, "that flight was as smooth as silk."[77]

After the stop at Southern Pines with more flowers and remarks, they traveled to Charlotte, North Carolina, the occasion commemorated there by a live broadcast on WSOC Radio. There was plenty of time for the interview. "Everything was going along nicely on that first flight, the first day, February 20, 1948, until we got to Charlotte," said Tom Davis. "Asheville, not unexpectedly, was socked in with fog. So we had to delay the flight in Charlotte for about an hour, hour and a half, something like that, which made me very nervous with all these dignitaries around. We were trying to show them what a great airline we were."[78] The growing entourage moved on to Asheville, where each passenger received a carnation. After a stop at the Tri-Cities Airport (Bristol, Kingsport, Johnson City, Tennessee) the flight moved on to Lexington, Kentucky. At Lexington, each passenger was presented with a hardcover book about the history of the state of Kentucky. Once the entourage reached the Greater Cincinnati Airport, Frank Jones took another photograph, this one of the assembled dignitaries in front of the Kanawha Pacemaker that had collected them from stations along the route as it journeyed successfully to the Ohio Valley.

Waiting for the group were city officials from Cincinnati, and also Piedmont's ground crew. Tom Cowan, Pete Jones, and Edward Best comprised the station personnel who first served Piedmont's western terminus. "It was an exciting time for us," said Edward Best, who well remembered the landing in Cincinnati because like his coworker Pete Jones, this was his first flight as a station agent. They hauled the first sack of mail and some cargo off the plane while Tom Davis and his assembled notables posed for pictures. In working the first flight, Best recalled, "We did everything," which included checking the oil on the engines of the DC-3 while it waited its return flight.[79]

Following a celebratory luncheon, the jubilant group boarded the DC-3 to return via a reverse of the same route. Leon Fox and Hoss Dobbins left the plane in Cincinnati, turning the controls over to another crew, equally anxious to fly their first official flight with the new company.[80] The only additional passengers were Piedmont's second and third paying customers, Mr. and Mrs. Emil Stemler, who were going as far as Charlotte. Officials who had boarded the plane that morning were returned to their hometowns as the flight hop-scotched its way back to Wilmington.

At the end of the day, Tom Davis wiped the

Captain Leon Fox many years after he piloted the first flight for Piedmont Airlines, as well as the last DC-3 flight. A 30 year veteran for the company, he began the airline with the first flight out of Wilmington, N.C., on February 20, 1948 (Leon Fox Collection).

sweat off his brow. He had done it! However temporary his certificates might be, as the court case then remained in litigation, he had seen the gears turn. Piedmont was an airline, though the irony of the first flight being designated as "41" was unknown to all who flew it. The symbolic significance of the number would only become apparent when a Piedmont plane flew its last passenger 41 years later.

3

Puddle Jumping, 1948–1958

After a successful maiden flight on February 20, 1948, Tom Davis and company performed a second set of initial flights over another set of cities. A week later, on February 27, the ride came in a different direction, from the Ohio Valley to the North Carolina coast as service was inaugurated over the northern portion of Piedmont's service area. Piedmont's *Appalachian Pacemaker* flight flew out of Louisville, Kentucky, again collecting dignitaries as it went. The Speedbird made its way back to the Tri-Cities of Tennessee, then stopped in North Carolina, at Winston-Salem, Raleigh and Goldsboro, before terminating the route in New Bern.[1] As Piedmont Airlines completed its first flights and settled down to the daily business of hauling passengers, a celebration was in order and the party was at home in Winston-Salem.

At Smith Reynolds Airport, crowds converged to see the official hometown launch. Tom Davis was bright and full of sunshine, even if the skies overhead were not. Throughout the afternoon, storm clouds threatened to disrupt the outdoor ceremony. By mid-afternoon, all was in place for the grand opening, which would occur once the Piedmont plane that made the run from Louisville to New Bern arrived in Winston-Salem. Earlier that day, North Carolina Governor R. Gregg Cherry and President Pro-tem of the Kentucky Senate Lewis Cox flew in onboard a special Piedmont aircraft to give congratulatory speeches at the event that welcomed Piedmont Airlines to service within their states.[2]

Spectators gathered behind a fence on the airport tarmac, ready to hear what these developments meant for the future of the Twin City. The nose of the DC-3 pointed with dignity toward the horizon, behind the official delegation that ascended a platform with a speaking stand at its center. Perhaps the most curious of the hosting group was a small child with curly hair. As radio reporter Lou Marsh described the action, Tom Davis escorted the young girl, Molly Norfleet, over to another platform, this one just under the nose of the proud plane. There he handed her a silver bowl, into which two bottles of water were poured. Mixing the two had symbolic significance, as one had come from the Ohio River and the other from the Atlantic Ocean, boundaries of Piedmont's Route 87. As water filled the bowl, Molly struggled to keep it steady, so as not to spill the liquid. After the second bottle of water filled the cup, she got the signal from Tom Davis to heave the bowl's contents onto the airplane, christening it the *Appalachian Pacemaker*. When the audience burst in enthusiastic applause, Tom Davis winked at little Molly for doing her part to launch his airline.[3] Among those clapping was Molly's father Charlie Norfleet, whose financial assistance and guidance had made the day possible.

Over the airwaves of Winston-Salem radio station WTOB, listeners of the event felt both relief and hope as speakers heralded a great future for Piedmont Airlines. Governor Cherry hailed the opportunities that came with air travel to most portions of his state. He said that the advantage Piedmont was bringing to North Carolinians "has been needed a long time." Tom Davis went further with his own comments, remarking that his new service area had "suffered miserably from a transportation point of view." With a feeling of boundless pride, the president of the company relished connecting a "community, a state, and a particular section of our great country which offers such unlimited possibilities to progressive individuals and institutions."[4] He lauded those intrepid souls willing to buy tickets on his Pacemakers.

Tom Davis was so proud of his new airline that he put it on display for all who wanted to see. From dignitaries to bystanders, everyone was treated to an extensive tour of company facilities, including Tom's own office. The renovated Army barracks were part of the walk-through, as were the communications and reservations offices, and hangars where equipped maintenance and repair facilities kept the Pacemakers in shape. Two additional twin engine DC-3s, just purchased, were also presented to onlookers. The company even threw open stock rooms for close inspection. It was all part of a plan to make the public comfortable with the new airline and to encourage Tom's "progressive individuals" to look at everything from the office where service records were kept to the engine test stands where mechanics readied the Pratt and Whitney motors on the DC-3s for service.[5]

The celebration culminated that night with a party at Winston-Salem's most elegant venue, the Hotel Robert E. Lee. Over two decades had passed since the city had celebrated a milestone in aviation like this one, the last being Lindbergh's 1927 visit. Keynote speaker for the dinner, Air Transport Association Vice-President Robert Ramseck, praised the company as an integral part of the national transportation network. The festivities marked the Piedmont Airline initiation into the community of local service, or feeder, airlines. According to Ramseck, Piedmont Airlines gave Midwesterner travelers "gateways to the great southeast." He extended his praise for the new carrier as a vital resource for manufacturers who could use Piedmont planes to take their products to market.[6]

Tom Davis smiled and accepted the plaudits of the speaker, knowing full well that his government certificate for operation was still just temporary. Nevertheless, that February night, Tom and his employees lifted a glass of champagne to toast their

(As Piedmont Airlines opened for business, Mr. Davis threw open the doors of his venture for public viewing. The event familiarized the public with all aspects of the airline and called upon employees to work very hard to accommodate sightseers. Shown here are three un-identified employees relaxing after the festivities (courtesy Piedmont Aviation Historical Society).

teamwork.[7] Piedmont had received its baptism and opened its routes, flying to a portion of the stations it was authorized to serve. There were still more towns in which to touch down and the Piedmont crew was anxious to get busy.

Unfortunately for those who carefully prepared the flight timetables, weather continued to play havoc with the schedule. Following the entourage who had departed Cincinnati back east a week before on the southern portion of the first flight was another snowstorm; the weather stranded Flight 41's two pilots. Leon Fox recalled that he and Harold Dobbins found themselves stuck in the southern Ohio city after their first flight. Their delay lasted a week. Fox said, "On the eighth day, we were able to leave Cincinnati." They then went back to Wilmington with another crew. The copilot added that the same thing happened again with their next flight. "Out of the first 15 days of operation, we got home a little over a 24-hour period," remembered Hoss Dobbins. But the big problem wasn't snow and ice for Leon Fox. It was the fact that he had to live in Cincinnati for a week without any money. As Fox acknowledged, he was broke. Reminiscing with his copilot, Fox told Dobbins, "If it hadn't been for your money, we wouldn't have made it."[8] Their difficulties weren't the only ones. Overall, the new airline and its employees found the winter of 1948 a tough time to stay in the air.

Flying across the mountains was tough enough, but getting through bad weather, even thick clouds, was temporarily impossible for the new airline. The government mandated such. In the provisional certificate to fly, the Civil Aeronautics Board restricted Piedmont to fly by Visual Flight Rules (VFR) for its first 90 days. Since instruments served as a way to combat elements like snow, fog, or thundershowers, the flight schedule had to dodge weather patterns until summer. The CAB wanted to make sure that pilots could see the Appalachian Mountains as they flew over them instead of relying on instruments. The governing body also wanted to make sure pilots would get used to the runways upon which they would be landing. For Piedmont and its passengers, this restriction almost continually disrupted schedules because it required reasonably clear days for flight or the skill to fly around turbulent weather patterns. Captain John Onoff, called "Switch" by some colleagues, remembered flying in poor conditions. "The weather can get pretty bad over the mountains, thunderstorms in summertime, ice in winter time and operating out of some of the airports we did back then, where the airports didn't have facilities."[9] Management accepted the constraint in the name of safety, understanding that revenue for the fledgling carrier would take time to build.[10]

Flying to cities and towns along Piedmont's designated route by VFR kept the pilot group on their toes. In the early days, they landed in a variety of conditions. Major metropolitan airports, like the one near Cincinnati, offered modern accommodations to pilots who could make Instrument Landing System (ILS) approaches, once the 90 day probation ended.[11] Those landings contrasted sharply with some stations like Southern Pines and Fayetteville, N.C., both of which were grass landing strips that required visual approaches. Some of the pilots who enjoyed the adventure of a more rugged style of flying actually preferred these cruder conditions. One such pilot was Zeke Saunders, who said, "Dirt is easier to land on than a concrete airport. On concrete you come in and your tires screech up on the concrete and have a tendency to dart with you. And on a dirt field you don't get that screeching and the grass slows you down a little."[12]

As much as Piedmont's early pilots may have liked landing on more natural surfaces, it was cause for alarm for some passengers. When Tory Vaughn captained a flight from Lexington, Kentucky, to Wilmington, North Carolina, he landed on grass fields in Pinehurst and Fayetteville. After the flight ended in Wilmington, a man came up to Vaughn and said, "You really scared the pants off me." When Vaughn inquired why, the passenger replied, "I looked out the

The first flight into Huntington, West Virginia. November 3, 1952. When Piedmont began service to many small communities, commercial flight was still a novelty and brought out many spectators to see their town connected to other cities by air (courtesy Piedmont Aviation Historical Society; from the collection of Zeke Saunders).

window and I saw all these cows grazing out there and we landed in this grass field and I thought we made a forced landing. Wait until I get back to California and tell the people about this."[13] What the passenger did not know was that Piedmont pilots routinely found Southern Pines by listening for a radio signal from a local AM station near the field.[14] Flying across rural North Carolina was a very different endeavor from that in other parts of the country.

In many ways, the early pilots were a unique breed of aviator, ones who knew their airplanes in much the same way as cowboys knew their horses. Piedmont flight trainer R.L. Gordon, known as "Spiderman" to his fellow employees, taught and observed many pilots. Years later, he divided them into two groups, saying, "You had the numbers pilots who flew the airplane by the numbers, by the book. Then you had the seat of the pants pilots. They could just feel that airplane. You could tell them in class, they hated the numbers, they just knew. They flew so much they just knew. They [would] get to 'feeling' that airplane, they knew what they were doing."[15]

On occasion, pilots demonstrated their ability with an airplane in challenging ways. When Chuck Meacham was a youngster, he remembered that his father flew right over their house as part of his regular flights between Southern Pines and Charlotte. One time Charlie Meacham went on a bombing mission. He took Piedmont paper cups, put wet towels in them for weight and dropped them out over his house in Rockingham, North Carolina. When he called his family to go look for the six cups he jettisoned from the DC-3 he was flying, his wife and kids found four of them near the house. "My mother and my sister were right there, we saw it all," recalled Chuck, who said when he told friends about the episode, they refused to believe him. They weren't the only ones. "When we told daddy about it he couldn't believe it. He said, 'I didn't have any idea those things would hit the house.'"[16]

Even Zeke Saunders, who served as chief pilot for the company and later as a Piedmont senior vice president, was something of a daredevil early on, leaving no doubt into which of Spiderman's categories he fit. One of the courses Zeke taught while an instructor for the Civilian Pilot Training program was acrobatics. After the war, Zeke took up stunt flying as something of a hobby, following in the tradition of Winston-Salem's first aerial entertainer, Shelly Charles. The suggestion to become an acrobatic pilot came from Tom Davis's wife Nancy. According to Zeke, "We — Tom Davis, his wife and I were in Miami at an air show. She said why don't you get you an airplane and get into that business and advertise for Piedmont. So I talked with Tom, and he agreed. We bought a Stearman."[17] In exchange for gasoline, Zeke put a Piedmont decal on the side of his plane and flew in air shows throughout the Southeast. "I always loved to do acrobatics. It was kind of fun for me," Zeke recalled.

He had only one close call. To make sure an engine didn't sputter during a loop when the plane would be upside down, a system had to be installed to assure the continued flow of gas to the carburetor. Once when Zeke was performing the feat with the Speedbird displayed on the side of the wing, he went into a roll and flipped the switch. "Well, I got the valve turned the wrong way. I did an outside loop and tried to come around the bottom about four hundred feet and got up to there and the half power wouldn't take it on up," said Zeke. "I couldn't get it to switch over and I just kept sliding back. I said 'oh shit.' Finally I kept fooling with it and got it kicked off and went on out." For his efforts, where he defied death even more than the audience realized, he won second place.[18]

The adventure of this "seat-of-the-pants" pilot was short lived, however. After about two years, Tom Davis had a change of heart and forced Zeke to give up the stunt show circuit. "They took my insurance away from me, because my personal insurance wouldn't cover air shows. So I figured it was better off to quit." Zeke admitted that the real reason he gave up stunts was "because Tom Davis told me he didn't want his chief pilot out there trying to kill himself while he was trying to sell safety to his airlines passengers."[19]

Safety was an overriding concern for Piedmont. Mr. Davis insisted upon it before anything else, even the comfort of the customer. He knew passengers could accept inconveniences if delays cropped up but, were a plane to crash, travelers might never trust the airline again. Harold Dobbins, co-pilot on the first flight, remembered the airlines president's visits to the Wilmington base to "talk shop." About Davis, Dobbins noted, "Being a pilot, he was very much interested in safety. He would spend money in the cockpit and leave passengers in a hard seat."[20] One of the most important measures that many pilots felt ensured safety was cockpit standardization. In order to make sure pilots were comfortable in their surroundings and therefore quick to act when necessary, instruments were placed in the same location for both captain and copilot in every plane. Piedmont was unique in the industry to spend the extra time and money to make all cockpits identical.[21] When the airline celebrated its tenth anniversary, it rightfully claimed a spotless record, with no crashes.

A number of World War II veterans joined the Piedmont ranks in all departments. Navy flight instructor Tory Vaughn jumped at the chance to work for the new airline because as he remembered "right after the war flying jobs were kind of scarce. They were hard to come by."

Each DC-3 was stripped to the metal and rebuilt by Piedmont mechanics to make sure each Pacemaker was safe for passengers and crew alike. Here mechanics reassemble the wing (courtesy Piedmont Aviation Historical Society).

Before he came to Winston-Salem, he remembered that some pilots were so desperate for a job, "They were all sitting around wishing for another war." When hired, he was number 42 on the seniority list of pilots and started as a copilot on the DC-3. The pay was meager. He recalled being paid $220 per month, which he described as "pretty hard to get by on" if you were a "family man."[22] Bob McAlphin agreed. He had secured a job with Delta Airlines in Chicago but longed to return to his home state of North Carolina. After a month with Delta, he signed on as a station agent for Piedmont Airlines in Charlotte in 1955 but admitted, "I had to take a pay cut."[23]

With about 3,000 hours flying time under his belt, Tory Vaughn became a member of a brotherhood of pilots that taught and supported each other, making them all better at the art of flying. Vaughn was flying as copilot with Captain Harold Brown out of Norfolk. After about their fifth trip with Brown in the left seat as captain and Vaughn in the right as copilot, or "first officer," as it was called, the captain said to Vaughn, "Tory, you notice I do all the flying?" The response of the first officer was "Captain Brown, I can ride as far as you can fly." After taxiing down to the end of the runway Brown asked, "You can ride as far I can fly?" and then barked, "OK, you fly the damn thing." According to Tory Vaughn, "There, we became good friends. And it wasn't two or three trips after that he said, 'You can have the left seat my friend.'"[24] The trust between pilots all over the Piedmont system served to increase their expertise and launched an important dynamic from which the airline would benefit for decades to come.

Pilots for the airline came with a variety of experience. Tommy Orrell went to work for Piedmont's fixed base operation while harboring a desire to fly. In July of 1949, he started as "a line boy pumping gas" and waited for an opportunity. After only a few months with the airline, his college training became better utilized when he began working as a flight instructor for the company's school, which was still in operation. By February 1950, Tommy Orrell attained his goal. He was offered a slot as a copilot on a DC-3. He felt that having a minimal number of flight hours actually helped his chances of becoming a commercial aviator. According to Orrell, "That didn't really bother them. You were going to be copilot for several years and they'll train you the way they wanted you to fly, so it was probably a good thing to hire young boys with low time and put them on as copilot and teach them the way you wanted." In four years, he checked out as captain and flew a DC-3 until 1960.[25]

As Piedmont pilots perfected their craft, the folks on the ground made sure the airplanes were reliable. Every DC-3 purchased went through rigorous refurbishing to make sure all parts were reliable. Superintendent of Airline Maintenance Howard Cartwright noted that "each

Piedmont mechanics prepare a Pratt and Whitney engine for mounting on a Pacemaker (courtesy Piedmont Aviation Historical Society).

plane we turn out is stripped right down to the skeleton and then some."[26] After choosing from a dwindling number of the aircraft and paying an average of $120,000 for them, Piedmont maintenance people put in over 12,000 man-hours rebuilding the planes, spending an additional $52,000 per plane. Cartwright asserted, "We set our standards as high as any can be and we stick to them like the Bible."[27] General Sales Manager Bill McGee described Piedmont's DC-3 restorations eloquently by saying, "Every airplane we fly is a highly specialized work of art."[28]

In re-crafting the DC-3 to be better than new, Piedmont made some improvements to an airplane that was no longer being manufactured but was still the company workhorse. One change dealt with seating. For maximum usefulness, Piedmont upgraded the seating capacity of the normally 21-passenger plane to 24. On one of the airline's earliest DC-3s, the extra space was found by removing the cargo box or "the coffin" as it was affectionately called by many Piedmont employees, since it looked amazingly like one. Besides providing more cabin room, the removal of the box kept passengers away from any gruesome ideas that might create questions about safety. By 1950, lounges became part of the DC-3 cabin. Inspired by the example of other airlines, Piedmont's addition of a lounge helped to create a more fashionable atmosphere and greater passenger comfort.[29]

Looking from the passenger area toward the cockpit of a DC-3, which could be icy in winter, hot in summer and very wet when it rained. Here, Captain Ed Clement (left) and First Officer Gene Smith await takeoff (Ronnie Macklin Collection).

Employees worked diligently to balance the pleasure of the customer with careful protection of company assets. On occasion, a judgment call had to be made between the two. Though rules like VFR were in effect at Piedmont's start up and were designed to protect the passenger from harm while pilots learned the terrain, the restriction also could prove very inconvenient to travelers whose plane had not reached their destination by sunset. Leon Fox remembered one such instance when he ran out of daylight before reaching his final stop in Charlotte. Landing in Asheville at dusk, he realized he would be unable to complete his run before dark without violating the CAB law. Ever the creative thinker, Fox informed his passengers of the problem and told them he was ending the "scheduled" flight. However, if they wanted to ride with him as he "ferried" the plane to Charlotte, they were welcome to do so. "Everybody got on board," Fox remembered.[30]

"It being a new airline, you were very interested in everything that was going on," said Edward Best, describing the keen attention employees paid to every departure and arrival throughout the system. A station agent in Cincinnati, Southern Pines, and Charlotte in the early years, Best kept abreast of everything happening at all the stations by reading the teletype machines located at every station. The teletype helped ground personnel stay informed about passengers, cargo, and mail coming in on the next flight. "You'd put your information on the teletype and it would go to every station on the system," said Best, "but it would only be addressed to the next station, the one you were wanting it to go to." Best remembered many employees, himself included, came in on their days off to see what was going on, and they did so by reading the teletype.[31]

One teletype message coming out of Winston-Salem regularly was a codified message to New Bern that some never understood. According to one employee, it was the liquor order. Since the cargo compartments usually had a bit of extra space on the run between the two cities, and since Winston-Salem was a "dry" community, a system was set up to place orders for various types of alcoholic beverages. One day, the employee was approached by the supervisor in charge of the headquarters teletype and asked point blank, "Are you placing orders for liquor on the teletype?" At first flustered the employee hemmed and hawed, thinking that a "yes" answer was grounds for dismissal. The cat and mouse game continued until the employee realized that the supervisor was interested in placing an order, at which time he finally admitted the scheme and added to his teletype message to New Bern. The practice continued until alcohol sales in Winston-Salem became legal.[32]

Most employees never dared used the teletype for jokes or liquor orders because they knew the folks in Winston-Salem could see the messages. In the early days of 1948, however, one purser wrote before he thought. Edward Best remembered when a message from Lee Golson came over the teletype inquiring as to the whereabouts of a purser coming in on a flight. It just so happened that the very same purser was reading the machine as Golson sent his query from headquarters to Cincinnati. As a joke, the purser typed back a message saying that the one they were looking for had dropped dead. "About two minutes later, the telephone rang and it was all the officials of the general office wanting to know what happened to that guy," said Best, who recollected, "It caused a roar." Best said when he told the home office that the purser they were looking for had jokingly written the message about his own death, "[It] didn't go over too well." From that point on, the teletype was used for very few pranks.[33]

From the creation of the Piedmont Airlines idea to the development of the company to this point, Mr. Davis (as he was now being called by his employees) was the personification of the airline. After the ceremonial takeoffs, focus shifted. Now the emphasis was on the people who got the planes up and down, the pilots, mechanics, stewards, station agents and managers, and the reservations and clerical workers who daily assured customers that their flights would be safe and on time. Mr. Davis remained the guiding force for the company, but his philosophy to hire good people and let them do their job had reached the point where the employees would determine if Piedmont would succeed. His people recognized the "hands off" approach, which spurred most to work even harder. Harold Dobbins noticed it: "He didn't mess with you much if you were doing right."[34]

The head of the company did not isolate himself in a corporate boardroom. Beyond his duties as president and treasurer of the Piedmont Aviation, Mr. Davis continued to promote and protect his company. One of his vice-presidents, Bill McGee, said that Mr. Davis was "available to anyone at any time." McGee pointed out that his accessibility included passengers. "If a customer had a complaint, they could call Mr. Davis directly."[35]

The toughest part of working for Mr. Davis, many employees later revealed, was his frugality. Harold Dobbins made the point directly when he asserted, "He wasn't easy to work for when it came to a buck."[36] Mr. Davis enjoyed the reputation. "We even watch pencils,"[37] joked the company president over his miserly habits which became legend. Dobbins appreciated how Mr. Davis made the most of company resources, as did just about everyone connected with the company. For a small, local service airline, Piedmont had "the highest credit ratings," said Harold Dobbins. "Piedmont's credit rating was good wherever you wanted to go."[38]

Thrift proved to be an important attribute for the airline, a quality retained long after the company ledgers moved firmly into the black. Mr. Davis took a lot of teasing for his parsimony. One event, recounted by Zeke Saunders, during the inaugural flight to Morehead City demonstrated the quality of frugality which kept the Pacemakers in the air. With Zeke in the cockpit and Mr. Davis in the cabin entertaining dignitaries on the flight, a problem occurred. "The landing gear handle broke off in the up position, so all the hydraulic pressure was holding the gear up, and I knew we had to get the line broken somewhere," said Zeke. Without tools aboard, Zeke was forced to kick the line in two to release the landing gear. The quick maneuver unleashed a rush of fluid, which seeped onto the carpet in the passenger area. A tense moment was made almost comical when Mr. Davis implored Zeke to find a way to save the plane's new carpet from the widening pool of hydraulic fluid. Asserted Zeke, "Here we were trying to get the gear down and he was wondering if we couldn't catch that hydraulic fluid somewhere so it wouldn't ruin the rugs in his airplane." The reaction of Mr. Davis to the story was characteristically candid. He said, "I frankly admit it. I have had a lot of, I think, friendly barbs thrown at me that I was too tight with a penny."[39]

Running a successful airline, as Piedmont was laying the groundwork to do, required getting the most out of available resources. Mr. Davis did that with everything he had, including his labor force. Many employees handled multiple jobs. Bill Barber was one of those employees. As he saw it, "I did it because they needed me." Bill was among the most versatile employees Tom Davis had and whenever an obstacle needed tackling, the president of Piedmont often tapped Bill. As Barber observed, "Tom never paid you for a job. He paid you for anything he wanted done."[40]

Mr. Davis got his money's worth out of Bill Barber (who started with the company on June 9, 1941, in the pre-airline days). Bill began his career as a stock clerk, remembering how he didn't make ten dollars a week until he got his first raise. "I worked from daylight till dark, five days a week," Barber recalled. As a new guy, Bill Barber ended up with a lot of jobs nobody wanted, and the veterans weren't above teasing him when they had the chance. "We had this rotating beacon between the number one and two hangers there and it was pretty high. We had to cut it off and rotate it and all this other stuff. I was there a week and they said how's about changing those light bulbs," said Barber. "Every time I'd start to unscrew them they would cut them things on. And of course that thing wasn't big enough to stand on. They were trying to knock me off. They would do crazy things down there."[41]

Bill Barber also knew how to fly, getting his instructor's rating and teaching during Civilian Pilot Training days. After a stint in the military, he came home and started short-lived Piedmont sidelines, which included building crop dusting kits for airplanes and overseeing a janitorial service. Tom Davis also gave Bill Barber the opportunity to fly as a pilot for the new airline but Bill chose instead to stay on the ground, handling a variety of jobs, including supervision of security, buildings, and purchasing. He later served the company as vice president of purchasing.

Along the way, Bill Barber served a number of useful functions for Mr. Davis, including telling his boss once that the company was making a mistake with its division that made crop dusting kits for sale. One day, Bill Barber, who worked in that area, noticed that sales of the crop dusting kits were tremendous. "We just got more business than we could do. I just got me a pencil and decided I would figure out what this stuff was costing in raw material. We were paying more money than we were selling them for. He took his discovery to Mr. Davis.

> "I went to Tom and said you know what, Mr. Davis. There is something wrong here. We are selling these things too cheap. He said, "no." I said, "Well you look at these figures." Tom was a mathematician. Anything to do with figures he could do in his head. He looked at those things. And he said, "Let's think about that thing until tomorrow." I pulled out all the invoices and everything and I gave them to him and he goes over it and says, "we'll have to up the price on them." I said, "oh no, we can't sell them then."[42]

Piedmont quickly got out of the crop dusting kit business. The head of the crop dusting kit division soon left Piedmont, going across town to another Winston-Salem enterprise, where he helped automate the donut making process of Krispy-Kreme.[43]

Anytime a need arose, Tom Davis called upon Bill Barber to help fix a problem, often asking for service beyond the normal call of duty. When a flight had to go and pilots were scarce, Bill sometimes climbed into the cockpit with Chief Pilot Zeke Saunders. Barber remembered one experience vividly:

> I know we had one flight that went from Winston to Roanoke to Charleston, West Virginia. I'd work all day then we'd go up there at night. I think we left here at 5 P.M. and got up there and spent the night. And of course, they had a purser, a flight attendant you know. We had one room with three cots in it and one bathroom. If you don't think that was a job trying to get all of them ready to go the next morning? Then we'd come back the next morning and work all day. But this is the way it was. I flew that flight for a while.[44]

Piedmont Airlines began to build a reputation as a proactive airline, thanks to the extracurricular efforts of many employees like Bill Barber, who went far beyond normal expectations. In addition to flying the line, Bill also flew periodic charter flights, once for the University of North Carolina football team during the days of Charlie "Choo-Choo" Justice.[45] Bill Barber and other early employees like him argued that it was their job to do all they could to ensure success for their employer. They felt they could do no less. Their efforts, in turn, set a precedent for all who followed, instilling in most every Piedmont employee an ethic of support to help build a company about which they could all be justifiably proud.

In the early days of the airline, Bill Barber's career reflected the spirit of the company.

The Piedmont hangar at Smith Reynolds Airport. Not long after construction the airline had outgrown the facility, necessitating even larger housing for newer planes (Ronnie Macklin Collection).

Everyone worked in enterprising ways to make Piedmont a winner. Every person hustled. Employees were known to hand deliver tickets to busy customers.[46] One counter person is credited with helping a tardy passenger delayed by traffic still make his flight by relaying the errant passenger's problem to the plane's crew. The captain, who had already taxied the plane to the runway, turned around and came back, saying, "Just two minutes [were] lost" and vowing, "We'll make it up in the air."[47] Chester B. Nutt, a Piedmont Station Manager in New Bern in 1948, acknowledged the juggling that was necessary to keep operations running. He admitted to wearing many hats: "We did ticket selling, reservations, obtained weather information for the flights, filed flight plans, and we loaded and fueled the planes."[48]

Scrambling for customers often required ingenious schemes. In between servicing flights as a station agent, Edward Best spent his time on the telephone calling businesses all over Cincinnati to tell them about the services Piedmont offered. "We had to work it up. They didn't come running out there to fly Piedmont right at first." Best and the two other station agents augmented newspaper and radio advertising with their phone contacts. As Best remembered, "We worked up quite a nice business doing it that way."[49]

Employees looked for any advantage that could secure passengers for Piedmont. If a competitor's flight was delayed or cancelled, Norfolk ticket agent Reggie Powell took one airline's misfortune and turned it into customers for his. He revealed that he would "get on the public address system and say [for example] 'Would Washington passenger John Smith please page Piedmont Airlines?'"[50] Powell had noticed that a Washington flight was delayed and concocted a mythical customer to alert stranded passengers that Piedmont had a flight going their way. He confessed that people would come to his counter to see if space were available, which he was happy to sell to them. Reggie Powell later became staff vice president for operations and control at Piedmont Airlines.[51]

Personnel kept close control of the inventory, making sure to get the maximum revenue out of each flight. Station agent, later Vice President of Airline Scheduling, Bob McAlphin revealed, "Sometimes we oversold it. I say not intentionally but we did oversell some of them intentionally because we kept records on them and we knew which flights were subject to fall apart." On a few instances where Piedmont had too many passengers for a flight, the airline went to extreme measures to accommodate the customers. "Most of the time we'd probably send a small private airplane with him to where he was going," said McAlphin, who remembered the important thing was to keep the passenger happy. "In Charlotte, for instance, we used to take them downtown to a movie if the flight was spaced several hours apart. Buy them lunch or dinner and it appeased them rather well. Hopefully they'd remember that and come back."[52]

Often station agents were asked to perform a myriad of jobs. Paul Snell remembered that many of the tasks he performed became separate jobs in later years. His list of various duties included

> "radio operator, weatherman, making weather observations and advising flights, Teletype Operator, checking fuel storage tanks for quantity as well as for water, direct parking, starting and exiting of aircraft, all loading of freight, mail, luggage & passengers, as well as unloading, keeping all station manuals [operations, freight, and passenger tariffs] etc. up to date, writing and selling passenger tickets plus handling air freight and US Mail, filling out all forms for departing flights and filing IFR flight plans, fuel slip, weather and clearance forms, plus figure weight and balance for each flight."[53]

Snell and the many other employees carried out these jobs daily, making sure each of them were executed to the standard they had set for themselves and their airline. The positive attitude and strong work ethic infused the company. The climate of camaraderie and mutual assistance began building itself to the point that many within the company felt sure of success, even though the operation was lean and the future was still unsure. L.J. Lambert spoke for many of his coworkers when he declared, "I felt it was my airline just as much as it was Tom Davis's. And that if I succeeded, it had to succeed. It was my company and that was just the way I felt. I think almost all our employees felt that way. And I think that's what made it more successful.... [The] fact is that we were all dedicated to help this company to succeed. It meant a great deal to us."[54]

This relationship between management and employees, while enviable, might seem impossibly idyllic were it not for the fact that so many in the ranks felt the same as L.J. Lambert. What president of a company would not want the kind of relationship that Mr. Davis had with his people? Some of the pictures employees paint might be attributed to nostalgia as many look back on their youth and good times. However, almost all admit that the work was hard, but they trusted Tom Davis to keep the operation thriving. Many felt like the one employee whose job it was to clean airplane toilets between flights. The story goes that one day, after 20 years of what was euphemistically referred to as "cleaning the honey pot," he went home to his wife "cussing" about the conditions under which he had to work. When his wife suggested he find other work, he turned to her in surprise and said, "QUIT? And get out of aviation?" He never gave up his job.[55]

The thrill of being part of a dynamic new type of business attracted many. Tom Davis understood their fascination; in fact, he shared their passion. He also cultivated his workforce. One knack he had was to greet employees on a first name basis, which was no little feat of recognition. By 1952, the company roster had grown to 683 employees in both the Airline Division (602) and Fixed Base Operations (81).[56] Many of those people he remembered by name have marveled as his ability to recall them as well as every other employee he saw on sight. Some believed Tom Davis had an innate ability to recognize a face and have a name readily associated with it. Others suspect he did his homework before venturing out, making sure he knew whomever he might encounter. Zeke Saunders revealed that Mr. Davis occasionally nudged him for a name when he saw what he thought to be an employee coming his way.[57] The gestures of recognition served Tom Davis well during the years, increasing his stature among employees to the point of reverence. Bill Barber perceived

Captain Paul Snell in uniform as a pilot with Piedmont Airlines. Beginning his career as a purser for the carrier, Snell retired the same year as Mr. Davis. He also was first on the scene flying another plane into Asheville-Hendersonville after the fatal crash of Flight 22 (courtesy Paul Snell).

that the admiration was mutual, saying Mr. Davis "loved his people and they loved him."[58] Part of his charm may well have been his ease with people. His charisma and friendliness relaxed any situation. The same skill that allowed him to interact fluently with politicians as he and his planes began arriving in city after southeastern city also allowed him to be outgoing with his people. Bill Barber liked to say that "he could relax with the guys over a scotch and soda" as easy as anyone.[59]

Mr. Davis demonstrated the respect he had for his workforce in a number of ways. Anytime the company faced a problem, he refrained from hiring outside consultants to come into the company and recommend improvements. Instead he sought the advice of his own people. It was a policy that paid dividends for the company. First, it saved the company from paying consulting fees, and it showed the employees that their opinion and knowledge mattered to Tom Davis. As a result, they gave him their complete loyalty.[60]

Tom Davis managed people with a deft hand, though at times it might have seemed more like babysitting, especially among his pilots, who were always considered a "breed apart." Once, when a group assembled for a meeting of the Quiet Birdman Society, a pilot fraternity supposedly founded by Charles Lindbergh, the idea for a prank emerged. After a few drinks, a number of Piedmont pilots began to scrutinize their surroundings. They found a large, blue marlin mounted to the wall. One of the "QBs" hit upon the idea of stealing the marlin as a worthwhile adventure. They quickly dismounted the fish. As they headed to the elevator, Mr. Davis caught the wayward boys in the act. In a stern, fatherly lecture tone, he reportedly said something like, "Boys, I believe I would take that back if I were you all." Sheepishly, they did.[61]

The adage of "once Piedmont, always Piedmont" applied to many who came to work for the aviation company. L.J. Lambert began right out of high school as a stock-boy for the company before the airline started. Like Bill Barber, he learned to fly but found his specialty after working in a number of areas. "I was offered a job to help start and create a parts department for the airlines. I was the one clerk with the person who organized the shop, two of us, and after about a year or so he left the company. I took it over and developed the parts department over the next twenty years, and supervised the operation of it. We just grew and grew and grew."[62]

Lambert's job required him to keep a full inventory of parts available not only in Winston-Salem where the airline's overhaul facilities existed, but also at sites along the Piedmont route where mechanics performed overnight maintenance. Stations included Cincinnati, Wilmington, and two locations in Virginia, Roanoke and Norfolk. Lambert detailed the maintenance process at these sites, saying, "We had some maintenance bases and when these airplanes were there overnight they had these routine inspections they performed. They had parts that we sent out from Winston-Salem. They had little miniature parts departments, you might say. If they didn't have what they needed and if we had an airplane down we'd just have to send another airplane to replace it or send the parts to fix it on another airplane."[63]

In subsequent years, most of Piedmont's management came from the ranks of those early employees. Tom Davis gave his people the chance to ascend as far as talent and the needs of the organization would take them. None better exemplify the opportunities at Piedmont better than Paul Snell. A Winston-Salem native, Snell returned home after a two-year stint in the Navy. He, like many others, remembered the day he started working for Piedmont. He joined the ranks on April 16, 1948. "I worked in the station. That way it gave me time to take flight training and ground school. They had a ground school course and I would go to ground school at night and then I would fly when the weather was good; when I wasn't working with Piedmont, I'd go fly."[64] Snell moved over to the job of steward, handling passenger needs on flights, before coming back to the Winston-Salem station. Since he could fly, he began handling small flying jobs for Piedmont, like hops around Winston-Salem. "They had a little airplane where you flew passengers over the city, you know. On the weekends people would come out to the airport and I would fly them around the city and I would come back. They would get out and then I would get another load and I'd take them sightseeing, just building up time."[65] Snell looked for any and every opportunity to fly. Director of Flight Operations Frank Nicholson believed in the young pilot and followed the Davis dictum to give young employees a break. Nicholson gave Snell a call whenever he needed a pilot. "If an airplane broke down somewhere in the middle of the night and they needed an airplane, say if they needed to take a plane to Norfolk, I'd meet him out at the airport and we'd take that airplane to where ever it had to go," recalled Snell. "At the time I hadn't been hired as a co-pilot but that gave me good training. He would let me fly to deliver that airplane to wherever we needed to go. So I had a lot of trips like that, so that helped build up my time and it gave me experience. I was always very appreciative of him giving me that opportunity. I had a lot of those flights." Snell waited patiently for an opening in the pilot ranks and eagerly accepted the chance to "fly the line" when it came available. From there he went on to fly for the airlines until his retirement in 1983, after logging over 25,000 hours.[66] He flew as first officer (copilot or second in command) for about ten years before ascending to captain, as there was no expansion during that decade.[67]

Even with Mr. Davis's "cool headed and warm hearted leadership,"[68] as it was sometimes described, some workers began to wonder how the airline could sustain itself with such little business. By the first anniversary of the airline operation, the legal battles with State Airlines had yet to reach a conclusive verdict. Flights were going out well short of capacity and the CAB continued to scrutinize Piedmont's performance. How could the company survive? The air carrier needed every customer it could get and then some. Even though 39,370 revenue passengers flew with Piedmont in that first year, over 72 percent of seats on flights went unfilled. The company showed a small profit for 1948, partially on the strength of 34,380 tons of express freight and 18,785 tons of mail hauled.[69] Uncertainty hung over Piedmont Airlines like some of the dark clouds its pilots tried to fly around. The company gave its all to cultivate a solid customer base, which remained elusive. Legitimacy of Piedmont's certificate to fly had still not been conclusively determined by a court ruling. Yet there was no giving up.

The key to profitability in the early days of feeder airlines was not passengers; it was the government subsidy. The lines were paid to carry the United States mail into smaller cities and towns in the Southeast and the calculations had already been made to determine how many seats needed to be filled to make a trip cost-effective. According to Captain John Onoff, "We needed seven passengers to break even with the subsidy. So, you know, back then, it was like, count passengers, got seven or eight, you might be making money if you had more than seven. But that was the kind of break even."[70] Many planes flew with fewer passengers than even John Onoff's break even number. Based in Wilmington, Harold Dobbins remembered flying practically empty planes. "We operated out of here, [Wilmington] day in and day out, sometimes hauling one passenger."[71]

If substantial revenue eluded flights, then Piedmont worked hard to control expenses, which required getting the most out of its planes. Unlike most feeder carriers, which operated their aircraft for about six hours each day, the DC-3s of the Piedmont fleet stayed in service up to eight hours each day. Most of that time was spent in the air. One thing Piedmont prided itself on, and at which it became very efficient, was fast "turnaround" of its flights, and getting off the ground as fast as possible after landing. Most personnel whose jobs were part of getting planes out of the terminal boasted that turnaround was often done in ten minutes, and some say less. Passenger Leslie Boney clocked the turnaround by recalling, "They would throw the baggage in the back and inside of three minutes you were off and running."[72] To get in and out of airports, or stations as the employees called them, captains of the flight would leave one engine turning while one set of passengers got off and another got on. Some co-pilots even got off the plane to help stewards load baggage.[73] Mr. Davis proudly proclaimed, "Not a minute of excess time was spent sitting at the dozens of airports Piedmont flew in and out of."[74]

As a first officer, Tommy Orrell believed he worked harder once the plane was on the ground than he did as the flight's copilot. At every stop he "would get out of the seat and they'd roll up a stand to the nose door. We'd load and unload the luggage that had to go into the nose compartment because of weight and balance." Orrell remembered getting hot and sweaty, especially in summer, as he "jumped out of that seat, loaded the luggage, closed that luggage bin and the door and then we started that engine and went on to the next stop and did the same thing on the next stop." Orrell called the three minute turnarounds a "great effort on everybody's part to do more than just fly and get your paycheck, it was an effort where everybody did what they could."[75]

Saving fuel costs and time motivated Captain J.L. "Pappy" Wilkes to stay on schedule,

A Piedmont DC-3 crew. From left, Purser Stan Brunt, First Officer Tommy Orrell and Captain Sam Parnell. This is the type of flight crew that handled everything in the air for Speedbird flights until the era of female flight attendants (courtesy Piedmont Aviation Historical Society; from the collection of Zeke Saunders).

even when some of his fellow employees were not. Fellow pilot Tory Vaughn remembered a flight Wilkes flew out of Wilmington one morning heading to Cincinnati. When Wilkes stopped in Pinehurst, he found "the agent had overslept or something and he didn't show up," said Vaughn. "But here's this one lone passenger standing out there so Pappy pulls up and gets the passenger, puts him on and leaves a note on operations, 'been here and left picked up one passenger, [signed] Poop-Deck Pappy."[76] Piedmont Airlines had a schedule to keep and Captain Wilkes refused to let any problem he could resolve stand in the way.

One way to ensure efficiency and safety was the five finger salute. Each finger represented one area that ground crew had specifically checked. Captain Howard Thompson remembered the salute, which was detailed in Piedmont's operations manual. "I think it came three pins, chocks and doors and that was when the agent held up the five fingers. He held up five fingers like that [gesturing with a flat palm] first. Then he saluted and that meant that you could depart."[77] The five finger salute became a regular sendoff for every Piedmont flight. Since airlines followed a pseudo-military code, including ranks and uniforms, and because many of the early pilots came from military backgrounds, the salute fit right in.

Piedmont flew between the small cities of the southeast, gathering passengers to head over the mountains on its east-west runs. As it did so, flights almost hopped from one terminal to the next. A regularly scheduled flight from Greensboro to Winston-Salem stayed airborne for only about ten minutes before landing.[78] One newspaper reporter said, "The plane hardly gets up before it starts to come down."[79] He likened stops to another form of ground transportation, saying, "After a couple of short hops, one gets the impression that the plane, like a downtown bus, will stop to let people on and off whenever someone pulls the cord."[80]

The major carriers were indifferent to the needs of the small town air traveler, but Piedmont, with its quick, friendly service, labored to make the enterprise profitable. The airline was derisively referred to as a "puddle jumper" because of the short-hop service it provided, but employees smiled and continued to enthusiastically serve a company that could get passengers from one city to the next faster than any other transportation source at the time. "It offended me, but not for long," Tom Davis said of the slightly deprecating tag. "As long as we are out there doing a job, providing a lot of good jobs, making some money, doing well by our stockholders, growing, call us puddle jumper if you want to."[81]

Captain Jim Taylor flew the stops and starts regularly for Piedmont. He remembered the jack-rabbit nature of trips, pointing out how flights "had to go from here [Winston-Salem] over to Greensboro, up to Danville, up to Roanoke and around the horn. We had to go from here up to Pulaski to go down. We couldn't go straight to Tri-city and cut about a third of the flying time off." Taylor recalled another nickname for the airlines. "They called us the Jack Rabbit airlines, you know. We had short and rapid stops."[82] Passenger Earl Wilcox often puddle jumped with Piedmont. A furniture industry analyst, Wilcox measured the trips like most of the other businessmen on the flights. "From the time smoking was permitted until we were preparing for landing, I only had time to smoke one cigarette."[83]

Tommy Orrell looked back on all the puddle jumping as a time when he gained valuable experience in handling a DC-3. Once he landed in Huntington, West Virginia, with a 45 mile per hour crosswind. He had the confidence to make that approach because of all the other landings he accomplished regularly. He said, "My schedule was I flew up to Columbus and back down to Norfolk and all the stops in between, so in one day I did 16 landings and I did that every third day. When you fly a route that gives you that number of landings, you're going to get a good feel of landings, because that's all kinds of experiences in different kinds of winds and different runways and approaches. So you get confidence."[84]

To make money on flights in the early days, the airline deemed nothing too bizarre to be transported. Tory Vaughn hauled everything from strawberries to snakes. He remembered that 15 boxes of strawberries could start to stink when shoved into a cargo bin just behind the cockpit. Even worse, one day a snake they were transporting to a zoo in Wilmington managed to escape. "They tore that airplane apart for two days. Never did find it," he said. He wondered on subsequent flights in that same airplane if the serpent would show up curled under his feet. While a station agent in Southern Pines, Edward Best recalled handling a shipment of baby chicks that managed to escape on their way to Morehead City. "They were all over the airplane. They were running up and down the aisles and everything," said Best. "We had the whole crew chasing baby chicks."[85] Tory Vaughn had a similar mishap in Hickory, N.C. Thinking they had all the chicks rounded up, the crew took off for their next stop in Charlotte. Upon arriving, a passenger came to Vaughn and said, "'Captain, do you mind? I found this little baby chick under the seat.' We'd missed it. 'Do you think it would be ok if I'd take it?'" Captain Vaughn told her that he thought it would be fine for her to have the chick.[86]

The air bridge that hauled passengers as well as all kinds of other cargo over the Appalachians slowly became a viable alternative to travelers. Zeke Saunders noted that ground "transportation across the mountains was kind of hard. It was a hard trip on a bus and it was a hard trip on a train. And we were the only service across the mountains from North Carolina and Virginia into Cincinnati, Louisville, and later Chicago. People used it."[87] One farmer found air travel actually cheaper than ground transportation that wound around crooked highways. For him the savings of time was decisive.[88] Many like him were new to flying. The airline estimated that around 15 percent of its passengers were first time flyers.[89] Piedmont Airlines had begun to shrink the world for folks in the Southeast; its Pacemakers reduced the time to get from one end of North Carolina and Virginia to another and points beyond.[90]

Every aspect of the early operation was manually driven. All paperwork was handwritten or typed. All processes were organized by the individuals within the departments. Even the tracking of flights took physical effort. To monitor where a plane was at any given time of the day, the traffic department built a device they called a "mouse" that crept along a daily path. It carried with it a "tail" that represented the current time in front of strips of paper denoting scheduled flights of the airline. As the tail moved across the strips of paper, they gave approximate placement of the flight. From the board, traffickers could tell which flight would be taking off or landing anywhere along the line. Though primitive, the mouse system worked well and effectively served Piedmont in its need to pinpoint events as they occurred along the system.[91]

Within the jurisdiction of Route 87, Mr. Davis added more stops in hopes of attracting the maximum number of passengers. By April of 1948, both Virginia towns of Roanoke and Danville received service. The following month, Morehead City was added to deliver vacationers to North Carolina beaches. Before summer, Piedmont touched down in even more cities and towns, including Charleston in West Virginia and Lynchburg, Richmond, and Norfolk in Virginia. The following year, planes made regular landings in Fayetteville, North Carolina, and Newport News, Virginia. However, as an ongoing business, finances remained rocky. Annual reports show Piedmont Aviation making a profit each year, although sometimes the margin was razor thin. According to a 1968 story in the magazine *Air Transport World*, "Only in three out of the first six years of the airline operation did Piedmont show an overall net loss. But this was offset those same six years by three good profit years which put Piedmont $91,000 to the good even for this early period."[92]

When the airline division was down, luckily the fixed base side was up, continually increasing sales after 1949 and often rescuing the bottom line for the company. Fixed base operations was the basis from which the airline blossomed. Activity continued to include small aircraft sales for Beech and Piper, maintenance of planes for various companies and individuals, flight training school, and wholesale parts distribution.

By 1955, the annual report noted a 376.7 percent increase in fixed base sales over the last five years. Also, a significant portion of the talent employed by the airline had gotten their training or served as trainers for fixed base operations.[93] Now selling Beechcraft airplanes as well as Piper, all under the name Piedmont, the fixed base division spread the company name farther throughout the South. In fact, the general aviation division reached farther than the airline division's planes flew, thanks to general aviation's position as a leader in sales, service and parts. The employees of the fixed base division adroitly continued to perform the same stellar service that the company originally did when it incorporated back in 1940. Twelve years later, some 375 pilots were receiving flight training from Piedmont, many on the G.I. Bill. Meanwhile, Piedmont mechanics continued to repair aircraft engines for a number of groups, including another feeder line that was then known as Allegheny Airlines, which would one day be known as USAir.[94]

The fixed base hangar from where Piedmont Aviation sold Piper and Beechcraft planes (courtesy Piedmont Aviation Historical Society; from the collection of Ed Culler).

As Piedmont Aviation labored to attract customers, Mr. Davis and a bevy of lawyers prepared to cross swords again with Hank Gilbert and State Airlines. After giving Piedmont the certificate to start the airline, the CAB found itself in court once more on the subject, as State asked for a review by the U.S. Court of Appeals for the District of Columbia. In 1949, the appeals court sided with State Airlines in its attempt to wrest away control of Piedmont's routes. Piedmont immediately appealed the decision and all pending decisions on Route 87 were folded into one case to be heard by the United States Supreme Court. The argument was mainly between State Airlines and the CAB, but the future of Piedmont Airlines loomed in the balance.

The Supreme Court heard the case of *Civil Aeronautics Board v. State Airlines, Inc.*, on December 12, 1949. Piedmont Airlines was not an official litigant in the case but had more to lose than anyone. Between 1944 and 1947, the CAB had deliberated extensively over which airline could best provide service to Route 87 and judged Tom Davis's application more convincing than that of Hank Gilbert. State Airlines argued conversely, maintaining that it had the stronger request and that Piedmont had skirted the application process by not specifying routes and being unclear about whether it would rather haul passengers or mail.

In a serious but restrained manner, the counsel for Piedmont, Charles Murchison, stood shoulder to shoulder with Emory T. Nunneley, representative of the CAB, in front of the highest court in the land. The argument they made centered around two main issues: whether

Congress intended to grant the CAB powers to select the airline it felt could do the best job and did Piedmont live up to the criteria set by the CAB. The Civil Aeronautics Board and Piedmont agreed on both points, each complementary to the other. The opposing argument was the assertion that Piedmont's application was vague, and in awarding Route 87 to Piedmont, the CAB had shirked its investigative duty.

The battle, while intense, was mercifully short. Less than two months after counsel argued their cases, a decision was rendered. Handed down on February 6, 1950, the Supreme Court, in a six to two decision, upheld the CAB's right to grant certificates for scheduled air service and with it, Piedmont's legitimacy as an air carrier. Writing for the majority, Justice Hugo Black opined that "Piedmont's applications were sufficient to permit certification of Piedmont for the routes awarded."[95] The court conceded that Piedmont's request had been hazy with respect to specific lines but said such was reasonable given that the CAB had grouped all the applicants together as the Southeastern States case and that "limiting all applications to the precise routes they describe would destroy necessary flexibility" of the CAB's decision-making process. Justice Black recognized that "the Board's decision as to what new routes are actually available is not reached until long after the applications are filed." In reviewing all the applicants, the court found that "Piedmont, like other airlines, inserted a so-called 'catchall clause' in its applications, broadly requesting authority to transport on 'the routes detailed herein, or such modification of such routes as the Board may find public convenience and necessity require.'"[96]

Concerning the CAB's authority to make such decisions, the Supreme Court found that "The flexible requirements set by the Board were reasonable."[97] Two justices, Felix Frankfurter and Harry Reed, who wrote the dissent, objected to the way the CAB disregarded the requirements Congress had established for the sanctioning body, referring to it as an "administrative absolutism."[98] While the two justices did not deny that Piedmont may have been the best applicant, they argued that the selection process employed by the CAB was flawed and should have required all carriers to amend their applications so that each of the contenders would know with whom they were competing. Luckily for Piedmont Airlines, this view was the minority opinion.

A second endorsement of Piedmont came in 1951 when the United States Postal Service recognized Piedmont's hard work and diligent efforts to maintain its scheduled flights (and transportation of the mail). The postal service supported renewal of Piedmont's local service certificate to carry letters and packages. In doing so, the U.S. Postal Service broke precedent, having never previously recommended continuation by the same carrier for an airline mail route.[99]

The next year Piedmont received astounding news. CAB examiner Ferdinand D. Moran recommended to the full CAB that Piedmont Airlines not be given a five year certificate to operate. He advocated instead a ten year extension. By saying "since the beginning of its operation, Piedmont has had an outstanding record of declining costs and rising revenue,"[100] Moran applauded the work of Mr. Davis's people as the example all other airlines should follow. While impressed, the full body of the CAB restrained itself somewhat and chose to award Piedmont a seven year certificate. Still, the award was significant. Not only had the CAB removed the carrier from a probationary status as a government sanctioned feeder line, but it also broke precedent, as the United States Postal Service had done. After review, most airlines got three or five year renewals, depending upon the CAB's judgment of their performance. In the case of Piedmont Airlines, the CAB went much farther. Its landmark decision read:

"The record achieved by Piedmont is so outstanding as to merit special recognition. By renewing Piedmont's certificate for seven years, we would reward the carrier for its achievement and thereby offer an incentive to other carriers to strive for comparable results."[101]

Never had an airline so impressed a governing agency as Piedmont Airlines had with the CAB. The praise, as well as the reward, was lavish. Beyond the fact that Piedmont was guaranteed a future of at least seven years, the recognition was unprecedented, especially among the newly created feeder carriers. In the same decision, the CAB extended Piedmont's routes by 1,000 miles, bringing its total to almost 2,900.[102] Obviously, the people of Piedmont impressed the CAB, as they handled jobs in an exemplary fashion. The seven-year certificate was a reward for all those employees keeping their heads up when times were trying. The CAB may have said it best when it acknowledged that the extended renewal was "fully warranted by our confidence in the carrier based on its outstanding record."[103] Taken with the Supreme Court decision that legitimized the airline and the U.S. Postal Service recommendation that hinted at the excellent performance of Piedmont, the blessing given by the CAB surpassed all expectations and reflected the exceptional job being performed by Piedmont's people. Mr. Davis agreed. He called it "a fitting tribute to the host of dedicated Piedmont employees who had established a record of being one of the most efficiently operated airlines in the country." [104]

The seven-year certificate for Piedmont was sweet, but ultimately unnecessary. By 1954, Congress considered the process of renewing certificates cumbersome and began deliberation on amending the Civil Aeronautics Act of 1938 to make Certificates of Public Convenience and Necessity permanent. As House Bill 8898 emerged from the Interstate and Foreign Commerce Committee and passed the full House of Representatives, Piedmont employees wasted no time making their feelings known about the impending law. Telegrams flooded North Carolina Senator Sam Ervin Jr.'s office urging him to vote yes for the bill when it came to the floor of the Senate. Division Chief Pilot L.W. McNames telegrammed from Western Union his view that "Piedmont Airlines carried 30,000 passengers last month [June 1954]. Over 700 employees feel they deserve a chance to continue building this fine record."[105] Another missive claimed to represent 50 pilots and urged "Senator Sam" to support his constituency. It observed: "Certification would greatly facilitate our planning and attaining a more self-sufficient operation which would better serve the public as well as our own future needs."[106]

Piedmont people need not have worried about the backing of the senator from Morganton, North Carolina. Later to become a national celebrity during the Watergate Hearings, Senator Ervin fully endorsed the legislation. In his reply to constituents, he assured them he was "glad to support legislation to make the Piedmont Airline Certificate of Convenience and Necessity permanent, when such legislation reaches the Senate." His opinion seemed to stem more from his experience as a passenger than as a legislator; he wrote, "I sometimes travel the Piedmont Airlines myself and know what fine service it is rendering."[107] The legislation passed and gave Piedmont the freedom its employees were asking for: to not be burdened by the constant certification uncertainty to which they had been subjected since startup.

As Tom Davis started formulating a long-term plan for his airline, he analyzed all his expenses, hoping to find areas in which he could save money. One point of scrutiny became Winston-Salem itself. The Twin City did not provide an abundance of passengers to the system. Smith Reynolds Airport had become virtually land-locked, leaving no room to expand, and other cities clamored for Piedmont to move its fixed base and airline operations to their airports. Among the forerunners was the Tri-City area of northeast Tennessee, which stood in the geographic center of the Piedmont route system. Mr. Davis remarked that if he were building the airline over from scratch, the temptation would be very strong to locate the headquarters in the Tri-Cities.[108] However, Winston-Salem fought hard to keep Piedmont Aviation centered just where it was. Just as the city outbid any competitors to attract Wake Forest College and the Bowman Gray School of Medicine, Forsyth County committed half a million dollars to keep Piedmont's headquarters in Winston-Salem.

The money, raised by revenue bonds, was earmarked for construction of a new hangar and office space across the street from Smith Reynolds Airport. Mr. Davis could exercise the option to buy the buildings after ten years. The move was controversial from the standpoint of spending money to keep an existing business from leaving, but the county pacified many by explaining that over a 20 year period, it stood to make $100,000 from the pact. The county banked on the supposition that Piedmont Aviation would still be flying 20 years down the road. Tom Davis banked on the same supposition.

With an infusion of money, Piedmont began to upgrade its plant. The old army barracks that served company purposes during World War II and into the early days of the airline was hopelessly inadequate as headquarters of a growing airline. In characteristic fashion, Mr. Davis grabbed his trusted assistant, Bill Barber, to oversee construction of a new facility. "Tom walked over and said I want you to be in charge of building this hanger. I said, yes sir." Barber fully admitted that "I'd never seen the drawing of a hanger before in my life." However, Tom Davis knew he could trust Bill Barber and assigned him the task anyway.[109] Barber tapped his friend Ronnie Macklin to help with construction. Macklin's father had been a noted architect in Winston-Salem and Barber had confidence in his childhood pal. After the project, Ronnie Macklin came to work for Piedmont, working in a number of areas until his retirement in 1989.[110]

The only inconvenience to the plan stemmed from the fact that Liberty Street bisected Piedmont's office and hangar from the runways of Smith Reynolds Airport. Whenever a plane needed to be brought into the new hangar for repair or maintenance, traffic had to stop. At first, a traffic-crossing arm was installed to signal oncoming cars and later a stop light warned motorists. Surprisingly, few accidents occurred as a result of the traffic disruption. In a 1954 question and answer session, Tom Davis saw the interruption as hardly a problem at all. He said, "Actually, this arrangement isn't as unusual as it may sound. National Airlines in Miami have their offices and shops across an eight-lane highway from the airport."[111] In the mid–1950s, Piedmont employees had only to contend with a two lane road.

The pieces of the puzzle began falling into place for Piedmont Airlines. Ridership continued to build. By 1950, the company had carried well over 100,000 passengers, and as the decade progressed, Piedmont added another 100,000 to their annual totals every two years. By 1959, over a half million passengers flew Piedmont. Plane occupancy rose from 27 percent in 1948 to over 50 percent eight years later. Plus, the CAB achievement gave Tom Davis the ability to find other potential passengers around the state, as the company applied for even more new stops in the Southeast. In doing so, Piedmont became increasingly capable of providing services at subsidy costs that were lower than any feeder airline in the country.[112]

World events also played a part in the rising numbers of passengers. In the summer of 1950, North Korea invaded U.S. backed South Korea, beginning the Korean Conflict. President Harry Truman vowed to contain communism and keep other nations from falling as China and North Korea had after World War II. With the war came soldiers, many who needed quick access to such locations as Fort Bragg, near Fayetteville, North Carolina, the Marine base at Camp Lejeune between Wilmington and Morehead City, North Carolina, and to Norfolk, Virginia's naval base. All three were within the route system of Piedmont Airlines. Harold Dobbins and other pilots began to notice how much fuller the planes were as

Overlooking the 1953 Piedmont headquarters located across Liberty Street from Smith Reynolds Airport. Within a decade the company needed larger accommodations and built an even larger facility at the north end of the airport (Piedmont Silver Eagles Collection).

a result. He remarked, "That meant their wives and them [the soldiers] were flying back and forth."[113]

Emboldened by the positive feedback the airline was receiving and the growing passenger lists, Mr. Davis began to expand the service area. He had already applied for and gotten permission to extend seasonal service to Myrtle Beach, South Carolina, in the late spring of 1950. Two years later, citizens in Beckley and Huntington, West Virginia, as well as Kinston, North Carolina, welcomed the Speedbird. By the mid-fifties, Piedmont prepared itself to tap into some larger markets. The CAB granted entry into its own hometown of Washington, D.C. Service was inaugurated on August 17, 1955, the same day Piedmont also began doing business in Charlottesville, Virginia. Several months before the CAB had given Piedmont Airlines even greater reach into the Ohio Valley, sanctioning passenger trade in Columbus, Ohio, and at Wood County Airport which served Parkersburg, West Virginia, and Marietta, Ohio, both along the big bend in the Ohio River.

Piedmont also sought to take over the service area underserved by Capital Airlines in the South. The addition offered a route from Norfolk, Virginia, to Knoxville, Tennessee, with North Carolina stops in Raleigh/Durham, Greensboro/High Point, Winston-Salem, Charlotte, Hickory, and Asheville.[114] The CAB ruled that the "tobacco road" route would be better served by a North Carolina carrier and kicked out the mid–Atlantic feeder in favor of Piedmont.[115] Zeke Saunders recalled the competitive edge Piedmont had over Capital Airlines. "They flew the same route. They had the little old 900 HP [horsepower] engines in their DC-3s. We had 1200 HP, so we always raced across there. They couldn't keep up with us with those 900 HP engines."[116] By 1960, Capital Airlines was gone completely, absorbed by United Airlines.[117]

Piedmont Airlines provided a range of services that accommodated the traveling needs of the communities into which the Pacemakers ventured, becoming a reliable friend. Thelma Davis flew into most of those stations to set up the new venues. "I would go into that station and attempt to help set up the reservation setup and the train agents there," said Davis, who was called "The First Lady of Piedmont."[118] Originally hired to create Piedmont's first reservation system, Davis remembered how she once helped book a "special" flight when she handled charter services for the company. "We had a couple that wanted to be married in the air, in an airplane.... They chartered a DC-3 and their wedding service was performed in the air. That was kind of interesting, unique."[119] As always, Piedmont had aimed to please.

For many of the communities into which Piedmont came, the celebration was like none

May 16, 1954 — Inside the Piedmont inaugural flight to Bluefield, West Virginia, Tom Davis chats with dignitaries who appreciate the service Piedmont Airlines was about to give their community (courtesy Piedmont Aviation Historical Society; from the collection of Ronnie Macklin).

seen before, especially in smaller towns. Huge crowds gathered to see a passenger airliner up close, many seeing one for the first time. Headlines blazed, "Fayetteville on World Airlines" as service came to the city on September 26, 1949, suggesting that citizens of Fayetteville, North Carolina, could now connect with the other cities of the world. To many, Piedmont's service gave their town recognition, putting them on the map in a way no other event could. Every civic leader wanted to ride on the inaugural flight. The town newspapers dutifully noted the guest lists, which sometimes got to be extensive.[120] It was common for the local citizenry of such cities as Hickory to include a trip to the airport on the weekend just to watch the big Piedmont plane land and take off.

Often, Piedmont improved the efficiency of the station where their aircraft landed. For example, when Piedmont planes started using kerosene, the company was uncertain if Hickory Airport personnel were adequately trained to handle the fuel. They sent Ronnie Macklin to make sure. When he got there, he was shocked. Macklin told Hickory's fuel man, "I don't think you know what the hell you are doing." The station man replied, "You're right. Seven days ago I was working for Baskin-Robbins," adding, "That's all I know. I don't know a damned thing about kerosene and I don't really want to know." Macklin immediately sent his people to train the Hickory people to help make the station better, not only for Piedmont, but for all subsequent carriers who flew into Hickory.[121]

Many of the airports into which the Pacemakers flew were small, almost rural locations that included their own unique hazards. Zeke Saunders recalled flying out of Charleston, West Virginia, where deer were a problem, "particularly in the morning.... They'll get on the runway."[122] But one of the most outrageous hazards for Zeke came one Saturday night. As chief pilot, he was performing what was called a "check-ride" where he regularly evaluated pilots while they flew the line. On a ride from Roanoke to Danville with Bob Nance and Bill Taylor, Zeke was in the jump seat behind the pilots in the cockpit when a duck crashed through the windshield of a DC-3. The bird hit Nance in the face. "He reached up there and he felt his face. It was all torn up. It had duck on it and it was covered up completely. We laid him down in the passageway and headed for the hospital in Winston-Salem. I held a piece [of the duck], and the checklist was in a plastic case. I held it up where the hole was in the windshield," Zeke said. "There wasn't anything but a bunch of little pinpricks where that glass had hit his face. There were duck-guts all over him. He thought he was dying. I remember he was lying on the floor and saying, 'I'm dying.' My face is all torn up.' You couldn't see his eyes or anything. It [the collision] just smattered that duck."[123]

As the man on the front line, Zeke Saunders handled a number of crises for the new airline. In the days before flight simulators, pilots had to prove their competence in the air with hands-on training. Because the planes were busy during the day hauling passengers, prospective pilots flew their "check rides," as they were called, at night. Zeke took one individual up several thousand feet, going through the routine of procedures necessary to complete a successful flight. To see how the student could handle an emergency, Zeke reached up and turned the right engine off. Instead of restarting the engine, the student mistakenly turned off the left engine. As the story goes Zeke moved pretty quickly to get those engines going again.[124] Problems as they cropped up required inventive and often quick solutions. Even under great adversity, Piedmont folks kept the planes flying.

Small airports presented a number of predicaments for pilots, including choosing the right one on which one to land. On a trip from the Tri-Cities, one pilot confused the Hickory and Statesville airports, which came into view at about the same time if, as Zeke Saunders put it, "you got a little bit to the right." The captain, thinking Statesville was Hickory, flew into the wrong airport. The worst part was that Tom Davis was on board the flight. The problem, while infrequent, occurred again when a pilot landed at the Morganton-Lenoir airport instead of Hickory. The pilot of that flight lost his license to fly for three months. Another had better luck when he started to land a flight bound for Kinston, North Carolina, in Goldsboro. Luckily, the pilot saw the error before he touched down. Zeke Saunders remembered getting a call one Saturday afternoon from a pilot who put down at the wrong field in Louisville, Kentucky, which was serviced by two airports separated by about three or four miles. He told Zeke, "I made a mistake," and asked Zeke what to do. Zeke replied, "If I were you I'd crank her up and go on over to Stanford [the correct airport]."[125]

Despite the miscalculations, Piedmont remained solvent even if its growth was skimpy. Tommy Orrell did not see slow growth necessarily as a hindrance. He cited Mr. Davis's conservative approach to growth as a prudent strategy for the airline. "He didn't expand rapidly and take a chance on things not working out. He just expanded the airline a little bit at a time each year, which was good strong growth," said Orrell, who watched incremental increases closely as a sign of progress. "We were just very proud of how the passenger count each month began to grow. We watched that for years."[126] So did Mr. Davis. As he looked for opportunities, he never bet on long shots.

Company stock sold for one dollar per share as the airline began in 1948. By the mid-fifties, shares traded over the counter at around three dollars. Also, passenger revenues continued to climb and government subsidies remained, averaging about 30 percent of airline revenues thanks to the increasing number of destinations reached by Piedmont planes. Some of those communities served, like London-Corbin, Kentucky, which was added in 1953, made Piedmont very little money. A big reason for the decision to serve the London-Corbin area was that it was home to the outgoing vice-president of the United States, Alben Barkley. Zeke Saunders pointed out, "There was absolutely not enough traffic to pay to operate into that airport. But he arranged through the government somehow that we would operate in there and I went up there and we picked out a spot to build an airport."[127] Zeke also pointed out that the same thing happened a year later when a member of the United States Congress wanted air access to Bluefield-Princeton, West Virginia. He remembered Bluefield being especially treacherous: "We wouldn't go in there at night because you couldn't see the trees. It was in the mountains. He [the congressman] finally had it lighted so he could come home on Saturday night."[128]

The pace of the Pacemakers quickened as the fifties progressed. Piedmont pilots joined the Airline Pilots Association (ALPA) in 1951 and threatened to strike a few years later over pay. Speedbird pilots were indeed making less than their industry counterparts, and periodically, the group threatened collective action if the situation did not improve. Even with the labor problem, Mr. Davis was fortunate in those days since ALPA was the only union with which he had to deal. All other Piedmont employees remained unorganized until much later. Negotiation in December 1953 brought the two sides together where a compromise was hammered out, keeping pilots satisfied while still under industry standard in pay and keeping airline schedules running on time.[129]

The speed of Piedmont's rise soon slowed because of its aging fleet of planes. The DC-3, once the economical answer to passenger service, had become a small, slow, costly liability. Harold Dobbins knew the plane well. "I put in 10 years and 10,000 hours on a DC-3.... You froze in the winter and boiled in the summer. If it rained outside, it used to come right in the windshield."[130] His condemnation of the plane was quickly becoming universal. Pilot Bill Kyle also suffered the conditions in the cockpit, saying, "You learned to fly with ice-cold

Piedmont company picnic, 1950. From left to right, front row, Milton Fare, Zeke Saunders, Ed Culler, Howard Cartwright, "Mom" Shouse, and Frank Nicholson. Back row, Tom Davis, Bill Barber, E.G. Warner, Jake Rowe, Norris Young, Red Willard and John Johnson (Zeke Saunders Collection).

feet."[131] He carried cans of antifreeze "so that in icy weather we could open the side window and reach around and squirt antifreeze on the windshield."[132] Tory Vaughn carried a putty knife as part of his tool kit so that he could scrape ice from the windshield. For him, summers were just as bad. "We kept the cabin door open and the two cockpit windows open," said Vaughn. "That set up a draft that would bring air right up through the cabin and out and it was pretty comfortable."[133]

The DC-3 was also cramped and uncomfortable. It had only a small baggage compartment at the rear of the plane, so luggage was sometimes stored in the cockpit. Since the aircraft had been altered to carry 24 passengers, space for kitchens was mostly unavailable. Pursers carried on jugs of coffee or crates of soft drinks as the only in-flight refreshment available, but they always made sure to have chewing gum. Since the DC-3 was not pressurized, chewing helped passengers handle altitude changes and the subsequent ear popping that accompanied their flight. The situation caused airsickness in some, including the pursers.[134] Since the cabin of the DC-3 did not pressurize in flight, it was restricted to lower altitudes. Pilots did not have the luxury of flying with radar and could not fly around very many storms since they couldn't see them coming.[135]

The discomfort of flying in a DC-3 could be substantial. One account of the ride declared, "It tossed, dipped, dropped, and crabbed all over the place, but it got you there."[136] Watching it fly was no better. "Someone once said it looked like it was limping along even if both engines were functioning perfectly."[137] Some passengers could not fly on the DC-3 at all. Those who suffered from "ear, heart or sinus trouble" generally could not "withstand the strain."[138]

Mr. Davis realized the time had come to modernize his fleet. As he put it, he knew that "short-haul air service for small and medium-sized cities could never be profitable without subsidy support unless a new modern aircraft more efficient than the DC-3 was available."[139] With over a dozen feeder carriers flying, Davis felt a market existed for a replacement, and he intended to spur the development of one. Piedmont engineers "developed detailed specifications which were outlined in a paper presented to the Society of Automotive and Aeronautical Engineers in New York in April 1951."[140] From there, Mr. Davis's people began visiting aircraft manufacturers, not only in the United States, but in Europe as well, to see who could build a new plane to his liking. Ultimately, it took two companies to design and build a replacement for the DC-3. Holland's Fokker Company and the U.S. manufacturer Fairchild combined to produce the F-27, a turbo-prop similar to what Piedmont had been seeking. After its initial creation for Piedmont and the other local service carriers, the aircraft had the distinction of remaining "in production for more than 25 years, proving itself to be efficient and economical short-haul air transportation."[141]

The real difficulty for Piedmont was not the decision to upgrade the fleet; it was how to pay for the new planes. Captain John Onoff remembered Mr. Davis being onboard one of his flights into Winston-Salem. Onoff went back to talk to the president of the company, noticing that Mr. Davis "was dejected and so he told me he'd been in Cincinnati, talking to bankers about money and hadn't been successful, so he was a little disappointed."[142] Onoff also recalled that it didn't take long for word to spread about the setback. "I remember that there were rumors at one time that we were going to maybe get paid with chips instead of money, or checks."[143] Moving the company forward required squeezing the finances at times to pay for improvements. R.L. Gordon, who came down from Pilot Mountain to work for the carrier in the late 50s, remembered similar times after he first came to work, when "our foreman told us that you may not get your check this Friday so you may have to wait until Monday."[144] Onoff summed up the feeling of uncertainty when he said, "I can remember occasions when Tom Davis was quite concerned about our finances, whether we were going to survive."[145] Tough times did not, however, cause the faith of employees to dwindle. Most vowed to work even harder.

Mr. Davis grappled with the issue of how to pay for the F-27s. He knew he absolutely needed the new aircraft to keep Piedmont on a path of progress. If the Speedbird expected to "set the pace" as its own slogan said, the fleet needed to modernize. However, $6.5 million was more than the company could reasonably borrow.[146] After all, Piedmont had begun airline operations with only $1 million. Having no specific collateral to offer for the loan, Tom Davis and Wachovia Bank president John Watlington fretted over how to finance the deal. They came up with the idea of offering "debentures," interest bearing bonds based upon the general good credit of the organization.[147] The company banked on the good name of Piedmont to attract investors. In June of 1956, Piedmont placed its order for the F-27. Delivery of the new plane came less than a year later.

The F-27 solved a number of problems for Piedmont. First, the newer airplane was pressurized, a point bound to please passengers who would be more comfortable on flights since the cabin could be climate controlled. Pressurization allowed the cockpit to be equipped with weather radar, giving pilots the convenience of knowing what conditions lay ahead. The F-27 could fly faster (280 mph), reducing travel time. These advances made the plane safer, especially in bad weather. An added benefit was its economy of operation, which improved upon the DC-3's costs considerably. Zeke Saunders pointed out one valuable factor favoring the F-27, the notable savings in fuel. "It used kerosene for fuel. That wasn't but about 8 cents per gallon," compared to gasoline prices of 20–30 cents per gallon.[148] Finally, the new model accommodated more passengers. The F-27 seated up to 36 people, a fifty percent increase over the maximum DC-3 capacity of 24.[149]

The president of Piedmont Aviation took a personal interest in the F-27 purchase. Mr. Davis insisted upon flying one before committing his company to buying. One account of that flight revealed, "When they got up into the air, Tom took over the controls, and he really wrung that plane out. A couple of times, he even frightened his chief pilot."[150] Mr. Davis's desire to take the plane to the limit was reported to come more from a concern for how the aircraft would hold up under stress than any desire to barnstorm. Piedmont purchased a total of eight planes from Fairchild.[151] Tom Davis was quite proud of the acquisition, noting it was "part of a long range program to replace the aging DC-3s. This was, at the time, the largest order for new aircraft by any local service airline."[152]

The F-27 was billed as a modern aircraft that could do it all. One description announced that the plane would fly itself after the pilot pushed a button. "The equipment takes over, brings the plane on course and altitude and then seeks radio signals from the airport to which it is flying." The plane is even credited with being able to land itself. General Sales Manager Bill McGee called it "the biggest advance in commercial aviation [Piedmont has] ever seen."[153]

Piedmont Airlines had weathered its first decade, and with the addition of the F-27, planned for a bright future. With its sister division, fixed base at its side, the air carrier had

The Fairchild F-27 (foreground from right tail area) became part of the Piedmont fleet in 1958 to begin the retirement of the DC-3. This F-27 stands in front of the hangar at Roanoke, Virginia, where a hole was cut to accommodate tails of larger aircraft (Larry Dudley Collection).

February 1958, Piedmont celebrates its tenth anniversary with a party and a cake. From right to left, Milton Fare, Bob Northington, Tom Davis, Zeke Saunders, Bill Turner (counting the years since he was the first paying customer) and Bob Turbyville, seated (courtesy Piedmont Aviation Historical Society; from the collection of Zeke Saunders).

emerged from uncertainty to become a strong, energetic organization that had proven itself in the post war economy. Against its feeder counterparts, Piedmont could claim several distinctions. By 1956, the airline was the largest company in passenger miles flown, clocking over 338 million, utilizing its planes the most at (on average) almost eight hours per day, and claiming the lowest operating cost per mile at just under 90 cents.

Tom Davis looked toward the future when he told a reporter, "We like to think of our operation as one that is not going to be stagnant. We have ideas and plans and we're trying to put them into effect as rapidly as we can, while keeping our present operation in a sound position."[154]

• 4 •

Speedy Petey, 1958–1968

When John F. Kennedy took office in January of 1961, he noted that "the torch has been passed to a new generation of Americans — born in this century" who could effect great change in the United States. As the new president gazed into the decade ahead, he saw endless opportunities for Americans. Born less than a year before Tom Davis, JFK epitomized the mood of the nation: optimism about a future bright with possibilities because of ever increasing technological advances. Both the president of the United States and the president of Piedmont Aviation were ready to harness progress for greater ends and both accepted the challenge of a "new frontier" and saw the sixties as a time of soaring opportunities ahead.

As Piedmont flew into and through the 1960s, passengers and observers alike teased the airline about its earnest, yet unsophisticated, service. Some replied "Pete who?" when the airline's name was mentioned, chiding the airline for its numerous stops. After Carroll Spencer began with the airline in 1966, he routinely made 13 stops en route from Wilmington to Cincinnati. Along the way he heard passengers complain about the number of landings their flight had to make. When they go aboard he typically heard them say, "I don't know why this damned airline stops everywhere, it stops in every cow pasture along here." After Spencer inquired as to where they got onboard and one said "Goldsboro," he just shook his head, since the passenger had no idea that his departure point was one of those cow pastures that he and the other passengers resented.[1]

Business from the "cow pasture" and the other small cities steadily improved. More people rode the puddle jumper every year. On the campus of Wake Forest College, which moved to Winston-Salem in the 1950s, students nicknamed the airline "Speedy Petey." Even though the name implied some derision, the undergraduates found the Piedmont Airlines to be an economical choice for getting to campus. Over the years, "Speedy Petey" became an affectionate moniker for Piedmont among the college crowd, who witnessed a significant growth of the airline in the 1960s.[2]

A makeover for Piedmont Airlines began when the company changed planes. In 1958, passengers began to climb into a new type of aircraft, one purchased new and designed to Piedmont specifications, ready to provide them with all the comforts of modern aviation. Eight Fokker-designed, Fairchild-built F-27s wore the red, white and blue paint scheme that proclaimed them to be part of the Piedmont fleet. After an arduous decision-making process, Zeke Saunders remembered, "The F-27 was not an ideal airplane but it was the best then, and Fairchild was going to build it in the United States. That was the only one in the U.S. that was going to be available."[3]

Piedmont management searched extensively for a new advanced aircraft and chose

Fairchild over a number of other models, including Beech, the company whose consumer planes were retailed by Piedmont Aviation's fixed base division and who also made a model under consideration. British and French planes were evaluated too, but were ultimately rejected.[4] The F-27 bested the DC-3 in speed, operation, and comfort, and it immediately helped the airline enhance its image with the flying public. The new aircraft also brought new problems to Piedmont, but mechanic Don Collins had straightforward answers. He remembered how "a pilot would come through Roanoke. He'd be raising cane about pressurization or have a problem with pressurization on an F-27. We said, 'We'll fix that. We'll give you a DC-3.' He'd say, 'That's all right.'"[5]

A number of older pilots appreciated the skill and finesse it took to fly a DC-3. Tommy Orrell commented, "I just believe that starting and getting a base of skill and knowledge with the DC-3, in a tail wheel type airplane, just really did teach me how to fly as far as controlling the airplane with the flight controls, not just steering it on the ground with a nose wheel."[6] But new airplanes like the F-27 with its nose wheel, in addition to its other modern conveniences, made the job of piloting an airplane much easier.

The DC-3 had become a liability to Piedmont Airlines. Though still reliable, the aircraft looked obsolete in an era that heralded the jet engine as the modern means of air travel. *Twin City Sentinel* reporter Cleta Covington spoke for her times when she wrote, "To the modern eye she looks fat. She's dumpy, a little drab and not at all chic by today's standards."[7] With only eight F-27s in the fleet, many Piedmont passengers still rode on the earlier Pacemakers as the fifties turned into the sixties. In a day when almost everyone marveled at advances in technology, flying an old airliner like the DC-3 kept Piedmont in "puddle jumping" status in the minds of passengers.

To completely replace his original fleet, Mr. Davis shopped for more substitutes. What he found was a bargain offered by one of the trunk carriers that helped Piedmont hasten the departure of the DC-3. TWA wanted to sell its entire fleet of 17 Martin 404s. Davis recalled buying those aircraft in 1961 "under very favorable terms."[8] In doing so, he also noted that Piedmont "became the first local service airline to be completely equipped with air-conditioned, pressurized aircraft."[9]

The opportunity presented by the purchase of the Martin 404s meant an early but welcomed retirement of the DC-3s. Some mourned the passing of the plane that had meant so much to the carrier during its fledgling days. The final flight for Piedmont's first workhorse came exactly fifteen years after its first. On February 20, 1963, following a run from Columbus, Ohio, to New Bern, North Carolina, the *Great Smokies Pacemaker* (N40V) returned to Winston-Salem. It was not the same plane that had flown the initial trip from Wilmington to Cincinnati back in 1948, but the aircraft had been a part of the fleet since 1949. The similarity of first and last flights existed by design. Just like Piedmont's initial flight, Tom Davis was there completing the career of the aging Piedmont DC-3. Along with him was Bill McGee, who now worked as general sales manager, and Bill Turner, Piedmont's first paying passenger. The crew completed the nostalgic trip. Leon Fox and Harold Dobbins, who were now captains on other aircraft, were asked to make the last journey, just as they had the first. Both Fox and Dobbins needed a refresher course to go back in time. Fox said, "They pulled us off [regular flights] and give us a crash course in the old DC-3 to re-qualify us and we flew the last scheduled flight of the DC-3."[10]

In the excitement over the new airplanes, retirement of the old ones was largely ignored. The Winston-Salem papers only mentioned the occasion. The editorial page of the *Twin City Sentinel* did, however, contain a "Lament for the DC-3," calling the plane an "aviation

Flying above Roanoke, Virginia, this Martin 404 (*Savannah River Pacemaker*) proved to be a much more reliable plane for Piedmont than the F-27s. From the mid to late 1960s, the Martin was the workhorse of the fleet (Larry Dudley Collection).

institution and a friend an aviator could trust."[11] The column, with a predilection for the oratory of Douglas MacArthur, intoned, "Old airplanes never die, they just fly away."[12] Like most of society at the time, Piedmont Airlines was looking forward, not backward. Fox watched as the DC-3 was quickly shunted away. He said, "That airplane was sold the next day."[13]

The trade for the newer Martin 404s proved to be beneficial to both the buyer and the seller. Trunk carrier TWA had grounded its fleet of 404s, referred to by the manufacturer as "Skyliners," in search of a buyer. Piedmont could only purchase the Martins if it could at the same time get rid of its own DC-3s. Once the Spanish government expressed an interest in Piedmont's planes, a three way deal could then be conducted to the satisfaction of everyone. Airplane wholesaler "Jinks" Caldwell arranged the particulars. Piedmont traded the DC-3s for Martin 404s to TWA, who in turn sold them to the Spanish government. TWA got rid of its Martins; the Spanish got 21 affordably priced DC-3s, and Piedmont upgraded its stable of aircraft. The Speedbird stepped forward in its efforts to modernize.[14]

The purchase of the Martin 404s gave employees a satisfaction like nothing since the inception of the airline. Piedmont people could now crow about the fine fleet of turbo props, or prop jets as they were sometimes called, that serviced the line. The investment had been tremendous; over twelve million dollars were spent to retire the DC-3 in favor of newer, more comfortable planes. Along with the rejoicing came a bit of anxiety as workers recognized that these new planes upped the stakes. They asked themselves, "Could the small airline, with the cities it served, earn the revenue needed to pay for these planes?" Leonard Martin got right to the point, answering the question soon after asking it. He said, "I recall that when we added the Martin 404 in 1961 we all wondered how we would fill up that huge cargo bin. By the aircraft's second flight out of Charlottesville, both the cargo bin and passenger seats were full."[15] Loads like those witnessed by Leonard Martin ensured the debt would be paid without a problem.

The Martins gave Piedmont the appearance of a more up-to-date carrier. Hauling 44 passengers gave the airline its biggest passenger payload to date. "The airplane was a pretty doggone good airplane," asserted maintenance chief Ronnie Macklin. "Of course it had an R-2800 engine, which was one of the best large piston engines ever made. It was just a good deal."[16] When the transaction was made, Piedmont got a lot more than just the 17 Martin 404s it purchased. Bill Barber remembered, "We got every spare part that would fit on that airplane, everything from floor sweepings on up."[17] According to Barber, it took an entire warehouse to hold all the parts received from TWA. In addition, Ronnie Macklin recalled another benefit: "Their technical manuals were, as far as we knew, the best in the industry. So we got those manuals and we used that as a guide to write our manuals after that."[18] In all, as Zeke Saunders put it, "That was probably one of the best buys any airline ever made, to buy whole complete parts and everything."[19]

Another reason the purchase of the Martins proved to be a "good deal" was because the previous acquisition of the Fairchild F-27s had not worked out as hoped. Ronnie Macklin called the Martin 404 "a proven airplane," meaning that all the bugs had been worked out of

Ronnie Macklin demonstrates an engine. Though a small regional carrier, Piedmont became an early adopter of new technology (courtesy Piedmont Aviation Historical Society, Piedmont Silver Eagles).

it. By contrast, the F-27 was new and as Macklin explained, "Fairchild had never fielded an airplane like that, so they had a lot of problems with what they did." One example was the use of hydraulic nose steering on the plane, which had to be dropped for the air operated system. "You name it. There was a problem somewhere," noted Macklin.[20] Even passengers disliked the plane. Frequent flyer Earl Wilcox said, "The F-27 was not the smoothest riding plane. Air turbulence in the mountains was cause for a lot of air sickness." For that reason, he and the other businessmen on his commute began to refer to the F-27 as the "vomit comet."[21] Wilcox remembered the interior of the aircraft vividly, saying, "The seats and aisle were small. About midway down the aisle it was necessary to lower one's head where the wing structure came through the top of the cabin. Because the wing was over the cabin, the fuselage was only a few steps above the ground."[22]

The F-27 remained a troublesome aircraft during its tenure with Piedmont. Zeke Saunders recalled a meeting attended by Mr. Davis and the head of trunk carrier American Airlines, C.R. Smith, where the subject of problems with the airplane came up. Smith was one of the giants of the industry, having led the nation's largest commercial carrier since 1934. Zeke remembered Tom Davis complaining about the bugs in the F-27s and the advice he received from one of aviation's elder statesmen. "I never will forget, C. R. said, 'Tiny, I want to tell you something. I have been in this business a long time and you've only had those a year or so. You add another year and a half to it and you will have the troubles worked out.'"[23] Mr. Davis ultimately found a way to work out his problems with the F-27. By the mid-sixties, he had his fill of trying to cope with what was sometimes referred to as a "squirrelly airplane." By 1967, all of them were liquidated.

Piedmont was not finished, however, with a Fairchild product. The airline got rid of the F-27 by trading for an "improved" model. Zeke Saunders remembered being adamantly opposed to the purchase of the second generation craft, the Fairchild-Hiller 227, a longer, more powerful aircraft. "Tom got talked into buying the thing," Zeke said. "I remember the head of the executive committee and one of the directors came and I had lunch with them. They told me they agreed with me but Tom was the president and he wanted that airplane and they thought they would let him get it, although they didn't agree with him."[24] A total of ten FH-227s joined the Piedmont fleet in November of 1966. The first three were retrofitted with structural reinforcements to allow heavier payloads and were officially designated FH-227B, same as the last seven purchased, which already had the upgrade. Tory Vaughn flew the Fairchild-Hillers and did not number them among his favorite planes. Of the FH-227 he said, "You had to be a pretty good pilot to fly that thing or you're going to get in trouble with it."[25] For ten years, Piedmont's best piloted the FH-227. The model remained in service until 1976.

To the chagrin of those who didn't like the Fairchild-Hiller, Tom's brother, Egbert, Jr. who was a member of the board, acknowledged the trust they had in the decisions of his younger brother. "Anything Tom wanted to do, well, we one hundred percent backed him up from the board's point of view. We didn't have to say much because none of us knew anything about an airline. But Tom knew it and Tom would tell us what he wanted to do. And we'd say, 'OK buddy, go ahead and do it.'"[26]

The need to be as up to date as possible was paramount because Piedmont Airlines suddenly gained a lot more territory. Mr. Davis continually petitioned the CAB for more routes, adding to his list of cities served almost every year. Always ambitious, the company president asked for more than he got, but each request netted the airline something and gave the carrier's crew new destinations. Along with small and midsized communities, the applications

Captain Johnny Flowers and First Officer Bill Morgan pose in uniform in front of an FH-227 at Kinston, N.C., before taking off on another flight (Bill Morgan Collection).

increasingly aimed for larger cities. By the early sixties, Piedmont reached for Chicago, Atlanta, Baltimore, and Nashville. In March of 1962, the CAB followed the precedent it had set in earlier decisions by giving Tom Davis some of what he wanted, but not all: Denying Piedmont the right to fly into Chicago and Nashville for the time being, the agency did grant service to Atlanta and Baltimore. This step was an important one for Piedmont Airlines.[27]

The extension of routes on both the northern and southern end gave the airline many more options for passengers. By July of 1962, air travelers could ride Piedmont on their choice of three daily flights out of Atlanta to Baltimore with a number of stops in between. In addition, Piedmont gained the right to stop along the way in Augusta, Georgia, as well as Columbia and Florence, both in South Carolina. The addition meant a 50 percent increase in the number of passenger service miles the Speedbird flew, from 4,000 to 6,000. By conservative estimates, revenue for the local service carrier was expected to increase 80 percent as a result. In the interest of profitability, the CAB bestowed another small gift on Piedmont Airlines. The 1962 decision also included privileges of "skip-stop," which meant that after serving small communities with a required number of stops, routes could be scheduled to skip those stations on the way to other locations if there was nothing or no one scheduled to pick up or deliver. The change meant that the airline did not need to fly into Fayetteville, for example, every time a flight flew from Wilmington to Charlotte as long as Fayetteville received the minimum number of landings and departures promised to the CAB.[28]

Schedulers went to work fine-tuning passenger service, creating greater efficiency. The F-27s and 404s assisted that effort greatly. In addition to fewer stops, the faster planes would

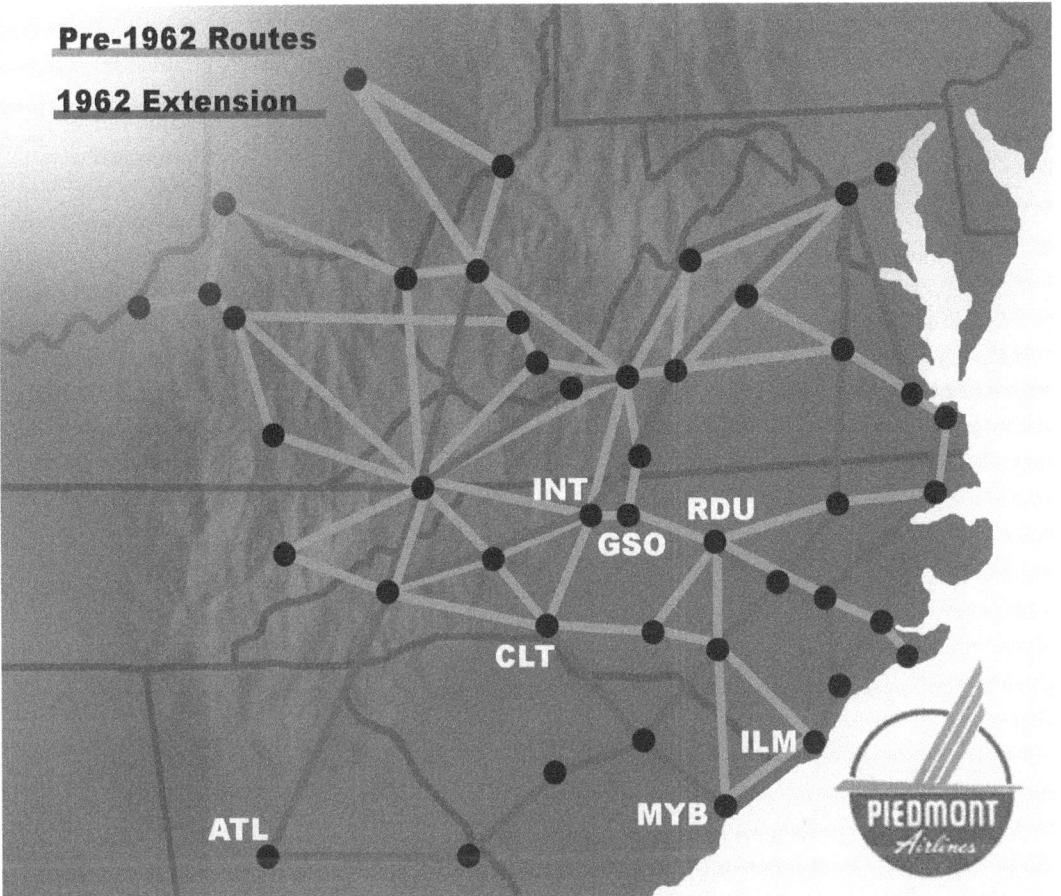

The 1962 award by the CAB increased Piedmont's route system by 50 percent and represented one of the most significant advances for the airline in its history (Author's Collection).

certainly cut travel time. Mr. Davis hoped the efficiency would cut costs while the higher capacity cabins would generate more revenue.

The real advantage of flying into Baltimore and Atlanta was that Piedmont could take its customers not only from city to city along its own line but to connections with the main trunk carriers so that passengers might travel far beyond the Southeast. Since Atlanta served as a major airport for carriers like Eastern and Delta, Piedmont's riders could link up easily and move on to wherever they wanted to go, be it San Francisco, Boston, or the Caribbean. As a result, passengers did just that. After 1962, business for Piedmont as a connector began a steady climb.[29] In building revenue, Piedmont people worked harder to connect passengers with their flights on the major carriers. As pilot Carroll Spencer pointed out, "We fed Eastern. We fed Delta. We fed American. We fed United. We fed Continental, so we gave a damn whether our passengers made their flight on their airline." Taking passengers from little airport to big, or vice versa, was the Piedmont mission. Even with delays caused by bad weather, the Speedbird made every effort to deliver customers to their next flight, even if the big airlines were indifferent to the work it took to get those passengers there. "It didn't make any difference to Delta, they'd shut the door in the people's face. They could care less," said Spencer, adding "They didn't cut us any ice. They said 'Delta pulls out on time.' They push back in the face of our people or we'd have the people on and the bags not on. But it didn't matter; we'd do the best we could."[30] The relationship with the larger carriers gave Piedmont even less room for error in its schedules.

Until the addition of Atlanta and Baltimore, the company struggled to stay out of the red. Profitability bounced back and forth between divisions. In 1959, airline revenue was meager, losing $91,517. General Aviation proved to be the salvation for the company that year with a $176,714 profit. The next year, the fixed base division fell $18,933 shy of breaking even, but the airline bounced back with a profit of $342,435.[31]

As the airline celebrated its tenth then fifteenth birthdays, the pace began to quicken, and Piedmont began banking on expansion. In 1958, the General Aviation division opened a facility in Alexandria, Virginia, just outside of Washington, D.C. Instead of servicing planes, the new branch sold only parts and accessories. It was the only Piedmont fixed base operation that did so.[32] By 1960, General Aviation had grown too large to remain a single division within the company. Operations were split, with General Aviation retaining sales and service of Beech Aircraft, as well as "engine and aircraft overhaul and maintenance."[33] The new division, called Central Piedmont Aero, handled distributorship of Piper Aircraft for the company, along with "flight training, aircraft storage, fuel service, and charter and air taxi service."[34] In Winston-Salem, Piedmont complemented its already large maintenance building with an engine overhaul shop in 1963.[35]

With new connector cities under his belt, Mr. Davis piloted his airline into clearer skies in 1963. After the retirement of the DC-3, his fleet was as modern as any local service

Piedmont employees celebrate the airline's 15th anniversary in 1963 with a cake and a copy of their internal company newsletter, the *Piedmonitor* (courtesy Piedmont Aviation Historical Society).

carrier's, and he accepted the plaudits and profits that came. October of 1964 brought the opportunity for Piedmont's board of directors to declare its first ever cash dividend, a ten cent per share bonus. Not only was the dividend a first for Piedmont shareholders, but it was a first for any publicly owned local service airline. Six months later, the board did it again, declaring another ten cent dividend. In the meantime, the airline recorded the boarding of its one-millionth passenger for the year of 1964. The second quarter of 1965 saw record boardings for three consecutive months.[36]

Piedmont reached the mark of one million passengers in a single year partially because of its pioneering use of promotional fares. In 1961, the "Xcursion Plan" offered discounted rates for weekend passengers, a first for a local service carrier. The fare helped increase revenue customers by 32 percent in 1962. The next year, Piedmont partnered with Allegheny Airlines and offered foreign customers the ability to travel on both systems for 30 days without limitations for $99. Called the "Visit USA" fare, it contributed to a 24 percent increase in passengers served during 1963.[37] In 1964, the airline served 1,078,028 people, which also included charter service.[38]

Piedmont's series of stations laid out along the east coast, called "the system" by employees, provided a number of bases from which flight crews flew in and out on a daily basis. Cities like Wilmington, Cincinnati, Louisville, Atlanta, Baltimore and Norfolk were termination points for routes, making several internal cities hub-like locations for the airline. Don Collins moved up to lead mechanic while in Roanoke during the sixties. He and his wife, Audrey, who worked as a secretary in the maintenance department, called Roanoke a hub before Piedmont actually had a designated one because most all flights went through Roanoke. As a result, Collins got to know many of the pilots flying through his facility. "If pilots had a problem with an airplane, we took it off the line and gave them another airplane," he said. "The next day a lot of them would come to the hangar and check on it, sit down and talk to us, buy us coffee. Several of them had light airplanes. We'd work on their airplanes for them. Fixed them [the personal aircraft] for them, give them sheet metal, give them rivets, give them wire, fix it for them, whatever."[39]

In turn, pilots reciprocated with help anytime they could. Saying that the mechanics and pilots "took care of each other." Don Collins added, "If we were out somewhere and needed a ride, we'd get a ride back even if the flight was full. I came out of Charleston, West Virginia, one night and there was six of us in the cockpit on a 737. In an F-27 the cargo bin was behind the pilot. It was the cockpit, then the cargo bin, then the cabin. I rode in the cargo bin a lot of times hanging onto the webbing."[40]

The larger Piedmont grew, the more it created opportunity for a smaller service to fly into many small towns that the Speedbird had. In 1963, a third line carrier, following in the footsteps of the trunk and feeder/local service airlines, emerged in Winston-Salem. The *Twin City Sentinel* screamed the headline, "New Airline is Established; To Have Headquarters Here" to announce the creation of South Central Airlines. The brainchild of St. Louis native Sam Coester, the new air transporter pledged to serve towns from 15,000 to 50,000, from Staunton, Virginia, to Savannah, Georgia. Many towns, like North Carolina's Lumberton, Statesville and Roanoke Rapids, as well as South Carolina's Sumter, Orangeburg and Newberry, were places Piedmont's Pacemakers did not venture. The new "airline" duplicated service to places like Charlotte, Norfolk, and Florence. After careful consideration by the CAB, where Piedmont justified need for access to all its cities, the intrusion of South Central might have seemed illegal. Indeed, the potential for taking away business from Piedmont looked likely on first glance. Several major differences existed between Piedmont and Coester's new carrier, though.

First, South Central did not fall directly under CAB jurisdiction because, even though it claimed "scheduled" status, flights were classified as an air taxi service, which meant they flew only when there was a need. Secondly, the plane of choice for SCA was a six-seat Piper Aztec, which made the company no real threat to Piedmont for moving large numbers of passengers. Finally, South Central was not in line for federal subsidy money since it planned no mail service.[41] Less than one year after its inception, the company was involved in an uproar caused by a fatal crash in Gainesville, Florida, and ceased operation after a short time. The threat to Piedmont Airlines never materialized.

Just in time for Piedmont's entry into Atlanta, the airline accepted further change dictated by shifting social tides. Since the late 1930s, airline passengers received assistance on their flights from male and female flight attendants. In fact, one of the first women to serve in this capacity came from Winston-Salem. United Airlines hired Virginia Davis, thanks in part to her medical training, to assist customers on Newark, New Jersey, to Chicago flights. United felt a nurse would have a calming effect on nervous or queasy travelers. However, Mr. Davis saw the issue differently. Male flight attendants, also called stewards or pursers, offered the more conservative Piedmont Airlines other advantages. Men could assist agents and even co-pilots on the ground with baggage handling, thus making three minute turnarounds possible. Also, rooming for three men on a flight was easier and cheaper to book, because they could all stay in the same room.

Piedmont Airlines bucked the trend among other airlines that were employing women as attendants. However, the airline did, on at least one occasion, use a woman to assist passengers, with their overwhelming approval. One evening on a flight that went through Charleston, West Virginia, a male purser became ill and was unable to continue his job. As captain of the flight, Tory Vaughn turned to station agent Betty Christo, who had been the first woman Piedmont hired in that capacity. Vaughn asked, "Betty, you want to take this thing on down to Norfolk with me?" When she answered, "Yeah, I'll do it," he said get in and away they flew. Vaughn said as they made their way to Norfolk, he kept thinking, "If this gets back to the company I might be in deep trouble." Later he found out that letters were indeed sent to Winston-Salem about the event. "Some of the passengers wrote the company about it," recalled Vaughn, adding, "Of course they were all positive."[42]

By the early sixties, Piedmont began to reconsider its all male policy. Female flight attendants, or stewardesses, as they were called at the time, were already recognized nationwide as an attraction unto themselves for frequent flyers, who were then mostly businessmen. As the liberating sixties began to flower, the job of stewardess became the symbol of a glamorous, exciting lifestyle to countless young women across the nation. At five years old, Connie Chalk Counts knew it the first time she saw a flight attendant. "We lived out in the country in Greenville [South Carolina]. My daddy had a big country church. He was a Baptist minister and we went to get him that night. He landed and the flight attendant opened the door and stepped out and that was my first exposure to anything like that, and I said, 'That's exactly what I want to do.'"[43] By 1968 she would land just such a job at Piedmont and stay with it for the next 34 years.

The early 1960s saw all the major carriers except Piedmont employ women to keep passengers comfortable during their flight. In the summer of 1961, management in Winston-Salem accepted the inevitable and began a feasibility study to determine how to implement the change. After nearly a year of weighing the pros and cons, considering "every angle, from the economy to customer service acceptance,"[44] Piedmont Airlines announced its intent to hire and train women as professional cabin crew personnel. The response netted "an almost instantaneous flood of letters and inquiries from young women all over the eastern half of the nation."⁴⁵ Out of 150 applications, 35 women were interviewed. Ultimately, five became members of the first class who got aboard just in time to help the system inaugurate the expanded route system that included Baltimore and Atlanta. One of them was Dottie Elmore Sain, who worked as a secretary in the Mercer County, West Virginia, Courthouse when she heard about an opening. She said, "They announced that they were going to start hiring females. They were probably the last airline to do that. So I got very interested in being a stewardess, as we were called back then."⁴⁶

Margaret Jenkins Queen joined Piedmont as one of eight flight attendants who worked regularly out of Atlanta. She was part of the third class of flight attendants hired and trained by the organization. Like all the early trainees, she received instruction from Harold Warner, Piedmont's director of flight services, and Thelma Taylor Davis. Davis was one of the airline's earliest female employees who had helped set up the reservation system for the company before tackling a number of other jobs, including stewardess instruction. Thelma Davis complimented Piedmont's newest employees, saying the women were "extremely enthusiastic and eager to learn. It was not difficult by any means to get this program off the ground because they had the Piedmont spirit also."⁴⁷

In full uniform, Carol Fair presents the company image of a flight attendant, known in the era as a stewardess. Women became part of the Piedmont flight crew in 1962 and quickly became an integral part of the operation (Carol Fair Collection).

Margaret Jenkins Queen recalled that much of her training for the job came while in flight:

> All we had were instant coffee and bottled Coca-Colas, and one type of cup, a paper cup that you put coffee in. The boys, the men flight attendants, they served them in the bottle. They wrapped a napkin around them and [said], "Here's your Coke." He would put them between his fingers. He'd serve four Cokes at a time. He'd take them out [to passengers] in his fingers and he'd say, "That's how you do it." And I thought, "Are you nuts, I can't do that." First of all, I don't think my fingers would be strong enough to hold them.⁴⁸

The world these women entered remained the domain of men. By later standards, treatment of stewardesses bordered upon what might be called sexual harassment. Connie Counts said, "They wanted you young, sexy and beautiful and that was the bottom line."⁴⁹ Through the sixties, stewardesses endured requirements centering primarily on their physical attributes. Standards dictated that hair had to conform with length and styling guidelines, a strict weight range had to be maintained, lipstick and fingernail polish had to be color coordinated with the uniform, and a foundation garment must be worn at all times. According to Margaret Queen, "They checked to see if you had on a girdle because they didn't want anybody pinching you. And if you had on a girdle, you couldn't be pinched. So you had to wear a girdle."[50] Connie Counts added with a smile, "Charlie Perry would check to see if you had a girdle on."[51] Presumably, he asked.

Female flight attendants were subjected to many rules that did not apply to their male counterparts. A stewardess had to remain single and couldn't work past her early thirties. Margaret Queen was one of many who agreed to the stipulations: "We signed a contract which said, 'I will retire upon being married or reaching age 32, which ever comes first.' And the reason age 32 came about was TWA. The president of TWA said, 'If these women are not married by the age of 32 and no man wants them, I don't want them either.'"[52]

Disagreeing with the double standard, Margaret Queen eventually circumvented the rules. Before she began training, she was already engaged. Then, in the summer of 1964 she wed, a clear violation of the rules for stewardesses. She simply said, "I didn't tell because you couldn't tell. If you told, you were going to be fired."[53] Eventually, however, she found her secret revealed, but with surprising results.

> My supervisor lived in Wilmington and he got on my plane in Winston-Salem one day and he said, "I've been to the home office and they've instructed me to ask you some questions." I said, "OK what are they?" I had no idea. He said, "come sit down right here beside me on the back of the airplane." He said, "I'm going to tell you the answer before I tell you the question. That's how they told me to ask you this question." Well, I am bewildered. What the heck is this? I had no idea. Another thing I did too, I went out alone to dinner with one of the Winston-Salem people who used to be my supervisor in Wilmington. His name was Al Huddleston. I did that purposely because I wanted people to think I was still single. So we made no bones about it that we went out to dinner. I thought well, if I'm going out to dinner with one of the honchos in Winston-Salem and having dinner, then they're never going to think I'm married. And it worked for a while. That's why Jack Doyle was on the airplane. He said Harold Warner told me to tell you to answer the question "No." And he finally got the question out and said "I have to ask you this. Are you married?" I said, "No, I'm not married."[54]

Thanks to an anonymous clipping about the wedding sent to Winston-Salem from Margaret's hometown paper, the *Littleton Observer*, management knew her circumstances and as she said, "They got it and looked at it and decided what they were going to do. Then they programmed how they were going to have me handle it."[55] Added Connie Counts, it was "because you were a good flight attendant and they didn't want to lose you."[56]

While Margaret Queen continued to work for Piedmont Airlines, others did not. When confronted with the issue, Virginia Lane made a different choice. On Saturday, June 23, 1966, she married G.F. Colvin. The following Monday a letter went out to her that said it was "company policy that a stewardess, upon marriage, resign from company employment." The letter went on to say, "Therefore, this verification of your marriage is considered as a resignation from company employment" and listed her resignation date as the day of her wedding. With "personal good wishes, "the letter was signed by C.L. Stewart, Jr., the division chief flight attendant for Washington, D.C., where the new Mrs. Colvin was based. Virginia Lane Colvin had made no attempt to hide marriage; in fact, she invited C.L. Stewart to attend the ceremony, a point he mentioned in the letter which Stewart used as verification of the new Mrs. Colvin's status. He closed by writing, "It is our wish that you will find happiness and contentment in your new life."[57] Contrasting the experience of Margaret Queen and Virginia

Colvin suggests that flight attendants who concealed their marital status demonstrated to the airline their desire to remain employed, which seemingly made all the difference.

For several years, rules on female flight attendant behavior and grooming remained stricter than it did for their male counterparts. At first women could not even join the union that represented male flight attendants. But as the equal rights movement of the 1960s progressed, restrictions on female flight attendants began to ease. They were allowed to have children and marry, as male flight attendants did. Women also gained the right to work past the former mandatory retirement age of 32; all these concessions were won during union negotiation after court litigation.[58] According to Carol Dobyns Fair, Dr. Martin Luther King was the reason. "When the civil rights act was passed, it made it against the law to fire us. Then it made it legal for you to be married."[59] Slowly, women began to erase the gender distinctions in their job.

Many female flight attendants chafed under the double standard but were powerless to change the rules and willing to adhere to the policy out of devotion to a profession they dearly loved. Carol Fair didn't hesitate a moment when given an ultimatum concerning her career as a stewardess. "I had a boyfriend that told me that I had to quit and come home and I told him bye, bye," said Fair, who added, "there was no question in my mind which one was going to go." However, she was always afraid that she might lose the job she cherished because of the restrictions. She revealed, "One of the worst things was the weight check thing because you were always under the gun. You were afraid you were going to be fired." With an ironic sense of humor about the situation, she recalled a common observation of the time, "The only time we ever lost weight was when we were running from the supervisor so we wouldn't be weighed in."[60] Carol Fair and numerous other female flight attendants persisted, dodging the scales, dieting when they couldn't, and ultimately served long careers with Piedmont Airlines.

Many pilots agreed that "seasoned" stewardesses were a greater asset on flights than younger, less experienced ones. An official of the Airline Pilots Association (to which Piedmont pilots belonged) said he would "much rather have an experienced gal back of me than some of the 'bunnies.'" In an *Atlanta Journal* column, Hugh Parks wrote that a veteran flight attendant was better in an emergency. "It wouldn't hurt a young pilot to have a good solid stewardess back there," remarked the columnist. "She might be able to teach him a few things." He went on to add that "some of the older girls are holding up fine. Some are real good looking."[61] The interest was apparently reciprocal. A number of female flight attendants ended up marrying pilots.

"It was just a welcomed sight," Captain Howard Thompson said of the addition of women to the flight crew. He acknowledged, "You had to conduct yourselves differently, and of course on overnight trips you had to kind of look out for the girls, as a gentleman."[62] Many of the pilots, especially the older ones, took a fatherly attitude toward their new workmates. Carol Dobyns Fair's first flight was to Winston-Salem for a job interview seeking to become a flight attendant. On her way back home, the 19-year-old resident of Johnson City, Tennessee, was summoned to the cockpit by Captain Hoss Dobbins. She admitted that she was "scared to death," wondering, "What does the captain want to see me for?" The captain quizzed the flight attendant about her name. When she told him, he broke out in a smile and said, "Good to know you, my name is Hoss Dobbins." And even though each spelled their last names differently, "My name is D-O-B-Y-N-S, His was D-O-B-B-I-N-S," a friendship had been cemented. There was no official family connection, but for the rest of her career with Piedmont, people sometimes mistook Carol Dobyns to be Hoss Dobbins's daughter. Among her fellow employees, she was nicknamed "Little Hoss."[63]

A flight crew gathers to commemorate the last flight of the Martin 404. Flight attendant Cindy Baldock hands a Piedmont passenger a flight bag as Captain Curly Bowden, First Officer Jerry Tate, and Purser Roger Dietz look on (Cyndee Baldock Peters Collection).

To Don Collins, the addition of females on the flight crew meant Piedmont had gained in stature. He said, "We hit the big time when we started hiring stews [stewardesses]," likening the advance to when Piedmont shed its DC-3s for the F-27.[64] The businessmen who flew regularly on the airline noticed female flight attendants too. Most found them to be helpful and attractive. Earl Wilcox described the stewardesses he saw as "very slim and trim. Their hair was above the collar with little pillbox hats as part of the uniform."[65]

The life of a stewardess seldom resembled the world Margaret Queen envisioned when she dreamed of getting onto an airliner. "I thought it was very glamorous. I thought, oh what pretty uniforms, you just stand around and look pretty and I thought, I can see the world. I can go anywhere and I can meet a lot of people."[66] Conversely, the job required many long days and constant exhibitions of patience. From the first class of stewardesses in 1962, Dottie Elmore Sain remembered 15 hour days and handling situations that were almost comic in their outlandishness. "Back in the good old days, people had a tendency to get airsick a whole lot more than they do now during the jet age.... So this lady got sick and her false teeth came out. The next stop we threw the bags away. So she realized they [the false teeth] were gone. We had to get an agent to get in the trash can.... Back in those days you did what you had to do."[67] Since Mr. Davis insisted on the needs of the customer coming first, sometimes employees were forced to dig deep to keep the passengers happy and willing to return to the airline the next time they needed to fly.

Flight attendants, male and female, were the face of the airline for most customers. They comforted, accommodated, refereed, policed, protected, and befriended passengers. Connie

Counts said, "We would absolutely go to any length. I would give them food out of my suitcase. I would call ahead. I brought them home with me."[68] The success of every flight depended in large part on the interpersonal skills of these stewardesses. For women in the early days, duties required them to handle tickets, as well as serve meals and refreshments, including alcoholic drinks for a dollar each. Flight attendants regularly passed out cigarette samples (always Reynolds brands since the cigarette company shared the same hometown with the airline). Most businessmen lit up soon after takeoff while the flight attendants had to breathe the secondhand smoke. "Society expected different then. They expected to get on an airplane and have a drink, a liquor drink. Everybody lit a cigarette, which was insane," recalled Counts. "As soon as the 'no smoking' sign came off, we wouldn't even be a thousand [feet] off the ground, they'd all light a cigarette, and you could not see the cockpit door."[69]

Over the years, female flight attendants witnessed a change in the type of passengers who flew. In their early days, flights almost exclusively hauled businessmen who traveled as a requirement of their jobs. Margaret Queen noted that women were an exception on a plane, saying, "Generally if it was a woman and two kids they were either very wealthy and had their nanny with them or it was kind of a military situation and that was kind of rare."[70] Many of the men who flew did so regularly. Flight attendant Ann S. Caudle said, "You used to have some of the same passengers back then. So we knew a lot of the people because at that time we flew the same routes."[71]

The job of flight attendant functioned as an intermediary between station agents, pilots, and passenger. It could be a very demanding job. Beyond the pressure while on duty, Dottie Elmore Sain also recalled the stress of having to work flight after flight: "They could fly as many hours as they wanted to, a hundred plus hours a month. That was over a month. If they needed you, you went."[72] "Piedmont worked the flight attendants to death," asserted Connie Counts. "They got every dime they could out of us. That's why they were so prosperous. And we felt like we were so small that if we didn't work ourselves to death we wouldn't make it. We took drink orders on the ground. We served drinks. We served dinner. We served breakfast on 40 minute flights from Atlanta to Asheville."[73]

Refreshments were relatively simple when women began to fill the role of flight attendant. Since most flights were short, passengers got a choice of two beverages, instant coffee or Coca-Cola. If a longer leg of a flight was in the air during lunchtime, Carol Dobyns Fair and her fellow flight attendants served sandwich trays. "The sandwiches were a sandwich cut into four pieces and put on a tray with some parsley or a few little pickles," said Fair, who noticed, "It was so funny because you would hand them a napkin and they'd finger all over their sandwiches before they picked the one they wanted. Back in those days that was the way you did it." In addition, passengers might also be offered a tidy dessert like "date nut bread with cream cheese in the middle" recalled Fair, who handed them out routinely on some of Piedmont's longer flights, like from Winston-Salem to Raleigh or Norfolk to Elizabeth City.[74]

As meals became more elaborate, their coordination often proved quite a task for personnel flying many short hops, especially when Piedmont upgraded its fleet to faster planes. Margaret Queen related a story about how busy those puddle jumping flights could be for a full service airline that made record time between New York and Dulles Airport in Washington, D.C.

> With tail winds the air time could be like 35 minutes for over a hundred people and you just cannot serve that many people. One night the gear went down and we didn't have all the meals served. So I went up and told the captain, Joe Fickling, I said Joe, the cabin is unsafe for landing. He said "What do you mean?" I said "all the meal trays are out, we haven't even

served everybody." So he told the co-pilot, "Gear up." And he said "Call the center and tell them we've got a light on and we need a couple of circles." He said, "Let me know when you're ready." He said, "do what you need to do." So we went back and served the rest of the meals and got everybody fed. They knew the gear had gone down, and I said, "Ladies and gentlemen, what we've just experienced is an early arrival but due to the fact that we haven't finished our meals, we're going to hold up here in the air just a little while, while you finish your meals. So enjoy your meal, and when we're ready to land I'll let the captain know." That was the best flight, everybody was so helpful. When it was time to clean up the cabin, they had them ready for you. It was beautiful. It was done in record time.[75]

Flight attendants were also expected to carry out plans for improved service made back in Winston-Salem by executives who aimed to make the flying experience for customers as inviting as possible. The Piedmont difference, though, meant that when the front line workers faced unexpected problems with a new procedure or new product, they could tell the home office and expect to be heard. Connie Counts and Margaret Queen both called Peter Van Duser, who was in charge of passenger services, "the flight attendant's best friend." He took their concerns and suggestions seriously. They told him when the chili was too messy or rolls fell off the plate, knowing he would find a way to improve the situation. In return, he knew that these women, who increasingly became flight attendants, were working creatively to make new services work. Connie Counts said, "Anything they wanted to instigate, any kind of different service, the flight attendants were real creative. The flight attendants would figure out how to do it."[76] They considered it part of the job. Both Margaret Queen and Connie Counts said they wanted the experience of flying with Piedmont to be a superior one for the customer. Years later, when both worked for USAir, Queen was recognized as a Piedmont veteran. She stated, "We enjoyed pleasing the passengers. Passengers would know. They'd get off the airplane and say, 'You were Piedmont weren't you'?"[77] The difference was in the attitude.

Female flight attendants became instantly popular on the airline, ultimately crowding out many males, although throughout the sixties and seventies, Piedmont customers were served by a substantial number of both men and women. Often, guys began their careers with Piedmont as flight attendants just to get their foot in the door. One example is David Caudle, who said the first six years he spent as a flight attendant were the best of his life, even though he eventually moved into the cockpit. "After I had been working for about two years, they started hiring the girls. Then I realized I can't be a purser all my life. I got to do something."[78] So the pilots who flew out of Wilmington with Caudle took him, quite literally, under their wings and gave him an education in flight. "The guys taught me how to do everything before I ever got hired. I knew how to do the flight plans. I knew the system. I knew the operation. The only thing they had to teach me how to do was land a Martin."[79] Occasionally the pilots would let the young trainee take off once they were sure he could handle the job. Caudle joked about the reason for helping him make the transition: "I always said they got me hired because they could get another female in the back. That's the reason they got me hired."[80]

Nurturing was how C.D. McLean described the airline. "It was a great time. Piedmont was a very nurturing carrier. If you wanted to do well you could do well there," said McLean, who started with the company as a wheels and brakes mechanic and left the company 28 years later as a staff vice president of flight training. "If you wanted to be successful the opportunity was presented to you because they didn't restrict you to one department if they saw you had the ability and you wanted to transfer just like so many flight attendants, so many mechan-

A 1970s graduating class of Piedmont stewardesses. The mini skirts were part of the ensemble for only a few years (Piedmont Silver Eagles Collection).

ics, so many ground workers transferred into flight ops. A lot of the pilots were just people who had started at the lowest level. They [management] always encouraged that and never hindered that process."[81]

Some of the early pilots went on to administration positions with the airline. Men like Zeke Saunders, Frank Nicholson, and Warren O. "Jack" Tadlock, who all once flew the line, moved over to management, overseeing the ranks of which they were once a part. By the 1960s, Jack Tadlock became chief pilot, a job that required evaluation of applicants who wanted to fly for the airline. He was tough and imposing. No pilot hired by Jack Tadlock ever forgot the experience. Captain James "Beetle" Bailey recalled engaging in a bit of trickery to get the attention of Captain Tadlock. Sauntering into his office on a Friday afternoon, Beetle Bailey had an answer when Tadlock told him rather vehemently that the airline wasn't hiring. Bailey replied, "I'm not really interested in a job. Can I just sit in your class? I ain't got no instrument rating." He did, however, promise to get one by Monday morning. Tadlock took the bait, saying that if he could obtain an instrument rating by Monday morning, Bailey could sit in the class. "I already had an appointment — unknown by him — to take my check ride for my instrument rating," Bailey remembered. "I passed that. I came in his class and waved a little ticket saying I had my instrument rating."[82] It was one of the few times an applicant got anything over on Jack Tadlock.

Often, the hiring experience could be a tedious one. After interviewing for a job in 1966, Larry Dudley went down from his home in Roanoke to Winston-Salem for six more weeks

Larry Dudley described himself as a "happy young man" on May 16, 1967, as he turned from his duties for a moment to pose in the cockpit of a Martin 404. Dudley persisted in seeking an interview with Jack Tadlock until he realized his dream, to wear the Speedbird and fly the route of the Pacemakers (Larry Dudley Collection).

with no appointment and sat outside Tadlock's office waiting for the chance to make another pitch for employment. "I knew he would come out sooner or later," said Dudley. "Every time he'd come out he'd talk to me a little bit. The seventh time he came out he said, 'What the hell are you doing back down here?'" Larry Dudley replied, "I came after a job." With usual bluster, Jack Tadlock shot back, "I'm going to give you my damned job. You're down here every time I turn around." The tactic proved successful. Dudley said, "We went in and talked, and I thought that was as close as I was getting. I didn't go back anymore until I got hired. I was in the first class after that."[83]

Prospective pilots generally had to hang out a lot to get noticed by Tadlock and his associate Jim Bradley, who also interviewed hopefuls. Jim Hamilton may have gotten his job for reasons that had little to do with his airplane handling abilities. When he came to Winston-Salem, he caught the attention of administrator Jim Bradley, who continually shooed away candidates who hung around his door. When the resume of Hamilton came across Bradley's desk, he found that the young pilot was well qualified and had a college degree. But the real topic of conversation between the two of them was an old house purchased by Bradley that had an uneven floor. Since Hamilton's father was a house mover, Hamilton gave Bradley some tips on shoring up the foundation. Then, the interview concluded. Three weeks later Bradley called Hamilton to say, "I don't know how you can fly and I don't really care but you sure did help me out with jacking up the floor."[84]

Chief Pilot Jack Tadlock kept a tight rein on his pilot group after they were hired. Captain Howard Thompson heard from Tadlock a couple of times after flying a particularly rough flight through thunderstorms between Washington, D.C., and Charlottesville, Virginia. Thompson recalled the conditions vividly: "It looked like the end of time. I'm out there holding. My airplane is half upside down. Everybody is sick and I can't do anything about it." After finding a "clear slot" through the clouds and landing, Thompson was in no mood to answer passenger questions about the weather on down the line when two riders asked. Both got off and rented cars for the rest of their journey after the encounter, writing Jack Tadlock about Thompson's abruptness. Tadlock sent Captain Thompson a letter berating him for his behavior. "I answered his letter, and then two days later I get a letter from Tadlock praising me. Two or three other people said they had been in weather but they'd never been in weather like that, even in World War II, and they praised me for what a good job I did." Thompson said he never quite understood Tadlock. "He was famous for sending you a letter about the bad part. Then after you answered him, he'd send you the good letter."[85]

When a situation called for a face to face meeting with the chief pilot in which some discrepancy had to be worked out, pilots quipped they were going to Winston-Salem to do the "Tadlock Shuffle." In Howard Thompson's words, "That meant you paced the floor in front of his desk until you wore a hole in it."[86]

No one was exempt from the scrutiny of the chief of flight operations, although at times, his bark was much worse than his bite. After the crash of Piedmont plane in New Bern, North Carolina, Jack Tadlock and a number of concerned employees flew down to help out. Among them was Captain J.Y. Spencer. While Tadlock hurried to the scene of the accident, Spencer helped out by relaying messages back to Winston-Salem from the station at New Bern. Later in the day, Mr. Davis returned from the crash scene and said to Spencer, "Let's go to Winston-Salem." Spencer's reply: "Yes, sir." So they climbed into a Piedmont F-27, with Mr. Davis in the captain's seat and Spencer as copilot. Mr. Davis asked Captain Spencer if he knew how to fly the Fairchild aircraft and when Spencer assured the president of the company that he did, they took off. "He [Mr. Davis] didn't have a type rating or much time in the Fairchild at that time," recalled Spencer. "He took off and just like a homing pigeon went right to the outer marker at Winston-Salem and he said now when we get ready in the landing pattern up there, he said, 'You tell me when to drop the gear and the flaps and the approach speed,' and I said 'yes, sir.'" Spencer reported the landing was as "slick as you could be." Since the flight was uneventful, J.Y. Spencer forgot about it until stopped in the hallway about a week later by Jack Tadlock, who wanted to know how he got back from New Bern. About his boss, J.Y. Spencer said, "Jack was a great guy to work for. You just didn't ever want to cross him because he wanted the truth out of you regardless of how bad it hurt. If you didn't tell him the truth, he would tack you to the wall." Forthrightly, Spencer told Jack Tadlock that he had flown back on the Fairchild. Quickly, Tadlock quizzed his pilot, "Who flew that airplane back?" When told that it was Mr. Davis, Jack Tadlock blurted out, "My goodness, didn't you know Mr. Davis didn't qualify in that airplane? He didn't have a type rating." Unaware of the situation, J.Y. Spencer told his boss, "No sir, I didn't know that." At that point Tadlock began to admonish Spencer, saying, "You shouldn't have let him do that." In reply, Spencer calmly explained the situation. "Mr. Tadlock, Mr. Davis told me he wanted to fly to Winston-Salem and I wasn't going to tell him he couldn't fly his own airplane to Winston-Salem." Jack Tadlock could only say, "Well, don't let it happen again." According to Spencer, he never heard another word about his flight with Mr. Davis.[87]

Years later, J.Y. Spencer had a similar clash with Jack Tadlock. Flying a charter flight for skiers to Colorado one December Saturday, bad weather conditions and repeated mistakes put the trip behind schedule more than three hours. In order to keep his customers happy, Captain Spencer devised a number of activities for the passengers, which included drawing straws to select someone for the privilege of getting to ride the jump seat, just behind the pilots, and a raffle where the pot went to whomever picked the right minute in the hour when the flight touched down in Denver. In addition, Spencer opened the bar for passengers and no one complained about the lateness of their arrival. A week later, the absence of any pilots with enough flight time left to fly another charter back to pick up the skiers forced Jack Tadlock to take the controls himself. When Tadlock picked up the same travelers that J.Y. Spencer had dropped off the previous weekend, they all asked who was going to get to ride the jump seat. Unknown to them, Captain Tadlock had just recently sent out a memo that stated because of a crackdown by the FAA, no passengers were to be allowed to ride up front with the pilots. Again, Tadlock jumped Spencer in the hall, saying, "You didn't, you didn't fly that charter out to Denver, Colorado Sunday a week ago, did you." When Spencer freely and honestly admitted that he did, Tadlock reminded him of the memo in no uncertain terms. Spencer responded:

> I said, "Wait a minute Captain Jack," after about two or three minutes. I said, "You picked that group up. Did you get a single complaint from anybody about the flight? The weather was terrible, we were late getting started, the de-icing truck didn't work. Then, it ran out of fuel. We had to stop in Oklahoma City and refuel. We had a good time and nobody complained when I got out there. Did you have any complaints when people got back on the plane coming back to Winston-Salem?" He thought about it a minute and then said, "I didn't have a single complaint but don't let it happen again."[88]

The two events ended with the same warning from the chief of flight operations. Both demonstrate how seriously Jack Tadlock took the business of flying commercial aircraft. He wanted a safe airline and at times would use his forceful personality to make the point. On the two flights where J.Y. Spencer came into conflict with Jack Tadlock, the pilot had considerations beyond which his boss knew. In the end, Tadlock trusted his pilots to do the right thing, and even though pilots were a hard group to handle, they obeyed their manager, when they could.

One of the legendary pilots that Jack Tadlock had to watch closely was Jim Brown. Characterizing him as a "seat of the pants flyer," R.L. Gordon remembered him well. Gordon recalled Jim was a deacon in his church and "could drink more beer than anybody."[89] Pilots like Jim Brown exemplified an indomitable spirit that could not be squashed. R.L. Gordon concurred, saying, "Pilots are the most outgoing people you'll ever meet in your life. I tell people, 'How would you like to be up there with a guy shooting a category two approach [difficult] that you can't see anything about a hundred foot off the ground and them saying I don't know if I can make this or not?'"[90] When intense situations arose, a pilot in the cockpit who felt he could handle the situation was something passengers wanted.

Jim Brown was just one of many Piedmont success stories. After a stint in the Navy during World War II, Brown worked in his hometown of Johnson City, Tennessee (part of the Tri-Cities that included Kingsport and Bristol, Tennessee), where Piedmont flew in and out

Maybe the most talked about pilot in Piedmont history, Captain Jim Brown is shown in the center joking with his fellow employees. Brown flew every kind of plane Piedmont owned. He retired in 1989 (Marilyn Brown Collection).

daily. In April of 1953, Jim Brown went to work for Piedmont as a purser. His intent was to become a pilot, which he later did. His daughter, Debbie, also went to work for the company at his insistence. "The minute I turned 20 and I was old enough to get on, he made me quit college and go to work because his children were going to work for the greatest airline that ever was," she said. "In fact, I've heard him say it a million times. I can hear him saying it to this day, that he would have paid them to let him fly."[91]

A larger than life personality, Jim Brown spawned a string of stories that defined the maverick days of pilots. Debbie remembered that he never told most of the things that happened to him when he came home. She said, "There had to be a whole crowd of people to listen to them [his stories]. We weren't privy to them until there was a crowd of people around." Along with being a character, Jim could also recreate the events with enthusiasm.

In the world of Jim Brown, no one was spared from a practical joke, not even a brand new employee. When Philip Beeson joined Piedmont as a purser, he had the "honor" of his first flight being with Jim Brown. As Beeson remembered, Irv Eisler served as captain and Brown assisted as first officer. As soon as Beeson stepped into the cabin of the DC-3, he "kept hearing this bird whistle so I went up to the cockpit and I told the crew." With a straight face, Eisler and Brown told the new flight attendant to "try to find it." Beeson searched everywhere on the flight to Cincinnati while trying to serve passengers their Cokes and cigarettes until it dawned on him that the noise was coming from a speaker. "It was Jim Brown whistling," said Beeson, who noted that there was "a little telephone in the back and interphone in the front and Jim was whistling over the interphone like a bird."[92] Philip Beeson had quickly learned about the antics of Jim Brown.

Things just had a way of happening to Jim Brown. When he spilled coffee on his socks, Brown asked his captain, Charlie Meacham, what to do. Meacham suggested hanging the socks out of the window of the DC-3 they were flying, as a way to dry them. The socks flapped in the wind as Jim shut the window on the dry end to hold the socks in place. While in the air, the socks stretched to stocking length of about four or five feet, thanks to the 200 mile per hour winds created by aircraft. But Jim Brown never got the chance to wear those socks. As he opened the window in mid-flight, Brown's socks flew away, leaving Brown technically out of uniform but with another story to tell.[93]

Brown's most famous incident has two versions. Piloting a charter flight to Freeport on a "gambling junket," Jim Brown felt he did not have enough expense money for the trip. He called Jack Tadlock back in Winston-Salem to send him more cash, asking Tadlock to pull money from Brown's own savings account at the company credit union. Tadlock, thinking Brown wanted a loan, refused and hung up on the pilot. By 3 o'clock the next morning, both Brown and his first officer on the flight were, in his daughter's words, "pretty ripped," and Brown told his copilot, "I'll show you how to get some money." They called Jack Tadlock at home asking him how much the plane they flew down was worth. When Tadlock asked why, Jim Brown informed his boss, "I just lost it in a poker game" and hung up on him. Debbie finished the story as she remembered her father telling it. "The next morning Tadlock had gone over and had gotten money out of Dad's savings account and Dad had the money. But the story that Dad wanted told was that he had really gambled away the airplane in a poker game, and put it up as collateral."[94] The story that Jim Brown actually lost and then won back the airplane he was flying became legend at Piedmont.

Jim told copilot and friend Dave Johnson that doing something for the first time was what mattered. After that, it just wasn't the same. So when other pilots later felt compelled to fly naked, they were flying in territory where Jim Brown had already gone. Like the gambling story, this feat has been bandied about among Piedmont folk for decades. The motivation for the exhibition or even its validity has only been conjectured and never proven. Dave Johnson was once told, "They got naked and they put their epaulets on their shoulders. So [Jim Brown] said, 'We were not technically naked.'"[95] Others claimed it was a necktie that kept them "technically" clothed. Whatever the circumstance, the story demonstrated the magnitude of daring and reputation Jim Brown held at Piedmont Airlines.

Jim Brown was in many ways a quintessential pilot for Piedmont. Perhaps more outlandish than most, he lived up to the expectation of an airplane pilot in the sixties as a larger-than-life figure. Fellow pilot Jim Hamilton observed Brown as a guy who "would try to act like he was a little bit dumb. Jim was a real smart man." Hamilton cited his financial acumen as an investor and his public service contributions as a city councilman in his hometown of Bristol, Tennessee, as well as his piloting skills as evidence of Brown's tremendous abilities.[96] Copilot and friend Dave Johnson agreed. He mentioned feats handled by Brown that very few other pilots could accomplish, including the ability to fly from Boeing's Seattle plant back to Winston-Salem without refueling. Brown used to say there were "trained pilots" and then there were "pilots."[97] What he meant was that some pilots were taught to fly like being trained for any given profession. Others seemed to understand how to handle an airplane instinctually. Everyone would put Captain Brown in the latter category.

Jim Brown also possessed the ability to "bring other pilots along" said Johnson, who noted that the captains held certain prerogatives in the cockpits for themselves. For example,

Johnson said, "If a copilot was to touch the seatbelt switch lightning would probably strike them dead." Instead of exercising his right to control the seatbelt switch, which was a traditional prerogative of the commander of the flight, Jim Brown as captain and Dave Johnson, his copilot, developed a shorthand language that gave the copilot, sitting in the right seat, the privilege. "I was flying with Jim with the FAA aboard and did our normal little deal," said Johnson. "We always ran our checklist but our answers were sometimes a little bit off. We were cruising at altitude. [Jim said] 'Hey boy, you want to let them shit?' I reached up and he'd let me turn the seatbelt sign off and whenever we'd start down it'd be, 'Hey boy, run them out of the shitter'" to the shock of the FAA man on board. The government official told the two pilots, "You two fly this airplane as well as anybody I've ever seen fly a 727, and it's obvious you all fly together a lot because I ain't never heard a seatbelt sign called a shitter switch."[98] In his own way, Jim Brown was passing along some of the job that he knew his copilot would one day fill. And though Brown was the consummate pilot, he never took himself too seriously.

Even with their sometimes crazy antics, pilots remained a key element in Piedmont Airlines. Since many within the management structure were pilots themselves, the relationship between the two was very close. Often, the leadership sought out the pilot group as a barometer of the company's success on the line. Bill Kyle, a Piedmont pilot who moved into management, remembered regular meetings conducted by Mr. Davis with his pilots. "We'd go to various bases and listen to the pilots and see what their thoughts and complaints and suggestions were," recalled Kyle, who said that over dinner, Mr. Davis wanted to know "how are things going and how do you think we can do it better." Calling it "one of the outstanding things about Piedmont,"[99] Kyle acknowledged a lot of improvements came out of those meetings.

Pilots formed the bonds of brotherhood, sharing conditions, experiences, even language among themselves. Many who flew for Piedmont joined a fraternity of pilots, known as the Quiet Birdmen, or "Q.B." for short. The organization required regular attendance to meetings, sponsorship by a member and a unique initiation to the organization. Zeke Saunders remembered his ceremony, which included wearing a prisoner's uniform. "My initiation was in Charlotte. [I had] to have an authentic uniform and they gave me a bag to carry. And in that bag, which I didn't know, was a half gallon of white liquor. I carried it 10 blocks. The police were supposed to arrest me and take me in. And I would speak to them and they'd just throw up their hand. I never got a hit. So when I got to the terminal they said I had to sweep the terminal."[100]

The interest and experience of flying created a strong bond of brotherhood in these men who came to Piedmont from a number of different backgrounds. Many of the early pilots flew during the war. Some logged enough hours in light planes to gain consideration. Some, like David Caudle, began as a purser for the airline. Maybe the most unusual jump to the cockpit came with the help of Bill Barber, who himself turned down the opportunity to fly. "I had a boy who was out marking lines for us in the parking lot. He said, 'Hey, I want a job with you all.' I said, 'Well what kind of job do you want?' He said, 'I want any kind of job.' So I put him in the print shop. And he ended up being a captain."[101] Pilots came from everywhere, including places Tom Davis never dreamed of when he hired his first one.

Philip Beeson had a similar kind of introduction to the cockpit. As a teenager, Beeson groomed horses for a living. On Saturday mornings, Zeke Saunders brought his daughters out to ride at the stables where Beeson worked. "When I turned 19 it dawned on me that I was not making any money in the horse riding business," said Beeson, who asked Saunders for a job with Piedmont. Saunders replied that he thought they could use Beeson since the airline was in the process of expanding into Frankfort, Kentucky. Saunders gave Philip Beeson his choice of jobs: station agent or purser. Unfamiliar with the duties of a flight attendant, Beeson asked Zeke what they did. Saunders said, "You serve cokes and cigarettes on a DC-3 and F-27." Beeson jumped at the chance. "I said I believe I would like to be a purser. Well, I went to work for Piedmont in November of 1960 as a purser and that was my first aviation experience."[102]

Beeson joined the ranks of a group of men who were unique among the Piedmont workforce. The responsibility of piloting an airplane required a special breed of individual. R.L. Gordon observed many of these individuals after he took over the job of training pilots. "I used to tell some of these women around, these pilots, they don't know the word 'no.' I don't care what you say, they're going to have another approach to you," he said, adding: "There's a lot of truth in that. Of course, they are so positive thinking. They think they can fly an airplane in the worst kind of situations."[103]

For their confidence and bravery, pilots were held in high esteem by their coworkers but occasionally, they were also resented. Thirty years before the era of personal cell phones, Captain Woody Bost carried around a telephone handset and cord in his coat pocket. As part of this practical joke, he wired up a ringer that he triggered to ring. When it did he pulled the phone out of his pocket and carried on imaginary yet convincing conversations to the chagrin of those around him. After seeing Bost's trick, Paul Snell got one for himself. One night in Atlanta after landing, the flight crew was on a bus at the terminal when Snell decided to spring his joke on his fellow riders. Leaning on his coat to activate the ringer, Captain Snell pulled the phone out of his pocket and began a conversation with his wife that included her request for bread and milk on his way home. Snell concluded his "phone call" and returned the phone handset to his pocket. No one commented on the event until Snell started to get off the bus. As he did, the Piedmont pilot heard the bus driver mutter under his breath, "Damned pilots got everything."[104]

As a fair minded individual, Mr. Davis gave equal opportunity to anyone who wanted to work for his company, including nonconformist pilots. While he never went out of his way to seek minorities for employment, he also never shied away from individuals for any reason if he thought they could be an asset. Warren Wheeler applied for a pilot's job in 1966. Like Tom Davis, Wheeler fell in love with airplanes as a kid and sported a private pilot's license by the time he graduated high school. The military did not accept him for service during the Vietnam era because of a physical disability, so he was free to pursue his love of flying. A flight instructor and charter pilot, Wheeler flew former North Carolina governor Terry Sanford around the state before sending his resume to Piedmont. "I don't know where the application went," said Wheeler. "I got the impression that it went into the drawer somewhere and that was where it was going to stay." Warren Wheeler wasn't sure if he would get a fair shot at Piedmont because he was an African-American. One day Mr. Davis got a call from Terry Sanford, who asked the Piedmont president to take a look at the 22 year old pilot. Mr. Davis called the Chief pilot and said, "If he's qualified hire him."

Warren Wheeler went to work for Piedmont in March of 1966, but knew there would probably be what he called "resistance." "It was a southern based airline and there were a lot of people there who didn't want me there, that's for sure. That didn't necessarily flow into the management. The president of the company, Tom Davis, couldn't have been a more fair-minded person. He was a jewel."[105]

Wheeler described his reception at Piedmont as "mixed." He noted, "There were some wonderful people there who did not participate in that resistance who were very supportive, and very easy to get along with and very helpful. And then there were just a few that were on the opposite side, resistant and totally opposed to it." Wheeler worked in that atmosphere for two years until he felt "the fun of it was out. I was prepared to quit. I had made up my mind that I was going to walk into Tom Davis's office and try to ask for a leave of absence just to catch my breath and if he didn't give it to me, I was going to quit." Wheeler found a sympathetic boss who understood the problem. "Tom Davis knew everything I was going through. He didn't hesitate for a minute. He said, 'Take the leave of absence. Let me know when you want to come back.' That's the only reason I made 28 years with Piedmont."[106]

Warren Wheeler shared more than a love of flying with Tom Davis. Both possessed an entrepreneurial spirit as well. While at Piedmont, Wheeler began his own flying business. Wheeler Flying Service was a charter carrier and later, a commuter airline flying Cessnas and Aerostars.[107] He balanced that operation with his work as a first officer for nine years, then captain on the YS-11 and the Boeing jets. Warren Wheeler felt such respect for the company president that he asked permission from Mr. Davis to begin the sideline business. "I went into Tom Davis's office and told him what I was going to do it and asked him what he thought of it." Wheeler remembered Mr. Davis's response. "He said he didn't see any benefit to Piedmont but he didn't see any problem either so if I wanted to do it, go ahead and do it." Warren Wheeler said he thought that Mr. Davis might have later regretted the decision to approve, but never went back on his word.[108]

Another move made by Mr. Davis that demonstrated his egalitarian nature also involved African-Americans. Many blacks who worked at Piedmont did so in the maintenance area as assistants and helpers. They were left out of the company's unwritten but recognized practice of helping workers move up within the company until the inequity was brought to the attention of Mr. Davis. Ronnie Macklin remembered that the company president instantly saw potential for both the company and its workers. Black mechanic assistants were given an opportunity to go to take classes that ultimately allowed them to move up to better jobs with better pay.[109]

By the mid-1960s, Mr. Davis employed a different type of managerial skill to hold his company together. No longer was the question being asked, "Would Piedmont Airlines be successful?" Instead, as confidence grew, the focus shifted to improvement. Management at all levels concerned itself with efficient operation as well as sustained growth, balancing the two in every budget, every purchase, every day of operation. By then Ronnie Macklin acknowledged that maintenance got enough to do its job but still, "If you had a truck and you had the option of buying one used and fixing it up or a new truck, we had to buy the old truck and fix it up."[110] In getting the resources to do his job, Macklin fared better than those who worked stations at the airports, bringing the Speedbirds in. Flying Martin 404s into airports along Piedmont routes, Carroll Spencer noticed that the support equipment for his airplane came from other airlines. Spencer remembered, "We borrowed Eastern, American, United, or anybody's ground equipment, power units to start our airplanes, and de-icing equipment." Since the big boys did not consider Piedmont a threat, they allowed the smaller airline to use their equipment. "We'd take a delay to get going, coming through Charlotte while our agents negotiated with other airlines to borrow their equipment," said Spencer, who pointed to the frugal nature of Mr. Davis as the reason Piedmont didn't have its own tugs and power carts. "He would buy a jet or two with subsidy, but he couldn't let go the money to buy ground service equipment."[111]

Mr. Davis got the most out of everything, including people. A 1967 story on the airline called the company "conservative," noting that "Davis runs Piedmont with a tight budget and with a tightly-knit management team. The entire $52 million operation has three VP's and four asst. VP's."[112] With Davis as both president and treasurer, officers for the company included Zeke Saunders, Bob Northington and Gordon Brown as vice presidents, with both Saunders and Northington also members of the board of directors. The assistant vice-presidents were Bill Barber in charge of purchasing, Howard Cartwright, who oversaw maintenance and engineering, Bill McGee, who handled sales, and Bob Turbyville, who directed traffic.[113]

Surprising as it might be for a company based in a southern city, Piedmont Airlines accepted unionization and prospered as a result. For union members during the 1960s though, it was an affiliation they played down. Calling Winston-Salem "a hotbed of anti-union personnel," Carroll Spencer asserted, "If we had a union organizer come down and walk down the street and the police recognized him as a union organizer, they were liable to arrest him. It was a very serious thing to be a union man in Winston-Salem in the 60s."[114]

Piedmonts pilots had joined the Airline Pilot's Association only a few years after the carrier took off. Male flight attendants also joined ALPA before starting a union of their own. Mechanics were the last main group to seek union representation. Don Collins worked on both sides of the issue, as a mechanic under union contracts, then later in management for Piedmont. He noted that introduction of the International Association of Machinists, which also included aerospace workers, aided the company as well as its employees. "Everybody had

Operations center, Winston-Salem, N.C. In order to keep track throughout the day each flight was represented by a strip of paper. As the day wore on a mouse glided across the board with its tail representing the current time so any flight could pinpointed if necessary (Piedmont Silver Eagles Collection).

their way," said Collins, who pointed out the fact that operating rules for mechanics varied from one facility to another. After a layoff, Collins asserted that the problem became acute. "The main thing that brought the IAM to Piedmont wasn't salary but it was seniority because they kept people here with lesser seniority than the people they laid off and people saw that." Union representation created a standardized work environment that provided clear expectations for every mechanic no matter where they worked. "The company prospered better as far as in the way they treated the people. You knew what to do because you had a contract to go by."[115]

Throughout the decade, the operation remained lean until growth demanded expansion. In 1968, it came in the form of a new headquarters at Smith Reynolds Airport in Winston-Salem. The mid-1950s command center for the company, located on Liberty Street across from the Smith Reynolds Airport terminal, could no longer contain the maturing business. In an effort to make sure Piedmont Aviation remained a Winston-Salem based enterprise, Forsyth County's Airport Commission first built Central Piedmont Aero a new $35,000 facility in 1965.[116] Two years later, the commission embarked on an $8.7 million bond program, which included the construction of a new headquarters building and hangar complex on the northern end of airport property for Piedmont Aviation. The $6.5 million structure was offered to Piedmont on a twenty year lease. It was three times larger than the facility it replaced and the hangar built behind the offices had the capacity to house six large aircraft. Newspaper reports of the time quoted Mr. Davis saying that the new facility would create as many as 300 additional jobs to the workforce of over 1,000 that planned to move into it in 1968. Along with strengthening runways for the coming of jets, Forsyth County Manager Robert House saw the expansion as a boon for both parties: "We can expect to fill all Piedmont's needs here."[117] Again the city of Winston-Salem had made a strong effort to keep aviation a part of its offering.

One particular event from the construction of the new headquarters conveyed the kind of leader Tom Davis had become to his people. Related by Tom Sharpe, who became a pilot after first doing charter work for the fixed base division in the seventies, the oft-told story defined the president of the company in the eyes of Piedmont employees:

> Mr. Davis apparently, from what I was told, had gone up to do a preliminary tour of the building all on his own, and he was getting prepared for the opening of the building, of the hangar. He called his general contractor and said we've got a problem out here and I would like to meet with you. So the guy comes out, and he says, "Mr. Davis, what's the problem?" Mr. Davis went around to the bathrooms and pointed to one of signs, and said, "There are no men and women who work for this company, only ladies and gentlemen." And that sort of summed up what we felt he felt about his employees. He didn't have men and women working for him but he had ladies and gentlemen. And he expected you to act accordingly. He looked at you as a gentleman and he expected you to act like one. At least that was the way I felt about it. I knew if I wanted to disappoint him, don't act like a gentleman.[118]

Until Mr. Davis entered into the deal with the airport for a new corporate office, apprehension remained (at least on the part of city and county officials) about whether Piedmont might move its headquarters to another location. Back in the fifties, the new home was rumored to be Bristol, Tennessee. By the mid-sixties, the alternate location ranged much closer, just 17 miles down the road in Greensboro. In 1963, Smith Reynolds Airport recorded almost 130,000 takeoffs and landings, making it North Carolina's busiest airport. In subsequent years, both Charlotte and Greensboro began to make inroads, soon eclipsing Winston-Salem's airport.[119]

Mr. Davis considered moving to be nearer his customer base. Much like his move earlier, the thought of losing Piedmont Airlines propelled municipal officials to keep Mr. Davis happy by again sweetening the pot, creating an even more comfortable home for the airline and fixed base operation. In the end, everyone breathed a sigh of relief. Davis got an impressive new building proudly displaying the Speedbird. The city of Winston-Salem kept the company, and more importantly, its jobs and employees avoided being uprooted.

The new headquarters facility revealed more about Piedmont Aviation than just the fact that it was a growing company. Years later pilot Dave Johnson pointed out that "the corporate office was in a hangar,"[120] demonstrating to him how important aviation was to everyone who worked for the company. Many employees agreed, including flight attendant Lynn Sass, who also came to work later for Piedmont. She said, "Everybody that was working for that company absolutely lived and breathed airplanes."[121] From conception to completion, the new facility revealed who the real stars at Piedmont were. They were the planes. Everyone else was just there to help them fly, including the company president.

Mr. Davis seemed to enjoy his position as company patriarch, watching over his employees as he did his own family, which had grown to five children — two sons and three daughters.[122] He paid meticulous attention to the company, answering every inquiry with a typed response. When he did occasionally partake of a hobby, it still centered on flying. If he had the time he flew himself to meetings in his own small plane. Periodically, he made trips back out to Tucson, Arizona, where he kept a house. Egbert Davis, Jr., noted that his younger

In 1968, Piedmont Aviation moved into a new set of offices across from its previous headquarters, just north of Smith Reynolds Airport. In keeping with Piedmont tradition to stay near the action, the offices fronted a spacious new hangar (courtesy Piedmont Aviation Historical Society; from the collection of Ronnie Macklin).

brother would still suffer from time to time with bouts of asthma. The elder Davis said Tom flew to Arizona "quite a bit for his health" to improve his breathing and take a respite from the responsibilities of corporate matters.[123]

On regular Sunday afternoons, Tom practiced quite a different type of flying back in Winston-Salem, one that required special skills as a pilot. L.J. Lambert remembered often lowering one of two gliders from the ceiling and taking Mr. Davis up in it. "They took up a lot of space on the hanger floor so we had block and tackle, and we kept them in the rafters of the hangar. Whenever he wanted to fly one, we would get the airplanes out of the hangar and drop it down on the floor and get it ready and let him go."[124]

Although the business of running a very successful local service carrier was a full time job, Tom Davis could now relax a bit as fortune continued to smile upon his operations. The company totaled over $1.5 million in net income for 1965, the airline division completing over 99 percent of its scheduled miles. The following year net income reached almost two million dollars. His company, while serving a more rural population than most other feeder airlines, operated at such efficiency that it demonstrated the ability to make a profit without taking government subsidies in 1966.[125] Other local service providers, now being called "regional" carriers, could not duplicate the feat, even with more potential passengers from which to draw. This success was both a blessing and a curse to Piedmont. While such profitability demonstrated the competence of the airline to provide good service and make money at it, the effectiveness meant the company could no longer rely on a source of income it had received since its inception. However, in 1967, Piedmont again qualified for subsidy, but it received a much lower amount than other local service carriers. Through November of 1967, Piedmont received exactly half of what the twelve other regional feeders got for the same period. Mr. Davis went on record objecting to the inequity, saying the CAB penalized Piedmont for superior performance, but he had to at least secretly smile at the position in which he found himself.[126]

Meanwhile, Mr. Davis continued to follow his plan, one that was proving to be astute. The tastes of large cities like Atlanta and Baltimore whetted his appetite for more. Four years after extending its destinations into Georgia and Maryland, Mr. Davis took a shot at the Big Apple. One of the world's most populous cities could give travelers from the southeastern United States unlimited connections, and Mr. Davis carried Piedmont's case to the CAB in another vigorous application for extension of service. After due consideration, the regulatory agency relented, allowing its first regional carrier in ten years the right to add New York to its offering of cities in late 1966. Calling the inaugural flight of November 16, 1966 "a great day for Piedmont,"[127] Tom Davis estimated that his company would carry 90,000 passengers to New York each year, while his marketing department bought advertising that proudly proclaimed, "Piedmont Puts New York City on the map." The new slogan demonstrated how comfortable Piedmont was as a David taking on the Goliath of the largest of all major metropolitan cities. However, flying into New York on Piedmont meant landing at La Guardia Airport instead of the newly renamed John F. Kennedy International Airport. Speedbird passengers who planned an international flight out of JFK had to transfer by helicopter or bus to the New York's premier airport of the time. In getting into the new market, Piedmont had to accept some hardships.

During the same period, Piedmont also began dropping off Washington, D.C., passengers at a newly constructed facility located west of the nation's capital. Dulles International Airport welcomed Piedmont as the first regional airline to its gates, hoping to become a preferable alternative to the district's downtown National Airport, which endured tremendous overcrowding. Piedmont now served both. Though the inaugural flight found the Dulles

International practically empty, Federal Aviation Administrator General William F. McKee praised Davis and Piedmont for being in "on the ground floor" of a facility that expected to be as busy as its downtown counterpart in ten years.

Tom Davis understood growth. He continually hammered away at the CAB for more cities to serve, trying again and again when refused. In the spring of 1968, he was granted two cities for which he had pitched a long time. Adding to his Tennessee destinations of Knoxville and the Tri-Cities of Bristol-Kingsport-Johnson City, Piedmont gained permission to extend its service to the central and western parts of the state with flights into Nashville and Memphis. The ceremonial ribbon cutting on February 2, 1968, capped off a twenty year expansion by the airline. The accomplishment only augured for even greater feats in the future.

The plan of Piedmont, however, was not to seek larger cities just for the sake of expansion. While some other regionals believed that new towns automatically meant new profits, even if each location already had good service and, therefore, stiff competition, Mr. Davis endorsed a different business model. He believed that each new destination should be immediately lucrative for Piedmont or else he refrained from making the jump. If trunk carriers like Eastern had been adequately providing transportation for cities throughout the southeast, Piedmont would have never gone after cities like Atlanta or Memphis. But his acumen told him that his airline had something to special to offer that could make the effort worthwhile.[128] C.D. McLean remembered an adage Mr. Davis often told his pilots: "Boys, we don't fly airplanes to fly airplanes. We fly airplanes to make money."[129]

As Piedmont flew through the 1960s, Tom Davis's entrepreneurial instinct spread farther. Since its pre-airline days, Piedmont had been in the business of training. In many ways, teaching was the life blood of the company. The Civilian Pilot Training program kept the company alive during World War II. When the airline came along, the company trained its pilots, mechanics, and even flight attendants to perform in the interest of the Speedbird. So, in 1966, when the idea of creating a school for airplane maintenance came about, Mr. Davis was willing to put his money into the Piedmont Aerospace Institute. The school found the perfect location in the old 1956 headquarters building and provided certification in maintenance, electronics and avionics. Within five years, the company graduated over 250 students from the school. Enrollees paid $1440 in tuition for a 14 month course designed to provide an FAA–approved certificate for aircraft mechanics and electronics technicians.[130]

Occasionally, some of the Tom Davis's hunches took him off the beaten path toward new business ventures that might at first seem to have no relationship to an airline. One of the lucrative services offered by fixed base operations was the sale and maintenance of corporate planes for a number of companies. Clients included Texaco, Alcoa, Champion Spark Plug, Proctor and Gamble, NASA, Norfolk and Western Railroad, and of course, Winston-Salem based R.J. Reynolds Corporation. Ronnie Macklin credited outfitting planes for a host of companies as the genesis of the Piedmont Fabricators Division. "We bought the airplane; put the interior in it, and so on. Those things are a lot of woodwork. We didn't have any woodshop, so we bought a carpenter's shop."[131] Working across town from Smith Reynolds Airport, the new enterprise custom crafted luxurious interiors for airplanes on demand as well as many of the airline's ticket counters at stations along the line.

The fabricator division followed an example set by the folks in fixed base operations. They often tackled assignments that had nothing to do with Piedmont Airlines. "I don't care how you run an airline," Ronnie Macklin explained. "The workload isn't consistent." In his area of business aircraft, when work slowed down because all Piedmont maintenance was up to date, his mechanics worked "on other people's airplanes so we could have continuity and keep everybody working." The carpenters with Piedmont Fabricators did much the same thing, except projects ranged far beyond aviation. Besides airplane interiors, these craftsmen constructed custom furniture for hotels and even barber shops. As Macklin described it, "Anything to do with woodwork, high quality woodwork, those people did that. They were exceptionally good people."[132]

Piedmont Aviation followed the Davis dictum to take care of the customer, which often necessitated going the extra mile. One way Piedmont people did so was to work closely as a liaison between companies and convention sites, helping to coordinate meetings, conventions, trade shows, tours, any event that meant more passengers on board a Piedmont Pacemaker. Here was another area that Thelma Taylor Davis pioneered, as director of charter and convention sales. She explained the process by example: "Say if General Electric is having an annual meeting then I would contact their transportation agent and mention two or three sites, such as the Greenbrier Hotel, such as the Hotel Roanoke [both in Roanoke, Virginia], trying to sell this company. The site of their convention would be on Piedmont Airlines and that would be of course additional revenue for us."[133]

The Speedbird spread its wings over much more than just commercial passengers. One big aspect of the fixed base operation was the lease of pilots and mechanics to transport company executives who owned their own planes. Among the most prominent of these was Norfolk and Western Railroad, which later merged with Southern Railroad to form Norfolk-Southern. Many of the pilots who flew for the airline jockeyed for the ability to bid the job of flying for the railroad. Howard Miller was one of those. A veteran Piedmont pilot, both he and his twin brother Harold went to work for Piedmont on April 15, 1954. Both applied to fly for the railroad through the pilot process of bidding to work in Roanoke, Virginia. Seniority usually gave older pilots their choice of assignments, but as Howard noted, "The bid at Norfolk and Western had some stipulations to it. Whoever bid it had to have an aircraft and engines mechanic license. There were very few of those on the airlines. Most of them just had pilot ratings. So it cut down the number of guys who could bid it." Howard's twin brother Harold went with the railroad first. "Harold did a terrific job there. He was a good person for that job." Meanwhile, Howard Miller worked for a while in Roanoke as chief pilot before moving over into his brother's position. "They paid Piedmont and then Piedmont would send us the check. Of course, they kept a percentage out of it," remembered Howard, who also recalled that Piedmont farmed out its pilots to more than just Norfolk and Western. "Piedmont loved us to be on these little contract jobs if we could get on them." Howard mentioned the L&N (Louisville and Nashville) Railroad and another company that owned a DC-3 in Charlottesville, Virginia, as examples of companies who hired Piedmont pilots.[134]

Mel Blocker also flew airplanes for the railroad. The nephew of Bonanza star Dan "Hoss" Blocker, Mel inherited a strong family resemblance. Blocker flew the line at Piedmont for three months when he got the opportunity to bid for the job at the railroad. His previous maintenance experience with Braniff earned him an A & E license which gave him an edge, just like the Miller brothers. According to Blocker, "I was the only copilot potential or otherwise that had that type license and they had heard about me. They came down and interviewed me and wanted to know if I'd be interested in joining Norfolk and Western."[135] He was quickly hired and flew his first flight for Norfolk and Western on Christmas Day of 1966. Like Howard Miller, with whom he was a longtime friend, Mel Blocker's ten year tenure as railroad pilot allowed him the chance to fly a Lear Jet, a Falcon 20 and Norfolk and Western's F-27.

Norfolk and Western Railroad typified the era, owning jets as well as propeller craft for

Mel Blocker and its other pilots to fly. During the sixties, Piedmont moved strongly into the jet era as well. "One of the most significant days in the history of this company was when we made the transition into the jet era," reflected longtime employee Bill McGee. He felt "from a marketing standpoint and an operational standpoint that it was time created by competitive activity that we get involved in the jet business." The airline found the Boeing 737 to its liking but was impatient for delivery, so two larger 727s were leased by the company so that Piedmont could quickly become a jet carrier, like many of the other airlines of the era. McGee, who ascended though the ranks at Piedmont to move even beyond his position as senior vice president of marketing, believed the beginning of the jet era marked a milestone for the company. He said, "I think aside from the original startup date, that probably was one of the most significant moves that the company has made, one that certainly was a dynamic move and a move that has set the pace for the progress of this company."[136]

As the airline marked its twentieth anniversary and Piedmont Aviation moved closer to its thirtieth, the company continued to spread its wings with new businesses, new planes, new employees, and new destinations as Mr. Davis continued to have an answer to suit any air traveler's need. The business found solvency in the sixties, experiencing steady growth in an unsteady decade. Piedmont met the challenge of the New Frontier and turned the puddle jumper into an "up and coming airline." Mr. Davis handled his people adeptly, and they performed well for the most part. The seventies, he felt, only afforded more opportunity to shine.

• 5 •

Experience Comes with Age, 1968–1977

"We've been extremely fortunate to get a high level of people. We have a better record of employee stability than any airline in the U.S.,"¹ said Tom Davis, obviously proud of his company and the employees who made it function. He lavished praise for "the people who run the shop — the mechanics, pilots, flight attendants, reservation clerks and other office and support staff who really make things move." Citing statistics to make the point, he noted that "forty-six percent of the company's employees have been there five years or more and twenty-six percent have ten years or more service."² After over 20 years of steering Piedmont Aviation toward success, Tom Davis heartily applauded those who shared the load with him, making his achievement seem so easy.

The 1968 awards luncheon illustrated all that Piedmont had become. When Mr. Davis fulfilled his role as company president by handing out service pins for his employees, he basked in the high level of employee morale his people displayed as they came to receive their recognition. The company rewarded 48 employees for their length of service, which totaled 635 years. Of that number, 17 sported 20-year pins. Those people had been with Mr. Davis since the first days of the airline.³

The appreciation flowed both ways. Tom Davis valued the ride on their shoulders as much as they loved putting him there. One observer wrote that he said he was like "a turtle found on a fence post. You know that somebody had to put him there, he would say, because he couldn't have done it by himself."⁴ "We felt like in our hearts that we were loved and appreciated," said Connie Counts, who worked as a flight attendant for 34 years. Awarding employees who had reached a benchmark was a special night in Winston-Salem, which was as Counts noted, "A nice dinner and a nice banquet and they recognized you." Employees thrived on the respect, appreciating the acknowledgment of their contribution to the success of the airline. Those recognized employees returned to their jobs, working even harder for the airline because as Connie Counts put it, "You felt like that you made a difference."⁵

Many of his early employees now helped Mr. Davis run the company. In addition to Zeke Saunders and Bill Barber, a number of others who had grown up with the company assumed positions of responsibility. Bill McGee started as a line boy. By the seventies, he had worked his way up to vice-president of sales.⁶ One day he would move into the president's chair that Mr. Davis then occupied. As Howard Miller commented, "Mr. Davis had a knack for getting the right people in the right jobs."⁷ Howard Cartwright worked from one end of the maintenance operation to the other, starting as a "grease monkey" and ending as the vice-president of maintenance.⁸ Paul Snell began work for the company at the age of 20 six weeks after the airline first flew, working as an agent. Before he was 26, he flew as a co-pilot for the

Company identification for Captain Bill Morgan. As Piedmont Airlines grew not everyone instantly recognized their fellow employees (Bill Morgan Collection).

airline.⁹ R.L. Gordon's brother got him on with the airline as a mechanic. According to Gordon, it was three months before they knew he was there. He ultimately became a ground school supervisor, training pilots.¹⁰ As the employees prospered, the company prospered and vice versa. Within ten years of the 1968 luncheon, 30 percent of the employee base owned company stock.¹¹

Devotion to Piedmont never flagged as the company marked one, two, and then three decades of operation. As far back as could be traced, Ed Culler never took a sick day. He remained "on the job" faithfully, even when he was once sick with pneumonia. His wife Elizabeth recalled, "They would come over there, some of the mechanics, and bring a piece of an airplane wing or something under their arm and ask him about it, how to fix it." She also recalled many instances when her husband, who had become assistant vice president for aircraft services for the General Aviation Group, was called at all hours of the night after a problem arose. As far as the disturbance went, Mrs. Culler said, "He didn't mind one bit."¹²

Piedmont grew into a family for many employees. The shared experiences of workers on a professional or social level, or often both, created a bond that meant supreme loyalty to the company and each other. R.L. Gordon described it best when he observed that his co-workers "worked hard when they worked and when they were off work they played hard. They played as hard as they worked. That's the way they were and that's what you saw and that's what made that airline go."¹³ At his retirement Howard Thompson admitted to Mr. Davis, "You don't know this, but I would have worked for you for room and board." Reportedly, the president of the company replied, "Well Howard, I did know that too." Likening the company to his family, Thompson remarked upon the all inclusive nature of Piedmont. He said that his fellow pilot Larry Dudley told him a number of times, "The worst employee we had, the person that no one liked, he was still part of Piedmont Airlines."¹⁴

Flight crews, like the company itself, frequently operated as a social unit. Since schedules changed only quarterly, many saw fellow employees often as they flew in and out of the same airports on a regular basis. Captain Harv Horrell was among many who remembered the setup in Norfolk, Virginia, one summer, saying, "Everybody had a good time." He recalled that there were approximately 30 crew members in and out of one wing of a motel reserved just for Piedmont people.

> The crews got in around 2 or 3 o'clock in the afternoons. They'd go over to the supermarket. They had a charcoal grill they'd bought. It stayed in one of the rooms all the time. Whoever

Employees spent many of their non-work hours together engaging in a variety of activities. Here the Piedmont bowling team poses with its trophies and Mr. Davis, seated. From left to right are Vestal Widener (prop shop), John Hall (parts department), Ed Culler (fixed base service manager), L.J. Lambert (parts), and C.W. Goth (VP of fixed base) (Ed Culler Collection).

used it last, they'd go to the Giant Supermarket and everybody would buy a steak and whatever needed to make salad with. They'd bring it back over there and they'd line the dresser drawers with aluminum foil and make the salad up in the dresser drawer. They'd drag the charcoal grill out on the, I call it the patio; [it was] one of these hotels where you had an inside hall plus you could pull up the cars on the outside. So you had two doors. And they'd drag the charcoal grill outside and everybody would cook their own steak, make a salad up, had paper plates, paper bowls and everybody had a fantastic steak for dinner and everybody got along great; a few cocktails before you ate. If it was raining, they dragged the charcoal grill in the room; smoke was pouring out everywhere. We just had fantastic time. Everybody was family.[15]

Pilot James "Beetle" Bailey added that someone always brought along a guitar, a surefire source of entertainment that had the crews singing late into the night.[16]

Invariably, practical jokes were also a part of the summer festivities. Bailey recalled that one pilot made a habit of leaving his liquor bottle hidden in the room. Upon returning, the pilot noticed his bottle a little emptier than when he left it. According to Beetle the pilot looked at the bottle and said, "I'll fix em." Beetle reported that "the pilot left a little note behind, writing on the side of the bottle, 'I have pissed in this bottle.'" Upon returning to the room Beetle's friend was chagrined to find even more liquor missing and another note on the bottle that simply said, "So did I."[17]

At times, pranks got very elaborate for the sake of a laugh. Harv Horrell went to his room one night to find "not a damn thing in there except a telephone and TV. They took every bit of my damn furniture and set it out in the parking lot, and left, and the only reason [my room] had a TV and the phone cord [was that it was] fastened to the wall with a wire."[18] Horrell's most vivid memory of a hoax was one in which he was just a spectator but nevertheless enjoyed. He said that it was an answer to an earlier prank played on a female flight attendant by a pilot.

> She got the co-pilot to dress up in her negligee and get in a bed and screwed all the light bulbs out and all where you might flip a light on and see who it is. And then they called up the captain that they were flying with and told him that one of his old friends from out of town was there. Got the man at the front desk to call him that one of his friends that he'd met up there a while back was in town and she wanted to see him. Well, now the co-pilot had one of the girl's wigs on [and] her negligee [on] in bed. So he goes down there and knocks on the door. Voice says come in. Well, he goes in, the light won't come on. He closes the door and comes on in. Well, the next thing you know, he's taking his clothes off and gets in bed with the co-pilot, and starts trying to, you know, massage him and all of a sudden his hand slips and slides down the man's arm. Well, his arm had more hair than I got on. And when he hits his arm, he knows he's been had and when he did the co-pilot jumps out of bed and runs and opens the door and 15 of us standing outside the door listening. We all come charging in there. Here's the captain standing there buck naked and his whole crew standing in the room just hee-hawing. Pranks like that. It was something.[19]

Complex tricks often took a while to spring and many of the perpetrators never saw the look on victim's face. Though done in good fun, some of these practical jokes were ingenious in their intricacy and were sometimes motivated by retaliation. Imagine how one employee felt after he drove a pickup to work filled with wood for traction following a snowstorm only to return and find a sign that said "free firewood" and all his wood gone. Another employee also drove his pickup to work one day and when he got back to it at the end of the day to drive home he found a sign too. He also discovered a toilet bolted to the bed of his truck. The sign explained the toilet. It read "Don's John. If you gotta go, let Donny know."[20]

"They played hardball," said Harv Horrell as he looked back on all the pranks perpetrated during his time with the airline. He remembered a fellow pilot who lived in Roanoke and owned a mobile home on nearby Smith Mountain Lake that he used for a weekend getaway. While Harv's friend was away, flying a trip, someone went to the expense of having an elaborate sign painted and placed it in front of the pilot's vacation spot. It said, "XXX massage parlor; all girl staff; our customers come first." Returning from his trip, the friend found the sign and a deputy waiting for him, saying the sheriff's department had received a number of calls inquiring about the business advertised by the sign.[21]

Tricks often had their points to make. When one purser finished his duties with the passengers, he eagerly sprinted to the cockpit to learn all he could, because he had ambitions toward becoming a pilot. Often he brought coffee for the pilots. The only problem was that sometimes he carried the paper cups with his fingers dipped down into the coffee. Captain Charlie Meacham expressed some dissatisfaction over the drink but was assured by the flight attendant that his hands were clean. Intent upon teaching the young man a lesson, Meacham pricked a minute hole in a cup and gave it to the purser to fill with coffee. The flight attendant's white shirt quickly became stained. The purser went on to become a pilot for Piedmont and eventually figured out the reason for the mishap.[22]

"Humor was always around," asserted Paul Snell, who believed that's why Piedmont folks

An example of the lengths to which Piedmont people would go to play a practical joke. One pilot was sorely surprised when he returned from a trip to find a toilet bolted to the bed of his truck (Don Martin Collection).

never minded coming to work "even in bad weather." Some went out of the way to have fun with practical jokes. Occasionally, amusing situations arose spontaneously. Once, a Mr. Herron, in charge of maintenance, called Lee Golson, in charge of tariffs for the company. Instead of reaching Golson, Herron got through to Mr. Golson's recently hired assistant. Disappointed when the assistant told him that Mr. Golson was out of the office, Herron then asked to whom he was talking. The reply was, "This is Abe Lincoln. Would you like to leave a message?" Thinking he was being fooled, Herron shot back, "Yeah, tell him Henry the Eighth called," and hung up the phone. In reality, Lee Golson had actually hired a new assistant named Abe Lincoln.[23]

Piedmont employees always remembered the jokes. When he was a lead mechanic in Roanoke, Don Collins always got to work early. "I was late if I didn't get there at least 30 minutes prior to going to work," said Collins, who never took a sick day for fear of missing something. "We'd sit around and drink coffee, mess with one another, get our tools ready. Sometimes we'd go to work before going to work time," meaning that if a task was pressing, the mechanics didn't wait until they were on the clock to get started.[24] Piedmont management knew the work ethic of their people and applauded the effort, whatever it took. Once in a while, leaders of the company went to bizarre lengths to keep their people going. Pilot Charlie Meacham told his son Chuck about how some pilots would call up Vice President Zeke Saunders, who played bluegrass with his own band as a sideline, and request that he sing "Beautiful Flower" over the phone, which they somehow managed to mistake as "Beautiful Flyer." With good nature, Zeke obliged the request. When asked by his wife why he repeatedly accommodated such a strange request, Zeke answered that if he refused, they'd just call back again and again.[25]

The camaraderie among employees was so good that every now and then, some expected a joke when there wasn't one. "Piedmont people are real big on jokes," said Dave Johnson, as he led into a story about a phone call he got just before Christmas one year. When he answered the phone, a voice said, "Captain Johnson, my name is Rick Miller, and I'm offering you a job as a check airman on a 727." Thinking one of his friends at the airline was pulling his leg, he said, "Yeah, right" and hung up the phone. Immediately the phone rang again. This time the voice said, "Listen; don't hang up on me again. Do you know I'm over the training department of the 727, and I'm offering you a good deal?" Dave Johnson quickly figured out that no joke was being played, and he accepted the job. He remained a check airman for Piedmont for the next four years.[26]

Employees played tricks on each other, but they also looked to each other for help in times of crisis. When one pilot's wife was stricken with cancer, the rest banded together to help. Larry Dudley recollected, "The rest of us made a schedule up and we flew his trips and we put his pay number in." Covering for the pilot for over three months, the extra work was, as Dudley revealed, "spread out over everybody. And he never came to Roanoke, never used a day of sick leave, or anything."[27] In the late sixties, the Chicago station manager's wife also suffered from cancer. The company found a way to relocate him back to Winston-Salem to give him an opportunity to be near her.[28] Dudley acknowledged the genuine love people felt for each other when he said, "Piedmont was a family, or a big family if you want to call it that. Everybody took care of most everybody."[29]

In less catastrophic times, the concern for fellow employees still existed, but in more subtle ways. Many attributed the ethic to Mr. Davis but remarked that it spread from one employee to another over the years, building into a truly unique corporate culture. Years later, Frank Davis saw it flow through the company. "It just snowballed and the new hires would see it in the old guys, staying over a little longer or working a little longer in the day. They just really paid a lot of attention to detail," said Frank, who also observed how each person tried to leave things in better shape for next guy who was just starting his day's work.[30]

The family atmosphere extended at times well beyond fellow employees. Howard Thompson recalled, "We fed more kids peanuts and I'm proud of it," referring to children who came to airports like the Shenandoah Valley Airport in Staunton, Virginia. From the cockpit Thompson and fellow pilot Larry Dudley saw groups of school kids with "their little hands sticking through the wire fence. They'd never seen an airplane." Dudley admitted, "We'd get boxes of peanuts and give to them." Oftentimes, the pilots enlisted the help of the flight attendants to hand out peanuts to children while passengers were getting off and on. Said Thompson, "We did that everywhere." The gesture did not, however, pass muster back in Winston-Salem. "I got in trouble with Tadlock, too, over them peanuts," Howard Thompson revealed. "Tadlock wanted me to pay for the peanuts. I said, 'Well, I'm going to write the Shenandoah Sentinel or whatever the name of the newspaper was, and I'm going to tell them, those little handicapped kids, you made me pay for the peanuts.' He soon relented, saying, 'Ah, I don't want you to do that.'"[31] Actually, Jack Tadlock cared very much for the welfare of children.

When not directing pilots at Piedmont, he and other Piedmont employees helped create SCAN, "Stop Child Abuse Now." Tadlock served the Winston-Salem organization for ten years and when he died, his ashes were scattered at the facility's courtyard.

Taking care of each other was a common thread that ran through all Piedmont relationships. Beyond company loyalty, personnel in various departments were incredibly dedicated to leaders in particular areas. One strong example was found in maintenance. Howard Cartwright joined the airline during its infancy, ultimately moving in to the position of assistant vice president of maintenance and engineering. Don Collins contended, "There was a lot of loyalty to that man, not just to the company but a lot of loyalty to him." Collins was one of those loyalists. Noting Cartwright had a "fatherly demeanor," Don Collins felt he owed much of his career to the helping hand of Howard Cartwright. After working in Roanoke, Virginia, for ten years, Collins was transferred to Winston-Salem, a tough transition considering his wife, Audrey, also a Piedmont employee, remained back in Roanoke. After 14 months, Collins went to Cartwright and said, "Boss man, I got to do one of two things. I got to either quit or get Audrey down here [to Winston-Salem]. I'm tired of running up and down the road on the weekends.... I'm wearing myself out. I said, 'Is there any way you can bring her down here?'" Cartwright told his mechanic yes. While Don Collins was looking for a house, someone up in Roanoke told Mrs. Collins, "Howard's not going to let you transfer to Winston." After a frantic call to her husband, Don went back to see Howard Cartwright to make sure that he was as good as his word. According to Audrey Collins, "He never did say what I was actually going to be doing until I got down here. I guess he was going to put me somewhere." She went to work in the accessory shop on her eleventh anniversary with Piedmont. "So many people owed him personally," she said. She and her husband were among many.[32]

When a member of the flight crew could not perform the tasks necessary, his or her associates covered for them. David Caudle gave an example:

> I can remember having a flight attendant that got on board that had been out the night before partying and had gotten drunk. She'd shown up the next morning for her trip and she was sick. I'd just lock her in the blue room and we'd take off and the flight attendants would take care of each other. If we had two back there then one would work the whole trip; if we had three back there two would work the whole trip. But you would kind of take care of each other.... Just occasionally you would have one that would kind of stray and so you would just take care of them.[33]

On occasion, employees were treated like members of the family even before they were in the family. Ronnie Macklin remembered having a stranded Martin 404 aircraft in Baltimore that needed a carburetor changed. Without a maintenance facility in Baltimore, Macklin contacted a mechanic who worked for Baltimore's fixed base operator, Henson Aviation, about the job. He agreed to do the work and a carburetor was shipped to Baltimore. It carried with it a tag that read, "Remove this plug before installation." The contract mechanic failed to follow the instruction on the tag. The plugged carburetor quickly burned up the engine because water could not get to the engine to cool it. Once the FAA inspector learned of the incident, he went to Baltimore to take the license of the mechanic. When Ronnie Macklin asked how long the mechanic would be without his license, the FAA inspector replied, "For good." Macklin said, "I don't know about that ... I'm the one who is supposed to be mad. He burned up my damned engine, but I don't think we need to do that. Hold on and I'll go with you."

When questioned about his training, the mechanic revealed he had been to Embry-Riddle, which Macklin noted was "pretty damned good. If you've been to Embry-Riddle, you're good." After explaining what the FAA had in mind for the mechanic, Ronnie Macklin offered him a job back in Winston-Salem, working as an instructor for Piedmont. Reluctantly, the mechanic took the job. As Macklin remembered, "He did a good job." After a year and a half, the mechanic-turned-instructor became interested in becoming a pilot and convinced Zeke Saunders to put him "on the line," said Macklin. "He retired as the third highest Boeing 767 captain in USAir, all because he was too damned dumb to change a carburetor on an R-2800. Every time he gets up to thank somebody he said, 'If it hadn't been for Piedmont Airlines taking care of me I would not be where I am today.'"[34] Most everyone who ever worked for Piedmont knew the feeling.

The Piedmont workforce could be described as protective, like a big brother. Many employees expressed only the most devoted respect for those who had come before them. T.D. Stanges came to Piedmont in 1981 and recognized the debt he owed to those pilots who exemplified the work environment he enjoyed. "Those pilots that came aboard during that time set the tone and pace of the company's future successes by sheer grit," said Stanges, who relished the opportunity to hear these pilots tell stories of their experiences. "They flew the most challenging routes and destinations in the Piedmont region and surrounding areas, often below 10,000 feet, in second-hand equipment, and out-dated navigational aids. It required unparalleled skill and judgment to survive it and for those of us who came aboard later, it was a great privilege and honor to have served under their command."[35]

The regard employees had for each other was phenomenal. Like all other pilots, Captain Calvin James Redburn received his copy of the agreement between ALPA (Airline Pilots Association) and Piedmont in the form of a book which also included the names of pilots listed by seniority. The issue was standard for pilots to make sure they were equipped with a manual detailing all facets of their job as a pilot for Piedmont Airlines. What makes Redburn's 1977 copy interesting and somewhat unique is the fact that he took the time to find out and write down the birthday for each of the pilots senior to him and quite a few of those below him on the list. Redburn recorded the birthdays of the first 123 pilots, suggesting he intended to offer his best wishes on their big day. The gesture demonstrated the regard he felt for the men who shared their seat with him on board the Pacemakers.[36]

No claim can be made that every employee loved working for Piedmont, but expressing discontent often drew reproach from fellow workers. Don Martin, who worked as station manager in several cities, witnessed a scene that he said he would never forget. He recalled a pilot who was constantly putting down the company. "I was back there in my office in the operations part of the terminal, and Bud Gilley was flying and he came in that morning, and he was just on a turnaround and this Washington based captain was just running down the airlines." Martin recalled, "Bud Gilley went over to him and pointed his finger at him and said, 'If I disliked this company as much as you claim to, I'd hunt me another job.' That shut him up pretty much."[37]

Another way employees showed their ultimate respect for the company and those who worked for it was to protect each other from harm. Since the business of flying is dangerous work, the jobs of everyone on the ground supported the efforts of everyone in the air. From reservations to luggage retrieval, many displayed devotion to the safety and ultimately success of their fellow employees by making sure everything was done right and everyone was properly trained. One group whose responsibility it was to make sure flight and ground crews stayed prepared for every contingency was the training department. Piedmont invested heavily in training, requiring "recurrent" training annually of all employees. By the late sixties, flight training had moved out of the planes and into simulators. That way, any trainee who could not handle the demands of their airplane would at least not die. Instead, they would simply have to perform the task again until they got it right. David Caudle remembered training with the help of Hop Hee "Hoppy" Dunne, a Chinese lady who "ferried planes back during World War II." According to Caudle, "If you went in there with a cocky attitude, she could turn you loose in that simulator. She could make a monkey out of anybody in that Link Trainer."[38] David Caudle knew better than to play the part of the arrogant pilot around Hoppy. "I'd go down there and I'd say 'I'm low time, I'm very minimum. Help me all you can.' She said 'OK.' So she would put me in that little Link simulator, and she'd lead me around and give me a lot of instruction and help me out."[39]

Training was intense for Piedmont employees. Knowing and performing their jobs was paramount, and the company spent immense resources on keeping everyone on their toes. For many new hires, employment hinged upon successful completion of training sessions specific to their job. Ground school supervisor R.L. Gordon put many though their paces. Describing pilot training, he said, "They had to learn the aircraft because when they came out of that ground school, they'd go in front of the FAA and they had to take a verbal exam from the FAA on the systems on that aircraft. And of course, they had to pass it." He also pointed out that beyond the government test, these employees had to "be able to operate the systems once they got to the aircraft." Gordon watched enough of these people come through ground school that he knew from their test scores if they were going to succeed. "Seventy was passing. We prided ourselves in trying to get everybody in that class to make 90 or better. We really did. If we saw somebody make 85, as ground school instructors on the test, we knew they were in trouble because they couldn't do the FAA."[40]

Even after overcoming the hurdles necessary to work for the airline, employees were required to return to the classroom annually for recurrent training. Everyone took the classes because failure meant probable job loss. However, the occasional prank helped liven up the classes and made them memorable. R.L. "Spiderman" Gordon remembered one such joke played on a pilot named Sonny.

> We gave him a maintenance exam. Everybody in the whole class was in on it, except Sonny. Of course I wasn't in class but I knew what was going on because I was supervisor at that time. Sonny was sitting there and he was looking and he was reading, and everybody else was just going down the paper and Sonny was sitting there and he started looking around. He said [to an] instructor, he said, "Jim I don't remember them talking about this right here in class." Of course Jim gets the paper up and says, "Oh yeah, Sonny, you know we talked about that in class." He said, "Oh yeah" and he asked another one of the other captains and they said, "Oh yeah, Sonny we talked about that." We let that go on for about 15 minutes. They couldn't stand it anymore and somebody said, "hey, are you about through, I don't lack but five more." He said, "Damn it, I ain't got the first ten answered. What in the hell is going on?" And of course, you know everybody laughed.[41]

R.L. Gordon made the best out of even bad situations, using humor and ingenuity as a training tool. He took the time to handle a cheater in a rather unique way. Everyone in the class was given a different test and when grades were returned, the offending pilot failed while everyone else passed. Suspecting foul play but unmindful of his own offense, Gordon recalled the culprit saying, "Ain't nobody leaving this damn room till I find out what's going on because I know I copied that guy's paper."[42]

Many pilots remembered Spiderman's signature line while training pilots. He could often be heard beginning a point by saying, "You're flying along in flight." The often used phrase caused Dave Johnson to wonder, "Where else would you be flying along if you weren't in flight?"[43]

Everyone trained because each depended on the other, so all links of the chain had to be strong. "The maintenance department was just like the flight department. They loved their job. They took pride in what they did, and we depended on one another. It was excellent. I don't think I ever had a problem with maintenance," commented Captain Buddy Counts. "They knew their job and when they went in training on a particular airplane, they worked just as hard as we did. Most of the trainers, as far as ground school, were maintenance to pilots. When we went into ground school, the maintenance department did the teaching. So we depended on them. We knew them all."[44]

Piedmont prided itself on its training. Without a tremendous effort to keep personnel up to date, the carrier might have gotten slack and looked at the process as more of the same. Instead, with its policy to promote from within, the company found some of the most dedicated and motivated trainers who kept employees readied on all aspects of their jobs. The effort paid off in the efficiency with which Piedmont ran and the stature of the airline among its peers. The company was hailed for its expertise in a 1971 magazine article which stated, "Many of Piedmont's pilots are considered among the most experienced and skilled in the business. In fact, one aircraft manufacturer has asked for film of their techniques for use in training."[45]

Throughout its existence, Piedmont Airlines had seldom led the industry in innovation. It proved itself in steady, reliable performance. Mostly, Piedmont followed the major carriers when it came to such changes as female flight attendants, food service, and plane upgrades. It came as a bit of shock when the airline found a new model in Japan. While most airlines in the late sixties had gone to jets, and though Piedmont was purchasing in that area as well, its most substantial buy in 1968 was a plane called the YS-11A, produced by the Nihon Aeroplane Manufacturing Company.[46] Zeke Saunders described the model as an improved copy of a Convair (an American made plane). Although built by the Japanese, the YS-11 was made with mostly American parts. He noted the aircraft better suited the needs of the airline to get into mountainous airports like Beckley, Bluefield and Charleston, West Virginia, and Shenandoah Airport in Virginia.[47] *American Aviation* magazine even quoted Zeke as saying, "The YS-11 can operate fully loaded from the smallest runway Piedmont uses, the 3,780-ft. strip at Rocky Mount, N.C."[48] "We searched the world over for a plane which would operate safely in and out of small mountainous airports," said Tom Davis. "The YS-11 was the only one we could find which would do it on an economical basis."[49]

Tom Sharpe, who flew the YS-11, revealed an extremely practical reason why the aircraft made sense for Piedmont. "The story is that they were out trying it out and they landed somewhere and blew some tires on it. They realized that the Martin tires would fit it, and said, 'Heck, that's a good deal.' We had those Martin 404s at the time, Piedmont did, and since some components fit right on the YS-11 they said, 'Hey, we got a lot of that,' so they thought it was a pretty good deal."[50] Debate has since raged over just how many parts were interchangeable, but most agreed with the purchase of the YS-11 to augment the Speedbird fleet.

Though a curious choice, the YS-11 helped bail out the airline after another choice made two years earlier revealed itself to be less than adequate. The FH-227, made by Fairchild-Hiller, was an improvement on the disappointing F-27 that Piedmont bought in the late fifties. However, the newer model also proved to be unsatisfactory. Flights to the West Virginia destinations required operating with less than full loads to get the planes up and down into those locations safely. As a result, the FH-227s were relegated to, as Zeke Saunders put

In a surprise move within the airline industry, Piedmont Airlines purchased the Japanese-made YS-11. The last propeller plane of the fleet flew for over a decade (Tom Sharpe Collection).

it, "places flatter than Roanoke," flying smaller groups of passengers heading to and from North Carolina's piedmont region to Washington, New York, and Atlanta.[51]

The YS-11 proved to be a good choice for Piedmont as the airline headed for the seventies, but the plane did have its limitations, especially seasonally. "In the hot summertime, we couldn't keep them going. In the wintertime, good airplane," observed mechanic Don Collins. The YS-11 was tough to cool and as a result flying the airplane on a typical summer day in the South was troublesome. "We left Roanoke and we were going to Richmond non stop," said Collins, recalling a particularly sluggish flight. "We finally got to 4,000 feet over Lynchburg on a hot day. It was fully loaded. I was on the jump seat; [the pilot] said, 'That's all it's going to do today.'" With a bit of understatement, Collins believed that if that particular YS-11 had lost an engine, they would have been "in kind of bad shape."[52]

Beyond its performance, the YS-11 made good financial sense for the folks in Winston-Salem. Financing the planes in Japan meant that Piedmont paid an interest rate two percent lower than it would have in the United States. Nihon was very interested in getting their planes into the U.S. because they felt that once introduced, the exposure would mean even greater sales in the American market. "If we couldn't make the payments, they wouldn't take but one airplane back. They couldn't take all the airplanes back. They also loaned us some money to build the reservation center, and they also loaned us some money to buy spare parts for the airplane," explained Zeke Saunders, as he remembered bargaining successfully with the Japanese company. As one industry trade magazine put it, "The blending of Far East and Old South has apparently been a success, or as Zeke-san Saunders is learning to say, 'Ichiban.'"[53]

Before the transaction was completed, Zeke Saunders returned the compliment, helping the Japanese to speak with a southern drawl. The only member of the foreign group who spoke any English asked Zeke to take them coon hunting. Zeke hunted regularly with a group that included Piedmont mechanics and pilots and agreed to take his guests on a night hunt. With guns in hand, the Japanese mounted mules to stalk wild raccoons. According to Zeke, they managed to bag a few that night, but the experience turned sour for them when the Japanese members of the party asked to partake of another southern tradition, tobacco chewing. "They wanted to chew tobacco, so we got some tobacco, and every one of them got sick as hell. But they never said anymore about going coon hunting after that."[54]

Mr. Davis and his management team had some concerns about buying the YS-11 before making the plunge. As Zeke admitted to *American Aviation*, "We were somewhat apprehensive about public reaction to the airplane." The choice to buy airplanes from a foreign manufacturer was risky, especially from Japan. Many of Piedmont's early employees fought against the Japanese, including Zeke Saunders himself. Though the United States and Japan were building a strong trade relationship, some still harbored resentment and the airline feared a backlash. After implementation of the craft into the fleet, Zeke proudly reported, "We've had almost no unfavorable reaction at all."[55] Every now and then, however, passenger reaction to the YS-11 was harsh. Once, Mr. Davis was accosted by a woman in Wilmington, North Carolina, who squealed at him, "I'm going to St. Louis this weekend, and I'm scared to death." Unsure of what his customer meant, he said nothing. She persisted, "But I'm glad I'm not going on one of those horrible Japanese things you people have put on your system." With a calm voice, Mr. Davis assured the woman that the YS-11 was an excellent plane and that she would "enjoy flying on it." Somewhat puzzled, Mr. Davis refrained from informing the lady that Piedmont didn't fly to St. Louis on a YS-11. In fact, Piedmont didn't fly to St. Louis at all.[56]

The other worry Piedmont had with the Japanese plane concerned the differences between the typical Japanese and American passenger. "The only problem we found with the airplane was the windows were low because the Japanese people are smaller. We finally bought some seats, had a British concern build us a seat that put the American passenger more in line with the window on it."[57] The new seats were also larger and softer than the standard Japanese seat. Nihon picked up the cost for the seat conversion.[58]

As the company made its decision to buy the YS-11, Piedmont examined the plane diligently to make sure it was the right purchase. Bill Barber accompanied Mr. Davis, Zeke Saunders and Howard Cartwright to Tokyo for inspection. Barber recalled the methodical manner in which Mr. Davis went about his assessment.

> He said, "OK, Zeke, I want you to find this out." He gave him about fifteen, twenty questions, said find this out about this for me today. Went to Cartwright, asked him about the same thing and came to me said, "I want you to find out this and that," warranties, repairs, that sort of stuff, about fifteen or twenty items. He said, "We'll meet back here in my room when we get back." There was five days of this. So, first day, came back in, sat down in his room, he asked, in the order in which he asked the questions, he wanted answers. No paper. No nothing. We didn't write nothing down. Of course I rushed back up in the room and wrote these cute little notes down [concerning] what he asked me to find out about. But anyway, we'd go through every one of them and [on] a couple of them I'd say, "You know I forgot about that" or "I couldn't get the answer." "That's OK, no problem." Just don't ever lie to that man though. So we did the thing for five days just like that. Then when we started doing the contracts, we did our portion of it. I had warranties and guarantees and I forget all the various things I had, support[ing] what we can do. We had the finest contract in the world.[59]

"Amazement" best described industry reaction to the purchase. Calling Piedmont "the most conservative [and consistently, the most profitable] of all U.S. regionals," *Air Transport World*, along with fellow trade magazine *American Aviation*, gave feature status to the purchase. Author Joseph Murphy characterized the switch as a "dramatic one."[60] The initial purchase of ten YS-11s proved immediately successful. The company exercised its option to buy ten more. The planes gave Piedmont an instant boost in the number of passengers it could haul. Since the government approved no more flights in and out of high traffic areas, use of the YS-11 gained the company a 36 percent increase in the number of passengers it flew. The model also remained part of the Pacemaker fleet until 1982, longer than any other propeller plane used by Piedmont. In that time, the plane performed remarkably, completing "99.74% of its assigned flights, the best average yet for any of Piedmont's airplanes."[61] In its 14 years of service, the airline got virtually free use out of the YS-11. The company ultimately sold the planes for more than their purchase price.[62]

The only aircraft that wore the Speedbird longer than the YS-11 was the Boeing 737-200. Introduced in 1968, the same year of the Japanese twin turboprop's debut, the twin engine 737 was procured for a very different reason. Traveling into large cities, the Boeing craft could haul over 100 passengers, making the YS-11's 36 percent increase seem small by comparison. The 737 increased capacity by 127 percent.[63] The pure jet had been a long time in coming to Piedmont. As early as 1962, TWA had upgraded its fleet to the exclusive use of jets, which made the Martin 404s available to Piedmont. Tom Davis waited on profits to accumulate, so the airline could be financially solvent, before buying the more up-to-date aircraft. Including the YS-11 purchases, Piedmont spent close to $100 million on modernizing its fleet in the late sixties. By contrast, the new planes allowed Mr. Davis the opportunity to retire all 33 of the Martin 404s.[64] Just as the changeover from DC-3 revolutionized operations for Piedmont, the 737s did it again. Flights were faster, more efficient and gave the conservative company the image of an "up and coming airline," a phrase later used in advertising.

Thus far, the growth had been steady and mostly upward. By 1970, Piedmont Aviation's thirtieth anniversary, over 2.7 million passengers boarded Pacemakers in a single year. As a result, the company had grown to the point that it could no longer count on the manual systems it had created when it started. There were more passengers, more airplanes, more everything. L. J. Lambert supervised inventories of airplane parts, a department he developed when the airline started. After 20 years, his manual system could no longer cope with the growing number of parts he needed to keep on hand to service the Fairchilds and Martins. With the help of a computer expert from Delta Airlines, Lambert helped create an automated system for inventories that he used for the rest of his 44 years with the airline.[65]

The puddle jumper had slowly evolved into a budding major company. Since the airline's first days, reservations were made at every airport station manned by Piedmont. While convenient for some customers, the system was inefficient and up to the minute availability was impossible. The system required the use of handwritten file cards for each reservation.[66] In 1971, Senior Vice President Gordon Brown inked a deal to consolidate Piedmont's booking operations with the Central Reservations Office (CRO). Housed "in a new million-dollar facility located just west of Winston-Salem" (and built with money borrowed from the Japanese), the new center employed 386 people who handled calls on a 24-hour per day basis. The new computers were expected to handle up to 300,000 reservations per month. The CRO not only allowed booking flights on Piedmont but also served passengers wanting to connect to other airlines by reserving seats on those flights as well. The massive computerization was linked to a computer center in Los Angeles. The IBM computers at the CRO gave operators flexibility to find the best routes for customers as well as instant access to flight schedules.[67]

Along with their facilities, the stature of Piedmont Airlines continued to grow. The advent of the YS-11 and the Boeing 737 forced changes along the line, not the least of which were the hangars that housed the planes. Early on, Roanoke had become a busy location for Piedmont. The airport accommodated repair facilities for the airline as well as up to 52 flights per day in and out. The hangar was originally designed during the days of the F-27, so when the much larger jets began to land in Roanoke, the opening entryway into the hangar was not large enough. To get the new planes inside, Ronnie Macklin noted, "We had to put a cutout" in the top of the hangar door to make room for 737 tail fins. Cut under the word "Fly" and between the words "Piedmont" and "Airlines," the alteration showed the airline at its productive and improvisational best.[68]

Pilots also proved to be an enterprising lot when it came to creating favorable publicity for the airline. When Atlanta's Hartsfield International Airport opened its large air passenger terminal complex, the airlines vied for the honor of being the first into the terminal, reported to be the largest in the world at the time. Upon hearing of Delta's plan to keep the other carriers blocked off so it could claim the distinction of being first, Piedmont pilot Jim Hamilton shifted into gear. A native Georgian with political ties from his days as a state senator, Hamilton realized the first one to land would gain, as he put it, "publicity you can't buy." A quick phone call to Winston-Salem found a free plane that could fly into Atlanta and take the prize. Tom Stancil was in Bristol after finishing a charter flight when Hamilton told him to get to Atlanta in a hurry. Arriving on a Sunday morning at 3:17 A.M., the empty Piedmont plane beat Delta, Eastern, and even President Carter's *Air Force One* to be the first at the $500 million facility. While the others cried foul and claimed an empty flight did not count, including Atlanta Mayor Maynard Jackson, whose plane was also inbound, Captain Stancil said, "If we weren't the first then we sure shook a lot of hands," referring to Newt Gingrich and an entourage of airport officials who came to welcome Stancil and his plane as the inaugural flight into Atlanta's Hartsfield International Airport.[69]

From the sixties to the seventies, Piedmont Airlines matured in substantial ways, although not all of them good. As an expanding carrier, the airline ultimately had to deal with some of the same problems plaguing nationwide carriers, like hijackings. Because regional airlines flew shorter runs than the trunk carriers, they were thought to be immune to the demands of hijackers; however, from time to time an attempt was made.

The first hijacking attempt never got off the ground. A 26-year-old Tennessee man decided to board a flight on the ground at Smith Reynolds Airport in Winston-Salem and force it to travel to the same location that most hijackers of the age wanted to go: Cuba. With an overnight bag in hand, Bobby White boarded a 737 after all the passengers had departed and only Captain Leon Fox was still aboard the plane. White claimed he had explosives in the bag and wanted to go to Havana to "kill Castro." Fox radioed the man's demands and stalled for time. Vice-President of Flight Operations Jack Tadlock was called. He quickly donned his captain's uniform and headed up the steps to board the 737. Tadlock asked permission from White to enter, at which time the hijacker answered, "Okay, if you want to go to Cuba." White forced Tadlock to enter on his knees but refused entry to Federal Sky Marshal Raymond Ciccollilli, who was also trying to fake his way inside. Tadlock had to crawl toward the cockpit with the "bag of explosives" on his back. Before engaging White, the Piedmont executive had talked to a man who claimed to have driven Bobby White to the airport. One key point Tadlock remembered from the conversation was that White had "carelessly tossed a small travel bag in the seat" of the car he rode to get to the airport. Jack Tadlock suspected his hijacker was bluffing. White followed Tadlock to the cockpit, where Leon Fox was waiting. The hijacker was surprised when Ciccollilli showed up at the cockpit door. White reportedly yelled, "I said only one could come in and you get off." With White's attention on

Ciccollilli and another federal marshal who had sneaked in a back access door, Tadlock sprang into action. He grabbed the bag while the sky marshals overtook White. In the bag, Jack Tadlock found "some shoes, a pair of trousers and a shaving kit." In foiling the hijack attempt, the VP of operations indicated that when he got there, he didn't know if he would be flying to Cuba that night or not. Tadlock commented that if he thought White really did have a bomb, he might have "complied with the demand."[70]

The next attempted hijacking occurred on a flight from Cincinnati to Wilmington in January of 1978. After a scheduled stop in Kinston, North Carolina, 49-year-old Sam Dawkins revealed his intention to disrupt the journey. Fellow passenger Sam Hinson witnessed the hijacker's move, saying, "We saw some guy run up to the cabin and start talking to the stewardess. I saw he had his hand in his pocket and when I saw the expression on the stewardess' face change, I sat down." Dawkins moved into the cockpit and told Captain Tom Stancil and First Officer Ed Dunn that he was hijacking the plane. According to press reports, he mentioned a number of destinations, although he ultimately settled on Bobby White's choice of Havana, Cuba. The flight made its next scheduled stop at New Bern and took on "a full load of fuel" before departing. None of the passengers were allowed to leave. Stancil reportedly announced that the plane was heading for Cuba and advised everyone to relax. Meanwhile, the flight's captain noted the behavior of the hijacker to be "very irrational" and suspected he was intoxicated. Sam Dawkins at one point threatened to take the controls of the plane himself. Stancil also noticed that Dawkins occasionally removed his hands from his pocket, a sure sign to the Captain that the hijacker did not have a gun.

Just south of Myrtle Beach, South Carolina, flight attendant Steve Adana made a move, throwing a drink in the hijacker's face. Adana pushed Dawkins out of the cockpit and onto the floor. A number of people then jumped on the perpetrator, subduing him. During the melee, Stancil yelled, "Hold that man down but don't hurt him," adding, "He doesn't have a gun." The plane returned to Wilmington, where Dawkins was taken into custody by FBI agent Joe Zimmerman, who assessed the flight crews' performance as "heroic," adding, "I can't say enough about them." The highjacker saw his performance as noteworthy as well. While in jail, waiting to be charged with the federal crime of air piracy, Sam Dawkins asked press photographers if they wanted him to pose for their pictures.[71]

The last hijacking attempt actually made it to the destination the previous two attempts only sought: Havana, Cuba. Piedmont Flight 451 began in Newark, New Jersey, with stops in Charlotte and Charleston, South Carolina, and was making its way toward the final destination of Miami when a lone hijacker who called himself "Lt. Spartacus" sent a note to a flight attendant claiming to have a bomb. He demanded that the plane fly to Havana and then a ransom of $5 million be paid. After speaking with the captain of the flight by intercom, the man, a proclaimed member of the Black Liberation Army, locked himself in the restroom for the rest of the flight. The pilot landed in Havana where Cuban authorities quickly took the man into custody and determined he had no explosives. The hijacker left a note in the bathroom of the 737 that said "I am sorry for this.... I have duties ... I am a soldier." All 52 passengers and the five-man crew returned to Miami safely following the March 1984 attempt.[72]

Beyond three failed attempts at air piracy, Piedmont Airlines also had a connection to another hijacking, this one the most spectacular in American aviation history. The successful hijacking of a Northwest Orient Airlines flight in November of 1971 by an air pirate known only as D.B. Cooper brought attention to the crime of hijacking like no other. The fact that he succeeded in the attempt, getting away with $200,000, and was never found was overshadowed by his method of escape. D.B. Cooper fled the Boeing 727 in midair using a rear

A Boeing 727-100, the *Mount Mitchell Pacemaker*. By the time Piedmont purchased this aircraft from Northwest Orient it had already witnessed drama. D.B. Cooper jumped from the back stairs, seen in the photograph, to fame and obscurity (Ronnie Macklin Collection).

ladder, parachuting to fame and freedom. Following the feat, Piedmont purchased the plane from Northwest Orient in June of 1978 and reregistered the aircraft as N838N. The plane remained part of the Speedbird fleet until Piedmont phased out the 727s. It served Piedmont as the *Mount Mitchell Pacemaker*.[73] Passengers generally never knew the history of the plane and the aircraft was never part of a similar event while in the Piedmont fleet. Ronnie Macklin suggested calling the plane *The D.B. Cooper Pacemaker*. The company vetoed the suggestion.[74]

Occasionally, humor broke up tense situations on Piedmont flights. Hoss Dobbins and Carroll Spencer were flying a Martin 404 out of Washington National Airport one night heading for Rocky Mount, North Carolina, when the Richmond, Virginia, airport notified them of a need to land. First Officer Spencer remembered that his captain was "a talkative fellow" who immediately insisted on wanting to know why Richmond made such a demand. At first hesitant, air traffic control finally told the crew that they had received a warning that a bomb was concealed on their flight. According to Spencer, Hoss Dobbins "didn't say anything all the way to the airport. I don't even remember him saying gear down." Upon landing, everyone was evacuated and all power on the airplane was shut down until the FBI informed the two pilots that they would have to go back on board and search for the bomb. With flashlights in hand, the pilot, copilot and the FBI agent entered the plane. It was then that Captain Dobbins decided to turn back on the plane's battery power.

"The FBI guy is standing there in the baggage compartment and that's where the coffee maker is and the coffee maker had been making coffee," said Spencer "When the coffee maker made coffee, it goes tick-tick-tick-tick, real loud." Both Dobbins and Spencer were familiar with the noise but the FBI man wasn't. Carroll Spencer remembered the agent blurted out, "What the hell is that?" which caused both pilots to roar with laughter. As he tried to regain his composure, Spencer noted, "That man's face was as white as a sheet and he was standing there right beside the coffee maker and it was going tick-tick-tick-tick and he's looking for a bomb." No bomb was ever found that night in Richmond.[75]

Piedmont knew it was growing up when it was forced to confront the same kind of headaches that were usually the domain of the trunk carriers. Throughout its history, Piedmont management enjoyed a cordial relationship with employees. But in the summer of 1969, pilots were forced to choose between their company and their union over a decision to man all 737 (model 200) cockpits with three crew members. Since the days of the DC-3, Piedmont Pacemakers flew with only two pilots, a captain and a first officer. However, across the industry, some airlines with four-engine planes (like a DC-6 or DC-7) employed a flight engineer, or "third man" as he came to be called, to monitor the engines, among other duties. Piedmont's announcement of plans to purchase Boeing 737s created something of a problem for the airline. First, Piedmont could not immediately get 737s, so Boeing leased the airline two 727s which required a third man as a flight engineer. However, the 737-200 was designed as a two-man craft to compete with Douglas's DC-9.

Though it made sense to revert back to a two-man crew when the 737s started coming in, the Airline Pilots Association (ALPA) objected. As an organization whose mission it was to protect pilot jobs, telling airline management it could reduce its workforce went against ALPA's reason for existence. The much larger United Airlines faced the same situation as Piedmont, having also bought 737s. United employed a much larger pilot base than Piedmont, and consequently had more pilot jobs at stake. "Featherbedding" was how Jim Hamilton described it. "Nobody wanted to get into a contest with United [Airline's pilots] at that particular time," was Hamilton's assessment of the situation. As a young pilot in 1969, he came to Piedmont as one of those third men. In the interest of its members, especially its United members, ALPA stood firm on keeping a third man on the new Boeing 737s.[76]

As 1969 came in and the 737s were delivered, Piedmont staffed the cockpit with three men, but the practice struck at the frugal heart of Speedbird management. By summer, the company insisted that the 737 be flown as Boeing had designed them, without a third man. The decision caught the pilot group between its management and its union. The pilots decided to strike. Some pilots, like Roscoe Goforth, saw a legitimate need of a third man on the Boeing 737. He observed that "at that time we were flying into a lot of uncontrolled airports, where they didn't have air traffic controllers, nobody to advise you of traffic. On takeoff especially, most pilots were busy inside the cockpit. I felt we needed somebody to observe outside." For the most part the FAA agreed, pressing a "see and be seen" policy, and since the captain of first officer were busy enough, a third man served the function of being a visual lookout.

With a family atmosphere at Piedmont, a strike might have seemed unlikely but among the pilots, tension was brewing. "Everybody was mad about something," said Captain Carroll Spencer. Calling the summer of 1969 "an intense time for Piedmont," he opined, "There would be a man on the moon before there would be a strike on Piedmont and it all happened on the same night."[77] When Neil Armstrong walked the moon's surface, Piedmont pilots walked off their jobs. At Fayetteville, North Carolina, a confrontation between 50 pilots and management took place. Almost everything came to a standstill, but a few planes remained outside of their home bases and needed to be returned for protection.

Roanoke's Chief Pilot Howard Miller had to weigh his respect for the stand made by the pilots and the needs of the company to protect its equipment. He said, "We had some airplanes on the ground in Lynchburg. We didn't know how long the strike would last and we needed to get the airplanes back to Roanoke. I had to get a co-pilot to go over there and fly a couple Martin 404s back to Roanoke," said Miller, who acknowledged that both he and his co-pilot took some heat for not leaving the planes where they were.[78]

The strike dragged on into August until a federal court order demanded that Piedmont's pilots return to work.[79] The first judge to hear the case sided with Speedbird management, but the pilots appealed. Pilot and union representative Carroll Spencer remembered, "Our attorneys took it to Richmond and the court of appeals immediately turned it around and said it's going back, but it's going back as it was."[80] By that time Piedmont's Executive Committee was getting jittery over the loss of revenue sustained by the work stoppage. Zeke Saunders vividly remembered the mandate handed down. "We got instructions from the executive committee that we didn't need to take this strike any longer. We could straighten it out or they would get rid of us."[81] Zeke also remembered the reluctance of Mr. Davis to make the first move to settle things with his pilots. Mr. Davis said he would have to eat a lot of crow. "I remember Charlie Norfleet telling him, 'Well, eat that crow. Put salt on it, that will help it,'" said Zeke.[82] Some believed political pressure from the towns along the airline's route weighed on Mr. Davis the most. Pilot Carroll Spencer argued, "It wasn't the pilots that bothered him and the other things, it was the mayors calling and raising hell because they weren't getting service in their cities."[83] The strike proved tough on both the company and the pilots. Piedmont Airlines made no money for the duration of the walkout. Strikers failed to avail themselves of the union's strike funds because union rules only paid for strikes of 30 days or more. The strike over the third man lasted 28 days.

Pilots went back to work with a third man in the 737 cockpit, temporarily. Most of the 737 captains and first officers had no use for the third man and just about all the flight engineers who flew for the "seven-three" for Piedmont did nothing. "It was just like riding a jump seat," said Jim Hamilton, about his new job at Piedmont. He added, "You got to ride in the cockpit and didn't do anything."[84] Raises intended for the two man crew subsidized the third man for the next several years. Ultimately, the membership of ALPA relented at their annual meeting and gave each airline the option to use a third man on the 737-200, after Delta and Eastern pilots voted with their Piedmont brothers against the practice. Also, in March of 1971, a deal was struck to rid Piedmont planes of the third man on the "seven-threes" and still cover the job Roscoe Goforth cited that made them worthwhile. The company approved the installation of collision avoidance systems in each of its jets. A published report on the agreement addressed the third man problem, stating, "By the time the systems are installed, the third men should have enough seniority to become first officers, or copilots. This means they will not lose their jobs."[85]

The strike episode had impact well beyond that of the pilots of the Pacemakers and their union. Had Piedmont not fought the issue to the point of a strike, the industry would have followed the United standard of three men in the cockpit on the two-man 737. In the heavily competitive world of airplane sales, the extra cost in manpower might have given advantage to Boeing competitor Douglas, which was producing the DC-9 as an alternative jet to the 737. The Douglas model was also designed as a two pilot aircraft. A third man in the 737 might have put Boeing at an economic disadvantage in terms of operating cost and reduced sales for the Seattle based manufacturer. Instead, Boeing ultimately dominated commercial jet productions so much that the public has made Boeing's model numbers synonymous with jet aircraft. People refer to jets as 747s and 767s as often as they use the generic word "jet." Piedmont played a significant part in that association, especially since it became the largest buyer of Boeing 737s for a time.

For Piedmont, the strike served as a turning point. "It seemed to me that something happened to the airline," said veteran pilot Tory Vaughn, who believed that a wedge existed between pilots and the management. In negotiations, he remembered pilots making their case to the company by saying, "Look, we're not here trying to break the company. We want to make this thing. But we want to make a decent wage. We want to be able to live fairly comfortably." After that the two sides came together, Vaughn noted, "It seemed like the wedge was pulled out ... and everybody got together. We worked for the company."[86]

Some in the union used the strike to explain to Mr. Davis the pitfalls of running an efficient airline. Pointing out that other regional carriers, who were less efficient, got significantly more money from the government and more routes to keep them going, union officials made the point that Piedmont consequently got very little as a reward for its resourceful operation. In their opinion, Mr. Davis's frugal approach had hurt potential growth for the airline. They clamored for more jets and more equipment with which to do their jobs and asked Mr. Davis to rethink his spending habits.[87] While it wasn't until Mr. Davis left the president's chair that Piedmont began a serious program of upgrading its equipment, one positive aspect to the strike was that it cleared the air between pilots and management and helped to break the tension so that, as Tory Vaughn noted, the two groups could move harmoniously forward to further the goals of the airline.

One important aspect of leadership at Piedmont was the emphasis on bringing employees into the decision making process whenever possible, which gave everyone a greater stake in the company. Don Collins, whose responsibility at Piedmont continued to rise, remembered his mentor's philosophy. While working maintenance control, he asked Howard Cartwright about how a decision should be made in the absence of the boss. Cartwright's answer was unambiguous.

> He said, "I don't give a damn what you do as long as you are trying and you make a decision." He said, "Don't ever let me come in here and you are sitting on your laurels for eight hours waiting for me to get here and not make a decision. Make a decision, right or wrong and then we will go on with that. Nobody will try to Monday morning quarterback you. At least make a decision. Don't say I got to wait on so and so." He said, "Because you are Mr. Davis and you are Howard Cartwright when we are not here."[88]

Howard Cartwright's viewpoint encapsulated much of what made Piedmont an exemplary company. He encouraged immediate solutions, which saved time and money since keeping planes going was the heart of an aviation company's business. By giving workers the power to make decisions in the absence of a superior, management demonstrated confidence in the know-how of its worker base. And maybe most importantly, by not threatening retaliation for decisions that might not have proved to be the most prudent choice, leadership demonstrated its trust. Employees appreciated the faith their bosses placed in them and tried diligently not to let them down.

On occasion, an employee resolution did not work out as the best alternative, but leaders like Howard Cartwright remained true to their word and did not reprove the decision-maker. Don Collins had an example of just such a situation. During the OPEC oil embargo of the mid-seventies, the word had gone out for Piedmont employees to conserve as much fuel as possible. One night, a problem developed with a Pacemaker in Memphis. Collins remembered,

> They told us fuel is scarce. Don't use any more than you have to and this type thing so I rounded up a bunch of mechanics and put them on a light airplane and sent them to Memphis. We missed the schedule next morning. It was a long way to Memphis in a light airplane,

especially when you start at one or two o'clock in the morning. And we missed the schedule coming out of Memphis with the airplane. Cartwright came in the next morning and said, "What happened in Memphis?" I said, "Boss man, you said you don't want to use more fuel than we have to." He said, "Don't worry about that. We're selling fuel to Delta and American."

Howard Cartwright helped his employee understand that flying out on schedule the next morning from Memphis outweighed saving fuel. The vice president of maintenance and engineering didn't seek to criticize the resolution. Cartwright knew that Don Collins could not have known about the fact that Piedmont had made fortuitous purchases of fuel (a closely held company secret). Instead, Cartwright dealt fairly and instructively with the situation. From then on, Don Collins understood that keeping the planes on schedule was the top priority. About the incident, Collins recalled, "They had more fuel than they were burning, and they were selling fuel to several other airlines, so we didn't worry about it anymore. We just ferried airplanes all around and did what we wanted to and all that sort of thing, and he never said anything. Nobody ever said anything as long as we made schedule."[89]

While Cartwright and his boys kept the fleet flying, Mr. Davis looked for more American cities to introduce to the Speedbird. In addition to Atlanta, Baltimore, New York and Memphis, Piedmont finished the decade of the sixties by gaining permission to serve Chicago. The deal was unlike any Piedmont had struck before. After asking for the link for years and being repeatedly turned down, Mr. Davis followed his success in gaining Nashville and Memphis with one more attempt. In 1967, he asked for a "show cause ruling" which would have given the airline instant access to Chicago until some other carrier could prove Piedmont was hurting their business. The CAB flatly rejected the request. Mr. Davis kept up the fight, arguing that Piedmont, the smallest carrier in contention for a North Carolina to Chicago route, could actually serve passengers better than major airlines like Eastern, Delta, and United. The rationale centered on passengers picked up along the way. Since Piedmont would make more stops between the two destinations, more travelers would be served than a non-stop flight by one of the big boys.[90] The argument worked, although not as thoroughly as Mr. Davis would have liked. Two years after filing its application, Piedmont won the right to serve Chicago but not at the city's prestigious O'Hare International Airport. Piedmont planes were directed into the much older and smaller Midway Airport. The limitation was reminiscent of Piedmont's entry into New York, where Pacemakers landed at LaGuardia, not JFK. Tom Davis rode in on the inaugural flight to Chicago, presenting Mayor Richard J. Daley with the keys to the cities that Piedmont flights out of Chicago planned to serve. The gesture was unusual. Most often, it was the mayors of towns who bestowed "keys to the city" to prominent visitors.[91]

A few years later, Piedmont finally got into O'Hare and as Zeke Saunders said, "Bill Magruder did that." William M. Magruder signed on in May of 1973 as executive vice president, a new position. When he joined Piedmont at age 50, Magruder had already enjoyed an eventful career in aviation. A test pilot for the DC-8, he held several aviation patents. During his tenure with Lockheed Corporation, he headed the Supersonic Transport (SST) program. In 1970, he went to Washington, D.C., to lead the government's stance on the SST, but Congress cut support for the program a year later, and Magruder became special consultant on aeronautics to President Richard Nixon. Like Tom Davis, Bill Magruder loved to fly. He shared the experience of being introduced to aviation by his father, who took him to see Charles Lindbergh on his triumphant return, just like Egbert Davis Sr. had done for his son.[92]

Magruder was hired specifically to be the ultimate successor to the current, long standing president. Zeke Saunders contrasted the styles of the two men: "Tom Davis was one never to offer any bribes and he didn't take any bribes. McGruder had different ideas." Zeke traveled with Bill Magruder to Chicago to appeal to Mayor Daley and the head of the airport for permission to land at O'Hare. They refused. According to Zeke, Magruder said, "I think I'll send you all a little present, a case of scotch if you will sign that." Saunders added, "The airport director was head of the umpires for the National Football League, and he later got killed. But we got the whiskey and sent it up there, and it wasn't but about a week or two we got permission to go in to O'Hare."[93] Bill Magruder's arrival at Piedmont signified changes for the airline's future. Although he demonstrated an ability to get what Piedmont needed, everyone waited to see if Magruder had the skill of leadership that the airline's founder possessed.

Bill Magruder and Piedmont were something of an odd couple. Certainly, his innovative outlook was expected to carry the airline to the next level, creating a future that built on the solid past created by Davis and company. However, Bill Magruder had landed at a small, penny-wise airline that knew its customers and place in the industry. Magruder's larger view caused some to wonder if he was the right man for the future job of president. Among the things he wanted to do was to buy an oil field, believing that if the airline engaged in a bit of vertical integration, it could cut its fuel costs and guarantee its supply. Those around him scoffed at the idea, saying that Piedmont lacked the resources necessary for such a purpose, plus whimsically spending money was not a Piedmont tradition. The idea, though visionary, quickly died.[94]

The ascension of William Magruder typified a change going on at Piedmont. The original cast had skillfully guided the airline for over 25 years, handling weather, new planes and destinations, and a regulated airline industry. As the seventies wore on, many of the pilots who originally strapped themselves into DC-3s had become the elder statesmen of Piedmont as they reached the end of their careers. The early seventies saw a full fledged transition begin with a new generation of pilots moving into the company and preparing themselves to take the place of their elders. One of those paternal figures was Woody Bost, a native of Catawba County, North Carolina, who, according to contemporaries and county historian Sylvia Ray, was a celebrity because he was a Piedmont pilot. Zeke Saunders also came from Catawba County, but since he had moved into a management role with the airline, he didn't command the same kind of awe. Woody Bost enjoyed the image. On one flight he found out that the son of fellow pilot and friend Charlie Meacham was on board. Bost made a point of going to the back and talking with Chuck, who was heading off on his honeymoon with his new bride. According to Chuck, Bost looked straight at him and said, "I want you to tell your daddy that you had the chance to fly with the best pilot who ever flew for Piedmont." When Chuck relayed they message, his father enjoyed the bravado of his brother in the air.[95]

But before this first generation of pilots ended their career, each had something to teach the new guys who were to follow. In his book *From Kid to Captain*, James Hanson described one such situation; it happened on a flight to Chicago, during which his younger first officer expressed some doubt about pilots over the age of 50 having the necessary reaction time and reflexes to handle the jets in an emergency. Hanson explained to his younger companion that experience often trumped speed, and when the first officer learned that Hanson was a year shy of 50, he quickly changed the subject. According to Hanson, the flight went well until

> we are taxiing up to the gate at the Midway Terminal I ease down on the brakes about a hundred feet away from the building, the brakes shudder and are completely gone. Our gate is on a ground level finger and we have to park nose into the building where there's a large plate glass window where there are passengers looking straight at us and the only thing between us and them is a large tractor type tug which is used to push us back when we leave. The ground

The 25th anniversary of airline operation found the company in a period of calm after the storm. By 1973 the bottom line had turned positive again after a period of upheaval in the late sixties and early seventies (courtesy Piedmont Aviation Historical Society; from the collection of Zeke Saunders).

agent, signaling me in, realizes something is wrong and tries to throw a wheel chock in front of the nose wheel, at the same time I call for the Anti-skid switches off. The First Officer turns off the wrong switches, so I reach across and flip the guards off the skid switches and turn them off. I get the brakes back as the tug disappears under the nose, hit the left brake steering the nose between the tug and a part of the building which sticks out, and come to a stop about three feet from the building. The First Officer is a bit shook up and asks, "How did you know to do that?" I tell him it's like I said, experience comes with age and it makes up for my "slow reaction." I asked him what he would have done and he said he would have used reverse thrust and I reminded him about that plate glass window with all the people behind it.[96]

The new generation who came onboard with Piedmont in the seventies was not generally as arrogant as Jim Hanson's first officer. Most of them wanted to work for Piedmont because of the reputation established by the first flyers. They also shared the older generation's love of flying. Tom Sharpe, who began his Piedmont career flying charters for the fixed base operation, noted, "It wasn't just a job for us. It was a sort of obsession. Piedmont people seem to be in love with aviation."[97]

Tom Sharpe was certainly one of those. Hired in 1975, he went "across the street" from general aviation to the airline division two years later, fulfilling a lifelong ambition. "My dream was always to fly for Piedmont. That was what I wanted to do. I applied for some of the other airlines, but my heart was in Piedmont."[98] Buddy Bowen was another who wanted to be part of the Piedmont organization. He started as a parts organizer for the base at Roanoke, Virginia, in 1975. When he came to Winston-Salem for his training, he unknowingly met Mr. Davis. Bowen remembered the encounter. "He asked me if I needed a haircut." Bowen said, "He gave me three dollars and told me where to go. After I got my hair cut and realized who this man was, I gave him his three dollars back."[99] Buddy Bowen went on to become a pilot for the airline.

Among the new hires for Piedmont came the children of Mr. Davis. Four of the five Davis children worked for their father's enterprise. Tom, Jr., known as Bo, started with his father's company in 1969 for the fixed base operation. In late 1972, Bo transferred to the airline division as a pilot. Daughter Nancy began in 1978 and worked as a flight attendant, followed by her sister Julie, who joined the company in 1981 working part-time as a ticket agent. She later moved into flight attendant scheduling before moving to Raleigh, where she worked as station agent.[100] In the meantime, the youngest son, Frank Davis, went to work for Piedmont — but getting a job was not easy.

"It took me a year to get on," said Frank, who revealed his father did not use special influence to get him a job. "I started at the general aviation group in '76, pumping gas, towing airplanes, washing airplanes out on the ramp," said the younger Davis. He worked for fixed base operations for four years before leaving to pursue other interests. He returned periodically, and in the mid-eighties, he went to work for the airline in the aircraft maintenance department. Frank remembered that working for Tom Davis could still be an exacting proposition.

> When he was in the hospital back in the mid-eighties he [had] started having more breathing and respiratory and asthma problems. I would leave work at lunch if it was kind of a slow day

```
         TBD271(1501)(2-032440E035) PD 02/04/77 1445
ICS IPMMTZZ CSP
9197675371 TDMT WINSTON SALEM NC 21 02-04 0245P EST
FOR 9194273675
THOMAS WESLEY SHARPE
RT 2
STOKESDALE NC 27357
YOU HAVE BEEN ACCEPTED FOR PILOT TRAINING COMMENCING MARCH 7 1977 AT
830AM CONFIRM ACCEPTANCE BY RETURN WIRE
    W O TADLOCK PIEDMONT AIRLINES WINSTON SALEM NC
NNNN
```

Every pilot applicant hoped to get a notice from Western Union like the one Tom Sharpe got telling him to when to begin training to become a Piedmont pilot. Sent by Jack Tadlock, the notice held special significance for those who received it (Tom Sharpe Collection).

or we were in good shape. If there wasn't a lot going on, I'd tell my supervisor I wanted to run by the hospital on my lunch break. Well, we got thirty minutes for our lunch break and it would take me thirty minutes to drive there and back. I said, "Would it be all right if I take an extra thirty minutes or so today? I want to go visit my dad in the hospital." "Yeah, be sure you're back by one o'clock." I'd say, "Fine."

I'd leave about 11 o'clock and go over to the hospital and sit with daddy and talk with him a little bit. After being there for about half an hour or forty-five minutes, he'd say, "Are you working today?" I'd say, "Yes, sir." He said, "You working the day shift? Are you on lunch break?" I'd say, "Yes, I'm on lunch break. I just came over here for lunch." "We'll how long do you get for lunch?" I said, "30 minutes." He said, "You've been here for an hour. They're going to find out that they don't need you down there." I said, "I told them I was going to go visit you and we're in pretty good shape." [Mr. Davis replied], "Well you better be getting back over there."

Even in the hospital Tom Davis was watching the clock.[101]

A number of sons and daughters joined their parents in the employ of Piedmont aviation. Like the Davis children, both of Ed Culler's sons and a daughter went to work for the company. Eldest son Danny Culler remarked about growing up in Winston-Salem, "That was everybody's desire; to go to work for either R.J. Reynolds Tobacco Company or Piedmont Airlines.... My dad's name was Eddie Culler, so I became a pilot."[102] Both Danny and Rick Culler became pilots. Rick flew for the airline while Danny flew for fixed base. Their sister, Susan, worked in the training center and with Piedmont's frequent flyer program. Danny Culler also followed his Uncle Joe Culler's footsteps into aircraft sales. The year Joe Culler was named Beech Aircraft's "Man of the Year" (the second time he had won the award),

The next generation of Piedmont employees. Danny and Jill Culler, children of Ed Culler, hold up a cardboard replica of a DC-3. Danny went on to work for fixed base as a pilot and salesman (Ed Culler Collection).

5. Experience Comes with Age, 1968–1977

Danny Culler was recognized for seven million dollars in sales.[103] "Our family, between my Uncle Joe, my dad, my brother, myself, my sister, we have over a hundred years of service with Piedmont," said Danny Culler.[104] Piedmont Aviation's roster many times included individuals with the same last name. It was no coincidence. Numerous people followed their family members into the ranks of another kinship group, the Piedmont family.

Robert Wall had actually planned to become a history teacher when the desire to work for Piedmont became irresistible. After earning his degree from Wake Forest, Wall shocked his parents by taking a job as a part-time station agent in Baltimore. They really shouldn't have been shocked, as the careers of both parents had been in aviation. "I had been around airports and airplanes my whole life and just wasn't ready to give up all of that excitement," said the younger Wall. His father, Larry Wall, began with Piedmont in 1950 as a station agent in Charleston, West Virginia, and finished his career at Kinston, North Carolina. Along the way, he met his wife and Robert's mother, Margaret, while in Raleigh-Durham. She worked there also as a station agent for Eastern. Robert Wall moved up through the ranks at Piedmont, eventually working in the "Schedules and Planning" department.[105]

A considerable number of families got their start as a result of the Piedmont workplace. After Philip Beeson came to Piedmont, he met and married Bill Barber's secretary, Ann, in March of 1962. Don Collins met his future wife, Audrey, while both worked at the Roanoke

Ed Culler poses in front of an F25 Bonanza at Beechcraft's manufacturing headquarters in Wichita, Kansas. Culler brought back this plane for a customer, as he did many (Ed Culler Collection).

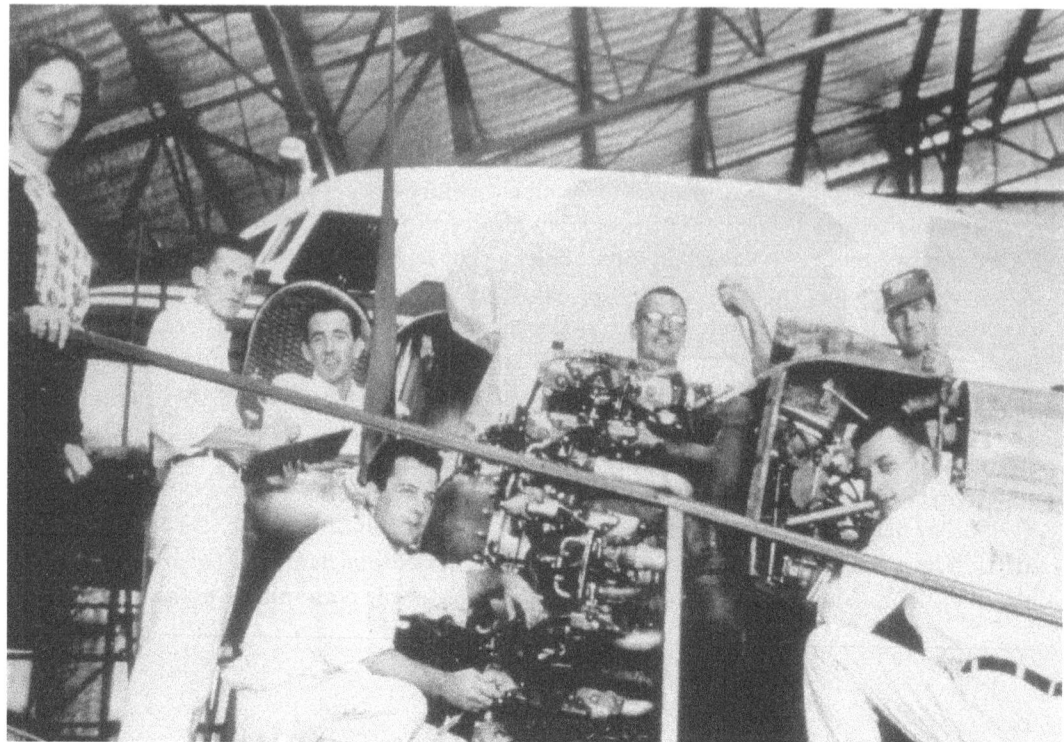

The maintenance crew at Roanoke in 1961, second, from left to right: T.E. Alley, Wallace Taylor (foreman), Kenny Atkinson, Roy Raines, Bobby Minter, and Don Collins. Don Collins' future wife, Audrey, an office assistant at the time, is pictured top left (Don and Audrey Collins Collection).

hangar, he as an aircraft electrician and she in the front office. "I worked there in the office I guess eight or nine months before I ever ventured out in the hangar to go down to the breakroom even," said Audrey. The concern was shared by everyone. "I was 19 when they hired me and about 20 years later, the man that hired me who lived here in Winston, he said, 'You know, Audrey. I really pondered that. You were so young ... and all those men.'"[106]

Women at Piedmont were not an unusual sight, but some jobs were strictly the domain of men. After women became part of the flight attendant corps in the sixties, further changes occurred. An unexpected addition to Piedmont's pilot group was Cheryl Peters. A former flight attendant with Eastern Airlines, Peters loved to fly to the point that she earned her commercial and instrument ratings and built up flight time in the late sixties and early seventies. When she interviewed in Winston-Salem, it was for a pilot's job. After a relaxed interview with Bill Kyle, she consented to a check ride in the flight simulator to see if she could handle a 727 "in what they called manual inversion," said Peters. As she explained, they wanted to know "if the airplane lost all hydraulics would a woman be able to physically handle the airplane." Less than a month later, Cheryl Peters joined the Piedmont organization. After several furloughs, she flew the YS-11 regularly, moving over to the left seat as captain in 1979. Several years later, she checked out on the 737.[107]

Given the fact that until the arrival of Cheryl Peters, the cockpit was a "men's only" club, the presence of a woman might have been at least awkward and at worst, hostile. From her perspective, the experience was neither. As she remembered, "The only thing that really broke down any barriers was once they realized that I could fly the airplane and do the job, then I was just another pilot to them." Actually it wasn't quite that simple, and Peters acknowledged that she was almost certainly a topic of discussion. "The talk in the crew room is always going to be something different, you know. 'Have you flown with that girl yet?'" But she noted the professionalism of her Piedmont coworkers, observing, "If it had been at another airline, it might have not been the same situation at all." Peters appreciated the family atmosphere in which she found herself and enjoyed the fact that she was able to pursue a career in commercial aviation without her gender being an issue. "They were just helpful and they were not resentful. They said, 'If you can do the job, have at it.'" She attributed much of her ease as Piedmont's first woman pilot to her ability with a plane. "I guess I just had a sense of confidence about what I was doing and they sensed that and they were not intimidated by me in any way."[108]

As Peters gained the acceptance of her co-pilots, she received the admiration of other employees on her flights. "Everyone adored her," said flight attendant Margaret Queen, who worked with Cheryl Peters on numerous trips. Ritchie's flying was "the smoothest in the air. There was never any jerking of the airplane. She was silk. Then after her came Denise Blankenship, and she was equally as good," Queen said.[109] The reference was to Piedmont's second woman pilot, who came aboard three years after Cheryl Peters.

One instructor also acknowledged the efforts of female pilots to whom he gave check rides, saying, "They were all excellent. They were probably 75 percentile or higher."[110] Piedmont

Cheryl Peters prepares for a flight not as a flight attendant but in the cockpit as Piedmont's first woman pilot. According to Flight Attendant Margaret Queen, her landings were "as smooth as silk" (Cheryl Peters Collection).

never took the initiative to break the gender barrier in the air. Male management in Winston-Salem had dragged their feet in employing female flight attendants earlier, but the acceptance of Cheryl and the other female pilots who came along after her demonstrated that the company was interested in hiring the best pilots available for their flights regardless of gender.

Most women who signed on to fly for Piedmont still did so as flight attendants. Among the new recruits was Lynn Shainberg Sass. She wanted to be a flight attendant so badly that she walked right into the crew room in Atlanta and told Ken Brock that Piedmont should hire her. They did. In February of 1972 she began a career that she characterized as a wonderful learning experience. "I felt like I got my education, my world wide education, that way and got to do things I probably would have never gotten to do," she said. "I thought it was extremely glamorous. It was hard work a lot of times but not all the time. It was a great pleasure to get on that airplane and go."[111]

Lynn Shainberg Sass's experiences as a flight attendant aboard Piedmont Pacemakers included meeting a number of celebrities who flew the airline, including Art Linkletter and Billy Graham, whom she remembered as "a much larger man than I expected. He had a wonderful handshake and he was just the sweetest person." One of her most memorable moments as a Piedmont flight attendant came only weeks after she started at the airline when she was tapped to fly a charter flight. Her supervisor in Winston-Salem, George Sack, called her one night and said, "I want you to start packing. I'm going to call you back in about thirty minutes, and I am going to give you some more details." She recalled, "I hung up and I pulled my suitcase out and realized that I didn't know where I was going." After being fingerprinted and going through a background check, her flight picked up 1972 presidential candidate George Wallace, whose campaign had chartered a Piedmont YS-11 for a swing through the Midwest. Lynn Shainberg got a firsthand look at the political process. "I did not necessarily agree with his politics but he was absolutely fascinating," said the flight attendant of the Alabama governor, "very charismatic personality — a terrific smile — the ultimate politician. He was very interesting and very friendly to the crew." Along with television reporters and campaign volunteers, Shainberg and the entire Piedmont crew took the Wallace entourage to numerous cities in the upper Midwest, just weeks before George Wallace was paralyzed by the bullet of a would-be assassin while campaigning in Maryland.[112]

As an energetic, petite flight attendant for twelve years, Lynn Shainberg Sass witnessed a lot of changes at Piedmont, including four uniform changes. In the mid-seventies flight attendants could wear hot pants as part of the ensemble. "That probably was in 1973 or '74," said Shainberg Sass, who remembered wearing them during the summer months for a few years until the next uniform change omitted the option. "They were polyester. A little bit longer shorts, was basically what it was."[113] Carol Dobyns Fair remembered wearing pantaloons under her uniform dress. "We had little pantaloons under them because the dress was so short that when we raised our arms up you could see your pants — so you had to have some protection under there so the gentlemen couldn't see up your dress."[114] Far from feeling objectified in the new attire that showed more leg, Sass said, "They were very comfortable.... It was probably the first time flight attendants didn't have to be dressed in dresses."[115] Flight attendant Pauline Fletcher Thomas remembered the wardrobe change fondly too, remarking, "I felt like we were finally in style with the times."[116]

In catching up, Piedmont made quite a leap. "We went from the old military look to a mod uniform that was yellow and orange," said Carol Dobyns Fair, pointing out that more than just the uniform had changed. "They went from the fact that you had to wear that hat all the time our you would be fired or reprimanded to no hat at all." The radical transformation Fair described as "crazy, but I understand that was Mrs. Davis's idea to bring us up to the new look."[117]

During the seventies, Lynn Shainberg Sass, Pauline Fletcher Thomas, Carol Dobyns Fair and all flight attendants all over the United States witnessed a change in their job title. Since the early days of Piedmont, men who assisted passengers in the cabin of the aircraft were known as pursers or stewards. When women joined the effort in 1962, they were called stewardesses, a titled that many shortened to "stews." During the sixties, the term carried overt sexual connotations with it, especially when some airlines used stewardesses in their advertising as an attraction. In late 1973, S&S (Steward and Stewardess) Division of the Air Line Pilots Union broke away to become the Association of Flight Attendants. The new union adopted the gender neutral term "flight attendant" to define those members of the cabin crew.[118] And while the union worked to take sexuality out of the job, the use of such wardrobe devices as hot pants further sexualized women in their role as flight attendants.

The company welcomed the changing times with its own new look. Since the late forties, Piedmont had adopted a Speedbird design and paint scheme that wore well through the fifties and sixties. By 1974, the design needed an update. That year, all aircraft in the fleet had some subtle changes made to their appearance. The word "Airlines" was officially dropped from the plane insignia,

Flight attendant Lynn Shainberg poses with Alabama Governor George Wallace during the 1972 campaign. The Wallace campaign chartered a Piedmont plane and crew to ferry them around the upper Midwest (Lynn Shainberg Sass Collection).

although a number of jets had already been painted with just the word "Piedmont" along the tube. In addition, the lettering was updated to a bolder version that was used by the company to its last day. Piedmont's 1974 annual report marked the renovation by stating, "We're now writing our name with more flair and color." A daring blue stripe adorned the side of each plane, leaving the pinstripe but a memory as "a reflection of our bold, bright outlook." Likewise, the Speedbird itself was altered in several ways. "Our streamlined 'bird' soars free — heading for tomorrow,"[119] the annual report declared. "The Piedmont symbol received a makeover that gave its wings a perpendicular edge to its body, which was also altered to look more like the jet aircraft that now carried passengers on many Piedmont routes.

The folks in Winston-Salem kept the color scheme for reasons that one Piedmont pilot

As a young flight attendant in the early 1970s, Pauline Fletcher Thomas sports the era's latest and most revealing uniform worn by Piedmont stewardesses. According to legend, all women's uniforms (including Pauline's) were designed by Mrs. Tom Davis (Pauline Fletcher Thomas Collection).

suggested were more practical than design oriented. "They painted the DC-3s, the top of the airplanes white," said Tory Vaughn, an early pilot for the airline. "A lot of people thought this was for looks but that's not true. They found it would drop the temperature in the cabin about six degrees."[120]

Piedmont Aviation created opportunities for many individuals. None benefited more from an association with the company than Bonnie McElveen-Hunter. In 1973, she almost single-handedly began publication of the first in flight magazine for the airline, called *Pace*. With a wide variety of stories, McElveen-Hunter took the opportunity provided by Mr. Davis to develop a regular publication and turned her company, Pace Communications, into "one of the largest woman-owned businesses in the country."[121] McElveen-Hunter, publisher and president of Pace Communications, writing for the last edition of the magazine fifteen years after the first, reflected on the relationship between her magazine and the airline which delivered it. "The airline had a vision for the future and a sincere desire for excellence, but most of all it was an airline with integrity. A Piedmont handshake was better than a signed contract. The commitment to quality and human values is what we have always held dear and tried to reflect in the pages of *Pace*."[122] After its association with Piedmont, the company went on to win numerous awards for its product and McElveen-Hunter became well known for her philanthropy and government service, which included appointments as ambassador to Finland and head of the American Red Cross.

As the new generation joined the airline and planes were given facelifts, Tom Davis weathered quite a bit of turbulence, not from the airline, but within his general aviation division. In November of 1975, Piedmont Aviation lost the lease as fixed base operator at Winston-Salem's Smith Reynolds Airport. The Forsyth County Airport Commission wanted greater revenue from Piedmont in negotiations for a new lease at Smith Reynolds. New York–based Baldwin Aviation quickly outbid Piedmont for the right to provide airport services to private pilots and companies that used the airport. The airport commission made the change after Pete Baldwin offered a substantial increase in payment to the commission for improvements to the areas used by operators other than the airline. When the commission accepted the offer, the folks from Piedmont were not happy. After 35 years of handling business for the airport, Mr. Davis and his company felt they had been brushed aside for empty promises on the part of Baldwin.

Both sides quickly drew battle lines. When the airport commission raised landing fees, Piedmont alleged the rate increase subsidized the poor decision to allow Baldwin in and pointed to decreased revenue from the new fixed base operator to prove it. Baldwin countered with an accusation that the wind created by passing Piedmont jets blew a private plane (belonging to a customer of Baldwin) off its tiedown. Further, Baldwin filed suit against Piedmont, making a number of charges of trespassing. "Baldwin claims Piedmont, in performing aircraft maintenance on the property, loading and unloading passengers and cargo on the property, taxiing across the property and driving heavy service vehicles across the property, is in violation of Baldwin's rights under the lease," said a news report.[123] Piedmont's access to portions of the Winston-Salem airport was being restricted. Piedmont fired back with a countersuit.

Those caught in the middle — private pilots and small companies that used airport facilities — felt themselves the real losers. Ed Lasley, who ran an air-taxi service, condemned the "mud-slinging" between Piedmont and Baldwin. He blamed the airport commission for allowing the controversy and said, "Airport officials have been remiss."[124] Private pilot G. Mackay Salley agreed with Lasley, saying that the airport commission was really to blame "for allowing things to run down under Piedmont to such a degree that they had to 'bail out' the airport at the expense of the private pilot." Salley called conditions at the airport under Piedmont "undesirable to say the least" but felt improvements made by Baldwin with the accompanying price tags for hangar fees, tie-downs and ramp parking were unreasonable.[125]

The controversy dragged on until the two parties settled the dispute out of court with the blessing of the airport commission. By the spring of 1977, an agreement had been worked out that allowed Piedmont to use "a back taxiway and a ramp" that Baldwin returned to the control of the airport authority in exchange for a five year extension on making capital improvements promised by Baldwin in its original lease agreement.[126] The two aviation companies lived uneasily together until Baldwin sold its operations at Smith Reynolds Airport to local businessman John Googe, who quickly renamed the operation Winston-Salem Air. After a year of operation, Winston-Salem Air, Inc., was quietly sold to Piedmont, returning control of the fixed base operation back to its old occupant.[127]

The trials of the mid-seventies caused the company to look for help from its employee base. Audrey Collins recollected a period in which the company asked for concessions from its workers. "Rather than cutting a salary they asked for a give back. It started out being eight hours a month," said Collins. "You didn't have to work. You could take a day off without pay. But then some of them [employees] were a little more generous. They give them the day and they worked too. It was company wide." Audrey Collins remembered many office employees willingly worked extra to help the company, efforts that were first monitored by the honor system. This pattern of assumption would change. "They found that sometimes some of the upper management wasn't doing that. They took it on their word to turn in the time. Then it became a mandatory thing, saying we're taking this time out of your check," Collins said. The pay reductions continued only a short time until budget constraints eased.[128]

Piedmont Airlines flew toward its 30th birthday having taken its share of lumps but still flying with more jets to more places than ever before. However, substantive changes for both Piedmont and the airline industry were brewing. Some of the company's management began to recognize that the future held potentially radical changes for the airline industry as a regulated body. Since the early seventies, cries had gone up to deregulate airlines in the hope that competition would drive down the price of tickets. Under the CAB, an airline was virtually guaranteed a profit. Consequently, all airlines were against deregulation. Mr. Davis saw Bill Magruder, who had been on the inside of government, as potentially helpful in the fight to remain a regulated industry and sustain the status quo. As the seventies progressed, the clamor rose even higher to force airlines into some competitive environment that would benefit the consumer. The fuel crisis of 1973–74 only exacerbated the problem. As the clamor grew, discussions on the state of the airline industry continued. Tom Davis speculated that if his protégée, Bill Magruder, could successfully navigate the troubled skies of deregulation, Piedmont Aviation would have a smooth ride into the 1980s. Magruder never got that opportunity.

On September 10, 1977, William M. Magruder died on the golf course of a massive heart attack. Ironically, Magruder had been the one to mandate that every employee learn cardio pulmonary resuscitation as part of their duties for Piedmont.[129] The untimely death of Bill Magruder left the company uncertain of its future during a period when tremendous change loomed within the airline industry.[130] Mr. Davis was just over five years from retirement and ready to wind down an extraordinary career with Piedmont. His executive vice president, whom he had thought would ascend to a position of leadership, was dead. With an avalanche of challenges ahead for the company and top management in transition, Piedmont Aviation had to find a successor to Tom Davis — fast.

· 6 ·

The Hazards of Flight, 1959–1988

> A recent study based on FAA reports identified Piedmont Airlines as the airline with the fewest malfunctions per 100,000 flights in three of the past five years: 1980, 1982, and 1984. Last year, Piedmont's malfunction rate was only .74 per 100,000 flights, compared with an industry average of 4.97.
> —*Winston-Salem Journal*, September 16, 1985

By the time of this newspaper article, Piedmont Airlines had hit its stride, flying mostly error free. For well over 15 years, Pacemakers had avoided accidents, adding safety to the company's laurels of efficiency and shrewdness. The words of the *Winston-Salem Journal* gratified the employees, many of whom worked hard to earn them. The safety record of Piedmont was the envy of the industry. However, the company suffered a number of earlier setbacks in the air. Piedmont Airlines was an exemplary air carrier but not flawless. Several tragic and occasionally bizarre incidents revealed the limits of the Speedbird in its quest to carry customers safely to their destination.

Of the millions of passengers carried by Piedmont Pacemakers, the overwhelming majority arrived reasonably satisfied. They enjoyed the ride and remained loyal customers when they had future air travel needs. Occasionally, turbulence or other factors caused difficulties that proved disruptive and were largely unavoidable. "If they have a smooth flight and the landing's nice, they will get off and say, 'Boy that was sure a nice trip,'" remarked Captain H.L. Mise during a television interview. But he added, "On the day where you have a beautiful day and you're not working very hard and if you come in and the landing is not quite so good, you'll have a few disgruntled people get off."[1] Employees worked hard to make experiences pleasurable for passengers but not every flight was comfortable, not every customer satisfied. Earl Wilcox flew Piedmont so much that his frequent flyer miles afforded vacation travel for his two children as well as himself and his wife. Like every passenger, he remembered the bad experiences much more than the good ones. He described a particularly bad flight aboard a Pacemaker.

> One of the worst flights I was ever on was a flight to Washington, D.C., with severe storms all the way from Hickory [North Carolina] to DC. By the time we reached D.C., I was half sick and was looking forward to a landing. I had already checked to see if I had a bag in the seat back. The storm over D.C. was so bad that flights were backed up and we were put in a holding pattern for a very long time. We were in the dark clouds and could not see anything. The plane was being tossed about, rising and then falling. My hands began to sweat and I got sicker and about ready to lose everything by the time we touched down. I made it without throwing up; how, I don't know.[2]

When flying as often as Earl Wilcox did, an unpleasant encounter was bound to occur. In a few situations, however, the outcome turned from the uncomfortable to the catastrophic. Over the 41 year history of Piedmont Airlines, a handful of disasters and near disasters took place that endangered the lives of passengers as well as the reputation of the airline. Though extensively investigated, these events have often left as many questions as answers. Many speculate what might have been at fault; some prefer to leave these incidences unexamined. However painful the tragedies may have been, their inclusion paints a fuller picture of Piedmont as an airline; they were an acknowledgement of failure that tempered success.

The telegram read, "Made an emergency landing three-quarters of a mile west of Tri-City. Because of excellent work of Captain [H.H.] Hutcheson, all of the 15 passengers were uninjured." Mr. Davis read those words three days after Christmas 1948, when he received the message. Flying to the scene immediately, he found the landing gear "shook loose" from the DC-3 that had come to rest on the uphill slope of a field only a few miles from the Bristol-Kingsport–Johnson City, Tennessee airport. According to press reports, one engine went out just after the 6:00 P.M. takeoff. The second engine quit almost immediately after. The succession of mishaps kept Hutcheson from returning to the airport and forced him to find a quick landing site. The pilot credited his copilot and purser, giving them 75 percent of the credit for a safe landing. "H.E. Moore, the purser, kept the passengers calm and the copilot James Craig was very cooperative," said Hutcheson. "There was no panic anywhere in the plane." The plane touched down at twilight and except for the landing gear, received only minor damage. The crew had the presence of mind to build a fire for everyone to keep them warm in the late December evening until help arrived. Passengers returned to the Tri-City airport, where they boarded another Piedmont plane to complete their flight to Cincinnati.[3] Everyone breathed a sigh of relief as the airline avoided calamity in its first mishap. They knew that in the future they might not be so fortunate.

"I heard a loud swoosh. Then it sounded like an explosion"[4] was how Luther Haynes described it to police. As caretaker of Zion Baptist Church in Shelby, North Carolina, Haynes was working in the church graveyard at about 6:15 P.M. when something fell from the sky and landed about 40 yards from him. The object had fallen 6,500 feet from a Piedmont flight on its way from Charlotte to Asheville, North Carolina. The object was passenger Oren Ase Pruitt, a 38-year-old chef turned surveyor from Charlotte. Pruitt died instantly upon impact. His body made a four-inch indentation in the ground, then "bounced into the air and rolled 27 feet"[5] before coming to rest in the graveyard. The episode launched a total of four investigations to try to determine why the Piedmont passenger fell from his flight on June 10, 1956.[6]

What happened onboard the *Tidewater Pacemaker* (N45V) remains a mystery. Oren Pruitt was a newlywed; married just 22 hours to Blandene Smith, a hostess at the same hotel were Pruitt worked as a chef. The couple missed their first flight to Asheville to meet her parents, so they boarded "Flight 5" which left Charlotte at 5:43 P.M., six minutes late on its way west. The DC-3 held its full complement of 24 passengers, which included the newly married Pruitts. Once the flight climbed to cruising altitude, Oren Pruitt got up from his seat and moved to the back of the plane, for reasons known only to him. Newspapers quoted his bride saying, "We were just sitting and talking." Blandene Pruitt told reporters, "He was telling me how pretty I looked, how much he loved me and wondering what my parents would think of him." She said he offered to get her water after noticing she looked "a little peaked."[7] Oren Pruitt walked to the back of the plane, found the restroom in use and apparently tried the other door in the rear. Inexplicably, he managed to exert enough pressure to open that door, the entryway to the plane.

When the door opened, only a few people on the plane knew it. Since the DC-3 was not pressurized, the airflow caused by the gaping passageway caused only minor commotion. Captain Baxter Slaughter and First Officer H.A. Schulze immediately realized that something had occurred, though. The flight of a DC-3 was so delicately balanced that a heavy flight attendant walking up the aisle from the front to the back of the plane caused a disruption in the plane's handling. Pruitt's opening of the door and the subsequent rush to the front by steward Bert Barnes caused the plane to "lurch" and slow down by 20 knots. "Pilot Baxter Slaughter thought motor trouble had developed. He reached for a mixture control and then spotted a warning light which showed the passenger door was open," explained Shelby reporter Bill Green. The copilot and steward rushed to the back of the plane to determine what happened. They found an open entry door, a terrified woman, and no sign of Oren Pruitt. The woman had been the occupant of the restroom at the time Pruitt made his error in judgment. She found the open, air-sucking door between herself and her seat. Afraid she might be pulled irresistibly out of the plane by the pressure, she waited until Purser Barnes and First Officer Schulze locked hands, forming a human chain to help her across the span so she could return to her seat.[8]

Captain Slaughter circled once then continued on to Asheville, landing with the passenger door open. Fred Smith waited at the airport to greet his daughter and new son-in-law. As the plane descended, he noticed the open door.[9] The Civil Aeronautics Administration, State Bureau of Investigation, North Carolina Highway Patrol, local law enforcement officers and Piedmont personnel all converged on the plane to determined what happened and why. The door was "wrenched slightly and out of line" due to the slipstream of air coursing across the plane in flight. "Heel marks were found alongside the plane's fuselage," reported the *Shelby Daily Star*.

The real question for Piedmont officials centered on how Oren Pruitt opened the door of the *Tidewater Pacemaker*. Bill McGee and Zeke Saunders headed the company investigation. McGee wondered out loud, "I do not understand how it was possible for Pruitt to open that door." Zeke added that it would take "considerable pressure" to do so.[10] After unlocking the door he said, "You had a tremendous amount of outward pressure on it."[11] Once passengers were questioned, one official said, "Most of them just thought Pruitt opened the wrong door." "When he opened that door, he went out," said Zeke Saunders. Looking back on the event, he surmised that "he hung on for a while to the side of the airplane."[12] At the time of the accident, Zeke believed that Pruitt probably "was conscious until he hit the earth" and that the hissing sound heard both in the air and on the ground was that of Oren Pruitt screaming.[13]

The investigation brought to light some observations that contradicted Mrs. Pruitt's assertion that all was well between the brand-new couple. Steward Bert Barnes alleged that Mr. Pruitt "had been drinking" because Barnes "smelled the odor of alcohol on Pruitt." When asked whether she and her husband had been drinking, the widow said flatly, "No."[14]

The interest in an event as out of the ordinary as this one intensified as the story circulated. The bizarre incident brought crowds to the Cleveland County cemetery where Oren Pruitt fell. Luther Haynes witnessed over 200 people coming to see the sight where the "freak death fall" landed. Well after dark, "community people and curiosity seekers" sought out the location, which was adjacent to Haynes's home. Gossip enlarged the depth of the impact of Pruitt's body from four inches to four feet.[15] The local funeral home that received the body reported thousands of calls throughout the night and into the next morning inquiring about the details of the affair. Callers included *Time Magazine* and the Associated Press.[16] R.D.

Hager of Piedmont Airlines quickly asserted, "Pruitt's death was the first fatality the line has had in 384,981,146 miles of flying,"[17] a total that covered over eight years. The next fatality would not be so long in coming.

Strangely enough, Zeke Saunders acknowledged flying a DC-3 where an eerily similar incident occurred, although this one did not render another lost passenger. On a flight out of Winston-Salem, Zeke noticed the same kind of warning light Baxter Slaughter saw when Oren Pruitt opened the passenger door. Going back to alert Purser T.L. Martin, who was standing next to the door, Zeke said, "Don't touch that door. It's not locked." Instead, Martin "reached and caught the handle of that door and it popped, so out he went. His shoulder hit the edge of the doorframe, and it threw his foot right in my hand," Zeke remembered. He grabbed the purser but admitted, "I couldn't hold him. He was fixing to pull me out too." Zeke had three choices: Let Martin go, be sucked out of the plane with him or get help pulling the terrified purser back in. "I hollered and the passengers formed a chain, five or six passengers. They got a hold of me and I had a hold of him and we pulled him back in."[18] The steward was saved from the fate of the unfortunate newlywed.

The next tragic flight for Piedmont occurred three years after the Pruitt fatality, on the day before Halloween in 1959. Flight 349 took off at 7:49 P.M. from Washington, D.C., a few minutes after its scheduled departure time because of heavy traffic at National Airport. With one stop to make at Charlottesville, Virginia, the plane was scheduled to terminate at

Flight 349 rests atop Buck's Elbow Mountain after the October 30, 1959, crash. Rescuers, which included local Boy Scouts, searched for 38 hours before discovering the DC-3 with only one survivor (Richard F. Gaya Collection).

Roanoke at approximately 9:12 P.M. At 8:24 P.M., the crew radioed the Charlottesville tower for landing instructions, advising that they were over Rochelle, Virginia, and flying at 150 miles per hour, putting them about six minutes away from the airport.[19] After that radio transmission, Flight 349 crashed into the side of Buck's Elbow Mountain, part of the Blue Ridge mountain range. The impact occurred less than 400 feet from the summit of the mountain.

For the next day and a half, Flight 349 was lost. One man from nearby Waynesboro, while at a Friday night high school football game, thought he saw a plane swerve "off to its left towards the mountain,"[20] but throughout the night and into the next day, no one had any clue as to what happened to the *Buckeye Pacemaker* (N55V). After "ricocheting off a huge boulder and coming to rest atop a rocky ledge amid a large number of trees,"[21] the wreckage lay silently near a microwave relay beam pilots used for navigation. Searchers looked within the general vicinity of the beam but did not venture far enough to find the plane's remains on Saturday. Since no explosion or fire lit the way to the wreckage, the exact location baffled everyone. A misty drizzle cut visibility, hampering rescue efforts throughout the day.

The search continued into Sunday. Planes and helicopters filled the air. The U.S. Air Force joined the Civil Air Patrol and Piedmont officials in the search for the downed plane. "We were just flying around when I happened to look at the side of the mountain," said Air Force Technical Sergeant Robert Mondragon. "I just happened to see what looked like a white tree, a dead tree. I asked the pilot to circle around. Then I spotted the tail. We could see no signs of life."[22] Thirty-five hours after impact, Flight 349 had been located.

The wreckage proved difficult to access. Rescuers reached the site by going down instead of up. Since the crash location was near the top of a hollow on the mountain, searchers climbed down from Skyline Drive, a national scenic highway, to get to the remains. They carried in blankets, rope, stretchers and first aid equipment, hoping to save at least some of the victims.[23]

Searchers found the spot littered with debris from the plane. The rear of the aircraft's cabin remained intact while the rest lay in pieces. Many of the plane's occupants had been thrown from the wreckage. The crew of three died at the scene along with almost every passenger. But the most amazing discovery made by the rescuers who sidled down the mountain was that one person was alive. Still sitting in his seat with a broken hip, E. Phillip Bradley withstood the plane's impact and weathered the wait until he was discovered at 7:45 A.M. on Sunday morning. He too had been jettisoned from the plane on impact.

Phil Bradley's position as the sole survivor of the first Piedmont Airline crash provided unique insight into the last few minutes of Flight 349. The day after his rescue Bradley began to tell the story of the crash, relating portions from a hospital stretcher in the emergency room. He continued his story over the years, culminating in an oral history told to Richard F. Gaya in the mid–1990s. He said the flight from Washington had gone smoothly until after passengers were instructed to fasten seat belts and extinguish cigarettes for the scheduled landing at Charlottesville. Having missed a flight earlier in the day, he eagerly took the last available seat on Flight 349. During the flight he saw several interesting sights as he sat looking out the window in the back row. First, a spotlight reached up from a Charlottesville shopping center to the DC-3. Bradley regarded the display as "unusual and unfamiliar" since, having flown this route many times, he had never seen such before.[24] He observed that the pilot seemed to "make one or more complete 360 degree circles" over the shopping center. Following that, he then "saw the reflection of the plane's anti-collision light on the rear of the aircraft bouncing off the clouds."[25] Suddenly Bradley felt "the lane's wings clipping the tree tops." He put his head

Local sheriff's deputies inspect the damage to the *Buckeye Pacemaker* following its crash. The interior can be plainly seen, including the air steps. The decision was made to leave the debris where it landed (Richard F. Gaya Collection).

down and looked at his watch. It was 8:40 P.M., ten minutes past scheduled arrival time at Charlottesville. He recalled,

> There was a tremendous crunching and tearing of metal and then everything went black. What I remembered next was a rushing, roaring sound of an ocean similar to the sounds we hear from a beach. This occurred while I was being propelled from my seat in the plane which had broken loose from the foundation bolts in the floor and was still fastened to my seat. The next thing I knew I was trying to get dirt and leaves out of my mouth.[26]

Then he waited. According to Phil Bradley, he did not move from his seat. He was in shock and had sustained severe injuries. He used a pole to reach blankets lodged in the trees to help protect him from the cold and a drizzle that began to fall. Bradley said he passed the time reflecting upon his military career, including his service during the D-Day invasion. During that time, he related seeing bears and turkey buzzards that were curious about the carnage around him. He also related seeing a vision of Jesus Christ, which comforted him through the long hours until rescuers came. When discovery of the crash site came on Sunday morning, Piedmont Vice President Zeke Saunders was among those who first surveyed the scene of the accident below Skyline Drive and offered help to the lone survivor.

The pieces of the puzzle fit together differently for Zeke Saunders, however. Believing that Bradley got up and moved around, Saunders noted, "You could tell by his cigarette butts.

6. *The Hazards of Flight, 1959–1988*   151

Emergency personnel observe E. Philip Bradley, the sole survivor from Piedmont's first crash. While recuperating, he described the aircraft's wings hitting the treetops before a "terrible lurching sound" (Richard F. Gaya Collection).

Apparently he just lit one right after another, and he threw them down."[27] Saunders speculated that Phil Bradley might have been more mobile than even the sole survivor himself believed. Upon arriving at the scene, Saunders saw evidence of partially smoked cigarettes all around the crash site. Zeke Saunders believed, "[Bradley] had moved down from where the accident site was, probably a hundred feet or so."[28] The implication was significant because of the speculation by the Piedmont Airlines vice president that several people might not have died instantly. "I remember when I got there the purser was laying face down. His toes had dug holes in the ground that deep [indicating four to six inches]. That would have taken him a long time for him to do that. He had been alive a long time. He was still warm," declared Saunders, who felt that Purser George Hicks and "one or two passengers" had not been dead long.[29] Phil Bradley was immediately sedated and prepped to be airlifted to the University of Virginia's Medical Center in Charlottesville. However, he refused. Bradley, having avoided death in one aircraft, said that he did not want to risk his life a second time. The rescue team carried him up the mountain on a stretcher. He was later flown to Charlottesville by helicopter after sedation took effect.

In the weeks and months that followed, authorities focused on the cause of the accident. Investigators removed the instruments from the plane, while CAB examiners conducted an extensive inquiry into the accident. A public hearing in Charlottesville convened for two days, December 10 and 11, 1959. In the view of Zeke Saunders, "[The pilot] flew a complete, perfect approach, just moved over about seven or eight miles."³⁰ Piedmont Airlines conducted extensive analysis where Saunders and Chief Pilot Frank Nicholson flew the same route "40 or 50 times," and from those flights, Zeke Saunders drew his conclusion. "The only thing we could find was that there was a homing beacon in Pennsylvania. We could pick that up once in a while and that could pull that needle off," said Zeke. "We think that's what happened that night. They got some skip and it pulled him off."³¹

The Civil Aeronautics Board reached a slightly different view. In April of 1961, the board issued its "Aircraft Accident Report." In it, they agreed with Zeke Saunders and Piedmont that the flight was off course at least eight miles. However, after extensive testing with the help of the Federal Communications Commission, investigators excluded the possibility of an "unauthorized homer rumored to be in operation" that might have pulled the pilots off course. Also, the board found "no malfunction of or failure of the aircraft prior to impact." Instead, CAB officials noted "navigational error" by the pilots as the reason Piedmont Flight 349 was off course in excess of eight miles. The board determined that the captain of the flight, George Lavrinc, was likely personally steering the *Buckeye Pacemaker* at the time of impact. The report pointed out, "Voice identification from the recordings showed the radio transmissions were made by First Officer [Lee] Haley, thus indicating that Captain Lavrinc was flying the aircraft."³²

Because of the navigational error, George Lavrinc was the subject of great scrutiny by the CAB in its effort to determine a cause for the crash. Such a mistake as that which doomed Flight 349 seemed inconsistent with Lavrinc's previous flight record. Lavrinc came to Piedmont Aviation in January of 1950 and worked in the radio department. He transferred over to the airline division in November of the following year. He had been a captain for Piedmont since May of 1957, flying almost 4,800 hours on a DC-3, many of them over the same route as the one in which the crash occurred. His last physical was performed two and a half weeks before the collision. He was 32 years old. Upon study, the board found that "there were numerous factors which were obviously inconsistent" with Captain Lavrinc's excellent record. Some were: "The apparent navigational omission, a non-adherence to precise tracking procedures, and a descent below the authorized procedure turn altitude."³³ Investigation by the board determined that George Lavrinc was under "severe mental strain." Finding that Lavrinc had received psychotherapy as well as psychotropic drugs for his condition, the CAB included in its conclusion the following statement.

> The consensus is that Captain Lavrinc was so heavily burdened with mental and emotional problems that he should have been relieved of the strain of flight duty while undergoing treatment for his condition. This condition was such that preoccupation with his problems could well have lowered his standard of performance during instrument flight. Further, with respect to this accident the consensus is that the emotional and mental problems were of far greater importance in causing the preoccupation than would have the use of psychotropic medication.³⁴

Like the Shelby graveyard where Oren Pruitt landed, the site of the Buck's Elbow Mountain crash, near Crozet, Virginia, has been the destination of curiosity seekers since the 1959 incident. Piedmont made the decision not to remove the wreckage, leaving it on the side of the mountain. Since then, hikers have traveled the approximately 2,000 foot incline, which at times reaches an incline of up to 30 degrees, to see the remnants of the *Buckeye Pacemaker*. Between Crozet and the ascent to Buck's Elbow Mountain, Phillip Bradley spearheaded construction of a monument to the 26 victims of the crash. Survivor Bradley designed and dedicated the memorial, putting much of his own time and money into the remembrance completed in 1999.³⁵

Less than six months after the Buck's Elbow crash, another Speedbird was involved in a mishap that resulted in fatalities, though none were Piedmont passengers. Just after 1:00 P.M. on Wednesday April 20, 1960, both a Piedmont F-27 and a private 310 Cessna approached the runway at the Hickory, North Carolina, airport. Approximately 600 feet above the ground the two planes collided. Pilots from both aircraft had been warned of the approach of the other and both were flying Visual Flight Rules (VFR). Eyewitness Robert Houston was on the roof of a nearby church when looked up and said, "The small plane moved over the top and I saw the propeller blade of the Piedmont plane chop off part of the wing. The small plane bobbled a couple of times then fell straight down at an angle with the good wing pointed straight down."[36]

The private plane had flown in over top of the Piedmont F-27, damaging the left wing and left engine propeller blades. Captain Lee Cottrell piloted the *Palmetto Pacemaker* (N2704R) and its 36 passengers to safety. Saying over and over again after landing that he never saw the private plane, Cottrell added, "I'm just sorry it happened." All four men on board the Cessna died instantly. Both flights were bringing buyers to the area's spring furniture show, held bi-annually by local furniture manufacturers. Describing the mid-air collision, Ed Manske, a passenger aboard the Piedmont flight, said he felt an "abrupt jolt with a lot of noise."[37] Don Collins worked on the Pacemaker after the accident and saw "tire marks right across the top of the wing."[38] As tragic as the collision proved to be for the group in the small plane, pilot training and alertness paid off for Piedmont's passengers, who landed safely.

A memorial to those who lost their lives aboard Flight 349 on October 30, 1959, erected by the sole survivor, Phil Bradley. The monument is located near Crozet, Virginia, and within sight of Buck's Elbow Mountain."

The same plane and the same pilot had gone through a previous ordeal together. On April 28, 1959, Cottrell ferried the *Palmetto Pacemaker* into the Greensboro–High Point Airport to pick up passengers for a 7:10 A.M. flight. When the plane landed, the wheels refused to lock into place and folded in as the F-27 touched down. Captain Cottrell and First Officer Pete Dickens steered the plane to a halt on its belly. Only Purser Bruce Clodfelter was with Cottrell and Dickens on the disabled plane. None of the three were injured in the crash landing. Published reports on the incident said that neither pilot had any indication that the landing gear had failed to lock into place when touchdown was made. About $50,000 in damage was done to the $700,000 aircraft as it skidded 1,400 feet before coming to a stop. In addition to the aluminum skin on its undercarriage, which left white skid marks on the black asphalt, both propellers were damaged in the incident. Passengers waiting for the plane's arrival were transported to Winston-Salem by limousine to catch a substitute aircraft for their expected trip to Cincinnati. The *Palmetto Pacemaker* was repaired and put back into service; eight days short of a year later it would be damaged again in the Hickory incident.[39]

Throughout its tenure, the F-27's landing gear failed a number of times. One landing in the summer of 1958 created panic as a nose wheel failed to deploy on a training flight in Winston-Salem. "The wheel finally came down after some maneuvering by the pilot," a news report said.[40] Likewise, flying acumen showed itself to be crucial to another F-27 flight in 1961. Captain Milt Browning and First Officer Pete Lindsay headed out of Winston-Salem en route to stops at Roanoke, Lynchburg, and Charlottesville, Virginia, before reaching a destination of Washington, D.C. Preparing to land in Charlottesville, both pilots noticed that the landing gear of the *James River Pacemaker* (N2707R) was down but it refused to lock in place. Unable to diagnose the problem, the crew informed the home base, which ordered the plane back to Winston-Salem. Upon return, the company sent another plane aloft to get a firsthand look at the malfunctioning gear the pilots themselves could not see. After a close look, the men from headquarters determined the landing gear could not be trusted to properly deploy.

Purser Bob Evans kept passengers calm as the company officials debated a way to bring the stranded airplane in safely. With full tanks of kerosene at the beginning of the flight, the folks in Winston-Salem had some time to decide the best way to solve the emergency that had not yet turned into a crisis. Looking for a place to attempt a "gears up, belly landing," the choice was made to cover a runway at Seymour Johnson Air Force Base in eastern North Carolina near Goldsboro with foam. Firemen laid a one-inch-thick strip of smelly spray down on the 3500-foot runway. Evans fulfilled the tasks of a flight attendant in an emergency situation well, preparing all 18 passengers onboard for the landing by strapping them to their seats at the rear of the plane, wrapping blankets around their legs and giving each a pillow. He instructed them to bury their heads in the pillows as the plane landed. Bob Evans reportedly commented after the event, "They were as fine a bunch of passengers as I've ever seen."[41]

The plane landed beautifully. Said copilot Pete Lindsay: "I've made wheel landings rougher than that one," Eyewitnesses agreed, saying that it was a perfect landing. Captain Milt Browning added, "I knew the gear would fold when we touched down. Then we would ride down the strip on the belly. That gear folded back and we sat down just as nice as you please." After landing, the pilots were interviewed. Evans admitted that he told the passengers "they wouldn't get a scratch," to which Browning quipped, "You sure were taking a lot for granted." Showing his complete confidence, Evans replied, "I trusted you guys up front." With a grin he added, "If I hadn't, I wouldn't have been on your plane." The trust was mutual. Neither Browning nor Lindsay ever went back to check on the passengers, knowing that Bob

Evans was taking care of them. When the substitute plane arrived to finish the trip, passengers showed their full trust in the flight crew. All 18 hopped aboard the flight to Washington, D.C.[42]

Another disabled Speedbird was landed successfully 18 months later after a most bizarre equipment malfunction. First Officer Bob Carter was getting his check ride, a procedure to demonstrate his competency with a newly purchased Martin 404, christened the *Tidewater Pacemaker* (N40401). Along to evaluate his handling of the plane were FAA official Paul Sills and Captain J.L. "Pappy" Wilkes. On his approach to Wilmington's New Hanover County Airport, the left propeller flew off, colliding with the fuselage just behind where Pappy Wilkes was sitting. Carter earned his endorsement as a pilot that day, holding the aircraft steady as he touched down on the runway. After traveling about 300 feet, the right engine "doubled back and caused the right wing to buckle." Instantly, the engine crashed through the skin of the plane in the area where passengers would have sat had the plane been carrying any, forcing Carter to further demonstrate his abilities. The plane stopped 150 feet from the runway and sustained extensive damage, but of the three men on the plane, only Wilkes received minor injuries.[43]

A Martin 404 proved unreliable on another occasion, this time as the plane readied for takeoff. A nearly full plane with 33 passengers boarded the *Buckeye* (namesake of the ill fated DC-3 crash on Buck's Elbow Mountain) *Pacemaker* (N40446) in Roanoke, Virginia, on their way to Cincinnati. As was customary, before takeoff the plane stopped for one final check, but this time, three of the aircraft's four wheels collapsed. One passenger reported "a sharp drop and a jolt" as the two main gear and the nose gear collapsed. The incident proved to be more awkward than dangerous, as passengers had to get out though an emergency window since the exit stair was wedged under the plane. The July 1966 mishap resulted in a few passengers being taken to the hospital, but none of the injuries were life-threatening.[44]

A succession of three bad years for Piedmont's safety record began in 1966. In November of that year, a Martin 404 went down, killing everyone aboard. A flight crew of three had been directed to ferry the *Appomattox Pacemaker* (NV40406) from Wilmington to New Bern, North Carolina, on Sunday morning, November 20, so the aircraft could begin service on Monday. Captained by World War II veteran pilot Joe Helsabeck, the flight also included a relatively new co-pilot, Ensley O. Adams, and flight attendant Pamela Sue Rumble. Though the trip carried no passengers, the 23 minute flight was designated as Flight 101.

As close as twelve miles outside of New Bern, the crew reported no trouble at all, according to Mr. Davis, when he was asked by the press to account for the crash. Like most at Piedmont, he was at a loss to explain how it happened. After takeoff from Wilmington at 5:40 A.M., last radio contact came from the doomed flight at 6:06 A.M. Four minutes later, the plane went down three miles from its destination. In Croatan National Forest, the aircraft bounced off the ground, then clipped tree tops before coming to rest in a swampy, heavily wooded area about a mile away from the nearest road. The plane did not explode but the tremendous impact proved fatal for all three crew members.[45]

Speculation abounded about the reason for the crash. Vice President Zeke Saunders scratched his head about the cause. He noted a couple of points that factored into the last moments of Flight 101, saying, "The copilot was a new boy I had hired. He flew for a lumber company in South Carolina," referring to Ensley Adams of Taylors. Saunders theorized that Adams may have been steering the aircraft, saying that Joe Helsabeck "had gone to the bathroom, and when he realized the guy was getting too low" he returned to the cockpit as quickly as possible. Zeke Saunders came to this conclusion because he said that Helsabeck "was in his seat, but his clothes were not all on and he didn't have a seat belt on. He got there a little late." According to Piedmont's vice president, "The boy [Adams] wasn't familiar with the thing. He [Helsabeck] shouldn't have ever let the boy make the approach like that."[46] Joe Helsabeck had been a World War II pilot flying 42 missions in North Africa and Italy, winning the Air Medal with seven oak leaf clusters and the Distinguished Flying Cross.[47] The flight held the infamous distinction of being the first to claim the life of a female flight attendant. Pamela Sue Rumble had worked for the airline a little over a year before the crash. She was 22 years old.

The worst crash in Piedmont's history followed on July 19, 1967. It tragically occurred as Piedmont inched into the jet age. By the mid–sixties, all of the major carriers and a few of the regionals already sported jets in their fleet. When Piedmont made the decision to buy jet aircraft, its choice was the Boeing 737 model 200. However, orders for the popular model could not be filled immediately and Boeing, eager to keep the airline interested, offered Piedmont a deal to keep it from looking at the Douglas DC-9. The manufacturer loaned Piedmont two 727 model 100s. The endeavor complicated life at Piedmont because the Boeing jet required three pilots in the cockpit, setting the stage for the third man issue. One of the two 727 loaners, the newest airplane Piedmont flew in 1967, became involved in a situation strangely reminiscent of the incident in Hickory, North Carolina, that had occurred seven years earlier.

"Piedmont To Inaugurate Jet Service Tomorrow" read the headline of the *Asheville Citizen* on March 14, 1967, as it revealed the startup of "the first scheduled jet airline service in Western North Carolina."[48] The Atlanta to Washington, D.C., run that stopped in Asheville began the next day with the 727. The move spelled progress for the area and gave the stop a certain prestige that fitted nicely with Asheville's reputation as a summer vacation destination. Its airport was located south of town, a facility Asheville shared with the nearby city of Hendersonville. At the time, the airport provided only one runway for its arrivals and departures. Many of those passengers were retreating to the North Carolina mountains to avoid the heat of summer.

Wednesday morning, July 19 dawned like many a lazy summer day along the Blue Ridge Mountains. The season was, however, an especially busy time because a number of summer camps for kids operated in the areas at full capacity while schools were out. A significant portion of Piedmont's passenger list included children bound to and from camp. The jet, still a novelty in the air to folks around Asheville, caught the attention of some on the ground.[49] Flying in from Atlanta, the *Manhattan Pacemaker* (N68650) was scheduled for a short stop at the Asheville Municipal Airport before departing for Roanoke, Virginia, and then Washington, D.C. Thirty-nine passengers got off in Asheville, including a number of children bound for camp.

Among those getting on were John T. McNaughton and his family. John and Sarah McNaughton flew to Asheville to pick up their only child, Theodore, who had just finished a five week stay at Camp Sequoyah. The McNaughtons had enjoyed the previous evening with friends at nearby Biltmore Forest but were anxious to get back to Washington, D.C., where John had a new job awaiting him. President Lyndon Johnson had recently picked McNaughton to serve as his secretary of the Navy. With his nomination confirmed by the United States Senate, Secretary-Designate McNaughton prepared to take the reins on August 1. Commenting on the area on the morning of the departure, McNaughton told reporters, "I think it's lovely here, except you gave us some rain yesterday."[50]

After a hearty breakfast, the McNaughtons boarded Flight 22. They joined 20 others

N68650, the *Manhattan Pacemaker*. This aircraft was one of two 727-100s acquired by Piedmont in 1967 as the airline raced into the jet age. On July 19, this jet collided with a small Cessna airplane in the skies over Hendersonville, N.C., killing all 79 people aboard, as well as 3 in the Cessna (Ronnie Macklin Collection).

flying out of Asheville, filling the aircraft with a total of 74 passengers. Twenty-four of those were food brokers from the Stokely–Van Camp Company, makers of canned vegetables, on their way to an annual sales meeting. They had all boarded in Atlanta. With Captain Ray F. Schulte at the helm, First Officer Thomas C. Conrad and Flight Engineer Lawrence C. Wilson manned the cockpit. Stewardesses Sandra Kay Cox and Deborah Davis attended to passenger needs.

The flight was about a half hour behind schedule. Slowed by a late departure from Atlanta, Schulte and the flight crew got the Boeing 727 off the ground in Asheville at one minute before noon. Scheduled departure time was 11:28 A.M. A local service station operator, Yates Pearson, saw the jet as it crawled into the sky. "I was watching him come across," said Pearson. "There goes that big plane again. It looked like he was going straight up [Interstate] 26," he said. From the vantage point of his service station located at the corner of the Interstate 26 and Highway 64,[51] Yates Pearson unsuspectingly watched a routine flight turn tragic.

Seemingly out of nowhere, and into the path of Flight 22, came a Cessna 310 private aircraft. As Thomas Conner labored in his yard digging a swimming pool, his twelve year old son Alden ran over to him and exclaimed, "Look Daddy, that little plane is gonna hit it." The father looked up and said he could "see the little plane coming up under the big one." Another eyewitness, Clarence Hyder remarked, "It looked like he stuck to the bottom of it," adding,

Flight 22 fell out of the air and barely to the right of Interstate 26 near Hendersonville, N.C. The land was owned by a summer day camp but no one on the ground was killed. No one on the flight survived (Author's Collection).

"It didn't seem like it moved the big plane at all." But the damage was done. Accounts vary on what happened next. Some said the Piedmont jet looked like it was trying to make an emergency landing on the interstate, remarking that the Pacemaker circled a few times before falling; others say it descended almost immediately. The National Transportation Safety Board, in its investigation, determined, "The jet continued straight ahead momentarily, then nosed over and fell rapidly to the ground. The twin-engine Cessna was not observed at any time following the collision."[52] Several eyewitnesses reported a second explosion in the sky. The Piedmont aircraft came down in several pieces. The main body of the plane fell nose first, hitting the ground about 200 feet from the recently completed Interstate 26. Smaller pieces and bodies thrown from the plane in the explosion landed in a number of locations around the main crash site.[53] One spectator witnessed a body smashing through his neighbor's roof.[54]

Thomas Conner immediately drove to the site. "It took me five minutes to get to the site in my jeepster," related Conner, who forgot all about digging his swimming pool. A member of the local rescue squad, he said, "There was no sign of life. I circled the area twice to see if there were any live bodies. There were none. It was a flaming mess."[55] Traffic on the Interstate stopped as some got out to help, and others to see the aftermath of the worst crash in the history of Piedmont Airlines. At the time it was the fourth largest loss of life in the U.S. resulting from a midair collision.[56] Over 400 other emergency personnel found the same thing as Thomas Conner. The crash left no survivors, and chaos reigned all afternoon as rescuers searched.[57]

Upon learning about the wreck, many parents frantically tied up phone lines to see if their children were on board the doomed flight. Three youngsters departed from Flight 22 when it landed that morning in Asheville and another 37 were aboard a charter flight that Piedmont had added to accommodate all the children coming to camp. Flight 1022 followed the 727 out of Atlanta and was piloted by Captain Paul Snell. Because both flights shared Asheville's one runway, Snell had to be within visual distance of the airport so the 727 could be cleared for takeoff. As Paul Snell prepared to land, Flight 22 took off. Parents from Atlanta to Florida (from where many of the children came) only knew a plane crashed in Asheville. In addition, there was further cause for concern because the plane crashed on land owned by the Blue Star Camp. Camp owner Herman Popkin spent all afternoon calling parents to assure them that no kids from his camp were near the scene of the crash. Commenting that the children "don't know anything about it," he admitted, "The parents are the ones who were caused anguish."[58] Luckily for them, the distress subsided when they learned their children were safe. For relatives of the passengers, the grief had just started.

Piedmont officials flew to Asheville immediately to deal with the crisis. Next of kin were notified immediately. By July 20, the local papers reported the names of those who perished. A feeling of "deep shock" consumed the Asheville-Hendersonville area as the pathos balanced with a strange "carnival air" as thousands swarmed to the scene.[59] No event in western North Carolina memory had consumed as many lives as were taken so quickly just eight miles from the Asheville Municipal Airport. The crash received national attention, partially because the flight carried Secretary of the Navy Designate McNaughton. Both Secretary of Defense Robert McNamara and President Lyndon Johnson lauded John T. McNaughton's contributions. Johnson honored all the victims when he remarked that the death of all those aboard Flight 22 "has made this a tragic afternoon for many American families."[60]

Questions about what caused the crash near Hendersonville began immediately. A total of 82 people died, including 74 passengers, the flight crew of five, and three aboard the Cessna flight. The National Transportation Safety Board (NTSB) had recently moved from control of the Civil Aeronautics Board (CAB) to the Federal Aviation Administration (FAA) and became the investigating authority on the accident. Analysis of the debris, including assembly of the "bits and pieces of two planes"[61] marked a critical part of the NTSB investigation, which was led by the board's chief investigator, Tom Saunders.[62] The NTSB held hearings in Asheville the following October to gather information on the crash.

But controversy began long before the inquiry held its first meeting. Less than one week after the crash, the Aircraft Owners and Pilot's Association (AOPA) took exception to early assessments of blame made by the FAA about the cause. The association telegrammed both the FAA and the NTSB protesting statements they regarded as "unfair and damaging to general aviation and create unwarranted prejudice in the eyes of the public." They were referring to statements that placed blame for the accident fully on the private plane. Even though a full investigation was held, including three days of hearings, the NTSB did not stray far from its original assessment. The report adopted by the NTSB upheld that belief, stating:

> The probable cause of this accident was the deviation of the Cessna from its IFR [Instrument Flight Rules] clearance resulting in a flight path into airspace allocated to the Piedmont Boeing 727. The reason for such deviation cannot be specifically or positively identified. The minimum control procedures utilized by the FAA in the handling of the Cessna were a contributing factor.[63]

The mystery that the NTSB was never able to solve was why the private plane made a southwesterly turn at the Asheville VOR (VHF Omni-directional Radio Range, a navigational guide) instead of continuing northwest, which would have put it in the proper position for its approach to the Asheville airport. As a result, the Cessna seemed to be heading to the runway from the opposite direction, which placed it in the path of the commercial Piedmont jet. The transcripts of the Cessna pilot's conversation with the Asheville Approach Center reveal that the Asheville tower made an error, then corrected itself, when it told the small plane "cleared over the VOR to the Broad River, correction, make that the Asheville Radio Beacon" and told David Addison to maintain an altitude of 7,000 feet. Instead of following the corrected course as ground control instructed, Addison's plane moved toward, but not to, the Broad River Radio Beacon. When Addison communicated his erroneous move toward Broad River, he was "rogered" by the Asheville tower. The "roger" was an affirmation of the Cessna's position, which meant that at the tower had no problem with the small plane's location at the time. As the subsequent investigation indicated, Addison was flying a pattern different from the flight plan he had earlier filed. During the hearing, control tower operators claimed the Cessna flew in a direction contrary to which it was directed, but conversations between the tower and the craft do not indicate any attempt to correct the error.

The NTSB arrived at the conclusion that the Cessna was out of position, although the investigating agency, by saying that "the failure of the ATC system to provide timely information which would have prevented the deviation or at least alerted the pilot to recognize his misunderstanding," held Asheville Approach Center personnel partially responsible.[64] The report readily admitted that there was confusion between the Cessna and the Asheville tower. As a result of the incident several changes were made in Asheville, including the re-designating of beacons used to give pilots bearing in relation to their approach to the Asheville runway. The implication was that the Asheville tower did not adequately assist the Cessna pilot to the runway, leaving the smaller plane on its own and in the path of the 727. Many Piedmont employees agreed, including Don Collins. He said, "Air traffic control didn't do their job there. It wasn't something that our people did. It wasn't something the 310 [Cessna] person did. They just let the two get together."[65] Given the fact that each pilot was talking with ground personnel on a different frequency, (a standard procedure to avoid confusion) it was impossible for each to know the location of the other. In addition, the Asheville Municipal Airport did not possess radar at the time, making the exact position of the Cessna 310 difficult to pinpoint as it headed for Piedmont airspace. Atlanta air traffic controllers released the private plane from their radar jurisdiction just before Addison made his calamitous turn.

The NTSB report struggled to answer the question of why the Cessna was so far from where it should have been, even if the Asheville tower did not catch the error. Many remained suspicious of what was going on aboard the private plane. During the hearings, questions arose about who in the Cessna was actually flying it at the time of impact. Personnel at the Charlotte airport testified that David Addison was not in the left seat, the pilot's seat, when Flight N3121S, as it was designated, took off. A line boy on duty in Charlotte testified that he witnessed the departure of the Cessna and said Ralph Reynolds was in the left seat. The investigation found that that "Mr. Reynolds held no airman certificates."[66] Since the Cessna 310 could be used as a pilot trainer, the plane could have been flown from both the left or right seat and the voice that communicated with ground personnel in Asheville was that of David Addison. Witnesses testified that Addison was "an experienced, careful pilot."[67] His qualifications, listed in the NTSB report, said he was a "rated flight instructor" but also revealed that Addison had less than eleven hours in the airplane he was flying that day.[68] The investigation report suggested that Addison, a Missourian, was unfamiliar with the area into which he was flying, saying the Cessna pilot had "inadequate knowledge of the Asheville area" and engaged in "poor flight planning."[69]

As pilot of the chartered Martin 404 that followed Flight 22 into Asheville, Paul Snell was the first Piedmont employee to witness the damage. He cast doubt on David Addison's certainty about being where he thought he needed to be in order to land safely. Snell emphasized Addison's use of profanity in relaying his position during one transmission to the Asheville tower, demonstrating some frustration with his understanding of the plane's proximity to the airport. At the crash site, remnants of maps and approach charts were found from the Cessna aircraft that indicated the information David Addison had available to him was three years out of date.[70]

The tragedy has provoked tremendous curiosity and some controversy in the years since. One interested individual was "amateur sleuth" Paul Houle, a history major who participated in traffic accident investigations during his military service.[71] "Commercial aviation has always fascinated me," said Houle. "And when I found out that there had been a crash in Hendersonville, which is about thirty miles up the road from me, I went to go to the crash site to see what was there and there was nothing there."[72] Houle decided to rectify the situation by spearheading the effort to erect a memorial to the eighty-two lives lost. He successfully led the campaign that raised the necessary funds and coordinated placement of a marker containing the names of all 82 persons who died in the mishap. In July of 2004, families of the victims gathered for a dedication where Houle served as keynote speaker. During his speech, he acknowledged pain caused by the collision but also found hope in what might otherwise have been written off as a random and inexplicable accident. Houle told the crowd:

> We must never forget the Flight 22 tragedy because of the lessons it has taught us and its impact on aviation safety. This tragedy was an impetus in mandating that all commercial airlines in the United States install a Collision Avoidance System aboard their craft. Since that mandate was announced and made effective in 1990, there has not been one mid-air collision involving a commercial jetliner in the United States. Flight 22 played a crucial part in that decision and we are grateful, at least, that their deaths were not wasted.[73]

Though Paul Houle had no training in the field of aviation accidents, he began to probe the evidence after talking the families of the victims, examining anew the circumstances of the 1967 crash. Spending his own money and working alone, he set out to test his thesis that "the federal government blamed the wrong person for the worst crash in N.C. history."[74] He reviewed the conclusions reached by the NTSB and its conduct in handling the investigation.

While the NTSB primarily blamed the position of the Cessna in its collision with the Piedmont Flight 22, Paul Houle questioned the procedures of the Piedmont 727 at the time of the accident. Houle discovered several factors that he felt would have possibly disrupted the Piedmont flight from keeping vigilant watch as it made its turn to head north toward Roanoke, its next stop. Instructed to fly according to its IFR (Instrument Flight Rules) the Piedmont plane had been allowed to navigate according to VFR (Visual Flight Rules) the NTSB noted. "The FAA and the NTSB cannot have it both ways here," Houle stated. "They can't sit there and say that this jet was on IFR and then go ahead and say that you don't have to follow IFR procedures, that it is not mandatory procedures to do so when you can effect it by visual means."[75] But as Piedmont pilot and early advocate of a collision avoidance system, Captain Carroll Spencer recalled, the byword of the FAA at the time was "see and be seen," suggesting that the flight, while on IFR, would have been encouraged to use all visual means possible to see oncoming traffic.[76] In this case, neither could see each other until it was too late.

As the Piedmont flight made its climb, Houle learned that noteworthy events were going

In 2004 a memorial to those who died in Piedmont's worst crash in history were honored. The 82 names on the plaque included all Piedmont passengers and crew as well as the occupants of the private plane (Author's Collection).

on in the cockpit that might have played a role in the crash. The cockpit voice recorder captured the conversation between the pilots of Flight 22 in the moments prior to the collision.

12:00:37	"Somebody got an ashtray on fire?"
12:00:39	"I do, I think."
12:00:41	"OK" [identified as spoken by the Flight Engineer]
12:00:42	"You know it couldn't be me."
12:00:43	[sound of a click]
12:00:49	"Ashtray isn't on fire. That's just the cigarette that's on fire."
12:00:52	[sound of muffled scraping] (third instance of same sound since takeoff)
12:00:54	"I'm sorry I f***ed up again, didn't I?"
12:00:58	"Just for that I burn your damn steak."
12:01:09	"Twenty one thousand, we got unrestricted."
12:01:11	"Yes sir"
12:01:13	"I guess he wants about on[e]t six doesn't he?"
12:01:16	"I expect he does. He didn't say it that way."
12:01:17	"[Pied]mont twenty two is"
12:01:18	"Ugh" [sound of loud noise][77]

Paul Houle held that the comments suggest a preoccupation of the pilots at a time when they were supposed to be looking for oncoming traffic. How big was the fire and how much of a distraction was it in the cockpit? None who witnessed it lived to describe the circumstance. Paul Snell argued that the attention given the fire in the cockpit has been overemphasized. He maintained that the pilot conversation might have been more from what they smelled than what they were watching, and in doing so the cockpit crew was not distracted from their duties. In fact, Captain Snell pointed to eight transmissions between Piedmont Flight 22 and Piedmont's incoming Flight 1022 as evidence of the attention given by Piedmont pilots to oncoming traffic.[78] Further, Snell believed that the scraping noise heard on the cockpit voice recorder just after mention of the burning cigarette in the cockpit ashtray was not necessarily a response. He argued that the noise should not indicate alarm at the situation. The same noise had been heard twice before in the minute and a half since takeoff.[79]

Other points of concern about the position of the Piedmont flight at the time of contact have also been raised by Paul Houle. Noting that the Piedmont flight began to turn east before it reached an altitude where he believed it was cleared to do so, Houle asserted that the NTSB report was inconsistent about reference to the height at which Flight 22 was allowed unrestricted movement. However, at one minute, six seconds into the flight, the Piedmont jet was given unrestricted clearance to the Asheville VOR, allowing the jet to make its turn toward Roanoke. Paul Snell insisted that "unrestricted means unrestricted" and the Piedmont flight was given new directives which revised all previous instructions, the ones which Paul Houle believed the Piedmont crew violated. Piedmont pilots, including Snell, have taken serious objection to Houle's suggestion that the crew of the ill-fated Piedmont flight was cutting corners. They insist that any effort to make up time would not have been attempted on the 727's climb. Instead, it has been the position of these pilots and the original finding of the FAA that the Piedmont plane was not out of position, and therefore not at fault in the incident.[80]

Another curious coincidence about the accident and its subsequent inquiry was never mentioned in the NTSB report. Only months before the crash of Flight 22, the NTSB had

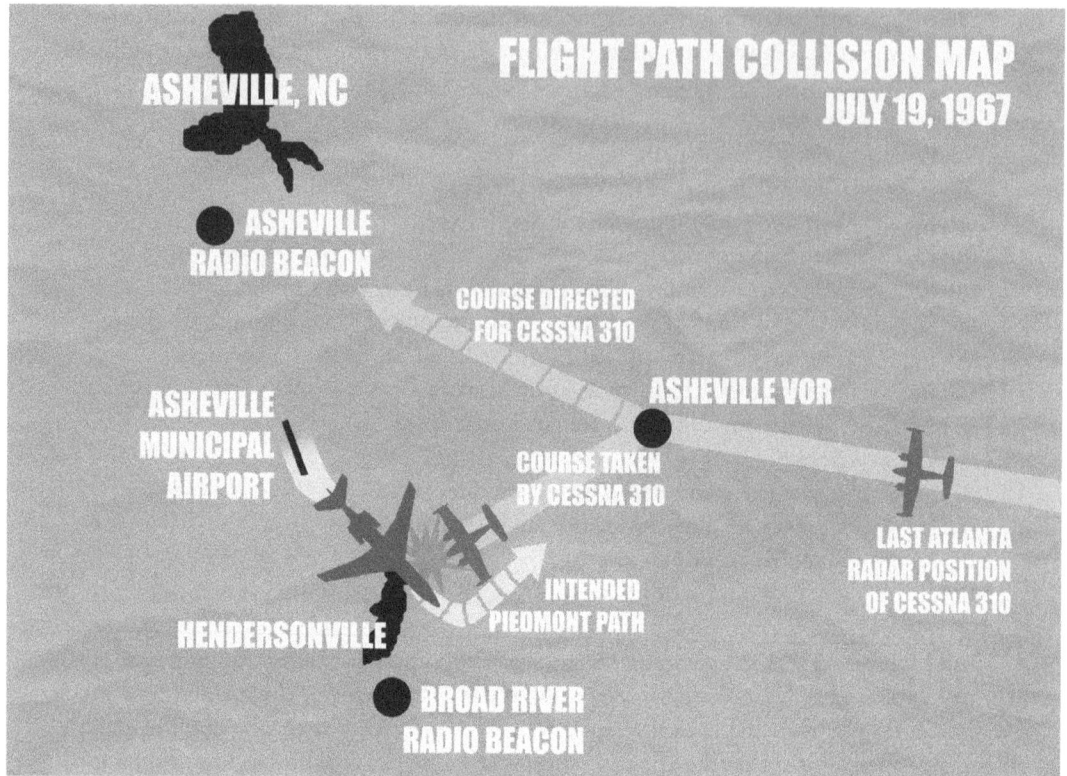

The flight of the Cessna 310 as it heads for Asheville, N.C., takes a wrong turn after flying over the Asheville VOR. The turn proved fatal to both the occupants of the private plane and 79 passengers and crew aboard Piedmont's *Manhattan Pacemaker* in both Piedmont's and North Carolina's worst air disaster (Author's Collection).

been formed as the accident examination arm of the FAA. The review of the Hendersonville wreck was the first major mishap investigated by the NTSB. Paul Houle noted that the assignment of Tom Saunders as lead investigator caused the appearance of partiality because of his relationship to Piedmont Vice President Zeke Saunders; the two men were brothers. Commenting on the disclosure, Houle said, "Even the appearance of impropriety was just as bad as impropriety."[81] Ronnie Macklin defended the appointment, stating that Tom Saunders had been assigned to the NTSB's next accident well before it occurred, making it coincidence that the crash he investigated involved an airline that employed his brother.[82] Zeke Saunders acknowledged that the situation might have looked as though a conflict of interest was likely. Concerning the investigation and his brother's role in it, Zeke said, "When they put him in charge of it I backed off and turned it over to Jack Tadlock and Jack Tadlock handled it for Piedmont."[83] During hearings on the crash held in Asheville in October, Director of Flight Operations Jack Tadlock answered questions as the representative of Piedmont Airlines.[84]

Paul Houle's crusade to revisit the conclusions of the NTSB on the 1967 crash stirred considerable resentment among the Piedmont family for his belief that "80 percent of the blame lies with the Asheville control tower and 20 percent with the Piedmont pilots," according to his assessment in a 2006 newspaper report on the effort. Very few applaud the work of Houle and most suggest that his efforts dredge up a particularly painful episode for the company without the likelihood of shedding new light on the circumstances of the crash. Despite the

Piedmont opposition, Houle remained undeterred and has made repeated requests to reopen documents relevant to the case, among which were a number of lawsuits that were brought against Piedmont for negligence after the crash.[85] To the dismay of Paul Houle, all judgments in the suits brought about as a result of the 1967 midair collision were settled by 1971 and the agreements sealed. Subsequent requests to unseal the records have been denied. Furthermore, Houle was disappointed with the final answer of the NTSB on his request to reopen its investigation of the midair collision. In February 2007, the governmental agency informed the amateur historian that "his arguments were unsubstantiated." In doing so, the NTSB called the disturbance in the cockpit "inconsequential" to the circumstances that resulted in Piedmont's greatest loss of life and a particularly bleak episode for the airline.[86]

The period after the crash was a critical time in the history of Piedmont Aviation as a company. Had bad publicity emerged from the findings of the NTSB surrounding the collision, public reaction might have turned extremely negative toward the airline, creating in one single event enough ill will to erase everything management and employees alike had worked over twenty years to build. The stakes were enormous. The Hendersonville crash took its toll on the bottom line almost immediately. As personnel struggled to move forward with efforts to purchase new aircraft and continued to wait upon delivery of the 737s, Piedmont faced filling the gap caused by the loss of one of its first jets. *American Aviation* pointed out less than a year later, "Not only did Piedmont have to apply all of the introductory costs of the two jets against the one remaining, but the schedules disrupted by the unexpected one-plane fleet cut deeply into traffic potential. And utilization on the single jet suffered, too."[87] Mr. Davis acknowledged "a sudden and dramatic drop in passenger revenue which continued throughout the rest of the year" in his portion of the 1967 Annual Report. He said, "It seemed to mark a major turning point during the year" and cited the "loss of this plane and its ability to produce, the torrent of spectacular publicity, together with a serious schedule disruption which followed" as reasons why the airline division showed a pre-tax income loss of $517,003. The year before the division showed a gain of over $2.6 million. The 1967 loss began a string of tough years for Piedmont Airlines. In each of the next three years, the company operated at a loss. Considering a pilots' strike in 1969 and extremely bad weather in the later months of 1967, crashes were not the only factor dragging down the bottom line. However, they left their mark. The crash took much more than profits from the airline; it also took fellow employees, as well as a bit of confidence. Audrey Collins characterized the legacy of Flight 22 best when she ruefully remarked, "That one lingered for an awfully long time."[88] While Mr. Davis composed his words carefully for 1967's year end report, two more accidents lay ahead: one on the airline and the other only minimally connected to a charter flight within his Central Piedmont Aero division.

Each of the fixed base divisions for Piedmont sold airplanes. General Aviation served as distributor for Beech and Central Piedmont Aero served for Piper. In January of 1968, a brand new Piper Navajo crashed shortly after takeoff from Smith Reynolds Airport in northwestern Forsyth County, killing all six aboard. Because Central Piedmont Aero sold the aircraft to Aero Flight Incorporated, a charter service in Winston-Salem, lawsuits brought by the families of the victims included Piedmont. The plane had been picked up directly from the manufacturer in Lock Haven, Pennsylvania, so no Piedmont personnel had ever touched the plane. Piedmont legal counsel argued that as a local dealer, they "never had access to the plane to determine its condition or to correct any defects." Two years after the crash, a judge agreed, freeing Piedmont from any further legal action taken regarding the crash.[89]

Fixed based operations later found itself involved in another potentially threatening event that originated from within. During a routine test of an engine in 1976 at the overhaul shop, a foreign object was found in the engine of one of the planes maintained by General Aviation. When no logical explanation presented itself, an investigation began. The company began testing all the work done on its planes and found a total of four engines had objects placed in either the carburetor intake or the interior walls. Quickly, all trails led back to one mechanic. An investigation determined the man had sabotaged one of Piedmont's non-airline planes, along with three owned by companies who contracted General Aviation for maintenance. The junior mechanic, who had been with the company for eleven years, was indicted in the case.[90]

Piedmont Airlines' last crash occurred just over a year after the Hendersonville accident. It was another lazy summer day in the upper South. By August, people began to count the foggy mornings, saying they could accurately predict the number of snowfalls for the upcoming winter. In the West Virginia capital of Charleston, the total of foggy August mornings was high, averaging 19 over the last few years.[91] On the morning of Saturday, August 10, 1968, the Kanawha Airport reported dense fog and smoke that made visual landings impossible until the sun burned away the obstruction late in the morning. The Charleston airport was especially vulnerable to fog because of its placement. The city of Charleston lies along the banks of the Kanawha River with mountains rising closely on either side. City officials constructed their airport on a leveled plateau of one of those mountains. Fog in the morning had to rise from the valley past the elevated airport before incoming pilots had a clear look at the runway. That morning the fog was estimated at 150 feet thick.[92]

Piedmont Flight 230 originated from Louisville, Kentucky, with stops scheduled for Cincinnati, Ohio, and Charleston before terminating in Roanoke, Virginia. In service for the flight was the *James River Pacemaker* (N712U) a Fairchild-Hiller 227B. The aircraft was only one year old and the last of the new models that replaced the F-27 in late 1967. Gene Sugg served as captain of the flight. He had recently celebrated his 13th anniversary with the airline on August 1. Accompanying Sugg was First Officer John A. Messick, a two year veteran with over 400 hours' experience on the Fairchilds. Twenty year old Anna Pearl worked the route to Roanoke as flight attendant.[93]

The flight departed Cincinnati routinely just after 8:00 A.M., cleared to fly an instrument approach into Charleston. On Runway 23, the Charleston Tower estimated visibility to the crew at about one-eighth mile, saying it might improve to about a half mile by the time they got there. It was no big deal to Gene Sugg. Over the last six months, he had flown into Charleston 35 times. The only tricky part of the descent for any pilot landing on Runway 23 was the drop off just in front of the runway. The plateau upon which Kanawha Airport had been built ended at the point where the runway began. As the morning wore on, the fog seemed to be clearing up, although a patchy spot stubbornly clung to the front of Runway 23 and down the mountain in front of it.[94]

Because under even the best of conditions a landing at Kanawha Airport was difficult, the FAA installed a "glide slope path" to guide pilots into the elevated airport. Sending out a "radio beam in the shape of a fan from the runway," the glide slope told a pilot if he was at the proper altitude during the approach.[95] However, on August 10, the glide slope had been turned off. Since June 18, this key part of the airport's instrument landing system had not been operational. The equipment, maintained and controlled by the FAA, had in testing been found to be "operating improperly" and declared the signal sent out by the glide slope as "too erratic to be reliable." Reports showed that Charleston, West Virginia, was among several airports that had lost use of this piece of equipment to assist landings. In both Pittsburgh and

Cincinnati, the glide slopes had also been shut down waiting for repairs. Both airports received priority over Charleston in the correction of their glide slopes. The Kanawha Airport's relative low priority would have devastating impact as Flight 230 sought Runway 23 for landing.[96]

As the *James River Pacemaker* approached Charleston, Gene Sugg and John Messick knew they did not have the services of the glide slope and would have to steer the flight using their skillfulness. They continually queried the Charleston Tower about the weather looking for any improvement. An American Airlines flight approached Charleston at about the same time as Flight 230, but Air Traffic Control in Indianapolis, Indiana, gave landing priority to Piedmont, and Sugg and Messick started down from 6,000 feet to make their approach. While descending, the flight crew asked the tower "Have you got the lights turned all the way up?" indicating that they were having some trouble seeing their way through the fog. Trying to give the pilots some encouragement, the tower responded, "Sure do, uh a little fog right off the end there, and it's wide open after you get by that."[97] The exchange proved to be the last between the flight and air traffic control. Within the cockpit, a few more comments were made about seeing the lights, followed by the sound of power decreasing in the plane. Then suddenly power increased, and someone exclaimed, "Watch it!"[98]

Less than 50 feet from the summit of the plateau where Runway 23 began, Piedmont Flight 230 crashed into the hillside. After impact, the plane "bounced high"[99] with debris being propelled onto the right side of the runway, demonstrating how close the aircraft had come to hitting its mark. Newspapers remarked that "the pieces of wreckage vaulted up the hill and spewed alongside the runway."[100] Ted Armbrecht was in a private plane waiting to take off when he heard the crash. He said, "I looked over; saw a great whoosh of flame, some debris flying around. I saw the tail break off. It seemed so unreal."[101]

Of the 37 people on board, 32 died instantly. Because the crash occurred at the airport, emergency personnel arrived quickly. Nineteen-year-old Barbara Schiller remembered waking up with "white stuff all over me and the plane." She was referring to the flame dousing chemical firemen used to put out the fire that burned from the crash. Rescuers found five survivors and quickly transferred them to Charleston Memorial Hospital for treatment.[102] Three later died from their injuries, leaving only Barbara Schiller and Thomas Voignier, age 27, as survivors of Flight 230. All five were "thrown clear of the aircraft cabin during the impact sequence."[103] The casualty list included seven servicemen, on leave.[104] Another soldier was scheduled to be onboard but missed his flight when his leave orders did not come through. The crash was the deadliest air disaster in West Virginia history up until that time.[105] One of the most poignant stories rescuers told about the effort to save lives came from L.C. Thaxton, a Charleston police officer who quickly arrived at the scene. In a newspaper interview, he said, "I picked up the little girl's body ... she was holding a doll in her lap ... the doll's head rolled off onto the ground."[106]

FAA investigators, along with Piedmont Aviation president Tom Davis, came quickly to the scene to try to determine the cause of the accident, the airline's third in three years. Hearings held in October consumed two days and issues surrounding the crash received close scrutiny. Examiners reviewed meteorological data and the glide slope issue, as well as every other aspect of the flight. In their report, they determined that Gene Sugg and/or John Messick saw the hill in front of them as they descended too far down in the fog and had only "3 or 4 seconds before impact,"[107] too little time to correct the problem. Examiners determined that the fog caused the accident. Regardless, the crash of Flight 230 was the last crash of a Piedmont Airline plane.

Coupled with the Hendersonville accident, the Charleston crash darkened the economic picture for the Speedbird. As the sixties ended, all nine of the regional carriers felt a pinch from a worsening economy that reduced business travel and added to expenses from inflation. In Piedmont's case, the mishaps only compounded the problem. In 1968, the Airline Division lost over $134,000 on total revenue of almost $47 million. The next year, the loss rose to $1.7 million as total revenue continued to rise. By 1970, the airline posted its biggest loss ever: $2.5 million. The bad publicity from the crashes coupled with the 1969 strike created a period of doubt not seen since the first uncertain days of the airline. Yet Piedmont Aviation continued to perform better than most of its contemporaries, who lost a "combined $70 million on total revenues of $725 million." Even with the adversity, Piedmont achieved a better profit and loss statement than all but two of the other regional airlines.[108]

One hundred fifty one people died as the result of accidents involving Piedmont Airlines. Those stories received significant attention, as most crashes and collisions do. Rarely, events also occurred that luckily did not result in fatalities and with them, headlines. Flight attendant Connie Counts looked back on a charter flight she manned that never made the papers, but barely avoided catastrophe.

> We took off and our engine was on fire. I had a college football team on there and I was sitting on the front jump seat and I looked back and you could see the big flame, poof. And we're climbing out and I'm sure we're overloaded. All football teams are overloaded. You've got all that equipment. You've got all those players and they're all overweight, big guys. I looked out the window, we had little peep hole over there and I saw the K-Mart parking lot. It was real bright and I thought "we are going to land in the K-Mart parking lot." I heard the captain say, "Son of a bitch won't climb, son of a bitch won't climb." It did climb enough that we turned immediately around we went back and we weren't far.[109]

It should be noted that none of the Piedmont fatalities ever occurred as the result of faulty equipment. On occasions where malfunctions did arise, pilots used their skill to bring the aircraft down safely, as in Connie Counts's situation. Pilots faced numerous situations where only their skill and a good reliable plane kept tragedy from occurring. The early aviators had gained that skill from their flying days in World War II. Captain Tory Vaughn recalled a situation in which he found himself that included elements from three of the four collisions. He was flying a DC-3, same as the plane involved in the 1959 accident. Like the crew in 1966, he was ferrying a plane without passengers and the episode happened at the site of the 1968 crash on the mountaintop airport in Charleston, West Virginia. After the weather prevented landing in Charleston on a flight out of Cincinnati, he was diverted to Roanoke. The next morning, dispatch told him to ferry the plane back to Charleston for resumption of the flight. Before he attempted to land, the tower informed him that they had checked the braking action of the runway with a car and except for some slush on the runway, everything was good for landing. Vaughn said that, as the plane touched down,

> Everything seemed to be fine and I went to put on the brakes and man, it was like on a pit of ball bearings. The airplane started sliding down the runway and I realized then I was in serious trouble. So I jerked the window open and looked out and snow and slush was piled all the way up over the top of the tires and the airplane was picking up speed. At that time I was halfway down the runway. About two weeks before that Capital Airlines had just put a Constellation off that same runway on the end and killed a few folks. In fact the wreckage was still down there. I had made up my mind I was not going to go off the airport. I was going to stay on the airport one way or another. In my flight training I used to fly sea planes off the

river there at Charleston. In the wintertime it would freeze and we would fly the sea planes off the ice and we would ground loop the airplane, so to speak, turn them around and slide backwards and apply power to stop. Well the first thing I thought about was that. So I said I'm going to do the same thing with this thing. When we got up to the intersection of Runway 33, I eased over to the side, got the tail up and poured the power to the left engine, brought the airplane around and was 90 degrees from the runway. We ended up sliding backwards on our butt. I applied both engine power and stopped. Taxied on in with the airplane, washed the snow and the ice off with a water hose, picked up our passengers and went on."[110]

For Tory Vaughn, it was "just another day at the office." The event could have spelled disaster for the crew if this veteran aviator had not relied on his experience to save the day. By doing so, he set a standard for future Piedmont pilots.

Most every Piedmont captain handled his aircraft deftly and could be counted upon to rise to the situation in case of crisis. Sometimes those emergencies were blown out of proportion. Captain Charlie Meacham took off from Atlanta one day heading for Fayetteville, North Carolina, when his inner tire blew after hitting a piece of concrete on the runway. He radioed the tower, which instructed him to fly around for a while to burn off jet fuel before making an approach. In the meantime, the runway was foamed to make the approach a smooth one. Meacham brought the 737 in without incident. Passengers got off the plane within three minutes of landing. Waiting for the captain of the flight was a television news reporter, who had been following the plight of the crippled plane. With microphone in hand and cameraman behind him, he asked Meacham about the "harrowing flight." Meacham's reply was "calm down," pointing up the fact that the reporter was more excited about the event than the pilot who brought it to a successful end. In the interview, Meacham told the TV newsman that the flight had been "boring." Like Tory Vaughn, Charlie Meacham took it in stride, even though later, he was named Atlanta "Man of the Month" for his boring flight.[111]

Throughout the seventies and into the eighties, Speedbirds flew safely through the air with no loss of life. In Piedmont's later days, a series of minor mishaps took place with only minor injuries. On one, a Saturday night flight from Newark to Charlotte turned anxious as the *Kanawha River Pacemaker* (N752N), a Boeing 737-200, lost its brakes during the landing. The plane skidded off the 7,845 foot runway at Charlotte-Douglas International Airport, through a field, and into an embankment. Air traffic controller Bill Price said, "He touched down but he did not slow down."[112] A news reporter from Charleston, West Virginia, who was on the plane asked the pilot what happened. "No damn brakes," was the succinct reply. The rainy night was thought to have kept the spilled fuel from igniting; as Fire Captain David McCallum noted, "There were fuel and fumes everywhere."[113]

After it came to a stop, real danger still awaited the Piedmont plane in Charlotte. The nose of the aircraft came to rest on tracks belonging to Southern Railway and a train was headed in the direction of the wreck. Emergency personnel contacted Southern dispatchers who got the locomotive stopped about a mile from the plane and avoided another collision. The Piedmont crew evacuated all 113 passengers from the plane immediately as they waited for the arrival of emergency teams in the rain.[114]

An almost comic turn of events took place in January of 1989 as the phrase "lost an engine" meant different things to the pilot of a flight out of Chicago and the control tower. Flight 1480 took off from O'Hare International only to be told frantically by an air traffic controller that he needed to return immediately. The pilot, somewhat irritated, came back to the airport with his 27 passengers believing the tower overreacted to an engine that had stopped working. Only after he landed did he understand that when the controller said, "You've lost an engine," he meant it, literally. Seconds after takeoff, the right engine had fallen from the Boeing 727-200 and landed in a field just beyond the runway. No one was injured and after investigating the incident, FAA spokesman Mort Edelstein complimented the captain on his return, saying, "The pilot was calm." He added, "I wonder how he would have felt if he'd known."[115]

Three months later, a flight leaving Charlotte developed a severe problem in the air. On April 14, 1988, a Fokker F-28 Fellowship 4000 (N110UR) was shaken by an immediate and unexpected explosion in its right jet engine. One passenger said it sounded like "a shotgun went off right behind my ear." The blast resulted from a frozen compressor that sent the turbine blades through the fuselage. Another passenger said the holes created in the blast were "big enough that I could crawl through it." A third individual on the flight got right to the point. He said, "My first thought was, 'This is it.'" Luckily for everyone onboard, it wasn't, although there were some very tense moments.[116] Once pierced, the cabin lost its pressurization, forcing the pilots to descend immediately to keep enough air in the cabin for passengers to breathe. Panic ensued among the passengers with some screaming and some praying. Oxygen masks dropped down but not all of them worked, according to those clutching for them. A few passengers reportedly passed out as the pilots dove down from 31,000 feet to reach an altitude where those in an un-pressurized cabin could get some air.[117] In less than ten minutes, the flight landed in Charleston, West Virginia, diverted from its original destination of Columbus, Ohio. The only people treated for injuries were two Piedmont flight attendants. Neither injury was considered serious.

The last Piedmont misfortune came during the airline's last days. On his approach to Greensboro's Triad Airport, Captain Larry Fuda engaged the landing gear on the *Kanawha Pacemaker* (N752N), a Boeing 737, to provide a smooth arrival for his passengers. The left set of wheels refused to lock into place, forcing Fuda to land with only the right landing gear in place. The cause of the malfunction proved hazardously simple. A black rubber wheel chock, used by ground crew to keep the airplane in place at the gate, was found in the wheel well. NTSB officials scratched their heads about how it got there. One investigator said, "Someone just flat forgot to take them out." Two mechanics from Washington, D.C., quickly came forward and admitted their error, but claimed they never intentionally put the rubber chocks onboard the 737. Both were suspended by the airline for causing the accident, which did extensive damage to the left jet engine.[118]

Although most hazards occurred in the air, planes did not have to be in flight to be dangerous. On rare occasions, Piedmont's propjets posed threats to individuals who walked into the path of propeller blades. Don Martin remembered an employee in Roanoke who did just that and was cut severely.[119] Mercifully, the wounds proved not to be mortal. The same situation occurred with Captain Paul Snell as he piloted the *Roanoke Valley Pacemaker* on the tarmac at Friendship Airport in Baltimore, Maryland. A pedestrian walked right into the spinning blades of the YS-11 in December of 1969. From the cockpit, Snell saw the man coming and quickly applied brakes to the propellers, thus minimizing injury and sparing the life of the wandering man. For his actions, Snell received commendation from both the NTSB investigator and Piedmont president Tom Davis.[120]

Numerous incidents, mishaps, and freak occurrences targeted Piedmont's Pacemakers, as they did most airlines. A June 1988 flight was hit by lightning that burned a hole in the wing of a 737 as it made its way to Charlotte. However, no one was injured, and the wing was repaired in less than an hour and a half.[121] On another flight into Charlotte five months later, a flight attendant suffered minor burns after hot coffee she was serving splashed her in the face. Reportedly, turbulence caused the accident. She was taken to an area hospital, where she was treated and released.[122]

Even with the mishaps, the airline assembled a safety record better than most. With thorough, systematic maintenance, Piedmont built its standing in the industry and with the Federal Aviation Administration. As safety inspector Ronnie Macklin said in reference to the FAA, "They trusted us." As an example, he described the relationship between the company and the government oversight agency.

> If you go back and check out the YS-11, when it came out it didn't have any airframe, A.D. notes. A.D. notes means there is something wrong with the airplane that is serious and the FAA will tell you what you have to do to correct it and give you a time limit. The FAA, when the A.D. notes would come from Japan, to them — they'd come over and ask us what are you going to do about this? We'd tell them either it wasn't worth a damn and forget about it, or it was a serious problem and we would put on it an engineering authorization, which modified the airplane. So they wouldn't issue an A.D. note. So this airplane, I guess for five or six years had no A.D. notes on it in the U.S. It was one of the only airplanes in the world like that. It was only because the FAA trusted Piedmont to do what was right in the first place. So when the airplanes were sold to Airbourne and PBA, they didn't trust either one of them. So they put the A.D. notes on the airplane. They both screamed. They said we bought these without any A.D. notes. I said, "Don't get onto us because we don't have anything to do with it."[123]

The FAA's trust in Piedmont was well founded, despite the accidents. The company followed Mr. Davis's early lead to put safety first. Piedmont Airlines launched a number of initiatives to protect planes from unforeseen occurrences. For example, when Piedmont bought the YS-11, it also announced that it would add two hours of additional training time to "qualify its pilots for Category 2 all-weather operations."[124] "Cat2," as it was called, gave pilots tools to better judge weather conditions beyond "100 feet altitude and a quarter mile radius."[125] Adding another first to its list, Piedmont became the first airline to install ACARS, the "Aeronautical Radio Inc. Communications and Reporting System," in 1976. The system housed a computer in each Piedmont plane that collected and stored data continuously about every facet of a flight. Captain Carroll Spencer called the move one of the most significant efforts by the airline. He noted the collision avoidance system grew out of the controversy over the third man on the 737 which caused the 1969 strike. "We wrote language to the effect that if there's ever a collision avoidance system that can replace the eyes of a man sitting on the jump seat, we will opt to go to two men. The pilots loved it. The union hated it. The company said, 'Well, we'll consider it,'" said Spencer, who pushed strongly and was instrumental in Piedmont's pursuit of the technology's development.[126]

As part of its commitment to being a safety conscious airline and, though the problem of wind shear had never been knowingly fatal to a Piedmont flight, the company also placed wind shear detectors on all of its planes to warn pilots of sudden changes in wind direction beginning in 1985.[127] Four years later, Piedmont helped the FAA test the "Traffic Alert and Collision Avoidance System" (TCAS). The system gave early warnings to pilots of the presence of nearby craft so evasive methods could be taken and events like those of Hickory or Hendersonville could be avoided.[128]

Even with all the assistance provided by equipment to help ensure a safe flight, the human element always remained. Training was always a vital component to flight operations for ground personnel as well as flight crews. Among the enhancements made by the airline were ever more realistic flight simulators than the old "Link" simulators that Hoppy Dunne trained pilots on in the 1960s. The new generation of simulators included "McDonnell-Douglas Vital 7," which came in time for the introduction of the Boeing 737-400. This computer driven simulator gave instructors the ability to replicate conditions at any airport into which Piedmont flew whether it was rain, ice, snow or technical malfunction. Instructor Dwight Corbello pointed out, "It's much easier here because I can give them something on the order of 39 or 40 different landing gear problems that we wouldn't dare simulate in the airplane."[129] Tom Miller saw the value for himself as well as his fellow pilots when he observed, "With the realism that we're creating with the new simulator here, we can take a pilot to his limitations. We can take him beyond his limitations. We can show him what can happen to him if he tries to overextend his abilities."[130] Trainers saw the immeasurable advantage of showing pilots their mistakes in a simulator so that on the line, they were prepared for any situation.

The pain of wrecks in Charlottesville, New Bern, Hendersonville and Charleston kept everyone connected to the airline very conscious about the lurking danger that awaited one simple mistake. A 1985 study by the *St. Petersburg* (Florida) *Times* noted the diligence of Piedmont Airlines, calling it "potentially the safest major airline in the United States." The report looked at malfunctions for a four year period and came to its conclusion after examination of every incident that put passengers at risk. The study found that in 1980, "Piedmont had 2.97 mechanical or structural malfunctions per 100,000 flights. The industry average that year was 10.20 malfunctions. The highest was 22.54 malfunctions by American Airlines." By 1984, Piedmont's rate dropped to the remarkable rate of .74. The industry average that year was 4.97. Piedmont Vice President Don McGuire remained cautious about the praise. When the study was released in 1985, he said, "We had 950 flights yesterday, and they all arrived safely. We're working on 950 more flights today, and then we'll have another 950 flights tomorrow. One incident that causes a plane to go down ruins every day of safety before it. As far as I'm concerned, one incident is too many."[131]

Every flight flown by any aircraft held the potential to end badly. For Piedmont Airlines, a few did. Crashes have remained a void for many, as they struggled to understand why such catastrophes occurred. There remains no answer to the questions. Piedmont's employees worked hard to make sure nothing would harm the many passengers who entrusted their lives to them every time they boarded a Pacemaker. When they weren't successful, they often cried right along with family members. After all, they too lost some of their own in the tragedies they tried so hard to prevent.

· 7 ·

The Great Outfit, 1978–1984

For the ten years after the Charleston crash, Piedmont Airlines kept to itself, announcing few developments, content to operate from its new 320,000-square-foot headquarters in Winston-Salem.[1] Mr. Davis focused the attention of the company away from new destinations, concentrating instead on growth in the markets already served. For most of the seventies, the airline retrenched, quietly building its standing after a series of unfortunate crashes. As a man in his fifties, Mr. Davis had managed the airline conservatively, keeping to what he knew his company did best: serving customers in the southeastern United States.

Outside the service area, few knew that an air carrier called "Piedmont" even existed. At that time, Piedmont Airlines may have been the best-kept secret in the airline industry, little more than a curiosity for any commercial aviation observer who lived outside the service area. Some couldn't get the name right. On a trip to Hawaii, Don Collins asked for an airline discount at the Hilton on Maui. His answer caused the desk clerk to say, "Pete who?" With a clear voice, he proudly said, "Piedmont," causing a manager to emerge and ask again, which airline. When Collins again said "Piedmont," the man asked more specifically where he worked. Don Collins's answer of Winston-Salem drew the admission that the hotel official in Maui was from Beckley, West Virginia. He knew Piedmont Airlines well, saying, "Fly them all the time." Collins remembered the instructions to the desk clerk. "Give them anything they want, just take care of them." The experience of Don Collins demonstrated that even far from home, Piedmont had a following, but still the reputation of the company was not universally known.[2] However, the thirtieth anniversary year of 1978 marked an awakening of the Speedbird from its obscurity, freeing the airline to fly higher and farther than even Mr. Davis had ever thought possible. Soon Piedmont would go from Pete-who? to the "up and coming airline."

The shakeup that started Piedmont down this new path concerned both the business climate in which the airline operated and the way Tom Davis ran his company. For some years, the idea of deregulating sectors like banking and transportation had been gaining currency. Free market capitalists sought to put government protected industries on a competitive footing so the companies could prove their value in the marketplace. They argued that customer support, not federal handouts, should determine the success of an enterprise. Deregulation proponents believed the move would save money in two ways. First and foremost, the end of government subsidies cancelled the need for billions of taxpayer dollars that had been going to support airline routes of debatable viability. The federal government also reduced its level of bureaucracy, opting instead to let market forces determine where an airline like Piedmont should fly. The selection of deregulation proponent Alfred Kahn as chairman of the Civil Aeronautics Board in 1977 signaled a move toward relaxation of the restrictive rules on American air carriers.³ Soon, Kahn and political conservatives in Washington joined forces to end the controlling hand of government in the passenger airline business. The policy fit well with concerns about depletion of the federal budget in that era and a growing mood that wanted government, and the politics that went along with it, out of business. Besides, deregulation proponents argued, who could best judge the worthiness of an airline to provide service, a government agency or air travelers? The Carter Administration backed the Airline Deregulation Act of 1978, supporting the effort to turn the business of air travel from a heavily regulated affair to a free market free-for-all. Most industry analysts applauded the move at the time. However, in Winston-Salem, the winds blew in the opposite direction.

Tom Davis's reaction to deregulation was to stop it. For help he went looking for an influential person with connections to help prevent the wave of deregulation flowing in Washington, D.C. The job description could well have said he wanted a bulldog to fend off a new set of laws that he felt would be detrimental to Piedmont. In an interview, Mr. Davis revealed, "We were not very happy when deregulation came along." He also admitted, "We could see all of the big boys coming in and swamping us."⁴ His words revealed that if fences came down between carriers, many of the other airlines would end up playing in his yard, a frightful prospect for a business owner who had always benefited from government protection. Thirty years ago, the government had given him his passenger and freight service. He understood how that game was played and had become accustomed to profiting from a regulated system, and while the government never gave him everything he sought, the government had kept him in business.

In the late seventies, Mr. Davis turned 60 and discussion of his successor also became a subject of interest. Zeke Saunders had always been the number two man at Piedmont and initially thought to be the one to succeed to the presidency, but when offered, Saunders declined, citing his own age as a factor. He was just a few years younger than Davis.⁵ The president of Piedmont Aviation, Inc. began to cast his net beyond the company for a replacement. Back in 1970, the first potential successor had climbed aboard. As senior vice president of administration, which was a new position, Bartlett M. Shaw was in charge of finance, accounting, personnel, industrial relations, purchasing and properties, but his tenure with the company was short. Bill Magruder followed Shaw as the heir apparent in 1973. Magruder's cardiac arrest on the Old Towne Golf Course spelled a second miss in filling the shoes of the president. Immediately, Tom Davis tried again.

When Piedmont's board of directors went looking for new leadership, they had some requirements of their own. Since the late sixties, in years when the airline was rebounding from three devastating crashes, growth had been minimal. The route system had not grown in the seventies and stockholders grew restive. The board's committee had put Mr. Davis in charge of finding his replacement, but circumstances had prevented a successor from emerging. Finally, between Davis and Wachovia Bank president and Piedmont board chairman John Watlington, a name came up for consideration: William R. Howard.

In 1977, Bill Howard was a 55 year old executive vice president with Eastern Airlines. A Midwesterner by birth, Howard earned his pilot's license at the age of 16 and flew for the 8th Air Force during World War II. He became a lawyer working for the Atlanta law firm of E. Smythe Gambrell, which represented Eastern Airlines. By 1967, Eastern persuaded Howard to join its legal department. He rose to a vice president's position with Eastern as the head of labor and customer relations. He also oversaw the medical and security departments as well as a number of hotels owned by Eastern Airlines. Howard's resume included a few interesting points. First, while getting his law degree from George Washington University, Howard worked for a senator from his native Nebraska; it was a political connection that could assist Piedmont's lobbying efforts to derail deregulation.[6] Also, while at Eastern Airlines, Bill Howard had honed his skills as a top negotiator. In one significant, yet odd, example, Eastern sent Howard to Honduras to retrieve a highjacked plane with over $300,000 in cash. Two FBI agents accompanied Howard but told him that they had "no authority" in the Latin American country. Single-handedly, Howard negotiated the return of the plane and the money.[7]

When Bill Howard received the invitation to come to Winston-Salem, he understood that he would eventually replace Tom Davis, "not because of any dissatisfaction with Tom," said Howard, "but the only thought maybe was that they could get some more aggressive blood." Howard started on January 1, 1978. He filled the position of executive vice president. "He really took that job to sort of get his feet wet, to get a feel of the company," observed Piedmont's Assistant Comptroller Jack Walker, who also noted that with Howard's previous legal experience, "It was just a familiarization process of learning the people."[8]

If Bill Howard came to Piedmont with impressive credentials that promised aggressiveness, he also brought with him a different attitude toward deregulation. Howard had observed that deregulation "was supported by the Republicans, the Democrats, the liberals, the conservatives, the ecologists and the consumerists, often for different and conflicting reasons."[9] He was sure it was going to pass. Yet before Congress voted, he had gone to work for an airline adamantly opposed to the prospect. "Tom repeatedly said to me and to the board that there weren't any good routes left, that all the good airline routes had been taken," remembered Howard from his first days at Piedmont. The viewpoint of Tom Davis, according to Howard, was that "Eastern had them or Delta had them or Northeast had them or American had them, that the good routes were gone. If you wanted to take the lesser routes you would die."[10] Further, Mr. Davis believed deregulation invited the big airlines to move into Piedmont's territory and take all the profitable routes that Tom Davis had labored so arduously for over the past 30 years. Howard quoted Davis as saying, "If this deregulation thing passes we're dead ducks. Eastern will come in, Delta will come in. They'll have a right to come red flagging our best routes. We'll be dead in the water." The fear was so great that upon coming to Piedmont, the current president told the future one that most of his time would be spent in Washington, D.C., where he would try to sway opinion in Congress. He was told that this effort was Bill Howard's first priority.

Many employees agreed with their chief. Pilots like Carroll Spencer felt that the era of deregulation would squeeze Piedmont into bankruptcy from two directions. He held that "the little cities: They're history. They can drive [to larger airports]. The interstate highway system is the way they'll connect to the medium cities." Without the small municipalities that Piedmont served so faithfully, the airline had no choice but to compete with the big carriers in the larger markets. Spencer saw an airline like Eastern, which already served those larger airports, as competition to formidable to beat. "We could never go forward because Eastern was on top of us," said Carroll Spencer. Under such a scenario, Piedmont had no place to go and a deregulated future spelled doom for Piedmont Airlines, especially with its leadership in transition.[11]

Scratching his head, Bill Howard questioned the logic of Piedmont's vehement stance against deregulation. The previous year, Howard had been part of the management at Eastern Airlines, and he knew a few things about what the "big boys" wanted. Eastern's plans for expansion did not include Piedmont routes. Howard asserted, "Service to the western half of the United States was what Eastern Airlines wanted, and I thought I knew what Delta wanted, and none of it would hurt Piedmont a bit. On the other hand, I thought that there were plenty of places that Eastern was going to get out of that would be good for us if they were nudged a little bit." He pointed out that while with Eastern, the trunk carrier had fought for years for permission to leave Roanoke, Virginia. He asserted that the large airlines would be even less interested in small cities like Roanoke in a deregulated environment and more interested in the most lucrative routes, like transport between major metropolitan areas in the United States. In Piedmont's territory of the southeastern United States, only Atlanta, Georgia, qualified as a major metropolitan area. Howard put forth a different viewpoint. He said, "It was something that we would have to look at closely, but I must say, I think that it would create as many opportunities as it would detriments. I think there are real opportunities." Besides, given the prevailing climate at the federal level of government, he thought opposing deregulation was futile. A newspaper reported Bill Howard as saying, "We were beating a dead horse."[12]

The new ideas of the new management at Piedmont took some time to evaluate and appreciate. However, as Bill Howard made his points, the logic slowly started to sink in. With passage almost certain, he suggested the airline take some time and look at the opportunities provided by deregulation. After some convincing, Howard recalled, "Then finally the board said OK, fair enough. Do that. Spend the next three months looking at how we are going to survive." The balance tipped when Tom Davis asked Bill Howard to craft a new letter to congressmen concerning Piedmont's stance on deregulation. As Howard remembered the letter, it said, in essence, "We're not asking that you support it. But we are withdrawing our previous objections and our previous request that you fight it. We think we can maneuver around and live with it if it passes." Giving the letter to the president of Piedmont, Howard noted, "Tom looked at it for a while and put in a paragraph and said this does not mean that we are for it. We are not for at it at all." Howard took what he called a "mishmash of our two views" and sent it out. A new course for the airline had been set.[13]

Looking back a few years later, Mr. Davis acknowledged, "Ironically, we originally had serious doubts that deregulation would be the panacea that its supporters predicted — from our own standpoint, and particularly from the standpoint of the traveling public." In that view, he proved prescient, predicting that deregulation was not the savior most had predicted at the time. Davis reasoned that if the Civil Aeronautics Board had operated properly, the need for deregulation might never have emerged. In a 1979 interview, he noted that it was the "self-styled administrative process" that caused the CAB to become its own victim. "If the CAB, during the past ten years or so, had processed route applications more promptly," Mr. Davis observed, "which the old law permitted, we would probably never had a clamor for airline deregulation."[14] Mr. Davis may have disagreed with need for a complete shift within his industry, but as a prudent businessman, he accepted the logic and the accomplished fact of deregulation. He went on to say, "It became clear to us that deregulation was going to be a fact of life and, importantly, our own analysis convinced us that we could indeed do very well in a deregulated environment."[15] With survival in mind, leading Piedmont's analytical charge was Bill Howard.

His first move was to begin cutting Piedmont's losses. His research department looked at every city served by the Speedbird for profitability. The study found a number of locations that drained Piedmont's resources. In towns like Beckley and Bluefield in West Virginia, Hickory and Rocky Mount in North Carolina, and Danville in Virginia, Piedmont lost money. Howard said, "We had never done in this company [Piedmont] anything like a route by route analysis of prosperity. It had been done bottom line and the airline was making a million or two million dollars a year, a rather meager return on investment. But at the same time, many airlines were losing money, so you couldn't knock it too much. They submitted to me an analysis of what cities were producing in terms of passengers." Howard took his findings to the president.[16]

Mr. Davis argued that just looking at who flew into and out of a city did not provide the whole picture. If a passenger connected to another flight on the Piedmont system, then some credit had to be given to the place from which that passenger started. Howard took his data back to the research department and weighted the results to acknowledge a city's value to other flights. He still found towns that did not carry their weight. "We came out with about a dozen cities that were losing money any way you looked at it, some of them quite substantial money," said Howard, who again went to Mr. Davis.

On his second trip, the defense for keeping these towns became more personal. "He named his good friends he knew who were the president of the bank, or the mayor or something. 'I couldn't tell Benny [an example] that we were going to get out. You can't do that,'" Bill Howard remembered Tom Davis saying. Howard replied, "Tom, they're businessmen. If we sat down with them and showed them the facts of life," Howard felt they would then understand. "What they really can support is a commuter," Bill Howard reasoned. "A commuter could go in there with smaller airplanes half that size and make some money but with our airplanes, we can't. I don't think there is any chance of getting the passenger flow up for most cities. They're doing reasonably well for the size city they are, but we really need to get out of them." Bill Howard had numbers on his side, figures that said if Piedmont dropped these unprofitable cities, profits would more than double. Mr. Davis listened. Although unsure about the reception he would get from his old friends, Tom Davis saw the logic and acquiesced.[17] Publicly, Mr. Davis acknowledged it as regrettable, citing "cost pressures" that forced the airline out of those towns. He noted that within an hour's drive of each of those locations, Piedmont continued to schedule flights at larger airports, making air travel still possible if coupled with a bit of automobile travel.[18]

Executive Vice President Howard began to make the rounds, telling cities running at a loss that his airline was leaving town. To some, he became "the prophet of doom." For a while, he scheduled a trip to relay the bad news every Monday. After a few trips, someone in fixed base operations who supplied the airplane figured out what was going on and warned those working in the stations about any upcoming trip Mr. Howard planned to take, thinking that every trip meant the end of Piedmont Airlines' service to that city. In among travels to unproductive Piedmont cities, Howard got an invitation to address the Asheville Chamber of Commerce. "When I flew into Asheville, it looked like every employee of Piedmont was standing by the airplane waiting for me to get off, said Howard as he shook hands with everybody. Few of them were smiling. Offering the "glum" station manager to be his guest, Howard and company took a car to his destination and delivered a speech about Piedmont's future. Once he got back to the airport, the station manager quizzed him. "Is that all you've got to say today?" Howard's answer was "Yeah. Why? What did you expect?" When told of what they anticipated, Howard called for an immediate general meeting. "We filled the terminal. Everybody on duty or not on duty had shown up," said Howard, who explained his reason for coming to Asheville was not to shut the place down, but instead to speak to community leaders.[19]

Bill Howard made the most significant operational changes that Piedmont had ever seen. For that, he was never loved in the way Mr. Davis was. However, he had a vision for the company that he intended to implement. The plans of Mr. Howard meant an airline that would soar far beyond where the Speedbird had previously gone. He did, however, "temper" his moves with caution. "My board was looking for aggressiveness in the new airline and I wanted to be moderately aggressive," said Bill Howard, "only because we didn't have a whole lot of money to do things with."

Slowly, the pieces in Bill Howard's puzzle began to come together. Once he freed up his fleet from old stops that did not produce profit, he focused on new ones that would. Prior to congressional deregulation, the CAB announced looser restrictions on the formerly cumbersome process to begin or end service to cities. While that announcement allowed Piedmont to shed some destinations, it also allowed the carrier to quickly move into others. The company had long seen routes to Florida as being lucrative, especially since the nature of air travel itself was changing. Vacationers started to vie with businessmen as airline customers and travel to cities like Jacksonville and Miami. Bill Howard proposed a flight from Greensboro to Miami with a stop in Jacksonville. At the time, Eastern offered six flights a day from Charlotte to Miami, nonstop. The logic escaped more than a few at Piedmont. Noting that "you wouldn't have to get off the airplane," Howard argued, "Jacksonville was a pretty good source of passengers for one thing, and Miami was even greater, and true, it was not nonstop but you presently have to connect with Eastern. With this, you don't have to connect, and it will take you right through. You can do it in an hour and 25 minutes less time." He made his presentation to the board, and they gave him their approval.[20]

Successor to Tom Davis, William R. Howard came to Piedmont from Eastern Airlines and proceeded to persuade the folks in Winston-Salem that deregulation could benefit the airline (Ronnie Macklin Collection).

Going to the board of directors with every move he intended to make was not something Bill Howard planned to keep up forever. While at Eastern, management made its decisions on how to operate and gave its board details about the results. Piedmont however, was a much smaller airline than Eastern, and Howard worked hard to gain the trust of the eleven member board of directors, especially when it involved decisions about which Mr. Davis, who was not only the president but also a board member, was hesitant. For each meeting, Howard came with a flip chart, prepared by his research department, and took board members through the steps of the Speedbird's expansion. "I didn't have to do anything but roll my pages that my girls made for me showing what was really happening." Early on, his numbers were not overwhelming, but they did show promise. He'd say, "This was the flight we had two months ago and you were concerned about and here it is. It still doesn't break even, but it will only take two more passengers to make it break even and look at the way its coming, and a month later or two months later I'd say here's where it is, here's where it's going. Here's where it crossed over." Also he never missed an opportunity to show that he was not worried about what the big airlines were going to do to him. He thought much more about what he was going to do to them. He'd add, "Did you know by the way, as a result, Eastern, dropped one of its flights to Miami."[21]

In taking away business from Eastern, Piedmont began to look more and more like a giant killer. Certainly, the Winston-Salem carrier proved itself to be brave in a competitive world. Bill Howard had used deregulation to his advantage. Without the cumbersome approval process, Piedmont Airlines could fly into anywhere it felt it could make a profit. Howard believed a flight to Boston would do so. "There was nobody flying it then," he noticed. Referring to the old CAB approval system, he believed, "We probably could have gotten it. But it would have taken a year and a half or two years to do. Eastern would have fought it tooth and nail all the way through, and it would have taken many months before we got the approval. After deregulation, you just do it. So the decision we would make one week, we would implement within the month." Before any of the other airlines knew it and could move to counter, Piedmont was in "Bean Town."[22]

By the time Congress made its move and officially enacted the Airline Deregulation Act, Piedmont Aviation, Inc., had already displayed another sign of a national prominence. Mr. Davis began the morning of September 25, 1978, on the floor of the New York Stock Exchange. He had come to make a ceremonial purchase of Piedmont stock in its first day being traded on the "big board." Since the airline's first days back in 1948, investors obtained stock in Piedmont through brokers on an "over the counter" basis. The offer to trade on the NYSE demonstrated the stability and potential of the North Carolina company just as it was beginning to feel its way beyond the Southeast. When the stock market opened at 10:00 A.M., Tom Davis bought 100 shares at $13 per share, putting his company in play with shareholders on a nationwide basis.[23]

Piedmont stock drew immediate interest, mostly because of a recent report by a New York investment firm that listed the aviation company among 22 of the nation's "most appetizing acquisition plums."[24] As a well run, efficient, and, most importantly, profitable business, the little known airline with the strong reputation attracted investors. However, as a publicly traded company, Piedmont ran the risk of being taken over by some other airline in an effort to bolster the buyers' sagging fortunes. Even though Mr. Davis had guided the company from its early days as president, he never owned a majority share of stock in the company and could not protect his company from takeover, especially once it hit the NYSE. Some estimates put his share of Piedmont as low as four percent. Since its first stock offering, Mr. Davis ran the risk of someone else obtaining a majority share, yet when the Goldman-Sachs report circulated, the president of Piedmont cautioned potential corporate raiders. Asked about the possibility of merger or buy out, Mr. Davis diplomatically said, "We want to continue to grow without going through the trauma of a merger." In more pointed words, he declared that far from an "acquisition plum," Piedmont Aviation was much more a "prickly pear," warning prospective buyers, "we'll stick you."[25] Interested parties heeded the message, at least for a while.

With a solid company and a new bullish attitude, Piedmont moved adroitly into a deregulated world. The strategy devised by the management team blended much of what Piedmont Airlines had stood for with exciting new possibilities for growth. They called it the "bypass strategy." Bill Howard was right when he said that the major airlines would look to the bigger markets to make their money, abandoning some small and mid-sized cities along the way once the government opened competition. Piedmont's plan did not involve going head to head with the large carriers for the most profitable runs of New York to Chicago or

Chicago to Atlanta. They chose instead to serve the needs of smaller cities; while Piedmont continued flights to New York, Chicago and Atlanta, the other end of the ride always went to a smaller city. Tom Davis characterized staying out of the ride between big towns: "We thought we'd be better served by not butting heads against a stone wall."[26] Bill Howard cited the specific problem of a directly competitive strategy when he said, "It takes a year to two years to get your share of the passengers in accordance to the share of seats you're offering. We would have had to offer $39 fares [on the New York–Chicago route] for six months just to gain some recognition."[27] Approving the strategy, Mr. Davis noted, "As a consequence, practically all of our new service has resulted in improved service to the public rather than simply expanding into markets that were already served by other very good airlines."[28] He called it a "rifle approach." He wanted markets overlooked by the other airlines. He felt profits could be guaranteed almost immediately in those situations. He said, "We don't plan to grow, just to get bigger." Looking for underserved markets in air travel, Mr. Davis wanted his company to grow, but for the right reasons: "We expect that growth to produce a profit."[29]

Piedmont relished the opportunities overlooked by the major carriers. In a deregulated environment, these markets meant less competition and, significantly, fewer debilitating price wars, since most of competition was out chasing denser routes. The strategy called for the Speedbird to go unnoticed by the other major airlines. While doing so, management planned to double their available seat miles from two and a half million to five million.[30] It may have been a mentality left over from the puddle jumping days, but Piedmont Airlines saw its niche under deregulation as a not-ready-for-prime-time carrier, but on the way up.

Piedmont expanded its destinations to serve a myriad of new cities, with all the routes leading back to the Southeast, the company home. Flights to locations like Boston, Houston, and Denver never connected to each other. They all stemmed from and returned to Piedmont's core service area, the same area served since its early days.[31] The mix of large and medium sized cities fit well into the new Piedmont approach. In essence, Mr. Davis saw each edition from the perspective of how it could accommodate southeastern customers. Flying to Denver gave them some exciting skiing options. As a seat of banking, Boston could serve the emerging New South banking center of Charlotte well. Plus, flights to Boston had the extra advantage of offering connecting flights to Europe on other airlines, giving Piedmont customers a choice instead of having to fly to New York for a connection overseas.[32] The emphasis remained primarily on Piedmont's base. Following the lead established by Davis, Bill Howard planned Piedmont's growth "with one foot in our traditional North Carolina–Virginia area."[33]

The company's expansion brought with it more contractions than expected. Perhaps the most surprising loss of service came to Piedmont's own hometown. Starting in 1978, Speedbird flights out of Smith Reynolds Airport began to dwindle as the company analyzed the profitability of each destination. Deregulation did not cut off subsidies cold turkey, but by 1982, only Winston-Salem and Greenbrier, West Virginia, were still serviced with government help.[34] When the money left, so did the service. Piedmont officials abandoned passenger service altogether in its native Winston-Salem, focusing instead on Greensboro's airport, just 17 miles east of Smith Reynolds Airport, the facility that still housed Piedmont Aviation's corporate headquarters. A Forsyth County commissioner summed up the loss by saying, "Old Piedmont has finally outgrown its birthplace."[35] Bob McAlphin saw the sadness that came with taking the Twin City off the schedule. He observed that the move "bothered Mr. Davis more than people will ever know. Because this was his hometown and he'd started service and had some generally good flights out of here. We continued service probably longer than anyone else would have to Winston-Salem. But there comes a time when you just got to use your airplanes more efficiently."[36]

7. The Great Outfit, 1978–1984

The mainstay of the Piedmont fleet in the jet age, the Boeing 737. Their size made 737s perfect for Piedmont's short and intermediate range flights (Ronnie Macklin Collection).

The growth of Piedmont Airlines demanded additional planes and the symbol of a modern airline at the dawn of the eighties was the jet. The enthusiastic choice for most Speedbird flights was the Boeing 737. During the first five years of deregulation, the airline doubled the number of planes it owned, ultimately operating the largest fleet of 737s of any airline in the world.[37] The company eventually acquired numerous models of the Boeing 737, including the series 200 and 300. The 737-400 became available in the later eighties. At a length of 100 feet, the 200 could carry 118 passengers up to 2,400 miles before refueling while the 300 was slightly larger, seating 138.[38] Most pilots flying the line in the late seventies enjoyed flying the 737s, and their size fit well with many of the destinations to which Piedmont flew. At the time of deregulation, the Pacemaker fleet of Boeing 737-200s had grown to 23. As historian Barry Lawing pointed out, Piedmont built its schedules around the 737s.[39]

The busy nature of keeping up with the demand hardly gave employees time to take pride in their expansion. In aircraft maintenance, Frank Davis explained, "Our job in maintenance picked up some because we were getting the new airplanes." With a plethora of new challenges, he remembered, there was always something new to learn. "We went from the 737-200s; then, Boeing started making the 300s, which were more fuel efficient. A larger airplane, it had the new glass cockpit. Real, neat avionics and electronics up in the cockpit, new high tech equipment that we were just real excited to see," Davis continued, noting the challenges that came with it. "Of course the flight crews were learning how to work them and maintenance was learning how to work with the new equipment."[40] The expansion meant new tests for everyone.

Unlike its early days when Tom Davis worried about funding for new planes, Piedmont had no problem when it went shopping for the additional 737s. At the time of purchase, Piedmont had increased profit by 445 percent since deregulation, making the airline the best of risks, especially in the face of the industry as a whole, which continued to make headlines with failing and struggling airlines. The company raised $404 million in a number of ways, including leases, new stock offerings and loans from New York's Chase Manhattan as well as hometown bank Wachovia. John G. Medlin succeeded John Watlington as both president of Wachovia and as a member of Piedmont's board of directors. Characterizing Wall Street's reaction to the carrier as responsive, he said, "Piedmont's performance has resulted in a more receptive equity market."[41] Airline analyst James Parker was more flattering, calling Piedmont's balance sheet "strong." Noting their large aircraft purchase in 1983, he said, "They've got all their money tied up in aircraft, but as long as they can meet their interest payments, they'll be fine. And the business is there."[42]

Everything Piedmont Airlines touched turned profitable as the eighties progressed. Even the 737-300s came to the airline at a bargain price. Many thought Piedmont was the launch customer for the 300 series because of the low price at which Piedmont made the purchase from Boeing. Captain Tom Sharpe remembered the reason for the confusion: "From what I understand, Zeke negotiated the deal that Piedmont actually got the Boeing cheaper than the launch customer, which is sort of unheard of. The launch customer is supposed to get a better deal. But somehow Zeke got a better deal than the launch customer did."[43] There was no apparent end to the "Midas touch" for Piedmont. Years later when the time came for introduction of the 737-400, the launch customer was Piedmont Airlines.

As Piedmont made its purchases of the "seven-threes," the last of the propeller planes was being phased out, giving the carrier claim to being an all jet airline. Throughout the sev-

A small ceremony was held to mark the last flight of a Piedmont YS-11 in scheduled service. The crew, headed by Captain Tom Sharpe, stood in front of the *Shenandoah Valley Pacemaker* and offered comments to the media about the passing of the last propeller plane in the fleet for Piedmont Airlines (Tom Sharpe Collection).

enties, many routes were still served by the Japanese made YS-11, referred to by Piedmont mechanic/pilot/executive C.D. McLean as the "Yokohama Mama."[44] Tom Sharpe flew what was acknowledged to be the last flight of the YS-11 in 1982. He characterized it as "a great airplane for what we were doing with it which was flying up and down and around all these mountains. We flew to Bluefield and Beckley, West Virginia, Tri-City, Tennessee, Asheville, North Carolina. It had the performance and the people carrying ability to do that."[45]

Deregulation ramped up the need for more aircraft quickly and while orders went out to Boeing for more 737s, Piedmont filled the immediate gap with six used 727-100s.[46] The Boeing 727-100 was not the first choice at Piedmont for reasons other than the fact that one of the first two acquired crashed in Hendersonville in 1967, and the three man cockpit requirement helped precipitate the unfortunate 1969 strike. Primarily, the tri-jet 727 was larger and less fuel efficient than the 737s with two jet engines. However, Bill Howard swam upstream yet again with enviable results. With all of its deficiencies, Howard wanted more 727s in his fleet, not fewer. Delta Airlines had 25 "seven-twos" for sale and Piedmont bought the entire lot. For Howard, they were just too good a deal to pass up. He asserted, "I was also looking at what they had paid for those airplanes. And they had paid like ten times as much for those airplanes as I was going to pay for those airplanes." So he bought them, but because it was a buyer's market, he wanted a few concessions. First, he insisted that he pay less per plane for buying the entire lot. Next he demanded that every airplane be sanded and scraped and that Delta pay to repaint them with Piedmont's colors and logos. Last, since pilots are trained to look in specific areas for a certain instrument (for quick action), Delta agreed to reconfigure every cockpit. Howard attributed winning such concessions from salesmen who were preoccupied with the sale. He took his feat back to the board, who was less enthused. They said, "Don't you know those are three jets? Those are big fuel consumers, and they have three pilots." Howard countered by saying, "Look at what those planes have cost Delta and what they'll cost us. And because of the low, low, low cost we have in them, we'll make money. Here's how we'll make money, and we did."[47]

For some pilots, the creation of an all jet fleet meant the end of an era for Piedmont. Phasing out propeller aircraft at Piedmont exemplified the changes going on within the company. Everything was speeding up. Original pilots like Leon Fox lamented the faster pace. At 500 miles per hour, the captain had no time for the kind of pleasantries typical of the propeller rides. "We were getting more preoccupied with technology and less with passengers,"[48]

Portrait of a Captain: Charlie Meacham in full uniform at the end of his career with Piedmont. He flew for 30 years with the airline, reaching the mandatory retirement age of 60 in September of 1979 (Chuck Meacham Collection).

September 13, 1979. Charlie Meacham going through a line of well-wishers that includes pilots, flight attendants and ground personnel, before his last flight. For many pilots the ride was special. In Meacham's case both his children flew their father's last flight and enjoyed the bittersweet celebration (Chuck Meacham Collection).

said Fox, who retired from the line in 1978.⁴⁹ With a mandatory retirement for pilots of age 60, many of Leon Fox's contemporaries were retiring too. Charlie Meacham flew his last flight on September 17, 1979. Both his son and daughter accompanied him and were surprised and awed by the many tributes to their father along the way. "He did not cut the autopilot on all day long. He manually flew it from chock to chock, from the time he left Atlanta until he got back," said his son Chuck. "Everywhere we stopped, he'd get off the plane and he would go in there, especially in Roanoke. They had candles lit and gave him gifts. He was at a loss for words, but he handled it better than I could have." On his last landing back in Atlanta, Chuck watched his dad's skill culminate with a perfect landing of his 727. "I've never seen anybody grease a landing like that," said Chuck with obvious admiration. He added that his father "was grinning, but his eyes were swimming in tears, so it was a pretty emotional day."⁵⁰

For the first generation of pilots, their career was capped just as the airline began a tremendous growth spurt. In many cases, the budding airline needed to buy and sell planes fast due to its rapid growth. The issue often centered on trading planes with little concern about who was buying or selling them. All the wheeling and dealing led to some strange and potentially dangerous places, like Iran just prior to the 1979 revolution. In searching for used

FH227s, the Fokker Company offered Piedmont the personal airplane of the Shah of Iran, one traded in by the Iranian leader for a new model. Later, in an effort to sell parts to the Iranian government, both Zeke Saunders and Howard Cartwright flew over to Tehran. "They let us use the Shah's sister's office at the airport, where we did our business for two weeks," Zeke said, recalling the trip took place just before the Islamic Revolution. "They were nice people, real nice people. You couldn't ask for better people than they treated us." [51] As a result, the two Piedmont officials worked out an arrangement to sell spare FH-227 parts to the Iranians. The exchange went well until the taking of American hostages in November of 1979, jeopardizing the deal. Zeke remarked, "During the hostage crisis, I talked to them several times on the phone. They were trying to figure some way to buy the parts to keep the airplanes going." The two business partners, Piedmont and the Iranian authorities, attempted to prevent the international incident from rupturing their symbiotic relationship. As they scratched their heads, the idea of an intermediary arose. "This company from Belgium wanted to buy them. Of course, I'm sure I knew what they were doing. They bought [the parts]. And I think they sold them to [Iran, however,] I didn't know that for sure." Even though Piedmont created a solution to their unfortunate problem, the deal ruptured for political reasons. "I remember our lawyer telling me, 'you sell [parts] to [the Iranians] and you'll be sitting up here explaining it to a bunch of congressmen,'" said Zeke. "I said 'I don't believe I want to do that.'"[52]

In the years since deregulation, most airlines suffered tremendously. The major carriers lost a collective $400 million in 1980. Competition among them forced better service and lower rates. The former substantially increased expenses while the latter pushed revenue down by 25 percent on average. One of the few exceptions was Piedmont Airlines, whose net income for the same year increased by 44 percent to $16 million. Clearly, the bypass strategy proved effective as ridership improved by 22 percent in 1980. Prior to deregulation, the *Wall Street Journal* said the only exciting thing at Piedmont was its landings on short, mountain runways. Bucking the industry trend gave the New York paper something else to talk about and it did, citing Piedmont's performance as "surprising."[53]

All of a sudden, this unexpected performance gave the previously small carrier a new problem. The company with a family atmosphere where the president knew most everyone's name had to cope with growing into a larger entity. The effort to keep the airline as the friendly, nurturing company its employees had come to know became difficult because of its tremendous growth. Vice President of Employee Relations Joe Wilson observed, "Size makes a big difference, and its hard to know as many people as you did in a smaller company and so on, but essentially that spirit sort of carried forth." Wilson came to Piedmont in 1974 to help build structure in the growing entity and soon took notice of the cohesion in the company. As the airline expanded, Wilson believed that employees had even greater cause for pride, as they realized, "This growth, look what it's doing for us. More of us are getting ahead, getting promotions, and we go to industry meetings and can point with pride to what we've accomplished."[54]

The increased stature of Piedmont threatened to disrupt the character of the company, but the effort was made to keep the familial atmosphere the airline had enjoyed all its life. In order to maintain close ties like the company had known in pre-deregulation days, Piedmont began its own "Olympics," born as a substitute for the 1980 boycott by the United States of the Moscow games. The company's internal newsletter, *The Piedmonitor*, put out the word to come to Winston-Salem for a cookout and various games where each employee represented the stations (cities) where they worked. Mr. Davis's son Frank characterized the event as a morale booster, serving to "get us together, have some fun, a little camaraderie and get [us] to put the name with the face. You've been talking to these people on the phone for a couple of years but never really knew who it was and now you're trying to outrun them."[55] Just because the family was growing larger did not mean that its members could become estranged. While Tom Davis had any control within Piedmont, he made sure they stayed close.

A natural extension of the new Piedmont approach was the establishment of its own hub and spoke system as a way to feed riders to its own longer haul flights. Bringing many of its flights into one of Piedmont's hubs meant travelers had numerous choices about where they could go, all on the Speedbird. Piedmont wanted to avoid the same connection points used by the already overcrowded major carriers. Major metropolitan areas like Chicago, used by United, or Atlanta, a major Delta hub, were to be avoided. Instead of banking on the establishment of one giant hub, thus creating chaos in a whole new location, Bill Howard considered the possibility of creating several. These regional hubs gave Piedmont passengers less congested airports in which to swap flights. The airline also gained the ability to build on its own strength, since it flew to an increasing number of cities. The new strategy called for Piedmont to feed itself passengers instead of its old "feeder" role of carrying them for part of their trip, then turning customers over to another airline for the completion of their journey. "Our schedules are totally devoted to our own connections," said Bill Howard succinctly.[56] When he took out a map of the east coast, he scoured it for under-utilized markets.

The first city upon which he zeroed in was Charlotte, North Carolina. Staff Vice President of Scheduling Bob McAlphin had worked on setting up flights for most of his career at Piedmont and as he remembered, "We kind of stumbled across getting the hub at Charlotte started." Said McAlphin, "I remember playing around with some flights at Charlotte coming from places like Fayetteville, Wilmington, Norfolk [and] Richmond with a morning airplane coming in to Charlotte and then [we'd] go out to larger points like Chicago, Dallas, Atlanta, Los Angeles and do that two or three times a day and it started to work. We saw we had something good there."[57] While L.A. was still a few years away, the system of short spokes and long spokes into a Charlotte hub began to appeal to the company as a means for growth. Charlotte was a fast growing New South city, and officials of North Carolina's largest city were eager to work with Piedmont to expand facilities at the city's Douglas Airport. When deregulation began, the Speedbird flew out of the Queen City just eight times a day. Six years later, the number rocketed to 145. Usage went from 7 percent to 79 percent of airport facilities. Located some 80 miles southwest from Winston-Salem, the inaugural hub of Charlotte tested the notion that Piedmont could develop its own network, and customers would patronize it.

The timing of flights in and out was crucial to the success of the Charlotte hub. Bob McAlphin scheduled arrivals only a couple minutes apart so passengers could move quickly to their departures. "Basically, they were all coming in at the same time and all leaving at the same time with just a little bit of spread in there, but it worked," he said, also mentioning that he heard minimal grumbles from customers who had to change planes or wait for the next leg of their trip. Piedmont helped those connections all it could, even occasionally holding outgoing flights a few extra minutes to allow passengers time to make the connection.[58]

In flying to all of Piedmont's new destinations, the airline banked on an unproven demand for these routes. Did people want to fly between Charlotte and a non-resort town like Dallas, Texas? A Piedmont vice president of corporate planning acknowledged the risk when he remembered people saying, "You'll starve to death — there aren't ten people a day going from Charlotte to Dallas."[59] But the strategy had some advantages.[60] Traditionally, a

7. *The Great Outfit, 1978–1984* 187

By the early eighties, Piedmont Airlines had made Charlotte's Douglas Airport a popular place. The airline began scheduling hundreds of flights into the Queen City daily in order to connect passengers between many places Piedmont had served for years, like Roanoke and Wilmington, with new destinations, such as Boston and Dallas (courtesy Piedmont Aviation Historical Society; from the collection of Ronnie Macklin).

Charlotte traveler heading to Dallas would have to fly to Atlanta before switching planes to head to "Big D." With the "by-pass strategy," the passenger could avoid the congestion of Atlanta and fly directly to their destination from Charlotte. Even if the passenger started in another city, Piedmont felt they might be lured to try a Speedbird and switch planes in Charlotte instead of amid the chaos of other connection points. "I was convinced that there were a lot of places that North Carolina could operate to and from," said Bill Howard, who credited the Charlotte to Dallas flight as the beginning of the Charlotte hub. With Eastern flying seven flights a day from Charlotte to Dallas, albeit through Atlanta, critics wondered out loud about Howard's sanity. "I said, 'We'll do it once a day and it will be the best service that Charlotte has to Dallas,'" Howard recalled. "There's a hell of a lot of passengers going there every day and I was convinced that one nonstop a day we would pretty well fill. And we did. We filled the second one too and the third one too."[61]

Establishment of the Charlotte hub started small and grew. For years, Bob McAlphin's office wall sported a picture that depicted how meager the beginnings were. He described the image which showed Piedmont's portion of "the Charlotte Airport with two gates, that's all we had and had 13 airplanes lined up out there ... they were all lined up in a row there with the two gates in front and we would have sufficient people to lead the passengers out and make sure they didn't get on the wrong flight or stumble into a jet engine or something." For McAlphin, the phenomenal part of the setup was the efficiency with which it operated. "We didn't have to have a $400,000 piece of equipment to push it back and turn it around and all that. That airplane would crank up its engine, hold one brake, spin around if he was ready to go before the rest of them, and go. It just worked beautifully." Bob McAlphin often wondered why all the money was spent on a new airport when what they had worked so beautifully.[62]

Some said the 1981 establishment of the Charlotte hub did as much for Charlotte as it did for Piedmont. Former mayor John Belk credited the move as significant to Charlotte's growth and its growing reputation as a prosperous metropolitan area. "Tom brought in Piedmont, and that really made Charlotte," commented Belk, who also headed a regional department store chain headquartered there.[63] Belk was a Piedmont supporter from then on, although the real success was more the work of Bill Howard than Tom Davis. The attention Piedmont showered on Charlotte helped create a whole new airport worthy of its premier status as a hub city. *Travel Weekly* magazine called Charlotte "The city deregulation built."[64] The choice of Charlotte as the first hub city for Piedmont made good business sense for several reasons. First, proximity to Piedmont's Winston-Salem headquarters meant close scrutiny of the expansion could be maintained. Second, Piedmont already had a presence in Douglas Airport, making expansion more comfortable. Third, the growth of Charlotte as a city had been tremendous, partially because of its development as a banking center. Piedmont invested its resources into a metropolitan area that had a lot to recommend itself.

Charlotte benefited too from the fact that it was no rival to Winston-Salem. In terms of airports, Greensboro's Triad Airport had long since eclipsed Smith Reynolds Airport in Winston-Salem. With the attributes of what was once the old Friendship Field, basing a hub for Piedmont a mere 17 miles away made some sense. However, in Tom Davis's view, the rivalry between the Twin City and the Gateway City, as Greensboro was called, still existed, and when the choice came for a selection of cities out of which to base most of its flights, Mr. Davis could not consent to giving in to Greensboro. Bill Howard observed, "Tom Davis grew up in Winston-Salem, and there had been heavy competition between Greensboro and Winston-Salem and Tom did not want to fly out of the Greensboro airport." Stanley Frank, manager of the Triad Airport and a friend of Bill Howard, was said to have believed that the choice robbed Greensboro of its preeminence among North Carolina cities. Said Howard, "He believed that Greensboro could have been what Charlotte is today." Piedmont based some flights out of Greensboro, but according to Howard, Charlotte did ten times more business than Greensboro.[65]

By the time Piedmont moved into Charlotte to become what Bill Howard called "the best choice"[66] among airlines serving the city, Howard himself had become the best choice as the anticipated successor to the company's presidency. Mr. Davis had always made it well known that he intended to retire in 1983 when he turned 65. Speculation centered on Bill Howard's eventual ascension to the top spot at Piedmont since his arrival. He edged toward it in 1981, taking the position of chief operating officer. Two years later Bill Howard moved into Davis's chair as president of the company. Davis remained as chairman of the board of directors' executive committee, but the daily running of the airline and fixed base operation became the concern of Bill Howard, who had been putting his stamp on the company ever since his arrival.

With a prospering company like Piedmont, it might have seemed like an awkward time for the transition of power. The momentum gained by several successful years under deregulation might have stalled if the exit of Mr. Davis had been perceived as damaging to the company. However, several reasons existed for the retirement of Piedmont Airlines' founder.

The problems he had as a child with asthma plagued him more often as he moved into his sixties, but his son suggested that more than his health was the cause. "Some of the health problems I think were bothering him but, more so, I think [it was] just trying to stay in line with the rules," said Frank Davis about his father's decision to leave the position of president and CEO of Piedmont. "He said that the directors and the officers had in their job descriptions that officers would retire at age 65. It was mandatory. It's like the pilots. I believe the pilots have to retire or quit flying at age 60. He was a nut for following the rules."[67] Tom Davis stepped down from the position he had occupied for 40 years on May 5, 1983, less than two months after his 65th birthday.[68]

Many in the company hated to see the retirement of the only boss they had ever known. Vice President of Marketing Dan Brock simply said, "He was revered." Brock was among many employees who recalled an extra special Christmas surprise from Mr. Davis in 1981. As thanks for all of their hard work, Davis gave each of his 6,600 employees a crisp new one hundred dollar bill.[69] Many who got that present say they never forgot it. Some even claimed to have kept theirs, never spending it.

They paid their boss back, though. In 1983, employees began a collection to buy Mr. Davis a present for his retirement. Everyone in the company was given the opportunity to contribute, including son Frank Davis. He remembered their goal, a brand new Mercedes-Benz. The younger Davis "chipped in" his part to buy a car, not for his father but for his boss. Said Frank, "At the Piedmont Olympics, they presented him with a 1983 380 Mercedes SL, a little two door sports car."[70] The Piedmont workforce raised more than $50,000, not only making the car possible, but also endowing a scholarship at Winston-Salem's Wake Forest University in the name of Tom Davis, where he sat as a trustee.[71] Probably the most sacrificial of gifts was a personalized "Piedmont" license tag owned by an employee who signed it over to Mr. Davis so it could adorn the bumper of the Mercedes-Benz.[72] Always a practical man, for years Davis had driven a station wagon to work daily because it suited his needs as a father of five. Frank Davis noted that the Mercedes became one of his most cherished possessions because of those who gave it to him. "It could have been a Hudson," remarked Frank, "but to be a big fancy Mercedes in 'Piedmont blue' colored paint and to think that the employees would think that much of him to chip in to get something like that for him for his retirement just overwhelmed him." He drove the car to work only on sunny days.[73]

Of the many personal tributes employees paid their boss, one demonstrated the respect workers had for the retiring president. It came from Flight Attendant Margaret Queen, who saw Mr. Davis when he often flew as a passenger on board one of the Speedbirds. "I remember sitting with him many times, and he was trying to pay me for a drink. He ordered a gin martini and tried to give me a dollar for it. I said, 'Mr. Davis, I think you've paid for this many times.' He said, 'What?' I said, 'Your drink is complimentary.'"[74] Captain Larry Dudley paid Tom Davis an equal compliment from the other end of the plane. He recalled that Davis reportedly always went to the cockpit and thanked whoever was there for their part in giving him the Mercedes. Dudley said, "I told him if he had half as much fun driving that Mercedes as I did flying his airplanes over all them years, he might as well hook his seat belt tight."[75]

The feeling of loyalty and the overwhelming sense of loss at the retirement of the company's "founder" was understandable among the Piedmont family, especially those of long standing. As men like Tom Davis and Zeke Saunders left the stage, others entered to take their place. The newer management team's frame of reference differed from the "old timers." Bill Barber noticed a change as the Davis era transitioned into the Howard era. The difference

At Tom Davis' retirement in 1983, the employees pooled their money to purchase a going away gift for their president of 40 years. Mr. Davis leans on the Mercedes convertible they bought. With the extra money they endowed a scholarship at Wake Forest University in his name. Behind Mr. Davis is a "Piedmont Pacemaker," a Boeing 737-200 (courtesy Piedmont Aviation Historical Society; from the collection of Paul Snell).

was so palpable that he chose to retire instead of finding his niche in the new group. "They called us Davis's boys, all of us, Zeke, Cartwright,"[76] said Barber, who sensed a certain amount of animosity between the two groups. According to Bill Barber, Mr. Davis tried to underplay the feeling and advised, "Don't you let those boys run you off. You can be here as long as you want." But Barber felt excluded from many of the jobs he handled for the company for so many years. "What they would do was take stuff away from me, like engine overhaul contracts," said Barber. "I'd been handling them for years and the first thing I knew they called me from Dallas and said, 'Hey did you know that you are not in charge of doing engine contracts any more?' I said, 'No, I didn't know that.' They said, 'Well, you're not.'"[77] Bill Barber retired from Piedmont Aviation in 1984.

The early eighties saw the retirement of many of the original Piedmont employees. Most had worked forty years or so, building Piedmont to the point where Mr. Davis called their combined efforts "the wonder of the industry."[78] People like Thelma Davis retired after handling a number of jobs skillfully and cheerfully. As she modestly remarked, "I did a little bit of everything, from sweeping floors to training stewardesses." At her farewell party, the note

After 46 years with Piedmont Aviation, Ed Culler (left) retired in 1986. Mr. Davis (center) was there to salute his long-time employee along with Culler's brother Joe (right), sales manager for fixed based operations (Ed Culler Collection).

from Mr. Davis expressed the value of her contribution to Piedmont. He wrote, "O, my dear Mrs. T. How in the world could I ever tell you what a great personal pleasure it has been to have the privilege of working with you over the years, both of us pulling together to make something out of our great outfit."[79]

Many of the early pilots were also leaving the Piedmont stage, in what they considered the prime of their lives. FAA requirements forced pilots to quit flying at age 60, well before the mandatory retirement age for other jobs. Tory Vaughn reflected on the end of his career as a pilot. He said, "I know it was a sad day for me when I walked off that 727 in Norfolk and said, 'Well, this is it.' I could have gone another ten years I know, or certainly at least another five." After 33 years and just over 33,000 hours in the air, he left the job he loved, saying, "I'd do it all over again if I could."[80]

Zeke Saunders had a particularly hard time leaving the organization, not due so much to sentiment but because Bill Howard wanted Zeke to hire his own replacement.

> I wanted to retire. The doc told me I couldn't work anymore after that heart attack, then they told me I could. Bill Howard said I had to find somebody to take my place before he would let me go. We had been talking to [Gordon] Bethune. The FAA had called me about Bethune. He had done a good job down at Boeing, where they had some trouble and he straightened it out. We talked about it. Then I called him and asked him if he wanted to

come take my job. He said yeah, he'd take it. So we called Bill and Bill said call him and hire him, and we did.[81]

Practically speaking, Zeke Saunders never completely left Piedmont. Davis seemed to misunderstand the meaning of the word "retire" and would periodically call Zeke in to solve one problem or another. "He never thought you were retired," said Zeke. "He'd call me up, and I had been retired two or three years. He'd say, 'How about getting your tail out here and get this airline on time?' I said, 'Tom, I've been retired for two years.'" Mr. Davis's answer: "That doesn't make any difference."[82]

While some within the company used the transition as an exit, its first leader stayed to have a somewhat invisible role in Piedmont's remarkable growth. By 1983, Mr. Davis relinquished his position as president, treasurer and CEO of Piedmont but stayed well connected to the pulse of the airline as chairman of the Executive Committee. Throughout the eighties he kept his office at Piedmont, and his continued presence in a decision making group afforded him considerable influence in the direction of the company, if he chose to exert it. Most still looked to the founder of Piedmont Airlines as the guiding force even though he had relinquished control of the company's day to day activities. Bill Howard noted that Tom Davis was kept on staff at Piedmont even after his retirement as a "consultant."[83] Keeping old friends like Zeke Saunders and Bill Barber around for occasional help was reminiscent of the old days.

Questions remained over the years about how much control Mr. Davis had over the direction of the company after his retirement. His continued presence meant he could have been decisive in any decision he opposed. His stature as founder of the airline gave him clout among the employees, which undoubtedly afforded him some opportunities to control from the shadows, but a member of the management team who arrived after Davis left the job contradicted those assertions. "He was still chairman and his office was adjacent to mine, so he was always a big factor," said Gordon Bethune, who observed the interplay of Tom Davis and Bill Howard. Bethune insisted that Howard charted the direction of the company. Of Mr. Davis, Bethune remarked, "A friend until the day he died, a wonderful man, but it was no question that he deferred to Bill and Bill was very much the chief executive officer of the company."[84]

Throughout his tenure with Piedmont, Mr. Bill Howard was a controversial figure. Some employees admit they were reluctant to support his efforts, especially as the new direction of the airline seemed to contradict the cherished beliefs Mr. Davis had voiced during his years as president. Howard's image of the company didn't seem to fit with the airline that Davis built. Plus, the style of the two presidents differed sharply. Carroll Spencer used the example of a full airliner to explain the dissimilarity.

> Mr. Davis [was] going through Goldsboro and the airplane fills up. Guess who gets off the airplane? On any other airline the last passenger would get off. On Piedmont, Mr. Davis got off the airplane, went and rented a car and drove to Winston-Salem. Mr. Howard did not do that. Mr. Howard drove around like he did at Eastern. [He] drove around when the jet was leaving, drives up, has his special car, drives up on the ramp, gets out, goes up, and gets in his special seat. That was a turnoff to our employees.[85]

As planes filled up and the results of moves made by Mr. Howard began to be felt, opinions changed. While some questioned the sanity of pouring money into sponsorship of a NASCAR racing team, Carroll Spencer looked back on it later as a smart move. "I suddenly realized after about three or four years that you take the NASCAR circuit and the Piedmont circuit and [put them together,] damned if it doesn't overlap and these people in NASCAR are brand conscious and loyal. They will ride your airplane if you have a racecar," said Spencer. "[Fans] may not make a lot of money but they will spend it on their racing. It suddenly dawned on me that the man was exactly right. He did a great job and he never got any recognition."[86] With or without the wholehearted support of his employee base, Bill Howard never shrunk from his effort to build a bigger and better airline, one that scarcely resembled the company of the Davis era.

Many felt strongly that Tom Davis could not walk away from Piedmont without employees acknowledging his leadership by creating some lasting memorial. As soon as a new training facility reached completion it was named the Thomas H. Davis Training Center. The building stood across Liberty Street from the Smith Reynolds Airport Terminal, beside the company headquarters built in the fifties. As Bill Barber remembered it, he made sure the building honored his old chief. "I think I just had the sign made," he said as he laughed about his audacity.[87] While there may have been more to it than Barber recalled, the honor stuck, appropriate for Thomas H. Davis, a man who turned a pilot training operation during World War II into one of the nation's best aviation companies.

The center gave training pilots the ability to become fully conversant with any Piedmont aircraft without ever stepping into an actual cockpit. A new era of training had also come along about that time with "Phase II" flight simulators. Though Piedmont had a simulator since the late sixties, the early eighties saw the company gain the ability to realistically replicate flight conditions on its seven-twos. Three simulators operated on a 24-hour a day schedule.

In 1982 Piedmont sponsored the number 3 car of Ricky Rudd. Since Piedmont was a southern airline, the connection to NASCAR was a logical choice. The year 1984 was triumphant for the airline after sponsorship was switched to Terry Labonte's car and he won the Winston Cup Championship (Ronnie Macklin Collection).

Even at a cost of six million dollars each, flight standards director Captain James Sifford said, "It's well worth its weight in gold."[88] With the flight simulators, pilots gained the ability to test their skills without possible tragic consequences. Sifford noted, "A pilot testing on this machine will be faced with more dangerous situations in one 'flight' than he probably would be faced with in his entire lifetime." Simulators even replicated various airports into which Piedmont flew. The T.H. Davis Training Center served as an important asset to Piedmont's mounting safety record. The company had flown since 1968 without a life threatening crash. When not used by Piedmont pilots, the simulators were contracted by numerous other airlines, including Iranian pilots who learned to fly 727s before the hostage crisis.[89]

In addition to a new facility for training, the burgeoning airline also required larger quarters to care for its fleet. With traffic in and out of Winston-Salem drying up, it made no financial sense to locate a new maintenance hangar at Smith Reynolds Airport. Instead of making costly "out of the way" flights to Winston-Salem for maintenance, the site needed to be at a more heavily utilized airport, but somewhere relatively close. Like the naming of the T.H. Davis Training Center, Bill Barber took part in selection process of the new maintenance hangar. He said, "They didn't know at first whether they were going to build the airplane hangar in Greensboro or Charlotte." Barber, along with Howard Cartwright and Zeke Saunders, visited both. "They drove us all over that place. They showed us what we could have and what we couldn't have," he recalled. Though he and Zeke voted for Charlotte, Barber said, "Cartwright had done made up his mind he wanted it in Greensboro because it was close. And that is where the first one was built. But the second one was at the place we picked out the first time."[90] Added Zeke Saunders, "We should have gone to Charlotte the first time. Bill Howard thought we should put it in Greensboro."[91] Despite the initial disagreement over locations, it spoke well of Piedmont's growth that both stations would find substantial use in the years to come.

An absolute necessity for pilots receiving recurrent training. By 1986, training operations had grown very sophisticated with flight simulators that could test pilots beyond their capabilities (Piedmont Silver Eagles Collection).

What they built in Greensboro cost over $11 million.[92] When the construction process started for the Charlotte facility, Ronnie Macklin and Ralph Hicks were called in to specify Piedmont's needs. Macklin remembered the question asked. "They said, 'Well, what do you want?' And I said, 'We want an airplane hangar big enough to hold six airplanes, and we want them bigger than 737s.' They said, 'That's all right.' That was the beginning of the hangar in Charlotte."[93]

7. The Great Outfit, 1978-1984

Generally, the Piedmont folks operated in a very straightforward manner. They were always plain about their needs and rarely considered factors beyond what would work best for the company. Those decisions always advanced the operations of the company, and as with Ronnie Macklin's quick summation of hangar needs in Charlotte, they were incredibly simple and to the point. Since the beginning, Piedmont believed in the "keep it simple" formula. Even with the incredible growth the company went through in the eighties, the maxim proved itself prudent again and again. It was not "rocket science" but good southern common sense that led Piedmont to many of its innovative decisions, like the choice to bypass Atlanta and filter its flights through Charlotte. As a result of a decision that made sense, air customers began to take advantage of the option right away, proving again that a winning business strategy did not have to be complicated; it just had to meet the need.

What Bill Howard began at Piedmont, he soon accelerated. Since Charlotte worked so well as a hub for the airline, the new Piedmont president searched his map for another location in hopes of duplicating his success. He found it in Dayton, Ohio. Never a Piedmont city, Dayton lost 36 percent of its service from other airlines in the early years of deregulation, as the major carriers pulled out looking for more profitable routes. In the early eighties, travelers from Dayton and other cities in the region often ended up driving to Detroit for a flight. Travel pattern data told Bill Howard that Dayton was just the kind of city overlooked by the likes of American and United, and could be profitably served by Piedmont. Situated in southwestern Ohio, Dayton showed potential as a gateway to the Great Lakes region, making hops to Detroit, Lansing and Grand Rapids, Michigan, as well as Fort Wayne, Indiana, and Toledo, Ohio, within easy reach.[94]

Piedmont approached Dayton city officials with a plan. The success of Charlotte as a hub provided a model that Howard felt could work in Dayton. With no other offers, officials jumped at the chance to give their city renewed stature as an airline destination. The city agreed to build new terminal space for Speedbird flights, just as Charlotte had done the year before. Actually, the Dayton city fathers did Charlotte officials one better. In addition to spending $15 million on airport improvements, Dayton told Piedmont that if the carrier did not find passengers in the Ohio city, they could "scrap the 10-year lease."[95] The concession surprised many in the industry since the entire region suffered the worst part of an economic slowdown in the early eighties. Both were confident the relationship could be worthwhile. With additional support from the upper Midwest cities served out of Dayton, Bill Howard could not refuse the offer. Plans called for feeder flights to arrive in Dayton each day before 8:00 A.M., giving commuters the opportunity to make their connection to longer haul flights like Boston, Dallas or even Charlotte without substantial wait time. The routine repeated around twelve noon, giving Midwestern passengers two chances to make their connection out of the Dayton hub daily. Piedmont scheduled return flights out of Dayton to the upper midwest cities each evening to give those customers who left earlier in the day a means to return home.[96]

The new operation came together quickly. After the 1981 establishment of the Charlotte hub, Bill Howard pushed for a July 1, 1982, debut in Dayton. Vice President of Flight Operations Gene Sharp took pride in the fact that, even though his people had short notice to make the Dayton hub operational, they worked diligently to meet the deadline and accomplish everything that went along with it.

> We opened up a Dayton hub and we got about 60 days' notice for our training people that we were going to Dayton with a hub and that we were going to put five more 727s on the line to take care of Dayton as a hub. All those 727s didn't go there, but five airplanes went to Dayton to make that a hub. You have to understand, once we bring a new airplane on, now

we have to check out a new captain to fly that airplane. Well it turns out to be five captains because it takes about five crews to fly an airplane. So we have five captains, those guys moved up from co-pilots seats, so now we've got to train five more copilots to replace those guys and now those copilots came from another airplane. So now we've got to train five more replacements for them and it's just a domino effect.

In addition to all that, now you have to come in with five new hire people to put into the seats that all these other people are moving up to, so it's a huge operation. We had about 60 days' notice that [the opening of the hub] was going to happen. We put five airplanes up there, ferried them in one night at midnight and the next day we were Dayton's largest carrier. And we did everything on time. Got it all done. Now we were running the simulator about 24 hours a day, all the simulators and the training people. They were pushed, ground school instructors bringing new people in, ordering new flight bags, ordering uniforms. It's a task. But everybody pitched in got the job done, nobody complained. People were at work at 7 o'clock the next morning ready to go again.[97]

The effort paid off. Even before July 1, "slot requirements" in Dallas compelled Piedmont to start flying a trip to and from Dayton. On the official launch date, Pacemakers flew out to 16 cities with more added by fall. If within the first 90 days, loads of Piedmont planes flying in and out of Dayton reached 45 percent, company officials had reached their goals. By August, the load factor was 53 percent above expectations.[98] Tom Heine, president of the Dayton Chamber of Commerce, admitted that most folks in his area had never heard of Piedmont before their arrival. "Let me tell you, people around here know what Piedmont is now," he said.[99] The fact that Dayton, Ohio, was hometown to the Wright Brothers and was now served by a North Carolina company did not escape the marketing minds in the Tar Heel State. The tie between the two areas as the place where the Wrights invented flight (Dayton) and where they first demonstrated it (North Carolina) received attention in advertisements that suggested Piedmont was returning the favor given by Orville and Wilbur when they trekked to Kitty Hawk, by providing service "better than anything Dayton has had before."[100] Score another strategic victory for aviation in North Carolina.

"After that worked, we said, 'Let's do that again — same strategy, same style.'" Bill Howard's words sent him back to the map to locate a third hub to build on the success of the other two. Looking again for an underserved market, Piedmont management probed the area around Washington, D.C., and began to eye with interest the Baltimore-Washington International Airport (BWI). Piedmont's Pacemakers had served the airport since 1962, but Bill Howard envisioned an operation larger than anything yet attempted by Piedmont. He went right to work wooing the city of Baltimore. "You've got to convince the city — the city fathers, the chamber of commerce — that you're doing something worthwhile. And then you've got to convince the travel agents, really put on a show for them."[101] Before the numbers were fully in on the Dayton hub, Bill Howard visited Maryland Department of Transportation officials about airport expansion. Having been ignored in favor of Washington's National Airport and the outlying Dulles in Virginia for air passengers to and from the nation's capital, the Maryland DOT eagerly listened to Piedmont's new hub plans and immediately opened their checkbooks. State aviation administrator Jim Turby, delighted by the offer, said the venture "will provide synergies to make BWI the dominant airport in the Baltimore-Washington area."[102]

Work began quickly on the Baltimore hub. An agreement was reached in late January of 1983 and construction began on March 1 for an anticipated July opening. Over 28 acres of concrete were poured in time to launch five new gates that provided space for 28 daily flights. By the end of the year, the number of gates would increase to twelve, with departures totaling over 50. Everyone marveled at the quick fruition of the Howard game plan, including

Maryland Secretary of Transportation Lowell Bridwell, who declared, "To my knowledge, this is the first time in the history of Maryland that a public agency has been able to create, from day one, in four and a half months, a $20 million project." Piedmont initially allocated eight 737s to the hub and expanded the airline's workforce in Baltimore to around 190 jobs.

When the Baltimore hub took off in usage, everyone was pleased, especially Bill Howard. Though he had been the architect of the new Piedmont system, the Baltimore effort was his first as chief executive officer of the company. After two years as chief operating officer, he finally stepped completely into the shoes of Tom Davis with a substantial triumph. It was a grand moment for the aviation lawyer turned airline visionary. His hunches about a deregulated world had paid off, and after 1983, he enjoyed the perks of taking over as head of Piedmont Aviation. When newspaper articles chronicled the success of one business gain or another for the airline, the face of William R. Howard was usually displayed prominently. Called "Piedmont's Pilot" in the *Winston-Salem Journal*, the not-so-subtle message went out to all that Tom Davis had passed the baton.[103]

Bill Howard grabbed hold with all his might. Assistant Comptroller Jack Walker said it best. "Bill Howard was determined to take Piedmont to higher ground, and quickly." He worked tirelessly to elevate Piedmont to the traveling public. While in Maryland for the Baltimore hub opening he accommodated the questions of a dozen reporters for as long as they wanted to ask them and did five phone interviews before leaving. He worked every angle of the next Piedmont move, even considering a name change for the company to demonstrate it larger horizons. He eventually gave up on renaming Piedmont, deciding instead that "the name was all right, but we needed to work on our image."[104]

His energy and enthusiasm for the task of leadership at Piedmont was best revealed when he became a victim of his own success. When he came to Winston-Salem, Bill Howard asserted that no "major" airline would be interested in the destinations to which Piedmont flew. For a while he was right, but after Piedmont posted double digit growth for a few years, major airlines like American began to take notice. The worst nightmare of Tom Davis had been realized. American Airlines moved to create a hub in Piedmont's territory, its home state, its capital: Raleigh. Jack Walker recounted how the new CEO relentlessly met the challenge spending "a good deal of time and effort convincing the Piedmont people that they were just as good and in many places better than people in any other airline. They were qualified. They were good. They fit the job." According to Walker,

> Bill Howard really went after our employees then, saying you are better than the people at American. You do a better job. You are more competent. And he said then we are going to run American out just as soon as they get in. And you know that he had people down at Raleigh when the American flight came in [the same tactic he used in Miami], who would count the number of people who got off. He teletyped that information back to Winston-Salem and as the route became profitable for American, Piedmont would put a flight on top of them, fifteen minutes before or something like that. I think the fare was cut too. American could not get to a profitable stance in Raleigh — was not being successful in Raleigh, so they eventually got out. By that time we had quite a number of planes going into Raleigh. Bill Howard just wanted to let the airline industry know — just don't step on Piedmont. We're little but we're mighty.[105]

Bill Howard was not averse to beating the larger airlines with their own tricks either. Since deregulation, many of the major carriers attempted to cut the throats of their rivals by reducing fares on flights between the same cities. Any time a carrier introduced a new lower fare, the other airlines immediately met it. Additionally, the early eighties saw a number of new airlines emerge as "low fare/low frill" operators, which also forced the bigger companies to reduce ticket prices. By staying out of flights between competitive markets, Piedmont often avoided the kind of hit on revenue that other airlines felt they had to take to stay competitive.

However, Piedmont could not always circumvent a challenge. In situations where the schedule called for flights between major centers with stops in between, Piedmont offered what it called the "hopscotch fare." If a passenger was willing to make a few stops along the way, they saved 40 percent on a one way ticket, 50 percent on a round trip. The fare appealed to bargain hunters who didn't mind the stops and the other major airlines almost always rushed to meet the price, even on their non-stop flights. The hopscotch fare was offered, as Vice President of Marketing Bill McGee explained, "Where we have a fractional piece of the market share." Piedmont kept its Pacemakers over half filled on flights from Atlanta to Washington with the stops it made in between. The hopscotchers only added to Speedbird flights that were already profitable. Carriers like Delta and Eastern who matched the fare eroded some of the hopscotch incentive, but not as much as Piedmont eroded their profitability for the trip. Vice President of Public Affairs Don McGuire politely refused to acknowledge the competitive factors involved when he remarked, "Our bottom line is not to outwit any other carrier, but to serve the people in our markets." His boss Bill Howard was much blunter. He said, "Somebody around here the other day said [the other airlines] had slit their wrists and tried to drown us in their blood. They may have picked up a few points on load factors, but they must have been seriously hurt."[106]

Piedmont Airlines had reached its maturity, playing the game like one of the majors. The Civil Aeronautics Board, still a nominal overseer of airline activity, defined "major" status (what used to be called a trunk carrier) as an airline with annual revenues totaling more than one billion dollars. In 1984 Piedmont broke the barrier and joined the group of airlines it once served as a feeder. For decades, Piedmont played a supporting role to the majors. Along the way, events had given Piedmont an opportunity to step up and make a name for itself. In the whirlwind of change brought by deregulation, Tom Davis recognized the tremendous growth experienced by his company. He gave a speech in 1982 where he noted that deregulation "has made possible greater expansion in only three years than we were able to achieve under the original Federal Aviation Act in 30 years. In this respect, Piedmont is unique since most of the airlines have not experienced the same result."[107]

The expansion had a profound impact on the employees of Piedmont. As each new hub opened, pride swelled when many contemplated how far the Speedbird had come from its earlier days. One tangible effect of the incredible growth was the prosperity that came along with it. Since its inception, Piedmont paid less than industry standard and though times were good, Bill Howard still hammered the 40 percent of Piedmont's workforce who were unionized for concessions.[108] Employees could, however, enjoy the fruits of their company's profitability by purchasing stock. Up to 30 percent of full time employees owned stock, and as it rose, their investment increased. The fate of one pilot resembled many when he revealed, "We could buy up to $500 worth and not pay any commission and get a little discount — a month. I bought $500 a month for years. When I retired, it was worth a fortune."[109] The history of Piedmont stock had been one of good risk for investors. It made them money. Tom Davis outlined just how good when he looked back from the perspective of 1982.

> An investor in our first public stock offering paid $1.00 per share. Since that time, our directors have declared four 10% and one 20% stock dividends. In addition, we have declared 30

cash dividends. If that early investor had bought 1,000 shares, he would now have 1,756 shares. Accordingly, the original $1,000 investment would now have a market value of approximately $44,000. And that's not all. In the meantime, that stockholder would have received $4,200 in cash dividends. To the best of my knowledge, none of the regional airlines and perhaps not more than two or three of the trunk airlines equal that record.[110]

With additional growth came additional employees. One important group with tremendous experience came from a casualty of the deregulation wars, Braniff Airways. After a distinguished and "colorful" career as an intercontinental airline, Braniff shut down operations abruptly in 1982, leaving thousands of employees high and dry. Luckily for many pilots, though, Piedmont needed trained personnel in the cockpit to facilitate its ever-increasing system. Because of the circumstances surrounding the bankruptcy, the federal government required airlines that intended to hire new pilots to first choose from the ones laid off by Braniff. The situation was a win-win for Piedmont and many Braniff pilots. Piedmont was expanding, and an experienced pool of pilots to choose from was fortuitous. Gene Sharp was among many who recognized the benefit for Piedmont. He commented, "From a safety standpoint and experience standpoint, I mean, we hit a home run when we hired those people, because we put experience in there, you couldn't go buy it. It wasn't available for sale. It just happened that that worked really great for us."[111]

Two hundred eighty Braniff pilots came to work for Piedmont. Bill Piper thought he would never fly again after the Braniff bankruptcy, but in less than a year, he joined the Speedbird force and found himself in an operation he described as "unique," saying that Piedmont was the kind of company "you rarely see." Piper added that Piedmont Airlines "opened their arms to all of the Braniff hirees that came in. We felt very welcomed." He noticed right away that Piedmont was "a people airline. They were interested in people that had the right attitude and work ethic and wanted to provide excellent service to their customers."[112] When asked why he thought Piedmont had developed into such a positive force, he cited the airline's founder, though Mr. Davis was moving out as Bill Piper was moving in. Piper said,

> Tom Davis was a very unique individual who was down to earth. And I think he chose people, I don't know if it was an accident or if it was his genius, but he chose people that had a good attitude and a good work ethic. He chose people that wanted to provide their customers with good customer service and he emphasized that people be friendly. And as a result of that, it was quite evident in the Piedmont operation. You could be walking down the hall and it didn't matter what level of person that you met, whether it was Mr. Davis himself or if it was the janitor, everybody would speak to you and he would speak to them and it was a friendly atmosphere, and that I think that has a lot to do with it.[113]

While most at the company made less than their industry counterparts, no one seemed to mind. Piedmont was known as a great place to work, not for the wages it paid, but for the atmosphere it created. Two examples of cost savings that matched up jobs needed with a ready workforce show Piedmont at its lean best. Peak flight times required the necessary personnel to meet the demand, but usually those times lasted for only a few hours, leaving some employees without anything to do for a substantial part of the day. Piedmont had just such a situation with tug drivers. They were the operators of small tractor type vehicles that backed planes out of the gate. After the morning rush of departures from Greensboro, Assistant Comptroller Jack Walker pointed out "a lag during the noon period until about 3:00 P.M., then it picks up again. Our regular people would start to work at 6:00 A.M. and they would be off at 2:30 or 3:00 P.M. and they were only working half the time." The solution was to bring in college students on a part-time basis. "We could bring them in at peak time, when you needed extra help. By 10:00 A.M. they were going back to Greensboro to go to school. They scheduled their classes around their work period." [114] Vice President of Flight Operations Gene Sharp added, "A lot of them were paying their college tuition"[115] with the money they made pulling planes in and pushing them out. As Jack Walker observed, there was a demand for the jobs Piedmont offered: "They wanted a job, and it was only $5 an hour but they could fly free. It paid us. We had a demand for those part time jobs. We could pick good people and it worked beautifully."[116] Explained Sharp, "We had a lot of people apply for those jobs because it benefited them and it benefited us."[117]

The fact that many of these workers were in college particularly interested Piedmont management. As Joe Wilson believed, "It gave us a leg up on being able to hire college graduates in these station agent, full time positions because they came with us as part-timers while they were in school and helped substantially to upgrade the education level in the company." In Wilson's opinion, the flying privileges offered by Piedmont made all the difference. "Particularly young people loved those flying privileges. We probably provided the most liberal free flying for part time agents of any airline in the industry, as I recall." Contrasted with other airlines that allowed only full time personnel the ability to fly for free on their planes, after stipulating that no employee could displace a paying customer, Piedmont felt it had nothing to lose and everything to gain by extending the offer to its part-time staff. Joe Wilson figured, "If people fly around on an airline on a space available basis, the only cost there was that you were filling a seat with an employee where it would otherwise have been empty, you've got the weight of the employee on there that uses up some fuel and maybe they get a free meal or something, and that's about all the cost to let them fly around."[118]

The same situation took place with reservation clerks who also experienced periods of peak demand, with some predictable rises and some that weren't. In much the same way that Piedmont had first made good use of student labor, reservations help was composed of seasonal workers and Winston-Salem housewives. According to Joe Wilson, "You had daily peaks, seasonal monthly peaks that you had to accommodate. What so many airlines did was they hired people who accommodated the peak periods and they still had them during their off periods, so they had a lot of lost productivity in not trying to tailor their staffing programs to their needs." Piedmont developed a way to plan for its periods of high demand without leaving workers idle during the slow times. Wilson formulated a staffing policy which added a new category between full time and part time worker. Under his guidance, the company "introduced the classification of intermediate agent, so what we wound up with in reservations was a full time agent, intermediate agent and a part time agent." The rationale for the new job was "that you had higher needs for six months of the year versus the other six months. So we created this intermediate agent which would work 40 hours a week half the year and 20 hours a week the other half. That took care of the seasonal swing. Then we took care of the daily swings by the way we staffed the part-timers."[119] For the daily spikes in demand, Gene Sharp recalled looking to women in the community who provided almost instant help. "If we needed to have two hundred more agents working the phones because we had a busy day or a bad weather day or something, they'd call them and they'd come right out. We could expand our reservations operation by twenty to thirty percent in a matter of thirty minutes. That was huge,"[120] said Sharp, who recalled paying those housewives roughly the same as the college kids and giving them the same perk of free airline travel.

While becoming one of the nation's top ten airlines, Piedmont endeavored to maintain its common sense approach to the business. Finding simple solutions to growth issues (like the use of part-timers) helped the company to maintain its momentum toward greater profitability and maintain a consistent attitude toward its business. Just as they did in the early years striving to keep the airline alive, Piedmont employees tried hard to find practical solutions to a new round of "growing pains." In June of 1983, Piedmont boarded over one million passengers in a single month. To handle the load, the Winston-Salem reservation center was invigorated with new computer equipment while new reservation centers went up in Nashville, Dayton and the Washington, D.C., suburb of Reston, Virginia.[121]

The milestones came quickly for Piedmont as the eighties rolled along. In March of 1983, a scheduling quirk "manned" a Piedmont flight departing Atlanta with an all female crew. In the cockpit were Captain Cheryl Peters Ritchie and First Officer Suzanne Alley, as well as an all female crew of flight attendants. *Atlanta Journal* columnist Ron Hudspeth noted the historic trip to Charlotte, then Washington "might be a first" in the airline industry. He called the flight "noteworthy," especially from Piedmont. With a much smaller workforce than either Delta or Eastern (he incorrectly numbered Piedmont at 900, instead of more accurately 9,000), which totaled 36,000 and 39,000 respectively; female pilots at Piedmont totaled eleven while Delta employed only three and Eastern had only two on its roster. Whether intended or not, Hudspeth argued that Piedmont Airlines deserved "gold star from pro–ERA [Equal Rights Amendment] groups."[122]

Coupled with new destinations and new employees, times were hectic for an airline that could no longer be deemed a "puddle jumper." But the Piedmont organization had plans for even greater expansion. Both Tom Davis and Bill Howard said that the Speedbird would never fly to the west coast just for the sake of calling Piedmont a continental airline. They always insisted that only when California destinations demonstrated that they would make money for the airline would they be added to the schedule. Flights to Denver, Colorado, began soon after deregulation, and that was as far as the airline reached for a while, but further expansion was impossible to resist. Piedmont folks found April Fools Day 1984 to be a joke on the big airlines. That day, the Speedbird began service into Los Angeles. Some industry analysts suggested that a North Carolina to L.A. flight would fly practically empty. Then again most of the moves made by the Winston-Salem carrier had confounded the airline industry, and this effort was no exception. The trip carried a full load to Los Angeles International Airport (LAX).

In preparation for the flight, everything was arranged except the planes themselves. According to Vice President of Operations Gene Sharp, "The airplanes that were supposed to be on that route did not have the extra fuel tanks so that they could go nonstop. Now fuel tanks were being added to the center section of the airplanes so that we could make it nonstop. But for the first few days we had to put what was called a short range 727 on there because they hadn't been modified."[123] These passengers had been promised nonstop service to L.A. and the inability to give them what had been advertised caused concern for the people of Piedmont, who went the extra mile to make it up to them. Gene Sharp recalled,

> In the seat back pocket, in front of the seat, where every passenger sits we told the people when we took off that we can't make it non stop today because we have a different airplane on here today and we're going to have to stop in Albuquerque for fuel and if you'll look in the seat back pocket in front of you, you'll find our appreciation for the fact that you're riding. We told you we'd make it nonstop but we just can't, so there is a little token of our appreciation for your taking us at our word, and there was a fifty dollar bill in the seat back pocket. That went on for about three of four days until we got the airplanes modified so we could do that.[124]

The move turned a potentially negative situation into an overwhelming positive. "You couldn't find anybody on that airplane that wasn't happy," commented Sharp, who also noted the airline did not have to make the concession but felt honor bound to compensate everyone who bought a ticket to fly Piedmont. With a chuckle he also remembered the lasting effect of the move. "We had people after a while looking in the seat back pocket to see if there was anything in there."[125]

Service to California had been a long time in coming. Since the advent of deregulation, planners at Piedmont eyed the west coast with eagerness, looking for the right time to offer flights. During that time, both Piedmont presidents played it close to the vest, never giving away their intentions until they were sure it was profitable to do so. "This effort began four and a half years ago, when we started seriously considering transcontinental service," said Vice President of Corporate Planning Richard James.[126] The interval required planners to consider an enhancement of services for the airline. First came the Piedmont Presidential Suites. Located in the terminals of major airports, the suites indulged members with a variety of services, like assistance in booking flights to "pouring complimentary soft drinks." Next, Piedmont reversed the decades old practice of identical treatment onboard no matter where passengers sat. First class service was inaugurated on the Charlotte to Los Angeles flight which included an enhanced variety of new entrées. Two years later, all Speedbirds offered first class service promoted by the slogan, "The company rated highest in service without even having First Class, introduces First Class."[127] Each of these moves followed the lead of what the larger airlines had been doing for some time. Piedmont accepted the need of such frills but implemented them in their own time, just like their larger business plan.

"A group of flight attendants pose for a quick shot before they perform the myriad tasks that keep passengers comfortable and happy during their flight. The uniforms are from the mid–80s. From top to bottom, Greg Miller, Tracey Silver, Carol Wright, and Pauline Fletcher (Pauline Thomas Collection).

Even with an occasional challenge, by all accounts, 1984 turned out to be a banner year for the Speedbird, the best in its history. Where the airline faced difficulties, the call to fix the problem brought the entire Piedmont family shoulder to shoulder. One example concerned flights arriving on time. For a year starting in September 1983, "on time" rates slipped for the airline. Even though "weather and air traffic control delays" accounted for much of the problem, Bill Howard focused attention on the trend with an "On Time in October" program. Implementing the initiative in the 62 airports served by Piedmont, Howard rallied employees to "restore the consumer's confidence in our ability to fly our schedule on time."[128] As a result, on time performance improved.

Most everything in the Speedbird game plan defied industry rules. Piedmont never connected the major metropolitan areas. Few in a deregulated world would have seen the wisdom in that, yet by 1984 Piedmont became the nation's ninth largest carrier with over 100 jet aircraft in its fleet. Nobody believed hubs in cities like Charlotte, Dayton, or Baltimore were advantageous, but a year after the three were established, 275 profitable flights left those cities each day. Many analysts complained that service from North Carolina to cities like Dallas and Los Angeles would starve Piedmont, but every year after deregulation, the airline increased earnings with over 58 million dollars to its credit in 1984, doubling its profit from the previous year.[129] If things weren't rosy enough, the General Aviation Group continued to expand with a facility in Monroe, North Carolina, and the corporation's aviation supply business planned to move west, just like the airline.

On many occasions, Piedmont decisions sounded "penny foolish" but turned out to be "pound wise." For instance, Piedmont cockpits were retrofitted to a uniform standard. The cost to standardize cockpits was expensive enough to keep other carriers from making the changes, but not Piedmont. C.D. McLean remembered, "We moved instruments; we moved controls; we moved a lot of stuff in the cockpit, just so that the pilot would feel comfortable stepping from one airplane to another." Alone in the industry, the folks in Winston-Salem felt standardization made sense on two levels, both of them advantageous to the company. First, pilots, who sometimes needed to make quick decisions, didn't have to search for switch and control locations. The sooner they found the switches to make their choices, the safer flights were. Secondly, the transition training time from one type of aircraft to another was reduced significantly as pilots, much more familiar with the controls the first time they entered a new plane's cockpit, were able to train quicker. "When you look at the savings as these pilots are progressing from one airplane to another and you look at the safety aspect of it, it's cheap, cheap, cheap," McLean asserted. "You cannot believe the savings that you realize from standardization." Remembering the fleet, he believed that Piedmont had in his opinion "the most standard cockpits in the world."[130]

At the end of five years of deregulation came an opportunity for the rest of the airline industry to catch up on what had been going on in a myriad of cities throughout the United States. One of the industry's most prestigious honors was *Air Transport World* magazine's Airline of the Year

In 1984 Piedmont Airlines was recognized for its tremendous growth and sterling reputation with the "Airline of the Year" award, given by *Air Transport World* magazine (Ronnie Macklin Collection).

Award. Piedmont Airlines received the award in 1984. In bestowing the prize upon Piedmont, *Air Transport World* defined its rationale in making the selection. "All during this expansion and traffic growth Piedmont has been able to make financial sense of it all, becoming a profit maker envied by most of the industry. Piedmont has also retained the qualities that it had all along, its friendly, courteous service and reasonable fare policies. In fact Piedmont has been one of the most successful in warding off threats for low-cost new entry operators, largely because of these qualities."[131]

The award shocked many in the airline industry but surprised few Piedmont employees. They knew how great their operation had been all along. The day after accepting the award, Bill Howard told employees, "This award was made possible because of a bond of faith we all have in one another."[132] That bond of faith had grown to include over 12,000 employees who worked collectively to generate one billion dollars in revenue.[133] Much was to be made of the award. The recognition served as both a beginning and an end. As the prize for the phenomenal growth and sterling reputation of the airline, many saw it as validation and thus as a way to reward everyone for the long climb to the top. After all, it was quite a transition in six years, to go from an efficient little airline making its daily bread on a hop across the Appalachians to Airline of the Year. Others saw the designation as a calling card to the rest of the world, heralding even greater things to come. Piedmont was now a player.

• 8 •

The Last Virgin, 1985–1987

As soon as deregulation became accomplished fact, airline management began to squirm. When CEOs finished toasting the prospect that the government would finally be off their backs, a new dread dawned, one more biting than anything ever possible in the regulated world. Instead of a straitjacket to confine their maneuverability in the marketplace, airlines suddenly gained enormous freedom to fly in any direction they chose, all directions if they wanted. Deregulation promised great possibilities for those who made the right moves, but the consequences would be painful for those who made the wrong ones. Under government control, even mediocre carriers could stay in business; without it, failure loomed as a very real option. Competition required new thinking, and luckily, Piedmont employed visionaries. Unfortunately, some competitors marched blindly into the future thinking their best in a regulated world would be good enough in a deregulated one. As the eighties dawned, so did aggressive forces that challenged carriers, major and minor, to vie for passengers. If they could not do so singularly, a last stop before total ruin was consolidation.

In those days, the newspapers were full of mergers. Pan-Am bought National Airlines. Southern, North Central, and Hughes Airwest came together as Republic. Frank Lorenzo went on a shopping spree buying Texas Air, Continental, People's Express and eventually Eastern Airlines. For the sake of profit, he ran them all into the ground.[1] The merger option gave airlines hope that if they could not make it on their own, a match up might save their company, at least in some form. Everyone in the airline business investigated partners for possible union, even Piedmont. And while Tom Davis publicly renounced the idea with his threat to "stick" takeover attempts via his "prickly pear" stance, Bill Howard had run the numbers on prospects. As early as 1981, he acknowledged an interest in building the airline through acquisition. When asked point blank by a North Carolina business publication reporter if Piedmont was looking to purchase another airline, Howard was forthright in saying, "No." He qualified that answer by adding, "I'd be less than candid, however, if I didn't admit that Piedmont continues to carefully examine the total airline industry for opportunities." He realized that many of his competitors suffered from competition and looked to mergers to bail them out of unprofitability. He concluded his observation by adding, "Under deregulation, it's clear that it will be easier to acquire airlines and easier to merge than it has been in the past. And as we expand, one of the things we'll carefully consider is acquisitions."[2] Later he played very coy about which airline Piedmont wanted to pair with, saying only "this mouse could have swallowed the elephant."[3] With the phenomenal growth Piedmont sustained in the years after deregulation, Bill Howard decided that the Speedbird would go it alone.

"Alone" hardly described the ownership structure of Piedmont Aviation, Inc. The company was publicly traded and thousands of people owned stock, including employees, investors, and anyone who wanted a good return on their money. One of the largest stockholders was also a customer of fixed base operations and also a transportation company. Based in the Piedmont city of Roanoke, Virginia, Norfolk and Western Railroad hired Piedmont to maintain two planes it owned as well as provide pilots for trips company officials wanted to take in those aircraft. Since railroads ceased to carry passengers (Norfolk and Western hauled a lot of coal) the two transportation sources did not directly compete with each other. Increasingly, Norfolk and Western expressed interest in Piedmont. In late 1981, Mr. Davis reached an agreement with the railroad. Piedmont issued new stock which Norfolk and Western bought, giving the railroad up to a 20.5 percent share of the airline. The signed document was called a "stand-still agreement" and remained in effect for the next five years. Terms of the agreement gave Piedmont time to grow without fear of takeover and with a significant infusion of capital from the sale of stock. Norfolk and Western expressed support of Piedmont's plan for growth and a strong belief that the investment would yield satisfactory results.[4]

Over the years, the relationship between Norfolk and Piedmont had been a good one for both carriers. Each company welcomed to its board officers from the other enterprise. Mel Blocker worked for both companies. A pilot for Piedmont, he flew the railroad's planes under the contract deal between the two. Blocker flew Norfolk Southern's management everywhere, mostly to meetings. The proximity to company leaders gave Mel Blocker the occasion to learn of the extent of the relationship between the railroad and the airline. "Sitting in a Lear Jet one time up in Washington D.C.," Blocker remembered N&W president Robert Claytor telling him about an ambitious strategy he had to create a "total transportation company" with Piedmont as part of the network. "He wanted a busing line. He wanted a freight line, a railroad, and an airline. He wanted them all. Well, he started out to get them," said Blocker.[5] As Norfolk-Southern expanded other transportation options, the management in Winston-Salem held the railroad to its promise of only one-fifth ownership in the airline, at least for the time being.

Tom Davis generally took a dim view of mergers, especially those involving Piedmont. In 1982, when the Newcomen Society recognized the carrier and asked Mr. Davis to present a brief overview, the airline founder took pride in the fact that his company's growth had been through its own effort. He told the group of business entrepreneurs,

> It might be of some interest to put in perspective Piedmont's size relative to its counterparts in the industry. In terms of revenue, passenger miles, number of passengers carried, route miles flown and other usual indices, there are only three of the eighteen originally certificated local service airlines — now referred to generally as regional airlines — that are larger. Those three, however, are larger only as the result of several mergers. In fact, Piedmont is one of only two of the original regional airlines whose growth has been entirely internal "boot strap" growth. And the other "virgin" is only about half as large as Piedmont.[6]

By that time Piedmont had already fended off one attempted takeover. In the first year of deregulation, Air Florida began to look at Piedmont with interest, as it did a number of other potential partners, including Air California, Emerald, and Western.[7] Piedmont avoided the offensive from other airlines but later looked with interest at the Florida market after Air Florida filed for bankruptcy following a deadly winter crash in Washington, D.C.

Piedmont Airlines was not interested in being on the acquired end of any purchase. Instead, management kept an ear to the ground for a smaller enterprise that might fit well with a growing airline. The first mating came in 1983 when Henson Airlines attracted some attention. Founded by aviation pioneer Richard Henson as a fixed base operation in Hagerstown, Maryland, the aviation company functioned as a small commuter line until 1962. For a time, Henson affiliated with Allegheny Airlines as a feeder to the larger carrier until after Allegheny changed its name to USAir in 1979. Flying between Washington, D.C., Baltimore and Philadelphia, Henson achieved a level of excellence that resulted in being awarded its own honor from *Air Transport World* magazine. In 1981, the publication cited Henson as the Regional Airline of the Year.[8]

Piedmont bought Henson and its fleet of Beech 99s, Shorts 3-30s, and Dehavilland Dash 7s.[9] Bill Howard negotiated the deal with Henson founder Richard Henson, throwing in a stipulation that almost broke the deal. "Dick and I made the Henson deal and were in complete agreement until I said the purchase price would be 10 percent cash and 90 percent stock," remembered Howard. Henson reacted negatively. "I said, 'Dick, do you realize our stock has gone from 5 dollars to 30 dollars since I've been here; it went up a dollar today.' He said, 'I don't know. I don't want stock.' But he eventually took it. He made a fortune. He made a fortune out of taking stock for his company."[10]

Keeping the Henson name, Piedmont added the designation "Piedmont Regional Airline" on the tailfin. Henson planes were repainted with a "Piedmont look" which included Piedmont colors and the Speedbird. Piedmont ramped up Henson's service area quickly to include Boston; Norfolk and Lynchburg, Virginia; Lewisburg, West Virginia; and Harrisburg, Allentown, and Wilkes-Barre, Pennsylvania. In Lewisburg, Piedmont filled a gap it had left during deregulation when it abandoned the town. Henson also beefed up its service to Long Island, New York, and Baltimore. In all, a total of 19 airports were served and under Piedmont's new wing. Henson upgraded its fleet to include eight new Dehavilland Dash 8 airplanes, seating 37 passengers.[11]

Two years later, Piedmont again looked north of the Mason-Dixon Line for an affiliate to feed passengers from smaller towns to the Speedbird's larger connecting points. In 1985, a small airline with the large sounding name of Jetstream International Airlines was targeted. Serving the western portion of Pennsylvania, Jetstream was originally known as Vee Neal Airlines, named after its owner, Vee Neal Frey. As another fixed base operator, Vee Neal Airlines began flying between Latrobe and Pittsburgh. Then, this small venture made a rather unusual aircraft buy, not unlike that of the Japanese YS-11 planes purchased in the late sixties. Vee Neal bought six Jetstream 31 planes, made by British Aerospace. With the acquisition came the name change to Jetstream International Airlines. The new identity reflected hopes for the company's future. The airline began flying east to New York, Washington, D.C., and Philadelphia but also spread its reach west to include cities of the upper Midwest like Cleveland, Detroit, and Chicago. In September of 1985, Jetstream International affiliated with Piedmont as another commuter feeding Speedbird flights. After less than a year, Piedmont chose to buy Jetstream outright, making it a "wholly-owned subsidiary" in August of 1986. In taking full control of the airline, Piedmont officials moved the Jetstream International fleet to Dayton, Ohio, to assist Britt Airways as another commuter line for the Dayton hub.[12]

The hub system created the need for a supporting commuter system. First, Britt Airways, and then Jetstream, supplied connections in Dayton, giving customers even more cities from which to start a journey in the air. Piedmont's first venture into a complementary commuter system centered around its first hub in Charlotte. CCAir, formerly Sunbird Airlines, fed Charlotte's Douglas Airport from surrounding cities like Kinston and Hickory, North Carolina, both of which had been part of the Piedmont system during the regulated era. Even Winston-Salem received service from CCAir, giving Piedmont's hometown a means to still fly Piedmont, if not from the origination point, at least to a destination. While CCAir did not return service to some of the smallest cities abandoned by Piedmont during deregulation, the commuter did add a number of locations. Of the twelve cities feeding into Charlotte daily, five were new sites for Piedmont via its affiliate.[13]

Like the hubs, commuters feeding Piedmont proved to be a very successful venture. Besides the fact that passengers gained a convenient way to make their connection, the relationship worked well for both Piedmont and the commuter line. The agreement between the two provided the commuter with enhanced status as their planes flew into the hub airports under Piedmont's designation of PI. Additionally, commuter flights were included within Piedmont's own schedule. Piedmont handled reservations for both, and incorporated the smaller airlines into its marketing plans. Piedmont exchanged this operational assistance for the right to direct the commuter's schedules as the larger airline needed, and to repaint all the commuter planes in the white and blue (with some red) Speedbird colors. With CCAir in Charlotte, and Britt and Jetstream in Dayton, the addition of two more carriers gave the trunk line (as Piedmont now was) even more flexibility. As Piedmont grew so did its affiliates. Winston-Salem management soon signed commuter deals with Trans Air in Florida and Brockway in New England, even though Piedmont had bigger plans for both markets.

The Florida market had always been an inviting one for Piedmont. One of the first cities to which Piedmont flew in the early days of deregulation was Miami. After a failed attempt to take over Piedmont in 1979, Air Florida slid into bankruptcy, leaving the Sunshine State without the kind of air service Bill Howard and company felt the market demanded. By 1985, Piedmont recognized Florida as "a burgeoning population with perhaps the most tourist travel of any state and a thriving business community with an economic vitality far greater than most states." Company analysis determined that Florida held enormous potential. Saying "It is a deceptively large state that lacked daily jet flights timed for morning out, evening return service between its major cites," Piedmont put together a covert plan to serve all of Florida in one grand sweep. They called it "Project Omaha" to keep the plan as top secret as possible.[14]

Bill Howard and company conceived a unique way to serve Florida. It might have been easy to apply the "hub mentality" to the state since it had worked so well in three previous situations. But to answer the air travel needs of a rather diverse market, they took a new approach. Instead of flying to one centralized location, the situation called for operations that spread service throughout the state, especially since a myriad of destinations were seen as likely vacation spots. In addition to Miami, the Speedbird also regularly flew into Orlando, Tampa, Jacksonville, Key West, and West Palm Beach. But analysis proffered that the state needed more.[15]

Once the plan became public, they christened it the "Florida Shuttle." It was the "largest, single expansion of service ever to occur in one state." Beginning October 1, 1985, the Speedbird launched 68 jet flights each day that connected ten Florida cities, including Naples, Gainesville, Tallahassee, Pensacola, Fort Lauderdale, and Daytona Beach, as well as those already served by Piedmont. The difference was that the Florida Shuttle was just what its name implied: an inter-state airline. Its affiliate, Trans Air, helped out with flights to even more communities in the Sunshine State—Sarasota, Melbourne, and Fort Myers among them. To further complement the Florida Shuttle, Trans Air flew daily routes to the islands of the Bahamas, giving passengers even more vacation destinations.[16]

Beyond the logistical issues associated with scheduling and executing so many flights, the most consequential decision concerning the Florida Shuttle was finding the right plane

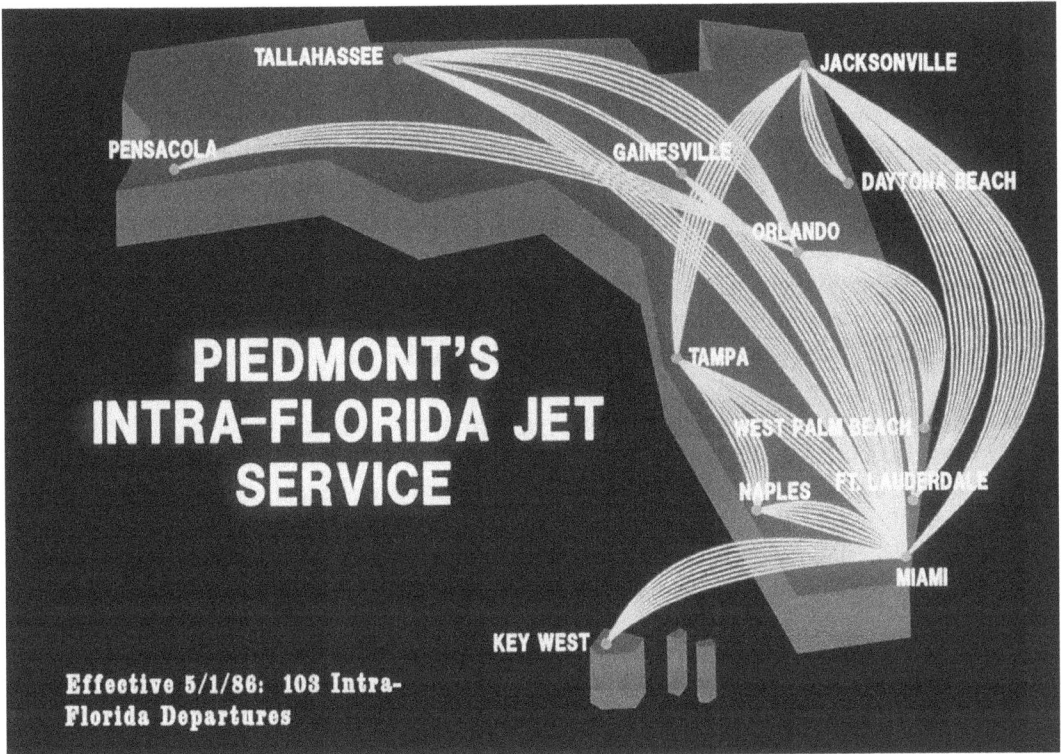

One of the most lucrative services was the Florida shuttle, which gave Piedmont instantaneous recognition in Florida as well as connecting points to the many cities already served. This slide showed employees the company's growth (Piedmont Silver Eagles Collection).

for the short hops. Explained Senior Vice President of Passenger Services Leonard Martin, an architect of the project, "We needed a smaller airplane for route development."[17] The Boeings were too large for flights that were sometimes as short as one hundred miles. The choice for the Florida routes was the Dutch-made Fokker F-28. Having had unsatisfactory experience with Fokker, like the American-made version of the F-27 in the late fifties, it seemed a questionable choice, but the new jet version provided an economy of flight that made the Florida Shuttle profitable, and again, like the 737-300s, the deal was a good one, as Gene Sharp explained: "We had an opportunity to buy some F-28s from Garuda [an Indonesian airline] and taking those airplanes back through Fokker in the Netherlands, just totally refurbishing the airplanes. They weren't quite new airplanes but they were about as close to it as you can get with an older airplane. They redid the fuselage, they redid the engines, they redid everything. They put a new interior in it. It was almost a brand new airplane."[18]

The F-28-1000 sat 65 passengers with an effective range of over 750 miles. At the same time the 20 Garuda planes were being refurbished, Piedmont also bought ten brand new models of the F-28, the 4000 series.[19] In support, over 1,000 employees were added to man the Florida Shuttle. Some went to the new maintenance facility and crew base in Miami. Others worked at the F-28 training center in Tampa. Meanwhile, a headquarters for reservations generated by the shuttle was built in Orlando at a cost of $4 million.[20] The growth at Piedmont had become exponential.

The refurbishing of the planes from Garuda Airlines took Piedmont officials to Europe to oversee the work. Don Collins went to Woensdrecht, Holland, as Piedmont's representative. "I had come home in each [F-28 and would] and turn around and go back [to get another when it was ready]," said Collins, who, off and on, spent about three years in Holland on the project while he also worked as a maintenance manager at the Greensboro facility. The purchase moved along smoothly until a problem developed on the F-28. During flight, the plane vibrated when the flaps were lowered. Fokker soon fixed the problem after Don Collins got the support he needed from back home. "We had a conference call. The pilots were there and they had Gene Sharp and Mr. Cartwright on [the U.S.] end. So Gene asked the pilots, 'Would you guys fly the airplane on the schedule if you brought it home?' They said, 'No, we'll fly it home but we won't fly it on schedule.' Mr. Cartwright said, 'Do you hear me?' I said, 'Yeah I hear you.' He said, 'Well tell them to fix the damn thing and we will buy them, understand?' 'Yes sir.'"[21]

Fokker listened to Don Collins's solution, corrected the problem and completed the sale. Perhaps the most pivotal issue in the whole enterprise was not the planes themselves but, instead, the pilots needed to fly the routes. The F-28 was a smaller plane than anything in the Piedmont fleet since the YS-11, and pay rates for flying them were going to be considerably less than what jet pilots were accustomed to. "We knew we couldn't pay the pilots the same thing to fly those airplanes that we were paying for the 737s," said Leonard Martin, who added,

> So Bill Howard and the flight operations people and the human resources people sat down with the pilots and said we've got these 20 airplanes and if we want to buy them Fokker Aircraft will run them through the factory and bring them out zero time on everything on the

The craftsmen who refurbished Piedmont's F-28s from Garuda. Taken to Fokker's headquarters in Woensdrecht, Holland, the last of the F-28s rolls off the assembly line ready to fly to the U.S. in September 1985. In the crowd is Don Collins, who oversaw the project for Piedmont (Don and Audrey Collins Collection).

airplanes. We can buy them, but we cannot pay more than 60 percent of the 737 rate for the front end crew. And if you'll agree to this, we'll buy the airplanes; if you don't, we're going to let them go. So they agreed to the contract. We bought the airplanes, and we set up what we called the Florida Shuttle.[22]

A number of the pilots who flew the Florida Shuttle came from Braniff. Even if they were not flying Piedmont's big jets, many were back in the cockpit much sooner than they had expected. Gene Sharp remembered, "That's where a lot of the Braniff guys ended up being captains on the airplane."[23] One of them was Bill Piper, who characterized his ascension to captaincy as "very rapid, almost unheard of." Piper came to work for Piedmont about a year after the Braniff bankruptcy and marveled at the success of Project Omaha. "Piedmont basically controlled the intrastate Florida market," he remarked, citing the precision with which the operation ran. "They had aircraft going clockwise and counterclockwise around the state servicing the various Florida cities and the reception of the customers was very positive." Bill Piper believed that because the Florida Shuttle confined its flying to Florida only, flights remained on time. He explained, "The airplanes were on time because we kept them in the state, and we didn't have to contend with traffic in places like New York or weather in other parts of the country that caused delay. So it was very much on time, which the people liked."[24]

The shuttle proved to be a triumph. A month after startup, flight capacity exceeded expectations, "surpassing the break-even level."[25] As Vice President of Operations Gene Sharp phrased it, "Piedmont, at one point, just basically owned Florida as an airline."[26] Leonard Martin pointed out how destitute Florida had become for air service before Piedmont arrived. He said, "Tallahassee had basically no air service at all to get around the state, which they needed very badly—and then we would feed the big airplanes for the long haul with those airplanes. It was an absolute instant success."[27] The feat was made all the sweeter by a point Gene Sharp made about some who still questioned the Piedmont methodology: "It was interesting to note that there were some—I guess I'll call them aviation reporters—that said they didn't think that was a wise move because they thought it would take a long time to be profitable. We were profitable 45 days after that operation started. And I mean a sizeable profit."[28]

The Florida Shuttle followed the pattern of the earlier hubs and the recent acquisitions. They all flourished. Each expansion complemented the other. Bill Piper noticed that a hub like Dayton brought a lot of travelers down from Michigan and Ohio into Florida. "When they got there, they could get on the Florida shuttle and go to any of the other towns in Florida," said Piper, adding, "The aircraft was small, but it served the purpose of serving towns like Pensacola and Tallahassee and Gainesville, the smaller towns. We had frequent service, and I think the people enjoyed it, and we enjoyed servicing them."[29] An astonished airline industry ate some crow and then waited to see if Piedmont could keep the streak alive and turn more secret projects into gold. Winston-Salem's gaze soon turned to the heavily competitive Northeast Corridor.

Speedbird officials made two moves in the industrial northeast, solidifying Piedmont as a viable airline competitor. In March of 1986, Brockway Air came onboard as an affiliated commuter service, and like TransAir in Florida, flew folks around New England, from Boston to Buffalo with quite a few smaller cities in between. The Brockway route included Burlington, Vermont; Poughkeepsie, New York; and Atlantic City, New Jersey. The move was designed to give Piedmont the assistance it needed to help strengthen its latest purchase. Unlike the Florida model, where Piedmont started its own air service, Bill Howard chose instead to take advantage of one that was already established. It was called Empire Airlines.

In the late seventies, Paul Quackenbush started Empire in upstate New York to serve smaller towns of the Mohawk Valley after deregulation made service for larger carriers optional. Initially, Quackenbush refused to even discuss the sale of his airline, and in Bill Howard's words, said, "Thank you, but no thank you." Refusing to take no for an answer, Howard promptly wrote members of Empire's board of directors. In his letter, he said that Piedmont was prepared to make a premium offer for shares of the company, "but thus far at least, Mr. Quackenbush has not been inclined to accept it nor has he let it be before the board. I just want you to know what's going on here." Quickly, board members contacted Howard about the offer. "They said, 'We've never heard of this, and we are very much interested,'" remembered Howard. He promptly sat down with the board and hammered out a deal. Bill Howard recalled the vote on Piedmont's final offer. "Eventually all voted for it except Quackenbush, who voted no, and we acquired them."[30] By the time Piedmont bought Empire, Paul Quackenbush had made his own deal with City of Syracuse officials to move the company's base from the nearby town of Utica. The plan called for 1,000 new jobs and renovations to Syracuse's Hamilton International Airport. Unfortunately for the city fathers and the deal, Empire's financial situation plummeted. The *Syracuse Herald-Journal* reported net revenue for Empire went from a $2.25 million in 1984 to a staggering loss of $5 million in 1985. Piedmont saw Empire as an appealing acquisition plum.[31]

The purchase of Empire Airlines would have gone smoothly if not for the promises made by Quackenbush in his move to Syracuse. When Piedmont announced its purchase of Empire for $42.5 million, Syracuse officials felt cheated, as if none of the earlier pledges would be honored. The city filed a $96 million suit against Piedmont. At issue was the thousand jobs and the airport upgrade promised, a point Piedmont officials were vague about when announcing the purchase. For six months, legal action threatened a good relationship between the new owner of Empire and the city into which it would be flying.[32] Conversely, Empire's board of directors overwhelmingly approved Piedmont's offer of $15 per share for a stock that was trading at $9.25 when the merger was announced.[33] Bill Howard soon understood that something had to happen to solve what was quickly becoming a public relations nightmare.

In late June of 1986, parties for all sides sat down and worked out an agreement. Piedmont's side proved to Syracuse Mayor Tom Young that had Empire remained in business, it could not possibly have fulfilled the provisions of its contract with the city. Once city officials accepted the position, they became amenable to Piedmont's offer of 625 new jobs (to go with the 475 already employed in Syracuse) and a $4 million effort to invigorate Hamilton International Airport. In exchange, Syracuse dropped its demand that Piedmont relocate a reservations center from Utica. "Litigation between the city and Piedmont should never have happened," said attorney William Clarke.[34] As Piedmont's legal counsel in the affair, he arranged meetings between the two sides to rectify the situation before the matter ended up in court. "It was based on a misunderstanding on both sides," he said. "It was really a question of getting people to see the other guy's point of view ... once the personalities got out of the way, things went well."[35]

Fears about the merger were not confined to the politicians of Syracuse. Empire employees uneasily waited to see what the takeover meant to them. Piedmont held numerous meetings to explain how management intended to blend the two companies, but one mechanic remained unconvinced. During a meeting in Utica with a blinding snowstorm raging outside, the mechanic told the senior vice president of operations that he believed "those boys from Greensboro are going to come up here and take [our] jobs." Looking outside at the wind blowing and the snow flying sideways, the vice president was stunned that anyone from upstate

New York would believe that someone from North Carolina would voluntarily give up a sunnier climate to seek a job there. He told the mechanic, "Nobody's coming up here to take your job, pal. You got it."[36]

With the purchase of Empire Airlines, Piedmont gained another 1,000 employees, 17 Fokker F-28 4000s, and a new Syracuse hub, as well as the Utica maintenance and reservations centers.[37] In return, Empire gave its new owner two Canadian destinations, Ottawa and Montreal. It also gave Piedmont 53 flights a day carrying about 130,000 passengers annually, with expectations of substantial growth in the coming years. The purchase netted Piedmont more arrivals and departures from airports in and around New York, including for the first time, JFK International Airport. The Speedbird's presence continued to grow in the Northeast, a region known for its fierce competition among airlines.

The acquisition of the new carrier also brought the daunting task of erasing the Empire identity and creating a Piedmont one. Prior to the official takeover, pilots and flight attendants from Empire flew to Winston-Salem for retraining so the new group would fit in seamlessly with the old Piedmont veterans. Station personnel also received instruction from a Piedmont point of view. The biggest obstacle to re-branding the airline was the changing everything that said "Empire" to "Piedmont" before opening for business on May 1. Leonard Martin headed up the operation and told local reporters, "If you see an Empire sign on the airport roadway or terminal building by May 1, we've messed up." He added, "If done properly every Empire sign should disappear by 1:30 [A.M.]." Employees spent over 3,000 man hours and $1 million to change 263 roadway signs and over 300 signs at terminals across the northeast. Additionally, every Empire plane got a makeover that included repainting, but also "new color radars, windshields, landing gear, controls, windshear equipment, galleys, coffee pots and closets," costing around half a million dollars per plane. A total of $14 million had been set aside for the conversion. This expense was significant, considering that the cost of buying the entire airline amounted to $42.5 million.[38] However, the company noted that the Empire's price was little more than the cost of two new Boeing 737-300s.[39]

Acquisitions for Piedmont came in many forms. Henson and Empire brought in a sizable number of employees, each an important component in helping the company to grow and prosper. But Piedmont also acquired some new ways of thinking thanks to the management structure that was coming onboard in the Bill Howard era. Among the most controversial was the replacement for Zeke Saunders. The new senior vice president of operations was a Navy veteran who came to Piedmont from Western Airlines by the name of Gordon Bethune. Coming from the west coast to the east, Bethune instantly felt the difference when he arrived in Winston-Salem in early 1984. When shown his office, Zeke's old one, he was shocked at the presence of a rotary dial telephone. "It was kind of like in a time warp, but at the same time in a classy way," he recalled. As they did when Bill Howard arrived, many wondered what contribution Gordon Bethune would make to Piedmont's future. As Bethune saw it, "I was there to help them do the things they wanted to do, not to redesign their product. They had a good product, and they had a good delivery."[40] He lent his expertise to helping the company work out problems and find ways to streamline the operation.

However, Bill Howard had bigger plans for Piedmont Airlines. Some of his goals had been reached by the time Gordon Bethune arrived, but Howard's agenda listed more. "He was the driver of innovation and change. Otherwise, [Piedmont] would not have taken off the way they did," acknowledged Bethune. "Piedmont was a great company, but it was Bill Howard who kind of kicked it in pants and got it going across the country, and into Florida and across the pond."[41] The expansion that Piedmont had experienced before the arrival of

Bethune and others brought during the Bill Howard era only foretold even more ambitious moves down the road. The head of the company needed this new blood to assist him in making it happen.

Gordon Bethune was part of a new generation of management for Piedmont. With industry connections and a pile of experience under their belts from other airlines, this new group brought fresh ideas to Piedmont. The phone system was just the beginning. "We needed to be able to talk to all the chief pilots or all the maintenance stations on a conference call without going through the operator downtown to set up a conference call," remembered Bethune. "So I got our communication people (I found out they worked for me) to go to Western and I got the people at Western to show them the switching networks. Western had to have a communications system within the company so that you could do those kinds of things." Gordon Bethune facilitated change in a way never seen before at Piedmont Airlines. When he asked how foremen in maintenance were chosen, the answer precipitated an overhaul of the system. Instead of department heads selecting who they thought might be the best choice from the available employee pool, Bethune sought to objectify the process and give workers who wanted to move up but had been overlooked a chance. He also removed a dearly cherished criterion for advancement. Among the job requirements for positions like foreman were longtime service with Piedmont, so people coming into those jobs knew the company way. As the new senior vice president of operations, Bethune pointed out that even he wasn't qualified for the job under those restrictions. He demanded such constraints be removed, saying, "You just had to break through those kind of barriers because that wasn't the way the company had been run or thought about."[42]

Gordon Bethune shook up the status quo at Piedmont. He admitted, "I think while Bill didn't always appreciate some of the sparks that flew, he knew that was what was needed. That's why he hired somebody from the outside like me ... he needed somebody to help him kind of do that 'cram down.'" Old ways could not carry the airline to its next step, Bethune felt. A more businesslike approach was needed. "While I admire and respect Tom Davis, he built the culture and the foundation, it's Bill who was really the second stage rocket that took off and that is why Piedmont did as well as it did."[43]

There were no sacred cows in Winston-Salem, as far as Gordon Bethune was concerned. He came to improve

After Mrs. Tom Davis died in 1985, her contribution to the success of Piedmont Airlines was honored by naming a 737-300 the *Nancy Davis Pacemaker*. There for the ceremony were (left to right) Gordon Bethune, Bill McGee, Bill Howard, Tom Davis, Zeke Saunders, and Bob Northington."

performance for his company and continued to strive for it as long as he was there. He liked a good idea wherever he saw it and had no trouble giving people his opinion about what he felt were bad ideas. During the Empire merger he went to Syracuse and found that Piedmont could benefit from what was going on there with the F-28. Realizing that the crews at Empire had been operating that airplane a lot longer than Piedmont, he asserted that they were "quite frankly more efficient and so one of my challenges in also overseeing the maintenance department there was not to have Piedmont rewrite the maintenance standards for the F-28 but to really follow the examples set by Empire on things like engine changes and the efficiency they were able to do." For example, he said, "We had traditionally taken two shifts to change an engine, but the people at Empire routinely did it in one. I said, 'We were going to learn how to do it in one, not to make Empire do it in two.'"[44] Gordon Bethune was tough and some did not like his style. They felt that his operational style and his ideas clashed with the Piedmont way. Certainly they had never seen anything like him in Winston-Salem. However, Piedmont, under Bill Howard, had ambitious goals. Bethune pushed people and even somewhat bullied them at times to get where he felt the airline needed to go — to the status of a major U.S. carrier.

A big airline needed a big time marketing plan that included an advertising campaign to bring more passengers to the seats. In the eighties, Piedmont gained for itself its own spokesman, one who truly believed in the product. Television personality McLean Stevenson, most well known for his role as Colonel Henry Blake on the CBS series, *M*A*S*H*, starred in a series of commercials pitching Piedmont as the "up and coming airline." The mating of Stevenson and Piedmont came quite by accident after the actor had an encounter with the airline. In 1980, the *M*A*S*H* star was in North Dakota making an appearance when he received word that his father was very ill, and that he needed to get to New York soon if he were to see him before he died. When he reached Cincinnati and found that his connecting flight had been cancelled, Stevenson said, "I was absolutely beside myself. I guess I made a real idiot of myself, jumping up and down and screaming at the ticket agent that I absolutely had to get to New York; that my father was dying. Well, while I was making a fool of myself, a young man in a blue jacket with this dippy little bird on the pocket came up and said, 'If you'll allow me, I'll help you get to New York.' He seemed eager to help so I gave him my baggage tickets and he said to go to such-and-such a gate, and he'd meet me there, and he'd take care of ... everything."

Stevenson went to the gate, where the Piedmont employee escorted he and his bags to the plane. "I didn't know I was on Piedmont until we were in flight. When we landed at LaGuardia in New York, here come another young man, and he had a blue jacket with a dippy bird on the pocket too. He offered to drive me to the hospital." ... He took me down to baggage claim, got my bags and carried them outside to his own car, which was illegally parked right outside the baggage claim."

The Piedmont employee drove Stevenson to the hospital and carried his bags to the lobby, and "before he left he gave me a piece of paper with his name and telephone number on it. He said, 'If you need me, just call. I'm only about half an hour away.' I didn't even think about it. I didn't even thank him. I just put the paper in my pocket and went up to my father's room.... I just had time to tell him I loved him, and say goodbye, and then he died."

A couple of weeks after this, Stevenson realized that I never would have been able to see my father at all if those two young men hadn't helped me get to him before he died." Unable to find the piece of paper that he'd been given by the second Piedmont employee, Stevenson called Piedmont headquarters in Winston-Salem. "This girl says, 'Piedmont Airlines,' and I said 'This is McLean Stevenson. I want to talk to the president.' She says, 'Just a minute.' And the man comes on the line and says, 'This is Bill Howard.' I told him the whole story. I said I wanted to thank these two guys, but I didn't know their names and I didn't know how to go about looking for them. He said he'd see what he could do."[45]

Bill Howard never determined which two of his employees helped the *M*A*S*H* star, but the relationship between McLean Stevenson and Piedmont Airlines bloomed to the point that Stevenson introduced much of the nation to the Winston-Salem based carrier through commercials.[46]

Piedmont looked for innovative and unique ways to advertise. For years, members of the company enjoyed the southern sport of stock car racing. In 1982, the Speedbird was affixed to the side of a stock car as Piedmont sponsored its first race team. Winston-Salem team owner Richard Childress secured Piedmont as a sponsor of his number three car with Ricky Rudd as the driver. The team won several races, including Riverside, California, and Martinsville, Virginia. Sponsorship moved to Terry Labonte's car in 1984. That season, the same year the company won "Airline of the Year," Piedmont's NASCAR team won the Winston Cup points championship, which referred to the cigarette brand, not the city.[47] The Piedmont name continued to spread, facilitating stupendous growth for the airline.

With the help of a myriad of employees and inventive marketing plans, Piedmont Airlines had grown into a large carrier. Everything seemed to be expanding, every indicator of performance setting a new record. In 1986, the Speedbird flew over 24 million passengers, 100,000 in a single day on November 30. Revenue for the year was $1.86 billion and net profit totaled over $72 million. Piedmont helped Boeing introduce the 737-400, signing on as a launch customer and buying 25 of them. The airline also moved up to the 767, taking delivery of six and placing options for six more. Both the Charlotte and Baltimore hubs were going through massive expansions, with the one in Charlotte estimated to cost $90 million.[48] And through "Henson, the Piedmont Regional Airline," Piedmont added flights to the Bahamas to augment those flown by the commuter. All the while, Piedmont Airlines made a substantial effort not to feel like a big airline in the mold of American or United. Kenneth Carlson noticed the attempt, once writing, "After Piedmont started its unprecedented growth following deregulation, the hometown feeling of a Piedmont flight remained. Even when things sometimes went wrong, when the airline made a mistake in booking or lost some luggage, the Piedmont people invariably were courteous and caring. They seemed to take pride in helping. They took the time to listen."[49]

One sure sign that demonstrated the company could not escape its size was the need to establish a new corporate headquarters. During the Davis years, space had always been found adjacent to Smith Reynolds Airport. However, by the mid–eighties, Piedmont had outgrown the facility both as a passenger destination and as a corporate headquarters. The search began for a new facility. Across town, Bill Howard commissioned the construction of two buildings to handle Piedmont's current and future needs. One Piedmont Plaza, provided 159,000 square feet of office space while the second building added another 132,000.[50] A large Speedbird and the name Piedmont were emblazoned across the top of the larger building, telling all of Winston-Salem that Piedmont had completely outgrown its hometown airport but not its hometown.

Eventually, the success grew to such enormity that cities came looking for Piedmont to serve them, quite a switch from the early days of the air carrier when it begged for new cities. The day had come when petitioning for airline service came from the opposite direction. One day in Winston-Salem, a curious billboard appeared along Liberty Street. All it said was "Wichita." As many drove up and down the road, where Piedmont's old headquarters were

Across town from Smith Reynolds Airport, Piedmont Aviation under Bill Howard constructed a new headquarters, more expansive than anything employees had yet witnessed. Unfortunately, the Piedmont name would not be affixed to the building for long (Ronnie Macklin Collection).

located, and saw the sign, some head scratching seemed in order. They wondered what the billboard was marketing and to whom. Piedmont folks caught on first. When asked by reporters, Vice President of Public Affairs Don McGuire quipped, "We suspect that somebody in Wichita had something to do with it." Jokingly, he added, "I don't think Omaha bought it." In truth, the billboard was just the latest ploy on the part of the Wichita Chamber of Commerce to attract the attention of the airline, and McGuire knew it. Earlier, the chamber had sent gifts, including popcorn and balloons to the Winston-Salem corporate headquarters to keep the name of Wichita in front of company officials looking for a new city to serve. Bill Howard had already met with both senators from the state. Senator Bob Dole even "popped in" twice to discuss Piedmont expansion in Kansas.[51]

Wichita, Kansas, was already served by eight other airlines as it made a play for Piedmont. However, getting to the east coast, especially North Carolina, was a chore for travelers from Wichita and city officials wanted to rectify the situation. Said economic development head for Wichita's chamber Larry Danielson, "It's no secret to Piedmont that we in Wichita are very actively seeking additional air service, and we know that Piedmont Airlines is a growing and healthy airline. And we would like to see them have a presence in our city."[52]

Everyone at Piedmont relished the attention. Don McGuire acknowledged the position in which it put the airline: "It's pretty appealing to be courted." He continued, "It's getting awfully hard to resist."[53] Now a star in the airline industry, Piedmont Airlines attracted a lot of attention. The efforts of the Sunflower State did not ultimately pay off. Wichita, Kansas, never became a Piedmont city, except as an alternate from Kansas City.

The rules of the airline industry had changed as a result of deregulation. The move of companies in the eighties was toward each other, with a number of significant mergers along the way. From time to time, Piedmont had played with the "bigger boys" and had created successful ventures for both parties. One such example was a marketing agreement with Trans World Airlines (TWA). Just after Eastern Airlines became part of Frank Lorenzo's monster Texas Air Corporation, Piedmont arranged with TWA to link domestic Piedmont flights with overseas trips on TWA, making transition from one airline to the next as seamless for the customer as possible. Piedmont promoted scheduled flights to New York's JFK Airport that allowed passengers to quickly board TWA flights to 20 cities in Europe and the Middle East. Commenting on the deal, Bill Howard said, "The two companies complement each other."[54]

Success for Piedmont came thanks to a combination of several factors. Timing had played a role as deregulation opened doors for the airline. A customer oriented workforce had given the company a solid foundation upon which the company had expanded. Much of that expansion relied on the southern work ethic of Piedmont's employees. Simply stated, Piedmont got more work out of its employees than other airlines. As Bill Howard phrased it, "We worked in such a way that the same man that signaled the airplane in could put the chocks in the wheels and could pull out the electric cart and plug it in to the air conditioner. It all could be done by one or two guys. Other airlines required a person for each job." As a result, Bill Howard could match his labor costs against any other airline with pride.[55] In reality, it was the same kind of can-do spirit that distinguished Piedmont Airlines from the beginning. Long-time employee Philip Beeson recognized what had changed, but more importantly, he saw what remained the same. "We were a trunk carrier now and with that you will have changes and different ideals, but we still had the major Piedmont Spirit we all grew up with."[56] Amid the changes, he still found the heart of the company intact and ready to serve.

The qualities that had always made Piedmont a special carrier were now displayed before a more national audience and the comparison pleased administrators like Gordon Bethune. Comparatively speaking, the Speedbird shined. "Piedmont had a customer service reputation and it was competing with—I would suspect you call them laggards—and it gave us a hell of an advantage," said Bethune as he took aim at some of the other major airlines in the mid–eighties. "Don't forget that we were advantaged because our main competitor was Delta. So you're already three steps ahead of the race when you were dealing with someone from Delta at the time."[57] Just as Gordon Bethune never minced words about how he wanted to improve Piedmont, he likewise evaluated his competition with brutal honesty. The industry tended to agree with Bethune's assessment and continued to bestow awards on Piedmont. In 1986, *Air Transportation World*, the same magazine that had recognized Piedmont as the "Airline of the Year" two years earlier, lauded the Winston-Salem company with its Financial Management Award.

Even with the spending sanctioned by Bill Howard, Piedmont Airlines remained a frugal operation as it grew in stature, like Mr. Davis first had taught his people. Personnel still sought out a good deal to save the Piedmont bottom line some money. C.D. McLean, having spent 28 years with the company, learned the lesson well. While overseeing operations and looking for flight simulators, he ran across a bargain. He remembered,

> I started looking for simulators and they were incredibly expensive. I found one that was up in Montreal in a food warehouse. Several African nations had gone together and bought this simulator. They were going to have a big flight training academy over in one of the countries there in West Africa, but nobody could ever come up with the money. So they put the simulator in a food warehouse. We needed a simulator really, really, really bad and Gordon

[Bethune] said go up there and take a look at that thing. I went up there and looked through the environment that sucker was in and the surroundings. We opened up a couple of panels, didn't see any corrosion or anything. I said Ok, Let's bid on this thing. We did and we got it for just a fraction of what a new simulator would cost. We moved that thing to Winston-Salem, and I guess it's still running in the Charlotte training center right now (2005). It was an incredible simulator, state of the art. We bought it for like ten cents on the dollar. But Piedmont was that way. They would look for a deal, and we found one because in that food environment, the environmental conditions have got to be absolutely perfect. Otherwise, you'll have the food spoilage and I said if food can survive in here, I think a piece of metal can, and it did.[58]

The austerity of Piedmont's operation did not keep the airline from developing a reputation that attracted people who wanted to come to work for the carrier. Richard Smith took a pay cut as chief pilot for Lowe's Corporation (the home improvement chain) to fly a 727 for Piedmont, a plane for which he had a great affinity. In 1984, he brought a Piedmont annual report to the comptroller at Lowe's and asked for an opinion. Smith was told, "If you're interested in buying stock in the company, buy it, but if you've been offered a job, take it." At age 40, Smith knew he would be junior to pilots younger than he. He joined Piedmont anyway, saying that from the first day, he was treated like family. Though he knew the 727 very well, Richard Smith appreciated the excellent training he received from Piedmont's ground school when he first arrived. "Piedmont taught you the airplane and the systems much more so than

As Piedmont moved aggressively into the deregulated world, it needed larger jets like this Boeing 727-200. With a range of 2800 miles, until the later advent of the 767s this was the largest of Piedmont's jets, able to carry 164 passengers (Tom Sharpe Collection).

most airlines did," said Smith. He pointed out that the instructors at Piedmont "were the mechanics that came into the classroom. The electricians taught us the electrical system. The people that dealt with the fuel system taught us the fuel system." Smith added to his already considerable knowledge of the 727 and looked forward to a long career in the "seven-two" cockpit.[59] What he and most of his fellow employees did not know was that the climate of acquisitions that had so permeated the airline industry would soon include Piedmont as well.

To some, it seemed like a fairy tale existence that might never end as long as good people kept the airplanes flying. However, the seeds of Piedmont's demise were sown back in the early days of deregulation in the Speedbird's relationship with Norfolk-Southern Railroad. As Piedmont stock continued to rise, and the railroad reaped the profit of its roughly 20 percent ownership of the company, the relationship naturally became a point of speculation. Explaining the relationship, Mr. Davis commented to the press, "We had worked so harmoniously with them for so many years and they continued to express a great interest in Piedmont."[60] The "stand-still" agreement signed in late 1981 gave Piedmont time to grow while the railroad weighed its options.[61] Registered with the Securities and Exchange Commission, the formal pact allowed Norfolk and Western to increase its share of the company if another investor started buying up Piedmont stock. The deal went into effect in late January of 1982 and gave management in Winston-Salem the opportunity to conduct its business plan with a free hand, without the threat of takeover for the next five years. The arrangement allowed Mr. Davis to assert, "Our position was that they were very much encouraged about our future opportunity just like we were."[62]

During the five year span, a number of things had changed for both the airline and the railroad. While Piedmont's growth during the period exceeded 25 percent every year, Norfolk and Western had grown also. The company merged with Southern Railroad to form Norfolk-Southern Corporation. The combined powerhouse east coast railroad also bought the fifth largest trucking firm in the United States, North American Van Lines. As late as 1986, Norfolk-Southern attempted to increase its railroad interests, making a play for government owned Conrail. After a backlash to the purchase nixed the deal in Congress, the railroad found itself with a wad of cash and the agreement with Piedmont coming to an end. It was time to become more than a passive investor in the airline.[63]

Early 1987 was a crucial period for the Speedbird. Not only did the railroad agreement expire on January 26, but Piedmont faced its stiffest competition yet in its home territory of North Carolina. The nightmare scenario Tom Davis dreamed when he opposed deregulation finally came true. After fantastic profits made for seven years, the other major American carriers had at last realized the lucrative nature of airline travel in the Southeast. They were invading North Carolina. The previous November, low cost carrier People's Express announced its intention to serve Greensboro. A month later, American Airlines revealed its plan to heighten service in the Tar Heel state, especially in the capital city of Raleigh. In January, Trans-World Airlines (TWA) announced flights scheduled for Charlotte and Raleigh.[64]

Other issues loomed on the horizon for Piedmont as well. In 1984, the Speedbird flew to the west coast for the first time, taking in Los Angeles and eventually San Francisco. Since that time, Piedmont had made no further efforts to establish itself out west. Industry analysts questioned the strategy since a number of competitors were buying up airlines in that direction for a more balanced presence across the continental United States.[65] In reality Piedmont had investigated the possibility. The Board of directors approved an effort to buy Western Airlines. Zeke Saunders had retired from Piedmont by that time but was still on the board. He remembered that Bill Howard "sent Bill McGee and somebody out there to look at it.

They said, 'The union is too strong. We can't handle it.' Bill told the board of directors that they couldn't handle the union and Delta bought it in the next two days."[66] Another source said that Piedmont considered Western Airlines overpriced but confided, "In retrospect it was a bargain. It would have taken us out of play."[67] Gordon Bethune agreed. Having worked for Western prior to coming to Piedmont, he said, "I was the one urging that to happen. I talked to Jerry Grinstein about it a couple of times while he was CEO. But I couldn't get Bill Howard interested."[68] In addition to the Delta/Western merger for $680 million, American Airlines snapped up AirCal for $225 million and northeastern carrier USAir negotiated purchase of Pacific Southwest Airlines for $400 million, leaving Piedmont, in the estimation of many observers, vulnerable. Instead of increasing its western presence with a new hub or airline acquisition, Piedmont announced that its focus in 1987 would be to strengthen its established hubs in Charlotte, Dayton, Baltimore, and Syracuse. It wasn't the first time airline analysts scratched their heads over a Piedmont decision that ran counter to industry advice.

The management at Piedmont had some understanding of where the expiration of the stand-still agreement with Norfolk-Southern would put the airline on the open market as a takeover target. As the date drew near, Piedmont officials talked informally with several carriers lining up to offer deals once Norfolk-Southern's investment arrangement had lapsed. Bill Howard's research people ran a number of scenarios trying to determine compatibility between Piedmont and another airline. Among those available were TWA and USAir. As a piece in the puzzle of the other two airlines, Piedmont fit each in unique ways. TWA had for some time been looking for a domestic airline to balance its primary offering as an international carrier. With its hubs in St. Louis and New York, the match up would produce no substantive conflicts. TWA had just recently bought Ozark Airlines, taking care of its needs in the Midwest, but Piedmont had grown into one of the largest carriers on the east coast, which would have been a welcome addition. Likewise, a mating with USAir was mostly complementary since the airline formerly known as Allegheny Airlines centered its service in the industrial northeast. The proximity of the Dayton hub to USAir's hubs in Indianapolis and Pittsburgh were the only potential conflicts.[69] In looking back on the analysis of USAir and Piedmont, CEO Howard recalled, "USAir was making a little money. We were making a lot of money and the two put together as one airline would be lucky to break even. That's what we concluded. And we went around the table and 100 percent of the people agreed. 'We sure don't want any part of that.'"[70]

The most likely scenario for the future, Piedmont management believed, was that the company would be bought by the railroad. When Norfolk-Southern's management came down to Winston-Salem, they told Bill Howard, "We would like to buy Piedmont, but we would agree to certain things. We would agree first of all that management and employees of Piedmont shall remain exactly as it is." In addition, the new owners planned to provide enough cash for Piedmont to "buy a big airline of your choice." In the meantime Norfolk planned continued purchases of Piedmont stock, which was moving toward thirty dollars per share. According to Howard, the railroad was prepared to go 20 percent beyond the thirty threshold, up to as high as $36, maybe as high as $40. As Howard put it, "We think we can buy the whole damned thing, particularly if you will nod appropriately and say this is good for the airline and you recommend its approval, you like it and think that the Norfolk-Southern people will be good to work with."[71] Bill Howard liked what he heard and nodded appropriately.

Once the Piedmont/Norfolk-Southern agreement officially lapsed, however, a mad scramble began. On January 27, the day after the pact had ended, the railroad filed with the Securities and Exchange Commission signaling its intent to buy Piedmont. Norfolk-Southern retained an investment firm to handle the offer. Meanwhile, Piedmont's board of directors formed a "Special Committee" of board members not employed by the airline to scrutinize any offers received as well as asking First Boston Bank to "assist the Special Committee."[72] As newspaper accounts later stated, "Once Piedmont was put into play, there was no turning back."[73]

The same day the Special Committee was formed, its members sat down with representatives from Norfolk-Southern to listen to the first offer. The railroad proposed to buy the airline for $63 per share in cash. The previous year Piedmont stockholders had approved a resolution that called for any tender for the company to be "all cash." The railroad's first offer fell right into line with investor requirements. The Special Committee members expressed satisfaction with the proposition.

Generally, everyone supported a Norfolk-Southern takeover. The deal would give Piedmont the ability to keep its organizational structure and identity intact. In essence, the Speedbird would remain much the same as it had been, a stand alone aviation company. The only difference was that Norfolk-Southern would increase its share of ownership from 19.44 percent (at the time of the offer) to full ownership.[74] It had been the kind of transportation super company that Mel Blocker heard Robert Claytor speak of years before. In fact, the ultimate plan called for an airline much bigger than just Piedmont. According to Gordon Bethune, Norfolk-Southern intended to also buy another airline, in all likelihood Delta, and have the entire operation managed by Piedmont personnel. Concerning Mr. Claytor's plan, Bethune said, "His whole idea was that he liked Delta, he liked the scale and the market presence. He just didn't like Delta management. He said the real combo was to put the Piedmont management in charge of the franchise."[75]

At first, the fact that the airline was "on the block" seemed of no real concern to Piedmont folks. The railroad offer eased anxiety since it looked like the Speedbird would continue in the future much as it had in the past. Norfolk-Southern was buying stock in the effort to build its share of Piedmont. Inexplicably, as the railroad was buying chunks of stock, so was someone else. Bill Howard remembered being told by Norfolk, "Do you know yesterday we bought 2000 shares; somebody else bought 3000. The day before we bought 1000, and somebody else bought 5000." Piedmont stock sales began attracting attention on Wall Street and the price rose. It didn't take long to figure out who the mystery buyer was. It was USAir. The railroad plan began to shake like a wooden trestle under a fast moving freight train. Piedmont's president, Bill Howard, urged forbearance, hoping Norfolk-Southern would continue to work its plan, but the stakes were getting high.[76]

On February 5, a substantial offer from USAir arrived for consideration. In it, the carrier offered the same price per share that Norfolk-Southern had, but instead of an all cash deal, USAir proposed to buy Piedmont stock with a mixture of cash and common stock from USAir. Left unsaid but fully realized by all who knew about the offer was the understanding that if accepted, Piedmont Airlines would be folded into the structure of USAir and cease to operate as an independent company. While the Special Committee evaluated both offers on the table, one Piedmont employee quipped, "There was one too many roosters in the hen house and one had to go."[77] The emergence of USAir struck some as curious. They suggested that the offer was borne out of more than just their admiration for a competitor. More likely, USAir wanted Piedmont for other reasons. When informal merger talks between Piedmont and USAir went nowhere in the fall of 1986, TWA began to consider the possible purchase of USAir. Just as Piedmont's routes fit well with TWA's, so did USAir's. TWA chief stockholder and corporate raider Carl Icahn was willing to consider any viable airline to help out his ailing carrier. Analysts called USAir's interest in Piedmont defensive, a way to avoid possible takeover by TWA.

Quickly, the bidding escalated. USAir delivered a new offer that gave stockholders $68 per share, $34 in cash and $34 in company stock. Although it was much higher than the price Norfolk-Southern had told Bill Howard they wanted to pay, the railroad countered, making a formal proposal to the company with a lower price, $65. Like the previous railroad proposal, the deal was all cash. However, not everyone endorsed the offer. Among Norfolk-Southern's board, one "no" vote kept the offer of purchase from being unanimous and showed some reluctance by the railroad of getting into the airline business.[78] That day Piedmont traded at $65.38 per share on the stock market. The day after receiving the revised offer from Norfolk Southern, the Special Committee announced its support of the deal and advised Piedmont's board to accept the second railroad proposal.[79]

It took USAir less than a day to sweeten the pot in its favor. In the most complicated proposition yet, the carrier said it would buy out Piedmont by obtaining 50.1 percent of Speedbird stock for $71 in cash while giving $73 in USAir stock for the remaining 49.9 percent of the outstanding shares. The new deal immediately prompted the Special Committee to retract its support of Norfolk-Southern while it and First Boston considered the alternative. The news continued an ascent for Piedmont's stock, sending it to $70, an almost $20 per share rise from late 1986. The board of directors met all day behind closed doors in Winston-Salem to consider the wrinkle USAir had created. Was the extra money to be gained from the higher price worth the company's loss of identity? Quietly, Norfolk-Southern board members told their Piedmont counterparts that the railroad would not raise its bid, nor would it withdraw it. The board held the fate of the company in their hands.[80]

With two offers on the table, Piedmont's board began to fish for more. While deliberating, the directors put out the word that they were "interested in hearing other offers to buy Piedmont."[81] The invitation made clear that the airline was for sale to the highest bidder. The only thing that seemed certain in the rapid succession of events was that Piedmont Aviation would soon be acquired by someone. One stock analyst commented that Piedmont "seemed amenable to the idea" of no longer being an independent company.[82] The ploy by Piedmont's board brought one more player to the table, TWA's Carl Icahn. Four days after the last USAir offer, TWA expressed interest in Piedmont, "either acquiring the company or being acquired by Piedmont." The prospect gave Piedmont the possibility to emerge from the bidding war as a larger entity with much of its identity intact but without a specific proposal to consider. First Boston quickly dismissed the suggestion and determined the USAir proposal superior to TWA's.[83]

The railroad executives could hold a poker face no longer. Their last visit to Winston-Salem carried the news that they "would rather a seller than a buyer be." Stock Norfolk-Southern purchased at $20 was trading for up to $80 per share. They did not have enough of an interest to buy at the higher rate and liked the prospect of a financial windfall if they sold what they had. Many Piedmont workers had put their hopes in Norfolk-Southern as savior, one that would have left the Speedbird with the same management structure, facilities and schedules that employees had always known. As they watched, a different scenario took place. "The bid got so high that the railroad figured it was cheaper just to sell," said pilot Howard Miller. "It was more profitable for them, and that is what they ended up doing."[84] One analyst estimated that the Norfolk-Southern made a profit of $100 million from the sale.

Carl Icahn continued to look for ways to disrupt a potential Piedmont/USAir union. He put in a bid to buy USAir for $52 per share, hinting that Piedmont join the new entity as well. In what seemed a game of corporate brinksmanship, Icahn attempted to force his airline into some combination with other smaller but more profitable carriers. Some analysts speculated that he was trying to get rid of TWA and get out of the airline business, while others thought he was searching for a way to save TWA from bankruptcy.[85] In the end, he drove Piedmont and USAir into each other's arms.

USAir made one final offer to Piedmont, as Carl Icahn tossed about his latest takeover plans of a possible triumvirate of the three airlines. Piedmont would receive a total of $69 a share in cash for its stock. The board of directors, already leaning toward the fourth USAir proposal but waiting to see what TWA might offer, accepted the offer to merge with USAir on March 9, 1987. The final bid brought $1.6 billion for Tom Davis's company, recently controlled by Bill Howard. In less than six weeks after the deal that gave Piedmont Airlines much of its flexibility during deregulation ended, the company was owned by another airline. Most took small satisfaction in the fact that the price of the airline was the highest ever paid up to that time for buyout in the history of aviation.

The news hit employees the hardest. Many were stunned, and some were angry at the outcome. A question echoed across the company and subsequently across the years — how could this have happened to our great company? "It was a powerful blow to Piedmont people because they were led to believe by Howard and others that we're great and nobody's ever going to take us over and if there's any acquiring done, we'll be the acquirer," said Piedmont's former Vice President of Employee Relations Joe Wilson. "Then the thing just suddenly collapsed around us overnight."[86] Audrey Collins was in shock over the turn of events. Discussing the buyout with a colleague, she was surprised at the reaction. When the fellow employee distressed over the need to change the letterhead, Collins exclaimed, "Change the letterhead, your whole life just changed."[87]

Countless Piedmont personnel took their cue from Mr. Davis. Publicly, Mr. Davis called the marriage the first since deregulation between two financially strong airlines. Son Frank Davis gauged his father's reaction to the upheaval after the reporter's questions and noted, "He'd kind of squint or frown a little bit but he would always come back with a positive remark in favor of USAir, in favor of the merger. He would always keep it positive. I can't remember ever hearing him say anything negative about the merger."[88] That was typical Tom Davis. Knowing the airline business as he did, he understood the merger climate that threatened to eat his company up if left on the market by itself. He seemed to take some pride in the fact that Piedmont had remained independent as long as it did. In an interview, he said, "Piedmont is the last virgin."[89]

A few others remained hopeful that the future might be as bright as USAir President and CEO Ed Colodny pictured it for the two airlines that were soon to become one. Bill McGee held the company line, telling employees: "I think there are tremendous opportunities in front of us when you think of the end product of what this merged company can look like, you see a company that's over 40,000 people strong, that will generate passage of some 60 to 70 million people in the course of a given year and will be and certainly could be the most profitable combination of airlines in the entire industry."[90]

Some saw no benefit to Piedmont or its employees. In his book *From Worst to First* Gordon Bethune revealed his feelings concerning the sale. He spoke for many at Piedmont when he wrote: "I was devastated, as were a lot of other employees, because I'm like anybody else — I was working at Piedmont for more than just wages. I thought I was making an investment in the company. I loved that company, and I loved the people in it. Even though I had a five-year contract with Piedmont and all kinds of stock options that the takeover was going to make worth a lot of money, I wasn't happy. I felt betrayed."[91]

Gordon Bethune's contact with employees in the days after the sale confirmed his assertion that a lot of people were angry. He reportedly walked into a hangar and found a corporate executive hung in effigy. When one mechanic apologized for the display, Bethune replied, "Sometime in the next couple of weeks, you get that down. You guys look like you're pretty busy getting airplanes fixed. That's what I'd focus on for now."[92] Piedmont's senior vice president of operations freely admitted his anger over the sale to what he termed "a bunch of second string management like USAir," and when asked how it could have happened he commented, "It was mismanaged by us. We had put ourselves in play without having done the work, the necessary foundation to make sure that the company we wanted to become, a subsidiary of Norfolk-Southern, was going to get done in spite of what should have been anticipated, a life and death struggle with a competitor." To explain where the responsibility rested for the circumstance into which Piedmont found itself, he used an aviation analogy. "When you have an airplane accident you don't talk to the flight attendant, you talk to the pilot, the captain, and that's the same way we wrecked that company which was acquired by USAir and was the destruction of Piedmont. You only have to talk to the guy in charge."[93]

The series of events that led to the demise of Piedmont may have stretched much further back than anyone realized at the time. While deregulation had brought the once small Winston-Salem based airline to the attention of a more national audience, it was one particular acquisition made by Piedmont that sealed its fate, believed Speedbird pilot Carroll Spencer. He pointed out that the purchase of Empire Airlines and the establishment of Syracuse, New York, as a hub for the North Carolina airline was a key component in its buyout by USAir. "We bought Empire and that woke Allegheny [later USAir] up," said Spencer, who asserted that Ed Colodny viewed the acquisition as threat to the security of his own Northeast-based airline. "We were going to take over Syracuse, we were going to put a base up there. That woke them up. Otherwise, they would have never woke up because they weren't too swift anyway."[94]

Suddenly, those people who "weren't too swift" were in charge.

· 9 ·

Another Airline,
1987–1989

Employees, nervous and excited, scurried about completing last minute details for the flight, a takeoff unlike any undertaken by Piedmont Airlines in its four decade history. Television news crews queried passengers and set up live shots for their evening newscasts because every station in town was making this event their lead story. The management team flew in from Winston-Salem to take part in the festivities heralded by billboards, balloons, even a cake. The flight attracted the presence of North Carolina's governor, a feat unseen since the first flight back in 1948. Giving a short speech, Governor Jim Martin cut the ribbon and wished the Speedbird well, saying in the way only a southerner can, "We're just as proud of you as we can be."[1] They had all come to Charlotte, Piedmont's first hub, to congratulate the airline as it took a momentous step. Piedmont Airlines was inaugurating regular service to London, England.

The takeover by USAir, still not official, had not dampened the spirits of the Piedmont team as they rallied once more to prove that a little airline from North Carolina could do big things. The rush of activity brought perspiration to the foreheads of the Piedmont workforce that toiled to make their first transatlantic flight "over the pond" as perfect as possible. Douglas International Airport earned its designation that day when the Boeing 767ER (extended range) jet named the *Pride of Piedmont* arrived just after 4:00 P.M. from Tampa, Florida, ready to continue on to Europe. Most of the Tampa passengers deplaned. A few stayed on and were joined by a host of Piedmont officials, dignitaries and customers anxious to be on the first trip to London. For years, Mr. Davis liked to joke that he always enjoyed flying into the London-Corbin, Kentucky, airport in the early days because that way he could say that his airline served London. As of June 15, 1987, he could make the claim without deception. With Charlotte as the last stop before spanning the Atlantic, the celebration centered first in the Queen City before it moved on to London. The pomp and ceremony associated with the grand feat, somewhat understandably, disrupted the schedule. The wide bodied Boeing took off 17 minutes late, but as it did, a nostalgic companion accompanied passengers bound for Britain. As a symbolic gesture, a refurbished DC-3 in Piedmont's original insignia escorted the newest Piedmont plane from Charlotte and on its way to writing the next chapter in the history of the Speedbird.[2]

Waiting for the arrival was a celebration even larger. English bands and American officials for the company welcomed the flight, which touched down just six minutes after its scheduled 6:40 A.M. arrival time at London's Gatwick Airport. Charlotte news reporter David Hains summed up the excitement as he covered the flight from London, quipping, "A lot of people really full of pride, really happy here, who work for Piedmont." Hains and other Charlotte

9. Another Airline, 1987–1989

"The first Boeing 767 for Piedmont to be brought to the hometown of Winston-Salem, N.C. The aircraft was christened the *City of London* because that was exactly where Piedmont planned to fly the jumbo jet that seated up to 210 passengers. The occasion also brought out an original Piedmont DC-3 and the red Waco Tom Davis used to fly as a kid." Another 767ER, the *Pride of the Piedmont*, would make the first flight to London on June 15, 1987 (Ronnie Macklin Collection).

journalists interviewed numerous individuals connected with Piedmont in London, including one flight attendant who, when asked about his feelings as the *Pride of Piedmont* took off from Charlotte, said only, "Excited." When it touched down he could only add that he was "more excited." "We couldn't sleep the night before we were so excited," said flight attendant for the inaugural trip Carol Dobyns Fair, whose adrenalin kept her going during the fourteen hour flight. The sense of accomplishment was strong for her, as it was with her fellow employees. "To go to London, England, after being on a puddle hopper for all those years" was an accomplishment Fair remembered with great pride. It contrasted sharply with her first days onboard a Piedmont Pacemaker that "had 22 landings in one day." The flight to London was, as she put it, "one hello and one goodbye."[3] Reporter Brian Thompson captured the mood and the meaning of the event by saying, "Most of all, this moment, this historic passage meant the most to Piedmont's employees."[4] They took pride in one more accomplishment for their airline, even if the days of the Speedbird were winding down.

During the summer of 1987, Piedmont did not act like a company that was on the verge of losing its identity. Prior to the first London flight, commercials aired on British television introducing the Piedmont name to the U.K. One spot began, "In 1903 in North Carolina, this was the only way to fly," showing early footage of the Wright Brothers. It continued with a switch to a jet flying overhead as it intoned, "In 1987, in North Carolina this is ... Piedmont, Trans-Atlantic daily." The carrier's British advertising agency asserted very plainly that their mission was "to establish not only the name, to establish Piedmont with the U.K. audience, but also give a reason to fly."[5] Name recognition for a carrier about to be absorbed into another company might not have seemed to be long term thinking, but as with many other Piedmont efforts, the company remained proud of its name as well as its accomplishment and wanted all of England to know that Piedmont had come to town.

Competition for the right to fly to London had been hotly contested. In July of 1986, well before sale of the company became an issue, Bill Howard and his management team filed with the U.S. Department of Transportation (DOT) for the right to begin service to the capital city of United Kingdom. The process resembled the old days before deregulation when Mr. Davis trekked to Washington, D.C., to gain permission to fly into American cities like Atlanta and Baltimore from the Civil Aeronautics Board. Part of an agreement between the U.S. and the U.K. allowed only twelve American cities to receive the designation of "gateway" to Britain. Ten had been assigned. Two gateways were up for grabs and Piedmont vied for a route from Charlotte with several other carriers. Delta Airlines wanted a London gateway to originate from Cincinnati; Pan Am applied for service from Pittsburgh, and American Airlines sought London passage from its upcoming hub in Raleigh-Durham, North Carolina, another sign that the major carrier itched to compete with Piedmont in the Speedbird's own back yard.

Among the competitors, the American-Piedmont contest proved to be especially contentious. Since the two origination points for these requests were relatively close, both in the state of North Carolina, expectations were that one award would go to either the Cincinnati or Pittsburgh carrier while the other was a battle between cities in the Tar Heel state. American Airlines immediately attacked Piedmont's plan, saying the North Carolina based airline simply could not possibly provide international service based on the grounds that the carrier had never flown internationally before, while American had. Gordon Bethune called the American assault "scurrilous" and said the larger airline "showed a tremendous amount of arrogance in the way that they approached it, criticizing our operational plans and talking about their own." Bethune welcomed the opportunity to challenge the accusations made by American. "We decimated their arguments in the courtroom. We showed that we had a great operation; we had a great airplane; we had a better product and could find London with our own professionalism and own airplane. We made a pretty good case and won the route." He relished the opportunity to be a David taking on the Goliath of the industry and winning. With some satisfaction he disclosed, "You get that arrogant, you might get taken to the cleaners. It was kind of fun. I enjoyed my time on the witness stand."[6]

In fighting the airline battle with London as its prize, Piedmont made a shrewd move to enhance its chances. A month and a half after filing its first gateway application, the airline amended its request to a joint petition that included the city of Tampa, Florida. Previous approval to fly from Tampa to London had been given to another carrier but that route had been dormant for some time. The new Piedmont request advocated the starting point for any trans–Atlantic flight to originate in Tampa, stopping in Charlotte before heading to London. Return flights would terminate in the Florida city as well. The new plan showed an intense desire on Piedmont's part to serve all three cities, as well as make better use of existing resources.[7]

The Department of Transportation's administrative law judge agreed with Piedmont, calling the airline the "clear choice" for the London route. Deputy Assistant Transportation Secretary for Policy and Administrative Affairs Vance Fort concurred, adding, "The strongest factor favoring the selection of Piedmont is its proven ability to serve the Southeast through its substantial hub at Charlotte."[8] Delta won the other award, leaving Pan Am, and more significantly, American Airlines, out in the cold. Seemingly, in an attempt to steal some of the Piedmont thunder after being beaten for the London route, American Airlines officially opened the Raleigh-Durham hub on the same day Piedmont took off to London for the first time. American Airlines President Robert Crandall cut the ribbon to launch a North Carolina hub in Raleigh while 180 miles away Piedmont officials toasted a transatlantic flight in Charlotte.[9]

The selection of Piedmont to fly non-stop from Charlotte to London was greeted with elation, not only by airline employees but also by anyone connected to the city of Charlotte. The prize came just days after the city learned that it had secured its first major league sports team, the Charlotte Hornets; Charlotteans could not believe their string of luck. About the gateway award, Charlotte Chamber of Commerce President Carroll Gray remarked, "This makes us an international city, just like the NBA announcement made us a national city."[10] Charlotte television news anchors Bill Walker and Meg MacDonald broadcasted live from London on the days leading up to the flight, cashing in on the excitement surrounding the gateway of which Charlotte was so proud.[11]

When the decision came, Piedmont had little time to spare in making London service a reality by its intended target date. Speedbird officials learned on April 23 that their request had won. "We would have liked to have started a little earlier," admitted London Director of Operations Larry Brooks. "We're where we think we should be considering when we knew we were coming here,"[12] he said as the day approached. With a projected first flight listed for the middle of June, everyone in the company again worked diligently to make the scheduled premier. Gordon Bethune revealed, "We did that sometimes by the skin of our teeth, but we did it." Among the last minute problems he mentioned, one seemingly minor issue had the potential to disrupt everything. While at Boeing in Seattle to pick up the plane, small issues concerning engine and aircraft compatibility emerged. Failure to gain official certification threatened to rob the airline of the use of the wide body jet. Since no other Piedmont plane had a comfortable range to fly across the Atlantic, they needed the 767. Boeing worked right

The billboard announced the feat. The little airline from Winston-Salem won the right to provide trans-Atlantic service to London, England, in 1987 after a struggle with rival American Airlines. According to some, the new owner was not happy with the Piedmont plan (Ronnie Macklin Collection).

up until the night before the plane was to be brought back to Winston-Salem, getting paperwork squared away so everything would be in order and Piedmont would have its big jet for the inaugural flight.[13]

Another obstacle overcome by the airline while waiting for the government to announce its decision was the National Aviation Safety Inspection Program (NASIP). The "white glove inspection" program had been instituted in 1986 by the Federal Aviation Administration (FAA) and, as Ronnie Macklin noted, "was established to insure that all FAA controlled airlines were operating safely." Teams of inspectors went out to all the carriers and checked compliance with every FAA rule that concerned flight operations, maintenance, and purchasing. Macklin joked that the motto of the teams was, "We are not happy unless you are unhappy."

The FAA announced its arrival in Winston-Salem for the fall of 1986. However, a lack of government funding delayed auditors until February of 1987, just as the battle between American and Piedmont heated up.[14] Serious violations by the airline would have likely damaged its efforts to secure the London route. Feeling his company had nothing to hide, Gordon Bethune said, "We welcomed the FAA with open arms and were very accommodating with them." Piedmont personnel worked diligently to get everything in order for examination, because as Bethune revealed personally, "having been a product of the Navy we always got ready for inspection. Why wouldn't you shine your shoes knowing the admiral's coming?"[15] C.D. McLean, part of the team preparing for the inspection, remembered Bethune telling Piedmont people that "next to breathing, it was the most important thing they had ever done. People got the message. People hunkered down. People did it."[16] Two large teams of investigators, one for maintenance, the other for operations, were set up with their own office at the company headquarters and given complete access to thoroughly inspect the airline.

The results amazed the FAA but not the Piedmont folks. The audit found that maintenance had two violations and flight operations had 19, reported Ronnie Macklin, who said, "Most of these were minor items."[17] Gordon Bethune remembered one of the violations. "They only found one airplane whose weight and balance hadn't been renewed. I think you had to do a re-inspection every three years to document the way you balanced the airplane. They had gone over the three year time limit, although it had been done, but late and when it was done, it was exactly the same as it was, so it had never been a factor."[18] Other violations included two incidents where flight crew members had worked beyond the maximum allowed hours.[19] At the end of the inspection, the fine for Piedmont was $30,000, the lowest of any FAA controlled airline. Comparatively, in the nine audits conducted by the FAA before coming to Winston-Salem, other airlines had been fined a total of $15.6 million. When the airline was notified of the results, Ronnie Macklin said Gordon Bethune asked him "to go to accounting and get a check for that amount and send it overnight delivery before anyone changed their mind." Macklin mailed the check and the audit was closed.[20]

Looking back on the experience, Gordon Bethune recalled, "I wasn't amazed. We did a very good preparation with very professional people getting ready for an unprecedented inspection." In fact, Bethune was not particularly satisfied with the fine. Asserting that the results indicated that Piedmont was running "probably one of the most professional operations in the United States," the senior vice president of operations believed his company should have been recognized for the feat. He asserted, "I thought we ought to get a medal instead of a fine. I was kind of pissed off about the fine." Gordon Bethune explained his rationale by saying, "Life is sometimes relative. It's not all absolutes. Let's say there were ten horses in the race, and they were all farm animals so there's nothing to write home about as far as speed, but there's still going to be a winner. Shouldn't the winner get acknowledged? Then why shouldn't they give us a ribbon? We beat everybody else."[21] Piedmont did not get a ribbon, but ultimately, the inspection did help the carrier get a much more prized possession: the London route.

One obstacle to flying into London turned out to be the new owners. Six weeks before the FAA awarded Piedmont the trans-Atlantic flight came the sale of the airline to USAir. Though transition would take some time, USAir CEO Ed Colodny expected to call the shots immediately. He called Bill Howard, telling him to cancel Piedmont's order for the 767ER. Howard told Colodny, "It's already too late. We bought them. We paid for them." Not to be outdone, the CEO of USAir then ordered his Piedmont counterpart, "For God's sake, do not start your transcontinental." At that order, Bill Howard had to stand up to his new boss. "I said in effect, 'Ed, my attorneys tell me that under the board rules and the law you cannot dictate how we run this company at all until the board has approved the acquisition,' which they had not done. 'Any effort on your part to influence how this is run in the mean time is, I believe, a violation of federal law.'" Since both were attorneys, Howard made his point and Colodny acceded, if only temporarily. In Howard's opinion, USAir's board of directors did not want Piedmont flying to London. "Colodny told them it was the worst move we ever made," said Howard, noting that it turned out to be one of Piedmont's best.[22]

London constituted Piedmont's furthest reach, but the airline continued to seek new destinations even in its final days and without the blessing of Ed Colodny. As buyout talk swirled around Winston-Salem, the company began service to the Bahamas through Henson Airlines. Commuter affiliate TransAir had been serving points off the coast of Florida since the Florida Shuttle began, but as part of an increase in service in Florida, the resort destinations of Treasure Cay and Marsh Harbour were added to the mix.[23] Later in 1987, Piedmont planes flew into Nassau from both Charlotte and Baltimore.[24] To the existing list of cities, Piedmont also added Phoenix, Arizona, and San Diego, California, later in the year as well, topping off a forty year history of ever expanding service for the "puddle jumper."

To serve those cities and many more Piedmont had on the drawing board before the merger became an issue, the airline planned to purchase new Boeing jets. Though the folks in Winston-Salem had bought a few Boeing 767ERs, the company put most of its trust into a new version of the plane that had served it so well for so many years, the 737. Boeing planned a new version of the seven-three, designated the 400 series. Piedmont Airlines became the launch customer for the 737-400. In the summer of 1988, Piedmont began to take delivery of 25 Boeing 737-400s with options on another 30. When the later ones arrived, they were painted in USAir colors. The aircraft was a stretched version of the earlier 737-300, able to haul more passengers and cover greater distances thanks to an engine upgrade that had been used on some later 300 models.[25] One unfortunate consequence for Boeing in the merger came when USAir discovered that though they had been promised by Boeing that they had received the lowest price as launch customer for the 737-300, a look at Piedmont records (which came to them as part of the sale) indicated that the folks in Winston-Salem had actually negotiated a lower price for the same airplane. USAir sued and reportedly bought Fokkers the next time they went shopping for aircraft to spite Boeing.[26]

For years, Piedmont had also planned for expansion of facilities in Charlotte. It began when Charlotte voters passed a $90 million bond to improve their airport in 1985. Construction soon began on a 300,000 square foot hangar complex twice as large as the Winston-Salem operation. Because the Queen City had emerged as Piedmont's largest hub, employing almost 5,000, the decision to base most everything connected with the company there came

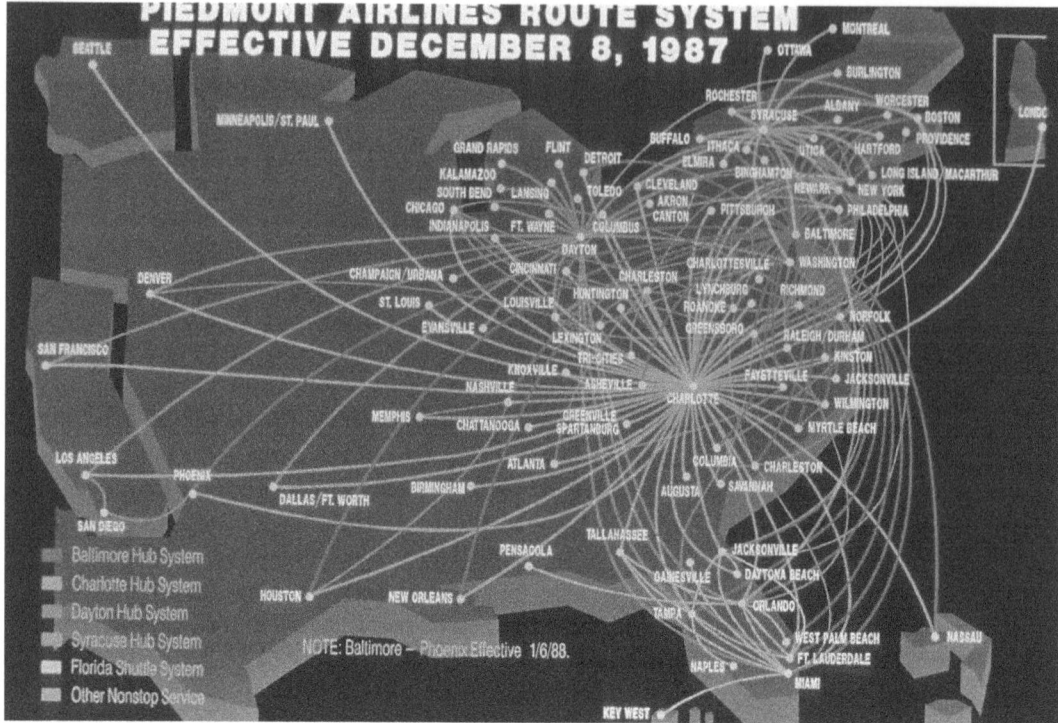

As the Speedbird neared the end of its flight, its reach continued to grow. From its east coast hubs, Piedmont flew to the west coast and across the Atlantic (courtesy Piedmont Aviation Historical Society; from the collection of Ronnie Macklin).

easy. As one of the biggest facilities of its kind in the nation, Piedmont housed planes, parts, as well as maintenance, training and operations centers at Charlotte with expectations to further expand after the complex opened in 1989. Unfortunately, the Piedmont logo and Speedbird would never be hoisted on the side of the building. Instead the letters "USAir" were affixed.

Like the letters, the impending merger hung over all that Piedmont did. In the preceding years, numerous mergers in the airline industry had occurred, all ultimately getting government approval. USAir President and CEO Ed Colodny expected this one to be no different. Within a few weeks, the United States Department of Transportation gave USAir approval to buy 51 percent of Piedmont's stock but held the buyer there while a full formal inquiry was made to determine how the union of the two companies might restrict competition. After all, both carriers flew into many of the same locations, and without the two in direct competition, the consumer could possibly suffer higher prices. Colodny decried lengthy hearings on the merger, saying, "It would be a tragedy to turn down this opportunity to let this combination be a much stronger competitor."[27] The formal hearing promised to slow down finalization on the merger for up to six months. Immediately, problems began to threaten the deal.

Protests emerged from several states that asserted the combined airline would cost their air travelers more. Attorneys general from New York, West Virginia, and Massachusetts each asked the DOT to reject the merger based on a restriction of competition which, in turn, they felt would produce high fares and cost jobs in their respective states. Of concern were nine pairs of cities where Piedmont and USAir were the only operators. Consolidation, the states argued, would erase any competition with those connections. The DOT listened, at least to some degree, and scheduled a pre-hearing conference for April 22, with arguments to begin in front of an administrative law judge by late June so all sides could be heard.[28]

Objections by the three states were in sharp contrast to the actions of the stockholders as they came to Winston-Salem on July 23, 1987, to vote their preference for the future of the company. "Several dozen shareholders" showed up to pass judgment on the board of directors' decision to sell the company made four months earlier. The vote was really a formality because by the time of the meeting, the outcome had been assured. A majority of Piedmont already belonged to USAir. Numerous stockholders had already tendered their shares to USAir for the $69 dollar offer. With 55 percent of the outstanding shares in their hands, USAir marked their ballot in favor of the merger. Those who hadn't sold stood to make even more money by approving the deal, since the provisions included interest paid to those who waited until government approval came. Shares were estimated to be worth over $70 per share if an affirmative decision came by October 1 from the DOT. If the answer was no, which no one expected, USAir would have to divest itself of the stock already attained.

Some employees might have hoped for a shareholder revolt, preventing Colodny and company from taking over Piedmont, but in reality, the group that assembled to vote had the most to gain from the sale. In an increasingly litigious business climate, had the board of directors acted differently back in March and rejected the higher USAir offer while accepting Norfolk-Southern's bid, they might have opened themselves up to a lawsuit by the stockholders. It was shareholder money the board would have turned away. Such litigation was avoided, however, and in an atmosphere described as "subdued," Tom Davis watched as fellow stockholders made their choice. The company he had helped to create back in 1940, the airline he envisioned and cultivated, was fading from existence. In a later interview, he likened the demise of the airline to losing a child. He said, "Everything is for sale except your wife and children. And Piedmont was one of my children." Looking back at the whirlwind of events that wrested control of the company into the hands of another airline, Mr. Davis remarked, "We felt we could maintain relative independence with the strength of the Norfolk-Southern deal," adding, "We would have preferred to have worked that out." Instead, he now found himself voting to sell his company. Despite his wistfulness, he joked, "There are a lot of happy shareholders." He was one of them. With his 165,000 shares, estimates were that Mr. Davis stood to reap $11.4 million from the deal.[29] Balloting took only minutes, and the decision was a unanimous vote in favor of the sale.[30]

Although saddened by the death of his airline, Tom Davis defended the move to merge. In a television interview, his motivations harkened back to his purpose for starting the airline in the first place. "With all the other airlines merging in order to stand up to the biggies and take full advantage of deregulation, keep all of our people employed, provide good service to our communities, the best thing to do was merge,"[31] Mr. Davis said, stressing employment for his workers just as he had in 1944 when the Civilian Pilot Training Program came to an end, and he looked for a profitable way to keep his people on the job.

Many Piedmont employees listened and waited. Early on, the deal got a bit of good news as the U.S. Department of Justice announced that it would not protest on antitrust grounds.[32] USAir's head, Ed Colodny, made the rounds, promoting the new entity and detailing how it would far outstrip the old. "Our objective is to marry the two strengths of airlines that exist." As he spoke to employee groups and governmental leaders in Piedmont cities, he attempted to allay fears, saying that few jobs would be hurt by the merger. To the contrary, he predicted more jobs in the service cities as the combined airline continued to grow. Only among upper management and their staffs in Winston-Salem would cuts be felt.[33] Time and time again Ed Colodny stressed, "We didn't buy Piedmont to disassemble what's been built."[34] Colodny, who planned to retire in a few years, even made the gesture of naming Bill Howard as president of the new, combined USAir as he retained his position as CEO and chairman of the board for a bit longer. Apparently, the dispute over the London route and the 767s held no lingering animosity.

No matter what Colodny had to say, some at Piedmont saw the handwriting on the wall immediately. One of them was C.D. McLean. "I was devastated," he said. "I was building a home up in Walnut Cove, right outside Winston-Salem. I had bought a farm up there. In fact I had just excavated the hole for the basement, and the day that they announced the sale, I told the bulldozer to fill the hole up, and I put the farm up for sale because I said this will never ever work."[35] Other Piedmont folks agreed and began to look for ways out. "It was all over. I don't need to see the last reel of that movie," remembered Gordon Bethune, who was among the first to leave Piedmont's upper management because of the coming merger. "Mr. Howard asked me to hold my resignation for two weeks so he could get his done," said Bethune. "He didn't want me to be the first. I was gone. And so I agreed to wait. I left the same day he did but only on his request." According to Gordon Bethune, Bill Howard had indicated that he might bring his management team with him in a move to TWA where a group of employees were trying to buy out Carl Icahn.[36] With Bethune definitely not a part of that effort, Howard instead stalled his senior vice president of operations for a bit, then announced that he was leaving Piedmont to join an effort to help a group of pilots at United Airlines buy their company.[37] Headquarters in Winston-Salem began to look like a lonely place.

In the years since the merger, some Piedmont employees pointed to the fact that Bill Howard's quick departure from Winston-Salem suggested that he orchestrated the USAir deal because he personally had a better offer. Offered a million dollars to head up the United pilots' effort, Howard took the job and exited Piedmont. "Some of them assumed that I had been part of the deal that sold out to USAir," said Howard. "God knows I didn't. God knows I didn't want it. I didn't engineer it. I didn't like it. I didn't think it was good. I knew it would not be good for me personally. When it was done, I had no clue that I would be hired the next week for a million dollars a year."[38]

Like Bill Howard, some chose to leave instead of working for USAir. C.D. McLean decided to quit without another position secured. The situation became so untenable for him that he finally said, "'I can get my lump sum. Also, I [can] get my pilot retirement.' I said, 'I think I better get out of here.'" After he made his choice, announced his decision and got his going away party, he began to wonder. "I got in my car and I drove away and about halfway down here to the eastern part of the state, I said, 'I think I let my mockingbird mouth overload my hummingbird ass here today.' I didn't know it was the best move I ever made in my life. At the time, though, I really said, 'What have I done?'"[39] Piedmont continued to lose many good people as the exodus continued.

Even the advertising agency that helped to make Piedmont an identifiable brand mourned publicly about the loss of the Speedbird. In a full page newspaper ad titled "The Toughest Ad We Ever Wrote," the firm of McKinney and Silver offered a fond farewell. The announcement said in part, "For ten years you made our job easy. Today, you are making it difficult." Saying the firm "cherished" its time serving Piedmont as its advertising agency, the folks at McKinney and Silver employed some of its own branding phrases for the airline by adding, "To us, you'll always be — not just a model of how good an airline can be — but a model of how good people can be. And we thank you for it."[40]

After the exit of Bill Howard, longtime Piedmont employee Bill McGee was named president and CEO. He had been on the first flight with Mr. Davis in February of 1948 and had risen through the company in the ensuing years. As a vice president of sales and marketing for many years, he gained a seat on the board of directors in 1984.[41] With Howard and Bethune gone, McGee spoke hopefully about the merger, as a new leader might be expected to do. He looked at the situation pragmatically as a lifelong member of the Piedmont culture would and reasoned, "The fact of life is that Mr. Colodny bought the company." He added, "Ed Colodny needs to have the continued expertise of all the Piedmont people in order for him to regain the biggest investment anyone's ever made in a company in the history of commercial aviation."[42] Many of the remaining employees clung to the belief that McGee was right.

By the time Bill Howard left the company, the position of president stood in the shadow of the buyout. "Once USAir bought us, that was it," said former Vice President of Employee Relations Joe Wilson. "Who was sitting in the [president's] chair was of little importance. At that point, Piedmont people weren't concerned with any of that. Their lot in life depended on what USAir was doing, what Colodny was doing."[43]

Piedmont's "de facto" leader made the rounds at Piedmont, talking to the workforce about the new union. One employee he ran into was Richard Smith, who remembered an encounter at the Piedmont gift shop.

> At the time they were selling a plastic license plate for $3.50 that said USAir on the front of it. He asked me what I thought of USAir. I said, "I can't tell you what I think about USAir yet but I can tell you what I think about Piedmont." I said, "The first day I went in for class at Piedmont they gave me an all leather flight bag and a pen and pencil set with Piedmont on it and they gave us a metal license plate as well. All of us proudly put that plate on the front of our automobile. You still see them running around today. I see that USAir has chosen to replace that nice metal license plate with a plastic one," and I said, "If the plastic license plate is any indication, I'm not going to like USAir."

According to Richard Smith, Colodny said he found the comment "interesting."[44]

Ed Colodny kept a smile on his face for Piedmont workers as the confirmation process got rocky. In addition to objections raised by the states, competitor America West Airlines protested the merger, saying basically the same thing the attorneys general were arguing, that the merger restricted competition in the east. America West contended that the new company should have to give up gate space at New York's La Guardia and Washington's National Airport. Colodny's answer: Let them fly into JFK or Dulles, airports that also serve New York and Washington, D.C.[45] In hearings, America West maintained that since La Guardia and National were "more desirable for most travelers," the administrative law judge hearing the case should treat those destinations as separate markets. Lawyers for the Department of Transportation advised Judge Ronnie Yoder to reject the accusations made by America West and send the case on to Transportation Secretary Elizabeth Dole for quick approval. Critics of the America West argument charged that the Arizona based airline cut its own throat when it indicated that it would be willing to drop the objection if space were made available for the west coast carrier at the contested airports, making America West look like it was jockeying for east coast position.

In September, Judge Yoder rendered his opinion. Everyone was shocked as Yoder recommended that the largest cash buyout in aviation history be rejected. The administrative law judge who heard arguments from interested parties all summer long concluded that a combination of USAir and Piedmont might "monopolize a number of eastern U.S. markets and would deny smaller carriers equal access to lucrative but tightly controlled airports in Washington and New York."[46] Colodny lost his smile over the verdict. Calling the decision "incomprehensible," he pointed out that the same judge approved a merger of Northwest and Republic Airlines a year earlier. He continued by saying in a prepared statement, "It would be a travesty if USAir and Piedmont were not allowed to merge after the DOT has approved far larger mergers that created some of the airline industry giants that are USAir's and Piedmont's major competitors. It would be an outrage if this acquisition, which has been carefully planned to avoid the consumer and labor problems that were caused by a few earlier airline mergers, were prejudiced by an overreaction to those mergers."[47]

Piedmont reacted less angrily than Colodny. In Winston-Salem, spokesman Don McGuire said they were "surprised by the judge's recommendation and cannot imagine the reasoning that would support his decision, which is contrary to the findings of both the Department of Transportation public counsel and the Department of Justice."[48] For those wanting a disruption in the merger, Ronnie Yoder gave a ray of hope. At this point, Piedmont Airlines was not a unified group. Many employees openly cheered the news of Yoder's opinion, causing company president Bill McGee to send out a letter to all Piedmont personnel insisting on a united front. He lectured his workforce: "Any action taken by any employee which is designed to undermine the merger, or obstruct its approval, would constitute a serious conflict of interest." In no uncertain terms, he demanded that everyone at the airline honor "corporate policy," even though "mixed emotions" permeated the company.[49] This seemed a heavy handed requirement for support of a move many felt ran counter to everything they had come to believe about Piedmont, and it sent employee morale plummeting. In less than a year, Bill McGee would be gone as well, replaced by former USAir-turned-Piedmont executive Tom Schick. In the McGee departure, four senior vice presidents went with him to attempt a resurrection of Braniff Airlines.[50]

The Yoder decision did not bind the DOT, but it did put the transportation department in an awkward situation. As Colodny stated, public counsel for the DOT had endorsed the merger earlier in the year and urged Yoder to do the same. However, the judge found enough unsettling questions brought about by Massachusetts, West Virginia and Maryland officials, along with the America West challenge, to conclude that a union of Piedmont and USAir would result in restricted competition and potentially higher airfares for some cities. It was Yoder's job to offer opinion based on the arguments he heard. Once the decision was made public, the DOT would have to countermand the judge if it let the deal go through. On the other hand, stopping a $1.59 billion cash buyout presented a myriad of problems, not just for the carriers but also for the look of inconsistency by the government that had rubber stamped a score of mergers during the era of deregulation. USAir applied political pressure where it could and waited for a favorable result.[51]

An unfavorable decision by the DOT would bring its own set of unintended consequences for Piedmont Airlines. By the time of the Yoder opinion in September of 1987, a number of key people had departed from Winston-Salem, leaving the carrier without the kind of leadership it had enjoyed during its prosperous days. Remaining independent meant that the Speedbird might be scooped up by some other airline like TWA or Pan Am, whose solvency was questionable. At the very least, Piedmont had lost momentum in days after the London inauguration as it waited to be taken over. As business reporter Larry Parnass wrote in a news analysis piece for the *Winston-Salem Journal*, Piedmont had much to lose if the merger were halted.[52] U.S. Representative Alex McMillan agreed. A strong supporter of Piedmont (he publicly announced the London award), McMillan was also a proponent of the merger, saying a disruption "would create uncertainties for Piedmont's employees and for the N.C. community Piedmont serves." McMillan's ninth congressional district included Charlotte. Over in the fifth district, representing Winston-Salem, Congressman Steven Neal spoke more for many of the employees who dreaded a merger. "Our preference would be for Piedmont to remain independent," said the representative. Acknowledging that such was unlikely, he added, "The deal with USAir is probably better than the unknown. And that unknown could be bad."[53]

The Department of Transportation got a lot more help in its decision making process than it ever intended. Lawyers for the DOT filed briefs reaffirming their earlier claim that the merger would not restrict competition. Both Piedmont and USAir did the same. The airlines charged that Yoder held the merger to "an unfair standard," one to which previous mergers had not been subjected. DOT lawyers maintained that Yoder's recommendation departed "from the department's consistent merger precedent and practices" to the point that if applied to previous mergers they too might have been disallowed. Given the laissez-faire approach the transportation department had taken in past mergers, disruption of USAir/Piedmont would signal a sea change in the government's attitude about airline industry consolidation.[54]

While waiting for the Department of Transportation's decision, a cultural anthropologist weighed in on the merger. W. Gerald Glover examined the recent Delta/Western Airlines merger in his book *World Class Service* and offered some observations about the USAir/Piedmont union. His points proved to be insightful. Glover pointed out that the two companies, while similarly sized, had very different ways of reaching decisions on issues. Also, employees at each airline looked at their jobs differently. Piedmont personnel were generally more willing to cross the lines of job duties than their USAir counterparts. Unless issues could be worked out and "managed properly" the way they were at Delta, Glover said problems loomed for the new USAir.[55] Those difficulties were the same ones that Piedmont management had identified when they analyzed a possible USAir acquisition a year earlier.

Then the decision arrived. On October 30, 28 years to the day after Piedmont's first plane crashed, came another disappointment for some Piedmont employees. The Department of Transportation approved the USAir acquisition of Piedmont Airlines. Speaking for the DOT, Assistant Transportation Secretary for Policy and International Affairs, Matthew Scocozza ruled, "We do not find that the acquisition of Piedmont is likely to reduce competition substantially."[56] Rejecting the Yoder view, the government seemed comfortable with another mega-carrier in the sky that could compete with the likes of United and Texas Air. Taking the number eight and nine sized carriers and putting them together created the nation's seventh largest airline with combined revenue passenger miles of 21.4 billion.[57] A final desperate appeal by America West for an injunction against the decision was quickly dismissed.

Reaction in Winston-Salem was mixed. Some looked forward to a new airline. Mayor Wayne Corpening asserted, "This will make us more competitive." The president of Wachovia agreed, adding, "The important thing was to keep a broad base and large number of jobs in the community."[58] Some Piedmont people took it in stride. Station agent Debora LaMoure said, "We've been waiting so long. I guess the announcement wasn't that big a deal." One pilot, when told after completing a flight, simply acknowledged what he had heard and said, "OK, I'll see you tomorrow."[59] With the die now cast, they waited to see how Ed Colodny would put into practice all he had promised.

"The day DOT approved it," C.D. McLean remembered, "It was 'by God, we [USAir] bought you and this is the way it is.'"[60] To the folks wearing the Speedbird, the change seemed to come overnight. "I'll never forget them telling us that they were going to change the dress codes for the pilots at Piedmont, and we were going to have to start wearing socks [a stereotype that everyone in the South walked around barefooted]. That kind of attitude just permeated the entire work group and everybody just started to hate USAir."[61] Many from the Piedmont side noticed a drastic drop in morale. Joe Wilson explained the Piedmont mind frame. "You've been acquired by a company you didn't have much respect for to start with and the more you were exposed to their management the respect went down hill. The CEO [was] coming around telling you the best of the two companies would win out on the job and suddenly [you] realize that regardless of how good they [Piedmont] were, if it was USAir, they were going to come out on top."[62]

The Piedmont workforce remained wary of the pronouncements made by USAir executives. However, many people had no choice other than to hope for the best. Joe Wilson captured the feeling when he observed, "Most of them had to face up to the fact that 'I got to have a job. I'm better off sticking around here than starting over somewhere else' and a lot of them were at ages where that would have been difficult to do anyhow."[63]

Throughout 1988, the Speedbird continued to fly and Piedmont looked to some like the company of old, but with USAir as the owner, things were vastly different on the inside. Immediately, the FAA wanted every airline under ownership of USAir Group, Inc., which also included California-based Pacific Southwest Airlines (PSA) purchased prior to Piedmont, to operate in the same manner. USAir's answer was a program called "Mirror Image." Since the other airlines now operated under the same certificate from the government, all policies and procedures needed to be the same. The Mirror Image program retrained Piedmont workers so they could function in the USAir way. Many from Piedmont resented the change, especially since they felt their way of operating superior to the USAir way. "USAir had people up there in Arlington and Pittsburgh that would come out with forms, one of the biggest wastes of my time as a station manager," said Don Martin. "In Lynchburg, I was working on a form and a report called the Overtime Budget Control Report, and I remember calling up there one day and asking them if they realized how much they were paying me to do that overtime budget control report."[64] Frank Davis was working with mechanics in Winston-Salem when the program was implemented. He remembered, "The guys in maintenance used to say well a mirror image is a reverse. If you look in the mirror it's actually not the same. What you see in the mirror is a reverse image of what you see. So it was kind of a snicker about that. We said we're doing the mirror image because we're doing it completely backwards from the way we used to do it."[65]

Many felt the new way of doing business was counterproductive. In the days as an independent company, if an employee felt he had a better way, he could suggest it and feel confident it would be considered, but now the folks at Piedmont felt powerless to change new procedures they believed were wasteful and time consuming. Bob McAlphin said he played a lot of golf those last two years because "they did not really want our ideas or our help, so we basically turned it all over to them, and for a couple of years there, we didn't have a whole lot to do."[66] Don Collins put it plainly: "Nobody from USAir liked anybody from Piedmont."[67] Joe Wilson saw the pride slipping away from his coworkers. He ruefully remembered, "As time went by, they threw out one Piedmont system after the other because they didn't want to take time to understand it and see if it was better than what they were doing. It was easier to keep doing what you were doing and that's pretty much what they did. So it was a sad time."[68] Bob McAlphin finally concluded, "They didn't want to do anything that Piedmont had looked good at."[69]

Richard Smith called the mirror image program "a joke" and noted sharp differences between the USAir workforce and that of Piedmont. One experience in the cockpit highlighted the dissimilarity. Usually the pilot who took the controls on one leg of the flight agreed to let the other pilot make the public address (PA) announcements to the passengers as a way to share duties. On one of his first flights with a USAir pilot, Smith was told, "I don't want any hicks like you talking on my PA." Smith, who grew up in western North Carolina, told his northern counterpart, "You don't have to worry." At the end of the trip, however, Smith did have something to say. "I told him 'I'm going to show you what a dialect and a hick is. When I get you in the parking lot and you don't have your uniform and I don't have my uniform on,' I said 'I'm going to show you what we boys down south do to you Long Island guys.'" Reportedly, from that point on, the USAir pilot became much friendlier. Richard Smith said, "I've run into that so many times and after that they want to be your best friends."[70]

One of the things Piedmont employees regretted bitterly was the loss of the reputation they had built over decades. Even though most planned to continue their career with USAir, passengers, neighbors, everyone knew them as Piedmont, giving workers a pride and self satisfaction that made them walk taller and smile more than their industry counterparts. In the days before the merger, if one said they worked for Piedmont, it meant they were part of a team that worked together and had built, along with their coworkers, an airline that had gone from a very frugal and uncertain beginning to becoming what most liked to call "a darling of the airline industry." To lose that reputation and be forced to start from scratch seemed to them unfair.

Years later, an analyst looking at airline marketing and management discussed the importance of branding, an industry term that refers to a distinctive identity, much like what Piedmont people cherished. During takeovers, Stephen Shaw noted that the purchasing airline most commonly dumps the brand being purchased "in the shortest possible time." He used the Piedmont sale as an example, suggesting that USAir might have done better to adopt the name "Piedmont" for the new company, giving Speedbird employees more to hold on to. He said, "The Piedmont brand was abandoned completely, despite the fact that its reputation had been a good one—probably better than that of USAirways [a name adopted by USAir after its first bankruptcy]."[71]

Conversely, some employees looked forward to union with USAir. One of them was flight attendant Marianne Moore. A 13 year veteran with Piedmont, she left Roanoke, Virginia, when the company quit using the city as a base. She had barely moved to Miami, her new base, when she learned that USAir had acquired her airline. Saying, "We're better off with the merger," she welcomed one significant benefit of working for USAir, higher pay. On average, Piedmont flight attendants made $33,100, far below the industry average of $42,600 and also under what Moore would make with USAir, which paid $46,800 in wages and benefits. However, since USAir would soon go through two bankruptcies, wages never reached the level promised during the merger. "After the initial sadness, most employees should feel a tinge of excitement," she said, asserting that USAir was the stronger airline. She also observed how some of her fellow employees were stopping USAir workers in airports to say they looked forward to working with them.[72] There was no report on the reception these workers received from their future colleagues.

Customer and spokesman McLean Stevenson recognized the "esprit de corps" of the Piedmont organization. In fact, through television commercials advertising the airline, he helped promote the name of which employees were so proud. When the merger came McLean Stevenson told USAir CEO Ed Colodny, "If you don't take the Piedmont spirit along with all the other assets, then all you will have accomplished is to have bought the most expensive airline in the history of aviation." Reportedly, Ed Colodny agreed with him.[73] As a demonstration of respect, USAir made an exception to its rule that discontinued the practice of naming each plane as Piedmont had done with its Pacemakers. The first USAir plane painted in colors to represent the new entity created out of the union of Piedmont, Pacific Southwest Airlines (PSA), and USAir was named like the Piedmont aircraft of old, the designation on the exterior just under the captain's seat. The 737 carried the title the *Thomas H. Davis Pacemaker*.[74]

The undertaking to merge USAir's 16,000 employees with Piedmont's 22,000 into one new happy family was a massive undertaking. Ed Colodny had no illusions that the marriage would be an instantly harmonious one. After seeing other airline mergers and going through the acquisition of PSA, he knew the key to building an airline passengers would love was based on the employee group. Saying, "If employee groups are in conflict with management, service is what ultimately suffers," he intended to win over the Piedmont workers and add them to the column already populated by folks like Marianne Moore.[75] C.D. McLean agreed with Ed Colodny on the importance of the workforce in keeping the airline moving ahead. Where he and other employees disagreed with the USAir approach was in its execution. "The employee makes the company, regardless of what company it is," said McLean, as he watched the Piedmont culture take a beating at the hands of the new owners. "And when a company like USAir comes in and they browbeat and they intimidate, and they treat the acquired carrier like they are a bunch of dog crap, you know what happens to the morale right there. And that's what happened."[76]

While the two airlines were getting used to each other, folks from Piedmont got a look inside how USAir worked. Joe Wilson made several trips to USAir headquarters as the plans for folding Piedmont into USAir progressed. What he witnessed was an operation run radically different from anything he saw in Winston-Salem. "One of USAir's problems was that there were no major decisions of any kind made without Colodny approving it," said Wilson. The USAir CEO had a similar ability to Tom Davis in that he could call people by name even if he only met them once. "But amongst the management people, they were scared to death of him. He'd raise hell if somebody did something he didn't think was right or whatever, so you were just constantly trying to guess whether this was the right thing to do. Will Colodny approve it or what? An unbelievable amount of merger decisions had to be made by him personally."[77] As a result, the plan to operate under one banner quickly bogged down.

As soon as the merger was approved, things began to slip for Piedmont Airlines. Trying to marry computer systems led to delay and frustration in Charlotte as flights on both Piedmont and USAir were interrupted.[78] Budgets took instant losses, as Joe Wilson remembered. "When we merged with USAir, we overnight doubled, for example, the labor cost in the maintenance area by converting over to provisions in USAir's maintenance contract and the same was true maybe to a little lesser extent with the flight crews."[79] In Bill Howard's earlier analysis of the two airlines, he anticipated the problem. "Our people never forced rules that they thought were ridiculous," asserted Howard. "USAir had a lot of rules that did nothing but pad their membership numbers."[80]

Piedmont's proven means of saving money were discarded by the new owner. In addition to his duties as maintenance manager in Greensboro, Don Collins ran a dry cleaning shop for Piedmont. The company had determined that buying the equipment necessary to clean seat covers for the entire fleet was significantly cheaper than farming out the job. Collins remarked, "We were running a dry cleaning shop with three people, and the first year we saved over two million dollars just in dry cleaning alone." Once the merger came, USAir discontinued the service no matter how much they stood to save. "They went back to dry cleaning by turning it over to somebody else."[81]

Pilot Richard Smith saw the same kind of waste. While flying the line, Smith noticed that when mechanical problems occurred, solutions were unwieldy and some USAir pilots had no commitment to staying with the plane until it was repaired. Instead, they left, flying back to Pittsburgh, which created even greater expense to get the airplane back into service. "That would never happen at Piedmont," said Smith. On a flight out of Denver a flap problem developed that was noticed before the plane took off. Smith's copilot departed immediately, leaving the Piedmont pilot with the plane. Calling maintenance control in Pittsburgh, Smith explained the problem. He also consulted with maintenance crews from another airline in Denver, who said the flaps could be fixed in about three hours. The folks in Pittsburgh were incredulous. Declaring that the airplane could not possibly be fixed in such a short amount of time, they sent out their own crew. When the plane was still not in working order the next day, Smith went over to the maintenance crew who claimed they could have the aircraft operating in three hours and inquired. The mechanics he talked to said a flap cable was broken. They would have strung new cable through the wing and then put the ends on it. Instead, USAir mechanics bought their cables from Boeing with the ends already attached, which required taking the wing apart to install. When Smith called maintenance control the next day to report that the problem had not been resolved, he also informed them of the method the other crew planned to use to fix the jet within three hours. According to Richard Smith, the folks in Pittsburgh had never considered such a solution.[82]

Weaving a new airline from the threads of three old ones (including PSA) took time. Though USAir was quick to urge the approval of the merger, they were slow to implement it. After the late October 1987 endorsement of the Department of Transportation cleared the way for folding Piedmont into USAir, Ed Colodny set a date of January 1, 1989, for completion. Then the date was moved back to the spring of that year. The uncertainty kept employees anxious. In a series of meetings with employees in early February 1989, Colodny set a final date, August 5. By that point, Piedmont had existed for 29 months as a lame duck airline before the Speedbird was erased from the tailfins.

Challenges loomed all around the merger landscape. One contentious issue for pilots was the debate over how to best fuse the seniority lists of the two groups. As Piedmont pilot and merger representative Richard Wallis explained it, "Seniority for pilots is everything. It is your pay; it is the base that you fly out of, the equipment you fly, whether captain or copilot, and primarily pay and working conditions, and it is all determined by seniority."[83] A lot was at stake when the two sides came together to create a combined list. Serving with Dick Wallis on the committee for Piedmont was Bob Kirch and Bob Koontz, who chaired. In negotiations, they argued that seniority be determined by "straight relative ratio," meaning that a pilot in the top 25 percent with Piedmont would roughly remain in that percentile in any merged seniority list. On the other hand, the USAir representatives advocated a straight date of hire arrangement that the Airline Pilot's Association (ALPA) recognized as standard. The two sides went through both negotiation and mediation phases with no agreement. As Piedmont pilots saw the issue, they had much to lose. Since Piedmont was growing much faster than USAir, Speedbird pilots moved up their seniority list quicker. That experience gave Piedmont pilots greater proficiency on aircraft than many USAir pilots hired at the same time.[84] Dick Wallis used his own situation as an example.

I had been a captain over six years and I was put in a list with captains on the other side that came from USAir that had two and three years, in length of service and grade. Now you become equal for bidding trips, vacation and everything else. It wasn't so bad if you are a captain. Your pay was not affected so much but people on the cusp, a very junior captain would wind up with pay cuts, and stayed junior for years and years as it turned out. So they get the worst choice of trips to fly, the worst choice of airplanes to fly, the worst choice of vacations. They have to fly all holidays, that kind of thing.[85]

With no consensus between the two positions, the issue went to arbitration. After study, arbitrator Sam Kagel sided with the USAir position since it was also the standard supported by the union and both groups of pilots were members of ALPA. Dick Wallis remembered reaction to the decision. "It seemed like most of the Piedmont people weren't terribly happy, but they got over it fairly quickly and went about doing their job and doing it well."[86]

Next came a controversy about when to implement the new seniority list. Again, the issue went to arbitration. Only this time, the Piedmont rationale was successful. USAir pilots wanted to put the list into practice seven months prior to the official merge date. As a result of the second arbitration, Piedmont pilots delayed operating under a combined list until the day Piedmont Airlines ceased to exist. Again, Dick Wallis explained the significance. "What was important about that is that there was seat protection language in that award, and we were able to upgrade about a hundred captains in that period."[87] The merger continued to move along bumpily.

As the final months loomed before the Speedbird folded into USAir, service on the Piedmont began to suffer. Unlike its pre-purchase performance, flights increasingly failed to arrive on time, and some were cancelled. Complaints soared. By the time the end arrived, news reports quoted passengers who were disgusted with the airline. USAir's answer pointed to the challenges of blending two airlines into one and promised better service in the future. In the last days, the once proud name of Piedmont got dragged through the mud as U.S. Department of Transportation data showed the company was dead last among carriers in on-time performance and baggage handling. The superior service given by Piedmont left long before the name. Captain Elmo Torres saw the change take place in front of his eyes. He described it by saying, "The goodwill that we had all worked for at Piedmont Airlines which was all focused on the treatment of passengers — that just disappeared."[88]

Others agreed, pointing to the DOT figures as proof. The month before Piedmont became USAir, only 62.8 percent of Speedbird flights arrived within 15 minutes of the scheduled time. Almost one out of every 100 passengers complained of lost baggage, an astoundingly high figure even for a sluggish industry.[89] Beyond weather delays, both Piedmont employees and USAir officials agreed on the source of the problem: USAir procedures. Spokespeople for USAir said Piedmont workers were adjusting to the new style of doing business, which they concluded caused the delays. On the other side, Piedmont employees pointed out that USAir policy prevented them from fixing problems that led to delays. One Piedmont pilot said, "It's been a mess." Anonymously, he explained that since all spare parts for airplanes were shipped to Pittsburgh (USAir's main hub) mechanics were left without the inventories they needed to fix planes and get them back on line.[90]

Along the way, USAir moved some of their personnel, with a portion of them going to Winston-Salem. As departments were combined, over 600 employees were relocated from the Washington, D.C., area to North Carolina. During the summer of 1988, USAir moved its consumer affairs department and frequent flier program, as well as revenue accounting, audit, management information systems, and credit and collection departments.[91] When interviewed,

Ed Colodny continually pointed out that merger meant more jobs for North Carolinians. While in Charlotte, he declared, "I think everything from Charlotte's standpoint is extremely positive."[92]

Throughout 1988, USAir proceeded to take firmer control of Piedmont. Issues remained to be worked out, such as whether or not USAir planned to keep Piedmont's first class service. Initiated systemwide in 1986, Piedmont offered a higher level of amenities than USAir. Eventually, USAir made the choice to follow the Piedmont lead and also provide the service on its planes. Likewise, differences in frequent flyer programs required attention. During the interim before complete takeover, the awards Piedmont gave for frequent fliers began to be trimmed. While Piedmont had gotten into the frequent flier program later than most other carriers, the rewards offered for flying the Speedbird were more generous. Passengers received credit for 1,000 miles on any Piedmont flight, however short, before the change. Under USAir, minimum credit was reduced to 750. Also, the prize for benchmarks like 50,000 miles diminished from two round trip coach tickets to any Piedmont destination in North America to one first class ticket under USAir.[93]

In the public eye, the greatest misstep made by USAir in its attempt to take over Piedmont's customer base came from a can of Coca-Cola. As long as a Speedbird had flown, flight attendants gave passengers a full bottle, and later on, can of Coke when they poured a soft drink. As with many policies, Piedmont's differed from USAir. Before the final consolidation, USAir policy dictated that flight attendants pour a cup full and remove the can unless the passenger specifically asked to keep the soda. A commotion erupted, more vocal than anything seen in the merger process previously. Piedmont passengers wanted their full can of Coke, and they began to complain loudly. The news media picked up on the story and used it as an indicator of the difference between the two airlines. USAir eventually altered its policy and instructed flight attendants to leave the can with the passenger. Most observers agreed it had been an unfortunate brouhaha for USAir. One airline analyst said, "There's no reason to have a customer dissatisfied over something that costs so little." Meanwhile, another writer pointed out, "There's no real economic consequence to it, but it does speak to style of service."[94] The *Charlotte Observer* could not help but take a bit of a shot at Colodny and company with a short editorial piece that addressed the situation. Under the title "Piedmont's Pacifier," the paper said the revised policy was both nice and necessary because "Piedmont's on-time record is so awful since USAir acquired it (second-worst among the largest U.S. airlines) that passengers who don't get enough cool drink might really be steaming by the time their flights finally unloaded."[95] Ed Colodny had no trouble discerning the cause of his company's black eye: A can of Coke blackened it.

When the time came to switch from being a Piedmont employee to working for USAir, Jim Brown could not bring himself to make the jump. Brown flew the line until just a week before the Speedbird came off the side of the planes forever, telling his daughter, "If I had wanted to fly for them [USAir] I would have sent them a resume."[96] He died of a massive heart attack just two years later. Other pilots, like Howard Miller, took early retirement. Instead of flying passengers under the USAir banner, Miller went to work for United Coal Company, which owned a plush 737 that it leased regularly to musical acts for tours. Miller flew the likes of Bruce Springsteen, Fleetwood Mac, Madonna, and Neil Diamond on tour. When additional crews were needed, he called on his old friend Mel Blocker, who flew one leg of Michael Jackson's European tour.[97] Beau Fields told television reporter Steve Gasque he had to leave, saying, "I didn't have any choice other than to retire under the good Piedmont benefits that we had worked for all these years." After a 20 year career in the cockpit for Piedmont, Gasque reported that Fields chose to "pilot" a 32-foot motor home in retirement.[98]

The exodus of pilots caused a shortage. As many World War II pilots retired at the mandatory age of 60 from commercial flying, fewer pilots were there to replace them. The trend began in the late seventies when pilots like Leon Fox, who flew the first flight, stepped down, and a shortage of trained pilots continued to grow throughout the eighties. However, Piedmont had an answer. Through the years, fixed base continued to operate its flight school which turned out 50 to 100 pilots per year. The fixed base division — owned by USAir but still called Piedmont Aviation — promised to continue supplying pilots well after the airline no longer carried the Piedmont name. In essence, Piedmont Aviation continued to operate pretty much as it did when Tom Davis helped incorporate the Piedmont name almost 50 years back.[99]

The last days of Piedmont Airlines left a bad taste in the mouths of customers. A lifetime of hustle and hard work had dissipated in less than 18 months. Every news media outlet had no trouble finding passengers whose flights were cancelled or significantly delayed. One particular flight from New York to Charlotte took twelve hours to complete, which included multiple delays and a bus ride from Greensboro to finally get passengers to Charlotte. The mother of a 15-year-old on that flight declared, "We've always had a lot of faith and trust in Piedmont.... We've completely lost our confidence."[100] Her lament rang through airport concourses all over the U.S.

Even with poor morale rampant at Piedmont, many employees still cried the day Piedmont flew its last flight, August 4, 1989. One mechanic spoke for many of his coworkers when he said simply, "It's just sad to see it go."[101] Other employees grabbed mementos of their past work life. On flights like the last one out of Charlotte into Myrtle Beach, South Carolina, flight attendants asked their fellow employees, even passengers to sign Piedmont posters as remembrances of shared experiences.[102] Just like Piedmont had engineered to quickly erase the Empire Airlines signs on the night of the official takeover, the same was done by USAir in the early morning hours of August 5. "15,000 Piedmont signs will be taken down. Every billboard, every ticket envelope, gone," intoned Steve Gasque as he reported the final hours.[103]

Debate raged for years afterward about which flight was actually the

Robert Wall and his father meet in front of a 737 just before the aircraft was repainted in USAir colors. Both had worked for the airline and both wanted a picture in front of a Speedbird before the company was gone (Robert Wall Collection).

last. In reality, every Piedmont employee had their own. "Nobody wanted this to happen and when it did happen the way they did it, none of the Piedmont people liked it," said Warren Wheeler about the end of an airline he joined 21 years before. He recalled of his last flight, "The night it was all switched over and there was no more Piedmont left, they made a gigantic effort to get all the cups and napkins or anything that said Piedmont off those airplanes. They didn't want anything on there the next day that said 'Piedmont Airlines,' which I thought was overkill. They seemed threatened by it — anything that was left that indicated or seemed to be a part of Piedmont and the Piedmont management style."[104]

The flight of the Speedbird had ended. It had been a phenomenal ride. From a cold winter morning in Wilmington to final flights all over the United States, Piedmont Airlines had come a long way. At the time of deregulation Piedmont ranked as the 18th largest carrier in the country. When USAir purchased the company, it ranked 9th and threatened to overtake its purchaser. Together, the two became the 7th biggest airline in the U.S. and counted themselves among the "big boys."[105] On the morning of August 5 Piedmont Airlines ceased to exist, except in the hearts of those who learned the airline business from a special breed of individual, many now retired and watching events from the sideline. Some continued on as USAir workers. The ones who did could not hide their Piedmont roots. Connie Counts worked a USAir flight years later and remembered being approached by "one of the big guys with BA [British Airways]." After handling her workload on the flight, the BA official asked her to "sit down and chat with him." In conversation, he asked, "'You were Piedmont, weren't you?' I said, 'Yes.' He said, 'If we could figure out how to combine our efficiency with Piedmont's personality, we would have an airline that nobody in the world could beat.'"[106] She smiled at the prospect.

Many wonder about what might have been for Piedmont Airlines. Don Collins conjectured, "If Mr. Davis could have done this, let's say the day of merger walked over somewhere and said, "Guys, we'll take all you retirees and anybody that wants to give us any time; we're going to start another airline, we could have built another one."[107] Could lightning have struck twice? Many determined souls say yes.

Afterword: Last Flight Out

Fifteen years after the last Speedbird landed, passengers still called for another takeoff. In the *Charlotte Observer* "Forum," a letters to the editor section, a vexed reader shook his head at the deplorable condition into which air travel had lapsed. Under the bold faced banner "Piedmont Airlines, we need you now!" Ralph S. McNatt of Charlotte wrote, "US Airways wouldn't be having all this trouble if Piedmont Airlines people were in charge. 'Northern efficiency' doesn't work."[1]

The trouble to which he referred was USAir's second bankruptcy since its 1989 merger/buyout of Piedmont Airlines. Many who remembered Piedmont, even from its early puddle jumping days, agreed. A once proud, efficient airline had allowed itself to become part of an organization mired in debt with no appreciable plan for resurrection and no one willing to accept responsibility for how it got there. When USAir bought Piedmont, the rhetoric of everyone associated with the deal, even that of Piedmont executives, boasted how the union of two strong companies would make for one superior airline. The merger was supposed to meld the northern efficiency of USAir, headquartered near Washington, D.C., with the southern hospitality of Piedmont Airlines, from down below the Mason-Dixon Line, in the piedmont of central North Carolina, into one great airline.

On the surface, the self congratulatory happy talk about the merger made sense. The eighth and ninth largest carriers in the United States combined to form a powerhouse enterprise that together could teach the rest of an ailing industry a thing or two about performance. True, both airlines prospered under deregulation. Both offered something to the other in marriage. They looked like chocolate and peanut butter, "two great tastes that taste great together," as the old slogan went. But far from being a sweet treat where one delight encased the other, the mix turned sour. The chemistry failed. Some USAir people snidely referred to their new coworkers from Piedmont as "the Southern division," with all the redneck, hillbilly connotations that being from the South could muster. Former Piedmont employees shot back with references to working for "Useless Air." The marriage went forward but with none of the élan predicted.

Often in a marriage when the two become one, a fair question becomes "who is the one the two become?" No matter how profitable USAir might have been in the decade after deregulation (and in some quarters it was very profitable), the company's success and its name has forever been overshadowed by its 1990s decline into insolvency. As the dominant partner in the wedding ceremony and the one who kept the name, USAir remained a tangible entity and, at least to some degree, answered the marriage question of identity. As the bride, Piedmont lost much more than its name. The company forsook the vast majority of its character and when the last flight landed in the wee hours of the morning on August 5, 1989, a persona was relegated to history as "Piedmont." To any visible degree, the Speedbird ceased to exist. There was nothing more for the company to do. It was, as a tangible entity, dead. The planes got new paint jobs; ticket counters were re-branded, old uniforms were shed for new ones; and all that was Piedmont was frozen in time as nothing more than memories.

The only thing left to do for the dearly departed Piedmont was to bury it and write the obituary. In the effort to be "on the same team" with the new company, much of the memorabilia was simply tossed away. The old made way for the new, but as memories have a tendency to do, the old was never completely forgotten. When the slide began down its slippery slope, not only were the memories of Piedmont rekindled as a nostalgic nod to better days, but also the ones doing the remembering began to appreciate the unconventional wisdom that collectively built what was acknowledged to be a superior airline. They mourned the fact that the likes of an airline such as Piedmont was never to be seen again. Some told themselves the new would be stronger than the old, hoping that indeed it would be. Others had the foresight to recognize that wishing was no recipe for success. Having seen more than their share of "lost causes," southerners took it all in stride.

Writing the obituary took a little longer. History, like Greek tragedy, sees the fall coming and orients the story to give the crash maximum impact. As theatrical as it might be to include the gory details filled with enough recriminations to make a divorce lawyer salivate, this obit does not follow the stormy ride down to the red ink. Instead, the story starts when there was no cliff from which to drop, only a city that embraced the new technology of flight as men were learning to use it for thrill and profit. In that respect, what ultimately came to be chronicled as Piedmont Aviation's story was no obituary at all. Instead, it has become a tribute to a group who worked hard, took pride, mentored the next generation, and expected that to be enough in the world of business.

Along the way the early Piedmont people witnessed uncertain times, including a societal and technological revolution that had them at times wondering if people really would pay to get across the Appalachians by air. The ride had its dips, even a few calamitous last moments about which some would rather not think. The tragedy and the triumph balanced each other out in a steady climb that ultimately afforded some dizzying heights. No one really knew where it would go. They just signed on and held on, trusting a balding, but gracious and friendly man named Tom Davis. He was a pilot who flew an airline. He knew them by name. He made one prudent decision after another until his company became larger than he, and the reins went to those in his shadow. They flew it out of the shadow and up the mountain of prosperity to the summit, never knowing that on the other side lay the cliff.

And that's where the ride stops. Looking over, a few rocks are kicked off, and we watch the long fall. We pause. William Faulkner wrote about the moment before the third day charge at Gettysburg (the pinnacle of the American Civil War and a pivotal moment for many southerners) when every southern boy could linger "not once but whenever he wants it" before the carnage of the inevitable, when life turns a corner and a once comfortable skin is shed never to be worn again. And while the chapter can never be rewritten, it can be reread, and like Faulkner's young man on Seminary Ridge, the outcome can be imagined differently: "*This time. Maybe this time* with all this much to lose and all this much to gain." Changing the outcome is, of course impossible, but there are places we all go and long for a decision made differently here, a reevaluation there, all leading up to the where we are now. Still, we are left with the consequences of decisions made as best they could be at the time. Since the future is a constant, new frontier, judging the decisions of the past might be too harsh. At the time, the foresight of those guiding the airline was 20/20. Ours is now considerably better. Reflection is not a wasted task. It's just sometimes uncomfortable.

There were as many different histories of Piedmont Airlines as there were employees, passengers, and observers, each correct from their own perspective, none that could completely take all viewpoints into account. This volume pulls together some of those sources, including many who held strong beliefs about the company, and who were not always in agreement with others. And therein lay the secret of this subject. To call this a business history is to so strip the subject of its passion, its essence, its blood, so much so that the experience is rendered empty. Yes, planes flew and passengers got to their destinations and the next day the same was completed again, but in that process something else happened, something almost unexplainable, except to say that without it, Piedmont would never have risen to the altitude it did. Even before the first flight, elements acted upon each other to bring opportunity to the remarkable circumstances. Trying to capture the spirit of these people, undertaking the work that called them, has been the goal of this narrative. If one can sense their motivations from reading their words, then the reader will have an inkling of what it was like to join a venture that provided more than a paycheck, one that provided a sense of self, a network for relationship, and a common cause. Adventure like this comes along seldom, but when it does, those along for the ride have little choice but to experience it to the fullest.

Everyone acknowledges that the likes of Piedmont Aviation could never be recaptured. The reason is twofold. First, the workforce is populated by very few people who would drag themselves into work avoiding a sick day because they think they might miss something. Still fewer would forfeit hours worked as a means to help insure the perpetuation of the company. Before the generation who started Piedmont faced a World War, they endured a Great Depression. A job was a precious commodity, one so valuable that if an extra measure were requested, the employee would give it. Affluence has killed notions of sacrifice. Secondly, as Jim Brown was quoted saying, "Doing something for the first time is the only time that counts."[2] Though another Piedmont Airlines might be a godsend to the airline industry, the fact remains that the environment for another airline like Piedmont could never be recreated, either by retracing the steps of Tom Davis or by getting a former Piedmont employee to guide the flight path personally. The forces that allowed Piedmont to prosper no longer exist. The second time around feels repetitive, and clearly, it would be.

But before the wake begins in earnest, consider that history builds on its own foundations. At one time, skeptics wondered if Piedmont would even remain solvent, much less become an industry darling. As Tom Davis might say, it was no sure thing. The people who are now rightly credited with building the airline had nothing heroic in mind as they came to work every day. They just wanted to pursue a rewarding career, make money for their families and leave their employer a little better off each day than they found it. Modest goals to be sure, but along the way, they built something significant, that they themselves recognized as such only when they stepped back to evaluate. Just as surely as employees who came to Piedmont in the seventies and eighties admired those before them, the original pilots had their own heroes, through Lindbergh, the Wright Brothers, all the way back to Icarus. The group that made the first flight for Piedmont has been called in other arenas "the greatest generation." They assume much the same role for this story. Though their wartime experiences are only mentioned, these people were part of the effort that made American prosperity possible after 1945. As the dips came in the sixties, seventies, and eighties they realized that life had been worse and more importantly, they calmly knew they'd get through circumstances as they had before. Their optimism built Piedmont Aviation.

So the airline came and went. Is there a lesson to be learned? For anyone who wasn't looking, there isn't one, but then again individuals with such a mind frame would never have lasted at Piedmont. The confidence each applied to their respective tasks was not an outward boast but an inner smile. Some will tell you they worked harder than they wanted to — tackled tasks that sometimes tackled them — but then got up the next morning and did it again, gladly. No matter what the job, notice should be given to the manner in which they carried out the task. The work ethic may not have been one hundred percent all the time, but it was so much better than just about any other airline of its time. Unfortunately, the effort was not enough to sustain it.

If Piedmont was such a perfect entity, how could it be just a memory now? Various people have various answers. George Washington never meant to catch cold and die as the minutes ticked away on 1799. His death was a consequence of his life. So too, perhaps, was this entity. A less profitable airline might still be in business but that would not be Piedmont's story. Life and business reflect each other often in that both take unexpected and unfortunate turns; the difference is how each handled the change. In Winston-Salem, more than a few Piedmont employees took the loss personally, not that they could be blamed. Throughout any career, one yearns for a career where the work is challenging but enjoyable. Coworkers can be relied upon and everyone's effort makes a difference. Most have been in jobs where that kind of satisfaction is never found. Imagine the plight of an employee for Piedmont. Most are eager to say that they found an agreeable work environment with people they liked and trusted. Their collective work ethic paid off in the success Piedmont achieved, whether we measure the early days of sustaining operation or the later days when the airline was an industry meteor, an unpretentious, energetic success in a sky with few bright stars. Then, all of a sudden, like a meteor, it was gone. The disappearance seemed counterintuitive. Wasn't success supposed to be rewarded? The Piedmont employee could rightly ask, "What happened?" And it they took it personally, but such feelings only signified how much they cared. The inability of USAir, with all its best intentions and bright shiny assurances to build a better airline, even with many of those same employees trying very hard to make it work, took away some of the joy of going to work each day, but it only heightened the moment in time when they wore the Speedbird.

For as long as the "great outfit" flew, most thought nothing of what made this airline tick. Everyone in Winston-Salem assumed that, like R.J. Reynolds and Hanes Knitting, Piedmont thrived because the rest of the world embraced that which came from the Twin City. Only after its demise did it occur to them what had really been lost. We seldom seem to realize the good time while we're having it, being caught up too much in the euphoria. This is not to suggest that Piedmont folks were euphoric every day of their lives, but they were fulfilled, which is an outlook that can be sustained for much longer. Bill McGee summed it up well when he said, "What it all gets down to is the fact that this company has in its success story been blessed by a unique group of people that had a willingness from the very start to work together toward a common cause."[3] Dave Johnson got to heart of the matter though when he evaluated his time with Piedmont: "It was the greatest thing I've ever experienced in life. It was right up there with watching your first child being born."[4]

As the decades pass since the last flight, the aura of Piedmont Airlines has grown. A stellar record of success in an era when the rest were mediocre begs the question of what could Piedmont have achieved if it had bought USAir instead of being bought. We will never know. Not only was the company a product of its time, but it was also a delicate mix of individuals. Most of those folks do not see their counterpart in today's airline industry. If there were comparisons drawn in the years that followed, the majority point to Southwest Airlines, a company with a strong guiding force, a willingness to defy industry analysts, and a growth strategy that was mapped out in decades, not months.

Some overriding principles distinguish Piedmont's approach as a service oriented company, ones that are deceptively simple, but are often overlooked in corporate America. Worry about the customers, not the budgets. Put the needs of the employees ahead of the stockholders. After all, if the workers take care of the daily business, the stockholders will profit. Never assume that growth solves every problem.

When Ivan Boesky declared "greed is healthy," he cursed the business world with an ethic that doomed capitalism to the status of deflating balloon. Open season was declared on taking whatever could be snatched from an executive position. Unlike later USAir presidents who found their company in bankruptcy for the second time, Tom Davis would have shouldered the burden for survival right along with his people, furthering the communal spirit that made Piedmont a cherished airline. Significant leadership is defined by sacrifice, not perks. Throughout history, as kings demonstrated their unconcern for the masses, they were either overthrown or marginalized. Corporate management runs the same risk. If workers feel CEOs and the VP staff are only out for their own needs, then employees refuse to heed the call to pull together for a common cause. Who wants to work solely for the profit of another and to their own personal detriment? Tom Davis shared a love of aviation with his people, not a desire to make money off them. He gave them respect, and they gave him devotion. His station wagon spoke volumes to Piedmont personnel about his priorities. Remember, it was the workers who put him in a Mercedes, and, in essence, said to him, "As our prudent leader, we want you to enjoy some of the fruits of success." Frank Davis said the car was one of his father's most cherished possessions, not because he could cruise around town with the top down, but because of the bond it represented with his people. Other than the kind of corporate suck ups that Don Collins called "hay boys," few corporate presidents have engendered such feeling, though they all secretly covet it.

The Davis era at Piedmont contrasts rather sharply with that of Bill Howard, but in many ways they complement each other. An energetic man of great ability, Howard came in fresh and took a well run but conservative airline and pushed it forward. He put meat on good bones and gave Piedmont visibility, something it lacked up until that time. The very idea that most outside the upper South had never heard of the Speedbird before Howard took the helm pays tribute to his abilities. He pushed and pulled, cajoled and barked until he had an air carrier that the rest of the nation had to recognize, and recognize they did. The summit may have been the "Airline of the Year" award that fulfilled the advertising promise of "how good an airline can be." Bill Howard gained for every Piedmont employee the admiration that was long in coming from a growing network of passengers, as well as their peers in the industry. The Speedbird flew high in those days. Some look back and say it was too high. The trouble with visibility is that while Piedmont was admired, it was also envied. With only so many passengers out there, flying on Piedmont meant not flying with another carrier. Other CEOs of other airlines were not willing to sit still and watch Piedmont overshadow them. Instead, they laid plans to snare Piedmont. In the end they stirred with greater alacrity than Piedmont, and Bill Howard's exemplary airline moved beyond his control.

Over time, Piedmont employees quit, worked, retired, and otherwise left the new airline that quickly grew old. In 2005, USAir suffered the same fate as Piedmont, and was merged with America West to form a true two coast airline. As a tip of the hat to all the old airlines that had come together over the years, America West management commissioned aircraft commemorative of the foundations upon which the "new" USAir was built. One more time a hurrah (or should I say a rebel yell) went up for Piedmont, now one of several grandfathers to a new airline trying to make its way in a more complex and competitive flying environment. Unfortunately, there are no tickets available to board an original Pacemaker and see for ourselves what kind of airline really flew the skies of first the Southeast, then up and down the East Coast, and finally to the Pacific Coast and London. All we have left now are the memories, but they tell a fantastic story.

As the flight attendants said when the ride was over, "Thank you for flying Piedmont Airlines."

Epilogue: Flying West

When a Piedmont pilot breathes his or her last, comrades euphemistically say that he or she has "flown west." The phrase conjures up notions about where all good people with aviation in their blood can be found on that last day, heading off to a new horizon. The Piedmont family takes it hard whenever a brother or sister has flown west, noticing how the circle grows ever smaller. With stories about the good times, those that remain reflect on the meaning of it all and where it all went. One might think that since 1989 the family dispersed to other jobs in other regions and only fond memories lingered. Certainly, some stayed with USAir, some left, some retired, but the bonds were not easily broken. In cafeterias and convention centers up and down the east coast, those family members have met regularly in the ensuing years to stay a part of each others lives, getting together for a meal, sometimes even spending a few days together. They talk, relive and reaffirm their shared experience as part of the Piedmont family.

Realizing that all must "fly west" one day, many of the Piedmont alumni have endeavored to leave lasting, tangible proof that the Speedbird did one day fly before it too was called west. Individual shrines can be found in the homes of family members, but as they too fly west, the biggest recipient of the artifacts that tell the Piedmont story are being accumulated at the North Carolina Transportation Museum (NCTM) in Spencer, near Salisbury. The museum has made a strong commitment to telling the history of this unique airline so that one day when all those who worked for Piedmont, as well as those who flew aboard one of the Pacemakers, are gone; the story remains.

Beyond housing memorabilia like flight attendants' uniforms and tickets, the NCTM has gone a step further. As part of an ongoing effort to bring the transportation story to its visitors, the museum plans restoration of an actual Piedmont DC-3. In 2004, volunteers hauled in the *Potomac Pacemaker* (N56V) and began the arduous process to bring the Speedbird back to life. When restored, the aircraft will be part of a display in the museum's "back shop" that details all aspects of North Carolina's varied transportation landscape. As usual, former Piedmont employees led the charge. Among them were Ronnie Macklin and Howard Miller, who looked for the most cost effective way to restore the Piedmont aircraft (not so different from their days with the airline). Their effort to resurrect a plane that has not flown for over 40 years marks one last tribute to their former employer.

The *Potomac Pacemaker* had a long career of service with the airline. Purchased in 1956 from Western Airlines, the *Potomac* flew the line until all DC-3s were phased out in 1963. This particular airplane held on to the very end, being the very last DC-3 operated by the airline. By then, it had logged of 48,000 hours of service. Prior to the plane's commercial usage, the aircraft was part of the war effort. Coming off the assembly line on March 20,

Epilogue: Flying West 253

A gathering of the Piedmont Silver Eagles in 2006. From left to right, Capt. Buddy Bowen/President, Piedmont Silver Eagles, Capt. H.K. (Zeke) Saunders, Capt. Stephanie Hamilton/President, Piedmont Silver Eagles Charitable Funds, Inc., Capt. Susan Dusenbury (ABX Air), and Capt. David Foster/Treasurer, Piedmont Silver Eagles Charitable Funds Inc. In front, Capt. Jim Hamilton (Piedmont Silver Eagles Collection).

1942, the C-53 (military designation) with serial number 4900 and Air Corps number 41-20130 remained stateside during World War II and was reassigned to the U.S. Government's Reconstruction Finance Corporation until sold to Western. Purchased in 1963 by a company known as Charlotte Aircraft, the *Potomac* remained grounded and fell into disrepair until it was discovered by Dick Wescott of the Nature Science Museum in Durham in 1978. The *Potomac Pacemaker* was given fresh paint in Piedmont's red, white and blue (provided by the airline) and hoisted up on pylons as an outdoor museum piece. Piedmont Aviation supplied an additional $20,000 in parts and technical expertise. Ronnie Macklin headed that restoration effort too. The effort required him to futilely search through the Piedmont files back in Winston-Salem for the specifications on the original paint scheme for the original Pacemakers. Eventually, old photographs had to be used. In addition, a number of parts had to be located to give the aircraft the look of a real Piedmont airplane. Already by the late 1970s, DC-3s were dinosaurs on the aviation landscape. Refurbishment required some creative engineering for Macklin and his crew. At the time only one other DC-3 had been restored for display. It was part of the Smithsonian's Air and Space Museum display, so when the *Potomac Pacemaker* needed a nose cone, called a radome, another DC-3's radome had to be used to make a mold, so one could be crafted for the antique aircraft. After fix-up, the *Potomac Pacemaker* stood on display at the Museum of Life and Science for close to 25 years, deteriorating gradually under the elements.[1]

The NCTM purchased the aircraft and brought it to Spencer in April of 2004. Since then, considerable study and preparation have gone into a restoration plan for the airplane. Now in a much more controlled environment, the airplane awaits another makeover to be presentable again. As Ronnie Macklin and Howard Miller hunt down parts that are even harder to find than they were almost 30 years ago, they have found a few partners willing to donate assistance. Guilford Technical Community College sponsors an Aviation Systems Technology Program at the T.H. Davis/GTCC Aviation Center located at the Piedmont Triad International Airport near Greensboro. Students in the program have been working with the North Carolina Transportation Museum to craft the necessary sheet metal repairs that will once again make the Potomac Pacemaker a show piece.[2] Likewise, a varied group of individuals are volunteering their help to get the Piedmont plane in shape for the unveiling of the backshop display, sometime before 2010. When completed, it will be the only airplane that actually flew the line for Piedmont to wear the colors of the former airline.[3]

Choosing a DC-3 for restoration was no accident. Piedmont flew other planes more miles for longer stretches, but the DC-3 represents something distinctive about the airline that a Martin 404, or a Boeing 737, loved though they were by those who flew and fixed them, did not. One anonymous pilot from a bygone era expressed a strong preference for the round engine planes like the DC-3 over the jet turbines of later years. He wrote:

The *Potomac Pacemaker* arrives at the North Carolina Transportation Museum. The plane, once part of the Piedmont fleet, is being readied to go through restoration at the North Carolina Transportation Museum in Spencer, N.C. as part of a large display that will note advances in transportation (Ronnie Macklin Collection).

We gotta get rid of those turbines; they're ruining aviation and our hearing.... A turbine is too simple minded, it has no mystery. The air travels through it in a straight line and doesn't pick up any of the pungent fragrance of engine oil or pilot sweat. Anybody can start a turbine. You just need to move a switch from "OFF" to "START" and then remember to move it back to "ON" after a while. My PC is harder to start.

Cranking a round engine requires skill, finesse and style. You have to seduce it into starting. It's like waking up a horny mistress. On some planes, the pilots aren't even allowed to do it.... Turbines start by whining for a while, then give a lady-like poof and start whining a little louder. Round engines give a satisfying rattle-rattle, click-click, BANG, more rattles, another BANG, a big macho FART or two, more clicks, a lot more smoke and finally a serious low pitched roar. We like that. It's a GUY thing.... When you start a round engine, your mind is engaged and you can concentrate on the flight ahead. Starting a turbine is like flicking on a ceiling fan: Useful, but, hardly exciting. When you have started his round engine successfully your Crew Chief looks up at you like he'd let you kiss his girl, too!

Turbines don't break or catch fire often enough, which leads to aircrew boredom, complacency and inattention. A round engine at speed looks and sounds like it's going to blow any minute. This helps concentrate the mind! Turbines don't have enough control levers or gauges to keep a pilot's attention. There's nothing to fiddle with during long flights. Turbines smell like a Boy Scout camp full of Coleman Lamps. Round engines smell like God intended machines to smell."[4]

The restoration of the *Potomac Pacemaker* represents a move to herald the contribution of Piedmont Airlines, North Carolina's largest, as part of the dynamic transportation history of the state.

Beyond seeing a real DC-3, students who visit the NCTM are getting the experience of what it was like to fly one. A former Piedmont employee has donated a General Aviation Trainer, called a GAT3 simulator, as an educational tool for children visiting the museum. Nicknamed the "Piedmonster," the flight simulator was the first generation of training devices used by the airline. The term Piedmonster has been more widely used to describe Piedmont employees who have remained fiercely loyal to their former company, but in subsequent years, it has been used to also include those loyal customers who miss the air carrier, as well as anyone who is intrigued by the unique history of Piedmont Airlines. The Piedmonster joins a collection of over 500 other items detailing the story to which Piedmonsters are so attracted.

Integral to the story of Piedmont Airlines was its people. The North Carolina Transportation Hall of Fame includes sev-

The man and his airline. Mr. Tom Davis poses behind a model of the first pressurized aircraft for Piedmont, the F-27. He was the obvious choice for induction into the first class of the North Carolina Transportation Museum Hall of Fame (courtesy Piedmont Aviation Historical Society; from the collection of the Piedmont Silver Eagles).

Left: The enthusiasm of his sister Mary for flight directed Frank Nicholson into the air as well. As an early Piedmont pilot, he helped set the standard that all fellow employees followed (courtesy Jan N. Assimos). *Right:* Though she never worked for Piedmont Aviation, Mary Nicholson was a pioneer in flight and an example of how enthusiasm for flying knew no gender bounds. Her brother, Frank flew for Piedmont as one of the first twelve pilots (courtesy of Mary Walton).

eral individuals connected with the airline. Mr. Tom Davis was part of the first class of inductees, demonstrating his profound impact on transportation in his native state. The contribution of Tom Davis to transportation and to his state and his nation is largely told in these pages. No other North Carolinian has been more important to aviation.

Joining Mr. Davis in the North Carolina Transportation Hall of Fame is Mary Nicholson, an early aviation pioneer who never flew for Piedmont. She was an accomplished pilot in the days when women flyers were few. As part of a women's flying group that included Amelia Earhart, she performed as a barnstormer before joining the war effort in Britain. Nicholson helped deliver planes from British factories to the Royal Air Force (RAF), which freed combat fighters for their missions against Germany in World War II. She might actually have come back to her native North Carolina after the war and flown a Speedbird had not she died tragically in a crash on May 22, 1943, while ferrying a plane.[5] Her connection to Piedmont stems from the fact that she was the older sister to one of Piedmont's original pilots, Frank Nicholson. His long and distinguished career with the airline might never have been possible if not for the formative influence of his big sister who gave her life serving the Allies during the war. Who knows, she might have become a Piedmont pilot well before other women became Piedmont flight attendants.

Another Piedmont person slated for initiation is Zeke Saunders. A pivotal figure in Pied-

Above: A country boy who loved and played bluegrass music, Zeke Saunders (right) embodied the spirit of Piedmont Airlines. He worked right beside Tom Davis to build the airline into an efficient family. Pictured here in the early days of the airline, Zeke points out John "Pappy" Wilkes's "Fly Piedmont" tie (Zeke Saunders Collection). *Right:* Reeve Lindbergh, daughter of Charles Lindbergh, the inspirational figure who captured Tom Davis's imagination, is shown receiving a pair of Piedmont wings from Ronnie Macklin at the North Carolina Transportation Museum in Spencer, N.C. (Chick Ayers Collection).

mont's history, Zeke, at 84, still garners the awe of those who worked with and for him in Winston-Salem. His contributions to the success of Piedmont (and aviation in North Carolina) stand with that of Mr. Davis as worthy of inclusion.

Interest in the story of Piedmont Airlines continues to grow long after the company folded its wings. First and foremost, the employees and their customers lead the charge with enthusiasm and always an interesting or funny story to tell. But the legend has spread much farther. Actually, it has come full circle.

Back in 1927, Tom Davis credited Charles Lindbergh's visit to Winston-Salem after his celebrated flight as the impetus to make all that later became Piedmont possible. Both Davis and Lindbergh have "flown west" but the admiration of Tom Davis for "Lucky Lindy" has been returned by the daughter of Charles Lindbergh, Reeve. Though Reeve never flew on Piedmont, she remembered that her father had once received a Piedmont pin. During a visit to the North Carolina Transportation Museum, Ronnie Macklin offered the youngest child of Charles Lindbergh her own Piedmont pin, which she eagerly accepted and asked that he pin it on her. She wore the pin to a meeting of the Lindbergh Foundation, where she explained to airline presidents from some of the nation's largest carriers that she was an honorary member of Piedmont Airlines.[6] Ironically, the first Piedmont Pacemaker ever named for an individual was to honor the contribution of Reeve's father. The journey has come full circle.

Appendix A:
The Piedmont Fleet, 1948–1989

Name	Type	PI	SN	Info
(Trainer)	DC-3	N8820	13041	Leased from Southern Airlines
Great Smokies Pacemaker	DC-3	N40V	3287	Last DC-3 flight
Blue Ridge Pacemaker	DC-3	N41V	2227	
Appalachian Pacemaker	DC-3	N42V	42974	
Kanawha River Pacemaker	DC-3	N43V	42958	
Commonwealth Pacemaker	DC-3	N44V	9914	
Tidewater Pacemaker	DC-3	N45V	18984	
Ohio Valley Pacemaker	DC-3	N46V	19402	
Blue Grass Pacemaker	DC-3	N47V	20471	
Piedmont Pacemaker	DC-3	N48V	13835	
Tennessee Valley Pacemaker	DC-3	N49V	20002	
Chesapeake Pacemaker	DC-3	N50V	19288	
Yadkin Valley Pacemaker	DC-3	N51V	19975	Preserved as C-47 at AAM
Shenandoah Valley Pacemaker	DC-3	N52V	19649	
Hampton Roads Pacemaker	DC-3	N53V	12717	
Sand Hills Pacemaker	DC-3	N54V	13998/25443	
Buckeye Pacemaker	DC-3	N55V	20447	Crashed, Crozet, Va. 10/30/59
Potomac Pacemaker	DC-3	N56V	4900	Preserved at NCTM
Tarheel Pacemaker	DC-3	N57V	4225	
Peninsula Pacemaker	DC-3	N58V	9856	
James River Pacemaker	DC-3	N59V	12336	
Catawba Pacemaker	DC-3	N60V	12555	
	DC-3	N145A	6098	Leased from Northeast Airlines
Piedmont Pacemaker	DC-3	N9184R	12027	1986 Promotional plane
Peninsula Pacemaker	F-27	N2700R	4	
Old Dominion Pacemaker	F-27	N2701R	8	
Cape Fear Pacemaker	F-27	N2702R	9	
Catawba Pacemaker	F-27	N2703R	10	
Palmetto Pacemaker	F-27	N2704R	17	Damaged, Hickory, N.C. 4/20/60
Kitty Hawk Pacemaker	F-27	N2705R	18	
Cumberland Pacemaker	F-27	N2706R	19	
James River Pacemaker	F-27	N2707R	20	Damaged, Goldsboro, N.C. 2/17/61
Tidewater Pacemaker	404	N40401	14101	Damaged, Wilmington, N.C. 8/22/62
Great Smokies Pacemaker	404	N40402	14106	
Savannah River Pacemaker	404	N40402	14102	
Mount Mitchell Pacemaker	404	N40403	14174	
Ohio Valley Pacemaker	404	N40405	14105	
Appomattox Pacemaker	404	N40406	14170	Crashed, New Bern, N.C. 11/20/66
Blue Grass Pacemaker	404	N40407	14107	
Rappahannock Pacemaker	404	N40408	14108	
Shenandoah Valley Pacemaker	404	N40410	14110	

Appendix A

Name	Type	PI	SN	Info
Tennessee Valley Pacemaker	404	N40411	14115	
Sand Hills Pacemaker	404	N40413	14117	
Commonwealth Pacemaker	404	N40414	14118	
Yadkin Valley Pacemaker	404	N40415	14119	
Piedmont Pacemaker	404	N40417	14123	
Hampton Roads Pacemaker	404	N40418	14124	
Kanawha River Pacemaker	404	N40419	14125	
Tar Heel Pacemaker	404	N40420	14126	
Appalachian Pacemaker	404	N40421	14127	
Pamlico Pacemaker	404	N40423	14129	
Pee Dee Pacemaker	404	N40424	14130	
Manassa Pacemaker	404	N40425	14131	
Chesapeake Pacemaker	404	N40430	14136	
Peachtree Pacemaker	404	N40433	14168	
Santee Pacemaker	404	N40440	14166	
Blue Ridge Pacemaker	404	N40442	14225	
Tidewater Pacemaker	404	N40443	14228	Damaged, Wilmington, N.C. 8/22/62
New River Pacemaker	404	N40444	14229	
Potomac Pacemaker	404	N40445	14230	
Buckeye Pacemaker	404	N40446	14238	Damaged, Roanoke, Va. 7/9/66
Albemarle Pacemaker	404	N40448	14242	
York River Pacemaker	404	N40450	14146	
Long Island Pacemaker	404	N462M	14153	
Cherokee Pacemaker	404	N467M	14164	
Neuse River Pacemaker	404	N468M	14139	
Roanoke Valley Pacemaker	404	N472M	14234	
Appomattox Pacemaker	FH-227B	N701U	524	Converted from FH-227
Buckeye Pacemaker	FH-227B	N702U	523	Converted from FH-227
Peninsula Pacemaker	FH-227B	N703U	530	Converted from FH-227
Old Dominion Pacemaker	FH-227B	N704U	540	
Palmetto Pacemaker	FH-227B	N705U	545	
Cape Fear Pacemaker	FH-227B	N706U	566	
Catawba Pacemaker	FH-227B	N708U	549	
Kitty Hawk Pacemaker	FH-227B	N709U	552	
Cumberland Pacemaker	FH-227B	N710U	554	
James River Pacemaker	FH-227B	N712U	557	Crashed, Charleston, W.Va. 8/10/68
Manhattan Pacemaker	727-100	N68650	18295	Crashed, Hendersonville, N.C. 7/19/67
Empire State Pacemaker	727-100	N7270C	18897	
Kitty Hawk Pacemaker	727-100	N833N	18935	
Lindbergh Pacemaker	727-100	N834N	18838	
Cape Fear Pacemaker	727-100	N836N	18850	
Catawba Pacemaker	727-100	N837N	18802	
Mount Mitchell Pacemaker	727-100	N838N	18803	Airliner used in D.B. Cooper hijacking
Long Island Pacemaker	727-100	N841N	18324	
Blue Ridge Pacemaker	YS-11/A500	N156P	2050	Renamed *Cherry Blossom Pacemaker*
Tidewater Pacemaker	YS-11/A500	N158P	2051	
York River Pacemaker	YS-11/A500	N159P	2057	
New River Pacemaker	YS-11/A500	N162P	2052	
Potomac Pacemaker	YS-11/A500	N164P	2053	
Albemarle Pacemaker	YS-11/A500	N169P	2056	
Long Island Pacemaker	YS-11/A500	N187P	2061	
Cherokee Pacemaker	YS-11/A500	N189P	2062	
Neuse River Pacemaker	YS-11/A500	N214P	2075	
Roanoke Valley Pacemaker	YS-11/A500	N218P	2077	
Garden State Pacemaker	YS-11/A500	N219P	2109	Renamed *Pamlico Pacemaker*
Grand Strand Pacemaker	YS-11/A500	N224P	2112	
Manassa Pacemaker	YS-11/A500	N245P	2113	Renamed *Croatan Pacemaker*

The Piedmont Fleet, 1948–1989

Name	Type	PI	SN	Info
Old Hickory Pacemaker	YS-11/A500	N247P	2114	
Pee Dee Pacemaker	YS-11/A500	N254P	2117	
Santee Pacemaker	YS-11/A500	N257P	2118	
Shenandoah Valley Pacemaker	YS-11/A500	N259P	2119	
Yajima Pacemaker	YS-11/100	N264P	2040	Used as spare only
Ito Tai Pacemaker	YS-11/100	N265P	2046	Used as spare only
Great Smokies Pacemaker	YS-11/A500	N268P	2120	
Ohio Valley Pacemaker	YS-11/A500	N269P	2121	
Peachtree Pacemaker	YS-11/A500	N273P	2122	
Tennessee Valley Pacemaker	YS-11/A500	N274P	2126	
Pee Dee Pacemaker	727–200	N1639	19444	
Kitty Hawk Pacemaker	727–200	N1640	19445	
Grand River Pacemaker	727–200	N1641	19446	
St. John's River Pacemaker	727–200	N1642	19447	
Savannah River Pacemaker	727–200	N1643	19448	
Keystone Pacemaker	727–200	N1644	19449	
Neuse River Pacemaker	727–200	N1645	20139	
Wolverine Pacemaker	727–200	N1646	20140	
Appomattox Pacemaker	727–200	N1647	20141	
Catawba Pacemaker	727–200	N1648	19994	
Monongahela Pacemaker	727–200	N1649	19995	
City of Grand Rapids	727–200	N2828W	21393	From Western Airlines, Long Range
Pride of Flint	727–200	N555PS	21512	From Pacific Southwest, Long Range
City of Los Angeles	727–200	N556PS	21513	From Pacific Southwest, Long Range
City of Fort Wayne	727–200	N557PS	21691	From Pacific Southwest, Long Range
City of San Francisco	727–200	N558PS	21692	From Pacific Southwest, Long Range
Pride of Kalamazoo	727–200	N559PS	21958	From Pacific Southwest, Long Range
Dixie Pacemaker	727–200	N855N	20163	
Delaware Bay Pacemaker	727–200	N856N	20164	
Independence Pacemaker	727–200	N857N	20165	
Valley Forge Pacemaker	727–200	N858N	20161	
Great Plains Pacemaker	727–200	N859N	20366	
Everglades Pacemaker	727–200	N860N	20166	
Tennessee Valley Pacemaker	727–200	N861N	20167	
Pride of Baltimore	727–200	N862N	20568	Renamed *City of Akron*
Pride of Dayton	727–200	N863N	20510	
City of New Orleans	727–200	N864N	20286	
Pride of Rochester	727–200	N865N	20570	
City of Denver	727–200	N866N	20569	
City of Lansing	727–200	N867N	20509	
City of Detroit	727–200	N869N	20367	
City of Evansville	727–200	N870N	20285	
Cape Cod Pacemaker	727–200	N895N	20168	
Tampa Bay Pacemaker	727–200	N896N	20367	
Piedmont Pacemaker	737–200	N734N	19418	
Appalachian Pacemaker	737–200	N735N	19419	
Mount Mitchell Pacemaker	737–200	N736N	19420	Renamed *Sunshine State*
Chesapeake Pacemaker	737–200	N737N	19421	
Hampton Roads Pacemaker	737–200	N738N	19422	
Empire State Pacemaker	737–200	N740N	19423	
Research Triangle Pacemaker	737–200	N741N	20211	
Garden State Pacemaker	737–200	N743N	20212	
Tar Heel Pacemaker	737–200	N744N	20213	
Blue Ridge Pacemaker	737–200	N745N	20214	
Manassa Pacemaker	737–200	N746N	20215	Renamed *Great Lakes*
Outer Banks Pacemaker	737–200	N747N	20216	
Manhattan Pacemaker	737–200	N749N	19547	

Appendix A

Name	Type	PI	SN	Info
Commonwealth Pacemaker	737–200	N751N	19548	
Kanawha River Pacemaker	737–200	N752N	19073	Damaged, Charlotte, N.C. 10/25/86
Yadkin Valley Pacemaker	737–200	N753N	20453	
James River Pacemaker	737–200	N754N	20454	
Buckeye Pacemaker	737–200	N758N	19603	
Bicentennial Pacemaker	737–200	N759N	19954	
New England Pacemaker	737–200	N761N	21665	
Old Dominion Pacemaker	737–200	N762N	21666	
Palmetto Pacemaker	737–200	N763N	21667	
Rocky Mountain Pacemaker	737–200	N767N	20095	
Gulf Coast Pacemaker	737–200	N768N	21815	
Volunteer Pacemaker	737–200	N769N	21816	
Peninsula Pacemaker	737–200	N772N	21817	
Tidewater Pacemaker	737–200	N773N	21818	
Great Smokies Pacemaker	737–200	N774N	21975	
Potomac Pacemaker	737–200	N775N	21976	
New River Pacemaker	737–200	N776N	20414	
Sand Hills Pacemaker	737–200	N778N	22018	
Rappahannock Pacemaker	737–200	N779N	22273	
Pisgah Pacemaker	737–200	N780N	22274	
Longhorn Pacemaker	737–200	N781N	22275	
Lone Star Pacemaker	737–200	N782N	22352	
Seminole Pacemaker	737–200	N783N	22353	
San Jacinto Pacemaker	737–200	N784N	22354	
Grand Strand Pacemaker	737–200	N785N	22355	
Roanoke Valley Pacemaker	737–200	N786N	22443	
Careline Pacemaker	737–200	N787N	22444	
Quaker State Pacemaker	737–200	N789N	22398	
Mountain State Pacemaker	737–200	N788N	22445	
Albemarle Pacemaker	737–200	N791N	22752	
Queen City Pacemaker	737–200	N792N	22753	
Suwanee Pacemaker	737–200	N793N	22754	
Wright Brothers Pacemaker	737–200	N794N	22755	
Shenandoah Pacemaker	737–200	N795N	22756	
Pamlico Pacemaker	737–200	N796N	22757	
Ohio Valley Pacemaker	737–200	N797N	22758	
Peach Tree Pacemaker	737–200	N798N	22751	
Mississippi Valley Pacemaker	737–200	N799N	22795	
Triad Pacemaker	737–200	N802N	22796	
Stone Mountain Pacemaker	737–200	N803N	22797	
Santee Pacemaker	737–200	N804N	22798	
York River Pacemaker	737–200	N805N	22799	
Cumberland Pacemaker	737–200	N806N	22806	
Cherry Blossom Pacemaker	737–200	N807N	22866	
Hudson River Pacemaker	737–200	N809N	22867	
Lindbergh Pacemaker	737–200	N810N	22868	
Cape Fear Pacemaker	737–200	N811N	22869	
Long Island Pacemaker	737–200	N813N	22961	
Hoosier Pacemaker	737–200	N814N	22962	
Bluegrass Pacemaker	737–200	N9049U	19555	
City of Dallas	737–300	N301P	23228	
City of St. Louis	737–300	N303P	23229	
Nancy Davis Pacemaker	737–300	N304P	23230	
City of Houston	737–300	N305P	23257	
City of Fort Worth	737–300	N306P	23258	
City of Minneapolis	737–300	N307P	23259	
City of Boston	737–300	N309P	23260	

Name	Type	PI	SN	Info
City of New York	737–300	N312P	23261	
City of Philadelphia	737–300	N313P	23231	
City of Cincinnati	737–300	N314P	23323	
City of Orlando	737–300	N315P	23233	
City of Richmond	737–300	N316P	23234	
City of Knoxville	737–300	N317P	23235	
City of Fort Lauderdale	737–300	N319P	23236	
City of Chattanooga	737–300	N320P	23237	
City of Buffalo	737–300	N321P	23510	
City of Providence	737–300	N322P	23511	
City of Harford	737–300	N323P	23512	
City of Syracuse	737–300	N324P	23513	
City of Asheville	737–300	N325P	23514	
City of Miami	737–300	N326P	23515	
City of Memphis	737–300	N327P	23550	
City of Louisville	737–300	N328P	23551	
City of Seattle	737–300	N334P	23552	
City of West Palm Beach	737–300	N335P	23553	
City of Jacksonville	737–300	N336P	23554	
City of Atlanta	737–300	N337P	23555	
City of Winston-Salem	737–300	N340P	23556	
City of Greensboro	737–300	N341P	23557	
City of Birmingham	737–300	N342P	23558	
City of Columbus	737–300	N348P	23559	
City of Indianapolis	737–300	N349P	23560	
	737–300	N350P	23739	
City of Phoenix	737–300	N352P	23740	
City of Fort Myers	737–300	N353P	23741	
City of Fayetteville	737–300	N354P	23742	
City of Nashville	737–300	N355P	23743	
City of Augusta	737–300	N357P	23930	
City of Charlottesville	737–300	N358P	23931	
City of Chicago	737–300	N359P	23932	
	737–300	N360P	23933	
	737–300	N361P	23934	
	737–300	N362P	23935	
	737–300	N364P	23936	
	737–300	N365P	23937	
City of Greenville	737–300	N397P	23256	
City of Charleston	737–300	N399P	23255	
Pride of Piedmont	767–201ER	N603P	23897	
City of London	767–201ER	N604P	23898	
City of Charlotte	767–201ER	N607P	23899	
City of Tampa	767–201ER	N608P	23900	
City of Los Angeles	767–201ER	N614P	23901	
	767–201ER	N617P	23902	
	F-28 1000	N271N	11105	
	F-28 1000	N272N	11095	
	F-28 1000	N273N	11106	
	F-28 1000	N274N	11107	
	F-28 1000	N280N	11061	
	F-28 1000	N281N	11075	
	F-28 1000	N282N	11032	
	F-28 1000	N283N	11035	
	F-28 1000	N284N	11036	
	F-28 1000	N286N	11044	
	F-28 1000	N287N	11087	

Name	Type	PI	SN	Info
	F-28 1000	N288N	11054	
	F-28 1000	N289N	11064	
	F-28 1000	N290N	11063	
	F-28 1000	N291N	11043	
	F-28 1000	N293N	11037	
	F-28 1000	N294N	11101	
	F-28 1000	N296N	11096	
	F-28 1000	N297N	11098	
	F-28 1000	N298N	11103	
	F-28 4000	N106UR	11149	From Empire Airlines
	F-28 4000	N107UR	11159	From Empire Airlines
	F-28 4000	N108UR	11173	From Empire Airlines
	F-28 4000	N109UR	11181	From Empire Airlines
	F-28 4000	N110UR	11182	From Empire Airlines
	F-28 4000	N117UR	11222	From Empire Airlines
	F-28 4000	N118UR	11224	From Empire Airlines
	F-28 4000	N119UR	11226	From Empire Airlines
	F-28 4000	N120UR	11231	From Empire Airlines
	F-28 4000	N121UR	11237	From Empire Airlines
	F-28 4000	N122UR	11238	From Empire Airlines
	F-28 4000	N204P	11227	
	F-28 4000	N205P	11228	
	F-28 4000	N206P	11229	
	F-28 4000	N207P	11230	
	F-28 4000	N208P	11233	
	F-28 4000	N209P	11234	
	F-28 4000	N214P	11235	
	F-28 4000	N215P	11240	
	F-28 4000	N504	11152	From Empire Airlines
	F-28 4000	N505	11156	From Empire Airlines
	F-28 4000	N509	11161	From Empire Airlines
	F-28 4000	N510	11167	From Empire Airlines
	F-28 4000	N512	11168	From Empire Airlines
	F-28 4000	N513	11169	From Empire Airlines
	737–400	N404US	23886	
	737–400	N405US	23885	
Thomas H. Davis Pacemaker	737–400	N406US	23876	
	737–400	N407US	23877	
	737–400	N408US	23878	
	737–400	N409US	23879	
	737–400	N411US	23880	
	737–400	N412US	23881	
	737–400	N413US	23882	
	737–400	N415US	23883	
	737–400	N416US	23884	
	737–400	N417US	23984	
	737–400	N418US	23985	
	737–400	N419US	23986	
	737–400	N420US	23987	
	737–400	N421US	23988	
	737–400	N422US	23989	
	737–400	N423US	23990	
	737–400	N424US	23991	
	737–400	N425US	23992	

Appendix B:
Piedmont Destinations, 1948–1989

Airport Code — City	Inaugural Service	Info
ILM — Wilmington, N.C.	February 20, 1948	Inaugural Flight Takeoff
SOP — Southern Pines, N.C.	February 20, 1948	Service discontinued 1972
CLT — Charlotte, N.C.	February 20, 1948	
AVL — Asheville, N.C.	February 20, 1948	
TRI — Tri-Cities, Tenn.	February 20, 1948	Bristol-Kingsport-Johnson City
LEX — Lexington, Ky.	February 20, 1948	
CVG — Cincinnati, Oh.	February 20, 1948	Inaugural Flight Destination
EWN — New Bern, N.C.	February 27, 1948	Later served by Henson Airlines
GSB — Goldsboro, N.C.	February 27, 1948	
RDU — Raleigh-Durham, N.C.	February 27, 1948	
GSO — Greensboro-High Point, N.C.	February 27, 1948	
INT — Winston-Salem, N.C.	February 27, 1948	Later served by CCAir
SDF — Louisville, Ky.	February 27, 1948	
DAN — Danville, Va.	April 16, 1948	
ROA — Roanoke, Va.	April 16, 1948	
MHR — Morehead City, N.C.	May 5, 1948	Service discontinued later
CRW — Charleston, W.Va.	May 14, 1948	
LYH — Lynchburg, Va.	May 14, 1948	
RIC — Richmond, Va.	May 14, 1948	
ORF — Norfolk, Va.	May 14, 1948	
FAY — Fayetteville, N.C.	September 25, 1949	
PHF — Newport News-Hampton-Williamsburg-Yorktown, Va.	November 14, 1949	Later served by Henson Airlines
MYR — Myrtle Beach, S.C.	May 14, 1950	Year round service began June 25, 1962
BKW — Beckley, W.Va.	July 15, 1952	Service discontinued later
HKY — Hickory, N.C.	August 25, 1952	Later serviced by CCAir
TYS — Knoxville, Tenn.	August 25, 1952	
ISO — Kinston, N.C.	September 10, 1952	Later serviced by CCAir
HTS — Ashland, Ky.-Huntington, W.Va.-Ironton, Oh.	November 3, 1952	Service discontinued later
LOZ — London-Corbin, Ky.	October 1, 1953	Service discontinued later
BLF — Bluefield-Princeton, W.Va.	May 16, 1954	Service discontinued later
CMH — Columbus, Oh.	March 18, 1955	
PKB — Parkersburg, W.Va.-Marietta, Oh.	March 18, 1955	
CHO — Charlottesville, Va.	August 17, 1955	
DCA/IAD — Washington, D.C.	August 17, 1955	National/Dulles
SHD — Harrisonburg-Staunton-Waynesboro, Va.	February 1, 1960	
FFT — Frankfort, Ky.	December 1, 1960	Service discontinued later
ECG — Elizabeth City, N.C.	March 30, 1961	Service discontinued 1972

Appendix B

Airport Code — City	Inaugural Service	Info
RWI — Rocky Mount, N.C.	March 30, 1961	Service discontinued later
ATL — Atlanta, Ga.	June 25, 1962	
BWI — Baltimore, Md.	June 25, 1962	
OAJ — Jacksonville-Camp Lejeune, N.C.	June 25, 1962	
FLO — Florence, S.C.	June 25, 1962	Later serviced by Henson Airlines
CAE — Columbia, S.C.	June 25, 1962	
ASG — Augusta, Ga.	June 25, 1962	
BCB — Pulaski-Radford-Blacksburg, Va.	June 25, 1962	Service discontinued 1972
HSP — Hot Springs, Va.	April 26, 1964	Service discontinued later
LGA — New York, N.Y.	November 15, 1966	LaGuardia
GSP — Greenville-Spartanburg, S.C.	April 1, 1967	
BNA — Nashville, Tenn.	February 1, 1968	
MEM — Memphis, Tenn.	February 1, 1968	
MDW/ORD — Chicago, Ill.	December 1, 1969	Midway/O'Hare
CHS — Charleston, S.C.	April 26, 1970	
LWB — Greenbrier-White Sulphur Springs-Lewisburg, Va.	September 15, 1970	
MIA — Miami, Fla.	June 15, 1978	
PIT — Pittsburgh, Pa.	October 25, 1978	
BOS — Boston, Mass.	December 1, 1978	
DEN — Denver, Colo.	December 15, 1978	
TPA — Tampa-St. Petersburg-Clearwater, Fla.	April 1, 1979	
DFW — Dallas-Fort Worth, Tex.	April 29, 1979	
ERW — Newark, N.J.	1979	
HOU — Houston, Tex.	1979	
ORL — Orlando, Fla.	January 1981	
PHL — Philadelphia, Pa.-Wilmington, Del.	March 1, 1981	
JAX — Jacksonville, Fla.	February 1982	
DAY — Dayton, Oh.	July 1, 1982	
CAK — Canton-Akron, Oh.	July 1, 1982	
TOL — Toledo, Oh.	July 1, 1982	
FWA — Ft. Wayne, Ind.	July 1, 1982	
SBN — South Bend, Ind.	July 1, 1982	
LAN — Lansing, Mich.	July 1, 1982	
FNT — Flint, Mich.	July 1, 1982	
GRR — Grand Rapids, Mich.	July 1, 1982	
DAB — Daytona Beach, Fla.	1982	
DTW — Detroit, Mich.	1983	
MSY — New Orleans, La.	1983	
CHA — Chattanooga, Tenn.	1983	
SAV — Savannah, Ga.	1983	
ALB — Albany, N.Y.	1984	
PVD — Providence, R.I.	1983	
BDL — Hartford, Conn.-Springfield, Mass.	1983	
CLE — Cleveland, Oh.	1983	
CMI — Champagne-Urbana, Ill.	1983	
HGR — Hagerstown, Md.	October 3, 1983	Henson Airlines
ISP — Long Island, N.Y.	October 3, 1983	Henson Airlines
JFK — New York	October 3, 1983	Henson Airlines, later served by Piedmont
SBY — Salisbury-Ocean City, Md.	October 3, 1983	Henson Airlines
MDT — Harrisburg, Pa.	October 3, 1983	Henson Airlines
LAX — Los Angeles-San Jose, Calif.	April 1, 1984	
SFO — San Francisco-Oakland, Calif.	November 1, 1984	
EVV — Evansville, Ill.	1984	
ABE — Allentown, Pa.	1984	

Piedmont Destinations, 1948–1989

Airport Code — City	Inaugural Service	Info
AZO — Kalamazoo/Battle Creek, Mich.	1984	
ROC — Rochester, N.Y.	1984	
ERI — Erie, Pa.	1985	Jetstream
YNG — Youngstown, Oh.	1985	Jetstream
PGV — Greenville, N.C.	Early 1985	CCAir
AHN — Athens, Ga.	Early 1985	CCAir
AND — Anderson, S.C.	Early 1985	CCAir
MSP — Minneapolis/St. Paul, Minn.	1985	
STL — St. Louis, Miss.	May 1, 1985	
ORH — Worcester, Mass.	1985	
GNV — Gainesville, Fla.	October 1, 1985	
EYW — Key West, Fla.	October 1, 1985	
APF — Naples, Fla.	October 1, 1985	
TLH — Tallahassee, Fla.	October 1, 1985	
PNS — Pensacola, Fla.	October 1, 1985	
PBI — West Palm Beach, Fla.	October 1, 1985	
LAF — Lafayette, Ind.	November 1985	Britt Airways
HUF — Terre Haute, Ind.	November 1985	Britt Airways
MIE — Muncie, Ind.	November 1985	Britt Airways
BUF — Buffalo, N.Y.	December 15, 1985	
MSS — Massena, N.Y.	March 1986	Brockway Air
ART — Watertown, N.Y.	March 1986	Brockway Air
PLB — Plattsburgh, N.Y.	March 1986	Brockway Air
SLK — Saranac Lake, N.Y.	March 1986	Brockway Air
ACY — Atlantic City, N.Y.	March 1986	Brockway Air
MVY — Martha's Vineyard, Mass.	March 1986	Brockway Air
ACK — Nantucket, Mass.	March 1986	Brockway Air
AVP — Wilkes-Barre-Scranton, Pa.	March 1986	Brockway Air
POU — Poughkeepsie, N.Y.	March 1986	Brockway Air
HPN — White Plains, N.Y.	March 1986	Brockway Air
RSW — Ft. Myers, Fla.	1986	TransAir
SRQ — Sarasota-Bradenton, Fla.	1986	TransAir
MLB — Melbourne, Fla.	1986	TransAir
FPO — Freeport, Bahamas	1986	TransAir
GGT — Georgetown, Bahamas	1986	TransAir
NAS — Nassau, Bahamas	1986	TransAir, Served by Piedmont 11/15/87
TCB — Treasure Cay, Bahamas	1986	TransAir
MHH — Marsh Harbor, Bahamas	1986	TransAir
ELH — North Eleuthera, Bahamas	1986	TransAir
GHB — Governor's Harbor, Bahamas	1986	TransAir
RSD — Rock Sound, Bahamas	1986	TransAir
BDR — Bridgeport, Conn.	1986	Henson Airlines
ELM — Elmira, N.Y.	May 1, 1986	Empire Airlines
ITH — Ithaca, N.Y.	May 1, 1986	Empire Airlines
SYR — Syracuse, N.Y.	May 1, 1986	Empire Airlines
BGM — Binghamton, N.Y.	May 1, 1986	Empire Airlines
UCA — Utica-Rome, N.Y.	May 1, 1986	Empire Airlines
BTV — Burlington, Vt.	May 1, 1986	Empire Airlines
YUL/YMX — Montreal, Canada	May 1, 1986	Empire Airlines
YOW — Ottawa, Canada	May 1, 1986	Empire Airlines
SEA — Seattle, Wash.	May 1987	
LGW — London, England	June 15, 1987	Gatwick Airport
BHM — Birmingham, Ala.	September 1987	
PHX — Phoenix, Ariz.	December 8, 1987	
SAN — San Diego, Calif.	December 8, 1987	

Chapter Notes

Introduction
1. Barbara Jamieson Adams, "The Piedmontster," unpublished essay.

Chapter 1
1. "Exhibition Successful," *Winston-Salem Journal*, April 9, 1911, p. 1.
2. "The Journal Will Hold Great Aviation Meet in This City on Thanksgiving Day," *Winston-Salem Journal*, November 8, 1911, p. 1.
3. "Flights Are Excellent," *Winston-Salem Journal*, December 1, 1911.
4. Bill East, "Winston-Salem's First Family of Flying," *Twin City Sentinel*, January 19, 1971, p. 16.
5. Martin Caidin, *Barnstorming*, New York: Duell, Sloan and Pearce, 1965.
6. "Girl is Killed When Plane was Forced to Land," *Winston-Salem Journal*, October 14, 1922.
7. Bill East, "Winston-Salem's First Family of Flying," *Twin City Sentinel*, January 19, 1971, p. 16.
8. "Five Citizens Own Private Ships for Own Sport Business," *Winston-Salem Journal*, June 22, 1930.
9. Reynolds and Tom Shachtman, *The Gilded Leaf*, Boston: Little, Brown and Company, 1989, p. vii
10. Ibid., p. 125.
11. Patrick Reynolds and Tom Shachtman, *The Gilded Leaf*, Boston: Little, Brown and Company, 1989, p. 127–128; "Resolution in Memory of Thomas Henry Davis," Rotary Club of Winston-Salem, May 16, 2000, p. 1.
12. Egbert Davis, Jr., interview, Winston-Salem, N.C., March 22, 2005.
13. Z. Smith Reynolds, *Log of Aeroplane NR-898W*, Reynolda House, Museum of American Art, 2003, Introduction by Barbara Babcock Millhouse, p. x.
14. "Aviation Co. Formed 1928," *Winston-Salem Journal & Sentinel*, June 22, 1930, p. 1.
15. Z. Smith Reynolds, *Log of Aeroplane NR-898W*, Reynolda House, Museum of American Art, 2003, Introduction by Barbara Babcock Millhouse, p. vii.
16. Z. Smith Reynolds, *Log of Aeroplane NR-898W*, Reynolda House, Museum of American Art, 2003, Introduction by Barbara Babcock Millhouse, p. x.
17. Patrick Reynolds and Tom Shachtman, *The Gilded Leaf*, Boston: Little, Brown and Company, 1989.
18. Patrick Reynolds and Tom Shachtman, p. 128.
19. Z. Smith Reynolds, *Log of Aeroplane NR-898W*, Reynolda House, Museum of American Art, 2003, Introduction by Barbara Babcock Millhouse, p. v.
20. E-mail from Ronnie Macklin to author, 8/6/05.
21. Richard Murdoch, interview, Reynolda House, Winston-Salem, N.C., January 11, 2005.
22. "McGinnis, Aviation Pioneer, Dies," *Winston-Salem Journal*, March 16, 1954.
23. "Lindbergh Will Visit Winston-Salem in October: To Fly Spirit of St. Louis," *Winston-Salem Journal*, July 12, 1927, p. 1.
24. "Winston-Salem Accords Lindbergh Great Ovation: Lone Eagle is Received Here with Open Arms," *Winston-Salem Journal*, October 15, 1927, p. 1.
25. Tom Wood, "'Good People' built Piedmont Aviation," *The Suburbanite*, Vol. X, No. 42, September 15, 1977, p. 1.
26. "Resolution in Memory of Thomas Henry Davis," Rotary Club of Winston-Salem, May 16, 2000, p. 1.
27. J.A.C. Dunn, "History," p. 54.
28. Clifton Daniel, "Ascent of a Dream: Businessman's 60-year love affair with the air is still climbing," *Wilmington Sunday Star News*, p. 1D, 3D.
29. Conrad Paysour, "Into the Wild Blue Yonder," *The State*, December 15, 1965, p. 15.
30. David Purlmutt, "Tom Davis and Piedmont Airlines: Carolina's Milestones in Flight," http://www.ncdot.org/news/dailyclips/2003-12-17gg.html.
31. Egbert Davis, Jr., interview, Winston-Salem, N.C., March 22, 2005.
32. Conrad Paysour, "Into the Wild Blue Yonder," *The State*, December 15, 1965, p. 15.
33. Jim Schlosser, "Davis Flies Piedmont from Puddle Jumping to Making Profit," *Greensboro News & Record*, May 15, 1983.
34. Egbert Davis, Jr., interview, Winston-Salem, N.C., March 22, 2005.
35. "Resolution in Memory of Thomas Henry Davis," Rotary Club of Winston-Salem, May 16, 2000, p. 1.
36. Thomas H. Davis, "The History of Piedmont: Setting a Special Pace," Newcomen Society, p. 7–8.
37. Egbert Davis, Jr., interview, Winston-Salem, N.C., March 22, 2005.
38. "Resolution in Memory of Thomas Henry Davis," Rotary Club of Winston-Salem, May 16, 2000, p. 1.
39. "Resolution in Memory of Thomas Henry Davis," Rotary Club of Winston-Salem, May 16, 2000, p. 1.
40. Tom Wood, "Good People," p. 1. Clifton Daniel, "Ascent of a Dream," *Wilmington Star News*, January 22, 1995, p. 5D.
41. "Tom Davis: Pioneer Aviator," Piedmont Triad Airport Anniversary Publication.
42. Joseph S. Murphy, "Conservative Piedmont Shifts to Turbines," *Air Transport World*, April 1968, p. 21.
43. Nannie M. Tilley, *The R.J. Reynolds Tobacco Company*, Chapel Hill: University of North Carolina Press, p. 287.
44. Egbert Davis, Jr., interview, Winston-Salem, N.C., March 22, 2005; Michael Wade, "From the Ground Up," *The Sentinel*, May 7, 1983, p. 1, 12.

Notes — Chapter 1

45. Egbert Davis, Jr., interview, Winston-Salem, N.C., March 22, 2005.
46. "The History of Sunnynoll," brochure from Allen Tate Realtors, 2599 Reynolda Road, Winston-Salem, N.C.
47. "The History of Sunnynoll," brochure from Allen Tate Realtors, 2599 Reynolda Road, Winston-Salem, N.C.
48. Egbert Davis, Jr., interview, Winston-Salem, N.C., March 22, 2005; Martin Kady, "Piedmont's Thomas H. Davis dies," *Winston-Salem Journal*, April 23, 1999, p. A1, A14.
49. Egbert Davis, Jr., interview, Winston-Salem, N.C., March 22, 2005.
50. Egbert Davis, Jr., interview, Winston-Salem, N.C., March 22, 2005.
51. "Resolution in Memory of Thomas Henry Davis," Rotary Club of Winston-Salem, May 16, 2000, p. 1.
52. Clifton Daniel, "Ascent of a Dream," *Wilmington News-Star*, January 22, 1995, p. D1.
53. J.A.C. Dunn, "The History of Piedmont Airlines," *Pace* magazine, December 1988, p. 54.
54. "Founder," *North Carolina*, p. 22; "Resolution in Memory of Thomas Henry Davis," Rotary Club of Winston-Salem, May 16, 2000, p. 1.
55. Jim Schlosser, "Davis Flies Piedmont from Puddle Jumping to Making Profit," *Greensboro News & Record*, May 15, 1983.
56. Thomas H. Davis, "The History of Piedmont: Setting a Special Pace," Newcomen Society, p. 8.
57. Tom Wood, "Good People," *Suburbanite*, p. 1.
58. Thomas H. Davis, "The History of Piedmont: Setting a Special Pace," Newcomen Society, p. 10.
59. "Founder," *North Carolina*, p. 22.; Thom Wood, "Piedmont's People & Planes," *Wachovia*, September/October 1971, p. 14.
60. *1937 Official Aviation Guide*, p. 98.
61. Walter R. Turner, "Flying the Blue Skies," *Our State*, March 2000, p. 71.
62. Patrick Reynolds and Tom Shachtman, p. 128.
63. "Resolution in Memory of Thomas Henry Davis," Rotary Club of Winston-Salem, May 16, 2000, p. 2.
64. Thomas H. Davis, "The History of Piedmont: Setting a Special Pace," Newcomen Society, p. 9.
65. Walter Turner, "The Home Grown Airline," http://www.businessnc.com/archives/2003/03/aviation_piedmont.html.
66. Jim Schlosser, "Davis Flies Piedmont from Puddle Jumping to Making Profit," *Greensboro News & Record*, May 15, 1983. Walter R. Turner, "A Brief History of Piedmont Airlines," *Carolina Comments*, September 2001, p. 105.
67. "Culler's Watched PI Grow Since Company's Early Days," *Piedmonitor*, October 1985.
68. Ed Culler, interview, Winston-Salem, N.C., September 22, 2005.
69. Michael Wade, "From the Ground Up," *The Sentinel*, May 7, 1983, p. 12.
70. Egbert Davis, Jr., interview, Winston-Salem, N.C., March 22, 2005.
71. Walter R. Turner, "Flying the Blue Skies," *Our State*, March 2000.
72. Zeke Saunders, interview, December 28, 2004.
73. Martin Kady, "Piedmont's Thomas H. Davis dies," *Winston-Salem Journal*, April 23, 1999, p. A1, A14; Walter R. Turner, "A Brief History of Piedmont Airlines," Carolina Comments, September 2001, p. 105.
74. Martin Kady, "Piedmont's Thomas H. Davis dies," *Winston-Salem Journal*, April 23, 1999, p. A1, A14.
75. Jim Schlosser, "Davis Flies Piedmont from Puddle Jumping to Making Profit," *Greensboro News & Record*, May 15, 1983.
76. "Founder," *North Carolina*, p. 22.
77. Zeke Saunders, interview, May 11, 2004, Winston-Salem, N.C.
78. Zeke Saunders, interview, May 11, 2004, Winston-Salem, N.C.
79. Bill Barber, phone interview, December 27, 2004.
80. Ibid.
81. Ibid.
82. Walter R. Turner, "Flying the Blue Skies," *Our State*, March 2000.
83. Bill Barber, phone interview, December 27, 2004.
84. Walter R. Turner, "Flying the Blue Skies," *Our State*, March 2000.
85. Zeke Saunders, interview, December 28, 2004, Winston-Salem, N.C.
86. Thomas H. Davis, "The History of Piedmont: Setting a Special Pace," Newcomen Society, p. 9.
87. "Resolution in Memory of Thomas Henry Davis," Rotary Club of Winston-Salem, May 16, 2000, p. 2.
88. Thomas H. Davis, "The History of Piedmont: Setting a Special Pace," Newcomen Society, p. 9.
89. Walter R. Turner, "Flying the Blue Skies," *Our State*, March 2000.
90. Thom Wood, "Piedmont's People & Planes," *Wachovia*, September/October 1971, p. 14.
91. Egbert Davis, Jr., interview, Winston-Salem, N.C., March 22, 2005.
92. Barry Alan Lawing, "History of Aviation," p. 44.
93. "Resolution in Memory of Thomas Henry Davis," Rotary Club of Winston-Salem, May 16, 2000, p. 2.
94. Zeke Saunders, interview, May 11, 2004, Winston-Salem, N.C.
95. Ibid.
96. Ibid.
97. Ibid.
98. R. Turner, "Flying the Blue Skies," *Our State*, March 2000, p. 72.
99. J.A.C. Dunn, "The History of Piedmont Airlines," *Pace* magazine, December 1988, p. 54.
100. Walter R. Turner, "Flying the Blue Skies," *Our State*, March 2000.
101. Barry Alan Lawing, "A History of Aviation in Winston-Salem," Thesis, Wake Forest University, 1984, p. 47.
102. Zeke Saunders, interview, December 28, 2004, Winston-Salem, N.C.
103. "Founder," *North Carolina*, p. 22.
104. "Culler's Watched PI Grow Since Company's Early Days," *Piedmonitor*, October 1985.
105. Letter from Frank E. Dawson to T.H. Davis, North Carolina Wing, Civil Air Patrol, Charlotte, N.C., September 21, 1944.
106. "Fire Destroys 14 Planes at Airport," *Winston-Salem Journal*, August 14, 1941, p. 1; "Cause of Airport Fire is Unknown," *Winston-Salem Journal*, August 15, 1941, p. 14.
107. Thomas H. Davis, "The History of Piedmont: Setting a Special Pace," Newcomen Society, p. 10–11.
108. "Good People," *Suburbanite*, p. 1.
109. Barry Alan Lawing, "A History of Aviation in Winston-Salem," Thesis, Wake Forest University, 1984, p. 46.
110. Barry Alan Lawing, "A History of Aviation in Winston-Salem," Thesis, Wake Forest University, 1984, p. 45.
111. Zeke Saunders, interview, May 11, 2004, Winston-Salem, N.C.
112. "Piedmont Aviation: Its Origins and Growth," *Winston-Salem Journal*, September 27, 1954. p. 1.; Barry Alan Lawing, "A History of Aviation in Winston-Salem," Thesis, Wake Forest University, 1984, p. 43.
113. "Good People," *Suburbanite*, p. 1.

114. Thomas H. Davis, "The History of Piedmont: Setting a Special Pace," Newcomen Society, p. 11.
115. Zeke Saunders, interview, May 11, 2004, Winston-Salem, N.C.
116. Martin Kady, "Piedmont's Thomas H. Davis dies," *Winston-Salem Journal*, April 23, 1999, p. A14.
117. Zeke Saunders, interview, May 11, 2004, Winston-Salem, N.C.
118. Ibid.
119. Thomas H. Davis, "The History of Piedmont: Setting a Special Pace," Newcomen Society, p. 11.
120. Walter R. Turner, "A Brief History of Piedmont Airlines," *Carolina Comments*, September 2001, p. 105.
121. "Resolution in Memory of Thomas Henry Davis," Rotary Club of Winston-Salem, May 16, 2000, p. 2.

Chapter 2

1. "Piedmont Airlines Plane Off to Inaugurate Its New Flight," *Twin City Sentinel*, February 21, 1948, p. 3.
2. Dudley Price, "'Puddle Jumper' Piedmont on last leg," *Raleigh News and Observer*, July 16, 1989.
3. Conrad Paysour, "Into the Wild Blue Yonder," *The State*, December 15, 1965, p. 15.
4. "Annual Meeting Board of Directors," Piedmont Aviation, Inc., January 18, 1944.
5. "Founder," *North Carolina*, p. 23.
6. Harold Dobbins, interview with Walter Turner, Wilmington, N.C., June 13, 1996.
7. "Piedmont Aviation Seeks Permit for 9 Local and Feeder Lines," *Winston-Salem Journal*, June 5, 1944, p. 1.
8. "Piedmont Aviation Seeks Permit for 9 Local and Feeder Lines," *Winston-Salem Journal*, June 5, 1944, p. 1.
9. Roger Mola, "Economic Regulation of Airlines," http://www.centennialofflight.gov/essay/Government_Role/Econ_Reg/POL16.htm.
10. *Civil Aeronautics Board v. State Airlines*, 338 U.S. 572 (1950), decision of the court.
11. Chester Davis, "A Big Step Forward by Piedmont Airlines," *Winston-Salem Journal/Sentinel*, June 24, 1962, p. D1.
12. Chester Davis, "Piedmont Airlines Success is the Best Argument for County's Working, Spending to Keep it Here," *Winston-Salem Journal/Sentinel*, June 28, 1953, p. C1.
13. Ted Vaden, "Airline and Its President Have Become Synonymous," *Raleigh News and Observer*, February 18, 1979.
14. Jim Schlosser, "Davis Flies Piedmont from Puddle Jumping to Making Profit," *Greensboro News & Record*, May 15, 1983, p. E5.
15. "Piedmont Aviation Seeks Permit for 9 Local and Feeder Lines," *Winston-Salem Journal*, June 5, 1944, p. 1.
16. Annual Report, Piedmont Aviation, Inc., 1949; Rixie Hunter, "Piedmont Airlines May Make Inaugural Flight This Week," *Winston-Salem Journal-Sentinel*, February 15, 1948, p. 3B.
17. Keith Saunders, "Route, Experience Favor Piedmont in Feeder Test," *American Aviation*, June 15, 1948, p. 18.
18. Thelma Davis, interview, Winston-Salem, N.C., September 15, 2004.
19. Ibid.
20. Thom Wood, "Piedmont's People & Planes," *Wachovia*, September/October 1971, p. 14.
21. Walter R. Turner, "A Brief History of Piedmont Airlines," *Carolina Comments*, September 2001, p. 105.
22. Martin Kady, "Piedmont's Thomas H. Davis dies," *Winston-Salem Journal*, April 23, 1999, p. A14; "Piedmont Airlines Off to Inaugurate Its New Flight," *Winston-Salem Journal*, February 20, 1948, p. 1.
23. James William Taylor, telephone interview, June 2004.
24. Jack Tadlock, interview with Walter Turner, Winston-Salem, N.C., date unknown.
25. Zeke Saunders, interview, Winston-Salem, N.C., May 11, 2004.
26. Ibid.
27. Ibid.
28. Thomas H. Davis, "The History of Piedmont: Setting a Special Pace," Newcomen Society, p. 13.
29. Patrick Reynolds and Tom Shachtman, *The Gilded Leaf*, Boston: Little, Brown and Company, 1989, p. 127–128.
30. Chester Davis, "A Big Step Forward by Piedmont Airlines," *Winston-Salem Journal/Sentinel*, June 24, 1962, p. D1.
31. Thom Wood, "Piedmont's People & Planes," *Wachovia*, September/October 1971, p. 15.
32. Zeke Saunders, interview, Winston-Salem, N.C., May 11, 2004.
33. "Piedmont, A Model of How Good an Airline Can Be," Slide/Video Presentation, 1987.
34. Zeke Saunders, interview, May 11, 2004.
35. Ed Jablonski, *Man with Wings*, Garden City, N.J.: Doubleday, 1980, p. 245.
36. Ibid.
37. "Miscellaneous Notes on N42V-NC 34978," Papers of Ronnie Macklin.
38. Thomas H. Davis, "The History of Piedmont: Setting a Special Pace," Newcomen Society, p. 12.
39. Chester Davis, "A Big Step Forward by Piedmont Airlines," *Winston-Salem Journal & Sentinel*, June 24, 1962, p. D1.
40. Chester Davis, "Piedmont Airlines Success is the Best Argument for County's Working, Spending to Keep it Here," *Winston-Salem Journal/Sentinel*, June 28, 1953, p. C1.
41. Hoke Norris, "They Wouldn't Stay Grounded," *The State*, January 19, 1952, p. 16.
42. Chester Davis, "A Big Step Forward by Piedmont Airlines," *Winston-Salem Journal & Sentinel*, June 24, 1962, p. D1.
43. Zeke Saunders interview, May 11, 2004.
44. http://caselaw.lp.findlaw.com/scripts/getcase.pl?court=us&vol=338&invol=572; "CAB Refuses 'Stay' of Piedmont Award," *Wilmington Morning Star*, January 30, 1948; Hoke Norris, "They Wouldn't Stay Grounded," *The State*, January 19, 1952, p. 16.
45. Thomas H. Davis, "The History of Piedmont: Setting a Special Pace," Newcomen Society, p. 14.
46. Zeke Saunders, interview, May 11, 2004.
47. Leon Fox, interview, June 1, 2004, by phone from Wilmington, N.C.
48. "The Little Puddle Jumper Who Could and Did," http://www.aahs-online.org/BackIssues/V45N4.htm.
49. "Culler Chosen Beech's 'Man of the Year,'" *Piedmonitor*, p. 10, Eddie Culler Collection.
50. Thomas H. Davis, "The History of Piedmont: Setting a Special Pace," Newcomen Society, p. 12.
51. Joseph S. Murphy, "Conservative Piedmont Shifts to Turbines," *Air Transport World*, April 1968, p. 19.
52. *The Piedmont Air-Line*, published by Jas. W. Nagle, Philadelphia, date unknown, in the collection of the North Carolina Room, Wilson Library, University of North Carolina, Chapel Hill, N.C.
53. "Piedmont Aviation Offers 675,000 Common Stock Shares," *Winston-Salem Journal*, February 17, 1948, p. 7.

54. "State Airlines Asks Service Stay Against Piedmont in New Petition, *Wilmington Morning Star*, January 19, 1948, p. 1; Hoke Norris, "They Wouldn't Stay Grounded," *The State*, January 19, 1952, p. 16.
55. "CAB Refuses 'Stay' of Piedmont Award," *Wilmington Morning Star*, January 30, 1948; Hoke Norris, "They Wouldn't Stay Grounded," *The State*, January 19, 1952, p. 16.
56. Michael Wade, "From the Ground Up," *The Sentinel*, May 7, 1983, p. 12.
57. Ibid.
58. Thomas H. Davis, "The History of Piedmont: Setting a Special Pace," Newcomen Society, p. 13–14.
59. Rixie Hunter, "Piedmont Airlines May Make Inaugural Flight This Week," *Winston-Salem Journal-Sentinel*, February 15, 1948, p. 3B.
60. "CAB Refuses 'Stay' of Piedmont Award," *Wilmington Morning Star*, January 30, 1948; Hoke Norris, "They Wouldn't Stay Grounded," *The State*, January 19, 1952, p. 16.
61. Keith Saunders, "Route, Experience Favor Piedmont in Feeder Test," American Aviation, June 15, 1948, p. 18.
62. Rixie Hunter, "Piedmont Airlines May Make Inaugural Flight This Week," *Winston-Salem Journal-Sentinel*, February 15, 1948, p. 3B.
63. Thom Wood, "Piedmont's People & Planes," *Wachovia*, September/October 1971, p. 14; Rixie Hunter, "Piedmont Airlines May Make Inaugural Flight This Week," *Winston-Salem Journal-Sentinel*, February 15, 1948, p. 3B.
64. "Eastern Carolina Digging Out from Worst Storm in 15 Years," *Wilmington Morning Star*, February 3, 1948, p. 1.
65. Josiah Cantwell, "Off the Ground," *Wilmington Star*, February 15, 1998, p. 6A.
66. Rixie Hunter, "Piedmont Airlines May Make Inaugural Flight This Week," *Winston-Salem Journal-Sentinel*, February 15, 1948, p. 3B.
67. "Rivers Hit Flood Stage In East N.C.," *Twin City Sentinel*, February 12, 1948, p. 1; "Court Refuses Stay of Airline Service," *Twin City Sentinel*, p. 12.
68. Thomas H. Davis, "The History of Piedmont: Setting a Special Pace," *Newcomen Society*, p. 9.
69. Zeke Saunders, interview, May 11, 2004, Winston-Salem, N.C.
70. Walter Turner, "The Home Grown Airline," http://www.airsider.net/files/2002/0902/002/pi_page1.htm.
71. See Appendix B for Pacemaker names.
72. "Last Rites Tomorrow for Wright; Man Who Aided Wrights in First Flight Dies," *Winston-Salem Journal and Sentinel*, February 1, 1948, p.10A.
73. http://www.centennialofflight.gov/essay/Explorers_Record_Setters_and_Daredevils/turner/EX22.htm.
74. Walter R. Turner, "A Brief History of Piedmont Airlines," *Carolina Comments*, September 2001, p. 105.
75. Leon Fox, interview, June 1, 2004, by phone from Wilmington, N.C.
76. "Piedmont Begins First Flight to Cincinnati," *Wilmington Star*, February 20, 1948, Bill Reaves Collection, New Hanover Public Library.
77. Josiah Cantwell, "Off the Ground," *Wilmington Sunday News-Star*, February 15, 1989, p. 6A.
78. Steve Gasque, "Goodbye Piedmont," News Package, WSOC-TV 6:00 P.M. Newscast, Charlotte, N.C., August 1, 1989.
79. Edward Best, telephone interview, August 30, 2005.
80. "Piedmont Airlines Makes First Wilmington-Cincinnati Flight," *Winston-Salem Journal*, February 21, 1948, p. 1.

Chapter 3

1. "Piedmont Starts Route Today from New Bern to Louisville," *Winston-Salem Journal*, February 27, 1948, p. 22.
2. Ibid.
3. "Ceremony Marks Launching of Louisville–New Bern Route," *Winston Salem Journal & Sentinel*, February 28, 1948, p. 1, 12.
4. Ibid.
5. "Piedmont Airlines Open House," tour handout, February 27, 1948.
6. "A.T.A. Chief Views Value of Air Power," *Winston-Salem Journal & Sentinel*, February 28, 1948, p. 1, 12.
7. Ibid., p. 1.
8. "First Flight Recalled," *Wilmington Star*, February 14, 1988, p. A1.
9. Interview with John Onoff, October 20, 2004, Charleston, S.C.
10. Merton Vance, "First Flight Recalled," *Wilmington Star*, February 14, 1988, p. A1.
11. Richard J. Hurley, "The Passing of the Pacemaker," *Airliners*, Fall 1988, p. 42.
12. Zeke Saunders, interview, Winston-Salem, N.C., February 8, 2005.
13. Tory Vaughn, telephone interview, July 6, 2005.
14. Chuck Meacham, interview, Rockingham, N.C., August 20, 2006.
15. R.L. Gordon, interview, Charleston, S.C., October 18, 2004.
16. Chuck Meacham, interview, Rockingham, N.C., August 20, 2006.
17. Zeke Saunders, interview, Winston-Salem, N.C., May 11, 2004.
18. Zeke Saunders, interview, Winston-Salem, N.C., March 1, 2005.
19. Zeke Saunders, interview, Winston-Salem, N.C., May 11, 2004.
20. Dudley Price, "'Puddle Jumper Piedmont on last leg," *Raleigh News & Observer*, July 16, 1989, p. 13A.
21. C.D. McLean, telephone interview, September 3, 2005.
22. Tory Vaughn, telephone interview, July 6, 2005.
23. Bob McAlpin, interview, Clemmons, N.C., September 13, 2005.
24. Tory Vaughn, telephone interview, July 6, 2005.
25. Tommy Orrell, telephone interview, September 12, 2005.
26. Ed Robins, "Turning Airliners Out 'Better Than New;' That's What Piedmont Aviation Experts Do," *Winston-Salem Journal-Sentinel*, January 29, 1956.
27. Ibid.
28. Ibid.
29. Ken Otterbourg, "Piedmont's Life Story," *Winston-Salem Journal*, March 10, 1987.
30. J.A.C. Dunn, "The History of Piedmont Airlines," *Pace* magazine, December 1988, p. 64, 66; Clifton Daniel, "Ascent of a Dream: Businessman's 60-year love affair with the air is still climbing," *Wilmington Star-News*, January 22, 1995, p. D3.
31. Edward Best, telephone interview, August 30, 2005.
32. Paul Snell, telephone interview, October 30, 2006.
33. Edward Best, telephone interview, August 30, 2005.
34. Clifton Daniel, "Ascent of a Dream: Businessman's 60-year love affair with the air is still climbing," *Wilmington Star-News*, January 22, 1995, p. D3.
35. Martin Kady, "Piedmont's Thomas H. Davis dies," *Winston-Salem Journal*, April 23, 1999, p. A14.
36. Clifton Daniel, "Ascent of a Dream: Businessman's

60-year love affair with the air is still climbing," *Wilmington Star-News*, January 22, 1995, p. D1.

37. "Piedmont's Progress," *Time*, June 9, 1952.

38. Clifton Daniel, "Ascent of a Dream: Businessman's 60-year love affair with the air is still climbing," *Wilmington Star-News*, January 22, 1995, p. D3.

39. Floyd Rogers, "Tarheel Sketch: Tom Davis," *Winston-Salem Journal*, July 30, 1989, p. A13.

40. Bill Barber, telephone interview, December 20, 2004.

41. Bill Barber, interview, Winston-Salem, N.C., March 1, 2005.

42. Ibid.

43. Zeke Saunders, interview, Winston-Salem, N.C., March 1, 2005.

44. Bill Barber, telephone interview, December 20, 2004.

45. Ibid.

46. J.A.C. Dunn, "The History of Piedmont Airlines," *Pace* magazine, December 1988, p. 66.

47. "Air Service for 500 Cities," reprint from *The Lamp*, from Winston-Salem Library North Carolina Room, Airline file.

48. Dudley Price, "'Puddle Jumper Piedmont on last leg," *Raleigh News & Observer*, July 16, 1989, p. 13A.

49. Edward Best, telephone interview, August 30, 2005.

50. Dudley Price, "'Puddle Jumper Piedmont on last leg," *Raleigh News & Observer*, July 16, 1989, p. 13A.

51. Ibid.

52. Bob McAlphin, interview, Clemmons, N.C., September 13, 2005.

53. Paul Snell, e-mail interview, February 24, 2005.

54. L.J. Lambert, telephone interview, January 22, 2005.

55. James Bailey, interview, Charleston, S.C., October 17, 2005.

56. Piedmont Aviation, Inc., 12th Annual Report (1952).

57. Zeke Saunders, interview, February 8, 2005.

58. Walter Turner, "The Home-Grown Airline," *Business North Carolina*, March 2003, http://www.businessnc.com/archives/2003/03/aviation_piedmont.html

59. Ibid.

60. J.A.C. Dunn, "The History of Piedmont Airlines," *Pace* magazine, December 1988, p. 62.

61. Debbie Brown, telephone interview, March 15, 2005.

62. L.J. Lambert, telephone interview, January 22, 2005.

63. Ibid.

64. Paul Snell, telephone interview, November 8, 2004.

65. Ibid.

66. Paul Snell, telephone interview, November 8, 2004; Paul Snell, e-mail to the author, August 25, 2005.

67. Paul Snell, telephone interview, November 8, 2004.

68. J.A.C. Dunn, "The History of Piedmont Airlines," *Pace* magazine, December 1988, p. 59.

69. Chester Davis, "A Big Step Forward by Piedmont Airlines," *Winston-Salem Journal-Sentinel*, June 24, 1962.

70. John Onoff, interview, Charleston, S.C., October 18, 2004.

71. Merton Vance, "First Flight Recalled," *Wilmington Star*, February 14, 1988, p. A9.

72. Josiah Cantwell, "Off the Ground," *Wilmington Star*, February 15, 1998, p. A6.

73. J.A.C. Dunn, "The History of Piedmont Airlines," *Pace* magazine, December 1988, p. 62.

74. "Founder," *North Carolina*, p. 22.

75. Tommy Orrell, telephone interview, September 12, 2005.

76. Tory Vaughn, telephone interview, July 6, 2005.

77. Howard Thompson, interview, Roanoke, Va., January 18, 2005.

78. Jim Schlosser, "Vintage DC-3 Takes What May Be Its Last Journey; A Former Piedmont Airlines Aircraft is Trucked from Durham to Spencer," *Greensboro News and Record*, April 17, 2004, p. B1.

79. "Just Like an 'Up' Elevator," Winston-Salem/Forsyth County Library Aviation Clipping File, date unknown.

80. "Just Like an 'Up' Elevator," Winston-Salem/Forsyth County Library Aviation Clipping File, date unknown.

81. Steve Gasque, "Goodbye Piedmont," News Package, WSOC-TV 6:00 P.M. Newscast, Charlotte, N.C., August 1, 1989; See also Jim Schlosser, "Davis Flies Piedmont from Puddle Jumping to Profit Making," *Greensboro News and Record*, May 15, 1983, p. 1E.

82. James Taylor, phone interview, September 29, 2004.

83. Earl Wilcox, interview, Hudson, N.C., March 29, 2005.

84. Tommy Orrell, telephone interview, September 12, 2005.

85. Edward Best, telephone interview, August 30, 2005.

86. Tory Vaughn, telephone interview, July 6, 2005.

87. Zeke Saunders, interview, Winston-Salem, N.C., May 4, 2004.

88. "Air Service for 500 Cities," reprint from *The Lamp*, from Winston-Salem Library North Carolina Room Airline file.

89. Chester Davis, "Piedmont Airlines' Success is the Best Argument For County's Working, Spending to Keep it Here," *Winston-Salem Journal & Sentinel*, June 28, 1953, p. C1.

90. "Founder," *North Carolina*, p. 22.

91. Jim Hamilton, Mooresville, N.C., July 14, 2004.

92. Joseph S. Murphy, "Conservative Piedmont Shifts to Turbines," *Air Transport World*, April 1968, p. 19–20.

93. Piedmont Aviation, Inc., 1955 Annual Report and 8 Year Picture of Progress.

94. "Piedmont Aviation: Its Origin and Growth," *Winston-Salem Journal*, September 27, 1954, p. 6.

95. http://caselaw.lp.findlaw.com/scripts/getcase.pl?court=us&vol=338&invol=572.

96. Ibid.

97. Ibid.

98. Ibid.

99. J.A.C. Dunn, "The History of Piedmont Airlines," *Pace* magazine, December 1988, p. 63.

100. Chester Davis, "Piedmont Airlines' Success is the Best Argument For County's Working, Spending to Keep it Here," *Winston-Salem Journal & Sentinel*, June 28, 1953, p. C1.

101. Thomas H. Davis, "The History of Piedmont: Setting a Special Pace," *Newcomen Society*, p. 14.

102. Chester Davis, "Piedmont Airlines' Success is the Best Argument for County's Working, Spending to Keep it Here," *Winston-Salem Journal & Sentinel*, June 28, 1953, p. C1.

103. Thomas H. Davis, "The History of Piedmont: Setting a Special Pace" (New York: Newcomen Society, 1982), p. 14.

104. Thomas H. Davis, "The History of Piedmont: Setting a Special Pace" (New York: Newcomen Society, 1982), p. 15.

105. Papers of Samuel J. Ervin, Jr. (3847), Manuscripts Department, Southern Historical Collection, Wilson Library, University of North Carolina at Chapel Hill.

106. Papers of Samuel J. Ervin, Jr. (3847), Manuscripts Department, Southern Historical Collection, Wilson Library, University of North Carolina at Chapel Hill.
107. Papers of Samuel J. Ervin, Jr. (3847), Manuscripts Department, Southern Historical Collection, Wilson Library, University of North Carolina at Chapel Hill.
108. Ronnie Macklin, interview, Statesville, N.C., August 12, 2005.
109. Bill Barber, interview, Winston-Salem, N.C., March 1, 2005.
110. Ronnie Macklin, interview, Statesville, N.C., August 12, 2005.
111. "Piedmont Aviation: Its Origin and Growth, *Winston-Salem Journal*, September 26, 1954, p. 6.
112. Thomas H. Davis, "The History of Piedmont: Setting a Special Pace," p. 15.
113. Merton Vance, "First Flight Recalled," *Wilmington Star*, February 14, 1988, p. 1A.
114. Thomas H. Davis, "The History of Piedmont: Setting a Special Pace," p. 14.
115. Charles Preslar, Jr., "Piedmont Air Service Welcomed," *Hickory Daily Record*, August 25, 1952.
116. Zeke Saunders, interview, Winston-Salem, N.C., February 8, 2005.
117. http://airlines.afriqonline.com/airlines/547.htm.
118. Thelma Taylor Davis, interview, Winston-Salem, N.C., September 28, 2004.
119. Thelma Taylor Davis, interview, Winston-Salem, N.C., September 28, 2004.
120. "Fayetteville on World Airlines," *Fayetteville Observer*, September 26, 1949, p. 1.; Commercial Air Service Comes to City," *Kinston Daily Free Press*, September 10, 1949, p. 1.
121. Ronnie Macklin, interview, Winston-Salem, N.C., March 1, 2005.
122. Zeke Saunders, interview, Winston-Salem, N.C., March 1, 2005.
123. Ibid.
124. Jack Walker, telephone interview, September 2, 2004.
125. Zeke Saunders, interview, Winston-Salem, N.C., March 1, 2005.
126. Tommy Orrell, telephone interview, September 12, 2005.
127. Zeke Saunders, interview, Winston-Salem, N.C., May 11, 2004.
128. Ibid.
129. "PAI Pilots Plan to Strike December 12 Over Contract," *The Piedmonitor*, Volume 5, Number 12, p. 1.
130. Clifton Daniel, "Ascent of a Dream: Businessman's 60-year love affair with the air is still climbing," *Wilmington Star-News*, January 22, 1995, p. D1.
131. J.A.C. Dunn, "The History of Piedmont Airlines," *Pace* magazine, December 1988, p. 61.
132. Ibid.
133. Tory Vaughn, telephone interview, July 6, 2005.
134. J.A.C. Dunn, "The History of Piedmont Airlines," *Pace* magazine, December 1988, p. 61.
135. Ibid.
136. "A Lament for the DC-3," *Twin City Sentinel*, February 21, 1965.
137. Ibid.
138. Cleta Covington, "Piedmont Bids Good-by to Its DC-3s," *Twin City Sentinel*, February 23, 1963.
139. Thomas H. Davis, "The History of Piedmont: Setting a Special Pace," p. 14–15.
140. Ibid.
141. Ibid.
142. Interview with John Onoff, October 20, 2004, Charleston, S.C.
143. Ibid.
144. Interview, Robert Gordon, Charleston, S.C., October 18, 2004.
145. John Onoff, interview, Charleston, S.C., October 18, 2004.
146. Ted Vaden, "Airline and its president have become synonymous," *Raleigh News & Observer*, February 18, 1980.
147. J.A.C. Dunn, "The History of Piedmont Airlines," *Pace* magazine, December 1988, p. 67.
148. Zeke Saunders, interview, Winston-Salem, N.C., February 8, 2005.
149. J.A.C. Dunn, "The History of Piedmont Airlines," *Pace* magazine, December 1988, p. 66.
150. Conrad Paysour, "Into the Wild Blue Yonder," *The State*, December 16, 1965, p. 16.
151. Richard J. Hurley, "The Passing of the Pacemaker," *Airliners*, Fall 1988, p. 42.
152. Thomas H. Davis, "The History of Piedmont: Setting a Special Pace," Newcomen Society, p. 15–16.
153. Joseph C. Koenenn, "Airline Spreads Its Wings," *Durham Morning Herald*, June 27, 1955.
154. Piedmont Aviation: Its Origin and Growth, *Winston-Salem Journal*, September 26, 1954, p. 6.

Chapter 4

1. Carroll Spencer, interview, Charlotte, N.C., September 5, 2006.
2. Chuck Meacham, interview, Rockingham, N.C., August 20, 2006.
3. Zeke Saunders, interview, Winston-Salem, N.C., February 9, 2005.
4. Ibid.
5. Don Collins, interview, Winston-Salem, N.C., September 13, 2005.
6. Tommy Orrell, telephone interview, September 12, 2005.
7. Cleta Covington, "Piedmont Bids Good-by to Its DC-3s," *Twin City Sentinel*, February 23, 1963.
8. Thomas H. Davis, "The History of Piedmont: Setting a Special Pace," p. 15–16.
9. Thomas H. Davis, "The History of Piedmont: Setting a Special Pace," p. 15–16.
10. Leon Fox, telephone interview.
11. "A Lament for the DC-3," *Twin City Sentinel*, February 21, 1963.
12. "A Lament for the DC-3," *Twin City Sentinel*, February 21, 1963.
13. Leon Fox, telephone interview.
14. Zeke Saunders, interview, Winston-Salem, N.C., March 1, 2005.
15. "Martin Leaves Piedmont," *The Piedmonitor*, December 1988, Volume 39, Number 11, p. 2.
16. Ronnie Macklin, interview, Winston-Salem, N.C., March 1, 2005.
17. Bill Barber, interview, Winston-Salem, N.C., March 1, 2005.
18. Ronnie Macklin, interview, Winston-Salem, N.C., March 1, 2005.
19. Zeke Saunders, interview, Winston-Salem, N.C., March 1, 2005.
20. Ronnie Macklin, interview, Winston-Salem, N.C., March 1, 2005.
21. Earl Wilcox, interview, Hudson, N.C., March 29, 2005.

22. Earl Wilcox, interview, Hudson, N.C., March 29, 2005.
23. Zeke Saunders, interview, Winston-Salem, N.C., March 1, 2005.
24. Zeke Saunders, interview, Winston-Salem, N.C., March 1, 2005.
25. Tory Vaughn, telephone interview, July 6, 2005.
26. Egbert Davis, Jr., interview, Winston-Salem, N.C., March 22, 2005.
27. Chester Davis, "A Big Step Forward by Piedmont Airlines," *Winston-Salem Journal & Sentinel*, June 24, 1962.
28. Chester Davis, "A Big Step Forward by Piedmont Airlines," *Winston-Salem Journal & Sentinel*, June 24, 1962.
29. "From 1940 to 1965...," *The Piedmonitor*, June 1965, p. 4.
30. Carroll Spencer, interview, Charlotte, N.C., September 5, 2006.
31. Joseph S. Murphy, "Conservative Piedmont Shifts to Turbines," *Air Transport World*, April 1968, p. 19.
32. "From 1940 to 1965...," *The Piedmonitor*, June 1965, p. 4.
33. "Piedmont Aviation Forms Division to Handle Piper Distributorship," *Twin City Sentinel*, May 31, 1960.
34. "Piedmont Aviation Forms Division to Handle Piper Distributorship," *Twin City Sentinel*, May 31, 1960.
35. "From 1940 to 1965...," *The Piedmonitor*, June 1965, p. 4.
36. "From 1940 to 1965...," *The Piedmonitor*, June 1965, p. 4.
37. Richard J. Hurley, "The Passing of the Pacemaker," *Airliners*, p. 43.
38. Annual Report, Piedmont Aviation, Inc., 1964, p. 3.
39. Don Collins, interview, Winston-Salem, N.C., September 13, 2005.
40. Don Collins, interview, Winston-Salem, N.C., September 13, 2005.
41. Ed Robins, "New Airline is Established; To Have Headquarters Here," *Twin City Sentinel*, April 9, 1963, p. 1.
42. Tory Vaughn, telephone interview, July 6, 2005.
43. Connie Chalk Counts, interview, Charleston, S.C., October 18, 2004.
44. Ed Robins, "Piedmont Begins Training Stewardesses," *Twin City Sentinel*, p. 16.
45. Ed Robins, "Piedmont Begins Training Stewardesses," *Twin City Sentinel*, p. 16.
46. Dottie Sain, telephone interview, August 12, 2004.
47. Thelma Taylor Davis, interview, Winston-Salem, N.C., September 28, 2004.
48. Margaret J. Queen, interview, Charleston, S.C., October 18, 2004.
49. Connie C. Counts, interview, Charleston, S.C., October 18, 2004.
50. Margaret J. Queen, interview, Charleston, S.C., October 18, 2004.
51. Connie C. Counts, interview, Charleston, S.C., October 18, 2004.
52. Margaret J. Queen, interview, Charleston, S.C., October 18, 2004.
53. Margaret J. Queen, interview, Charleston, S.C., October 18, 2004.
54. Margaret J. Queen, interview, Charleston, S.C., October 18, 2004.
55. Margaret J. Queen, interview, Charleston, S.C., October 18, 2004.
56. Connie C. Counts, interview, Charleston, S.C., October 18, 2004.
57. Letter to Virginia Lane Colvin from C.L. Stewart, July 25, 1966, courtesy of Mrs. Colvin and the North Carolina Transportation Museum.
58. Connie C. Counts, interview, Charleston, S.C., October 18, 2004.
59. Carol Dobyns Fair, telephone interview, September 24, 2006.
60. Carol Dobyns Fair, telephone interview, September 24, 2006.
61. Hugh Parks, "Pilots View of 'Old' Girls," *Atlanta Journal*, date unknown.
62. Howard Thompson, interview, Roanoke, Va., January 18, 2005.
63. Carol Dobyns Fair, telephone interview, September 24, 2006.
64. Don Collins, interview, Winston-Salem, N.C., September 13, 2005.
65. Earl Wilcox, interview, Hudson, N.C., March 29, 2005.
66. Margaret J. Queen, interview, Charleston, S.C., October 18, 2004.
67. Dottie E. Sain, telephone interview, August 12, 2004.
68. Connie C. Counts, interview, Charleston, S.C., October 18, 2004.
69. Connie C. Counts, interview, Charleston, S.C., October 18, 2004.
70. Margaret J. Queen, interview, Charleston, S.C., October 18, 2004.
71. Ann Caudle, interview, Charleston, S.C., October 18, 2004.
72. Dottie Sain, telephone interview, August 12, 2004.
73. Connie C. Counts, interview, Charleston, S.C., October 18, 2004.
74. Carol Dobyns Fair, telephone interview, September 24, 2006.
75. Margaret J. Queen, interview, Charleston, S.C., October 18, 2004.
76. Connie C. Counts, interview, Charleston, S.C., October 18, 2004.
77. Margaret J. Queen, interview, Charleston, S.C., October 18, 2004.
78. David Caudle, interview, Charleston, S.C., October 18, 2004.
79. David Caudle, interview, Charleston, S.C., October 18, 2004.
80. David Caudle, interview, Charleston, S.C., October 18, 2004.
81. C.D. McLean, telephone interview, September 5, 2005.
82. James Bailey, interview, Charleston, S.C., October 17, 2004.
83. Larry Dudley, interview, Roanoke, Va., January 18, 2005.
84. Jim Hamilton, interview, Mooresville, N.C., August 14, 2004.
85. Howard Thompson, interview, Roanoke, Va., January 18, 2005.
86. Howard Thompson, interview, Roanoke, Va., January 18, 2005.
87. J.Y. Spencer, telephone interview, October 29, 2006.
88. J.Y. Spencer, telephone interview, October 29, 2006.
89. Robert Gordon, interview, Charleston, S.C., October 18, 2004.
90. Robert Gordon, interview, Charleston, S.C., October 18, 2004.
91. Debbie Brown, telephone interview, March 15, 2005.
92. Philip Beeson, interview, June 23, 2005.
93. Chuck Meacham, interview, Rockingham, N.C., August 20, 2006.
94. Debbie Brown, telephone interview, March 15, 2005.
95. Dave Johnson, telephone interview, July 7, 2005.

96. Jim Hamilton, interview, Mooresville, N.C., June 17, 2005.
97. Dave Johnson, telephone interview, July 7, 2005.
98. Dave Johnson, telephone interview, July 7, 2005.
99. Bill Kyle, telephone interview, September 14, 2006.
100. Zeke Saunders, interview, Winston-Salem, N.C., March 1, 2005.
101. Bill Barber, telephone interview, December 20, 2004.
102. Philip Beeson, interview, June 23, 2005.
103. Robert Gordon, interview, Charleston, S.C., October 18, 2004.
104. Paul Snell, telephone interview, October 23, 2006.
105. Warren Wheeler, telephone interview, August 25, 2005.
106. Warren Wheeler, telephone interview, August 25, 2005.
107. http://avstop.com/History/History/CommuterAir.htm.
108. Warren Wheeler, telephone interview, August 25, 2005.
109. Ronnie Macklin, interview, Statesville, N.C., August 13, 2005.
110. Ronnie Macklin, interview, Winston-Salem, N.C., March 1, 2005.
111. Carroll Spencer, interview, Charlotte, N.C., September 5, 2006.
112. Joseph S. Murphy, "Conservative Piedmont Shifts to Turbines," *Air Transport World*, April 1968, p. 20.
113. Piedmont Aviation, Inc., 1967 Annual Report, p. 8.
114. Carroll Spencer, interview, Charlotte, N.C., September 5, 2006.
115. Don Collins, interview, Winston-Salem, N.C., September 13, 2005.
116. "Aviation Operations Building Opens," *Twin City Sentinel*, January 16, 1965, p. 16.
117. "Joint Airport Project Planned," *Winston-Salem Journal*, December, 13, 1966, p. 1; "Airline Complex Taking Shape," *Twin City Sentinel*, July 13, 1967.
118. Tom Sharpe, interview, Bristol, Tenn., August 13, 2004.
119. Blanche Carter, "Executive Airport," *Winston-Salem Business and Community Life* magazine, April/May 1997, p. 19.
120. Dave Johnson, telephone interview, July 7, 2005.
121. Lynn Sass, telephone interview, August 10, 2005.
122. Martin Kady, "Piedmont's Thomas H. Davis dies," *Winston-Salem Journal*, April 23, 1999, p. A14.
123. Egbert Davis, Jr., interview, Winston-Salem, N.C., March 25, 2005.
124. L.J. Lambert, phone interview.
125. Thomas H. Davis, "The History of Piedmont: Setting a Special Pace," Newcomen Society, p. 16.
126. Joseph S. Murphy, "Conservative Piedmont Shifts to Turbines," *Air Transport World*, April 1968, p. 20.
127. Ed Campbell, "Piedmont Inaugurates N.Y. Flight," *Twin City Sentinel*, November 15, 1966, p. 4.
128. Joseph S. Murphy, "Conservative Piedmont Shifts to Turbines," *Air Transport World*, April 1968, p. 21.
129. C.D. McLean, telephone interview, September 3, 2005.
130. Thom Wood, "Piedmont's People & Planes," *Wachovia*, September/October 1971, p. 15; Joseph S. Murphy, "Conservative Piedmont Shifts to Turbines," *Air Transport World*, April 1968, p. 21.
131. Ronnie Macklin, interview, Hickory, N.C., October 4, 2004.
132. Ronnie Macklin, interview, Hickory, N.C., October 4, 2004; Joseph S. Murphy, "Conservative Piedmont Shifts to Turbines," *Air Transport World*, April 1968, p. 21.
133. Thelma Taylor Davis, interview, Winston-Salem, N.C., September 28, 2004.
134. Howard Miller, telephone interview, November 11, 2004.
135. Mel Blocker, telephone interview, July 10, 2004.
136. "Piedmont: A Model of How Good an Airline Can Be," Slide/Video Presentation, 1987.

Chapter 5

1. "'Good People' Built Piedmont Aviation," *The Suburbanite*, September 15, 1977, p. 1.
2. Thom Wood, "Piedmont's People & Planes," *Wachovia*, September/October 1971, p. 15.
3. Joseph S. Murphy, "Conservative Piedmont Shifts to Turbines," *Air Transport World*, April 1968, p. 20.
4. "Resolution in Memory of Thomas Henry Davis," Rotary Club of Winston-Salem, May 16, 2000, p. 3.
5. Connie C. Counts, interview, Charleston, S.C., October 18, 2004.
6. 1973 Annual Report, Piedmont Aviation, Inc.
7. Howard Miller, telephone interview, November 11, 2004.
8. "Good People," *Suburbanite*, p. 1, September 15, 1977.
9. Paul Snell, telephone interview, November 1, 2004.
10. R.L. Gordon, interview, Charleston, S.C., October 18, 2004.
11. "Good People," *Suburbanite*, September 15, 1977, p. 12.
12. Elizabeth Culler, interview, Winston-Salem, N.C., September 22, 2005.
13. R.L. Gordon, interview, Charleston, S.C., October 18, 2004.
14. Howard Thompson, interview, Roanoke, Va., January 18, 2005.
15. Harvel Horrell, interview, Charleston, S.C., October 17, 2004.
16. James Bailey, interview, Charleston, S.C., October 17, 2005.
17. James Bailey, interview, Charleston, S.C., October 17, 2004.
18. Harvel Horrell, interview, Charleston, S.C., October 17, 2004.
19. Harvel Horrell, interview, Charleston, S.C., October 17, 2004.
20. Harvel Horrell, interview, Charleston, S.C., October 17, 2004.
21. Harvel Horrell, interview, Charleston, S.C., October 17, 2004.
22. Chuck Meacham, interview, Rockingham, N.C., August 20, 2006.
23. Paul Snell, private letter, May 1, 2004.
24. Don Collins, interview, September 19, 2005.
25. Chuck Meacham, interview, Rockingham, N.C., August 20, 2006.
26. Dave Johnson, telephone interview, July 7, 2005.
27. Larry Dudley, interview, Roanoke, Va., January 18, 2005.
28. Larry Dudley, interview, Roanoke, Va., January 18, 2005.
29. Larry Dudley, interview, Roanoke, Va., January 18, 2005.
30. Frank Davis, interview, Hickory, N.C., July 19, 2005.
31. Howard Thompson, interview, Roanoke, Va., January 18, 2005.

32. Don Collins, Audrey Collins, interview, Winston-Salem, September 13, 2005.
33. David Caudle, interview, Charleston, S.C., October 18, 2004.
34. Ronnie Macklin, interview, Winston-Salem, N.C., March 1, 2005.
35. E-mail from T.D. Stanges to the author, July 30, 2005.
36. Calvin James Redburn, copy of Airline Pilot Agreement Manual, Piedmont Aviation, Inc. Edition: Effective April 1, 1977 to October 1, 1979, p. i-v.
37. Don Martin, interview, Roanoke, Va., January 18, 2005.
38. David Caudle, interview, Charleston, S.C., October 18, 2004.
39. David Caudle, interview, Charleston, S.C., October 18, 2004.
40. R.L. Gordon, interview, Charleston, S.C., October 18, 2004.
41. R.L. Gordon, interview, Charleston, S.C., October 18, 2004.
42. R.L. Gordon, interview, Charleston, S.C., October 18, 2004.
43. Dave Johnson, telephone interview, July 7, 2005.
44. Buddy Counts, interview, Charleston, S.C., October 18, 2004.
45. Thom Wood, "Piedmont's People & Planes," *Wachovia*, September/October 1971, p. 15.
46. James P. Woolsey, "Piedmont Likes Nihon YS-11A," *American Aviation*, January 6, 1969, p. 36.
47. Zeke Saunders, interview, Winston-Salem, N.C., March 1, 2005.
48. James P. Woolsey, "Piedmont Likes Nihon YS-11A," *American Aviation*, January 6, 1969, p. 36; Joseph S. Murphy, "Conservative Piedmont Shifts to Turbines," *Air Transport World*, April 1968, p. 20.
49. Gene Whitman, "Piedmont Likes New Plane," *Twin City Sentinel*, June 12, 1970.
50. Tom Sharpe, interview, Bristol, Tenn., July 24, 2004.
51. Zeke Saunders, interview, Winston-Salem, N.C., March 1, 2005.
52. Don Collins, interview, Winston-Salem, N.C., September 13, 2005.
53. James P. Woolsey, "Piedmont Likes Nihon YS-11A," *American Aviation*, January 6, 1969, p. 38.
54. Zeke Saunders, telephone interview, December 28, 2004.
55. James P. Woolsey, "Piedmont Likes Nihon YS-11A," *American Aviation*, January 6, 1969, p. 36.
56. "Just Like an 'Up' Elevator," Winston-Salem Public Library Aviation File, date unknown.
57. Zeke Saunders, interview, Winston-Salem, N.C., March 1, 2005.
58. James P. Woolsey, "Piedmont Likes Nihon YS-11A," *American Aviation*, January 6, 1969, p. 36, 38.
59. Bill Barber, phone interview, January 20, 2005.
60. Joseph S. Murphy, "Conservative Piedmont Shifts to Turbines," *Air Transport World*, April 1968, p. 19.
61. James P. Woolsey, "Piedmont Likes Nihon YS-11A," *American Aviation*, January 6, 1969, p. 36.
62. Joseph S. Murphy, "Conservative Piedmont Shifts to Turbines," *Air Transport World*, April 1968, p. 19; Zeke Saunders, interview, Winston-Salem, N.C., March 1, 2005.
63. Joseph S. Murphy, "Conservative Piedmont Shifts to Turbines," *Air Transport World*, April 1968, p. 20.
64. Joseph S. Murphy, "Conservative Piedmont Shifts to Turbines," *Air Transport World*, April 1968, p. 19.
65. L.J. Lambert, telephone interview.
66. "Piedmont: A Model of How Good an Airline Can Be," slide/video presentation, 1987.
67. 1971 Annual Report, Piedmont Aviation, Inc., p. 5; "Piedmont Airlines Adopts Computer Reservation Plan," *Twin City Sentinel*, September 25, 1970; "Center to Handle All Air Reservations," *Winston-Salem Journal*.
68. Ronnie Macklin, interview, Winston-Salem, N.C., March 1, 2005.
69. Tom Barry, "Local Pilot at New Terminal But Last for Credit," *Atlanta Constitution*, supplied by Tom Stancil; Jim Hamilton, telephone interview, August 16, 2005.
70. Tom Beavers, "Man Tries Hijack, Seized at Airport," *Twin City Sentinel*, June 18, 1971; Bill Stracener, "Piedmont Hijacking is Foiled," *Winston-Salem Journal*, June 19, 1971; Rick Edmonds, "Cuba: Yes or No?" *Twin City Sentinel*, June 18, 1971.
71. John Meyer, "Piedmont crew foils hijack here, city man held," *Wilmington Star*, Forsyth County Public Library Aviation file, date unknown.
72. "Hijacker of Piedmont jet claims Black Liberation membership," *Greensboro Daily News and Record*, March 28, 1984, p. A2.
73. "D.B. Cooper and N838N, the *Mount Mitchell Pacemaker*," unpublished history by Ronnie Macklin.
74. Ronnie Macklin, interview, Statesville, N.C., August 13, 2005.
75. Carroll Spencer, interview, Charlotte, N.C., September 5, 2006.
76. Jim Hamilton, interview, Mooresville, N.C., September 10, 2004.
77. Carroll Spencer, interview, Charlotte, N.C., September 5, 2006.
78. Howard Miller, telephone interview, November 11, 2004.
79. "'Good People' Built Piedmont Aviation," *The Suburbanite*, September 15, 1977, p.12.
80. Carroll Spencer, interview, Charlotte, N.C., September 5, 2006.
81. Zeke Saunders, interview, Winston-Salem, N.C., February 11, 2005.
82. Zeke Saunders, interview, Winston-Salem, N.C., September 30, 2005.
83. Carroll Spencer, interview, Charlotte, N.C., September 5, 2006.
84. Jim Hamilton, interview, Mooresville, N.C., September 10, 2004.
85. Brad Rochester, "Piedmont Agrees to 3 in Cockpit," *Winston-Salem Journal*, March 25, 1971.
86. Tory Vaughn, telephone interview, July 6, 2005.
87. Carroll Spencer, interview, Charlotte, N.C., September 5, 2006.
88. Don Collins, interview, Winston-Salem, N.C., September 13, 1005.
89. Don Collins, interview, Winston-Salem, N.C., September 13, 1005.
90. Brad Rochester, "Airline Working for More Routes," *Winston-Salem Journal*, April 27, 1968.
91. Sid Bost, "Chicago Has High Hopes for New Piedmont Service," *Twin City Sentinel*, November 26, 1969, p. 12.
92. "William Magruder Dies at 54; Was Piedmont Aviation Official," *Winston-Salem Journal*, September 11, 1977.
93. Zeke Saunders, interview, Winston-Salem, N.C., March 1, 2005.
94. Carroll Spencer, interview, Charlotte, N.C., September 5, 2006.
95. Chuck Meacham, interview, Rockingham, N.C., August 20, 2006.
96. James R. Hanson, *From Kid to Captain*, p. 121.

97. Tom Sharpe, interview, Bristol, Tenn., July 24, 2004.
98. Tom Sharpe, interview, Bristol, Tenn., July 24, 2004.
99. Buddy Bowen, interview, Charleston, S.C., October 17, 2004.
100. E-mail from Frank Davis to the author, July 29, 2005.
101. Frank Davis, interview, Hickory, N.C., July 19, 2005.
102. Danny Culler, interview, Winston-Salem, N.C., September 22, 2005.
103. "Culler chosen Beech's 'Man of the Year,'" *Piedmonitor*, p. 10, Ed Culler Collection.
104. Danny Culler, interview, Winston-Salem, N.C., September 22, 2005.
105. Robert L. Wall, e-mail to the author, July 24, 2006.
106. Audrey Collins, interview, September 19, 2005.
107. Cheryl Peters, telephone interview, May 24, 2005.
108. Cheryl Peters, telephone interview, May 24, 2005.
109. Margaret Queen, interview, Charleston, S.C., October 18, 2004.
110. Dave Johnson, telephone interview, July 7, 2005.
111. Lynn Sass, telephone interview, August 10, 2005.
112. Lynn Sass, telephone interview, August 10, 2005.
113. Lynn Sass, telephone interview, August 10, 2005.
114. Carol Dobyns Fair, telephone interview, September 24, 2006.
115. Lynn Sass, telephone interview, August 10, 2005.
116. Pauline Fletcher Thomas, e-mail to the author, July 31, 2006.
117. Carol Dobyns Fair, telephone interview, September 24, 2006.
118. Pauline Fletcher Thomas, email to the author, July 28, 2006.
119. 1974 Annual Report, Piedmont Aviation Inc., p. 2.
120. Tory Vaughn, telephone interview, July 6, 2005.
121. Parker Lee Nash, "Bonnie McElveen-Hunter is the new U.S. Ambassador to Finland," *Greensboro News & Record*, Nov. 25, 2001, reprinted by http://www.unitedwaygso.org/whats_new_item.xml?id=137&page=10; Marsha Turner, Pace Communications CEO is March 29 Boyles Lecturer, March 21, 2001, http://www.news.appstate.edu/releases/info/032101mcelveenhunter.html.
122. Bonnie McElveen-Hunter, *Pace* magazine, December 1988, p. 12.
123. "Suit Filed Against Piedmont in Dispute Over Land Lease," *Winston-Salem Journal*, June 9, 1976, p. 8.
124. Paul Slater, "Air Taxi Veteran Deplores 'Mud-Slinging,'" *The Sentinel*, December 11, 1975.
125. "Some Pilots Unhappy," *The Sentinel*, November 8, 1975.
126. Ronald Jordan, "Airport Dispute With Piedmont and Baldwin Ended," *Winston-Salem Journal*, May 3, 1977.
127. Barry Alan Lawing, "A History of Aviation in Winston-Salem," Thesis, Wake Forest University, 1984, p. 140–1.
128. Audrey Collins, interview, Winston-Salem, N.C., September 13, 2005.
129. Carroll Spencer, interview, Charlotte, N.C., September 5, 2006.
130. 1977 Annual Report, Piedmont Aviation, Inc.

Chapter 6

1. Alan Taylor, "I'd Trust You with My Life," news segment, WBTV News, date unknown.
2. Earl Wilcox, interview, Hudson, N.C., March 29, 2005.
3. "Piedmont DC-3 Forced Down: Passengers, Crew Uninjured," *Winston-Salem Journal*, December 29, 1948, p. 1; "Pilot Gives Crew Members Credit for Safe Landing," *Winston-Salem Journal*, December 30, 1948, p. 1.
4. Bob Myers, "'Heard Swoosh ... Then Noise Like Explosion," *Shelby Daily Star*, June 11, 1956, p. 1.
5. Bob Myers, "'Heard Swoosh ... Then Noise Like Explosion," *Shelby Daily Star*, June 11, 1956, p. 1.
6. Bill Green, "Airlines Officials Reconstruct What Happened on Flight," *Shelby Daily Star*, June 11, 1956, p. 1.
7. John Martin "The Pruitts' Last Conversation," *Shelby Daily Star*, June 11, 1956, p. 1.
8. Bill Green, "Airlines Officials Reconstruct What Happened on Flight," *Shelby Daily Star*, June 11, 1956, p. 1.
9. John Martin, "The Pruitts' Last Conversation," *Shelby Daily Star*, June 11, 1956, p. 1.
10. Bill Green, "Airlines Officials Reconstruct What Happened on Flight," *Shelby Daily Star*, June 11, 1956, p. 2.
11. Zeke Saunders, interview, Winston-Salem, N.C., March 1, 2005.
12. Zeke Saunders, interview, Winston-Salem, N.C., February 9, 2005.
13. Bill Green, "Airlines Officials Reconstruct What Happened on Flight," *Shelby Daily Star*, June 11, 1956, p. 2.
14. Bill Green, "Airlines Officials Reconstruct What Happened on Flight," *Shelby Daily Star*, June 11, 1956, p. 2.
15. Myers, "'Heard Swoosh ... Then Noise Like Explosion," *Shelby Daily Star*, June 11, 1956, p. 2.
16. "Astonishing Accident Brings Many Calls to Funeral Home," *Shelby Daily Star*, June 11, 1956, p. 1.
17. Bill Green, "Airlines Officials Reconstruct What Happened on Flight," *Shelby Daily Star*, June 11, 1956, p. 2.
18. Zeke Saunders, interview, Winston-Salem, N.C., March 1, 2005.
19. Brower York, Jr., "Four Area Men on Downed Plane," *Waynesboro News-Virginian*, October 31, 1959, p. 1.
20. "Waynesborian May Have Spotted Plane," *Waynesboro News-Virginian*, November 2, 1959, p. 3.
21. Woodrow W. Stone, "Three Du Ponters Among 26 Dead; Clifton Forge Man Sole Survivor," *Waynesboro News-Virginian*, November 2, 1959, p. 1.
22. Woodrow W. Stone, "Three Du Ponters Among 26 Dead; Clifton Forge Man Sole Survivor," *Waynesboro News-Virginian*, November 2, 1959, p. 1.
23. "Local Aid Crew First on Scene," *Waynesboro News-Virginian*, November 2, 1959, p. 1.
24. "Sole Survivor Describes Crash 'Like the Roaring of the Ocean,'" *Daily Progress*, November 2, 1959, from Richard F. Gaya, Sr., "The Crash of Piedmont Flight 349 into Buck's Elbow Mountain as Told by the Sole Survivor, E. Phillip Bradley," author's manuscript.
25. Richard F. Gaya, Sr., "The Crash of Piedmont Flight 349 into Buck's Elbow Mountain as Told by the Sole Survivor, E. Phillip Bradley," author's manuscript.
26. Richard F. Gaya, Sr., "The Crash of Piedmont Flight 349 into Buck's Elbow Mountain as Told by the Sole Survivor, E. Phillip Bradley," author's manuscript.
27. Zeke Saunders, interview, Winston-Salem, N.C., March 1, 2005.
28. Ibid.
29. Ibid.
30. Zeke Saunders, interview, Winston-Salem, N.C., February 9, 2005.
31. Ibid.
32. CAB "Aircraft Accident Report," SA-348, File No. 1–0065, Adopted April 18, 1961, "Piedmont Airlines, Doug-

las DC-3, N55V, on Buck's Elbow Mountain, Near Charlottesville, Virginia, October 30, 1959," p. 2, n. 3.

33. CAB "Aircraft Accident Report," SA-348, File No. 1-0065, Adopted April 18, 1961, "Piedmont Airlines, Douglas DC-3, N55V, on Buck's Elbow Mountain, Near Charlottesville, Virginia, October 30, 1959," p. 11.

34. CAB "Aircraft Accident Report," SA-348, File No. 1-0065, Adopted April 18, 1961, "Piedmont Airlines, Douglas DC-3, N55V, on Buck's Elbow Mountain, Near Charlottesville, Virginia, October 30, 1959," p. 31.

35. John Bacheller, "Sole Survivor of DC-3 crash attends monument dedication," *Waynesboro News-Virginian*, October 3, 1999, p. 1; Carlos Santos, "Sole Survivor: 'Miracle man' builds memorial to crash victims," *Richmond Times-Dispatch*, October 2, 1999, p. C1.

36. Paul Fogleman, "Victim's Son Visiting Here Learns Early of Dad's Death," *Hickory Daily Record*, April 21, 1960, p. 1.

37. Paul Fogleman, "Piedmont Lands Safely Despite Clipped Wing," *Hickory Daily Record*, April 20, 1960, p. 1.

38. Don Collins, interview, Winston-Salem, N.C., September 13, 2005.

39. Bob Upton, "Piedmont Airliner in Crash Landing," *Twin City Sentinel*, April 28, 1959, p. 1; "Crash Landed Plane to Fly Again, Piedmont Says Damage Was Slight," *Winston-Salem Journal*, April 29, 1959, p. 5.

40. Bob Upton, "Piedmont Airliner in Crash Landing," *Twin City Sentinel*, April 28, 1959, p. 1.

41. Marjorie Hunter, "Plane Safe in Belly Landing," *Winston-Salem Journal*, February 18, 1961, p. 1.

42. Chester Davis, "Routine Flight, Almost," *Winston-Salem Journal*, February 18, 1961, p. 1.

43. "Airliner is Damaged When Propeller Lost," *Winston-Salem Journal*, August 23, 1962, p. 2.

44. "Landing Gear Folds in Roanoke, 1 Hurt," *Winston-Salem Journal*, July 10, 1966, p. A2.

45. "Piedmont Plane Crash Kills Crew of Three; No Passengers Aboard," *Winston-Salem Journal*, November 21, 1966, p. 1.

46. Zeke Saunders, interview, Winston-Salem, N.C., February 9, 2005.

47. "Helsabeck, Airline Pilot, Flew 42 Missions in War," *Winston-Salem Journal*, November 21, 1966, p. 1.

48. "Piedmont to Inaugurate Jet Service Tomorrow," *Asheville Citizen*, March 14, 1967, Pack Memorial Public Library, Airports File.

49. Bill Mebane, "Hundreds Watched as Planes Crashed," *Asheville Citizen*, July 20, 1967, p. 52.

50. Bruce Gourlay, "And Only a Few Hours Before," *Asheville Citizen*, July 20, 1967, p. 20.

51. Bill Mebane, "Hundreds Watched as Planes Crashed," *Asheville Citizen*, July 20, 1967, p. 52.

52. Aircraft Accident Report, Piedmont Aviation, Inc., Piedmont Airlines Division, Boeing 727, N68650, Lanseair Inc., Cessna 310 N3121S Midair Collision, Hendersonville, North Carolina, July 19, 1967, p. 6.

53. Bill Mebane, "From I-26 They Came to See," *Asheville Citizen*, July 20, 1967, p. 52.

54. "Where Body Fell," *Asheville Citizen*, July 20, 1967, p. 1.

55. "Horror of Plane Crash is Told," *Asheville Citizen*, July 20, 1967, p. 11.

56. "Worst Crash Ever Came From a Midair Collision," *Asheville Citizen* (AP), July 20, 1967, p. 52.

57. "400 Search Crash Area for Victims," *Asheville Citizen*, July 20, 1967, p. 13.

58. "Anxious Hours for Parents," *Asheville Citizen*, July 20, 1967, p. 13.

59. Lewis W. Green, "Deep Shock, Carnival Air Noted at Scene of Crash," *Asheville Citizen*, July 20, 1967, p. 8.

60. "President Johnson, McNamara Pay Tribute to McNaughton," *Asheville Citizen*, July 20, 1967, p. 8.

61. "Only the Pieces Remain," *Asheville Citizen*, July 25, 1967, Section 2, p. 1.

62. "Air Crash Probe Pace is Rapid," *Asheville Citizen*, July 25, 1967, Section 2, p. 1.

63. Aircraft Accident Report, Piedmont Aviation, Inc., Piedmont Airlines Division, Boeing 727, N68650, Lanseair Inc., Cessna 310 N3121S Midair Collision, Hendersonville, North Carolina, July 19, 1967, p. 45.

64. Aircraft Accident Report, Piedmont Aviation, Inc., Piedmont Airlines Division, Boeing 727, N68650, Lanseair Inc., Cessna 310 N3121S Midair Collision, Hendersonville, North Carolina, July 19, 1967, p. 45.

65. Don Collins, interview, Winston-Salem, N.C., September 13, 2005.

66. Aircraft Accident Report, Piedmont Aviation, Inc., Piedmont Airlines Division, Boeing 727, N68650, Lanseair Inc., Cessna 310 N3121S Midair Collision, Hendersonville, North Carolina, July 19, 1967, p. 20.

67. Sid Bost, "Corporation Pilot Called Careful Man," *Twin City Sentinel*, July 20, 1967, p. 1.

68. Aircraft Accident Report, Piedmont Aviation, Inc., Piedmont Airlines Division, Boeing 727, N68650, Lanseair Inc., Cessna 310 N3121S Midair Collision, Hendersonville, North Carolina, July 19, 1967, p. iii.

69. Aircraft Accident Report, Piedmont Aviation, Inc., Piedmont Airlines Division, Boeing 727, N68650, Lanseair Inc., Cessna 310 N3121S Midair Collision, Hendersonville, North Carolina, July 19, 1967, p. 38.

70. Paul Snell, telephone interview, October 16, 2006.

71. Steve Harrison, "Amateur sleuth disputes crash report," *Charlotte Observer*, November 13, 2006, p. 1.

72. Paul Houle, interview, Spartanburg, S.C., February 12, 2005.

73. http://www.flight22memorial.com/.

74. Steve Harrison, "Amateur sleuth disputes crash report," *Charlotte Observer*, November 13, 2006, p. 1.

75. Paul Houle, interview, Spartanburg, S.C., February 12, 2005.

76. Carroll Spencer, interview, Charlotte, N.C., September 5, 2006.

77. Transcript of Flight 22 Cockpit Voice Recorder, Reproduced at NARA, courtesy Paul Houle.

78. Paul Snell, telephone interview, September 13, 2006.

79. Paul Snell, telephone interview, October 16, 2006; e-mail from Paul Snell to the author, November 13, 2006.

80. Ibid.

81. Paul Houle, interview, Spartanburg, S.C., February 12, 2005.

82. Ronnie Macklin, interview, Statesville, N.C., August 13, 2005.

83. Zeke Saunders, interview, Winston-Salem, N.C., September 30, 2005.

84. Lawrence Irby, "Record Indicates Jet Crew Never Knew What Hit Them," *Asheville Citizen*, October 10, 1967, p. 6.

85. Paul Houle, interview, Spartanburg, S.C., February 12, 2005.

86. http://www.airportbusiness.com/web/online/General-Aviation-News/NTSB-Stands-by-1967-Report-of-Crash-that-Claimed-82-Lives/18$10324

87. Joseph S. Murphy, "Conservative Piedmont Shifts to Turbines," *Air Transport World*, April 1968, p. 20.

88. Audrey Collins, interview, Winston-Salem, N.C., September 13, 2005.

89. Tom Dillon and Lloyd Brinson, "Airplane Crash

Kills 5 from City, Virginian," *Winston-Salem Journal & Sentinel*, January 21, 1968, p. 1; "Piedmont Wins Suit Over 1968 Crash," *Winston-Salem Journal*, January 7, 1971, p. 2.

90. Joe Pichirallo, "Ex-Piedmont Mechanic Indicted in Engine Case," *Winston-Salem Journal*, September 8, 1976.

91. Aircraft Accident Report, "Piedmont Airlines Fairchild Hiller 2276, N712U, Charleston, West Virginia, August 10, 1968," p. 8.

92. Aircraft Accident Report, "Piedmont Airlines Fairchild Hiller 2276, N712U, Charleston, West Virginia, August 10, 1968," p. 1.

93. Aircraft Accident Report, "Piedmont Airlines Fairchild Hiller 2276, N712U, Charleston, West Virginia, August 10, 1968," appendix A and B; "Pilot Misses Strip in Thick Fog Bank: Fire Sweeps Ruins," *Charleston Daily Mail*, August 10, 1968, p. 1.

94. Aircraft Accident Report, "Piedmont Airlines Fairchild Hiller 2276, N712U, Charleston, West Virginia, August 10, 1968," p. 8.

95. John W. Yago, "Propjet's Approach Found Not Unusual," *Charleston Gazette*, August 13, 1968, p. 1.

96. John W. Yago, "Glide Slope Out at Other Airports," *Charleston Gazette*, August 15, 1968.

97. George Lawless, "Patch of Fog Called Major Factor in Aug. 10 Plane Crash," *Charleston Gazette*, October 23, 1968, p. 1.

98. George Lawless, "Patch of Fog Called Major Factor in Aug. 10 Plane Crash," *Charleston Gazette*, October 23, 1968, p. 1.

99. "Plane Bounces High After Impact, Strewing Wreckage," *Charleston Daily Mail* (Extra), August 10, 1968, p. 3.

100. "Death Path," *Charleston Gazette*, August 13, 1968.

101. George Lawless, "The Doll's Head Rolled Off Onto the Ground," *Charleston Sunday Gazette-Mail*, August 11, 1968, p. 11A.

102. Niles Jackson, "No Warning, Tearful Survivor Says," *Charleston Sunday Gazette-Mail*, August 11, 1968, p. 15A.

103. Aircraft Accident Report, "Piedmont Airlines Fairchild Hiller 2276, N712U, Charleston, West Virginia, August 10, 1968," p. 19.

104. "Snafu Keeps County Pair off Airliner," *Charleston Sunday Gazette-Mail*, August 11, 1968, p. 14A.

105. "32-Fatality Air Disaster State's Worst," *Charleston Sunday Gazette-Mail*, August 11, 1968.

106. George Lawless, "The Doll's Head Rolled Off Onto the Ground," *Charleston Sunday Gazette-Mail*, August 11, 1968, p. 11A.

107. Aircraft Accident Report, "Piedmont Airlines Fairchild Hiller 2276, N712U, Charleston, West Virginia, August 10, 1968," p. 34.

108. Thom Wood, "Piedmont's People and Planes," *Wachovia*, September/October 1971, p. 15.

109. Connie Counts, interview, Charleston, S.C., October 18, 2004.

110. Tory Vaughn, telephone interview, July 6, 2005.

111. Chuck Meacham, interview, Rockingham, N.C., August 20, 2006; "Local Airliner Pilot Lands Crippled Craft," *Atlanta Constitution*, date unknown, from the collection of Chuck Meacham, son of Charlie Meacham.

112. Tex O'Neill, "Jet Skids Off Runway in Charlotte," *Charlotte Observer*, October 26, 1986, p. 1A.

113. Jeri Fischer, "Transportation Board Begins Probe of Wrecked Piedmont Jet," *Charlotte Observer*, October 27, 1986, p. 4A.

114. Tex O'Neill, "Jet Skids Off Runway in Charlotte," *Charlotte Observer*, October 26, 1986, p. 1A.

115. "Piedmont Pilot Unaware Engine Had Fallen Off," *Winston-Salem Journal*, January 25, 1989.

116. "Engine Disintegrates in Flight, Blowing 2 Holes in Piedmont Jet," *Winston-Salem Journal*, April 15, 1988, p. 1.

117. "Engine Disintegrates in Flight, Blowing 2 Holes in Piedmont Jet," *Winston-Salem Journal*, April 15, 1988, p. 1.

118. Paul F. Conley, "Position of Chock Puzzling Officials," *Winston-Salem Journal*, August 4, 1989; WSOC-TV, Charlotte, N.C., 11:00 P.M. newscast; WBTV, Charlotte, N.C.

119. Don Martin, interview, Roanoke, Va., January 18, 2005.

120. Letter to T.H. Davis from C. Eugene Searle, Supervisory Air Safety Investigator, Dept. of Transportation, NTSB, January 20, 1970; Letter to C. Eugene Searle from T.H. Davis, President of Piedmont Aviation, January 23, 1970.

121. Kevin O'Brien, "Lightning Hits Piedmont Jet," *Charlotte Observer*, June 24, 1988, p. 1B; "Lightning, Winds Kill 5," *Los Angeles Times*, June 27, 1988, p. 2.

122. "Coffee Burns Flight Attendant," *Charlotte Observer*, November 2, 1988, p. 2B.

123. Ronnie Macklin, interview, Winston-Salem, N.C., March 1, 2005.

124. Joseph S. Murphy, "Conservative Piedmont Shifts to Turbines," *Air Transport World*, April 1968, p. 20.

125. J.A.C. Dunn, "The History of Piedmont Airlines," *Pace* magazine, December 1988, p. 66.

126. Carroll Spencer, interview, Charlotte, N.C., September 5, 2006.

127. J.A.C. Dunn, "The History of Piedmont Airlines," *Pace* magazine, December 1988, p. 66.

128. Alan Willis, "Piedmont Picked for First Testing of Safety System," *Winston-Salem Journal*, November 26, 1989.

129. Ray Boylan Report, WSOC-TV newscast, Charlotte, N.C., date unknown.

130. Bill Coy Report, WSOC-TV newscast, Charlotte, N.C., date unknown.

131. Bill East, "Safe Flying: Piedmont' Airline's Malfunction Rate Lower than Most," *Winston-Salem Journal*, August 21, 1985.

Chapter 7

1. Ted Vaden, "Piedmont Expansion Takes Off," *Raleigh News and Observer*, October 22, 1978.

2. Ted Shelsby, "'Pete Who?' Still Up And Coming," *The Chapel Hill Newspaper*, Airline File, Forsyth County Public Library, Winston-Salem, N.C., p. 1D; Don Collins, interview, Winston-Salem, N.C., September 13, 2005.

3. Richard J. Hurley, "The Passing of Piedmont," *Airliners*, p. 45.

4. Thom Hill, "Piedmont Inc. a homegrown, thick-skinned 'prickly pear,'" *Raleigh News and Observer*, February 15, 1981.

5. Zeke Saunders, interview, Winston-Salem, N.C., March 1, 2005.

6. John Byrd, "Piedmont's Pilot: Bill Howard Leading Airline into New Styles of Business," *Winston-Salem Journal*, June 12, 1883, p. G1.

7. John Byrd, "Piedmont's Pilot: Bill Howard Leading Airline into New Styles of Business," *Winston-Salem Journal*, June 12, 1883, p. G1.

8. Jack Walker, telephone interview, September 2, 2004.

9. John Byrd, "Piedmont's Pilot: Bill Howard Leading Airline into New Styles of Business," *Winston-Salem Journal*, June 12, 1883, p. G1.

10. William R. Howard, interview, Wilmington, N.C., July 14, 2006.
11. Carroll Spencer, interview, Charlotte, N.C., September 5, 2006.
12. John Byrd, "Piedmont's Pilot: Bill Howard Leading Airline into New Styles of Business," *Winston-Salem Journal*, June 12, 1883, p. G1.
13. William R. Howard, interview, Wilmington, N.C., July 14, 2006.
14. Charles K. Woodruff, "An interview with Thomas H. Davis," *North Carolina Review of Business and Economics*, October 1979, vol. 1, no. 6, p. 2.
15. Thomas H. Davis, "The History of Piedmont: Setting a Special Pace," Newcomen Society, p. 17.
16. William R. Howard, interview, Wilmington, N.C., July 14, 2006.
17. William R. Howard, interview, Wilmington, N.C., July 14, 2006.
18. Charles K. Woodruff, "An interview with Thomas H. Davis," *North Carolina Review of Business and Economics*, October 1979, vol. 1, no. 6, p. 4.
19. William R. Howard, interview, Wilmington, N.C., July 14, 2006.
20. Richard J. Hurley, "The Passing of Piedmont," *Airliners*, p. 45; William R. Howard, interview, Wilmington, N.C., July 14, 2006.
21. William R. Howard, interview, Wilmington, N.C., July 14, 2006.
22. William R. Howard, interview, Wilmington, N.C., July 14, 2006.
23. Thomas H. Davis, "The History of Piedmont: Setting a Special Pace," Newcomen Society, p. 16; Charlotte Hays, "Piedmont is Ready to Take Off," *Winston-Salem Journal*, September 24, 1978, p. A1.
24. Charlotte Hays, "Piedmont is Ready to Take Off," *Winston-Salem Journal*, September 24, 1978, p. A2.
25. Thom Hill, "Piedmont Inc. a homegrown, thick-skinned 'prickly pear,'" *Raleigh News and Observer*, February 15, 1981.
26. Susan Harrigan, "Piedmont Rises by Landing in Small Cities," *Wall Street Journal*, April 9, 1981, p. 1.
27. Ted Shelsby, "'Pete Who?' Still Up and Coming," *The Chapel Hill Newspaper*, Airline File, Forsyth County Public Library, Winston-Salem, N.C., p. 3D.
28. Thomas H. Davis, "The History of Piedmont: Setting a Special Pace," Newcomen Society, p. 17.
29. Don Bedwell, "What's Behind Piedmont Airline's Unlimited Visibility?" *Business North Carolina*, p. 28.
30. Ted Vaden, "Piedmont Expansion Takes Off," *Raleigh News and Observer*, October 22, 1978.
31. Doug McInnis "Piedmont capitalizing on deregulation vacuum," *New York Times News Service*, Forsyth County Public Library Airlines File, Winston-Salem, N.C.
32. Barry Alan Lawing, "A History of Aviation in Winston-Salem," Thesis, Wake Forest University, 1984, p. 85.
33. "William R. Howard: Q & A," *Business North Carolina*, Forsyth County Public Library, Airline File, Winston-Salem, N.C.
34. Richard J. Hurley, "The Passing of Piedmont," *Airliners*, p. 45.
35. Tuck Thompson, "Airport Confident it Will Find a Replacement for Piedmont," *The Sentinel*, July 30, 1983, p. 1.
36. Bob McAlphin, interview, Clemmons, N.C., September 13, 2005.
37. Barry Alan Lawing, "A History of Aviation in Winston-Salem," Thesis, Wake Forest University, 1984, p. 86.
38. Piedmont Pilots' Merger Analysis, Volume 1: History, cover information.
39. Barry Alan Lawing, "A History of Aviation in Winston-Salem," Thesis, Wake Forest University, 1984, p. 87.
40. Frank Davis, interview, Hickory, N.C., July 19, 2005.
41. Pete Mantius, "Debts No Threat to Piedmont: Financed Air Fleet Expansion," *Winston-Salem Journal*, September 11, 1983, p. G1–2.
42. 1982 Annual Report, Piedmont Aviation Inc., p. 11.
43. Tom Sharpe, interview, Bristol, Tenn., July 24, 2004.
44. C.D. McLean, telephone interview, September 3, 2005.
45. Tom Sharpe, interview, Bristol, Tenn., July 24, 2004.
46. Richard J. Hurley, "The Passing of Piedmont," *Airliners*, p. 45.
47. William R. Howard, interview, Wilmington, N.C., July 14, 2006.
48. J.A.C. Dunn, "The History of Piedmont Airlines," *Pace* magazine, December 1988, p. 69.
49. Leon Fox interview, June 1, 2004, by phone from Wilmington, N.C.
50. Chuck Meacham, interview, Rockingham, N.C., August 20, 2006.
51. Zeke Saunders, interview, Winston-Salem, N.C., March 1, 2005.
52. Zeke Saunders, interview, Winston-Salem, N.C., March 1, 2005.
53. Susan Harrigan, "Piedmont Rises By Landing in Small Cities," *Wall Street Journal*, April 9, 1981.
54. Joe Wilson, telephone interview, August 3, 2005.
55. Frank Davis, interview, Hickory, N.C., July 19, 2005.
56. Kay Pinckney, "Why Piedmont Succeeds Where Others Fail," *Airline Executive*, January 1983, p. 23.
57. Bob McAlphin, interview, Clemmons, N.C., September 13, 2005.
58. Bob McAlphin, interview, Clemmons, N.C., September 13, 2005.
59. Gaylord Shaw, "First in Flight Again: The Secrets Behind Piedmont Airlines' Climb to the Top," *Business North Carolina*, Forsyth County Public Library Airlines File, Winston-Salem, N.C.
60. Charlie Lehman, "Piedmont Takes Flight From Unique Hubs," *High Point Enterprise*, Forsyth County Public Library Airline File, Winston Salem, N.C.
61. William R. Howard, interview, Wilmington, N.C., July 14, 2006.
62. Bob McAlphin, interview, Clemmons, N.C., September 13, 2005.
63. Ted Reed & Stella Hopkins, "Piedmont Airlines Founder Dead at 81," *Charlotte Observer,* April 22, 1999.
64. Ernest Blum, "The City That Deregulation Built," *Travel Weekly*, January 31, 1987, p. 36.
65. William R. Howard, interview, Wilmington, N.C., July 14, 2006.
66. Don Bedwell, "What's Behind Piedmont Airline's Unlimited Visibility?" *Business North Carolina*, p. 28.
67. Frank Davis, interview, Hickory, N.C., July 19, 2005.
68. Jim Schlosser, "Davis Flies Piedmont from Puddle Jumping to Profit Making," *Greensboro Daily News*, May 15, 1983.
69. Gene Sharp, interview, Charleston, S.C., October 18, 2004.
70. Frank Davis, interview, Hickory, N.C., July 19, 2005.
71. Ted Reed & Stella Hopkins, "Piedmont Airlines Founder Dead at 81," *Charlotte Observer,* April 21, 1999, p. 1.
72. J. David Johnson, telephone interview, July 7, 2005.
73. Frank Davis, interview, Hickory, N.C., July 19, 2005.

74. Margaret Queen, interview, Charleston, S.C., October 18, 2004.
75. Larry Dudley, interview, Roanoke, Va., January 18, 2005.
76. Bill Barber, telephone interview, January 20, 2005.
77. Bill Barber, interview, Winston-Salem, N.C., March 1, 2005.
78. "Founder of Piedmont Airlines Receives the Honor of His Peers," *We the People of North Carolina*, p. 23.
79. Thelma Davis, interview, Winston-Salem, N.C., September 28, 2004.
80. Tory Vaughn, telephone interview, July 6, 2005.
81. Zeke Saunders, interview, Winston-Salem, N.C., March 1, 2005.
82. Zeke Saunders, interview, Winston-Salem, N.C., March 1, 2005.
83. William R. Howard, interview, Wilmington, N.C., July 14, 2006.
84. Gordon Bethune, telephone interview, August 18, 2005.
85. Carroll Spencer, interview, Charlotte, N.C., September 5, 2006.
86. Carroll Spencer, interview, Charlotte, N.C., September 5, 2006.
87. Bill Barber, interview, Winston-Salem, N.C., March 1, 2005.
88. John Lowe, "Piedmont Simulators Give Pilots Safe Lessons," *High Point Enterprise*, March 27, 1983.
89. John Lowe, "Piedmont Simulators Give Pilots Safe Lessons," *High Point Enterprise*, March 27, 1983.
90. Bill Barber, interview, Winston-Salem, N.C., March 1, 2005.
91. Zeke Saunders, interview, Winston-Salem, N.C., March 1, 2005.
92. Kay Pinckney, "Why Piedmont Succeeds Where Others Fail," *Airline Executive*, January 1983, p. 26.
93. Ronnie Macklin, interview, Winston-Salem, N.C., March 1, 2005.
94. Doug McInnis, "Piedmont Capitalizing on Deregulation Vacuum," *New York Times News Service*, Forsyth County Public Library Airline File, Winston-Salem, N.C.; Kay Pinckney, "Why Piedmont Succeeds Where Others Fail," *Airline Executive*, January 1983, p. 24.
95. Doug McInnis, "Piedmont Capitalizing on Deregulation Vacuum," *New York Times News Service*, Forsyth County Public Library Airline File, Winston-Salem, N.C.
96. Kay Pinckney, "Why Piedmont Succeeds Where Others Fail," *Airline Executive*, January 1983, p. 25.
97. Gene Sharp, interview, Charleston, S.C., October 18, 2004.
98. Kay Pinckney, "Why Piedmont Succeeds Where Others Fail," *Airline Executive*, January 1983, p. 25.
99. Charlie Lehman, "Piedmont Takes Flight From Unique Hubs," *High Point Enterprise*, Forsyth County Public Library Airline File, Winston-Salem, N.C.
100. Kay Pinckney, "Why Piedmont Succeeds Where Others Fail," *Airline Executive*, January 1983, p. 25.
101. John Byrd, "Piedmont's Pilot," *Winston-Salem Journal*, June 12, 1983.
102. Janice Westmoreland, "Off and Running in Maryland," *Winston-Salem Journal*, July 15, 1983.
103. John Byrd, "Piedmont's Pilot: Bill Howard Leading Airline into New Styles of Business," *Winston-Salem Journal*, June 12, 1883, p. G1.
104. "William R. Howard," Q&A Section, *Business North Carolina*, Forsyth County Public Library Airline File, Winston-Salem, N.C.
105. Jack Walker, telephone interview, September 2, 2004.
106. Kay Pinckney, "Why Piedmont Succeeds Where Others Fail," *Airline Executive*, January 1983, p. 24.
107. Thomas H. Davis, "The History of Piedmont: Setting a Special Pace," Newcomen Society, p. 17.
108. Jack Scism, "Airline is flying high since deregulation," *Greensboro News and Record*, April 15, 1984.
109. Howard Miller, telephone interview.
110. Thomas H. Davis, "The History of Piedmont: Setting a Special Pace," Newcomen Society, p. 22.
111. Gene Sharp, interview, Charleston, S.C., October 18, 2004.
112. Bill Piper, telephone interview, August 4, 2005.
113. Bill Piper, telephone interview, August 4, 2005.
114. Jack Walker, telephone interview, September 2, 2004.
115. Gene Sharp, interview, Charleston, S.C., October 18, 2004.
116. Jack Walker, telephone interview, September 2, 2004.
117. Gene Sharp, interview, Charleston, S.C., October 18, 2004.
118. Joe Wilson, telephone interview, August 3, 2005.
119. Joe Wilson, telephone interview, August 3, 2005.
120. Gene Sharp, interview, Charleston, S.C., October 18, 2004.
121. "Piedmont: A Model of How Good an Airline Can Be," slide/video presentation, 1987.
122. Ron Hudspeth, "Piedmont takes off with females flying," *Atlanta Journal*, March 22, 1983, p. C1; Cheryl Peters, telephone interview, May 24, 2005.
123. Gene Sharp, interview, Charleston, S.C., October 18, 2004.
124. Gene Sharp, interview, Charleston, S.C., October 18, 2004.
125. Gene Sharp, interview, Charleston, S.C., October 18, 2004.
126. Janice Westmoreland, "More to Flying to L.A. than Meets the Eye," *The Sentinel*, March 28, 1984.
127. "A History of Piedmont Airlines," video presentation, 1985, contained in history section of Piedmont Airlines Arbitration Presentation.
128. Piedmont internal memo, September 25, 1984.
129. 1984 Annual Report, Piedmont Aviation, Inc., p. 3–4.
130. C.D. McLean, telephone interview, September 3, 2005.
131. 1984 Annual Report, Piedmont Aviation, Inc., p. 4.
132. Piedmont internal memo, January 25, 1985, Johnny Privette Collection.
133. 1984 Annual Report, Piedmont Aviation, Inc., p. 4.

Chapter 8

1. Aaron Bernstein, *Grounded: Frank Lorenzo and the Destruction of Eastern Airlines*, 1990.
2. "William R. Howard," Q&A Section, *Business North Carolina*, Forsyth County Public Library Airline File, Winston-Salem, N.C., p. 56.
3. Gaylord Shaw, "First in Flight Again," *Business North Carolina*, Forsyth County Public Library Airline File, Winston-Salem, N.C.
4. David Mildenburg, "Norfolk Southern Exploring Piedmont Airlines Takeover," *Charlotte Observer*, January 28, 1987, p. 1.
5. Mel Blocker, telephone interview, July 10, 2004.
6. Thomas H. Davis, "The History of Piedmont: Setting a Special Pace," Newcomen Society, p. 17–18.

7. Patrick Mondout, http://www.super70s.com/Super70s/Tech/Aviation/Airlines/Air-Florida.asp.
8. http://www.alleghenyairlines.com/history.htm.
9. http://www.alleghenyairlines.com/history.htm.
10. William R. Howard, interview, Wilmington, N.C., July 14, 2006.
11. 1984 Annual Report, Piedmont Aviation Inc., pp. 16, 32.
12. http://www.psaairlines.com/cohist.asp.
13. 1985 Annual Report, Piedmont Aviation Inc., pp. 5–6.
14. 1985 Annual Report, Piedmont Aviation Inc., p. 11.
15. Leonard Martin, telephone interview, January 22, 2005.
16. 1985 Annual Report, Piedmont Aviation Inc., p. 6, 11–12.
17. Leonard Martin, telephone interview, January 22, 2005.
18. Gene Sharp, interview, Charleston, S.C., October 18, 2004.
19. Gene Sharp, e-mail to author, August 5, 2005.
20. "Piedmont: A Model of How Good an Airline Can Be," slide/video presentation, 1987.
21. Don Collins, interview, Winston-Salem, N.C., September 13, 2005.
22. Leonard Martin, telephone interview, January 22, 2005.
23. Gene Sharp, interview, Charleston, S.C., October 18, 2004.
24. Bill Piper, telephone interview, August 4, 2005.
25. 1985 Annual Report, Piedmont Aviation Inc., p. 6, 11.
26. Gene Sharp, interview, Charleston, S.C., October 18, 2004.
27. Leonard Martin, telephone interview, January 22, 2005.
28. Gene Sharp, interview, Charleston, S.C., October 18, 2004.
29. Bill Piper, telephone interview, August 4, 2005.
30. William R. Howard, interview, Wilmington, N.C., July 14, 2006.
31. Penny Sori, "Piedmont, city, kiss and make up," *Syracuse Herald-Journal,* July 1, 1986, p. A1.
32. Penny Sori, "Piedmont, city, kiss and make up," *Syracuse Herald-Journal,* July 1, 1986, p. A12.
33. James T. Mulder, "Piedmont's signs rise, signaling Empire's fall," *Syracuse Herald-Journal,* January 15, 1986, p. C7.
34. James T. Mulder, "Piedmont's signs rise, signaling Empire's fall," *Syracuse Herald-Journal,* January 15, 1986, p. C7.
35. James T. Mulder, "Piedmont's signs rise, signaling Empire's fall," *Syracuse Herald-Journal,* January 15, 1986, p. C7.
36. Gordon Bethune, telephone interview, August 18, 2005.
37. 1986 Annual Report, Piedmont Aviation, Inc., p. 4, 12; "Piedmont: A Model of How Good an Airline Can Be," slide/video presentation, 1987.
38. "Empire Airlines' visual image fading out," *Syracuse Herald-Journal,* April 28, 1986, p. D6.
39. 1986 Annual Report, Piedmont Aviation, Inc., p. 13.
40. Gordon Bethune, telephone interview, August 18, 2005.
41. Gordon Bethune, telephone interview, August 18, 2005.
42. Gordon Bethune, telephone interview, August 18, 2005.
43. Gordon Bethune, telephone interview, August 18, 2005.
44. Gordon Bethune, telephone interview, August 18, 2005.
45. J.A.C. Dunn, "The History of Piedmont Airlines," *Pace* magazine, December 1988, p. 60–73.
46. J.A.C. Dunn, "The History of Piedmont Airlines," *Pace* magazine, December 1988, p. 78.
47. Danny Culler, interview, Winston-Salem, N.C., September 22, 2005.
48. "1986 Annual Report," Piedmont Aviation, Inc. p. 4–5.
49. Kenneth Carlson, "Piedmont's final days evoke memories," Triad Business, June 26, 1989, p. 7.
50. 1986 Annual Report, Piedmont Aviation, Inc., p. 12.
51. Richard M. Barron, "Wichita's Chamber of Commerce is Wooing Piedmont in a Big Way," *Winston-Salem Journal,* March 21, 1986, p. 23.
52. Richard M. Barron, "Wichita's Chamber of Commerce is Wooing Piedmont in a Big Way," *Winston-Salem Journal,* March 21, 1986, p. 23.
53. Richard M. Barron, "Wichita's Chamber of Commerce is Wooing Piedmont in a Big Way," *Winston-Salem Journal,* March 21, 1986, p. 23.
54. "TWA, Piedmont Join Forces in Agreement for Marketing," *Oklahoma City Journal Record,* February 27, 1986.
55. William R. Howard, interview, Wilmington, N.C., July 14, 2006.
56. Philip Beeson, interview, June 23, 2005.
57. Gordon Bethune, telephone interview, August 25, 2005.
58. C.D. McLean, telephone interview, September 3, 2005.
59. Richard Smith, telephone interview, September 19, 2005.
60. Ann Corrigan, "White Knight," *Winston-Salem Journal,* May 4, 1986, p. G1.
61. Ken Otterbourg, "Norfolk-Southern Tells SEC It Might Try to Buy Piedmont," *Winston-Salem Journal,* January 28, 1987, p. 1.
62. Ann Corrigan, "White Knight," *Winston-Salem Journal,* May 4, 1986, p. G1.
63. Ken Otterbourg, "Norfolk Southern Corp. Reports Record Income: *Winston-Salem Journal,* January 28, 1987, p. 3.
64. Ann Corrigan, "Piedmont Facing Invasion of Competing Airlines," *Winston-Salem Journal,* February 3, 1987, p. G1, 3.
65. Ken Otterbourg, "Piedmont Follows Its Own Route to Expand," *Winston-Salem Journal,* December 14, 1986, p. 1.
66. Zeke Saunders, interview, Winston-Salem, N.C., March 1, 2005.
67. Ken Otterbourg, "Most Thought Piedmont Immune to Merger Mania," *Winston-Salem Journal,* March 15, 1987, p. 1.
68. Gordon Bethune, telephone interview, August 18, 2005.
69. Ken Otterbourg, "Most Thought Piedmont Immune to Merger Mania," *Winston-Salem Journal,* March 15, 1987, p. 1.
70. William R. Howard, interview, Wilmington, N.C., July 14, 2006.
71. William R. Howard, interview, Wilmington, N.C., July 14, 2006.
72. Larry Brian Worrell, "The Piedmont and USAir Merger," Honors Thesis, University of North Carolina at Chapel Hill; 1992, p. 26.
73. Ken Otterbourg, "Most Thought Piedmont

Immune to Merger Mania," *Winston-Salem Journal*, March 15, 1987, p. 1.
74. Larry Brian Worrell, "The Piedmont and USAir Merger," Honors Thesis, University of North Carolina at Chapel Hill; 1992, p. 25-6.
75. Gordon Bethune, telephone interview, August 18, 2005.
76. William R. Howard, interview, Wilmington, N.C., July 14, 2006.
77. Larry Brian Worrell, "The Piedmont and USAir Merger," Honors Thesis, University of North Carolina at Chapel Hill; 1992, p. 26.
78. Gordon Bethune, telephone interview, August 18, 2005.
79. Ken Otterbourg, "Piedmont Considers USAir Bid," *Winston-Salem Journal*, February 19, 1987, p. 1.
80. Ken Otterbourg, "Break in Bidding War Gives Piedmont Time to Think About Offers," *Winston-Salem Journal*, February 22, 1987, p. A1, A8.
81. "Piedmont Stock Rises as Investors Watch for Bids," *Winston-Salem Journal*, February 21, 1987, p. 1.
82. Ken Otterbourg, "Break in Bidding War Gives Piedmont Time to Think About Offers," Winston-*Salem Journal*, February 22, 1987, p. A1, A8.
83. Larry Brian Worrell, "The Piedmont and USAir Merger," Honors Thesis, University of North Carolina at Chapel Hill; 1992, p. 26.
84. Howard Miller, telephone interview, November 11, 2004.
85. Ken Otterbourg, "TWA Offer is Rejected," *Winston-Salem Journal*, March 5, 1987, p. 1; Ken Otterbourg, "Piedmont Deal Complicated by TWA's Offer for USAir," *Winston-Salem Journal*, March 5, 1987, p. 1.
86. Joe Wilson, telephone interview, September 1, 2005.
87. Audrey Collins, interview, September 13, 2005.
88. Frank Davis, interview, Hickory, N.C., July 19, 2005.
89. Valerie Reitman, "Piedmont's Davis Loses a Child," *Charlotte Observer*, June 22, 1987, p. 4A.
90. "Piedmont: A Model of How Good an Airline Can Be," slide/video presentation, 1987.
91. Gordon Bethune with Scott Huler, *From Worst to First*, John Wiley and Sons, New York, 1998, p. 161.
92. Gordon Bethune with Scott Huler, *From Worst to First*, John Wiley and Sons, New York, 1998, p. 162.
93. Gordon Bethune, telephone interview, August 18, 2005.
94. Carroll Spencer, interview, Charlotte, N.C., September 5, 2006.

Chapter 9

1. Brian Thompson reporting, WBTV News, 6:00 P.M. newscast, contained in "Piedmont Airlines: A Model of How Good an Airline Can Be," slide/video presentation, 1989.
2. Jeff Sonier reporting, WSOC News, 5:30 P.M. newscast, June 15, 1987.
3. Carol Dobyns Fair, telephone interview, September 14, 2006.
4. Brian Thompson reporting, WBTV News, 6:00 P.M. newscast, contained in "Piedmont Airlines: A Model of How Good an Airline Can Be," slide/video presentation, 1989.
5. David Hains reporting, segment from 11:00 P.M. news program, June 15, 1987, WSOC-TV, Charlotte, N.C.
6. Gordon Bethune, telephone interview, August 18, 2005.
7. http://www.ifrance.com/atbusiness/PI767.html.
8. Bill Arthur, "Piedmont Wins London Gateway for Charlotte," *Charlotte Observer*, April 24, 1987, p. 10A.
9. "American Opens Raleigh-Durham Hub," *Charlotte Observer*, July 16, 1987, p. 11A.
10. M.S. Van Hecke, "London Flight Causes Spirits to Soar in Charlotte," *Charlotte Observer*, April 24, 1987, p. C1.
11. Jeff Borden, "WSOC's Walker, MacDonald to Broadcast From London," *Charlotte Observer*, May 11, 1987, p. 9A.
12. David Hains reporting, WSOC-TV 5:30 P.M. Newscast, Charlotte, N.C., June 15, 1987.
13. Gordon Bethune, telephone interview, August 18, 2005.
14. Ronnie Macklin, e-mail to the author, August 9, 2005.
15. Gordon Bethune, telephone interview, August 18, 2005.
16. C.D. McLean, telephone interview, September 3, 2005.
17. Ronnie Macklin, e-mail to the author, August 9, 2005.
18. Gordon Bethune, telephone interview, August 18, 2005.
19. "Piedmont Fined $30,000," *Charlotte Observer*, July 15, 1987, p. 13A.
20. Ronnie Macklin, e-mail to the author, August 9, 2005.
21. Gordon Bethune, telephone interview, August 18, 2005.
22. William R. Howard, interview, Wilmington, N.C., July 14, 2006.
23. Valerie Reitman, "Piedmont to Start Bahamas' Service," *Charlotte Observer*, January 25, 1987, p. 25A.
24. David Dykes, "Piedmont Flights Link Charlotte to the Bahamas," *Charlotte Observer*, November 16, 1987, p. B1.
25. Ed Martin, "Piedmont Says 737–400s Perform Well," *Charlotte Observer*, January 10, 1989.
26. Ronnie Macklin, e-mail to author, September 11, 2005.
27. Valerie Reitman, "Colodny Committed to Expansion," *Charlotte Observer*, April 24, 1987, p. 1.
28. David Mildenberg, "3 States Try to Stop USAir-Piedmont Merger," *Charlotte Observer*, April 1, 1987, p. 7A; Ken Otterbourg, "DOT Plans Long Hearing on Piedmont Merger," *Winston-Salem Journal*, April 16, 1987, Airline File, Forsyth County Public Library.
29. Valerie Reitman, "Piedmont's Davis Loses a Child," *Charlotte Observer*, June 22, 1987, p. 1A, 4A.
30. Larry Parnass, "Piedmont Shareholders Approve USAir Merger," *Winston Salem Journal*, July 24, 1987, p. 1; "Business Briefly," *Charlotte Observer*, July 24, 1987, p. 5C.
31. Steve Gasque Reporting, WSOC-TV 6:00 P.M. news, August 2, 1989.
32. "Business Briefly," *Charlotte Observer*, May 23, 1987.
33. Ken Otterbourg, "Merger Would Hurt Few Jobs, Colodny Says," *Winston-Salem Journal*, April 24, 1987, p. 1.
34. Valerie Reitman, "Colodny Committed to Expansion," *Charlotte Observer*, April 24, 1987, p. 1.
35. C.D. McLean, telephone interview, September 3, 2005.
36. Gordon Bethune, telephone interview, August 18, 2005.
37. Ken Otterbourg and Larry Parnass, "Piedmont's Howard Quits to Join Effort to Buy United," *Winston-Salem Journal*, August 14, 1987, p. 1.
38. William R. Howard, interview, Wilmington, N.C., July 14, 2004.

39. C.D. McLean, telephone interview, September 3, 2005.
40. McKinney and Silver advertisement, date unknown, from the collection of Ronnie Macklin.
41. 1984 Annual Report, Piedmont Aviation, Inc.
42. Ken Otterbourg, "USAir Wants to Make 'Whole New Airline,'" *Winston-Salem Journal*, November 3, 1987, p. 4.
43. Joe Wilson, telephone interview, September 1, 2005.
44. Richard Smith, telephone interview, September 19, 2005.
45. Larry Parnass "Piedmont Shareholders Approve USAir Merger," *Winston-Salem Journal*, July 24, 1987, p. 1.
46. Paul Haskins, "Hearing Judge Rejects Piedmont-USAir Plan," *Winston-Salem Journal*, September 22, 1987, p. 1.
47. "Colodny: Ruling Incomprehensible," *Charlotte Observer*, September 22, 1987, p. 11A.
48. "DOT Law Judge Urges Rejection of USAir's Takeover of Piedmont," *Charlotte Observer*, September 22, 1987, p. 11A.
49. David Dykes, "Piedmont Cautions Workers," *Charlotte Observer*, September 30, 1987, p. 8C.
50. David Dykes, "Piedmont Names President," *Charlotte Observer*, June 25, 1988, p. 6B.
51. Paul Haskins, "Federal Lawyers Support Merger of Piedmont and USAir," *Winston-Salem Journal*, October 6, 1987, p. 1.
52. Larry Parnass, "Piedmont and USAir Stand to Lose Much if Merger is Not Approved," *Winston-Salem Journal*, September 23, 1987, p. 1.
53. Dykes, "Piedmont Cautions Workers," *Charlotte Observer*, September 30, 1987, p. 9C.
54. Paul Haskins, "Federal Lawyers Support Merger of Piedmont and USAir," *Winston-Salem Journal*, October 6, 1987, p. 1.
55. Larry Parnass, "Cultural Anthropologist Examines Marital Health of Airline Mergers," *Winston-Salem Journal*, October 26, 1987, p. 12, 17.
56. Bill Arthur and David Dykes, "Government OKs USAir Acquisition of Piedmont," *Charlotte Observer*, October 31, 1987, p. 1.
57. John Cleghorn, "Piedmont Employees Greet Word of Approval Warmly," *Charlotte Observer*, October 31, 1987, p. 8C.
58. Ron Strodghill II, "Winston-Salem Home Folks Have Mixed Emotions," *Charlotte Observer*, October 31, 1987, p. 8C.
59. John Cleghorn, "Piedmont Employees Greet Word of Approval Warmly," *Charlotte Observer*, October 31, 1987, p. 8C.
60. C.D. McLean, telephone interview, September 3, 2005.
61. C.D. McLean, telephone interview, September 3, 2005.
62. Joe Wilson, telephone interview, September 1, 2005.
63. Joe Wilson, telephone interview, September 1, 2005.
64. Don Martin, interview, Roanoke, Virginia, January 18, 2005.
65. Frank Davis, interview, Hickory, N.C., July 19, 2005.
66. Bob McAlphin, interview, Clemmons, N.C., September 13, 2005.
67. Don Collins, interview, Winston-Salem, N.C., September 13, 2005.
68. Joe Wilson, telephone interview, September 1, 2005.
69. Bob McAlphin, interview, Clemmons, N.C., September 13, 2005.
70. Richard Smith, telephone interview, September 19, 2005.
71. Stephen Shaw, *Airline Marketing and Management*, Fifth Edition, Ashgate Publishing, Burlington, Vt., p. 224.
72. David J. Morrow, *Business North Carolina*, May 1987, p. 7.
73. J.A.C. Dunn, "The History of Piedmont Airlines," *Pace* magazine, December 1988, p. 78.
74. Steve Gasque Reporting, WSOC-TV 6:00 P.M. News, August 2, 1989.
75. Robert L. Rose, *Wall Street Journal*, November 2, 1987, p. 1.
76. C.D. McLean, telephone interview, September 3, 2005.
77. Joe Wilson, telephone interview, September 1, 2005.
78. Ed Martin, "Computer Glitch Delays Piedmont, USAir Flights," *Charlotte Observer*, March 29, 1989, 2B.
79. Joe Wilson, telephone interview, September 1, 2005.
80. William R. Howard, interview, Wilmington, July 14, 2006.
81. Don Collins, interview, Winston-Salem, N.C., September 13, 2005.
82. Richard Smith, telephone interview, September 19, 2005.
83. Dick Wallis, telephone interview, August 15, 2005.
84. Piedmont Pilots' Merger Analysis, Volume 1, pp. 1–9.
85. Piedmont Pilots' Merger Analysis, Volume 1, pp. 1–9; Dick Wallis, telephone interview, August 15, 2005.
86. Dick Wallis, telephone interview, August 15, 2005.
87. Dick Wallis, telephone interview, August 15, 2005.
88. Elmo Torres, telephone interview, August 13, 2005.
89. "Piedmont's Service Suffering in Merger," *Winston-Salem Journal*, August 4, 1989, p. 1, 16.
90. "Piedmont's Service Suffering in Merger," *Winston-Salem Journal*, August 4, 1989, p. 16.
91. "USAir Moving 100 to Piedmont's Town," Business Briefly section, *Charlotte Observer*, July 2, 1988.
92. Steve Gasque Reporting, WSOC-TV 6:00 P.M. news, August 2, 1989.
93. "Piedmont to Reduce Frequent-Flier Mileage," *Charlotte Observer*, August 5, 1988, p. 17D; David Dykes, "Piedmont Changing Flier Plan," October 28, 1988; Steve Gasque Reporting, WSOC-TV 6:00 P.M. news, August 3, 1989.
94. John Cleghorn, "USAir Considers Canning Piedmont's Soft Drink Policy," *Charlotte Observer*, June 12, 1989, p. 1; Linda Bosley, "Fliers Keep the Can," *Charlotte Observer*, July 19, 1989, p. 6C.
95. "Piedmont's Pacifier," *Charlotte Observer*, July 20, 1989, p. 20A.
96. Debbie Brown, telephone interview, March 15, 2005.
97. Howard Miller, telephone interview, November 11, 2004.
98. Steve Gasque reporting, "Piedmont, Up, Up and Away," news package, 6:00 P.M. newscast, WSOC-TV, Charlotte, N.C.
99. Ed Martin, "Who'll Fly Our Planes?" *Charlotte Observer*, June 24, 1989, p. A1-A6.
100. Ed Martin, "USAir Faces Challenges as Piedmont Name Fades," *Charlotte Observer*, July 31, 1989, p. 1.
101. Phoebe Zerwick, "Winston-Salem's Home-Grown Airline Comes to an End," *Winston-Salem Journal*, August 5, 1989, p. 1.
102. Rick Jackson Reporting, WCNC-TV Morning News, August 5, 1989.
103. Steve Gasque Reporting, WSOC-TV 6:00 P.M. News, August 1, 1989.
104. Warren Wheeler, telephone interview, August 25, 2005.

105. Ed Martin, "Folding its Wings," *Charlotte Observer*, August 5, 1989, p. 16A.
106. Connie Counts, interview, Charleston, S.C., October 18, 2004.
107. Don Collins, interview, Winston-Salem, N.C., September 13, 2005.

Afterword

1. "Piedmont Airlines, we need you now," Observer Forum, *Charlotte Observer*, January 4, 2005, p. 10A.
2. Dave Johnson, telephone interview, July 7, 2005.
3. "Piedmont: A Model of How Good an Airline Can Be," slide/video presentation, 1987.
4. Dave Johnson, telephone interview, July 7, 2005.

Epilogue

1. Martha M. Haswell, "Saved from the Scrapheap," *Tarheel* magazine, date unknown; Ronnie Macklin, "Piedmont Airlines DC-3 N56V — *Potomac Pacemaker*," unpublished document, May 21, 2005; "Piedmont Airlines CD-3 N56V Background History," Museum of Life and Science press release, date unknown.
2. Interview, Ronnie Macklin and Howard Miller, Statesville, N.C., August 17, 2006.
3. NCTM. A plane commissioned by Mr. Davis after the airline merged with USAir is part of a flying display, housed at Charlotte's Douglas International Airport. However, that plane was never a part of the fleet originally flown by Piedmont prior to 1963.
4. Buddy Bowen, e-mail to the author, September 4, 2006.
5. http://www.newsobserver.com/543/story/296624.html.
6. E-mail from Ronnie Macklin to author, September 14, 2006.

Bibliography

Interviews

Bailey, James (Beetle). Charleston, S.C., October 17, 2004.
Barber, Bill. Telephone, December 20, 2004.
_____. Winston-Salem, N.C., March 1, 2005.
Beeson, Philip. Telephone, June 23, 2005.
Best, Edward. Telephone, August 30, 2005.
Bethune, Gordon. Telephone, August 18, 2005.
Blocker, Mel. Telephone, July 10, 2004.
Bowen, Buddy. Charleston, S.C., October 18, 2004.
Brown, Debbie. Telephone, March 15, 2005.
Caudle, Ann S. Charleston, S.C., October 18, 2004.
Caudle, David. Charleston, S.C., October 18, 2004.
Collins, Audrey. Winston-Salem, N.C., September 13, 2005.
Collins, Don. Winston-Salem, N.C., September 13, 2005.
Counts, Connie. Charleston, S.C., October 18, 2004.
Counts, Edward. Charleston, S.C., October 18, 2004.
Culler, Danny. Winston-Salem, N.C., September 22, 2005.
Culler, Ed. Winston-Salem, N.C., September 22, 2005.
Davis, Egbert, Jr. Winston-Salem, N.C., March 22, 2005.
Davis, Frank. Hickory, N.C., July 19, 2005.
Davis, Thelma. Winston-Salem, N.C., September 28, 2004.
Dudley, Larry. Roanoke, Va., January 18, 2005.
Fair, Carol Dobyns. Telephone, September 24, 2006.
Fisher, Randy. Charleston, S.C., October 19, 2004.
Fox, Leon. Telephone, June 1, 2004.
Gibson, Joe. Charleston, N.C., October 19, 2004.
Goforth, Roscoe. Charleston, S.C., October 17, 2004.
Gordon, Robert. Charleston, S.C., October 17, 2004.
Hamilton, Jim. Lake Norman, N.C., August 14, 2004.
Hamilton, Stephanie. Lake Norman, N.C., August 14, 2004.
Horrell, Harvel G. Charleston, S.C., October 18, 2004.
Houle, Paul. Boiling Springs, S.C., February 13, 2005.
Howard, William R. Wilmington, N.C., July 14, 2006.
Johnson, David. Telephone, July 7, 2005.
Lambert, L.J. Telephone, January 22, 2005.
Macklin, Ronald. Hickory, N.C., October 7, 2004.
_____. Winston-Salem, N.C., March 1, 2005.
Martin, Don. Roanoke, Va., January 18, 2005.
Martin, Leonard. Telephone, January 22, 2005.
McAlphin, Bob. Clemmons, N.C., September 13, 2005.
McLean, C.D. Telephone, September 3, 2005.
Meacham, Chuck. Rockingham, N.C., August 20, 2006.
Miller, Howard. Telephone, November 14, 2004.
Onoff, John. Charleston, S.C.. October 19, 2004.
Orrell, Tommy. Telephone, September 12, 2005.
Parnell, Samuel M. Charleston, S.C., October 18, 2004.
Peters, Cheryl. Telephone, May 24, 2005.
Piper, William. Telephone, August 4, 2005.
Queen, Margaret. Charleston, S.C., October 18, 2004.
Sain, Dottie. Telephone, August 12, 2004.
Sass, Lynn. Telephone, August 10, 2005.
Saunders, Harold (Zeke). Telephone, May 4, 2004.
_____. Winston-Salem, N.C. May 11, 2004; December 28, 2004; March 1, 2005; September 30, 2005; February 8, 2006.
Sharp, Gene. Charleston, S.C., October 18, 2004.
Sharpe, Tom. Bristol, Tenn., May 2004.
Smith, Richard. Telephone, September 19, 2005; November 8, 2004; February 24, 2005; October 30, 2006.
_____. E-mail to the Author, August 25, 2005.
Spencer, Carroll. Charlotte, N.C., September 5, 2006.
Spencer, J.Y. Telephone, October 29, 2006.
Taylor, James. Telephone, September 29, 2004.
Thomas, Pauline Fletcher. E-mail to the Author, July 28, 2006, July 31, 2006.
Thompson, Howard. Roanoke, Va., January 18, 2005.
Torres, Elmo. Telephone, August 13, 2005.
Vaughn, Tory. Telephone, July 6, 2005.
Walker, Jack. Telephone, September 2, 2004.
Wallis, Richard. Telephone, August 15, 2005.
Wilcox, Earl. Hudson, N.C., March 29, 2005.
Wilson, Joe. Telephone, September 1, 2005.
Wheeler, Warren. Telephone, August 24, 2005.

Government Documents

City of Winston-Salem, North Carolina, "An Ordinance Amending the Zoning Ordinance to Provide Airport Zoning Regulations Under the Model Airport Zoning Act," April 1, 1958.
Civil Aeronautics Board, *Aircraft Accident Report*, "Piedmont Airlines, Douglas DC-3, N55V, On Buck's Elbow Mountain, Near Charlottesville, Virginia, October 30, 1959. File No. 1-0065, Adopted: April 18, 1961, Released: April 24, 1961.
Civil Air Patrol, Letter to Major T.H. Davis, September 21, 1944.
U.S. Department of Transportation, NTSB, Letter to T.H. Davis, January 20, 1970.

Company Documents

Annual Reports
Annual Meeting Board of Directors, 1944.
1948 Annual Report to Stockholders, "Home Office and Operations Base, Smith-Reynolds Airport, Winston-Salem, N.C.," Piedmont Aviation, Inc.
1949 Annual Report, Piedmont Aviation, Inc.
Tenth Annual Report (1950), Piedmont Aviation, Inc.
Eleventh Annual Report (1951), Piedmont Aviation, Inc.
12th Annual Report (1952), Piedmont Aviation, Inc.
1953 Annual Report, "A Picture of Progress," Piedmont Aviation, Inc.
1954 Annual Report, Piedmont Aviation, Inc.
1955 Annual Report and 8-Year Picture of Progress, Piedmont Aviation, Inc.
1956 Annual Report, "The Shape of Wings to Come," Piedmont Aviation, Inc.
1957 Annual Report, Piedmont Aviation, Inc.
1958 Annual Report, Piedmont Aviation, Inc.
1959 Annual Report, Piedmont Aviation, Inc.
1960 Annual Report, "The World of Piedmont Airlines," Piedmont Aviation, Inc.
1962 Annual Report, Piedmont Aviation, Inc.
1963 Annual Report, Piedmont Aviation, Inc.
1965 Annual Report, Piedmont Aviation, Inc.
1966 Annual Report, Piedmont Aviation, Inc.
1967 Annual Report, Piedmont Aviation, Inc.
1968 Annual Report, Piedmont Aviation, Inc.
1969 Annual Report, Piedmont Aviation, Inc.
1970 Annual Report, Piedmont Aviation, Inc.
1971 Annual Report, Piedmont Aviation, Inc.
1972 Annual Report, Piedmont Aviation, Inc.
1973 Annual Report, Piedmont Aviation, Inc.
1974 Annual Report, Piedmont Aviation, Inc.
1975 Annual Report, Piedmont Aviation, Inc.
1976 Annual Report, Piedmont Aviation, Inc.
1977 Annual Report, Piedmont Aviation, Inc.
1978 Annual Report, Piedmont Aviation, Inc.
1979 Annual Report, Piedmont Aviation, Inc.
1980 Annual Report, Piedmont Aviation, Inc.
1981 Annual Report, Piedmont Aviation, Inc.
1982 Annual Report, Piedmont Aviation, Inc.
1983 Annual Report, Piedmont Aviation, Inc.
1984 Annual Report, Piedmont Aviation, Inc.
1985 Annual Report, Piedmont Aviation, Inc.
1986 Annual Report, Piedmont Aviation, Inc.
"Flight Times: A Publication for Piedmont Flight Attendants," April-May 1989.
Hurley, Dick, "Piedmont Airlines: A Company History," Piedmont Airlines company publication, date unknown.
Piedmonitor, December 1953.
Piedmonitor, 1987 Special Edition, company publication.
"Piedmont Airlines and the DC-3," Piedmont Airlines company brochure, 1987.
"The Piedmont Airlines Story," company publication, December 1, 1969.
"Piedmont Open House," handout. February 27, 1948.
Southern Bell Telephone and Telegraph Company, letter to Mr. F.R. Daniels from T.H. Davis, September 5, 1946.
"Welcome Aboard the 727," Boeing Commercial Airplane Division, Renton, Washington, October 5, 1965.

Newspapers

Adams, Jerry. "Airport's Financial Situation is Unclear Till Ink Dries," *Winston-Salem Journal*, May 12, 1976.
Adams, Jerry. "Deficit Continues as Airport; Subsidy to Be Requested," *Winston-Salem Journal*, January 13, 1976.
Adams, Jerry. "Local Airport Lost $24,266," *Winston-Salem Journal*, November 11, 1975.
"Air fare cuts have restrictions," *Roanoke Times & World News*, March 17, 1983.
"Air Mail Service Over New Route to Begin February 14," *Wilmington Morning Star*, February 6, 1948.
"Air Service for 500 Cities," *Winston-Salem Journal & Sentinel*, November 26, 1956.
"Air Service Inaugurated Here Today," *Wilmington Morning Star*, February 20, 1948.
"Air Traffic Threat is Blamed on FAA," *Winston-Salem Journal*, July 20, 1967.
"Airline Buys Anticrash System," *Winston-Salem Journal*, June 23, 1971.
"Airline Complex Taking Shape," *Twin City Sentinel*, July 13, 1967.
"Airline Carries Record Number of Passengers," *Winston-Salem Journal*, July 8, 1966.
"Airline Gripes Take Off," *Charlotte Observer*, July 16, 1987.
"Airline Strike Hearing Date Postponed Two Days," *Winston-Salem Journal*, August 7, 1969.
"Airline Takes Plea to Court," *Wilmington Morning Star*, January 20, 1948.
"Airline Will Start February 14," *Wilmington Morning Star*, January 29, 1948.
"Airliner is Damaged When Propeller Lost," *Winston-Salem Journal*, August 23, 1962.
"Airlines' Performance," *Charlotte Observer*, April 24, 1989.
"Airlines Ruffle Fliers With Tighter Rules," *Charlotte Observer*, April 22, 1987.
"Airplane Explosion Probed," *Charleston Daily Mail*, April 15, 1988.
"Airport Here Shows Profit of $34,094," *Twin City Sentinel*, August 27, 1965.
"Airport ILS Failure Known, Board Says," *Charleston Gazette*, August 12, 1968.
"Airport is Second Busiest," *Winston-Salem Journal*, January 28, 1969.
"Airport Mural Being Restored," *Twin City Sentinel*, December 16, 1961.
"Airport Revenue Increases," *Twin City Sentinel*, August 4, 1964.
"Airport Tenants Roles Described," *Twin City Sentinel*, May 15, 1964.
"America West Asks Court For Delay," *Charlotte Observer*, November 3, 1987.
"American Opens Raleigh-Durham Hub," *Charlotte Observer*, June 16, 1987.
Armstrong, Steve. "Friendship Airport Almost Empty," *Twin City Sentinel*, July 8, 1966.
Arthur, Bill. "Charlotte-Raleigh Rivalry for London Air

Gateway Soaring," *Charlotte Observer*, January 5, 1987.
Arthur, Bill. "DOT Staff Favoring Piedmont," *Charlotte Observer*, January 27, 1987.
Arthur, Bill. "Piedmont 'Gratified' at DOT's London Recommendation," *Charlotte Observer*, January 28, 1987.
Arthur, Bill. "Piedmont, USAir Make Final Pitch," *Charlotte Observer*, October 6, 1987.
Arthur, Bill. "Piedmont Wins London Gateway for Charlotte," *Charlotte Observer*, April 24, 1987.
Arthur, Bill, and David Dykes. "Government OKs USAir Acquisition of Piedmont," *Charlotte Observer*, October 31, 1987.
"A.T.A. Chief Views Value of Air Power," *Winston-Salem Journal*, February 28, 1948.
"A.T.A.A. Executive Will Speak at Piedmont Airlines Banquet," *Winston-Salem Journal*, February 26, 1948.
"Automobile Races and Band Concert at Big Aviation Meet," *Winston-Salem Journal*, January 16, 1911.
"Aviation Co. Formed 1928," *Winston-Salem Journal*, June 22, 1930.
"Aviation Meet Great Success," *Winston-Salem Journal*, November 30, 1911.
Bailey, David. "Lindbergh Fostered Airport," *Winston-Salem Journal & Sentinel*, May 1, 1977.
Barber, Karen. "Piedmont Return Comes Early," *Charlotte Observer*, June 17, 1987.
Barron, Richard M. "Airline to Expand its Offices Here," *Winston-Salem Journal*, January 13, 1987.
Barron, Richard M. "Eyes and Voices Show Worry on 'Blue Monday,'" *Winston-Salem Journal*, March 10, 1987.
Barron, Richard M. "Wichita's Chamber of Commerce is Wooing Piedmont in a Big Way," *Winston-Salem Journal*, March 21, 1986.
Barry, Tom. "Local Pilot First at New Terminal but Last For Credit," *Atlanta Constitution*, Sept. 22, 1980.
Bauguess, Bernard. "Phone Calls Flood Office," *Winston-Salem Journal*, July 20, 1967.
Beavers, Tom. "Man Tries Hijack, Seized at Airport," *Twin City Sentinel*, June 18, 1971.
Belden, Tom. "USAir Shuns Turbulence, Eases into Merger," *Charlotte Observer*, September 11, 1988.
Bennett, Steve. "'Metal Bent Over the Edge ... Like a Burnt Cigar,'" *Winston-Salem Journal*, July 20, 1967.
"Big Crowd Expected," *Winston-Salem Journal*, March 31, 1911.
"Bobby White is Two Men, Friends Say," *Winston-Salem Journal*, June 19, 1971.
"Bodies in Crash Are Recovered," *Winston-Salem Journal*, July 21, 1967.
Borden, Jeff. "WSOC's Walker, MacDonald to Broadcast from London," *Charlotte Observer*, May 11, 1987.
Bosley, Linda. "Fliers Keep the Can," *Charlotte Observer*, July 19, 1989.
Bost, Sid. "Chicago Has High Hopes for New Piedmont Service," *Twin City Sentinel*, November 26, 1969.
Bost, Sid. "Corporation Pilot Called Careful Man," *Twin City Sentinel*, July 20, 1967.
Bost, Sid. "Piedmont Asks for Philadelphia," *The Sentinel*, September 25, 1979.
"Both Aviators Here with Their Flyers," *Winston-Salem Journal*, November 18, 1911.

"Building a Great Air Line," *Twin City Sentinel*, February 19, 1948.
Burks, Ed. "City Airport Now Rates as Major Industry," *Winston-Salem Journal*, August 24, 1952.
Byrd, John. "Piedmont's Pilot," *Winston-Salem Journal*, June 12, 1983.
"CAA Officials Join Piedmont in Flight Over New Air Route," *Twin City Sentinel*, February 16, 1948.
"CAA Reduces Requirements at Bluethenthal," *Wilmington Morning Star*, January 29, 1948.
"CAB Refuses 'Stay' of Piedmont Award," *Wilmington Morning Star*, January 30, 1948.
Campbell, Ed. "Piedmont Inaugurates N.Y. Flight," *Twin City Sentinel*, November 15, 1966.
Cantwell, Josiah. "Off the Ground," *Wilmington Star-News*, February 15, 1989.
Carlson, Kenneth. "Piedmont-USAir merger means change in the Triad," *Triad Business*, June 26, 1989.
Carlson, Kenneth. "Piedmont's final days evoke memories," *Triad Business*, June 26, 1989.
Carlton, Caroline. "Many Stranded Here by Walkout," *Twin City Sentinel*, July 8, 1966.
"Cause of Airport Fire is Unknown," *Winston-Salem Journal*, August 15, 1941.
"Ceremony Marks Launching of Louisville–New Bern Route," *Winston-Salem Journal*, February 28, 1948.
Chamis, Eleni. "Piedmont has its hands in many businesses," *Winston-Salem Business Journal*, n.d. (Forsyth County Public Library Collection).
"Charlotte is Called Front-Runner for Gateway," *Winston-Salem Journal*, December 21, 1986.
"Chunks of Piedmont Flowing to USAir," *Winston-Salem Journal*, April 7, 1987.
"City, County Men to Take Flight," *Wilmington Morning Star*, February 12, 1948.
"City Storm Damage Heavy; Neighboring Towns Dig Out," *Wilmington Morning Star*, February 3, 1948.
Cleghorn, John. "As USAir Grapples with Reversing Rocky Ratings," *Charlotte Observer*, August 5, 1989.
____. "Charlotte Off to England," *Charlotte Observer*, June 16, 1987.
____. "Piedmont Employees Greet Word of Approval Warmly," *Charlotte Observer*, October 31, 1987.
____. "Piedmont's Last Arrival Record Barely Better," *Charlotte Observer*, September 9, 1989.
Clifford, Frank. "Airline Expected to Begin Full Operations Next Week," *Twin City Sentinel*, August 16, 1969.
Coble, Marvin. "Boys Glad to be Alive," *Twin City Sentinel*, July 20, 1967.
"Coffee Burns Flight Attendant," *Charlotte Observer*, November 2, 1988.
"Colodny: Ruling Incomprehensible," *Charlotte Observer*, September 22, 1987.
"Commercial Air Service Comes to City," *Kinston Daily Free Press*, September 10, 1949.
"Congress Alarmed Over Mid-Air Crash," *Winston-Salem Journal*, July 21, 1967.
"Congressmen Urge Limiting Small Planes," *Winston-Salem Journal*, July 20, 1967.
Conley, Paul. "Mechanics Left Wheel Chocks in Plane, Board Says," *Winston-Salem Journal*, August 5, 1989.
Conley, Paul F. "Fasten Seat Belts," *Winston-Salem Business Journal*, October 10, 1989.
____. "Position of Chock Puzzling Officials," *Winston-Salem Journal*, August 4, 1989.

Corrigan, Ann. "Cinderella Story: After Midnight Wednesday, All Empire Airlines Planes Will Turn into Piedmonts,'" *Winston-Salem Journal*, April 27, 1986.
_____. "Piedmont Aviation to Move Its Offices to McLean Building," *Winston-Salem Journal*, February 13, 1986.
_____. "Piedmont Facing Invasion of Competing Airlines," *Winston-Salem Journal*, February 2, 1985.
_____. "USAir Barely Survived Its Earlier Years," *Winston-Salem Business Journal*, July 31, 1989.
_____. "White Knight," *Winston-Salem Journal*, May 4, 1986.
Coupe, Mary. "Air passengers light up with smoking ban reactions," *Charleston Daily Mail*, April 22, 1988.
"Court Refuses 'Stay' of Airline Service," *Twin City Sentinel*, February 16, 1948.
"Court Won't Delay Piedmont Merger," *Charlotte Observer*, November 4, 1987.
"The Courting of Piedmont," *Roanoke Times & World News*, March 15, 1987.
Covington, Cleta. "Piedmont Bids Good-bye to Its DC-3s," *Twin City Sentinel*, February 23, 1963.
Cralidis, Ann. "Yes, Winston-Salem does have airport," *The Suburbanite*, August 29, 1984.
"Crash Dealt Airlines Heavy Blow," *Twin City Sentinel*, March 28, 1968.
"Crash is 3rd and Worst for Piedmont," *Twin City Sentinel*, July 20, 1967.
"Crash-landed Plane to Fly Again, Piedmont Says Damage Was Slight," *Winston-Salem Journal*, April 29, 1959.
Crawley, Oliver. "Huge Throng Sees Airport Dedication; Still More Expansion Announced," *Winston-Salem Journal*, June 14, 1942.
Creed, Dick. "Jet Had a Festive Beginning with Jokes at 14,000 Feet," *Winston-Salem Journal*, July 20, 1967.
Cummings, Tom. "Air Crash Probers Seek to Determine Fog Patch Effects," *Charleston Daily Mail*, October 23, 1968.
_____. "Heard Explosion, Then Lighter Sound, Crash Witness Reveals," *Charleston Daily Mail*, October 22, 1968.
_____. "Sorrowing Kinfolk Claiming Air Dead," *Charleston Daily Mail*, August 12, 1968.
"Curiosity Turns to Grim Silence," *Winston-Salem Journal*, July 20, 1967.
Curry, Kathleen. "Airline Wants More Runways Late at Night," *Charlotte Observer*, May 11, 1988.
Daniel, Clifton. "Ascent of a Dream," *Wilmington Star-News*, January 22, 1995.
_____. "Piedmont's first flight left Wilmington almost 47 years ago," *Wilmington Star-News*, January 22, 1995.
Davis, Chester. "A Big Step Forward by Piedmont Airlines," *Winston-Salem Journal & Sentinel*, June 24, 1962.
_____. "Piedmont Airlines' Success is the Best Argument for County's Working, Spending to Keep it Here," *Winston-Salem Journal & Sentinel*, June 28, 1953.
_____. "Routine Flight, Almost," *Winston-Salem Journal*, February 18, 1961.
"DC-3 Nose-Dives When Wing Falls," *Wilmington Morning Star*, January 29, 1948.

"Delay in Repair of Glide Slope by FAA Inexcusable," *Charleston Gazette*, August 12, 1968.
Dillon, Mark. "Airline grew too big, some say," *Winston-Salem Journal*, November 28, 1994.
Dillon, Tom. "Appeals Court Orders Pilots Back to Work," *Winston-Salem Journal*, August 16, 1969.
_____, and Lloyd Brinson. "Airplane Crash Kills 5 from City, Virginian," *Winston-Salem Journal and Sentinel*, January 21, 1968.
Dumbell, Jim. "Travelers Skirt Atlanta in Style," *Charlotte Observer*, June 17, 1987.
"Due for a change...," *Twin City Sentinel*, October 30, 1961.
Dykes, David. "Airline: We're Left Holding the Bag," *Charlotte Observer*, March 4, 1988.
_____. "Charlotte Will be Vital to USAir, Analysts Say," *Charlotte Observer*, October 31, 1987.
_____. "Piedmont Airlines Flight Attendants OK Contract," *Charlotte Observer*, November 4, 1987.
_____. "Piedmont Airlines Reports Big Jump in March Traffic," *Charlotte Observer*, April 5, 1988.
_____. "Piedmont Cautions Workers," *Charlotte Observer*, September 30, 1987.
_____. "Piedmont Changing Flier Plans," *Charlotte Observer*, October 28, 1987.
_____. "Piedmont Chief Sees More Expansion," *Charlotte Observer*, November 3, 1987.
_____. "Piedmont Departs, But Ad Agency Lands Braniff," *Charlotte Observer*, Jan. 3, 1989.
_____. "Piedmont Flights Link Charlotte to the Bahamas," *Charlotte Observer*, November 16, 1987.
_____. "Piedmont Machinists Vote for Higher Pay, Against 2-Tier Scale," *Charlotte Observer*, August 16, 1987.
_____. "Piedmont Names President," *Charlotte Observer*, June 25, 1988.
_____. "Piedmont, USAir Have to Decide: Your Way or Mine?" *Charlotte Observer*, November 9, 1987.
_____. "Piedmont-USAir: Making the Merger Mesh," *Charlotte Observer*, November 9, 1987.
_____. "USAir Chief: Merged Airline's Future Lies in U.S.," *Charlotte Observer*, April 4, 1988.
_____. "USAir, Piedmont to Trim Overlapping Air Service in 6 Markets," *Charlotte Observer*, March 1, 1988.
"Early Figures Show Airport Deficit," *Twin City Sentinel*, August 10, 1976.
East, Bill. "Do You Remember ... Airport Here 'Made' for Lindbergh," *Twin City Sentinel*, June 11, 1958.
_____. "Lindbergh's Visit Spurred Growth of Aviation," *Twin City Sentinel*, May 24, 1976.
_____. "Lindy Fathered Airport," *Twin City Sentinel*, August 28, 1974.
_____. "Safe Flying," *Winston-Salem Journal*, August 21, 1985.
_____. "Winston-Salem's First Family of Flying," *Twin City Sentinel*, January 19, 1971.
"Eastern Carolina Digging Out from Worst Storm in 15 Years," *Wilmington Morning Star*, February 3, 1948.
Edmonds, Rick. "Cuba: Yes or No?" *Twin City Sentinel*, June 18, 1971.
"82 Listed as Dead in Plane Collision," *Twin City Sentinel*, July 20, 1967.
"Empire Airlines' visual image fading out," *Syracuse Herald-Journal*, April 28, 1986.

"Engine Disintegrates in Flight, Blowing 2 Holes in Piedmont Jet," *Winston-Salem Journal*, April 15, 1988.

"Engine Falls Off Piedmont Jet; No One Injured," *Winston-Salem Journal*, January 21, 1989.

"Ex-Employees Have Fond Memories of the Time Spent with Piedmont," *Winston-Salem Business Journal*, July 31, 1989.

"Fake Memo at Piedmont Fails to Fly," *Winston-Salem Journal*, March 3, 1987.

Falk, Lawrence C. "Light Plane, Jet Collide in Midair," *Winston-Salem Journal*, July 20, 1967.

"Fayetteville on World Airlines," *Fayetteville Observer*, September 26, 1949.

"58 Planned to Leave Jet at Roanoke," *Winston-Salem Journal*, July 20, 1967.

"Fire Destroys 14 Planes at Airport," *Winston-Salem Journal*, August 14, 1941.

"The First Paying Passenger," *Twin City Sentinel*, February 21, 1948.

"First Piedmont Flight Slated for Friday A.M.," *Wilmington Morning Star*, February 17, 1948.

Fischer, Jeri. "Transportation Board Begins Probe of Wrecked Piedmont Jet," *Charlotte Observer*, October 28, 1986.

"Five Citizens Own Private Ships for Own Sport, Business," *Winston-Salem Journal*, June 22, 1930.

"Fly USAir's routes to your roots" (advertisement) *Winston-Salem Journal*, May 26, 1987.

"Fog-Created Illusion Caused Piedmont Plane Crash Here," *Charleston Daily Mail*, August 10, 1968.

Frankel, Jonathan. "USAir is Planning to Eliminate 2,100 More Jobs," *Winston-Salem Journal*, August 25, 1990.

"Funerals Arranged for 7 Servicemen Killed at Airport," *Charleston Daily Mail*, August 12, 1968.

Garber, Mary. "Circle of Guards Watches Twisted Wreckage of Plane," *Twin City Sentinel*, July 20, 1967.

"Gateway is Awarded to Piedmont Airlines and Charlotte," *Winston-Salem Journal*, April 24, 1987.

"Girl is Killed When Plane was Forced to Land," *Winston-Salem Journal*, October 14, 1922.

Goodykoontz, Bill. "'I Saw the Terminal, and It Just Flew By,' Flier Says," *Charlotte Observer*, October 27, 1988.

Gourlay, Bruce. "McNaughtons Came to Pick Up Son," *Twin City Sentinel*, July 20, 1967.

"Government Hears Fewer Airline Gripes," *Charlotte Observer*, June 7, 1988.

Graettinger, Robert S. "Piedmont Flights Heading West," *The Sentinel*, December 22, 1983.

Gray, Jim. "Airport Expansion: Report Needed," *Winston-Salem Journal*, November 21, 1971.

Griffin, Frances. "Piedmont Will Give Public 'Inside' View of Air Line," *Winston-Salem Journal*, February 27, 1948.

Gubbins, Pat. "Plane's Landing Began Smoothly," *Charlotte Observer*, October 26, 1986.

Harper-Evans, Cindy. "Despite best-laid plans, airlines' merger rocky," *Roanoke Times & World News*, April 1, 1990.

Harrigan, Susan. "Piedmont Rises by Landing in Small Cities," *Wall Street Journal*, April 9, 1981.

Harrison, Steve. "Amateur sleuth disputes crash report," *Charlotte Observer*, November 13, 2006.

Haskins, Paul. "Federal Judge Favors Piedmont Airlines for London Service," *Winston-Salem Journal*, February 26, 1987.

Haskins, Paul. "Federal Lawyers Support Merger of Piedmont and USAir," *Winston-Salem Journal*, October 6, 1987.

Haskins, Paul. "Hearing Judge Rejects Piedmont-USAir Plan," *Winston-Salem Journal*, September 22, 1987.

Haskins, Paul. "Judge is Urged to OK Merger of Piedmont," *Winston-Salem Journal*, August 22, 1987.

Haskins, Paul. "Piedmont and USAir Merger Gets Final Approval," *Winston-Salem Journal*, October 31, 1987.

Haskins, Paul. "Piedmont's Gateway Plan Endorsed," *Winston-Salem Journal*, January 28, 1987.

Haugland, Vern. "Air Traffic is Growing Problem," *Winston-Salem Journal*, July 21, 1967.

"'Have You Got Light All Up?' Pilot's Last Words," *Charleston Gazette*, August 14, 1968.

Hayden, Wes. "New Piedmont Routes Urged by 10 Virginia Cities," *Winston-Salem Journal*, April 28, 1959.

Hays, Charlotte. "Piedmont is Ready to Take Off," *Winston-Salem Journal*, September 24, 1979.

"Hearing in Air Crash Slated Here October 22," *Charleston Gazette*, October 3, 1968.

"Hearing on Merger Ordered," *Charlotte Observer*, April 16, 1987.

"Helsabeck, Airline Pilot, Flew 42 Missions in War," *Winston-Salem Journal*, November 21, 1966.

Henderson, Bruce, and Ed Martin. "Misplaced Block Jammed Landing Gear, Officials Say," *Charlotte Observer*, August 3, 1989.

Hill, Thom. "Piedmont Inc. a homegrown, thick-skinned 'prickly pear,'" *Raleigh News and Observer*, February 15, 1981.

Hoar, Steve. "Downed Jet was Plagued by Troubles," *Winston-Salem Journal*, July 20, 1967.

"How Will Charlotte Fare With USAir?" *Charlotte Observer*, April 25, 1987.

Hudspeth, Ron. "Piedmont Takes Off with Females Flying," *Atlanta Journal*, March 22, 1983.

Hunter, Marjorie. "Plane Safe in Belly Landing," *Winston-Salem Journal*, February 18, 1961.

Hunter, Rixie. "Piedmont Airlines May Make Inaugural Flight This Week," *Winston-Salem Journal & Sentinel*, February 15, 1948.

"Inaugural Flight Will Start Here," *Wilmington Morning Star*, January 27, 1948.

"Increased Revenue Listed by Airport," *Twin City Sentinel*, n.d.

"Injuries Kill 3 of 5 Piedmont Survivors," *Charleston Daily Mail*, August 12, 1968.

"Investigator Hits Tower Instructions," *Winston-Salem Journal*, July 21, 1967.

"Investigators Seeking Plane Crash Cause," *Winston-Salem Journal*, November 22, 1966.

"Investigators Unsure if Failure of Bolts Caused Engine to Fall Off Piedmont Jet," *Winston-Salem Journal*, January 22, 1989.

Jackson, Niles. "No Warning, Girl Relates," *Charleston Daily Mail*, August 10, 1968.

Jackson, Niles. "No Warning, Tearful Survivor Says," *Charleston Daily Mail*, August 11, 1968.

Jenkins, Bernice. "Second Sleet Storm Again Isolates Wilmington Area; Power Lines Sag Under Ice Loads," *Wilmington Morning Star*, February 10, 1948.

Johnson, Bradley. "Wall Street sees Piedmont as prime

takeover candidate," *Roanoke Times & World News*, March 3, 1987.

Johnston, Steve. "London Flight Generates Flood of Calls," *Charlotte Observer*, April 25, 1987.

Johnston, Steve. "Piedmont Complaints Pile Up," *Charlotte Observer*, April 1, 1989.

"Joint Airport Project Planned," *Winston-Salem Journal*, December 13, 1966.

Jordan, Ronald. "Airport Dispute with Piedmont, Baldwin Ended," *Winston-Salem Journal*, May 3, 1977.

"The Journal Will Hold Great Aviation Meet in This City on Thanksgiving Day," *Winston-Salem Journal*, November 8, 1911.

"Journal's Air Circus Stirs City's Interest," *Winston-Salem Journal*, February 24, 1925.

"Just Like an 'Up' Elevator" (Forsyth County Public Library Collection), publication and date unknown.

Kady, Martin. "Piedmont's Thomas H. Davis dies," *Winston-Salem Journal*, April 23, 1999.

Kegley, George. "Piedmont changes colors," *Roanoke Times & World News*, July 30, 1989.

_____. "Piedmont panel favors accepting $1 billion buyout offer from NS," *Roanoke Times & World News*, February 17, 1987.

_____. "Piedmont shifting 198 from Roanoke," *Roanoke Times & World News*, February 7, 1987.

_____. "Piedmont to drop flights from Roanoke to Atlanta," *Roanoke Times & World News*, August 29, 1987.

_____. "USAir service assailed," *Roanoke Times & World News*, August 27, 1989.

Kinney, David. "Trade Talk," *Winston-Salem Journal*, September 9, 1979.

Klein, Gil. "Airline Files for a Rehearing," *Winston-Salem Journal*, March 21, 1987.

Kline, Bob. "Wilmington Can Expect Thaw Today," *Wilmington Morning Star*, February 1, 1948.

Knox, Joe. "Piedmont Making Most of Deregulation," *Greensboro Daily News*, June 3, 1979.

Knox, Joe. "Piedmont Seeks Major Expansion," *Greensboro Daily News*, January 8, 1978.

Koenenn, Joseph C. "Airline Spreads Its Wings," *Durham Morning Herald*, July 27, 1955.

"A Lament for the DC-3," *Twin City Sentinel*, February 21, 1963.

"Landing Charge Up for Piedmont," *Winston-Salem Journal*, June 9, 1976.

"Landing Fee Compromise on Agenda," *Twin City Sentinel*, September 20, 1976.

"Landing Gear Folds in Roanoke, 1 Hurt," *Winston-Salem Journal*, July 10, 1966.

Lanning, Clydie. "Airport Commission," *The Forsythian*. April 1966.

"Lassiter Gives Airport to Winston-Salem; Winston-Salem Accords Lindbergh," *Winston-Salem Journal*, October 15, 1927.

Lassiter, Wingate. "One Piedmont Flight Restored; Full Situation Remains Confused; Appeal Decision Awaited," *Twin City Sentinel*, August 15, 1969.

"Last Rites Tomorrow for Wright," *Winston-Salem Journal & Sentinel*, February 1, 1948.

Lawless, George. "Fog-Caused Illusion Cited as Likelihood in Air Crash," *Charleston Gazette*, October 24, 1968.

_____. "Patch of Fog Called Major Factor in August 10 Plane Crash," *Charleston Daily Mail*, October 23, 1968.

_____. "Plane Crash Toll Includes 4 from State," *Charleston Sunday Gazette-Mail*, August 11, 1968.

_____. "The Doll's Head Rolled Off Onto the Ground," *Charleston Sunday Gazette-Mail*, August 11, 1968.

Layman, Mark. "Piedmont cuts round-trip fares 30–40% on its Roanoke flights," *Roanoke Times & World News*, March 11, 1983.

Lehman, Charlie. "Piedmont Takes Flight from Unique Hubs," *High Point Enterprise*, November 11, 1984.

"Lindbergh Banquet was a Great Boost for Aviation," *Twin City Sentinel*, October 15, 1927.

"Lindbergh Will Visit Winston-Salem in October," *Winston-Salem Journal*, July 12, 1927.

"Lindy's Boyish Heart is Full of Sympathy," *Twin City Sentinel*, October 15, 1927.

Lowe, John. "Piedmont's Simulators Give Pilots Safe Lesson," High Point Enterprise, March 27, 1983.

Mackay, Mike. "Piedmont Jet Makes Emergency Landing," *Winston-Salem Journal*, August 3, 1989.

"Mail on Plane Forwarded," *Charleston Daily Mail*, August 12, 1968.

Mantius, Pete. "Debts No Threat to Piedmont," *Winston-Salem Journal*, September 11, 1983.

_____. "Piedmont to Cut Last 5 Flights Out of Winston," *Winston-Salem Journal*, July 30, 1983.

Marion, Debbie. "People Manager," *Winston-Salem Business Journal*, August 1, 1988.

Martin, Ed. "Baldwin's Charges Hogwash, Piedmont Retorts," *Winston-Salem Journal*, June 11, 1976.

_____. "Boeing 737 Mishaps: Pilot Error or Design Flaw?" *Charlotte Observer*, November 15, 1987.

_____. "Computer Glitch Delays Piedmont, USAir Flights," *Charlotte Observer*, March 29, 1989.

_____. "Folding Its Wings," *Charlotte Observer*, August 5, 1989.

_____. "Jet Makes Emergency Landing," *Charlotte Observer*, April 15, 1988.

_____. "Piedmont Airlines Readies New Facility at Charlotte," *Charlotte Observer*, March 6, 1988.

_____. "Piedmont 1st to Test Collision Warning System," *Charlotte Observer*, January 13, 1987.

_____. "Piedmont Jet Climbs Near Level Of Another," *Charlotte Observer*, August 1, 1987.

_____. "Piedmont Keeps Policy on Late Planes," *Charlotte Observer*, July 19, 1989.

_____. "Piedmont Says 737-400s Perform Well," *Charlotte Observer*, January 10, 1989.

_____. "Piedmont to Install Anti-Collision Systems," *Charlotte Observer*, November 20, 1987.

_____. "Pilots Get Down-to-Earth Training," *Charlotte Observer*, March 6, 1988.

_____. "Tense Passengers Could Only Brace — and Wait for Crash," *Charlotte Observer*, August 3, 1989.

_____. "USAir Faces Challenges as Piedmont Name Fades," *Charlotte Observer*, July 31, 1989.

_____. "USAir left behind as airline stocks ride updraft of investor confidence," *Charlotte Observer*, May 26, 1991.

_____. "Was 2nd Landing Gear Obstructed?" *Charlotte Observer*, August 4, 1989.

_____. "Who'll Fly Our Planes?" *Charlotte Observer*, June 24, 1989.

Matthews, Steve. "Colodny Soothes Piedmont Employees," *Charlotte Observer*, February 1, 1989.
"Mayor White, Gardner Plan Trip Saturday," *Wilmington Morning Star*, February 11, 1948. (Bill Reaves Collection, New Hanover Public Library).
McCrary, Elissa. "Piedmont's hub in Ohio pays off with profit sooner than expected," *Raleigh News and Observer*, August 29, 1982.
"McGinnis, Aviation Pioneer, Dies," *Winston-Salem Journal*, March 16, 1954.
McIlwain, Bill. "Many Factors Cause Delays in Airline Flights," *Winston-Salem Journal*, August 7, 1987.
McInnis, Doug. "Piedmont capitalizing on deregulation vacuum" (Forsyth County Public Library Collection, clipping [n.d., n.p.], Winston-Salem Airlines clippings file).
McNatt, Ralph. "Piedmont Airlines, we need you now!" *Charlotte Observer*, January 4, 2005.
"McNaughton Built Reputation in Arms Control Post," *Winston-Salem Journal*, July 20, 1967.
"Meet Will Begin Promptly at 2:30 O'Clock," *Winston-Salem Journal*, November 28, 1911.
"Midair Crash is Worst N.C. Air Disaster," *Winston-Salem Journal*, July 20, 1967.
Mildenberg, David. "Agreement Stalls TWA Bid," *Charlotte Observer*, March 10, 1987.
_____. "'86 Passenger Traffic Up 14% at Airport," *Charlotte Observer*, February 1987.
_____. "Norfolk Southern Exploring Piedmont Airlines Takeover," *Charlotte Observer*, January 28, 1987.
_____. "Piedmont Airlines' Dominance to Grow at Charlotte Airport," *Charlotte Observer*, January 18, 1987.
_____. "Piedmont Earnings Up 8.5% In 1986; Revenues Rise 22%," *Charlotte Observer*, February 5, 1987.
_____. "Piedmont Pooh-Poohs TWA Merger Talk," *Charlotte Observer*, January 14, 1987.
_____. "Piedmont Requests Flight to Bahamas," *Charlotte Observer*, February 5, 1987.
_____. "Railroad Hungrily Eyes Piedmont," *Charlotte Observer*, February 2, 1987.
_____. "3 States Try to Stop USAir-Piedmont Merger," *Charlotte Observer*, April 1, 1987.
_____. "What's Railroad's Interest in Piedmont?" *Charlotte Observer*, January 29, 1987.
"Miller Field in New Hands," *Winston-Salem Journal*, July 2, 1932.
"Miller Municipal Airport Preparing for Ten Years of Continued Progress," *Winston-Salem Journal & Sentinel*, December 26, 1937.
Millikan, Diane, and Brad Rochester. "Airline Requests Injunction to Start Propeller Service," *Winston-Salem Journal*, August 6, 1969.
Mitchell, Steve. "Extending Runway for Jets is Planned at Airport," *Winston-Salem Journal*, September 15, 1966.
Moe, Susan Spence. "Rigorous tests on the ground keep Piedmont jets in the air," *Raleigh News and Observer*, October 14, 1979.
Moore, Pamela. "Analysts Expect USAir to Report Loss," *Winston-Salem Journal*, December 9, 1990.
_____. "USAir Cuts Less Severe in Winston, Chief Says," *Winston-Salem Journal*, February 14, 1991.
_____. "USAir President Talks About Restructuring with Area Employees," *Winston-Salem Journal*, February 16, 1991.
_____. "USAir to Fire 1,500 Workers," *Winston-Salem Journal*, August 22, 1990.
Morrison, Mark. "Piedmont remembered," *Roanoke Times & World News*, July 5, 1989.
Mulder, James T. "Piedmont signs rise, signaling Empire's fall," *Syracuse Herald-Journal*, January 15, 1986.
"NAL Planes Carried 300 Passengers in December," *Wilmington Morning Star*, January 6, 1948.
"National Airline Quits Service Here," *Wilmington Morning Star*, February 10, 1948. (Bill Reaves Collection, New Hanover Public Library).
"N.C. Commuter Airline to Serve Smith Reynolds," *Rural Hall Independent*, April 10, 1980.
"New Airline Planning 1st Runs Wednesday," *Winston-Salem Journal*, May 27, 1963.
"New Boss at Airport Lists Needs," *Twin City Sentinel*, May 23, 1967.
"New Plane Arrives," *Twin City Sentinel*, May 16, 1968.
"New York Flights to Begin," *Twin City Sentinel*, November 14, 1966.
"No Hint of Trouble in Pilot-Tower Talk," *Charleston Daily Mail*, August 14, 1968.
"No Merger Plans, Piedmont Says," *Twin City Sentinel*, July 26, 1969.
"No Strikebreakers, Says Airline Here," *Winston-Salem Journal*, August 5, 1969.
Nomani, Asra Q., and Judith Valente. "USAir comes down from clouds," *Wall Street Journal*, reprinted in Raleigh *News and Observer*, Sept. 2, 1990, 1F.
"Nonstrikers May Sue Piedmont Pilots," *Winston-Salem Journal*, August 12, 1969.
"Non-Striking Employees Sue Pilot Union," *Winston-Salem Journal*, August 13, 1969.
O'Brien, Kevin. "Lightning Hits Piedmont Jet," *Charlotte Observer*, June 24, 1988.
"Officials at Piedmont Adjusting Schedules," *Winston-Salem Journal*, July 21, 1967.
"Officials Honor Piedmont Flight," *Wilmington Morning Star*, February 21, 1948.
"On Piedmont and USAir," *Winston-Salem Journal*, March 11, 1987.
O'Neil, Tex. "Jet Skids Off Runway in Charlotte," *Charlotte Observer*, October 26, 1986.
"Opening Set by Piedmont for Second Air Route," *Winston-Salem Journal & Sentinel*, February 22, 1948.
"Other Airlines Join Spreading Fare War," *Charlotte Observer*, January 31, 1987.
Otterbourg, Ken. "Break in Bidding War Gives Piedmont Time to Think About Offers," *Winston-Salem Journal*, February 22, 1987.
_____. "Buyout" *Winston-Salem Journal*, March 21, 1987.
_____. "DOT Plans Long Hearing on Piedmont Merger," *Winston-Salem Journal*, April 16, 1987.
_____. "Government Gives USAir Go-Ahead," *Winston-Salem Journal*, March 21, 1987.
_____. "Job-Protection Plan Covers Piedmont Employees," *Winston-Salem Journal*, March 13, 1987.
_____. "Merger Would Hurt Few Jobs, Colodny Says," *Winston-Salem Journal*, April 24, 1987.
_____. "Most Thought Piedmont Immune to Merger Mania," *Winston-Salem Journal*, March 15, 1987.

———. "Norfolk Southern Corp. Reports Record Income," *Winston-Salem Journal*, January 28, 1987.
———. "Norfolk Southern Tells SEC It Might Try to Buy Piedmont," *Winston-Salem Journal*, January 28, 1987.
———. "Piedmont Adding First-Class to Planes," *Winston-Salem Journal*, February 9, 1987.
———. "Piedmont Considers USAir Bid," *Winston-Salem Journal*, February 19, 1987.
———. "Piedmont Deal Complicated by TWA's Offer for USAir," *Winston-Salem Journal*, March 5, 1987.
———. "Piedmont Follows Its Own Route to Expand," *Winston-Salem Journal*, December 14, 1986.
———. "Piedmont Gets Offer by Railroad," *Winston-Salem Journal*, February 18, 1987.
———. "Piedmont, Pilots' Union Stop Negotiations," *Winston-Salem Journal*, February 2, 1987.
———. "Piedmont Tightens Inspection of Older Jets," *Winston-Salem Journal*, April 26, 1988, p.1A.
———. "Piedmont's Life Story," *Winston-Salem Journal*, March 10, 1987.
———. "Piedmont's Meeting Could Involve Final Approval of Sale to USAir," *Winston-Salem Journal*, March 4, 1987.
———. "TWA Offer is Rejected," *Winston-Salem Journal*, March 6, 1987.
———. "USAir to Buy Piedmont in Cash Deal," *Winston-Salem Journal*, March 10, 1987.
———. "USAir Wants to Make 'Whole New Airline,'" *Winston-Salem Journal*, November 3, 1987.
———. "USAir's 3rd Bid Causes Piedmont to Think Twice," *Winston-Salem Journal*, February 20, 1987.
———. "Winston May Bear Brunt of Merger," *Winston-Salem Journal*, March 11, 1987.
———, and Larry Parnass. "Piedmont's Howard Quits to Join Effort to Buy United," *Winston-Salem Journal*, August 14, 1987.
Parnass, Larry. "Airlines: Competition gets keener than ever as American and Piedmont up the ante with new flights from hubs in North Carolina," *Winston-Salem Business Journal*, January 31, 1988.
———. "Cultural Anthropologist Examines Marital Health of Airline Mergers," *Winston-Salem Journal*, October 26, 1987.
———. "Piedmont and USAir Stand to Lose Much if Merger is Not Approved," *Winston-Salem Journal*, September 23, 1987.
———. "Piedmont Jets Have Wind Shear Detectors," *Winston-Salem Journal*, August 20, 1987.
———. "Piedmont Shareholders Approve USAir Merger," *Winston-Salem Journal*, July 24, 1987.
———. "Piedmont-USAir Hearing is Ordered," *Winston-Salem Journal*, July 16, 1987.
———. "Piedmont's Collision Avoidance Systems Will Go on USAir Jets," *Winston-Salem Journal*, November 20, 1987.
———. "USAir Group to Move 370 Jobs to Piedmont Office in Winston," *Winston-Salem Journal*, Jan. 28, 1988, 1A.
———, and Ken Otterbourg. "Merger Work Gets More Difficult," *Winston-Salem Journal*, November 1, 1987.
"Passengers Evacuated from Plane," *Charlotte Observer*, April 24, 1989.
Pichirallo, Joe. "Ex-Piedmont Mechanic Indicted in Engine Case," *Winston-Salem Journal*, September 18, 1976.

"Piedmont Adding Charleston, S.C.," *Twin City Sentinel*, April 23, 1970.
"Piedmont Adds Two Cities," *Twin City Sentinel*, February 2, 1968.
"Piedmont Air Crash Unsolved," *Twin City Sentinel*, December 10, 1966.
"Piedmont Airline Readies Service," *Wilmington Morning Star*, January 17, 1948.
"Piedmont Airliner Crashes," *Twin City Sentinel*, August 22, 1962.
"Piedmont Airliner Crashes into West Virginia Mountain," *Twin City Sentinel*, August 10, 1968.
"Piedmont Airliner Safe in Emergency Landing," *Twin City Sentinel*, February 17, 1961.
"Piedmont Airlines Adopts Computer Reservation Plan," *Twin City Sentinel*, September 25, 1970.
"Piedmont Airlines Buys 10 Planes," *Twin City Sentinel*, April 20, 1966.
"Piedmont Airlines 'Consolidating,'" *Durham Morning Herald*, March 8, 1981.
"Piedmont Airlines Has Record December," *The Suburbanite*, January 14, 1981.
"Piedmont Airlines Hikes Fares $2–$20," *Charlotte Observer*, August 12, 1987.
"Piedmont Airlines Makes First Wilmington–Cincinnati Flight," *Winston-Salem Journal*, February 21, 1948.
"Piedmont Airlines Plane Off to Inaugurate its New Flight," *Winston-Salem Journal*, February 20, 1948.
"Piedmont Airlines Profiting from Northward Expansion," *Greensboro Daily News and Record*, August 29, 1982.
"Piedmont Airlines Readies Service," *Wilmington Morning Star*, January 17, 1948.
"Piedmont Airlines Signs as Madison Park's First Tenant," *Rural Hall Independent*, February 10, 1983.
"Piedmont Airlines to Raise Its Passenger Fares 6%," *Winston-Salem Journal*, April 14, 1971.
"Piedmont Airlines to Resume Runs with Prop Craft," *Twin City Sentinel*, July 29, 1969.
"Piedmont Aviation Forms Division to Handle Piper Distributorship," *Twin City Sentinel*, May 31, 1960.
"Piedmont Aviation Had Record Earnings in 1986," *Winston-Salem Journal*, February 5, 1987.
"Piedmont Aviation, Inc.," *Charlotte Observer*, July 24, 1987.
"Piedmont Aviation: Its Origin and Growth," *Winston-Salem Journal*, September 27, 1954.
"Piedmont Aviation Offers 675,000 Common Stock Shares," *Winston-Salem Journal*, February 17, 1948.
"Piedmont Aviation Officials Here," *Wilmington Morning Star*, January 5, 1948.
"Piedmont Aviation Seeks Permit for 9 Local and Feeder Lines," *Winston-Salem Journal*, June 6, 1944.
"Piedmont Awaits Date for First N.Y. Flight," *Twin City Sentinel*, September 24, 1966.
"Piedmont Awaits Formal Approval of First Flight," *Wilmington Morning Star*, February 18, 1948.
"Piedmont Begins First Flight to Cincinnati," *Wilmington Morning Star*, February 20, 1948.
"Piedmont Buys Adjacent Buildings," *Charlotte Observer*, January 13, 1989.
"Piedmont Captain Calm Following Belly Landing," *Twin City Sentinel*, February 18, 1961.
"Piedmont Clear for Inaugural," *Wilmington Morning Star*, February 19, 1948.

"Piedmont Considers Protection," *Twin City Sentinel*, September 11, 1970.
"Piedmont Continues to Expand and Prosper," *Winston-Salem Journal*, March 4, 1984.
"Piedmont DC-3 Forced Down, Passengers, Crew Uninjured," *Twin City Sentinel*, December 30, 1948.
"Piedmont Ends Runs by DC-3s," *Twin City Sentinel*, February 20, 1963.
"Piedmont Fined $30,000," *Charlotte Observer*, July 15, 1987.
"Piedmont Flies Steady Course Toward Profits," *Charlotte Observer*, February 14, 1980.
"Piedmont Flights Nearer," *Winston-Salem Journal*, February 16, 1948.
"Piedmont Gets Relief from $3 Million Suit," *Twin City Sentinel*, January 6, 1971.
"Piedmont Given N.Y. Flight Okay," *Winston-Salem Journal*, July 7, 1966.
"Piedmont Has Midair Flight Cancellation," *Charlotte Observer*, January 11, 1988.
"Piedmont Hires 15 New Pilots," *Twin City Sentinel*, March 5, 1965.
"Piedmont hunting site for maintenance," *Raleigh News and Observer*, March 8, 1981.
"Piedmont is Using Reservation System," *Winston-Salem Journal & Sentinel*, May 9, 1971.
"Piedmont Lines Will Inaugurate Flight Friday," *Asheville Citizen*, February 19, 1948.
"Piedmont Loss Hit $1.4 Million," *The Suburbanite*, May 5, 1977.
"Piedmont Names Top Executive," *Winston-Salem Journal & Sentinel*, November 8, 1970.
"Piedmont Officials Plan Visit," *Wilmington Morning Star*, January 2, 1948.
"Piedmont On-Time Rate Better, But Last Among Carriers," *Charlotte Observer*, June 7, 1989.
"Piedmont Opens New N.C.–Ohio Plane Service," *Asheville Citizen Times*, February 21, 1948.
"Piedmont Pilot Unaware Engine Had Fallen Off," *Winston-Salem Journal*, January 25, 1989.
"Piedmont Pilots Told to Meet," *Winston-Salem Journal*, August 1, 1969.
"Piedmont plan will give credits to frequent fliers," *Roanoke Times & World News*, November 13, 1984.
"Piedmont Plane Crash Kills Crew of Three; No Passengers Aboard," *Winston-Salem Journal*, November 21, 1966.
"Piedmont Plane Lands at New Port on Initial Trip Over Air Route," *Charleston Daily Mail*, May 13, 1948.
"Piedmont Plane Test Runs Today," *Wilmington Morning Star*, February 3, 1948.
"Piedmont President will be Honored," *Charlotte Observer*, January 22, 1987.
"Piedmont Purchases Airliners," *Twin City Sentinel*, October 27, 1967.
"Piedmont Ready for Inaugural," *Wilmington Morning Star*, February 18, 1948.
"Piedmont Ready on Mail Service," *Wilmington Morning Star*, February 7, 1948.
"Piedmont Recovers Last Year's Losses," *Rural Hall Independent*, August 2, 1984.
"Piedmont Reservation Desks Busy," *Winston-Salem Journal*, July 8, 1966.
"Piedmont Sets Maiden Flight for Saturday," *Winston-Salem Journal*, February 12, 1948.
"Piedmont Soars to Record Growth," *Winston-Salem Journal*, May 13, 1986.
"Piedmont Spending $101 Million to Build All-Turbine Air Fleet," *Winston-Salem Journal*, May 13, 1969.
"Piedmont Starts New Air Service," *Charleston Gazette*, May 13, 1948.
"Piedmont Starts Route Today from New Bern to Louisville," *Winston-Salem Journal*, February 27, 1948.
"Piedmont stock price holds steady as directors consider USAir's offer," *Roanoke Times & World News*, March 4, 1987.
"Piedmont Stock Rises as Investors Watch for Bids," *Winston-Salem Journal*, February 21, 1987.
"Piedmont Test Flight Scheduled," *Wilmington Morning Star*, February 2, 1948.
"Piedmont Test Flight Under Way," *Wilmington Morning Star*, February 3, 1948.
"Piedmont to Add 20 Flights," *Twin City Sentinel*, July 9, 1966.
"Piedmont to Begin Service Friday," *Wilmington Morning Star*, February 19, 1948.
"Piedmont to Reduce Frequent-Flier Mileage," *Charlotte Observer*, August 8, 1988.
"Piedmont to Start Using 404s," *Twin City Sentinel*, December 20, 1961.
"Piedmont Told It Cannot Quit Elizabeth City," *Winston-Salem Journal*, November 20, 1970.
"Piedmont traffic figures declined in Roanoke in '82," *Roanoke Times & World News*, January 11, 1983.
"The Piedmont Tragedy," *Winston-Salem Journal*, July 20, 1967.
"Piedmont Wins Suit Over 1968 Crash," *Winston-Salem Journal*, January 7, 1971.
"Piedmont's Profits take off through efficiency, traffic," *Raleigh News and Observer*, February 8, 1981.
"Piedmont's Service Suffering in Merger," *Winston-Salem Journal*, August 4, 1989.
"Pilot Gives Crew Members Credit for Safe Landing," *Winston-Salem Journal*, December 30, 1948.
"Pilot Learned Love of Planes from Dad, Piedmont Cofounder," *Charlotte Observer*, October 26, 1987.
"Pilot Warning Device Studied," *Twin City Sentinel*, July 20, 1967.
"Plan Complete for Aviation," *Winston-Salem Journal*, April 2, 1911.
"Plane Crash Hearing Slated Here October 22," *Charleston Daily Mail*, September 28, 1968.
Poff, Mag. "Airline shakeout," *Roanoke Times & World News*, March 3, 1985.
_____. "Piedmont drove USAir out of Roanoke in '70s," *Roanoke Times & World News*, March 5, 1987.
_____. "Piedmont to drop three more flights," *Roanoke Times & World News*, January 26, 1983.
_____. "USAir says merger won't hurt service," *Roanoke Times & World News*, April 25, 1987.
_____. "With or without the merger, fares are many and different," *Roanoke Times & World News*, July 30, 1989.
Poff, Mag. "You can get there from here," *Roanoke Times & World News*, November 13, 1984.
Poindexter, Jesse. "10 Towns Would Get Service," *Winston-Salem Journal*, July 8, 1966.

"Polluted Air Suspect in Crash Fatal to 35," *Charleston Gazette*, August 17, 1968.

"Power Lines Sag Under Ice Loads," *Wilmington Morning Star*, February 10, 1948.

Preslar, Charles, Jr. "Piedmont Air Service Welcomed," *Hickory Daily Record*, August 25, 1952.

Preslar, Lloyd. "Two Airlines Also Plagued by Single-Airport Issue," *Winston-Salem Journal & Sentinel*, April 16, 1961.

Price, Dudley. "'Puddle Jumper' Piedmont on last leg," *Raleigh News and Observer*, July 16, 1989.

"Propeller of Plane Beats Feeble Man to Death Near This City," *Winston-Salem Journal*, December 27, 1922.

"Q. Why do people have to travel…," *Twin City Sentinel*, October 10, 1966.

"Rain, Warmer Temperatures Help Remove Ice, Snow Here; More of Same is Present Forecast," *Winston-Salem Journal*, February 13, 1948.

"The realities of Better Air Service," *Roanoke Times & World News*, May 6, 1983.

Reitman, Valerie. "Charlotte Airport Takes On Foreign Accent Today," *Charlotte Observer*, June 15, 1987.

_____. "Colodny Committed to Expansion," *Charlotte Observer*, April 24, 1987.

_____. "Flights from London Average 58 Passengers," *Charlotte Observer*, June 18, 1987.

_____. "London-Charlotte Flight Ads Take Different Course," *Charlotte Observer*, June 17, 1987.

_____. "London Route to Bring Foreign Firms?" *Charlotte Observer*, June 15, 1987.

_____. "Londoners Haven't a Clue Where They'd End Up," *Charlotte Observer*, June 16, 1987.

_____. "Piedmont Earnings Increase 26.5%," *Charlotte Observer*, July 23, 1987.

_____. "Piedmont Merger Approval Delayed," *Charlotte Observer*, July 16, 1987.

_____. "Piedmont to Start Bahamas' Service," *Charlotte Observer*, January 22, 1987.

_____. "Piedmont Tops 5 Competitors in Completing Flights on Time," *Charlotte Observer*, May 19, 1987.

_____. "Piedmont, USAir Want to Rev Up Proposed Merger," *Charlotte Observer*, May 27, 1987.

_____. "Piedmont's Davis Loses a Child," *Charlotte Observer*, July 22, 1987.

_____. "Strong Airline Will Result From Merger, Analysts Say," *Charlotte Observer*, March 10, 1987.

Rice, David. "Airline's Renovation Plan Has $4.5 Million Price Tag," *Winston-Salem Journal*, February 20, 1987.

_____. "Board Approves $3 Million to Help Remodel Building," *Winston-Salem Journal*, n.d.

"Rivers Hit Flood Stage in Eastern N.C.," *Twin City Sentinel*, February 12, 1948.

"Roanoke Ready to Fly," *Roanoke Times & World News*, January 15, 1989.

"Roanoke to Fight for N.Y. Air Service," *Roanoke Times*, September 28, 1965.

Roberts, John. "Piedmont Taking Aim at Bigger Profits," *Greensboro Daily News*, May 16, 1980.

Robins, Ed. "Airport Opened in 1927," *Twin City Sentinel*, November 22, 1962.

_____. "First Air Mail-Passenger Service for this Area was Inaugurated by Eastern Just 25 Years Ago," *Winston-Salem Journal-Sentinel*.

_____. "Local Airport Again Leads State," *Twin City Sentinel*, January 10, 1964.

_____. "New Airline is Established; To Have Headquarters Here," *Twin City Sentinel*, April 9, 1963.

_____. "New Airline's Head Recognizes the Risk," *Twin City Sentinel*, April 10, 1963.

_____. "Piedmont Begins Training Stewardesses," *Twin City Sentinel*, May 26, 1962.

_____. "Stewardesses and Why They Fly," *Twin City Sentinel*, n.d.

_____. "Turning Airliners Out 'Better Than New;' That's What Piedmont Aviation Experts Do," *Winston-Salem Journal & Sentinel*, January 29, 1956.

_____. "Twin City Airport is Flying Center," *Winston-Salem Journal & Sentinel*, June 21, 1959.

Rochester, Brad. "Airline Working for More Routes," *Winston-Salem Journal*, April 27, 1968.

_____. "Piedmont Agrees to 3 in Cockpit," *Winston-Salem Journal*, March 25, 1971.

_____. "Piedmont Gets First 737," *Winston-Salem Journal*, May 31, 1965.

_____. "Piedmont Gets Route to Chicago," *Winston-Salem Journal*, June 19, 1969.

Rogers, Floyd. "Tarheel Sketch: Tom Davis," *Winston-Salem Journal*, July 30, 1989, p. A13.

_____. "Wachovia Helped Piedmont Get Off the Ground," *Winston-Salem Journal*, July 31, 1989.

Rosenthal, David. "Merger plans leave Piedmont workers reeling, confused," *Roanoke Times & World News*, March 7, 1987.

_____. "New bidders being sought by Piedmont," *Roanoke Times & World News*, February 20, 1987.

_____. "Piedmont employees trying to adjust to takeover by USAir," *Roanoke Times & World News*, March 11, 1987.

_____. "Piedmont maneuvers won't delay terminal, councilman says," *Roanoke Times & World News*, March 6, 1987.

_____. "Piedmont Takeover Bids Have Not Affected Plans at Roanoke Airport—Yet," *Roanoke Times & World News*, March 6, 1987.

_____. "USAir Gets Piedmont for $1.6 billion," *Roanoke Times & World News*, March 9, 1987.

_____, and George Kegley. "Piedmont Bid Would Be Largest Airline Buyout," *Roanoke Times & World News*, February 18, 1987.

Sawyer, Tom. "'Watch It' … Last Word from Plane," *Charleston Daily Mail*, August 13, 1968.

Schlosser, Jim. "Davis Flies Piedmont from Puddle Jumping to Profit Making," *Greensboro News and Record*, May 15, 1983.

"Scott Makes Appeal for End to Piedmont Airlines Strike," *Winston-Salem Journal*, August 9, 1969.

Scism, Jack. "Airline is Flying High since deregulation," Greensboro *Daily News*, April 15, 1984.

Shelsby, Ted. "'Pete Who?' Still Up and Coming," *Chapel Hill News*, March 20, 1983.

Sieg, Tom. "Across the Blue from Ground Up," *The Sentinel*, June 3, 1976.

"'69 Passengers Hit Record High for Piedmont," *Twin City Sentinel*, February 25, 1970.

Slater, Paul. "Air Taxi Veteran Deplores 'Mud Slinging,'" *The Sentinel*, December 11, 1975.

Slater, Paul. "Airport Forecast: 'Steady' Growth," *The Sentinel*, April 12, 1976.

Slater, Paul. "FAA Rejects Piedmont-Baldwin Plan," *The Sentinel*, December 13, 1976.
"Smith Reynolds Airport," *Winston-Salem Journal*, March 20, 1966.
"Snafu Keeps County Pair Off Airliner," *Charleston Sunday Gazette-Mail*, August 11, 1968.
"Some Pilots Unhappy," *The Sentinel*, November 8, 1975.
Sori, Penny. "Piedmont, city kiss and make up," *Syracuse Herald-Journal*, July 1, 1984.
Sparks, Jim. "A Piece of History," *Winston-Salem Journal*, October 9, 2006.
"Steady Course Toward Profits," *Charlotte Observer*, February 14, 1982.
Steele, George. "3 More Die, Push Crash Toll to 35," *Charleston Gazette*, August 12, 1968.
"Stewardess Once Lived in Twin City," *Winston-Salem Journal*, November 21, 1966.
Stinebaker, Joe. "FAA Considers Moving Inspectors to Main Office at Smith Reynolds," *Winston-Salem Journal*, August 14, 1987.
Stodghill II, Ron. "Winston-Salem Home Folks Have Mixed Emotions," *Charlotte Observer*, October 31, 1987.
Stracener, Bill. "Piedmont Hijacking is Foiled," *Winston-Salem Journal*, June 19, 1971.
"Strike Strands Jazz Pianist," *Winston-Salem Journal*, July 9, 1966.
Suchetka, Diane. "Piedmont Pilot has Real Reason to Celebrate," *Charlotte Observer*, August 3, 1989.
"Suit Filed Against Piedmont in Dispute Over Land Lease," *Winston-Salem Journal*, June 9, 1976. (Forsyth County Public Library Collection).
"Suitors Line Up at Piedmont," *Winston-Salem Journal*, February 22, 1987.
Swain, George T. "Now Who's to Blame at Airport," *Charleston Gazette*, August 14, 1968.
Syme, John. "Hometown Folks Tour Piedmont's New 'City of London,'" *Winston-Salem Journal*, June 10, 1987.
"Terminal Nearing Completion," *Twin City Sentinel*, May 30, 1966.
"$35,000 Facility Replaces Old One," *Twin City Sentinel*, January 16, 1965.
"32-Fatality Air Disaster State's Worst," *Charleston Sunday Gazette-Mail*, August 11, 1968.
"32 On Piedmont Plane Die, 5 Hurt in Flaming Plunge on Airport Strip; Pilot Misses Strip in Thick Fog Bank; Fire Sweeps Ruins," *Charleston Daily Mail*, August 10, 1968.
"Three Thousand Feet in the Air" (advertisement) *Winston-Salem Journal*, April 11, 1911.
Thompson, Clary. "Big Airliner Reaches City at 6:50 P.M. On Way North," *Winston-Salem Journal*, June 13, 1941.
Thompson, Deanna. "Up, Up and Gone," *Triad Business*, June 26, 1989.
Thompson, Lil. "'Merger Fever' Could Lead to Concern in Congress," *Winston-Salem Journal*, March 14, 1987.
Thompson, Roy. "Employees of Airline Feel the Cash Pinch," *Winston-Salem Journal*, August 9, 1969.
Thompson, Tuck. "Airport Confident It Will Find a Replacement for Piedmont," *The Sentinel*, July 30, 1983.

"To Test Aviation," *Winston-Salem Journal*, August 5, 1927.
"Today's Tragedy on Hilltop Worst in W. Va. Air History," *Charleston Daily Mail*, August 10, 1968.
"Triad Council Okays Plans for Airport," *Twin City Sentinel*, November 3, 1971.
Turner, Joel. "Airport chairman praises Piedmont fare cuts," *Roanoke Times & World News*, March 22, 1983.
_____. "Take complaints to Piedmont — Ewert," *Roanoke Times & World News*, January 26, 1983.
"TWA Won't Try to Buy USAir for Now," *Winston-Salem Journal*, March 17, 1987.
"TWA's USAir Bid Flawed, U.S. Says," *Winston-Salem Journal*, March 7, 1987.
"Twin Citians Among Piedmont Jet Crew," *Winston-Salem Journal*, July 20, 1967.
"Twin City Lad Makes Record," *Winston-Salem Journal*, June 22, 1930.
"$22 Million Signature," *Twin City Sentinel*, October 28, 1967.
"2 Local Air Crash Survivors Improve," *Charleston Daily Mail*, August 17, 1968.
"$280,000 Fund for Airport Frozen," *Twin City Sentinel*, August 9, 1967.
Upton, Bob. "Piedmont Airliner in Crash Landing," *Twin City Sentinel*, April 28, 1959.
_____. "Ready for the Worst," *Charlotte Observer*, August 3, 1989.
"U.S. Investigators Study Plane Crash," *Winston-Salem Journal*, January 22, 1968.
"The U.S. Justice Department," *Charlotte Observer*, May 23, 1987.
"U.S. Okays $265,000 for Airport," *Twin City Sentinel*, December 16, 1966.
"U.S. Team Will Study Traffic Plan," *Winston-Salem Journal*, July 20, 1967.
"USAir Delays Piedmont Plans Until Spring," *Charlotte Observer*, May 28, 1986.
"USAir Likes Pittsburgh for Frankfurt Flight," *Charlotte Observer*, July 7, 1987.
"USAir Moving 100 to Piedmont's Town," *Charlotte Observer*, July 2, 1988.
"USAir Will Lay Off 3,585 Workers," *Winston Salem Journal*, February 17, 1991.
"USAir's Cutbacks May Be the Start of Industrywide Trend," *Winston-Salem Journal*, September 4, 1990.
Vaden, Ted. "Airline and its president have become synonymous," *Raleigh News and Observer*, February 18, 1979.
_____. "Piedmont Expansion takes off," *Raleigh News and Observer*, October 22, 1978.
Vance, Merton. "First Flight Recalled," *Wilmington Star-News*, February 14, 1988.
Van Der Linden, Frank. "Charlotte Firm Files Court Suit," *Wilmington Morning Star*, January 20, 1948.
_____. "Piedmont Gets Mail Approval," *Wilmington Morning Star*, January 31, 1948.
_____. "State Airlines Suit May Halt Airmail Subsidy to Piedmont," *Wilmington Morning Star*, January 28, 1948.
Van Hecke, M.S. "London Flight Causes Spirits to Soar in Charlotte," *Charlotte Observer*, April 24, 1987.
"Vital Landing Link Out, FAA Confirms," *Charleston Sunday Gazette-Mail*, August 11, 1968.

Wade, Michael. "From the Ground Up," *The Sentinel*, May 7, 1983.
"Way Clear for Piedmont Acquisition," *Charlotte Observer*, March 21, 1987.
"Way to Go, Piedmont," *Charlotte Observer*, April 26, 1987.
Weatherman, Rom. "Jobs on the Wing," *Twin City Sentinel*, May 11, 1965.
_____. "Runway Extension Planned," *Twin City Sentinel*, April 24, 1964.
Wessels, Andy. "Compressor failure may have forced landing," *Charleston Gazette*, April 15, 1988.
West, Stephen. "Piedmont, American Fight Takes Off," *Charlotte Observer*, June 15, 1987.
_____, and David Mildenberg. "Piedmont Airlines Chief Quits," *Charlotte Observer*, August 14, 1987.
Westmoreland, Janice. "Meals Fit for a King ... er, a First-Class Passenger," *The Sentinel*, March 28, 1984.
_____. "More to Flying to L.A. than Meets the Eye," *The Sentinel*, March 28, 1984.
_____. "Off and Running in Maryland," *The Sentinel*, July 15, 1983.
_____. "Piedmont Among 10 Busiest U.S. Airlines During 1983," *The Sentinel*, July 17, 1984.
_____. "Piedmont Aviation Records Highest Earnings in its History," *The Sentinel*, July 23, 1982.
_____. "Piedmont Jet Lands in L.A. for First Time," *The Sentinel*, April 2, 1984.
"What About Cold Days?" *Roanoke Times & World News*, March 19, 1975.
Whitman, Gene. "Air Traffic Here Shows Big Gains," *Twin City Sentinel*, January 2, 1968.
_____. "Airport Business Shows Increase," *Twin City Sentinel*, January 27, 1969.
_____. "Airport Growth Nears Halt," *Twin City Sentinel*, August 22, 1967.
_____. "Business Winging Along," *Twin City Sentinel*, October 27, 1965.
_____. "Charlotte Flight to Close Era for Piedmont Airlines," *Twin City Sentinel*, February 13, 1970.
_____. "Forsyth Air Station Joins in Emergency Flight Plan," *Twin City Sentinel*, July 12, 1966.
_____. "Hey! We're Stewardesses!" *Twin City Sentinel*, August 6, 1966.
_____. "How Stewardesses Earn Wings," *Twin City Sentinel*, February 3, 1966.
_____. "Jetliner Section to be Reassembled," *Twin City Sentinel*, July 21, 1967.
_____. "New York Service Begins Tuesday," *Twin City Sentinel*, November 12, 1966.
_____. "No Pay for Piedmont Staff," *Twin City Sentinel*, July 23, 1969.
_____. "Off-Course Plane, Lack of Radar Called Key Factors in Jet Crash," *Twin City Sentinel*, July 20, 1967.
_____. "1-Engine Landing is Made," *Twin City Sentinel*, August 1 1966.
_____. "Piedmont Airlines is Idled by Strike," *Twin City Sentinel*, July 21, 1969.
_____. "Piedmont Airlines Lays Off 2,100," *Twin City Sentinel*, July 22, 1969.
_____. "Piedmont Airlines to Stay in Forsyth," *Twin City Sentinel*, November 29, 1968.
_____. "Piedmont Likes New Plane," *Twin City Sentinel*, June 12, 1970.
_____. "Piedmont Officials Find No Clues in Fatal Crash," *Twin City Sentinel*, November 21, 1966.
_____. "Piedmont Resumes 3 Flights; Full Service Due Thursday," *Twin City Sentinel*, August 18, 1969.
_____. "Planning Helps Restore Service," *Twin City Sentinel*, August 20, 1966.
_____. "Reynolds Gets 4-Jet Plane," *Twin City Sentinel*, January 17, 1967.
Whittington, Dennis. "Piedmont Airlines faces changes," *Triad Business*, March 16, 1987.
_____. "Piedmont's London route takes off," *Triad Business*, June 15, 1987.
"Why do black employees and USAir have problems?" *Winston-Salem Chronicle*, April 16, 1992.
"William Magruder Dies at 51; Was Piedmont Aviation Official," *Winston-Salem Journal*, September 11, 1977.
Willis, Alan. "Piedmont Picked for First Testing of Safety System," *Winston-Salem Journal*, November 26, 1985.
_____. "Piedmont: Unconventional Strategy Seems to be Key to Airline's Growth," *Winston-Salem Journal*, December 16, 1985.
"Wilmington is Cut Off by Ice Storm," *Winston-Salem Journal*, February 11, 1948.
"Winston-Salem Accords Colonel Lindbergh a Great Welcome," *Winston-Salem Journal*, October 15, 1927.
"Winston-Salem Aviation Pioneer in the South," *Twin City Sentinel*, May 4, 1935.
Woestendiek, Jo. "50 Years in the Air," *Winston-Salem Journal*, November 13, 1986.
Wood, Tom. "'Good People' Built Piedmont Aviation," *The Suburbanite*, Vol. X, No. 42, September 15, 1977.
Wright, Mark. "Piedmont Trying Fuel-Saving Ideas," *Twin City Sentinel*, April 14, 1981.
Wright, Phil. "Southeast Counties in Bad Way," *Wilmington Morning Star*, February 1, 1948.
Yago, John W. "Glide Slope Out at Other Airports," *Charleston Gazette*, August 15, 1968.
_____. "Propjet's Approach Found Not Unusual," *Charleston Gazette*, August 13, 1968.
Zerwick, Phoebe. "Airlines: Winston-Salem's beloved Piedmont faded into history as deregulation continued to put the squeeze on the industry," *Winston-Salem Journal*, January 28, 1999.
_____. "Colodny Introducing Piedmont to a New Style of Management," *Winston-Salem Journal*, July 31, 1989.
_____. "Harmony Was Illusion, Ex-Executives Say," *Winston-Salem Business Journal*, July 31, 1989.
_____. "Merger Will Mean Higher Wages for Union Workers," *Winston-Salem Business Journal*, July 31, 1989.
_____. "Piedmont Struggles to Fly Under USAir," *Winston-Salem Journal*, July 30, 1989.
_____. "Winston-Salem's Home-Grown Airline Comes to an End," *Winston-Salem Journal*, August 5, 1989.
_____, and Sharon Kebschull. "Ex Employees Have Fond Memories of the Time Spent With Piedmont," *Winston-Salem Journal*, July 31, 1989.

Books

Berg, A. Scott. *Lindbergh*. New York: G.P. Putnam's Sons, 1998.

Bernstein, Aaron. *Grounded: Frank Lorenzo and the Destruction of Eastern Airlines.* New York: Simon and Schuster, 1990.
Bethune, Gordon, with Scott Huler. *From Worst to First.* New York: John Wiley and Sons, Inc., 1998.
Biddle, Wayne. *Barons of the Sky: From Early Flight to Strategic Warfare, The Story of the Early American Aerospace Industry.* New York: Simon and Schuster, 1991.
Bilstein, Roger E. *Flight in America: 1900–1983.* Baltimore and London: Johns Hopkins University Press, 1984.
Bradley, E. Phil, and Richard F. Gaya, Sr. *The Crash of Piedmont Flight 349 Into Buck's Elbow Mountain as Told by the Sole Survivor, E. Philip Bradley.* 1997.
Caidin, Martin. *Barnstorming.* New York: Duell, Sloan and Pearce, 1965.
Captain X. *Safety Last: The Dangers of Commercial Aviation: An Indictment by an Airline Pilot.* New York: Dial Press, 1972.
Davies, R.E.G. *A History of the World's Airlines.* London: Oxford University Press, 1964.
Gunther, Max. *D.B. Cooper: What Really Happened.* Chicago: Contemporary Books, 1985.
Hanson, James R. *From Kid to Captain.* Norfolk, Virginia: Liskey and Sons Printing, publication date unknown.
Harrison, James P. *Mastering the Sky: A History of Aviation from Ancient Times to the Present.* New York: Sarpedon, 1996.
Hildreth, C.H., and Bernard C. Nalty. *1001 Questions Answered About Aviation History.* New York: Dodd, Mead and Company, 1969.
Jablonski, Edward. *Man with Wings.* Garden City, N.J.: Doubleday and Company, Inc., 1980.
Lopez, Donald S. *Smithsonian Guides—Aviation: From Our Earliest Attempts at Flight to Tomorrow's Advanced Designs.* New York: Macmillan, 1995.
Milton, Joyce. *Loss of Eden: A Biography of Charles and Anne Morrow Lindbergh.* New York: HarperCollins, 1993.
Petzinger Jr., Thomas. *Hard Landing: The Epic Contest for Power and Profits That Plunged the Airlines into Chaos.* New York: Times Books/Random House, 1995.
Rae, John B. *Climb to Greatness: The American Aircraft Industry, 1920–1960.* Cambridge, Mass.: MIT Press, 1968.
Reynolds, Patrick, and Tom Shachtman. *The Gilded Leaf.* Boston: Little, Brown and Company, 1989.
Reynolds, Z. Smith. *Log of Aeroplane NR-898W.* Winston-Salem, N.C.: Reynolda House, Museum of American Art, 2003.
Rhodes, Bernie. *D.B. Cooper: The Real McCoy.* Salt Lake City: University of Utah Press, 1991.
Tilley, Nannie M. *The R.J. Reynolds Tobacco Company.* Chapel Hill: University of North Carolina Press, 1985.
Tursi, Frank V. *Winston-Salem: A History.* Winston-Salem, N.C.: John F. Blair Publishing, 1994.
Winkowski, Fredric, and Frank D. Sullivan. *100 Planes, 100 Years: The First Century of Aviation.* New York: Smith Mark Publishing, 1988.

Dissertations, Theses, and Unpublished Papers

Samuel James Ervin Collection, 3847, Southern Historical Collection, University of North Carolina at Chapel Hill.
Galifianakis, Hon. Nick. "Piedmont Airlines 20th Anniversary," *Congressional Record,* February 20, 1968.
Lawing, Barry Alan. *A History of Aviation in Winston-Salem,* Master's Thesis, Wake Forest University, 1984.
Papers of Ronald S. Macklin.
"Miller Field and Smith Reynolds Airport," Molly G. Rawls, Forsyth County Public Library, July 1999.
Rogers, Dennis. "Buy-out of Piedmont Airlines is like losing an old friend." E-mail posting.
Worrell, Larry Brian. "The Piedmont and USAir Merger: A Case Study of Compensating Wage Differentials and Flight Attendant Labor Agreements," Bachelor's Thesis, University of North Carolina at Chapel Hill, 1992.

Magazine and Journal Articles

"Airlines earnings." *Travel Weekly,* September 1, 1986.
Banks, Howard. "Combat in the mid–Atlantic." *Forbes,* October 6, 1986.
Bedwell, Don. "What's Behind Piedmont Airline's Unlimited Visibility?" *South Magazine,* July 1980.
Blum, Ernest. "The city that deregulation built: Becoming a hub of Piedmont Airlines turned Charlotte, N.C., into a business and travel center." *Travel Weekly,* January 31, 1987.
Carter, Blanche. "Executive Airport." *Winston-Salem Business and Community Life Magazine,* April-May 1997.
Davies, R.E.G. "Tom Davis: Founder of Piedmont Airlines." *Airways,* Vol. 6, No. 6, August 1999.
Dunn, J.A.C. "The History of Piedmont Airlines." *Pace* magazine, Vol. 15, No. 7, December 1988.
"During the past 10 years, Delta has replaced USAir as the airline carrying the most passengers from Piedmont Triad International Airport. The number of airlines there has nearly doubled." *Business North Carolina,* August 2003.
Edelson, Sharon. "Holiday Inn's new advertising drive stakes chain's claim to winning edge." *Travel Weekly,* June 29, 1987.
"Founder of Piedmont Airlines Receives the Honor of His Peers." *We, The People of North Carolina,* Vol. 42, No. 4, April 1984.
Gold, Howard. "The visible airline." *Forbes,* May 20, 1985.
Golden, Fran. "Piedmont matches American cuts in new flurry of fare reductions." *Travel Weekly,* March 13, 1986.
Hurley, Richard J. "The Passing of the Pacemaker." *Airliners,* 1988.
Hutchins, Dexter. "Airline stocks: ready at last to climb?" *Time,* August 18, 1986.
Kohn, Bernie. "Piedmont Leasing Jetliner for Charters." *Knight Ridder/Tribune Business News,* March 28, 1996.

Murphy, Joseph S. "Conservative Piedmont Shifts to Turbines." *Air Transport World*, Vol. 5, No. 4, April 1968.

"New Air Route Starts Soon." *The State*, January 31, 1948.

Norris, Hoke. "They Wouldn't Stay Grounded." *The State* (North Carolina), January 19, 1952.

Paysour, Conrad. "Into the Wild Blue Yonder." *The State*, December 15, 1965.

"Piedmont Airlines Going Boeing Jet." *We, the People of North Carolina*, March 1966.

"Piedmont Airlines: Up and Coming with Style." *Southern Living*, August 1984.

"Piedmont Aviation, Inc.: Now Definitely a "Major" Carrier With a Fleet of New Jets On Order." *We, The People of North Carolina*, July 1986.

"Piedmont: Fast Growing Interstate Airline." *The Wachovia*, October 1952.

"Piedmont's Progress." *Time*, June 9, 1952.

Pinckney, Kay. "Why Piedmont Succeeds Where Others Fail." *Airline Executive*, January 1983.

Poling, Bill. "DOT approves USAir-Piedmont." *Travel Weekly*, November 9, 1987.

_____. "USAir to buy Piedmont; blocks TWA." *Travel Weekly*, March 16, 1987.

Reed, Ted, and Stella Hopkins. "Piedmont Airlines Founder Dead at 81." *Charlotte Observer*, April 22, 1999

Saunders, Keith. "Route, Experience Favor Piedmont in Feeder Test." *American Aviation*, June 15, 1948.

Shaw, Gaylord. "First in Flight Again: The Secrets Behind Piedmont Airlines' Climb to the Top." *Business North Carolina*, n.d.

Skolnik, Rayna. "Let Your Airline Do the Planning." *Sales & Marketing Management*, November 1986.

"Take the Train to the Plane." *Time*, February 9, 1987.

"Tom Davis: Pioneer Aviator." In "1941–1991, 50th Anniversary Commemorative Edition and Guide to Services, Piedmont Triad Airport," 1991.

"Traffic Stopper." *The State*, June 14, 1958.

"Transportation Department Defends USAir-Piedmont decision." *Travel Weekly*, December 21, 1987.

Turner, Walter R. "A Brief History of Piedmont Airlines" *Carolina Comments*, Vol. 49, No. 5, September 2001.

_____. "Airline with a Heart." Publisher and date unknown.

_____. "Flying the Blue Skies." *Our State*, March 2000.

_____. "In the Air." *Our State*, February 1999.

_____. "Piedmont Airlines Flies the Blue Skies." *Tarheel Junior Historian*, Fall 2003.

_____. "The Home-Grown Airline." *Business North Carolina*, March 2003.

"The Twenties." Piedmont Triad 50th Anniversary Publication.

"Two engines are better." *Time*, January 30, 1989.

"William R. Howard." *Business North Carolina*, November 1981.

Wood, Thom. "Piedmont's People and Planes." *Wachovia*, Vol. 58, No. 5, September-October 1971.

Woodruff, Charles K. "An Interview with Thomas H. Davis." *North Carolina Review of Business and Economics*, October 1979.

Woolsey, James P. "Piedmont Likes Nihon YS-11A." *American Aviation*, Vol. 32, No. 16, January 6, 1969.

Miscellaneous

Davis, Thomas H. *The History of Piedmont: Setting a Special Pace*, Piedmont Aviation, Inc., Newcomen Publication Number 1160, Copyright 1982.

The History of Sunnynoll, Publication of Allen Tate Realtors, 2599 Reynolda Road, Winston-Salem, N.C., n.d.

The Piedmont Air-Line. Published by Jas. W. Nagle, Philadelphia, publication date unknown.

Index

Aberdeen, NC 44
Adams, Ensley O. 155–156
Adana, Steve 127
Addison, David 160–161
Aeronautical Radio Inc. Communications and Reporting System (ACARS) 171
Air California 206, 221
Air Florida 206, 208
Air Force One 126
Aircraft Owners and Pilot's Association (AOPA) 159
Airline Deregulation Act of 1978 174, 179
Airline of the Year (Air Transport World Magazine) 203–204
Airline Pilots Association (ALPA) 76, 93, 106, 120, 129–130, 141, 241, 242
Albuquerque, NM 201
Alcoa Aluminum 110
Alexandria, VA 88
Allegheny Airlines 68, 89, 207
Allentown, PA 207
Alley, Suzanne 201
Alley, T.E. 138
America West Airlines 235–237, 250
American Airlines 33–34, 85, 87, 105, 132, 167, 172, 175, 195, 197, 216, 220, 221, 228, 230
Appalachian Pacemaker 46, 50
Appomattox Pacemaker 155
Arlington, VA 238
Armbrecht, Ted 167
Asheville, NC 44, 48, 58, 73, 95, 146, 156–165, 177, 183
Association of Flight Attendants 141
Atkinson, Kenny 138
Atlanta, GA 86, 87, 88, 89, 91, 95, 104, 109, 110, 123, 126, 140, 156, 157, 159, 160, 169, 176, 180, 184, 186, 187, 195, 198, 201, 228
Atlantic City, NJ 211
Augusta, GA 86, 90

Bailey, James "Beetle" 97, 115
Baldock, Cindy 94
Baldwin, Pete 143
Baldwin Aviation 143
Baltimore, MD 86, 87, 88, 89, 91, 109, 110, 119, 137, 170, 196–197, 203, 207, 216, 221, 228, 231
Barber, Bill 23, 25, 28, 35, 59–61, 63, 72, 84, 103, 106, 113, 124, 137, 189–190, 193, 194
Barkley, Alben 76
Barnes, Bert 147
Beachy, Lincoln 9
Beckley, WV 44, 73, 122, 173, 176, 183
Beeson, Ann 137
Beeson, Philip 101–102, 103–104, 137, 218
Belk, John 188
Best, Edward 48, 58, 61, 67
Bethune, Gordon 191–192, 213–215, 218–219, 221, 222, 224–225, 228–230, 234, 235
Black, Hugo 70
Blankenship, Denise 139
Blocker, Mel 111, 206, 222, 243
Bluefield, WV 44, 74, 76, 122, 176, 183
Boeing 727 103, 112, 127–128, 129, 138, 156, 170, 183, 201, 219–220
Boeing 737 89, 112, 125–126, 129–130, 138, 156, 165, 169, 170, 172, 181, 182, 183, 190, 194, 197, 209, 213, 216, 231, 240, 243, 254
Boeing 767 216, 226–227, 229, 231
Boesky, Ivan 250
Boney, Leslie 65
Bost, Woody 104, 133
Boston, MA 179, 180, 195, 207, 211
Bowden, Curly 94
Bowen, Buddy 135, 253
Boyle, Rockwell S. 27
Bradley, E. Phillip 149–153
Bradley, Jim 98
Braniff Airlines 111, 199, 211, 236
Bridwell, Lowell 197
British Aerospace 207
British Airways 245
Britt Airways 207, 208
Brock, Dan 189
Brock, Ken 140
Brockway Airlines 208, 211
Brooks, Larry 229
Brown, Debbie 101, 102
Brown, Gordon 34, 106, 125
Brown, Harold 55

Brown, Jim 100–103, 243, 248
Browning, Milt 154
Brunt, Stan 66
Buckeye Pacemaker 149, 152, 155
Buffalo, NY 211
Burlington, VT 211

Caldwell, "Jinks" 83
Capital Airlines 73–74, 168
Carlson, Kenneth 216
Carter, Bob 155
Cartwright, Howard 28, 56–57, 77, 106, 113, 119, 124, 131–132, 185, 194, 210
Caudle, Ann S. 95
Caudle, David 96, 103, 119, 121
CCAir (Sunbird Airlines) 207–208
Central Piedmont Aero 88, 165
Central Reservations Office (CRO) 125
Champion Spark Plug 110
Charles, Shelly 11, 42, 54
Charles Field 10
Charleston, SC 33, 127
Charleston, WV 44, 68, 75, 89, 90, 122, 137, 166–168, 169, 170
Charlotte, NC 48, 55, 58, 62, 73, 89, 105, 107, 127, 146, 160, 169, 178, 180, 186–188, 194–195, 201, 202, 203, 207–208, 216, 219, 220, 221, 226, 228–229, 231–232, 237, 240, 243, 244
Charlotte Aircraft 253
Charlotte Hornets 229
Charlottesville, NC 44, 73, 99, 111, 148–151, 154
Chase Manhattan Bank 182
Cherry, R. Gregg 50, 51
Chicago, IL 68, 86, 90, 118, 132, 133, 169, 179, 180, 186, 207
Childress, Richard 216
Christo, Betty 90
Ciccollilli, Raymond 126–127
Cincinnati, Ohio 44, 45, 48, 52, 58, 61, 64, 66, 68, 78, 81, 82, 89, 101, 127, 146, 154, 155, 166, 168, 215, 228
Civil Aeronautics Board 33, 35, 37–38, 39–41, 52, 58, 65, 69–71, 73, 85, 89–90, 109–110, 144, 147,

Index

151–152, 159, 173, 176, 178, 179, 198, 228
Civil Air Patrol 149
Civilian Pilot Training Program 23–29, 54, 110, 233
Clark, William 212
Claytor, Robert 206, 222
Clement, Ed 57
Cleveland, OH 207
Clodfelter, Bruce 154
Coca-Cola 243
Coester, Sam 89
Collins, Audrey 89, 119, 137–138, 144, 165, 224
Collins, Don 82, 89, 94, 106–107, 117, 119, 123, 131–132, 137–138, 153, 160, 173, 210, 238, 240–241, 245, 250
Collision Avoidance System 130, 161, 171
Colodny, Ed 224, 225, 231–233, 234–236, 239–241, 243
Colonial Airlines 38, 39, 40
Columbia, SC 86
Columbus, OH 67, 73, 82, 170
Colvin, Virginia Lane 92
Conner, Alden 157
Conner, Thomas 157–158
Conrad, Thomas C. 157
Conrail 220
Continental Airlines 87, 205
Cooper, D.B. 127–128
Corbello, Dwight 172
Corbin, KY 44, 76, 226
Corpening, Wayne 237
Cottrell, Lee 153, 154
Counts, Buddy 122
Counts, Connie Chalk 90, 91, 92, 95, 96, 113, 168, 245
Covington, Cleta 82
Cowan, Tom 48
Cox, Lewis 50
Cox, Sandra Kay 157
Craig, James 146
Crandall, Robert 228
Crozet, VA (Buck's Elbow Mountain) 148–153
Culler, Danny 136–137
Culler, Eddie 20, 21, 25, 28, 35, 42, 77, 114, 115, 136–137, 191
Culler, Elizabeth 114
Culler, Jill 136
Culler, Joe 42, 136–137, 191
Culler, Rick 136

Daley, Richard J. 132, 133
Dallas, TX 186, 187, 195, 196, 203
Danielson, Larry 217
Danville, VA 44, 67, 68, 75, 176
Davis, Deborah 157
Davis, Egbert, Jr. 13, 15, 17–18, 21, 22, 23, 32, 47, 85, 108
Davis, Egbert, Sr. 15, 16–17, 21, 132
Davis, Frank 118, 135–136, 181, 185–186, 189, 224, 238, 250
Davis, Julie 135
Davis, Nancy (daughter) 135

Davis, Nancy (wife) 40, 54, 141
Davis, Thelma Taylor 34–35, 74, 91, 111, 190–191
Davis, Thomas H., Jr. (Bo) 135
Davis, Thomas H., Sr. 5, 6, 15–16, 17–19, 19–23, 28–30, 31–34, 35, 37–52, 58–60, 63–64, 65, 68, 69, 71–72, 73, 74, 76–80, 82, 85, 88–89, 99–100, 103, 104–110, 112, 113, 115, 118, 124, 130–133, 135–136, 142–143, 144, 165, 167, 170, 173–181, 186, 188–193, 198, 199, 201, 205, 206, 214, 218, 220, 224, 228, 233, 235, 240, 244, 245, 247, 248, 250, 256, 258
Davis, Virginia 90
Dawkins, Sam 127
Dayton, OH 195–196, 201, 203, 207, 208, 211, 221
Daytona Beach, FL 208
Dehavilland Dash 8, 207
Delta Airlines 13, 41, 42, 55, 87, 125, 126, 130, 132, 175, 183, 186, 198, 201, 218, 221, 222, 228, 237
Denver, CO 180, 201, 241
Deregulation 173–183
Detroit, MI 195, 207
Dickens, Ed 154
Dietz, Roger 94
Dobbins, Harold "Hoss" 32, 47, 48, 52, 54, 59, 65, 72–73, 76, 82, 93, 128
Dole, Bob 217
Dole, Elizabeth 235
Douglas Commercial 3 (DC-3) 38–39, 46, 48, 51, 56–57, 65, 74, 76–78, 79, 82, 111, 142, 146–149, 168, 226, 252–255
Doyle, Jack 92
Dudley, Larry 97–98, 114, 118, 189
Dunn, Ed 127
Dunne, Hop Hee "Hoppy" 121, 171
Durham, NC 44, 73, 137, 228, 253
Dusenbury, Susan 253

Earhart, Amelia 256
Eastern Airlines 13, 33–34, 41, 42, 87, 105, 110, 126, 130, 132, 137, 138, 174–176, 178–179, 187, 198, 201, 205, 218
Edelstein, Mort 170
Eisler, Irv 101
Elizabeth City, NC 95
Emerald Airlines 206
Empire Airlines 211–213, 215, 225, 244
Ervin, Sam, Jr. 71
Evans, Bob 154–155

Fair, Carol Dobyns 91, 93, 95, 140–141, 227
Fairchild 27 (F-27) 78–79, 81–82, 84–85, 86, 122, 126, 153, 154
Fairchild-Hiller 227B (FH-227) 85, 122–123, 166, 185
Fare, Milton 21, 24, 77, 80
Farrell, John H. 47

Fayetteville, NC 52, 68, 72, 75, 129, 169, 186
Federal Aviation Administration (FAA) 100, 103, 119–120, 121, 145, 159, 161, 164, 166, 167, 171, 191, 230, 238
Federal Communications Commission 152
Fickling, Joe 95–96
Fields, Beau 243–244
Financial Management Award (Air Transportation World Magazine) 218
First Boston Bank 222, 223
First Class Service 202
Florence, SC 86, 89
Florida Shuttle "Project Omaha" 208–211, 231
Flowers, Johnny 86
Fokker F-28 170, 209–210, 213, 215
Forsyth Country Airport Commission 107, 143
Fort, Vance 228
Fort Lauderdale, FL 208
Fort Myers, FL 208
Fort Wayne, IN 195
Foster, David 253
Fox, Leon 31, 42, 47, 48, 52, 58, 82, 126, 183–184, 244
Frank, Stanley 188
Frankfort, KY 104
Frankfurter, Felix 70
Frequent Flyer Program 243
Fuda, Larry 170

Gainesville, FL 208, 211
Gambrel, E. Smythe (Law Firm) 174
Garuda Airlines 209–210
Gasque, Steve 243–244
Gaya, Richard F. 149
General Aviation (Fixed Base Operations) 29, 42–43, 68, 69, 88, 110, 111, 134–135, 143, 165–166, 177, 203, 244
General Aviation Trainer (GAT) aka "Piedmonster" 255
Gilbert, Hank 41, 68
Gilley, Bud 36, 38, 47, 120
Gingrich, Newt 126
Glover, W. Gerald 237
Goforth, Roscoe 129, 130
Goldsboro, NC 44, 50, 76, 81, 154, 192, 194
Golson, Lee 34, 45, 58, 117
Googe, John 143
Gordon, R.L. 53, 78, 100, 104, 113–114, 121
Goth, G.W. 115
Graham, Billy 140
Grand Rapids, MI 195
Gray, Carroll 229
Great Smokies Pacemaker 82
Green, Bill 147
Greenbrier, WV 180
Greensboro, NC 44, 67, 73, 107,

170, 178, 180, 188, 199–200, 210, 212, 220, 240, 244
Greenville, SC 90
Grinstein, Jerry 221
Groat, Frank 21, 24, 32
Guilford Technical Community College 254

Hager, R.D. 34, 47, 147–148
Hagerstown, MD 207
Hains, David 226
Haley, Lee 152
Hall, John 115
Hamilton, Jim 98, 102, 126, 129, 130, 253
Hamilton, Stephanie 253
Hanes Knitting 249
Hanson, James 133–134
Harlan, KY 44
Harrisburg, PA 207
Haynes, Luther 146, 147
Heine, Tom 196
Helsabeck, Joe 155–156
Hendrix, Glenn 36
Henson, Richard 207
Henson Airlines (Aviation) 119, 206–207, 213, 216, 231
Hickory, NC 67, 73, 75, 145, 153, 176, 207
Hicks, George 151
Hicks, Ralph 194
High Point, NC 44, 73
Hijackings 126–128
Hinson, Sam 127
Hopscotch Fare 198
Horrell, Harv 114–115, 116
Hotel Robert E. Lee 28, 51
Houle, Paul 161–165
House, Robert 107
Houston, Robert 153
Houston, TX 180
Howard, William (Bill) 174–180, 183, 186–188, 192–193, 195–198, 201, 202, 204, 205, 208, 210–218, 220–225, 228, 231, 234–235, 240, 250
Hubs 186–198
Huddleston, Al 92
Hudspeth, Ron 201
Hughes Airwest 205
Huntington, WV 44, 53, 67, 73
Hutchinson, H.H. 146
Hyder, Clarence 157–158

Icahn, Carl 222–224, 234
Indianapolis, Indiana 221
International Association of Machinists (IAM) 106

Jackson, Maynard 126
Jacksonville, FL 178, 208
James, Richard 202
James River Pacemaker 154, 166
Jetstream International Airlines (Vee Neal) 207, 208
Johnson, Dave 102–103, 108, 118, 122, 249

Johnson, John 77
Johnson, Lyndon B. 156, 159
Jones, Frank 47, 48
Jones, Pete 48
Justice, Charlie "Choo-Choo" 60

Kagel, Sam 242
Kahn, Alfred 173–174
Kanawha Pacemaker 170
Kanawha River Pacemaker 46, 47, 169
Kansas City, MO 217
Key West, FL 208
Kinston, NC 73, 76, 127, 137, 207
Kirch, Bob 241
Kirchoffer and Arnold Associates 44
Knoxville, TN 73, 110
Koontz, Bob 241
Kyle, Bill 76, 103, 138

Labonte, Terry 216
Lambert, L.J. 62, 64, 109, 115, 125
LaMoure, Debora 237
Lansing, MI 195
Lasley, Ed 143
Latrobe, PA 207
Lavrinc, George 152
Lawing, Barry 181
Lewisburg, WV 207
Lexington, KY 44, 48, 52
"Lt. Spartacus" 127
Lincoln, Abe 117
Lindbergh, Charles 14–15, 258
Lindbergh, Reeve 258
Lindsay, Pete 154
Link simulator 121, 171
Linkletter, Art 140
London, England 226, 228–231
London, KY 44, 76, 226
Long Island, NY 207
Lorenzo, Frank 205, 218
Los Angeles, CA 125, 186, 201, 202, 203, 220
Louisville, KY 46, 50, 68, 76, 89, 166
Louisville and Nashville Railroad (L&N) 111
Lumberton, NC 89
Lynchburg, VA 44, 68, 123, 129, 154, 207, 238

Macklin, Ronnie 39, 72, 75, 84–85, 105, 110–111, 119–120, 126, 128, 164, 171, 194, 195, 230, 252, 253, 254, 257–258
Magruder, William M. 132–133, 144
Manhattan Pacemaker 156–157
Manske, Ed 153
Marietta, OH 73
Marsh, Lou 50
Marsh Harbor, the Bahamas 231
Martin, Don 120, 170, 238
Martin, Leonard 84, 209, 210, 211, 213
Martin, T.L. 148
Martin 4-0-4 82–84, 86, 96, 105, 119, 122, 125, 155, 254

Martinsville, VA 216
Maynard Field 10
McAlphin, Bob 55, 62, 180, 186, 187–188, 238
McCallum, David 169
McDonald, Meg 229
McDonnell-Douglas Vital 7, 172
McElveen-Hunter, Bonnie 142–143
McGee, Bill 35, 45, 47, 57, 59, 79, 82, 106, 112, 113, 147, 198, 214, 220–221, 224, 235, 236, 249
McGinnis, Lewin S. "Mac" 13, 14, 15, 19, 20, 22–23, 24, 32
McGuire, Don 172, 198, 217, 236
McKee, William F. 110
McKinney and Silver Advertising 234
McLean, C.D. 96, 110, 183, 203, 218–219, 230, 234, 237, 240
McMillan, Alex 236–237
McNames, L.W. 71
McNatt, Ralph S. 246
McNaughton, John T. 156, 159
McNaughton, Sarah 156
McNaughton, Theodore 156
Meacham, Charlie 37, 53, 116, 118, 133, 169, 183, 184
Meacham, Chuck 53, 118, 133, 184
Medlin, John G 21, 182
Melbourne, FL 208
Memphis, TN 110, 131, 132
Messick, John A. 166–167
Miami, FL 127, 178, 179, 208, 239
Middlesboro, KY 44
Miller, Greg 202
Miller, Harold 111
Miller, Howard 111, 113, 129, 223, 243, 252, 254
Miller, Rick 118
Miller, Tom 172
Minter, Bobby 138
Mirror Image 238–239
Mise, H.L. 145
Mohammad Reza Pahlavi, Shah of Iran 185
Mondragon, Robert 149
Monroe, NC 203
Montreal, Canada 213
Moore, H.E. 146
Moore, Marianne 239, 240
Moran, Ferdinand D. 70
Morehead City, NC 67, 68
Morgan, Bill 86, 114
Morganton, NC 71, 76
Mount Mitchell Pacemaker 128
Murchison, Charles 69
Murphy, Joseph 124
Myrtle Beach, SC 73, 127, 244

Nance, Bob 75
Naples, FL 208
NASCAR 192–193, 216
Nashville, TN 86, 110, 132, 201
Nassau, the Bahamas 231
National Aeronautics and Space Administration (NASA) 110
National Airlines 205

Index

National Aviation Safety Inspection Program (NASIP) 230
National Transportation Safety Board (NTSB) 159–165, 170
Neal, Stephen 237
New Bern, NC 44, 46, 50, 58, 61, 82, 99, 127, 155
New York, NY 95, 109, 123, 179, 180, 207, 211, 213, 215, 218, 235, 236, 244
New York Stock Exchange 179
Newark, NJ 90, 127, 169
Newberry, SC 89
Newcomen Society 206
Newport News, VA 68
Nicholson, Frank 35, 64, 77, 97, 152, 256
Nicholson, Mary 256
Nihon YS-11 105, 122–125, 138, 140, 170, 171, 182–183, 207
Norfleet, Charlie 20, 37, 50, 130
Norfleet, Molly 50
Norfolk, VA 44, 64, 67, 68, 72, 73, 89, 90, 95, 114, 186, 207
Norfolk-Southern Railroad (Norfolk and Western) 110, 111, 206, 220–225, 233
North American Van Lines 220
North Carolina Highway Patrol 147
North Carolina Transportation Hall of Fame 255–256
North Carolina Transportation Museum 252, 254
North Central Airlines 205
Northington, Bob 21, 28, 80, 106, 214
Northwest Airlines 127–128, 236
Nunneley, Emory T. 69
Nutt, Chester B. 61

Oklahoma City, OK 100
One Piedmont Plaza 216, 217
Onoff, John 52, 65, 78
Orangeburg, SC 89
Orlando, FL 208, 209
Orrell, Tommy 56, 65, 66, 67, 76, 82
Ottawa, Canada 213
Ozark Airlines 221

PACE 142–143
Pacific Southwest Airlines 221, 238, 240, 241
Palmetto Pacemaker 153, 154
Pan-American Airlines 205, 228, 236
Parker, James 182
Parkersburg, WV 73
Parks, Hugh 93
Parnell, Sam 66
Parness, Larry 236
Pearl, Anna 166
Pearson, Yates 157
Pensacola, FL 208, 211
People's Express 205
Perry, Charlie 92
Peters, Cheryl 138–140, 201

Phase II Flight Simulators 193
Philadelphia, PA 207
Phoenix, AZ 231
Piedmonitor 185
Piedmont Aerospace Institute 110
Piedmont Air Line (railroad) 43
Piedmont Fabricators Division 110–111
Piedmont Olympics 185–186
Piedmont Presidential Suites 202
Pinehurst, NC 44, 66
Piper, Bill 199, 211
Pittsburgh, PA 207, 221, 228, 238, 241, 242
Popkin, Herman 159
Portsmouth, OH 44
Potomac Pacemaker 252–255
Poughkeepsie, NY 211
Powell, Reggie 61–62
Price, Bill 169
Pride of Piedmont 226–227
Princeton, WV 44, 76
Proctor and Gamble 110
Pruitt, Blandene Smith 146–147
Pruitt, Oren Ase 146–147
Pulaski, VA 67

Quackenbush, Paul 212
Queen, Margaret Jenkins 91, 92, 94, 95–96, 139, 189
Quiet Birdmen 63, 103

R.J. Reynolds Tobacco Co. 9, 16, 95, 110, 249
Raines, Roy 138
Raleigh, NC 44, 50, 73, 95, 135, 137, 197, 220, 228
Ramseck, Robert 51
Ray, Sylvia 133
Redburn, Calvin James 120
Reed, Harry 70
Republic Airlines 205, 236
Reston, VA 201
Reynolds, R.J. 10
Reynolds, R.J., Jr. (Dick) 10, 11, 12, 19, 20
Reynolds, Ralph 160
Reynolds, Smith 10, 11, 12–13
Reynolds Aviation (Airways) 12, 19
Richmond, VA 44, 68, 123, 128, 130, 186
Riverside, CA 216
Roanoke, VA 44, 64, 67, 68, 75, 89, 97, 111, 116, 117, 118, 119, 123, 126, 129–130, 135, 137–138, 154, 155, 156, 161, 166, 168, 170, 176, 184, 206, 239
Roanoke Rapids, NC 89
Roanoke Valley Pacemaker 170
Rochelle, VA 149
Rockingham, NC 54, 176
Rocky Mount, NC 122, 128
Rowe, Cliff 25
Rowe, Jake 77
Rowe, Jason 25
Rudd, Ricky 216
Rumble, Pamela Sue 155–156

Sack, George 140
Sain, Dottie Elmore 91, 94, 95
Salley, G. Mackay 143
Samuels, R.W. 47
San Diego, CA 231
San Francisco, CA 220
Sanford, Terry 104
Sarasota, FL 208
Sass, Lynn Shainberg 108, 140–141
Saunder, Tom 159, 164
Saunders, Harold K. "Zeke" 23, 24, 27, 28–29, 35, 36, 38, 42, 46, 47, 52, 54, 59, 63, 67, 74, 75, 76, 77, 78, 79, 80, 81, 84, 85, 97, 103–104, 106, 113, 118, 120, 122, 123–124, 130, 132–133, 147, 148, 150–152, 156, 174, 182, 185, 191–192, 194, 213, 214, 220–221, 253, 256–257
Savannah, GA 89
Schick, Tom 236
Schiller, Barbara 167
Schulte, Ray F. 157
Schulze, H.A. 147
Scocozza, Matthew 237
Seattle, WA 102, 229
Securities and Exchange Commission 220–221
Sharp, Gene 195–196, 199, 200, 201–202, 209, 210–211
Sharpe, Tom vii, 107, 122, 134–35, 182–183
Shaw, Bartlett M. 174
Shaw, Stephen 239
Shelby, NC 146
Shenandoah Valley Pacemaker 182
Shouse, "Mom" 77
Sifford, Jim 194
Silver, Tracy 202
Skip-Stop service 86
Skyline Drive, VA 149, 150
Slaughter, Baxter 147
Smith, C.R. 38, 85
Smith, Fred 147
Smith, Gene 57
Smith, Richard 219, 235, 238–239, 241
Snell, Paul 63, 64, 104, 113, 116–117, 159, 161, 163, 170
South Central Airlines 89–90
Southern Airways 38, 40
Southern Pines, NC 44, 48, 52, 53, 58, 67
Southwest Airlines 250
Spencer, Carroll 81, 87, 105, 106, 128, 161, 171, 175, 192–193, 225
Spencer, J.Y. 99–100
Stancil, Tom 126, 127
Stanges, Tom D. 120
State Airlines 41, 42, 44, 65, 69
State Bureau of Investigation, NC (SBI) 147
Statesville, NC 75, 89
Staunton, VA 89, 118
Stemler, Mr. & Mrs. Emil 48
Stevenson, McLean 215–216, 239–240

Stewart, C.L., Jr. 92
Stokely-Van Camp Company 157
Stop Child Abuse Now (SCAN) 119
Strike (Third Man Issue) 129–10
Sugg, Gene 166–167
Sumter, SC 89
Supersonic Transport Program (SST) 132
Swaim, Bill 25
Syracuse, NY 212–213, 215, 225

Tadlock, Warren O. "Jack" 36, 97, 98, 99–100, 102, 118–119, 126–127, 135, 164
Tallahassee, FL 208, 211
Tampa, FL 208, 209, 226, 228
Tate, Jerry 94
Taylor, Bill 35–36, 75
Taylor, Jim 67
Taylor, Wallace 138
Tehran, Iran 185
Texaco 110
Texas Air 205, 218, 237
Thaxton, L.C. 167
Thomas, Pauline Fletcher 140, 141, 142, 202
Thomas H. Davis Pacemaker 240
Thomas H. Davis Training Center 193, 194
Thompson, Brian 227
Thompson, Howard 66, 93, 99, 114, 118
Tidewater Pacemaker 146, 155
Toledo, OH 195
Torres, Elmo 242
Traffic Alert and Collision Avoidance System (TCAS) 171
Trans Air 208, 211, 231
Trans-World Airlines (TWA) 33–34, 82–83, 92, 125, 218, 220, 221, 222–224, 234, 236
Trask, George 47
Treasure Cay, the Bahamas 231
Tri-Cities, TN (Bristol, Kingsport, Johnson City) 44, 48, 50, 67, 71, 75, 93, 100, 102, 110, 146, 183
Tucson, AZ 17–19, 108–109
Turby, Jim 196
Turbyville, R.E. 34, 80, 106

Turner, Bill 47, 80, 82
Turner, Roscoe 10, 47

United Airlines 33–34, 74, 87, 90, 105, 129, 132, 186, 195, 216, 234, 237
United Coal Company 243
United States Air Force 149
United States Department of Justice 233, 236
United States Department of Transportation (DOT) 228, 232–233, 235–237, 241, 242
United States Postal Service 70
United States Supreme Court 41, 70–71
USAir 96, 207, 221–225, 232–245, 246, 249, 250
Utica, NY 212–213

Van Duser, Peter 96
Vaughn, Tory 52, 54–56, 66, 67, 77, 85, 90, 130–131, 142, 168–169, 191
Voignier, Thomas 167

Wachovia Bank 20, 37, 78, 174, 182, 237
Wagner, Othel 25
Wake Forest University 189–190
Walker, Bill 229
Walker, Jack 175, 197, 199–200
Wall, Larry 137, 244
Wall, Margaret 137
Wall, Robert 137, 244
Wallace, George 140, 141
Wallis, Richard 241–242
Walnut Cove, NC 234
Warner, E.G. 77
Warner, Harold 91, 92
Washington, DC 73, 95, 99, 109, 123, 128, 132, 145, 148, 149, 154, 156, 170, 175, 196, 198, 201, 206, 207, 228, 235, 236, 242, 246
Watlington, John 78, 174, 182
Waynesboro, VA 149
Wescott, Dick 253
West Palm Beach, FL 208

Western Airlines 206 213, 214, 220–221, 237, 252
Wheeler, Mr. 25
Wheeler, Warren 104–105, 245
White, Bobby 126
Wichita, KS 216–217
Widner, Vestal 115
Wilcox, Earl 67, 85, 94, 145–146
Wilkes, J.L. "Pappy" 65, 155, 257
Wilkes-Barre, PA 207
Willard, Red 25, 77
Wilmington, NC 31, 43, 45–47, 48, 52, 64, 65, 66, 67, 81, 82, 89, 92, 96, 124, 127, 155, 186, 245
Wilson, Joe 185, 200, 224, 235, 238, 240
Wilson, Lawrence C. 157
Winston-Salem, NC 1, 9, 10, 13, 28, 50, 58, 64, 67, 71–72, 73, 75, 78, 82, 88, 89, 90, 92, 93, 95, 96, 97, 98, 99, 100, 102, 106, 107–108, 109, 113, 118, 119, 120, 123, 125, 126, 135, 138, 140, 141, 148, 154, 165, 173, 174, 175, 180, 186, 188, 192, 194, 197, 200, 203, 206, 207, 211, 213, 215, 216, 219, 221, 223, 226, 229–230, 231, 233–234, 236, 237, 238, 240, 242, 249, 253, 258
Woensdrecht, Holland 210
Wright, Carol 202
Wright, Wilbur and Orville 9, 46–47, 196, 227
WSOC Radio 48
WTOB Radio 50

Xcursion Plan 89

Yoder, Ronnie 235–237
Young, Norris 77
Young, Tom 212

Z. Smith Reynolds Airport (Miller Field) 13, 14, 19, 20, 26, 50, 61, 71, 72, 73, 107–108, 110, 126, 143, 180, 188, 193, 194, 216
Zimmerman, Joe 127

www.ingramcontent.com/pod-product-compliance
Ingram Content Group UK Ltd.
Pitfield, Milton Keynes, MK11 3LW, UK
UKHW050542150426
5217IPUK00026B/2037